LITERATURE AND NATURE IN THE ENGLISH RENAISSANCE

Featuring over two hundred nature-themed texts that span the disciplines of literature, science and history, this sourcebook offers an accessible field guide to the environment of Renaissance England, revealing a nation at a crossroads between its pastoral heritage and industrialized future. Carefully selected primary sources, each modernized and prefaced with an introduction, survey an encyclopaedic array of topographies, species, and topics: from astrology to zoology, bear-baiting to bee-keeping, coal-mining to tree-planting, fen-draining to sheep-whispering. The familiar voices of Spenser, Shakespeare, Jonson, and Marvell mingle with a diverse chorus of farmers, herbalists, shepherds, hunters, foresters, philosophers, sailors, sky-watchers, and duchesses – as well as ventriloquized beasts, trees, and rivers. Lavishly illustrated, the anthology is supported by a lucid introduction that outlines and intervenes in key debates in Renaissance ecocriticism, a reflective essay on ecocritical editing, a bibliography of further reading, and a timeline of environmental history and legislation drawing on extensive archival research.

TODD ANDREW BORLIK is Senior Lecturer in English Literature at the University of Huddersfield and the author of *Ecocriticism and Early Modern English Literature* (2011).

LITERATURE AND NATURE IN THE ENGLISH RENAISSANCE

An Ecocritical Anthology

Edited by

TODD ANDREW BORLIK
UNIVERSITY OF HUDDERSFIELD

CAMBRIDGE
UNIVERSITY PRESS

University Printing House, Cambridge CB2 8BS, United Kingdom

One Liberty Plaza, 20th Floor, New York, NY 10006, USA

477 Williamstown Road, Port Melbourne, VIC 3207, Australia

314–321, 3rd Floor, Plot 3, Splendor Forum, Jasola District Centre, New Delhi – 110025, India

79 Anson Road, #06–04/06, Singapore 079906

Cambridge University Press is part of the University of Cambridge.

It furthers the University's mission by disseminating knowledge in the pursuit of education, learning, and research at the highest international levels of excellence.

www.cambridge.org
Information on this title: www.cambridge.org/9781316510155
DOI: 10.1017/9781108224901

First published 2019

Printed in the United Kingdom by TJ International Ltd, Padstow Cornwall

A catalogue record for this publication is available from the British Library.

ISBN 978-1-316-51015-5 Hardback

CONTENTS

List of Illustrations   *page* xv
Acknowledgements   xvi
Editorial Principles: Towards the Ecocritical Editing of
     Renaissance Texts   xviii

Introduction   1

PART I   *Cosmologies*   25

Creation and the State of Nature   27

"The Creation of the World," from Genesis (c. 900–500
     BCE; the Geneva translation 1560)   27
Ovid, "The Creation," "The Four Ages," and "The
     Oration of Pythagoras" (4 BCE – 2 CE; Arthur Golding
     translation 1567)   30
Lucretius, "That the World Was Not Created for
     Mankind's Sake" and "The First Productions of the
     Earth" (c. 55 BCE; Lucy Hutchinson translation c. 1650s)   36
Philip Sidney, "As I my little flock on Ister Bank" (c. 1580)   38
William Shakespeare, "Each thing's a Thief," from *Timon
     of Athens* (c. 1606)   43
John Norden, "The state of this island of Great Britain at
     the beginning" (1607)   44
Thomas Traherne, "Dumbness" (c. 1660)   46
Lucy Hutchinson, [The Third Day] and [The Naming of
     the Animals] (c. 1670s)   49

Natural Theologies   52
Psalm 104 (c. 900–400 BCE; Mary Sidney translation c. 1599)   52
Guillaume de Salluste Du Bartas, "The World's a Book in
     Folio" (1578; Joshua Sylvester translation 1605)   55
Giordano Bruno, "The World Soul" (1584)   57
Richard Hooker, "The Law Which Natural Agents Have
     Given Them to Observe" (1593)   60
John Donne, "Why are we by all Creatures waited on?" (c. 1609)   63

Walter Ralegh, "How It Is To Be Understood That the
Spirit of God Moved Upon the Waters" and "That
Nature Is No *Principium Per Se*" (1614)   63

George Wither, "Song for Rogation Week" (1623)   65

John Milton, "On the Morning of Christ's Nativity" (1629)   66

George Herbert, "Man" and "Providence" (1633)   70

Thomas Browne, "Nature is the Art of God" (c. 1635)   75

Thomasine Pendarves, [Embracing the Creatures] (1649)   77

Joseph Caryl, "To cause it to rain on the earth where no
man is" (1653)   79

John Ray, from *The Wisdom of God Manifested in the Works
of Creation* (1691)   81

PART II   *The Tangled Chain*   85

Hierarchy and the Human Animal   87

Ambroise Paré, "Of Monsters by the Confusion of Seed of
Diverse Kinds" (1572; Thomas Johnson translation 1634)   87

Reginald Scot, "That the Body of a Man Cannot Be
Turned into the Body of a Beast by a Witch" (1584)   89

Michel de Montaigne, "Apology for Raymond Sebond"
(c. 1580; John Florio translation c. 1603)   91

Francis Bacon, "Prometheus, or the State of Man" (1609;
Arthur Gorges translation 1619)   99

René Descartes, "The Animal Machine" (1637; anonymous
translation 1649)   102

Margaret Cavendish, [Animal Intelligence] (1664)   103

John Bulwer, "Man was at first but a kind of Ape" (1650)   105

Ann Conway, "This Transmutation of Things out of one
Species into another" (c. 1675)   107

from Anonymous, from *Scala Naturæ* (1695)   110

Beasts   113

Edward Topsell, [Dedicatory Epistle] and "Of the
Unicorn," from *A History of Four-Footed Beasts* (1607)   113

Thomas Heyrick, "On an Ape" (1691)   117

William Shakespeare, [The Courser and the Jennet], from
Venus and Adonis (1593)   118

John Harington, "My Dog Bungay" (1608)   121

William Baldwin, from *Beware the Cat* (c. 1553)   123

Kenelm Digby, "Concerning the Invention of Foxes and
Other Beasts" and "Of the Several Cryings and Tones of
Beasts" (1644)   126

Thomas Tryon, "Of the Language of Sheep" (1684)   129

Jacques Du Fouilloux, "The Badger" (1561; George
    Gascoigne translation 1575)   130
Richard Brathwaite, "The Squirrel" and "The Hedgehog"
    (1634)   132
Edward May, "On a Toad" (1633)   135
John Derricke, "[Why] the Irish ground … neither breedeth
    nor fostereth up any venomous beast or worm" (1581)   135

Birds   138
John Skelton, "Speak, Parrot" (c. 1521)   138
Henry Vaughan, "The Eagle" (1655)   140
George Morley, "The Nightingale" (c. 1633)   141
William Turner, [The Kite] (1555) and [The Robin
    and Redstart] (1544)   143
Henry Chillester, "A Commendation of the Robin
    Redbreast" (1579)   145
Richard Brathwaite, "The Lapwing" and
    "The Swallow" (1621)   147
Anonymous, *A Battle of Birds* (1621)   149
Hester Pulter, "The Lark" (c. 1655)   153
John Caius, "Of the Puffin" (1570)   155
William Harvey and Francis Willoughby, [Gannets at Bass
    Rock] (1633, 1661)   156

Fish   158
Edmund Spenser, "Huge Sea monsters" (1590)   158
Tomos Prys, "The Porpoise" (c. 1594–1600)   160
Michael Drayton, [Fish in the River Trent] (1622)   162
Izaak Walton, "Observations of the Salmon" and
    "Observations of the Eel" (1655)   163

Insects   167
Thomas Moffett, from *The Theatre of Insects* (1589)   167
Charles Butler, from *The Feminine Monarchy, or a Treatise
    Concerning Bees* (1609)   169
Richard Lovelace, "The Ant" (c. 1655)   172
Margaret Cavendish, "Of the Spider" (1653)   174
Anonymous, "Upon the biting of Fleas" (c. 1650)   174

Plants   177
Edmund Spenser, [The Oak and the Briar] (1579)   177
William Lawson, [The Size and Age of Trees] (1618)   181
William Strode, "On a Great Hollow Tree" (c. 1634)   183

Robert Herrick, "The Willow Tree," "The Vine,"
   "Parliament of Roses to Julia," and "Divination by a
   Daffodil" (1648)   186
Anonymous, [The Crab-tree's Lament] (1558)   188
William Turner, "Orobanche" (1568)   189
John Gerard, from *The Herbal* (1597)   191
John Donne, [The Mandrake] (1601)   194
John Heywood, "A Rose and a Nettle" (1550)   195
Francis Bacon, "Sympathy and Antipathy of Plants" (c. 1625)   196

Gems, Metals, Elements, Atoms   198
   John Maplet, "Sovereign Virtues in Stones" (1567)   198
   Anne Bradstreet, "The Four Elements" (1650)   201
   Margaret Cavendish, "Motion directs, while Atoms dance"
      and "A World in an Earring" (1653)   202

           PART III   *Time and Place*   205
Seasons   207

   Henry Howard, "Description of Spring" (c. 1535)   207
   Alexander Hume, "Of the Day Estival" (1599)   208
   Nicholas Breton, "Harvest" and "October" (1626)   213
   Alexander Barclay, "The winter snows, all covered is the
      ground" (c. 1518)   214

Country Houses   217
   George Gascoigne, [The Wild Man of Kenilworth] (1575)   217
   Aemelia Lanyer, "The Description of Cookham" (1610)   218
   Ben Jonson, "To Penshurst" (c. 1611)   222
   Thomas Carew, "To Saxham" (c. 1635)   225
   Andrew Marvell, "Upon Appleton House" (c. 1651)   226

Gardens   232
   Thomas Hill, "Rare inventions and defences for most
      seeds" (1577)   232
   Anonymous, "The Mole-catcher's Speech" (1591)   234
   William Shakespeare, [The Duke of York's Garden] from
      Richard II (c. 1595)   235
   Francis Bacon, "Of Gardens" (1625)   237
   Andrew Marvell, "The Garden" and "The Mower against
      Gardens" (c. 1651)   240
   Abraham Cowley, "The Garden" (1667)   243

Pastoral: Pastures, Meadows, Plains, Downs   246
   Philip Sidney, from *The Arcadia* (c. 1585)   246
   Richard Barnfield, from *The Affectionate Shepherd* (1594) 248
   Michael Drayton, "A Nice Description of Cotswold" (1612) 250
   William Browne, "The Swineherd" (1614)   252
   William Strode, "On Westwell Downs" (c. 1640)   253
   Robert Herrick, "To Meadows" (1648)   254
   John Aubrey, [Salisbury Plains and the Downs]
     (c. 1656–1685)   255

Georgic: Fields, Farms   258
   Virgil, from *Georgics* (c. 29 BCE; Thomas May
     translation 1628)   258
   Thomas Tusser, "The Praise of Husbandry" (1570)   260
   Hugh Plat, "A Philosophical Garden," "Gillyflowers," and
     "Grafting" (1608)   261
   Margaret Cavendish, "Earth's Complaint" (1653)   264

Forests, Woods, Parks   265
   William Harrison, "Of Parks and Warrens" (1577)   265
   Philip Sidney, "O sweet woods" (c. 1580)   266
   Nicholas Breton, "Now lies this walk along a wilderness"
     (1592)   268
   John Manwood, "The Definition of a Forest" (1598)   270
   Anthony Bradshaw, "A Friend's Due Commendation of
     Duffield Frith" (c. 1588–1608)   273
   Michael Drayton, "The Forest of Arden" (1612)   276
   Edward Herbert, "Made upon the Groves near Merlow
     Castle" (1620)   280
   Mary Wroth, [Pamphilia's Tree-Carving] (1621)   281
   William Habington, "To Castara, venturing to walk too far
     in the neighbouring wood" (1633)   284
   Katherine Philips, "Upon the graving of her Name upon a
     Tree in Barn Elms' Walks" (1669)   284

Heaths, Moors   286
   John Norden, "Heathy Ground" (1607)   286
   John Speed, [Norfolk Heaths and Yorkshire Dales] (1612) 287
   Tristram Risdon, [Dartmoor and the Devonshire
     Countryside] (c. 1633)   288
   Richard James, [Pendle Hill and the Wild Moorlands]
     (1636)   290
   Gerrard Winstanley, "The barren land shall be made
     fruitful" (1649)   291

Mountains, Hills, Vales   292
    Robert Southwell, "A Vale of Tears" (c. 1578)   292
    Thomas Churchyard, "A Discourse of Mountains" (1587)   294
    William Browne, "A Landscape" and "Description of a
        Solitary Vale" (1613)   297
    Thomas Hobbes, from *The Wonders of the Peak* (c. 1627)   299
    Anne Kemp, "A Contemplation on Basset's Down Hill"
        (c. 1658)   301
    Thomas Burnet, "Concerning the Mountains of the Earth"
        (1684)   303
    Jane Barker, "The Prospect of a Landscape, Beginning with
        a Grove" (1688)   305

Lakes, Rivers, Oceans   307
    Richard Brathwaite, "The Lake" (1634)   307
    William Browne, [Marina and the River-God] (1613)   308
    John Taylor, from *Taylor on Thame Isis* (1632)   310
    Henry Vaughan, "To the River Usk" (1651)   312
    John Donne, "The Storm" and "The Calm" (1597)   315
    Samuel Daniel, [Milford Haven] (1610)   317
    Anonymous, *A Poetical Sea-Piece* (1633)   320
    Margaret Cavendish, "Similarizing the Sea to Meadows
        and Pastures" (1653)   322
    Thomas Heyrick, from "The Submarine Voyage" (1691)   323

           PART IV   *Interactions*   327

Animal-Baiting   329
    Robert Laneham, [Bear-Baiting at Kenilworth] (1575)   329
    Philip Stubbes, "Bear-baiting and other Exercises Used
        Unlawfully in Ailgna" (1583)   330
    Robert Wild, "The Combat of the Cocks" (1637)   333

Hunting, Hawking   336
    John Caius, "Why there are no wolves in England" (1570)   336
    George Gascoigne, "The Woeful Words of the Hart to the
        Hunter" and "The Otter's Oration" (1575)   337
    Henry Porter, [Lady Smith's Denunciation of the Hunt] (1597) 341
    Jonas Poole, [Killing Polar Bears and Walrus in the Arctic]
        (1606, 1609)   343
    Margaret Cavendish, "The Hunting of the Hare" (1653)   347
    George Turberville, "In Commendation of Hawking" (1575)   350

Fishing   353

    John Dee, "Manifold disorder used about fry and spawn"
      (1577)   353
    Thomas Bastard, "There is no fish in brooks" and "De
      Piscatione" (1598)   354
    John Dennys, from *The Secrets of Angling* (1613)   355
    Timothy Granger, *Seventeen Monstrous Fishes Taken in
      Suffolk* (1568)   358
    Edmund Waller, from "The Battle of the Summer Islands"
      (1645)   359

Pet-Keeping   363

    John Caius, "Of the delicate, neat, and pretty kind of dogs
      called the Spaniel Gentle, or the Comforter" (1570)   363
    John Harington, "To His Wife, for striking her Dog"
      (c. 1600)   364
    Anonymous, "The Old Woman's Legacy to Her Cat" (1695)   364
    George Gifford, [Witches' Familiars] (1593)   365

Cooking, Feasting, Fasting, Healing   369

    Thomas Dawson, from *The Good Housewife's Jewel* (1587)   369
    Thomas Nashe, "Nature in England is But
      Plain Dame" (1592)   371
    John Harington, "Against Feasting" and "In Defence of
      Lent" (c. 1600)   372
    Thomas Middleton, from *A Chaste Maid
      in Cheapside* (c. 1613)   374
    Thomas Moffett, "Of Fatting of Meats" (1655)   377
    Thomas Tryon, "The Voice of the Dumb, or the
      Complaints of the Creatures" (1691)   379
    John Fletcher, "Enter Clorin the Shepherdess, sorting of
      herbs and telling the natures of them" (1610)   383
    Aletheia Talbot, from *Natura Exenterata* (1655)   385
    William Cole, "Of the Signatures of Plants" (1656)   390
    Margaret Baker, "Of Millefeuille or Yarrow and His Great
      Virtue" (c. 1675)   392

    PART V   *Environmental Problems in Early Modern England*   393

Population   395

    Thomas Harriot, "An estimable reckoning how many
      persons may inhabit the whole world" (c. 1590)   395
    Thomas Dekker and Thomas Middleton, "The Necessity
      of a Plague" (1603)   396

Thomas Freeman, "London's Progress" (1614)   397
Walter Ralegh, "Necessary War" (c. 1615)   398
Gabriel Plattes, from *A Discovery of Infinite Treasure* (1639)   400
William Petty, from *An Essay Concerning the Multiplication
    of Mankind* (1682)   401

Enclosure   403
Thomas More, "English Sheep Devourers of Men" (1516;
    Ralph Robinson translation 1551)   403
Thomas Bastard, "Sheep have eat up our meadows and our
    downs" and "When the great forests" dwelling was so
    wide" (1598)   405
John Harington, "Of Sheep Turned Wolves" (c. 1600)   405
John Taylor, from *Taylor's Pastoral* (1624)   406
Anonymous, "The Diggers of Warwickshire to all other
    Diggers" (1607)   408
Gerrard Winstanley *et al.,* from *The True Levellers' Standard
    Advanced* (1649)   409
Henry King, "Woe to the worldly men" (1657)   411

Deforestation   413
Robin Clidro, "Marchan Wood" (c. 1545–1580)   413
Anonymous, "Glyn Cynon Wood" (c. 1600)   414
William Harrison, "Of Woods" (1577)   416
John Lyly, "The Crime of Erysichthon" (c. 1588)   418
John Harington, "Of the Growth of Trees, to Sir Hugh
    Portman" (c. 1600)   422
John Norden, "Articles of Inquiry from a Court of Survey"
    and "Gentlemen Sell Their Woods too Fast" (1607)   422
Michael Drayton, [Deforestation in *Poly-Olbion*] (1612, 1622)   426
Michael Drayton, "The Tenth Nymphal" (1630)   430
Gerard Boate, "Woods much diminished in Ireland since
    the first coming in of the English" (1645)   434
Margaret Cavendish, "A Dialogue between an Oak and a
    Man cutting him down" (1653)   435
Abraham Cowley, [The Oak's Prophecy] (1662; Aphra
    Behn translation 1689)   441
John Aubrey, "This whole island was anciently one great
    forest" (c. 1656–1685)   445

The Draining of the Fens   448
Michael Drayton, "Holland Fen" (1622)   448
Ben Jonson, "The Duke of Drowned Land" (1616)   452
Penny of Wisbech, "The Pout's Complaint" (c. 1619)   454

Anonymous, "The Draining of the Fens" (c. 1620–1660) 457
Gerard Boate, "Draining of the Bogs practised by the
    English in Ireland" (1645) 458
John Bunyan, "The Slough of Despond" (c. 1660–1678) 460
Samuel Fortrey?, "A True and Natural Description of the
    Great Level of the Fens" (c. 1660–1680) 462

Pollution 469
Edmund Spenser, [Mammon's Delve] (1590) 469
Gawin Smith, "For the Cleansing and Clean Keeping and
    Continuing Sweet of the Ditches about the Walls of
    London" (c. 1610) 471
Ben Jonson, "On the Famous Voyage" (1616) 473
Patrick Hannay, "Croydon clothed in black" (1622) 477
Hugh Plat, "Sea-coal sweetened and multiplied" (1603) 479
Thomas Middleton, "The Mist of Error" (1613) 481
William Strode, [The Chimney-Sweeper's Song] (c. 1640) 483
Anonymous, "Upon the Foggy Air, Sea-coal Smoke, Dirt,
    Filth, and Mire of London," (c. 1640–1660) 486
William Davenant, "London is smothered with sulph'rous
    fires" (1656) 487
John Evelyn, from *Fumifugium* (1661) 488

    PART VI   *Disaster and Resilience in the Little Ice Age* 495
Extreme Weather, Disorder, Dearth 497
John Heywood, from *The Play of the Weather* (1533) 497
Roger Ascham, [The Wind on the Snow] (1545) 500
Thomas Hill, "The End, Effect, and Signification of
    Comets" (1567) 501
Abraham Fleming, "A Terrible Tempest in Norfolk" (1577) 503
Thomas Nashe, "Backwinter" (c. 1592–1600) 504
Ludwig Lavater and William Barlow, "Dearth" (1596) 510
John Stradling, "The Incredible Flooding of the Severn"
    and "Another Poem on the Flood" (1607) 515
William Browne, "As Tavy creeps" (1613) 517
Thomas Dekker?, *The Great Frost* (1608) 518
John Taylor, "The Frozen Age" (1621) 522
William Cartwright, "On the Great Frost, 1634" (1634) 524
Henry Coventry, "On the Dry Summer" (1636) 526
Gabriel Plattes, "Islands of Ice" (1639) 528
John Evelyn, "The Freezing of the Thames" (1684) 529

Decay   531
    John Lilliat, "Finding few fruit upon the Oak" (c. 1596)   531
    Thomas Bastard, "Our fathers did but use the world
       before" (1598)   531
    Edmund Spenser, "Two Cantos of Mutability" (c. 1598)   532
    John Donne, from *An Anatomy of the World* (1611)   547

Resilience   554
    Joachim Du Bellay, "Then I beheld the fair Dodonian tree"
       (1558; Edmund Spenser translation 1569)   554
    George Wither, "*A Posteritati*: He that delights to Plant and
       Set" (c. 1620)   555
    George Hakewill, "Of this Pretended Decay" (1627)   556
    Michael Drayton, from "Noah's Flood" (1630)   559

Appendix A   *Industrialization and Environmental Legislation
in the Early Anthropocene: A Timeline*   564
Appendix B   *Further Reading: A Bibliography of Environmental
Scholarship on the English Renaissance*   581

ILLUSTRATIONS

1 Johann Theodor de Bry, "Mirror of All Nature and
the Image of Art," from Robert Fludd, *Utriusque cosmi ...
historia* (1621). John Hay Library, Brown University.   *page* 14

2 Bacton Altar Cloth (c. 1590). © Historic Royal Palaces.   15

3 Mandrake, from *Hortus Sanitatus* (1491). © British Library Board.   18

4 Mandrake, from John Gerard, *Herbal* (1597). Wellcome Library.   18

5 Nathaniel Bacon, "Landscape" (c. 1610–1627). © Ashmolean
Museum, University of Oxford.   19

6 Isaac Oliver, "Edward Herbert" (c. 1610). National Trust.
Todd White Art Photography.   281

7 Clement Walker, "The Royal Oak of Britain" (1649). © Trustees
of the British Museum. Creative Commons licence
CC BY-NC-SA 4.0.   440

8 Jonas Moore, "Map of the Fens" (c. 1685). © British
Library Board.   468

9 The Chimney-Sweep Mulled-Sack (c. 1620). Wellcome Library.   484

10 The Bristol Channel Floods, from *Wonderful Overflowings
of Waters* (1607). © British Library Board.   516

11 Frost Fair, from *Wonders on the Deep* (1684). © Trustees of
the British Museum. Creative Commons licence
CC BY-NC-SA 4.0.   523

ACKNOWLEDGEMENTS

In a feverish effort to compile an exhaustive survey of England's topography and natural history, the Tudor antiquarian John Leland reportedly "fell beside his wits" (Smith xiv). There were moments during the preparation of this anthology when those around me may have wondered if I were destined to suffer the same fate. Fortunately, my mental balance was kept within a half bubble of plumb by the encouragement and advice of dozens of wonderful people. Thanks are due first of all to my former research assistant, Clare Egan, who helped unearth and transcribe several of the manuscripts. An ex-student, Clarissa Coffay, volunteered to assist with this project in its early days, and meticulously prepared extensive selections from Topsell and Gerard. This anthology would not have been possible without the generous support I received from the University of Huddersfield in funding many of my numerous trips to archives. I am particularly grateful to my colleague Jessica Malay, who has acted as both a sounding board and pillar of support.

The quality of this anthology was improved tenfold by the feedback of some fellow scholars who commented on the manuscript in its pupal stage: among them are Jennifer Munroe, Vin Nardizzi, Karen Raber, and Robert Watson. The following also kindly offered input on the selections or shared their expertise: Keith Botello, Lynne Bruckner, Rebecca Bushnell, Joe Campana, Jeffrey Cohen, Lowell Duckert, Gabriel Egan, James Ellis, Simon Estok, David Goldstein, Rose Hadshar, Bonnie Lander Johnson, Rebecca Laroche, Randall Martin, Tayler Meredith, John Morgan, Katharine Norbury, Peter Remien, Marjorie Swann, Jeffrey Theis, Amy Tigner, Rebecca Totaro, Bart van Es, and Tiffany Werth.

This book had its genesis in the classroom, and its contents have been tried and tested over the past decade by students at the University of Washington, Bloomsburg University, and the University of Huddersfield. I remain indebted to them for their willingness to root through some dense texts, as their comments and essays have helped me to package the selections for a wider readership. Thanks are also owed to the battalion of librarians who assisted with my requests at various archives: Bodleian Library, British Library, Brotherton Library, Cambridge University Library, Corpus Christi College (Oxford), Dulwich College, Folger Shakespeare Library, John Rylands Library, the National Archives (at Bradford, Derbyshire, Kew, Lincolnshire, and Northamptonshire), New York Public Library, Parker Library, Rosenbach, St John's College (Cambridge), and Wellcome Library.

I am much obliged to Gwydion Williams for permission to reproduce his father's mesmeric translations of some Welsh poems. Dana Sutton, Martin Wiggins, and the University of Birmingham also kindly granted permission to reprint translations of two Latin poems about the Bristol Channel flood. Thanks to the Syndics of Cambridge University Library for allowing me to cite manuscripts of "The Combat of the Cocks" and "The Draining of the Fens." Excerpts from Bruno's *Cause, Principle, Unity* appear courtesy of Cambridge University Press. Gratitude also prompts me to make a deep bow in the direction of my editors at Cambridge, Sarah Stanton and Emily Hockley, for championing this unorthodox project, coping with my panicked emails, and gently reminding me of the ecological principle that less is often more. The keen eye of Damian Love saved me from several embarrassing mistakes and helped bring the manuscript into publishable shape. As always, my profoundest thanks are to my family for their support and patience over the years. I am forever grateful to my parents, who nurtured my love of English culture at a young age and have heroically managed to overcome their displeasure at my decision to move to England. This anthology would not have been possible if my wife and two sons had not agreed to leap the pond with me in the fall of 2014. The countless hours spent at archives and before the computer have been relieved by their companionship, especially on long walks along the windswept footpaths of our hilltop Yorkshire village, gaining the acquaintance of the flora and fauna. While much energy (and yes, petrol) has been poured into this anthology, it is in essence, a labour-saving device: may the time I have spent blackberrying in dim archives free up more afternoons for its readers to go blackberrying outdoors. In the process of compiling these entries and then strolling out into the Yorkshire countryside, I have come to appreciate the wisdom in the paradox of the Victorian nature writer Richard Jefferies: "It seems as if the chief value of books is to give us something to unlearn" (44). If nothing else, this volume can fulfil that purpose. Insofar as the Renaissance marks the advancement of a purely human learning, to read between the lines of Francis Bacon's title, we have much to unlearn from it. But some of its greatest minds, such as Montaigne and Shakespeare, can also remind us of how much more we will never know. Like Thomas Wyatt trying to snare the wind in a net, perhaps this book is ultimately an awkward demonstration of the incapacity of the human intellect to capture the staggering complexity of our greater-than-human environment.

EDITORIAL PRINCIPLES:
TOWARDS THE ECOCRITICAL EDITING OF RENAISSANCE TEXTS

At the outset, some decisions were made to prepare this anthology in accordance with a few basic guidelines:

- Modernize spelling and punctuation (exceptions noted below).
- Annotate to define archaic words, explain obscure allusions, and record original spellings or textual variants where they may have added significance (particularly if they assist ecocritical interpretation).
- Preserve capitalization when it has rhetorical force, or may imply elevation to a proper noun.
- Preserve original punctuation when it may aid comprehension or enhance rhetorical impact.
- Deploy diacritical marks and syncope in verse to help with scansion.

Each of these choices has significant implications, and thus calls for a brief defence. Modernizing is of course a standard practice with editions intended for classroom use. Thanks to the growing accessibility of Renaissance books in digital format, the need for original spelling is no longer so pressing. Readability seems paramount. Moreover, modernizing should, if only on a subliminal level, help drive home the message that Elizabethan writers, while not exactly our contemporaries, were tussling with and can speak to problems not unfamiliar to twenty-first-century readers. As for punctuation, the plain fact is that in many early modern books it is not authorial but was often left to the whims of the compositors or printers. Sniffing at a modernized text thus seems as obstinate as refusing to attend a production of Shakespeare in modern dress or pronunciation.

Nevertheless, during the painstaking process of editing this anthology I became increasingly aware of the pitfalls of strict modernization. Due to the scope of the contents, implementing a rigid one-size-fits-all policy seemed far too constrictive. The verse of Skelton and the prose of Aubrey call for very different editorial interventions in both degree and kind. As its critics have observed, modernized spelling can blunt or efface the polysemous complexity of certain words. For instance, early modern readers encountering a "forrest" are subtly alerted to its status as a game preserve, a shelter where beasts go "for rest." When a tract by Winstanley spells

mankind as "Manking" and oppression as "oppresin," can one be confident that these are mere typos and silently emend them? Similarly, it seems
almost collusive to ignore that a royal hunt and bear-baiting took place at
"Killingworth" (instead of Kenilworth) Castle. Changing humane to human, fawn to faun, travailling to travelling, arguably diminishes some of
the lexical charge these words possessed in early modern usage. When confronted with such cruxes, I have followed Stanley Wells's advice to adopt
the modern spelling for the dominant meaning and to annotate to capture
additional resonances lurking in the original.

Capitalization presents a tougher challenge. Most modern-spelling editions today conform to current usage. In an ecocritical edition, however,
decapitalizing feels tantamount to decapitation. Beginning a noun with
an uppercase letter can endow it with a dignity or honorary subjectivity,
which is not necessarily the same thing as anthropomorphism. Texts by the
Sidneys, Drayton, Lanyer, Cavendish, and Tryon often – though madden-
ingly, not always – capitalize the names of animals or topographical features as they seek to transform our sense of nature's agency and the ethical
status of non-humans. Conversely, other writers like Herbert sometimes
deploy a capital M to puff Man up above the rest of creation. These nu-
ances matter. Unlike old spellings, they cannot be documented neatly in a
footnote. Consider, for instance, this specimen of Renaissance verse: "The
World's a Book in Folio, printed all / With God's great Works in Letters
Capital." Many Jacobean readers would have agreed with the insinuation
by the poet Du Bartas and his English translator that God's creatures deserve to be capitalized in the same way one capitalizes the title of a literary
work. The recent "materialist turn" makes the argument for preserving
original capitalization even more compelling since it seems to bestow a
greater existential stature on a word. In a note scrawled on the inside cover
of a collection of Thomas Traherne's manuscripts, his Edwardian editor
remarks, "in Traherne's handwriting there is an abundance of capital letters – so much so that this is a distinguishing feature" (Bodleian MS Eng.
poet c.42). With a writer like Traherne, this blitz of capitals is more than
an idiosyncrasy; it is symptomatic of the poet's quasi-animistic spirituality.
Admittedly, capitals at times do seemingly sprout up at random, but wrestling with these texts forced me to revise my initial policy and let readers
decide for themselves which instances are rhetorically significant. While
not every single capitalized letter can be assumed to be authorial or to deliver an animating jolt, this edition asks readers to entertain the possibility
that the liberal capitalization that prevailed during the Renaissance reflects
a pre-mechanistic worldview that was perhaps closer to what contemporary theorists would call object-oriented, and could, before we were modern, amplify the non-human voice in a Parliament of Things.

The prevalence of rhythm and rhyme in Renaissance literature, meanwhile, speaks to the cultural yearning for a cosmos (and polity) pervaded

by order. Consequently, editors should try to avoid interfering with these patterns, especially as deviations can coincide with outbursts of disorder, like the "swervings" that worried theologian Richard Hooker. The need to accommodate rhythm and rhyme also pushed Renaissance writers to employ a Latinate syntax which can shatter the subject-verb-object mould of modern English and thus allow for more flexible conceptions of agency. On related grounds, it seems worthwhile to differentiate (when possible) between an exclamatory "oh" voicing anguish or surprise and the vocative "O" which can address and personify the inhuman. Editors should also follow this commandment: thou shalt not tamper with "thou," which, as Martin Buber demonstrated, can bind humans and the environment in a more ethical rapport. For the same reason, it would be a distortion to introduce neutral pronouns, and textual apparatus should note variants in pronoun usage in different manuscripts or editions. When Macbeth gloats that none can "bid the tree unfix *his* earthbound root" (4.1.111) or Mary Wroth or George Morley refer to the nightingale as *her*, the pronouns betray the persistent anthropomorphizing and gendering of other species, offering precedents (albeit ambiguous ones) for the challenge to post-Enlightenment usage by some in animal studies and the new field of ecolinguistics.

Could one also argue that there is an ecological undercurrent in pre-modern punctuation? While modern usage prefers to slice and segment thought into tidy, discrete units, the loose-jointed, rambling syntax of the Renaissance seems to emphasize the ecological principle of connectivity: a fluidity of clauses encoding a fluidity of relations between subjects, objects, actions, consequences, and other subjects. Many seventeenth-century writers such as Mary Wroth and John Evelyn composed long sentences like meandering paths through a wood, or like Rube Goldberg devices, where causes trigger effects that in turn trigger other causes and so on. Even when the punctuation is not authorial, it still reflects reading habits of a culture accustomed to tease out complex relationships across grammatical and ontological divides. Since enhancing the perception of connnectivity is a cardinal duty of ecocritics there is some justification for retaining this rhetorical punctuation. Thus this edition, while weeding out many commas that retard the reading, preserves some long sentences when occasion demands, deploying the semicolon as a super comma for a brief pause and the colon for a longer pause or amplification.

By following a policy of selective modernization, this anthology could be accused of being "neither fish nor flesh," a complaint gracefully deflected by the editors of the Digital Renaissance Editions. Such a dish may not be to the taste of purists, but ecology is a discipline that pays little devotion to purity. It seems far more important to make texts accessible for modern readers while also enabling them to glimpse the vitalistic, pre-Enlightenment sensibility interwoven into the stylistic warp and woof of Renaissance texts. Instead of choosing to be either stringently historicist or stridently presentist, an ecocritical edition has a divided duty. If this anthology encourages more students and scholars to cross-pollinate the study of Renaissance literature and the environmental humanities, its chief ambition will have been fulfilled.

INTRODUCTION

Observing the population levels of 7,964 native species and cross-referencing the results with a Biodiversity Intactness Index, conservationists have pronounced the United Kingdom to be one of the most "nature-depleted countries in the world."[1] Not coincidentally, it also has the dubious distinction of being among the least forested in Europe: its 13 per cent wood cover (10 per cent in England) barely amounts to a third of the EU average of 38 per cent.[2] Since conservation biology trades in hard statistics gleaned from consistent observation, the 2016 State of Nature Report defines "long term" as the past forty years. But Britain was not de-wilded in a few decades. It has been a centuries-long saga, one of the most eventful chapters of which coincides with the great cultural flowering known as the Renaissance.

Despite the fact forty years is an eyeblink in geological terms, ecocriticism has tended to patrol a narrow strip of the recent past. While this is in part due to an admirable concern for the here and now, it also results from a myopia induced by crude narratives in cultural and environmental history. Surely, before Wordsworth gazed down upon the Wye Valley no one bothered to peer "into the life of things." Prior to Darwin's *Origin of Species*, humans fancied themselves the god-like overlords of creation. Only after the Industrial Revolution and post-war pesticides endangered it did the environment come into focus as a realm in need of protection. While puncturing such blithe assumptions is one of the objectives of this book, it has become abundantly clear that environmental criticism need not – and indeed should not – confine itself to anthems to a green and pleasant land. It bears remembering that the picturesque landscapes around Tintern Abbey and the Lake District that so enraptured Wordsworth were wrought by deforestation from ironworks and charcoal-making, and that much of the worst damage occurred in the sixteenth century.[3] The commitment of second-wave ecocritics to move "beyond nature writing" has given wings to a chronological leap beyond the contemporary and Romantic eras into earlier periods when prevailing attitudes towards the natural world were, by and large, not so eco-friendly but which demand all the more scrutiny by virtue of their difference.

---

[1] See Eaton's summary. Interestingly, the report argues that climate change's impact is ambiguous, helping some species while threatening others, and instead places most of the blame on intensive agriculture.

[2] Forest Research, "*Forestry Statistics 2017: International Forestry.*" www.forestresearch.gov.uk/ tools-and-resources/statistics/forestry-statistics/forestry-statistics-2017/international-forestry

[3] On "Tintern Abbey," see Levinson, 29–32, and the timeline in Appendix A.

At the turn of the millennium, excavating the ecological politics of Renaissance literature might have seemed a laughably anachronistic undertaking. Thanks to the diligent toils of a legion of scholars, whose insights I have sought to graft into this anthology, that is no longer the case.[4] Tudor England reformed more than its religion; it embarked on a vigorous campaign to "improve" its fields, woods, moors, waterways, and fens. Examining these developments would once have been considered the province of the small sub-discipline of agrarian history. Now that the Anthropocene, as Dipesh Chakrabarty powerfully argues, has both dissolved the boundaries between natural history and human history and exposed how modernity's freedoms have been purchased with the spoils of planetary conquest, investigating the roots of our species' emergence as a geological force has become an urgent task for the environmental humanities. Whether or not the scientific community accepts Lewis and Maslin's proposal that the "Orbis spike" of 1610 (coinciding roughly with the establishment of the first permanent English settlement in North America and the premiere of Shakespeare's *Tempest*) heralds the onset of this brave new era, the two centuries after Columbus's voyage indisputably represent a pivotal moment in the history of the earth. Of course tallying up the facts and figures of harvest yields, wool exports, and tree cover can only tell so much of the story; it is vital to probe the underlying beliefs and aesthetics that propelled, resisted, or adapted to these efforts to understand and colonize the natural world. Elizabethan poets, playwrights, and naturalists often bear witness to the changes unfolding around them, and the entries gathered here present something like a biocultural audit of the English Renaissance.

The past decade has produced a bumper crop of monographs and edited collections on Renaissance literature and the environment, yet the field still lacks a teachable compendium of primary texts. Since ecocriticism boasts a commitment to praxis, packaging and relaying research to students and the broader public is every bit as important as publishing an erudite article in a scholarly journal. This anthology is not targeted solely at undergraduates, however. It should also serve as a vade mecum or sourcebook to galvanize further critical research. It advances original interpretations of dozens of texts, and presents the fruits of painstaking archival labour on both sides of the Atlantic, sifting through hundreds of manuscripts: from forestry surveys to psalm translations to Star Chamber cases to poems about the weather to patents for clean coal. Collectively, these materials expose the eco-material muck that underlies literary production in Renaissance England.

Compiling a new anthology is always a cherry-picking, and a new theoretical movement nudges one to trawl through untrodden rows in the orchard, even if – as in Proserpina's Garden – not everything that grows there

---

[4] A thorough list of scholarship that has informed this anthology can be found in Appendix B, "Further Reading: A Bibliography of Environmental Scholarship on the English Renaissance."

is sweet. Just as feminism and post-colonial studies broadcast the voices of those marginalized or silenced due to gender and race, ecocriticism makes a place at (not just on) the table for the other species with whom we share the planet. The disturbing corollaries between the oppression of the Other and the exploitation of nature make ecocriticism a logical extension of, rather than a diversion from, these earlier critical insurgencies. It demands a radical shift in both how we read and what we read. It demands a change in how we teach and what we teach. It demands, in other words, a new anthology.

By unearthing over two hundred nature-themed texts and presenting them in accessible modern spelling, this book offers itself as a friendly field guide for ecocritical studies on Renaissance England. Spanning the disciplines of literature, science, and history, it unveils a radiant panorama of a nation at a crossroads between its pastoral heritage and industrialized future. Its contents comprise a *Wunderkammer* of primary sources on nature and natural history during a time of intense cultural ferment and dramatic environmental change. Readers will be escorted on a bracing tour of the nation's natural splendours and survey some pressing environmental concerns. Instead of a uniformly verdant and pleasant land, England is revealed to be coping with problems all too familiar to twenty-first-century readers: deforestation, pollution, resource scarcity, extinction, overpopulation, and a volatile climate. The selections cover an encyclopaedic range of topics: from astrology to zoology, bear-baiting to bee-keeping, coal-mining to tree-planting, fen-draining to sheep-whispering. Venturing beyond green spaces, the entries take stock of the recent critical turn to the "blue" and "brown" spectra of our terraqueous planet (and add the "white" of the Little Ice Age), sketching a more prismatic picture of the Renaissance.[5] Familiar voices like those of Spenser, Shakespeare, Jonson, and Marvell mingle with a chorus of unsung writers whose works are destined to become touchstones for ecocriticism. Its contributors include farmers, philosophers, herbalists, sailors, bishops, heretics, surveyors, shepherds, entomologists, duchesses, Diggers, hunters, vegetarians, and demographers – not to mention Orphic poets and a motley herd of talking rivers, trees, satyrs, and others animals. Here is nature's plenty.

In garnering the contents, an effort has been made to include writings by men and women from across the socio-economic spectrum and throughout the British Isles. This teeming variety should facilitate consideration of the ways in which gender, class, religion, and region factor into how humans relate to their surroundings. Although early modern England, the first industrialized society, remains its cynosure, the collection encompasses ancient creation myths and apocalyptic predictions of the future. It ranges from the sewers of London to the shrinking woodlands of Arden and the Weald, from Bass Rock in Scotland to the bogs of Ireland. It draws particular attention to the mountainous Welsh landscape – the Renaissance equivalent of the Lake

---

[5] See works by Cohen, Brayton, Mentz, and Eklund.

District – so admired by Churchyard, Drayton, and Vaughan, and the marginalized tradition of Welsh poetry to invite consideration of whether this culture was more eco-conscious than that of its Anglo-Saxon neighbours (or became so because it was being exploited more aggressively after the 1536 unification). Readers can even stow away on English expeditions to hunt walrus and polar bear in the Arctic and vicariously join in the "fun" of firing heavy artillery at a beached whale in Bermuda. Featuring scores of obscure or understudied works, and repotting familiar texts in new ecological contexts, this anthology reframes the landscape of early modern literary studies and sizeably extends the vista of the environmental humanities.

Needless to say, *Literature and Nature in the English Renaissance* does not pretend to be comprehensive. How could it be? There are simply so many texts that represent the non-human environment that to include them all would swell the book to backbreaking proportions. Nevertheless, the scope and diversity of the contents are hopefully rich enough that they can enable ecocritical readings of virtually any Renaissance text, empowering both novice students and seasoned researchers to probe what Lawrence Buell has called an "environmental unconscious" (2001, 18–22) in writings that do not overtly depict nature. It is not an attempt to delimit a green canon but creatively curate a heterogeneous collection of specimens – many of them tested out in the classroom over the past decade – showcasing some of the multifarious beliefs, literary tactics, and techno-material practices through which people in Tudor and Stuart England understood, represented, and impacted their environment. While this anthology does propose some new ways of conceptualizing the Renaissance, it does not champion a grand unified theory: rather its guiding premise is that a single master narrative seeking to impose unity and intelligibility on the chaotic realities of the ecosphere would be reductive and misleading. Instead of presuming to offer definitive answers and shut down critical debates, this anthology intends to dramatize them and open up pathways for further research.

Two Myths of Environmental History

By selecting texts from a range of authors and literary genres and thus making it difficult to spin pat, one-sided narratives, this anthology aims to steer a *via media* between two myths that plague environmental history, which, for brevity's sake, one might label neo-Ovidian primitivism and neo-Hobbesian barbarism. The first designates the tendency to idealize the past as an immaculate golden age when all humans lived in greater harmony with the environment, the seasons, and other creatures. The second myth is the bleak vision of all pre-moderns as figurative heathens oblivious of the gospel of ecology and hell-bent on dominating and enslaving nature. Evidence for each of these views is not far to seek, and often appears very seductive.

On behalf of Ovidian or soft primitivism, one might observe that the English population in 1600 was much closer to what environmentalists now consider sustainable: Elizabethan London was home to around 200,000 people – roughly the size today of a town like Akron, Ohio or Luton (which the megapolis of Greater London now threatens to engulf) – and much of the area outside the medieval city walls was still green space; in John Donne's day, St Martin-in-the-Fields, in what is now the bustling Trafalgar Square, was still located in actual fields, and Lambeth was still marsh. Moreover, the majority of the population grew or raised much of their own food, living in greater proximity to livestock and wildlife, and Elizabethan texts often assume a familiarity with flora and fauna that few twenty-first-century readers possess. Renaissance writers were also deeply enamoured with the more earth-centred spirituality of ancient Greece and Rome, and a residual animism enlivens much of the poetry of this era. Carolyn Merchant's ecofeminist classic, *The Death of Nature*, asserted that the modern scientific method pioneered in the seventeenth-century by Francis Bacon and his acolytes spelled the doom of this enchanted cosmology and reconstituted the universe as mechanistic and inert. Meanwhile, Gabriel Egan has proposed that the much-maligned "Elizabethan World Picture," with its sense of correspondences across species, could nurture a proto-ecological mentality.

If Shakespeare and his contemporaries did not have a vocabulary of ready-made phrases such as biotic equilibrium or carbon footprint, they possessed other words suggestive of their physical intimacy with the environment. In *Landmarks*, Robert Macfarlane calls for a revival of these obsolete terms – like "smeuse" (a gap in a hedge made by small animals) and "ungive" (an East Anglian coinage for thaw) – on the grounds that they can provide "a vast glossary of Enchantment … that would allow nature to talk back to us and would help us to listen" (32). This anthology includes hundreds of such archaic words, and the glosses are not intended as substitutes but as tools for salvaging and reactivating the ways of seeing they encode. Some of the entries offer snapshots of what are now rare or extinct species, and diminished or even lost ecologies. Consider, for instance, this description of how the English landscape would have appeared to a hypothetical Elizabethan traveller:

> In some parts [one] would see flocks of several thousand sheep grazing over nearly a quarter of a county; in other parts [one] would be confronted by huge stretches of woodland or waste that have all by now been either cut down or reclaimed or else reduced to comparatively insignificant dimensions. [Riding] between Brandon and Peterborough [one] would pass by … an enormous stretch of fen more than 3,000 acres in extent. [One] would find Lancashire three parts morass or "moss," and Cannock Chase in Staffordshire still a mighty oak forest covering, with Needwood, a third of the county. (Byrne 105)

Arguably, only an understanding of environmental history before large-scale industrialization affords the necessary perspective to discern the "slow violence" (Nixon) through which humans have transformed the earth over the past five centuries. In reviving a past less "smeared with trade" and tainted by "man's smudge," this brand of ecohistoricism has a surprising affinity with the contemporary movement known as "re-wilding."[6]

The underside of this apple, however, does not look so savoury. Raymond Williams famously documented an "escalator" effect in which each generation idealizes the previous one as living in greater concord with nature (9–11). In literary history, the glamorization of the Renaissance as the "Golden Age" of English literature can all too readily be compounded with Ovidian myths of an idyllic past. This tendency is already full-blown in Romantic critics such as Schiller and Gervinus, the latter of whom asserted, "in Shakespeare's time, nature had not yet become extinct" (881). Such elegiac historiography tends to yearn for a Merry Olde England and lament "The World We Have Lost." Even when based in fact, wistful visions of the pre-industrial landscape like the one cited in the preceding paragraph can quickly descend into spurious claims that medieval Britain was one pristine greenwood, which a squirrel could cross from the Severn to the Wash without setting its paws on the ground. Insofar as it imagines an almost prelapsarian vision of the past, this "redemptive mode" (Mackenzie) of ecohistoricism must be inspected warily for distortions.

To state the obvious, the people of Tudor England did not fret about greenhouse gases or dichlorodiphenyltrichloroethane. They did not conduct sustained inquiries into the population dynamics among species in an ecosystem. What looks like ecological sentiment is often enlightened economic self-interest rather than genuine ethical concern for the rights of non-humans. As Bruce Boehrer cautions, environmental protests in the Jacobean period are entangled within and subservient to "a much broader complex of political, social, and religious grievances" (2013, 167). Revealingly, one of the pioneering studies of Renaissance ecocriticsm traced the ways in which the pastoral's nostalgia for the "green" is rooted in epistemological anxieties over human alienation from the "real" (Watson 2006). To study early modern natural history is to encounter ways of seeing and inhabiting the world that can be alien to a post-Enlightenment and post-Darwinian mentality. If this makes "doing ecocriticism" with writers like Shakespeare more challenging, it also makes it more exhilarating. It also renders the need for a scholarly anthology with an explanatory apparatus all the more pressing.

Rather than a time of harmonious dwelling, the Tudor era can just as easily be pegged as a time of de-wilding. In early modern usage, the word "forest" signifies a royal hunting ground (which may or may not be wooded) and uncultivated land was not glorified as wilderness but decried as "waste." This betrays a profoundly human-centred view of the

---

[6] The best-known spokesperson for re-wilding in England is George Monbiot. For a representative critique of re-wilding as perpetuating the nature/culture split, see Jørgenson. Given that Europe has been densely populated for so much longer than North America, it has been suggested that "re-naturing" would be a more realistic ideal (Westphal et al.).

world which environmentalists today, following the lead of William Blake, would classify as a devil's proverb: "Where man is not, nature is barren." If the UK's tree cover now seems worrisomely low, it is probably higher now (by about 2 per cent) than it was during Drayton's lifetime. For many early moderns, the standard of living was too precarious to allow the luxury of concern for non-humans. Agricultural labourers – the vast majority of the populace – would have been too preoccupied keeping the proverbial wolf from the door to squander a thought on the well-being of other species. Indeed, actual wolves had been deliberately exterminated from England in the late Middle Ages as wool became the chief staple of the English economy. Tudor "Vermin Laws" rewarding the wholesale slaughter of species deemed to be pests were, moreover, endorsed by Christian scripture. In a notorious article, Lynn White argued that Genesis 1:26–8 provided European civilization with a biblical warrant to exploit the earth and commandeer its resources. To most people prior to the Industrial Revolution, untamed nature must have seemed a complex of hostile forces that God commanded humanity to subdue. Such views undergird Simon Estok's diagnosis that Shakespeare's era was afflicted with "ecophobia" – a fear and loathing of the otherness and unpredictability of the environment.

Rather than discredit these two narratives, this anthology seeks to moderate them by playing them against each other. If Christianity sanctioned dominion, its natural theology could foster a belief in the sanctity of the creation and all living things, as evident from Pope Francis's 2015 Encyclical, "On Care for our Common Home," which draws on the Renaissance commonplace of the earth as a "magnificent book in which God speaks to us." Crucially, anthropocentric apologists licensed material practices that soon exposed the unsustainability of their own dogma. Hence White's thesis that Christianity was eco-hostile must be qualified by the shrewd observation of historian Keith Thomas:

> It was out of the very contradictions of the old anthropocentric tradition that a new attitude would emerge. That, after all, is how most new ideas appear. Just as modern atheism is probably best understood as a conviction growing out of Christianity, rather than something encroaching upon it from an external source, so consideration of other species has its intellectual roots within the old man-centered doctrine itself. (156–7)

To highlight these contradictions, this anthology juxtaposes works espousing different viewpoints – for and against hunting, enclosure, animal-baiting, fen-draining, etc. – in the conviction that this best encapsulates the era's complexities. While historians who idealize the past should not be acquitted, the sternness of our sentence must be reduced in light of a mitigating factor recognized by Adorno: "So long as progress, deformed by utilitarianism, does violence to the surface of the earth, it will be impossible – in spite of all proof to the contrary – completely to counter the perceptions that what antedates the trend is in its backwardness better and more humane" (84). One of the tasks of this anthology is to dredge up that proof, while also presenting the opposing evidence that enables people – then and now – to discount it.

Renaissance as "Great Rebirth," Late Iron Age, Early Anthropocene, and Little Ice Age

In addition to resisting these two contrapuntal siren-songs, readers of this volume should also be aware of two other besetting temptations. The first is the presentist impulse to view the Tudor and Stuart eras retrospectively through the lens of Romanticism and modern environmentalism. The second is to overemphasize the historical ruptures and downplay the continuities. Again, this anthology does not reject either outright so much as make a bigamous commitment to both. It seeks, as Robert Watson has quipped (in a felicitous marriage of Emily Dickinson and Al Gore), to "tell inconvenient truths but tell them slant" (2015, 28).

This Janus-faced outlook is reflected in the brief introductions that accompany each selection. Depending on the text in question, these have one or more of the following aims: (1) to situate the excerpt in a larger work, author's oeuvre, or literary tradition; (2) to anchor it in early modern natural and environmental history; (3) to direct readers to relevant criticism; and (4) to spotlight issues for discussion or further research. Some of the introductions have the fifth objective of considering how later environmental developments – such as habitat destruction, species loss, and current conservation or restoration efforts – can drastically impact the way we interpret four-hundred-year-old texts. While it traces connections between past and present, this anthology remains dedicated to illuminating – rather than disregarding or greenwashing – the alterity of the Renaissance. This point needs belabouring because the environmental humanities have tended to be unabashedly present-oriented. Tellingly, the first selection in *The Norton Book of Nature Writing* comes from Gilbert White's *Natural History of Selborne*, published in 1789, often hailed as the inaugural year of modernity. Writing about nature, however, goes back at least to Aristotle if not to *Gilgamesh*, and White himself belongs to an eco-exegetical school of parson-naturalists that was already emergent in mid-Tudor times. Moreover, second-wave ecocriticism has expanded its purview beyond nature writing. The environmental humanities stand to benefit from a longue durée approach. Like ice core samples extracted from the heart of a glacier, the entries in this collection decant the environmental conditions (and mental habits) of preceding centuries. In order to understand the current predicament of industrial civilization, it is imperative to chart the road we traversed to get here. It might also be worthwhile to note what got discarded or paved over along the way by the juggernaut of technocratic capitalism, especially if, as some speculative fiction imagines (see Richard Jefferies's *After London* or Ursula Le Guin's *Always Coming Home*), we career towards a post-catastrophe future that resembles the pre- or semi-industrial past. Given Amitav Ghosh's complaint that the contemporary realist novel seems inadequate to tackle the moral tragedy of climate change, can Renaissance genres (such as tragedy, comedy, chorography, romance, utopia, or fable) furnish – by virtue of their different foci, shifting time-scales, or greater poetic licence – better alternatives? In studying Renaissance literature from an ecohistoricist angle, something more is at stake than satisfying antiquarian curiosity.

If the label "early modern" underscores continuity with the present, Renaissance might seem to look backward to Greece and Rome. One advantage of this old-fashioned period-concept is that it resists the teleological narrative of progress, while accommodating the idea of multiple, overlapping temporalities. This anthology captures the profound engagement of Tudor England with Greco-Roman antiquity and the Christian Middle Ages. Simultaneously, it invites readers to see how these received ideas were endorsed, qualified, or exploded by sixteenth- and seventeenth-century naturalists, divines, and poets. Did theocentric texts always promote human dominion, or could they foster a vision of the earth as a sacred creation that had been cursed by human malfeasance? How and why did the Renaissance revive elements of Greco-Roman culture that clashed with a human-centred worldview? How did these theories (mutability, metamorphosis, the animal soul, the World Soul, atomism, etc.) and classical tropes (such as personification and prosopopoeia) embolden some Renaissance thinkers and poets to challenge the anthropocentric orthodoxy? This book does not attempt to resurrect Jacob Burckhardt's vision of the Renaissance – itself shaped by nineteenth-century Rhine Romanticism – but to reframe it as a time of heightened appreciation of the beauty and fragility of the natural world. Inevitably, the influx of literature from sunny Italy and the Continent affected England's perceptions of its own temperate climate and natural history. Were these visions of a Mediterranean *locus amoenus* of timeless stability or perpetual spring a stultifying escape from environmental realities? Or could the bounteous Arcadian landscape provoke greater awareness of England as a far less fruitful northern island already suffering resource scarcity?

One of the crucial ways this anthology redefines the Renaissance is not merely as a cultural "rebirth" of the classical past but as an era of *resurgent birth rates* in which population levels culled in the late Middle Ages by bubonic plague catapulted upwards in an arc that continues to this day. Arguably, it was this demographic surge that fuelled more intensive resource extraction, technological innovation, and economic growth, creating more leisure for literary production and consumption. Of course Shakespeare's contemporaries did not see themselves as basking in a glamorous Renaissance; primed by Ovid, they would have been more likely to regard themselves as denizens of a squalid Iron Age, a perception that would have been strengthened by the booming iron industry in the sixteenth century. While one must be wary of technodeterminism, the development of a new contraption like the blast furnace (first

erected in England in 1490 and proliferating after the Reformation threatened iron imports from the Continent) may be just as momentous, as far as
the earth is concerned, as the coronation of a new monarch. Insofar as early
industrialization and the "Great Rebirth" ultimately pushed England ahead
of any other nation in embracing coal as its chief fuel source, the Renaissance
might be regarded as a synonym for "Early Anthropocene."

On the flip side, this portrayal of the Renaissance as a time when Homo
sapiens, like a conquistador planting his banner on newfound shores, asserted its dominion over the earth should be set against the acute sense of vul-
nerability to the climate. Indeed, the drive to reclaim wilderness and boost
food production was often motivated by recurrent harvest failures. This anthology presents ample testimony supporting the paleo-climatological evidence of this period as one of global cooling; in fact, one of its working titles
was "Literature and Nature in the Little Ice Age." Although this phenomenon or "hyperobject" (to borrow Timothy Morton's term for something so
spatially and temporally vast that it befuddles human comprehension) may
be more accurately imagined as an "increased variability of the climate"
(Mann 504) rather than a steady chill, average temperatures in northern
Europe seem to have dipped most notably throughout the seventeenth century, an occurrence that problematizes the tendency of historians to seize
on the Civil War or Interregnum as a stopping-point. Since this meteorological epoch is generally considered to stretch from 1300–1850, however, a
proper survey of it would need to run to several hefty volumes. Moreover,
defining the era solely by the weather might promote climatic determinism.
While no single label can do justice to all these co-existing and interrelated
developments, one conclusion can be drawn: ecocriticism demands that we
rethink the narrow periodization of literary history. As a modest contribu-
tion to that effort, this book encourages readers to see the authors as of their
time, while also asking what they might have to say to our time.

Anthology as Literary Compost

Since a core tenet of ecology is "everything is connected to everything else,"
the structural divisions in this anthology might seem at first glance coun-
terproductive. These divisions should not be regarded as airtight compart-
ments but as sieves; images or opinions found in Part I can trickle through
many other readings and bubble up again in, say, Part VI. True to Charles
Foster's definition of the animal as a "rolling conversation with the land from
which it comes and of which it consists" (20), Renaissance texts often recognize that certain species are entwined with specific places (e.g. Drayton's
catalogues of birds and fish in the fens; the gannets on Bass Rock), or even
with specific times (the swallows of summer). Consequently, readers should
resist the temptation to abstract fauna and flora from their ecology. For that
reason, one need not move through this book in a linear fashion. Editorial
asides often rip open wormholes, inviting readers to leap between sections.

Instead of curating a gallery of well-wrought urns, this anthology unfurls a more rhizomatic vision of the Renaissance, its eclectic contents tracing both assemblages and conflicts across lines of time, space, and species.

When the Soothsayer in *Antony and Cleopatra* refers to "nature's infinite book of secrecy" (1.2.8), the adjective signals the impossibility of circumscribing the earth's biodiversity, which the play's heroine embodies in her "infinite variety." Confessing he can only decipher a "little" of it, the Soothsayer presents the biosphere as "an untotalizable totality" (in Fredric Jameson's phrase) that defies efforts of scientists – and anthology editors – to fully understand or encompass it. Long before the environmental historian Oliver Rackham proposed that nature would be better compared to a library, in which careless students deface and lose some of the volumes as new ones take their place on the shelves (1986, 29–30), Shakespeare was already aware of the book as an imperfect metaphor for the cosmos. Does the format foster an illusion of spurious unity that belies the messy, contradictory philosophies and experiences recorded within it? In some respects, twenty-first-century hypertext – with its links to other links to other links ad infinitum – might seem a better loom on which to weave the ecological webs of interdependence. If so, the book still has advantages that justify the sacrifice of compressed wood pulp. There needs no neurolinguist to come from the lab to tell us that encountering ideas on the printed page instead of a screen demands a higher intensity of engagement. Close, slow, or "deep" reading can model the sustained attention and accommodation of complexity valued by deep ecology. This is especially true of Renaissance texts, which require great cognitive exertion, not to mention specialist knowledge and hence annotations that most online and public domain versions lack. In allowing for old-fashioned textual analysis while also catering to "the way we read now," this collection negotiates (as it does with its mixture of original capitalization and modern spelling) between the past and the present.

If this anthology distils the superabundance of information in the age of Big Data and the infinite archive, the practice has historical precedents. Inundated with publications from the London presses, many sixteenth-century readers kept commonplace books in which they jotted down passages for purposes of reference and recall. In an incisive essay, Frances Dolan urges ecocritics to make hay from the analogy between commonplacing and the composting or recycling advocated in Renaissance husbandry manuals. Instead of an impeccably neat library or garden, this anthology might be better compared to a kind of literary compost. Stirring together texts from different genres, disciplines, and eras, its "mixture of materials is simultaneously archive, method, and argument" (Dolan 38).

In defiance of typical practice, then, this anthology is not organized chronologically by author. No doubt single-author studies will continue to have their place, but the ecocritical assault on anthropocentric values must also apply corrosive pressure to the author as the focal point of criticism.

Shakespeare is no exception, especially since he can still insidiously function as a figurehead not only of Anglo-Saxon genius but also of human exceptionalism (as Joseph Campana provocatively argues). Of course his colossal stature makes him impossible to ignore; so while he makes room in these pages for some arguably less gifted writers, he often haunts them like an absent presence. Instead of foregrounding the author, I have chosen to group texts together to facilitate discussion of key issues in environmental criticism: creation myths and eco-spirituality; species and the rise of observation-based writing about nature; sense of time, place, and topography; material practices; environmental degradation; and narratives of catastrophe and resilience. These six parts intentionally mirror some of the historical categories and hierarchies by which humans have imposed order on the natural world. Importantly, however, the selections and the commentary often grate against these taxonomies, so that many entries sabotage or break free of the framework that strives to contain them. The parts are further divided into sub-parts, and while these sometimes unfold in chronological order to show how attitudes shifted in response to historical circumstances (such as the Reformation, the Great Dearth, the arrival of the Stuarts, the Civil War, the formation of the Royal Society, etc.), these changes do not always reveal a steady, linear progression towards modern environmental values.

Part 1 features biblical and classical sources on the creation of the universe and the relationship between prehistoric humans and primeval wilderness. It would be difficult to overstate the importance of these origin stories in inflating humanity's sense of its privileged niche in the universe, and influencing Western presentiments of our species' long-term impact on the planet. Apart from a few daring minds like Thomas Harriot and Christopher Marlowe, early modern Europeans (like 38 per cent of American adults today) were Young Earth creationists.[7] Theologians since the time of Bede had estimated the earth's age at around six thousand years (and a seventeenth-century Irish bishop would pinpoint its birthday to 23 October, 4004 BCE). Nevertheless, this did not preclude fears that it was already suffering from senescence, or could be destroyed by an imminent apocalypse. While we must now entertain the mind-bending thought that this planet existed for well over four billion years before the first human, many early moderns interpreted the "days" of creation as millennia, and would have been similarly humbled by God's admonition to Job: "Where wast thou when I laid the foundations of the earth?" (38:4). The excerpts from Lucy Hutchinson's "third day" and Joseph Caryl's commentary on Job demonstrate that seventeenth-century writers could conceive of an ecology before or without humans. Sidney's "Ister Bank" laments humanity's evolutionary ascendancy over other animals as tyranny, while Shakespeare's Timon even fantasizes of life after people.

---

[7] "In US, Belief in Creationist View of Humans at New Low." *Gallup.* 22 May 2017. Web.

Generally speaking, however, Tudor England inherited from the Judeo-Christian tradition a worldview that was geocentric and anthropocentric, and buttressed it with elements of Greco-Roman natural philosophy (mainly Aristotle and Pliny) compatible with scriptural teachings. An engraving from Robert Fludd's treatise on the macrocosm and microcosm illustrates how differently a Renaissance humanist might conceive of the universe and our place within it (Figure 1). It depicts an earth-centred cosmos in which astrological energy radiating from the planets engenders metals and affects human behaviour so that, for instance, men are swayed by the sun and women by the sun and moon. Human sciences (alchemy, botany, animal husbandry) are represented as "natural arts" through which a simian humanity both imitates (following the principle of monkey see, monkey do) and improves the art of Nature. Following a neo-Platonic tradition, it exalts a female Nature as a semi-deific force that mediates between humanity and God, but is, therefore – as Richard Hooker and Walter Ralegh maintain in excerpts from this section – not an autonomous agent. Despite the scholastic impulse to synthesize in order to arrive at universal truths, the Renaissance discovery of ancient texts espousing heretical ideas, the proliferating translations of and commentaries on the Bible after the Reformation, and the growing emphasis on empirical observation of nature made it increasingly difficult to weave together the various strands of human knowledge into a coherent world picture. Although they differ in several respects, Hooker's defence of natural law and Thomas Browne's ruminations on a physician's faith were both motivated by a nervous apprehension that the chain binding God and nature had become noticeably slack. Likewise, Fludd would later pit his mystical philosophy (compounded from the teachings of Moses, Hermes Trismegistus, and Plato) against Aristotelian naturalists who placed, he thought, too much trust in the senses and thus "presume … over-boldly on their terrene and animal wisdom" (1659, 40). Such arguments signal the opening of an ideological rift between religion and science that persists to this day. In the Renaissance, jumping into that rift could have lethal consequences, as the fate of Giordano Bruno exemplifies. While Fludd clung to a geocentric universe, insisted that the human soul was not part of nature, and held Nature subordinate to God, Bruno notoriously embraced the new Copernican cosmology, proclaimed the universe to be infinite, revived vitalistic teachings that all matter was ensouled, and defined God as *Natura naturans* (the active, creative principle within nature).[8] The Catholic Church burnt

---

[8] Since Bruno wrote in bombastic Italian, he seldom appears in surveys of English literature, an oversight that ecocriticism should rectify, especially given his influence (documented by Hillary Gatti) on Elizabethan writers such as Sidney, Daniel, Greville, Ralegh, Harriot, Marlowe, and Shakespeare. On Bruno's vitalism as a path to "re-enchantment," see Gruber. The temptation to canonize Bruno as ecological saint should be moderated, however, by Frances Yates's thesis that his Hermeticism promoted a techno-scientific "will to operate," audible in Faustus's grandiose soliloquies of "dominion" over the material world.

Bruno at the stake in Rome in 1600, but some English writers such as John Donne, Thomas Browne, and Margaret Cavendish would find literature a relatively safer laboratory in which to dissect received truths or weigh the latest scientific theories of the day.

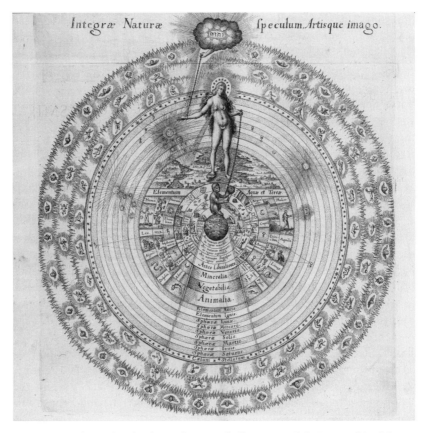

FIGURE 1 Johann Theodor de Bry, "Mirror of All Nature and the Image of Art," from Robert Fludd, *Utriusque cosmi ... historia* (1621). John Hay Library, Brown University.

Cavilling with this secular view of the Renaissance as driving a wedge between Christianity and nature, the sub-part entitled Natural Theologies offers some memorable examples of eco-inflected piety. Revealingly, many seventeenth-century writers who came the closest to composing what we would now regard as "nature poetry" were also extremely devout. Declaring the "mind is its own place," Milton's Satan voices his alienation from a hellscape that evokes the degradation and industrialization of England in the aftermath of the Civil War. In contrast, Henry Vaughan expresses a strong attachment to his native Wales, even imagining it as a heaven on earth in verses that ironically echo Satan's salute: "Hail crystal fountains and fresh shades" (1678, 62). Ecocritics must keep in mind that much seventeenth-century religious poetry grasps the environment as a Platonic ladder to ascend to heaven, and that Vaughan was "essentially of his age, not a Romantic born out of his time" (Pettet 98). Nevertheless, works like Herbert's "Providence" that envision nature as a holy temple seem to articulate – albeit with a theological rather than an ecological vocabulary – a commandment to see and treat the environment more holistically.

Of course this yearning for a unified, holistic cosmos overseen by God often has an ideological charge in a monarchical and imperialistic society. Evidence of these complex entanglements of religion, nature, and politics can be glimpsed in the Bacton Altar Cloth, recently identified as the only surviving piece of clothing worn by Queen Elizabeth (Figure 2). In a celebrated essay, Stephen Greenblatt interpreted the sale of an ecclesiastical cloak to a company of actors as symbolic of the post-Reformation transference of cultural energy from sacred ritual to secular art. The Bacton Altar Cloth presents almost the opposite trajectory: a vestment worn in the political theatre of the Tudor state (portraying Elizabeth as a Dame Nature figure or "Queen of Shepherds" with dominion over the resources of the realm) was recycled and repurposed to exalt God's grandeur through the splendid plenitude of nature. Its history complicates straightforward narratives of the Protestant Reformation as a time of disenchantment, a view represented in this anthology by Milton's "Nativity Ode."

FIGURE 2 Bacton Altar Cloth (c. 1590). © Historic Royal Palaces.

The cloth can also be contrasted with Elizabeth's translation of a song from Boethius's *Consolation of Philosophy*, which begins, "If wary, alone, of thund'ring God the laws thou wilt." Placing God before thou, the awkward Latinate syntax underscores its cosmological vision of order arising from universal submission to the laws of a divine ruler. If the queen sought to appropriate this neo-Platonic philosophy to bolster her authority, the altar cloth – like Spenser's "Mutability Cantos" and Drayton's personification of Albion – suggests how the worship devoted to Elizabeth's cult could be deflected back to God, nature, or the land.

Alert readers will notice that the organizational structure of Part II mirrors the hierarchical taxonomy characteristic of much Renaissance natural history: Human, Animal, Vegetable, and Mineral. The rationale for following this schema is to interrogate it, not endorse it. As the title "Tangled Chain" hints, the selections and commentaries expose vertical tendencies in the Elizabethan *Weltanschauung* while also revealing how they were checked or undermined by horizontal correspondences. In his 1966 study *The Order of Things*, the influential historian Michel Foucault sketched how the Renaissance "episteme" (or knowledge-system), which hinged on correspondence, analogy, and metaphor, was gradually replaced by Enlightenment taxonomies promoting categorization based on differences. Recently, ecocritics have begun to reappraise these analogical habits of mind and models – such as the Chain (Egan 2011) and the Scale (Werth) – since they in some ways presage the new episteme being shaped by ecology. This should not be misconstrued as calling for the wholesale revival of a decidedly musty worldview underpropped by a feudal social structure. In a 1503 poem by William Dunbar celebrating the marriage of James IV and Margaret Tudor, Dame Nature summons an assembly of creatures, and rewards the lion, eagle, and rose as the noblest of the beasts, birds, and plants. A century later, however, when King James VI ordered the actor Edward Alleyn to stage a lion-baiting at the Tower of London, the lion retreated and refused to fight the dogs. So much for the "king of beasts." Since nature is vast and unpredictable, ideologies and realities do not always align. Consequently, writers must foreground certain phenomena as "nature" and bracket off others. This book was prepared in full knowledge that the same applies to editors of literary anthologies; hence the choice and arrangement of texts was governed by a wish to gesture at the diversity not just of species in the biosphere but also of ideas in the public sphere. By pitting Montaigne against Bacon, Descartes against Cavendish, Digby against Tryon, it aims to provide students and researchers a first-hand glimpse of the complex, messy, and sometimes contradictory attitudes prevalent in the Long Renaissance: from curiosity to disgust, dominance to reverence.

Many of the selections in Part II illustrate the Renaissance "invention" of natural history – a discipline that arose from the synthesis of medicine, agriculture, and natural philosophy (Ogilvie), and the development of information networks among humanist intellectuals (Harkness). There was, nonetheless, still a robust market in the sixteenth century for medieval books on nature, as attested by works such as Bartholomew the Englishman's *On the Properties of Things* (translated and printed in 1495, 1533, and 1582), Laurence Andrew's *Noble Life and Natures of Man, Beasts, Serpents, Fowls, Fishes* (1527), and John Maplet's *Green Forest* (1567). These encyclopaedic tomes are heavily encrusted with fantastic material from the Roman naturalist Pliny, medieval bestiaries derived from Physiologus, and popular folklore. Just as Reformation theologians began to purge the Church of accumulated traditions, rituals, and the cult of the saints, Protestant naturalists such as William Turner, Thomas Penny, Charles L'Écluse, and Conrad Gesner started the gradual process of sifting out the ancient legends and folk beliefs in pre-modern texts on flora and fauna. This trend can be neatly illustrated by two different images of mandrakes. The first (Figure 3) is taken from Peter Schöffer's *Hortus Sanitatus* (1491). This humanoid plant appears (along with a female mandrake) in the first English herbal from 1526 – even though the accompanying text dismisses the anatomical resemblance as a myth! In contrast, John Gerard's 1597 herbal features a more faithful drawing (Figure 4) lifted from Matthias L'Obel's *Plantarum seu stirpium*. Similarly, the botanist John Parkinson juxtaposes two images of the passion fruit (1629, 394–5), one drawn by Jesuits to resemble Christ's crown of thorns and another more prosaic illustration intended to debunk the former. This demystifying of natural history, however, was by no means sudden and decisive. Edward Topsell's *Book of Four-Footed Beasts* – essentially a translation of Gesner – dispels many ancient legends and fables, yet also includes entries for mythical creatures like the unicorn and the lamia. As dramatized by several readings in Part II, Renaissance literature can veer nonchalantly from the natural to supernatural, the realistic to the fantastic, as these categories were not entirely discrete. Even members of the Royal Society, the first government-supported scientific institute founded in 1660, dabbled in occult studies like alchemy. So while it would be unwise to ignore the differences between John Ray and Topsell, between the more systematic inquiries of the Restoration and Tudor natural history, John Aubrey clearly overstated matters when he claimed that "till about 1649," when an experimental philosophy club formed at Oxford, "'twas held a Sin to make a Scrutiny into the Ways of Nature" (Aubrey MS 15ʳ).

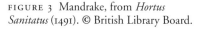

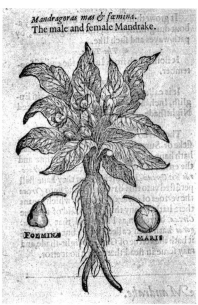

FIGURE 3 Mandrake, from *Hortus Sanitatus* (1491). © British Library Board.

FIGURE 4 Mandrake, from John Gerard, *Herbal* (1597). Wellcome Library.

If literature, natural history, and religion are not always discrete, could not the same be said of time and place, the two categories that structure Part III? Noting the relative scarcity of topographical verse in this period, Ken Hiltner has cleverly suggested that Renaissance poets preferred to "gesture" (2011, 21) or point at nature rather than attempt the presumptuous feat of a detailed mimetic depiction. Another feasible explanation is that early modern consciousness tended to prioritize time over place. As witnessed by James Thomson's *Seasons* (1730), one of the most popular poems of the eighteenth century, the pre-Romantics assumed that the drama of seasonal change would interest a larger number of readers than an autobiographical account of personal place attachment. Significantly, it is often religious writers who consider verse as a kind of private prayer who first articulate this love of place. While the four seasonal pieces included in this anthology represent the proverbial iceberg's tip, they will hopefully spur more critical reflection on the seasons not as a timeless, universal cycle, but as a human-crafted narrative, shaped by ever-changing cultural conditions and meteorological trends. Readers should remember that prior to the adoption of the Gregorian calendar in 1752, the year began on 25 March, around the time of the vernal equinox, and that the dates were eleven days behind what they are now. It would, however, be rash to focus exclusively on time and ignore place. An analysis of Hume's ode to summer, for example, cannot lose sight of the fact that it is set in Scotland; time and place are linked in a chronotopography.

On similar grounds, readers are warmly invited to knock down the place-based divisions in Part III: many of the texts simply refuse to stay rooted in one locale. Country house poems like "The Description of Cookham" and "Upon Appleton House" can wander past gardens, meadows, woods, streams, etc. The Renaissance admired a stylistic copiousness that encouraged some writers like Michael Drayton to catalogue the topographical variety and cornucopian abundance of the earth. This love of plenty may account for why Tudor poets often deemed gardens, copses, orchards, or productive land more congenial to their muse than genuine wilderness, and some pastoral lyrics can be seen as adopting an "encloser's eye view" (Norbrook 6) of the countryside. Nevertheless, several entries in this section do document the invention of landscape poetry in the seventeenth century, and even an aesthetic regard for untamed places. The focalization of landscape first occurred in Dutch painting, but English artists who imported the genre, such as Nathaniel Bacon (Figure 5), and English writers who appropriated this new way of seeing were also responding to economic developments within their native shores. The quest to "improve" and enclose wild spaces like mountains, moors, and fens prompted those who did benefit from these commons to argue that they had intrinsic beauty or purpose in their current state.

FIGURE 5 Nathaniel Bacon, "Landscape" (c. 1610–1627). © Ashmolean Museum, University of Oxford.

Part IV presents some disturbing reminders that audiences who could savour artistic masterpieces such as *Twelfth Night* or *Macbeth* also thrilled at the spectacle of bears, dogs, and roosters ripping each other to pieces. Hunting, hawking, birding, and fishing were fashionable recreations for the rural gentry. Many poorer families, meanwhile, relied on fowling and fishing for their subsistence. Although it may seem counterintuitive by contemporary standards, the people who enjoyed killing animals were often the most vocal about their preservation. King Henry VIII passed laws protecting raptor nests, while King James (in an early example of re-wilding) reintroduced boar back to England with the explicit purpose of someday hunting them. However, the selections from Philip Stubbes, George Gascoigne, and Margaret Cavendish reveal that some early moderns did find blood sports distasteful.

Modern readers may experience a similar reaction to some of the foods and medicines featured in this section – such as Talbot's prescription to cure plague sores by applying the plucked cloaca of a live chicken. When so many essential daily tasks depended on what was locally and seasonally available, early moderns could not be so squeamish. In addition to being resourceful, they had to be conscious of synchronizing their habits with cycles of plenty and scarcity. Beyond the Reformation assault on ritual, the growing disinclination to observe the Lenten fast, documented in the entries by Harington and Middleton, can be seen as symptomatic of an increasingly urban and capitalistic society's refusal to accept limitations on consumption. Other selections highlight the vital role of women as readers and writers of texts on cooking, healing, and household management – an important precursor of the modern concept of ecology (derived from the Greek for household, *oikos*). On the bright side, these material practices can be upheld as examples of eco-attunement or "transcorporeal domesticity," reminders that the threshold separating the inside/outside of both Tudor houses and bodies was much more porous than it is today (Laroche and Munroe 42). However, they also indicate that it was perfectly conscionable to torture other animals to relieve mild complaints in humans: a practice we outsource but still endorse today whenever we buy products tested on animals.

The Renaissance was a time of great scientific and industrial development, and in Part V the consequences of this become disconcertingly clear. Rampant deforestation threatens the habitat of game and whittles away timber supplies, triggering outcries that the present generation is overconsuming natural resources. Extractive mining practices contaminate waterways and pockmark the landscape. The burning of coal envelops urban areas in noxious clouds, and physicians blame air pollution for reducing life expectancy. Local communities protest the destruction of wetlands, even resorting to acts of sabotage against hydro-engineering projects. Over-fishing is depleting stocks of cod, salmon, and other marine species in the North Sea and the Atlantic Ocean, leading to strict regulation of the fishing industry. Profit-driven agricultural practices degrade soil quality, which in turn licenses more aggressive farming methods, while some condemn the crossbreeding of new species of plants as unnatural. The climate seems increasingly unstable, which some watchdogs blame on astronomical phenomena and others on the moral failures of human society. Cities are overcrowded and unsanitary, while rural areas are becoming depopulated, placing a strain on biomass resources that an island nation cannot support long-term.

The above might sound like a medley of alarmist headlines yanked from twenty-first-century media, but do in fact accurately sketch perceived environmental conditions in early modern Britain as reflected in many of the entries in this anthology. In the words of esteemed agricultural historian Joan Thirsk, "in the sixteenth and seventeenth centuries men made war upon the forests, moors, and fens with a zeal which they had not felt for some three hundred years. They cleared woods and drained wet, low-lying land to make new pastures; they turned old pastures into cornland, old cornland into grass" (1967, 2). In contrast to the pastoral fantasy of a tranquil, enamelled landscape – a vision currently being redeployed in the campaign to preserve the "green belt" – the English countryside has always been a site of change and tension, and development schemes incited controversies during Tudor times and long before.

Moreover, these issues were not remote from the lives of many Renaissance writers. The entries in this collection implicate figures like Sidney, Spenser, Ralegh, Sackville, Jonson, Middleton, Dekker, Greville, Milton, Cavendish, and Cowley in disputes over enclosure, mining, deforestation, fen-draining, and pollution. Nor were the noble patrons of these writers necessarily noble stewards of the environment. Henry Percy, the Earl of Northumberland, sold off most of his ancestral woodlands to pay off his debts. William Herbert, a dedicatee of Shakespeare's First Folio, was a major investor in the Society of Mines Royal, and founded lucrative ironworks in the Forest of Dean. Shakespeare's patron, the Earl of Southampton, managed iron forges and furnaces at Sowley and Titchfield. Charles Howard, the Lord Admiral, was a patron not only of an acting company but also of shipwrights, whose enterprises made him conscious of the need to replenish England's beleaguered woodlands. Philip Henslowe, the financier of the Admiral's acting company, profited from starch and woad production, and acquired much of his fortune from the family business of selling timber to ironmongers in Ashdown Forest. The Rose and Globe stood not only next to animal-baiting pits but also on top of reclaimed marshland, and the Bankside was becoming a semi-industrialized area in Jacobean times. Audiences entering the Blackfriars Theatre would have caught a whiff of smoke from the neighbouring glassworks, and the construction of Covent Garden, which became the heart of London's theatre district after the Restoration, was funded with money from the draining of the fens. The relationship between literature and nature in the Long Renaissance was often symbiotic, but sometimes more parasitic than most of us would care to admit.

The materials garnered in Part VI reveal that climatic instability and mounting concerns over resource scarcity spawned fears of environmental decay or apocalypse. Contrary to popular belief, climate change is not a modern notion: it was well documented in Aristotle's *Meteorology*, and was thus familiar to many Renaissance naturalists. In the sixteenth century, Bruno attributed these geoclimatic vicissitudes to variations in the earth's axial tilt, a phenomenon he adduced as proof that the earth is not stationary but orbits around the sun. Most people in the Little Ice Age, however, viewed inclement weather and natural disasters as divine punishments for the moral failures of society. Whether or not they placated God's wrath, the ensuing calls for communal penance (abstaining from meat and sex) did at least have the modest practical effect of reducing consumption in times of scarcity. Along with a dearth sermon, this part features meteorological laments and carnivalesque accounts of frost fairs. The anthology concludes on a slightly more upbeat note, with texts expressing a sense of resilience in the face of environmental degradation or calamity. Given the prominence of Michael Drayton in this collection it seems fitting that he have the last word, particularly as "Noah's Flood" loops back to the starting-point in the Book of Genesis, and seeks to revise the problematic covenant by which humans came to imagine themselves as petty gods on earth.

The first appendix features a timeline of industrialization and environmental policy in the Tudor and Stuart eras. It condenses and organizes a welter of archival material – such as letters, patents, proclamations, and parliamentary acts – to etch a granular picture of England in the Early Anthropocene. More precisely, it affords an unprecedented glimpse of the attempts by England's monarchs, Lord Treasurers, Privy Councils, Parliaments, and aldermen (particularly during the reigns of Queen Elizabeth and King James) to formulate legislative responses to environmental problems. The start and end dates have been chosen to bracket off an era in which charcoal-burning ironworks proliferated, feeding contemporary perceptions of the period as an Iron Age. Perusing this list should enable readers to situate literary texts in their ecological context more easily than ever before.

The book concludes with a bibliography of eco-themed scholarship on the English Renaissance. After a short list of recommended primers on ecocriticism, its structure mirrors the organization of this anthology. Like the timeline, it is not all-inclusive, but it does furnish a handy, up-to-date inventory of further reading to expedite critical research.

In the process of visiting many of the sites described in these pages and consulting original manuscripts, I have come to realize how much ecocritics and textual scholars still subscribe to the premium placed on immediacy and authenticity by the Renaissance and Reformation. Encountering both wild places and primary texts first-hand can maximize their emotional and ethical impact. In addition to speaking with the dead, this anthology both rehearses and springs from an atavistic desire to speak with the non-human. If we cannot confidently presume to "speak for" nature, as Jennifer Munroe reminds us, writers still "write-with" other species: and when they do it well we can hope to hear something more than us talking to ourselves about ourselves. Unless the environmental humanities is a mere oxymoron, we must believe that literature might help us listen, learn, and change.

PART I

Cosmologies

Creation and the State of Nature
"The Creation of the World,"
from Genesis (c. 900–500 BCE)

To understand modern attitudes towards the environment, one must begin "in the beginning," with the Judeo-Christian creation myth. In a now notorious article, Lynn White traced the roots of our environmental crisis back to the first chapter of Genesis, when God instates humans as the overlords of creation. The Renaissance regarded the Torah as a sacred text, dictated by God to Moses. Today, most biblical scholars believe the Genesis story was cobbled together from various sources that underwent mutations and embellishments as they circulated over a four-century span between 900 and 500 BCE. Cavilling with the White thesis, some eco-theologians observe that Adam derives from 'adamah, the Hebrew for earth, and insist that the "dominion mandate" stems from a Priestly version (the P-text) of the creation story, whereas the so-called Yahwist account (the J-text) in Chapter 2 promotes stewardship. The excerpt below is taken from the 1560 Protestant-slanted translation known as the Geneva Bible. This edition has been chosen for three reasons: (1) its monumental importance to Elizabethan culture and hence English literature; (2) the marginal glosses (excerpted in the footnotes) offer testimony of how Protestant theologians interpreted the scripture; and (3) the fact that the King James Version (published in 1611) is now far more widely available. Source: The Geneva Bible (1560), 1–2, 4.

Chapter 1

1 In the beginning God created the heaven and the earth. 2 And the earth was without form and void, and darkness was upon the deep, and the Spirit of God moved upon the waters.° 3 Then God said, Let there be light: and there was light.° 4 And God saw the light that it was good, and God separated the light from the darkness. 5 And God called the light Day, and the darkness he called Night. So the evening and the morning were the first day.

6 Again God said, Let there be a firmament° in the midst of the waters, and let it separate the waters from the waters. 7 Then God made the firmament, and parted the waters, which were under the firmament, from the

---

° **And ... waters**: according to the marginal gloss, God "maintaineth this confused heap by his secret power."

° **Then ... light**: "The light was made before either sun or moon was created; therefore, we must not attribute that to the creatures that are God's instruments, which only appertaineth to God." A warning against sun worship.

° **firmament**: ancient Israelites believed that a translucent dome (here translated as "firmament") arched over the earth, separating the blue ocean from the blue ether. The line was sometimes interpreted as implying that the earth was flat.

waters which were above the firmament: and it was so. 8 And God called the firmament Heaven. So the evening and the morning were the second day.

9 God said again, Let the waters under the heaven be gathered into one place, and let the dry land appear: and it was so. 10 And God called the dry land Earth, and he called the gathering together of the waters Seas. And God saw that it was good. 11 Then God said, Let the earth bud forth the bud of the herb that seedeth seed, the fruitful tree, which beareth fruit according to his kind, which may have his seed in itself upon the earth: and it was so.° 12 And the earth brought forth the bud of the herb that seedeth seed according to his kind, also the tree that yieldeth fruit, which hath his seed in itself according to his kind: and God saw that it was good.° 13 So the evening and the morning were the third day.

14 And God said, Let there be lights in the firmament of the heaven to separate the day from the night, and let them be for signs, and for seasons, and for days, and years.° 15 And let them be for lights in the firmament of the heaven to give light upon the earth: and it was so. 16 God then made two great lights: the greater light to rule the day and the lesser light to rule the night.° He made also the stars. 17 And God set them in the firmament of the heaven to shine upon the earth, 18 And to rule in the day and in the night, and to separate the light from the darkness: and God saw that it was good. 19 So the evening and the morning were the fourth day.

20 Afterward God said, Let the waters bring forth in abundance every creeping thing that hath life, and let the fowl fly upon the earth in the open firmament of the heaven. 21 Then God created the great whales, and every thing living and moving, which the waters brought forth in abundance according to their kind, and every feathered fowl according to his kind: and God saw that it was good.° 22 Then God blessed them, saying, Bring forth fruit and multiply, and fill the waters in the seas, and let the fowl multiply in the earth. 23 So the evening and the morning were the fifth day.

24 Moreover, God said, Let the earth bring forth the living thing according to his kind, cattle, and that which creepeth, and the beast of the earth according to his kind: and it was so. 25 And God made the beast of the earth according to his kind, and the cattle according to his kind, and every

---

° **And ... so**: "So we see that it is only the power of God's word that maketh the earth fruitful, which else naturally is barren."

° **And ... good**: "This sentence is so oft repeated to signify that God made all his creatures to serve to his glory, and to the profit of man; but for sin they were accursed, yet to the elect by Christ they are restored and serve to their wealth."

° **Let ... years**: The creation of the sun occurs on the fourth day. This has prompted biblical commentators to interpret the days of creation figuratively to mean "epoch."

° **God ... night**: in the anthropocentric worldview of the Geneva annotator, even the sun and moon are celestial lights installed for our convenience, "instruments ... to serve to man's use."

° **Then ... good**: for the Geneva annotator, the willingness of the sea and sky to receive the fish and fowl is proof "that nature giveth place to God's will."

creeping thing of the earth according to his kind: and God saw that it was good. 26 Furthermore God said, Let us make man in our image° according to our likeness, and let them rule over the fish of the sea, and over the fowl of the heaven, and over the beasts, and over all the earth, and over everything that creepeth and moveth on the earth. 27 Thus God created the man in his image: in the image of God created he him; he created them male and female. 28 And God blessed them, and God said to them, Bring forth fruit and multiply, and fill the earth, and subdue it, and rule over° the fish of the sea, and over the fowl of the heaven, and over every beast that moveth upon the earth. 29 And God said, Behold, I have given unto you every herb bearing seed, which is upon all the earth, and every tree, wherein is the fruit of a tree bearing seed: that shall be to you for meat.° 30 Likewise to every beast of the earth, and to every fowl of the heaven, and to everything that moveth upon the earth, which hath life in itself, every green herb shall be for meat: and it was so. 31 And God saw all that he had made, and lo, it was very good. So the evening and the morning were the sixth day ...

Chapter 2

4 The Lord God made the earth and heavens, 5 And every plant of the field before it was in the earth, and every herb of the field before it grew. For the Lord God had not caused it to rain upon the earth. Neither was there a man to till the ground, 6 But a mist went up from the earth and watered all the earth.

7 The Lord God also made the man of the dust of the ground,° and breathed in his face breath of life, and the man was a living soul. 8 And the Lord God planted a garden eastward in Eden ... 15 Then the Lord God took the man and put him into the Garden of Eden, that he might dress it and keep it.°

❧ ❧ ❧

° **image:** the Geneva commentary follows Jean Calvin in mocking the "Anthropomorphites" who interpreted this verse literally, but argues that "us" implies humans bear a spiritual resemblance to God.

° **rule over:** this controversial passage is known as the dominion mandate due to the King James Version's rendering of the Hebrew *radah*, to rule, as "dominion." *Radah* means to govern, but also has the harsher connotations of "tread upon, trample."

° **meat:** food. Genesis 1:29 implies that Adam and Eve were vegetarian, while the following verse declares that there is no predation in Eden.

° **dust ... ground:** the original Hebrew text plays on the similarity between *'adham* (man) and *'adamah* (ground or earth).

° **dress ... keep it:** this verse can be interpreted as promoting human stewardship rather than dominion. Calvin glosses it as appointing man "the Lord's steward," and ordering the "moderate and temprate use" of the earth's resources.

OVID

"The Creation," "The Four Ages," and "The Oration of Pythagoras" (4 BCE − 2 CE)

Weaving together a number of ancient Greek legends featuring transforma-
tions, the Roman poet Ovid produced one of the deathless works of Western
literature. In the Middle Ages and Renaissance, Ovid's pagan mythography was
heavily encrusted with commentary interpreting it in light of Christian dogma.
Encountering Book 1 on the heels of Genesis, it is easy to spy the parallels between the Greco-Roman and the Judeo-Christian creation myths. Both postulate
a divine creator bringing order to the universe, both glorify humans as quasi-
divine, both depict a primordial state of harmonious co-existence with the natural
world from which our early ancestors were expelled. In other respects, however,
the two traditions differ significantly. Ovid's universe is far more dynamic and
fluid, in which every creature can mutate into something else. Rather than being driven from paradise for eating forbidden fruit, the primitive humans in the
Metamorphoses experience a gradual fall, which manifests itself in an increasingly
antagonistic relationship to the earth and other creatures.

This is not entirely the hoary stuff of myth. If the imposition of order upon
chaos reflects the advent of the *Pax Romana* under Emperor Augustus, so, too,
the Iron Age can be interpreted as a pointed critique of environmental degradation in Ovid's day. Global conquest requires a tremendous amount of biomass
resources, and the weapon-forges, ships, and forts that built and maintained the
Roman Empire deforested much of the ancient Mediterranean (see Hughes), as
well as swathes of ancient Britannia. A similar dynamic was again unfolding in
early modern England due to rapid population growth and burgeoning industries
like mining, iron-manufacturing, glass-making, and ship-building. Rather than a
utopian fantasy, the Golden Age acquired a sudden topicality in the Renaissance
when Europeans discovered two new continents where people lived in conditions reminiscent of Ovid's prehistoric paradise. The great French writer Michel
de Montaigne and his English admirers saw Native Americans through Ovid's
gold-tinted glasses. Despite the considerable body of archaeological evidence to
contradict it, soft primitivism continues to exert an appeal. On a broader level, the
myth of the Four Ages outlines a powerful declensionist view of human history
that underlies many environmentalist narratives to this day.

The final extract from Book 15 consists of a sacred physics lecture by the Greek
sage Pythagoras. His vision of nature as a realm of perpetual flux lends the mytho-
poetic conceit of metamorphosis an aura of scientific credibility – a kind of precursor to the law of the conservation of energy. While many early moderns scoffed
at the idea of an animal soul and at vegetarianism, his philosophy spurred writers
such as Marlowe, Donne, and Shakespeare to question prevailing religious and
scientific orthodoxies. In its majestic revelation of the fundamental kinship of all
organic life, the speech deserves recognition as one of the great proto-ecological
texts in world literature.
Source: *The Fifteen Books of P. Ovidius Naso, Entitled Metamorphoses*, trans. Arthur
Golding (1567), 1ʳ–3ʳ, 189ʳ, 190ʳ⁻ᵛ, 193ʳ⁻ᵛ.

[The Creation]

Of shapes transformed to bodies strange I purpose to entreat,
Ye gods vouchsafe (for you are they ywrought° this wondrous feat)
To further this mine enterprise. And from the world begun,
Grant that my verse may to my time his course directly run.
Before the Sea and Land were made, and Heav'n that all doth hide,
In all the world one only face of nature did abide,
Which Chaos hight,° a huge rude heap, and nothing else but even
A heavy lump and clotted clod of seeds together driven,
Of things at strife among themselves, for want of order due.
No Sun as yet with lightsome beams the shapeless world did view.   10
No Moon in growing did repair her horns with borrowed light,
Nor yet the earth amidst the air did hang by wondrous sleight,°
Just peisèd° by her proper weight. Nor winding in and out
Did Amphitrite° with her arms embrace the earth about.
For where was earth was sea and air, so was the earth unstable.
The air all dark, the sea likewise, to bear a ship unable.
No kind of thing had proper shape, but each confounded other.
For in one selfsame body strove the hot and cold together,
The moist with dry, the soft with hard, the light with things of weight.
This strife did God and Nature° break and set in order straight.   20
The earth from heav'n, the sea from earth, he parted orderly,
And from the thick and foggy air he took the lightsome sky;
Which, when he once unfolded had and severed from the blind
And clodded heap, he setting each from other did them bind
In endless friendship to agree. The fire most pure and bright,
The substance of the heav'n itself, because it was so light,
Did mount aloft and set itself in highest place of all.
The second room of right, to air for lightness did befall.
The earth more gross drew down with it each weighty kind of matter,
And set itself in lowest place. Again the waving water   30
Did lastly challenge for his place, the utmost coast and bound
Of all the compass of the earth, to close the steadfast ground …
Above all these he set aloft the clear and lightsome sky,
Without all dregs of earthly filth or grossness utterly.
The bounds of things were scarcely yet by him thus pointed out,
But that appeared in the heaven stars glist'ring all about,   80
Which in the said confusèd heap had hidden been before.
And to th'intent with lively things each region for to store,
The heav'nly soil to Gods and Stars and Planets first he gave.
The waters next, both fresh and salt, he let the fishes have.
The subtle air to flick'ring° fowls and birds he hath assigned.
The earth to beasts, both wild and tame, of sundry sort and kind.
Howbeit yet of all this while the creature wanting was,
Far more divine, of nobler mind, which should the residue° pass

---

° **ywrought**: made.   ° **hight**: was called.   ° **sleight**: skill, artifice   ° **peised**: balanced.
° **Amphitrite**: Greek goddess of the ocean.
° **Nature**: In contrast to Genesis, Nature collaborates in the creation.   ° **flick'ring**: fluttering.
° **residue**: the rest.

90   In depth of knowledge, reason, wit, and high capacity,
        And which of all the residue should the Lord and ruler be.°
        Then either he that made the world, and things in order set,
        Of heav'nly seed engendered Man, or else the earth as yet
        Young, lusty, fresh, and in her flowers,° and parted from the sky
        But late before, the seed thereof as yet held inwardly.°
        The which Prometheus° temp'ring straight with water of the spring,
        Did make in likeness to the Gods that govern every thing.
        And where all other beasts behold the ground with grov'ling eye,
        He gave to Man a stately look replete with majesty,
        And willed him to behold the Heav'n with count'nance cast on high,
100   To mark and understand what things were in the starry sky.
        And thus the earth which late before had neither shape nor hue,
        Did take the noble shape of man, and was transformèd new.

[The Four Ages]

        Then sprang up first the Golden Age, which of itself maintained
        The truth and right of every thing unforced and unconstrained.
        There was no fear of punishment, there was no threat'ning law
        In brazen tables nailèd up to keep the folk in awe.
        There was no man would crouch or creep to Judge with cap in hand;
        They livèd safe without a Judge in every realm and land.
        The lofty Pine-tree was not hewn from mountains where it stood,
110   In seeking strange and foreign lands to rove upon the flood.
        Men knew none other countries yet than where themselves did keep.
        There was no town enclosèd yet with walls and ditches deep.
        No horn nor trumpet was in use, no sword nor helmet worn;
        The world was such that soldiers' help might eas'ly be forborne.
        The fertile earth as yet was free, untouched of spade or plough,
        And yet it yielded of itself of every thing enough.
        And men themselves, contented well with plain and simple food,
        That on the earth of nature's gift without their travail stood,
        Did live by rasps,° hips,° and haws,° by cornels,° plums and cherries,
120   By sloes° and apples, nuts and pears, and loathsome bramble berries,
        And by the acorns dropped on ground from Jove's broad tree in field.
        The Springtime lasted all the year, and Zephyr° with his mild
        And gentle blast did cherish things that grew of own accord;
        The ground untilled all kinds of fruits did plenteously afford.
        No muck° nor tillage was bestowed on lean and barren land,
        To make the corn of better head and ranker° for to stand.

° **ruler be**: compare with Genesis 1:26–28.
° **flowers**: prime, age of fertility.
° **either … inwardly**: Ovid leaves it ambiguous as to whether humans are heaven-born or fashioned from earth.
° **Prometheus**: mythological titan who later stole fire from the heavens to give it to humans.
° **rasps**: raspberries.   ° **hips**: wild-rose fruit.   ° **haws**: hawthorn berries.
° **cornels**: long cherries.   ° **sloes**: blackthorn fruit.   ° **Zephyr**: the west wind.
° **muck**: manure.   ° **ranker**: more abundant.

Then streams ran milk, then streams ran wine, and yellow honey flowed
From each green tree whereon the rays of fi'ry Phoebus glowed.
But when that into Limbo once Saturnus° being thrust,
The rule and charge of all the world was under Jove unjust, 130
And that the Silver Age came in (more somewhat base than gold,
More precious yet than freckled brass), immediately the old
And ancient Spring did Jove abridge and made thereof anon°
Four seasons: Winter, Summer, Spring, and Autumn off and on.
Then first of all began the air with fervent heat to swelt.°
Then Icicles hung roping down; then for the cold was felt
Men 'gan to shroud themselves in house. Their houses were the thicks°
And bushy queaches,° hollow caves, or hardels° made of sticks.
Then first of all were furrows drawn and corn was cast in ground.
The simple Ox with sorry sighs to heavy yoke was bound. 140
Next after this succeeded straight the third and Brazen Age:
More hard of nature, somewhat bent to cruèl wars and rage,
But yet not wholly past all grace. Of Iron is the last,
In no part good and tractable as former ages past.
For when that of this wicked Age once opened was the vein,
Therein all mischief rushèd forth; then Faith and Truth were fain°
(And honest Shame) to hide their heads, for whom crept stoutly in:
Craft, Treason, Violence, Envy, Pride, and wicked Lust to win.°
The shipman hoist his sails to winds whose names he did not know;
And ships, that erst in tops of hills and mountains had ygrow, 150
Did leap and dance on uncouth waves; and men began to bound
With dowels and ditches drawn in length the free and fertile ground,
Which was as common as the Air and light of Sun before.
Not only corn and other fruits, for sust'nance and for store,
Were now exacted of the Earth, but eft° they 'gan to dig,
And in the bowels of the ground insatiably to rig°
For Riches couched and hidden deep in places near to Hell:
The spurs and stirrers unto vice, and foes to doing well.
Then hurtful iron came abroad, then came forth yellow gold
(More hurtful than the iron far), then came forth battle bold, 160
That fights with both and shakes his sword in cruèl bloody hand.
Men live by ravine and by stealth; the wand'ring guest doth stand
In danger of his host, the host in danger of his guest;
And fathers of their son-in-laws—yea, seldom time doth rest
Between born brothers such accord and love as ought to be.
The goodman seeks the goodwife's° death, and his again seeks she.
The stepdames fell° their husbands' sons with poison do assail;
To see their fathers live so long the children do bewail.
All godliness lies underfoot. And Lady Astraea,° last
Of heav'nly virtues, from this earth in slaughter drownèd passed. 170

° **Saturnus**: primordial sky-god, overthrown by his son Jove. For a Lucretian reading of this myth,
  see Francis Bacon's "Coelum."
° **anon**: instantly.   ° **swelt**: swelter.   ° **thicks**: thickets.   ° **queaches**: undergrowth.
° **hardels**: hovels.   ° **fain**: obliged.   ° **win**: reside.   ° **eft**: then.   ° **rig**: ransack.
° **goodman ... goodwife's**: terms of respect for the male and female heads of household.
° **fell**: cruel.   ° **Astraea**: goddess of Justice.

[The Oration of Pythagoras]

"All things do change. But nothing sure doth perish. This same sprite
Doth fleet, and fisking° here and there doth swiftly take his flight
From one place to another place, and ent'reth every wight,
Removing out of man to beast, and out of beast to man.°
But yet it never perisheth, nor never perish can.
And e'en as supple wax with ease receiveth figures strange,
And keeps not ay° one shape, nor bides assurèd ay from change,
190   And yet continueth always wax in substance; so I say
The soul is ay the selfsame thing it was, and yet astray
It fleeteth into sundry shapes. Therefore lest Godliness
Be vanquished by outrageous lust of belly beastliness,
Forbear (I speak by prophecy) your kinsfolk's ghosts to chase
By slaughter: neither nourish blood with blood in any case.
And since on open sea the winds do blow my sails apace,
In all the world there is not that that standeth at a stay.
Things ebb and flow, and every shape is made to pass away, …
And these that we call Elements do never stand at stay.
The interchanging course of them I will before ye lay.
Give heed thereto. This endless world contains therein I say
Four substances of which all things are gendered. Of these four
The Earth and Water for their mass and weight are sunken lower.
The other couple, Air and Fire, the purer of the twain,
Mount up, and nought can keep them down. And though there do
    remain
A space between each one of them, yet every thing is made
Of themsame four, and into them at length again do fade.
270   The Earth resolving° leisurely doth melt to Water sheer.
The Water finèd° turns to Air. The Air eke purgèd clear
From grossness spireth up aloft, and there becometh Fire.
From thence in order contrary they back again retire.
Fire thickening passeth into Air, and Air waxing gross
Returns to Water. Water eke congealing into dross
Becometh Earth. No kind of thing keeps ay his shape and hue.
For nature loving ever change repairs one shape anew
Upon another. Neither doth there perish aught (trust me)
In all the world, but alt'ring takes new shape. For that which we
280   Do term by name of being born is for to 'gin to be
Another thing than that it was, and likewise for to die,
To cease to be the thing it was. And though that variably
Things pass perchance from place to place, yet all from whence they came
Returning, do unperishèd continue still the same.
But as for in one shape be sure that nothing long can last.
E'en so the ages of the world from Gold to Iron passed.
E'en so have places oftentimes exchangèd their estate.
For I have seen it sea which was substantial ground alate;

° **fisking**: whisking.
° **Removing … man**: metempsychosis, or the transmigration of souls across the species boundary.
° **ay**: always.   ° **resolving**: dissolving.   ° **fined**: refined.

Again where sea was, I have seen the same become dry land,
And shells and scales of sea-fish far have lain from any strand, 290
And in the tops of mountains high old anchors have been found.
Deep valleys have by water-shot° been made of level ground,
And hills by force of gulling° oft have into sea been worn.
Hard gravel ground is sometime seen where marris° was before,
And that that erst did suffer drought becometh standing lakes.
Here nature sendeth new springs out, and there the old intakes.
Full many rivers in the world through earthquakes heretofore
Have either changed their former course, or dried and run no more. ...
Men say that Sicil° also hath been joined to Italy,
Until the sea consumed the bound between, and did supply 320
The room with water. If ye go to seek for Helike
And Boura,° which were cities of Achaea, you shall see
Them hidden under water, and the shipmen yet do show
The walls and steeples of the towns drowned under as they row. ...
And we that of the world are part (consid'ring how we be
Not only flesh but also souls, which may with passage free
Remove them into every kind of beast both tame and wild),
Let live in safety honestly with slaughter undefiled, 510
The bodies which perchance may have the spirits of our brothers,
Our sisters, or our parents, or the spirits of some others
Allied to us either by some friendship or some kin,
Or at the least the souls of men abiding them within.
And let us not Thyestes-like° thus furnish up our boards
With bloody bowels. Oh, how lewd example he affords,
How wickedly prepareth he himself to murder man
That with a cruèl knife doth cut the throat of Calf, and can
Unmovably give hearing to the lowing of the dam,
Or stick the kid that waileth like the little babe, or eat 520
The fowl that he himself before had often fed with meat.
What wants of utter wickedness in working such a feat?
What may he after pass to do? Well, either let your steers
Wear out themselves with work, or else impute their death to years.
Against the wind and weather cold let Wethers yield ye coats,
And udders full of battling° milk receive ye of the Goats.
Away with springes, snares, and gins;° away with risp° and net;
Away with guileful feats; for fowls no lime-twigs see ye set.
No fearèd feathers° pitch ye up to keep the Red Deer in,
Nor with deceitful baited hook seek fishes for to win. 530
If aught do harm, destroy it, but destroy't and do no more.
Forbear the flesh and feed your mouths with fitter food therefore."

⁊ℭ ⁊ℭ ⁊ℭ

° **water-shot**: erosion.   ° **gulling**: channelling.   ° **marris**: marsh.   ° **Sicil**: Sicily.
° **Helike and Boura**: Cities in Greece (Achaea) submerged by a tsunami in 373 BCE.
° **Thysestes**: a Mycenean king whose sons were butchered by his brother and then served to their
   father to eat.
° **battling**: nourishing.   ° **gins**: traps.   ° **risp**: limed twigs.
° **feathers**: adorning nets used by Roman hunters.

LUCRETIUS

"That the World Was Not Created for Mankind's Sake" and "The First Productions of the Earth" (c. 55 BCE)

Few attempts to transmute physics into poetry can rival the brilliance of Lucretius's *De rerum natura* (*On the Nature of Things*). Little is known of its author, apart from the fact that he was a Roman devotee of Epicurus, whose atomist philosophy informs and electrifies Lucretius's poem. Like the Bible and the *Metamorphoses, On the Nature of Things* subscribes to a declensionist view of human and environmental history. In almost every other respect, however, Lucretius's account of creation differs dramatically from Genesis and Ovid. Atoms pinball through the universe, colliding and combining at random in "casual congressions" until, through trial and error, life forms arise that become capable of reproducing themselves. No transcendent deity forges the cosmos out of chaos. Instead Venus acts as a figurehead for the generative powers of nature, and the earth becomes a quasi-divine Great Mother; human beings enjoy no prerogative over the rest of the natural world.

While contemporary ecocritics may find much to admire in this worldview, Lucretius's atheism did not endear him to the Christian Church. His poem was all but forgotten during the Middle Ages; the 1417 rediscovery of a manuscript of it in a German monastery has been hailed as one of the events that ignited the Renaissance. Edmund Spenser, Walter Ralegh, John Davies, Francis Bacon, Nicholas Hill, Ben Jonson, Margaret Cavendish, and Aphra Behn were all acquainted with it. The proto-environmentalist John Evelyn translated Book 1 in 1656 and Thomas Creech published the first complete English version in 1682. Three decades earlier, however, Lucy Hutchinson had penned a translation, from which the extracts below are taken. Although she later claimed that reading Lucretius taught her to "abhor him, and dread a wanton dalliance with impious books"(4ᵛ), it might be more accurate to say that Hutchinson (whose own poem on the creation is also excerpted in this anthology) was both disturbed and exhilarated by the musings of this iconoclastic Roman poet.

Source: *On the Nature of* Things, trans. Lucy Hutchinson (c. 1650s). British Library MS 19333, 104ʳ, 115ᵛ–116ᵛ (Book 5).

"That the World Was Not Created for Mankind's Sake"

170   Next Memmius,° 'tis a senseless thing to hold
          That the gods only did for mankind's sake
          The goodly fabric of this great world make;
          That we must honour what they did create
          With an eternal and immortal state;
          That 'tis a sin to say foundations laid
          By sovereign powers, fair buildings made
          To be by men eternally enjoyed,

° **Memmius**: Lucretius's patron.

Must be overwhelmed and utterly destroyed°
(With many other fictions of this kind).
For what advantage can th'immortals find   180
That they, to gain poor mankind's favour thus,
Should undertake such mighty tasks for us? ...

[The First Productions of the Earth]

I now return to that young age when earth,
Impregnated with her first various birth,
Exposed her offspring to th'uncertain air.   820
Green herbs and grass her first-born issue were;
These clothed the mountains, graced the lower field,
Where mixed flowers did a various lustre yield.
The several kinds of trees advanced their heads,
While each in strifeful growth full branches spreads,
As the first downy plumes, bristles, and hair,
Which on young beasts and new-hatched birds appear,
So these fresh plants upon the new earth showed.
Next she produced the various multitude
Of living creatures, whose original   830
Did neither from the upper heaven fall,
Nor from th'inferior briny Ocean came,
But from th'earth's fruitful womb, who hence the name
Of the great mother° gained, since whatso'er
Enjoys a life, received it first from her ...
                              Then in the ground,
Moisture and heat did very much abound,
Which whereso'er earth yielded them fit place
Impregnated her womb with human race.
When the ripe infant births disclosèd were,
Leaving the moisture, now they sucked in air,
For whom nature through th'earth's disclosed veins sent   850
A pleasant, juicy, milk-like nourishment,
As new-delivered women's breasts, being filled
With sweet milk, food for their young infants yield.
The warm air clothed, the earth these children fed,
The downy moss and soft grass was their bed.
No rigid frosts assailed the world's young age,
No scorching heat, no wind's tempestuous rage;
All things at once full growth and strength attained,

° **destroyed**: Lucretius believed that the universe would decay and perish (see Part VI).

° **great mother**: the Magna Mater, an earth goddess worshipped throughout the ancient world in various guises, such as Cybele, Tellus, Maia, Rhea, and Isis. Whereas Lucretius treats the Magna Mater and Tellus as primitive metaphors, Augustine would criticize them in *City of God*, arguing "if the earth were held no goddess, men would lay their hands upon her and strengthen themselves by her" (7.24).

Whence justly th'earth a mother's title gained,
860   Since she in her due seasons mankind made,
And every beast which in the mountains strayed,
And all the kinds of airy birds. At last,
As women when their teeming days are past,
She ceased her numerous births, for age doth bring
A change to the whole world; and every thing
Which flowing time in any one state leaves,
A new condition the next age receives.
No creature its own likeness still retains,
For nature universal change constrains.°
870   Some waste and languish, weakened with long time;
Some to full growth, from low beginnings climb.
Thus change, by age, is through the whole world wrought,
And earth from one state to another brought.
What might of old have been can be no more,
What may be now could not have been before.

ᴈᴇ ᴈᴇ ᴈᴇ

° **No ... constrains**: these lines propose the mutability of species 1,900 years before Darwin.

PHILIP SIDNEY
"As I my little flock on Ister bank" (c. 1580)

In his *Defence of Poesy*, Sidney famously proclaims how the poet "lifted up with the vigour of his invention doth grow, in effect, another nature" better than anything found on earth. The pastoral urge to forge such "golden" worlds, however, can be regarded as a compensatory backlash against the grim environmental realities of an author's own "brazen" age. In the following eclogue, a dejected shepherd named Philisides (a stand-in for Sidney) spins an Aesopian fable (cf. "The Frogs that asked Jupiter for a King") that voices acute misgivings towards the authority humans wield over the natural world. Although it has often been deciphered as a political allegory, its tirade against the abuses of absolute monarchy only gains rhetorical force to the extent the reader is also appalled by its portrait of human tyranny over other species. The eclogue is also noteworthy for its almost evolutionary view of Homo sapiens as derived from the physical and mental attributes of other animals. It concludes with a poignant plea for their humane treatment. In short, Sidney's fable reveals how the classical tradition might embolden authors to imagine alternatives to the Genesis myth.
Source: *The Countess of Pembroke's Arcadia* (1593), 197ᵛ–199ᵛ.

As I my little flock on Ister° bank
(A little flock, but well my pipe they couthe)°
Did piping lead, the sun already sank

° **Ister**: Latin name for the Danube River.   ° **couthe**: knew.

Beyond our world, and ere I got my booth,°
Each thing with mantle black the night doth scothe,°
Saving the glow-worm, which would courteous be
Of that small light oft watching shepherds see.

The welkin° had full niggardly enclosed
In coffer of dim clouds his silver groats,°
Yclepèd° stars; each thing to rest disposed: 10
The caves were full, the mountains void of goats;
The birds' eyes closed, closed their chirping notes.
As for the nightingale, wood-music's king,
It August was, he deigned not then to sing.

Amid my sheep, though I saw naught to fear,
Yet (for I nothing saw) I fearèd° sore;
Then found I which thing is a charge to bear.
As for my sheep I dreaded mickle° more
Than ever for myself since I was bore.°
I sat me down, for see to go ne could, 20
And sang unto my sheep lest stray they should.

The song I sang old Lanquet° had me taught,
Lanquet, the shepherd best swift Ister knew
For clerkly reed,° and hating what is naught,
For faithful heart, clean hands, and mouth as true.
With his sweet skill my skilless youth he drew
To have a feeling taste of him that sits
Beyond the heav'n, far more beyond our° wits.

He said the music best thilke° powers pleased
Was jump° concord between our wit and will, 30
Where highest notes to godliness are raised,
And lowest sink not down to jot of ill.
With old true tales he wont mine ears to fill:
How shepherds did of yore, how now they thrive,
Spoiling their flock, or while 'twixt them they strive.

He likèd me, but pitied lustful youth;
His good strong staff my slipp'ry years upbore.
He still hoped well, because I lovèd truth;
Till forced to part with heart and eyes e'en sore,
To worthy Corydon° he gave me o'er. 40

° **booth**: shelter.   ° **scothe**: enscarf.   ° **welkin**: sky.   ° **groats**: small coins.
° **Ycleped**: called.   ° **feared**: scared] 1590.   ° **mickle**: much.   ° **bore**: born.
° **Lanquet**: Hubert Languet, Sidney's mentor and companion on his European travels, and a
    candidate for the authorship of *Vindiciae contra tyrannos* (*Vengeance Against Tyrants*), which
    advocates the assassination of unjust rulers.
° **clerkly reed**: scholarly learning.
° **our**: Duncan-Jones' emendation; the 1593 text reads "your".   ° **thilke**: these.   ° **jump**: precise.
° **Corydon**: stock name for shepherd in Renaissance pastoral. Presumably Edward Dyer, a courtier-
    poet who befriended Sidney.

But thus in oak's true shade recounted he
Which now in night's deep shade sheep heard of me.

Such manner time there was (what time I not°)
When all this Earth, this dam° or mould° of ours,
Was only woned° with such as beasts begot;
Unknown as then were they that builded towers.
The cattle, wild or tame, in nature's bowers
Might freely roam or rest, as seemèd them:
Man was not man their dwellings in to hem.

50 The beasts had sure some beastly policy;
For nothing can endure where order n'is.°
For once the Lion by the Lamb did lie;°
The fearful Hind the Leopard did kiss;
Hurtless was Tiger's paw and Serpent's hiss.
This think I well: the beasts with courage clad,
Like Senators, a harmless empire had.

At which, whether the others did repine
(For envy harb'reth most in feeblest hearts),
Or that they all to changing did incline
60 (As e'en in beasts their dams leave changing parts),
The multitude to Jove a suit imparts,
With neighing, blaying,° braying, and barking,
Roaring and howling, for to have a King.

A King in language theirs they said they would
(For then their language was a perfect speech).
The birds likewise with chirps and pewing° could,
Cackling and chatt'ring, that of Jove beseech.
Only the owl still warned them not to seech°
So hastily that which they would repent;
70 But saw they would, and he to deserts went.

Jove wisely said (for wisdom wisely says):
"O beasts, take heed what you of me desire.
Rulers will think all things made them to please,
And soon forget the swink° due to their hire.
But since you will, part of my heav'nly fire
I will you lend; the rest yourself must give,
That it both seen and felt may with you live."

Full glad they were, and took the naked sprite,
Which straight the Earth yclothèd in his clay.
80 The Lion, heart; the Ounce° gave active might;

° **not**: know not.   ° **dam**: mother.   ° **mould**: soil.   ° **woned**: inhabited.   ° **n'is**: is not.
° **Lion ... lie**: Isaiah 11:6.   ° **blaying**: bleating   ° **pewing**: screeching.   ° **seech**: seek.
° **swink**: labour.   ° **Ounce**: lynx.

The Horse, good shape; the Sparrow, lust to play;
Nightingale, voice, enticing songs to say;
Elephant gave a perfect memory;
And Parrot, ready tongue, that to apply.

The Fox gave craft; the Dog gave flattery;
Ass, patience; the Mole, a working thought;
Eagle, high look; Wolf, secret cruelty;
Monkey, sweet breath; the Cow, her fair eyes brought;
The Ermine, whitest skin spotted with naught;
The Sheep, mild-seeming face; climbing, the Bear;   90
The Stag did give the harm-eschewing fear.

The Hare her sleights; the Cat his melancholy;
Ant, industry; and Cony, skill to build;
Cranes, order; Storks, to be appearing holy;
Chameleon, ease to change; Duck, ease to yield;
Crocodile, tears, which might be falsely spilled;
Ape great thing gave, though he did mowing° stand:
The instrument of instruments, the hand.

Each other beast likewise his present brings;
And (but they drad° their Prince they oft should want)   100
They all consented were to give him wings.
And ay more awe towards him for to plant,°
To their own work this privilege they grant:
That from henceforth to all eternity,
No beast should freely speak, but only he.

Thus Man was made; thus Man their Lord became;
Who at the first, wanting or hiding pride,
He did to beasts' best use his cunning frame;
With water drink, herbs meat, and naked hide,
And fellow-like let his dominion slide,   110
Not in his sayings saying I, but we;
As if he meant his lordship common be.

But when his seat so rooted he had found
That they now skilled not how from him to wend,°
Then 'gan in guiltless earth full many a wound,
Iron to seek, which 'gainst itself should bend,
To tear the bowels that good corn should send.
But yet the common Dam none did bemoan,
Because (though hurt) they never heard her groan.

Then 'gan the° factions in the beasts to breed;   120
Where helping weaker sort, the nobler beasts

° **mowing**: grimacing.   ° **drad**: dreaded.
° **plant**: implant.   ° **wend**: go.   ° **the**: possible misprint for "he."

(As Tigers, Leopards, Bears, and Lions' seed)
Disdained with this, in deserts sought their rests;
Where famine ravin° taught their hungry chests,
That craftily he forced them to do ill,
Which, being done, he afterwards would kill

For murders done, which never erst was seen,
By those great beasts. As for the weakers' good,
He chose themselves his guarders for to been
'Gainst those of might of whom in fear they stood,
As horse and dog: not great, but gentle blood.
Blithe were the commons, cattle of the field,
Though, when they saw their foes of greatness killed.

But they, or° spent or made of slender might,
Then quickly did the meaner cattle find
The great beams gone, the house on shoulders light;
For by and by the horse fair bits did bind;
The dog was in a collar taught his kind.
As for the gentle birds, like case might rue,
When falcon they, and goshawk, saw in mew.°

Worst fell to smallest birds and meanest° herd,
Whom now his own, full like his own he used.
Yet first but wool or feathers off he teared;
And when they were well used° to be abused,
For hungry throat their flesh with teeth he bruised;
At length for glutton taste he did them kill;
At last for sport their silly° lives did spill.°

But yet, O man, rage not beyond thy need;
Deem it no gloire° to swell in tyranny.
Thou art of blood; joy not to make things bleed.
Thou fearest death; think they are loath to die.
A plaint° of guiltless hurt doth pierce the sky.
And you, poor beasts, in patience bide your hell,
Or know your strengths, and then you shall do well.

Thus did I sing and pipe eight sullen hours
To sheep, whom love not knowledge made to hear:
Now fancy's fits, now fortune's baleful stours.°
But then I homeward called my lambkins dear;
For to my dimmèd eyes began t'appear
The night grown old, her black head waxen gray,
Sure shepherd's sign that morn would soon fetch day.

130
140
150
160

❧ ❧ ❧

° **ravin**: predation.　　° **or**: either.　　° **in mew**: encaged.　　° **meanest**: lowest.
° **used**: accustomed.　　° **silly**: innocent.　　° **spill**: destroy.　　° **gloire**: glory (French).
° **plaint**: complaint.　　° **stours**: clashes.

WILLIAM SHAKESPEARE
"Each thing's a Thief," from Timon of Athens (*c.* 1606)

This passage from one of Shakespeare's neglected tragedies presents two conflicting views of the state of nature. The first envisions it as a feudal gift economy, in which the earth, like a free-handed hostess, dispenses her bounty to grateful humans. In the first three acts of the play (co-written with Thomas Middleton), the compulsively generous Timon disburses his fortune in the naïve belief that the human economy operates along similar principles. Hounded out of the city by his creditors, he now lives a hardscrabble existence in the wild that debunks idyllic fantasies of the primeval Golden Age. Surviving off "mere necessities," he aims to escape economic relations, until his accidental discovery of gold lures thieves to his den, leading him to perceive the natural world as always already functioning like a predatory capitalist economy, defined not by trade but outright piracy. Human rapacity simply imitates nature; ecological flow is not gift exchange but perpetual theft. The speech anticipates Thomas Hobbes's view of the state of nature as a nightmarish *bellum omnium contra omnes* (war of all against all), but stretches beyond the political to envisage what philosopher Timothy Morton calls "dark ecology" – a painful awareness of the negativity of co-existence.
Source: *Mr. William Shakespeare's Comedies, Histories, and Tragedies* (1623), 94.

4.3

BANDITTI   We are not Thieves, but men that much do want.°
TIMON   Your greatest want is you want much of meat.°
Why should you want? Behold, the Earth hath Roots.
Within this Mile break forth a hundred Springs.   420
The Oaks bear Mast,° the Briars Scarlet Hips:°
The bounteous Housewife Nature on each bush
Lays her full Mess° before you. Want? Why want?
FIRST BANDIT   We cannot live on Grass, on Berries, Water,
As Beasts and Birds and Fishes.
TIMON   Nor on the Beasts themselves, the Birds, and Fishes;
You must eat men. Yet thanks I must you con°
That you are Thieves professed, that you work not
In holier shapes: for there is boundless Theft
In limited° Professions. Rascal Thieves,   430
Here's Gold. Go, suck the subtle blood o' the Grape
Till the high Fever seethe your blood to froth,
And so 'scape hanging. Trust not the Physician;
His antidotes are poison and he slays
More than you Rob. Take wealth and lives together.
Do Villainy, do, since you protest to do't,
Like Workmen. I'll example you with Thievery:

° **want**: lack, crave.   ° **meat**: food, but with the specific connotation of animal flesh.
° **Mast**: acorns.   ° **Hips**: wild-rose fruit.   ° **Mess**: meal.   ° **con**: acknowledge.
° **limited**: licensed.

The Sun's a Thief, and with his great attraction
Robs the vast Sea; the Moon's an arrant Thief,
440   And her pale fire she snatches from the Sun;
The Sea's a Thief, whose liquid surge resolves°
The Moon into salt tears; the Earth's a Thief,
That feeds and breeds by a composture° stol'n
From general excrement: each thing's a Thief.°
The Laws, your curb and whip, in their rough power
Have unchecked Theft. Love not yourselves. Away!
Rob one another; there's more Gold. Cut throats;
All that you meet are Thieves. To Athens go,
Break open shops; nothing can you steal
450   But Thieves do lose it. Steal no less for this
I give you, and Gold confound you howsoe'er! Amen.

ӿ ӿ ӿ

° **resolves**: dissolves. The observation that tides were synchronized with lunar phases led natural
   philosophers to speculate that that the ocean absorbed watery vapours from the moon.
° **composture**: fertilizer.
° **each ... Thief**: see also Timon's vision of the animal kingdom as a vicious arena of mutual
   predation (4.3.330–47).

JOHN NORDEN
"The state of this island of Great Britain at the beginning"
(1607)

As the human impact on the landscape became more noticeable, Tudor historians
grew curious about the environment of prehistoric Britain. Roman accounts from
the first century BCE tend to depict it as a desolate backwater at the edge of the
earth, and the twelfth-century chronicle of Geoffrey of Monmouth had imagined
its original inhabitants as a race of giants. While challenging mythical historiography, antiquarians such as Raphael Holinshed and William Camden agreed that
ancient Albion – especially after the flooding of the land bridge across the English
Channel (now known to geologists as Doggerland) – must have been, as Edmund
Spenser calls it, a "salvage wilderness" (*Faerie Queene*, 2.10.5). The picture drawn
by the Jacobean surveyor John Norden is not much sunnier. Only the strenuous
efforts over the centuries of enterprising ancestors had made the land habitable.
Environmental historians now think a sizeable portion (around 50 per cent) of
the primeval wildwood was destroyed by the early Iron Age (c. 500 BCE), and it
was further whittled away by the Romans and Anglo-Saxons. Only around 15 per
cent of the English lands surveyed in the Domesday Book of 1086 were still wooded (Rackham 1986, 74–6). Even at the dawn of the seventeenth century, people
were aware that the English landscape had been dramatically altered by human

intervention and that many indigenous species had been extirpated. Rather than preserve what remains, Norden – despite his concerns over deforestation (see Part v) – upholds the ancestral taming of the wilderness as a precedent for more aggressive development and smarter resource management.

Source: *The Surveyor's Dialogue* (1607), 223–5.

BAILEY How then was the state of this island of Great Britain at the beginning, when it was first peopled?

SURVEYOR A very desert° and wilderness, full of woods, fells, moors, bogs, heaths, and all kind of forlorn places. And howsoever we find the state of this island now, records do witness unto us that it was for the most part a universal wilderness, until people finding it a place desolate and forlorn began to set footing here, and by degrees grew into multitudes. Though for the time brutish and rude, Time taught them and Nature drew them to find the means how to stock up trees, bushes, briars, and thorns, and in stead thereof, to plough the land, to sow, set, and plant, to build cities for defence as well against the force of wild beasts, then plentiful in these grounds which now we manure ... After cities (as the land became [224] more and more peopled), they built lesser Towns, Villages, and Dorps,° and after more security, Country Farms and Granges. And as these increased, wild beasts, as Bears, Boars, Wolves, and such like decreased. For when their shelters, great woods, were cut down and the country made more and more champaign,° then the people more and more increased, and more and more decreasing the inconveniences that offended them.

BAILEY I observe in this your discourse some doubts as whether all this island, now Great Britain, were a Wilderness and Desert, and whether there were ever such wild beasts in it as you speak of.

SURVEYOR If you will be satisfied by records, you may find that most of the shires in England were *Forestae*.° And as for the wild beasts, Authors very authentic report of the Caledonian Bear, Boar, Bull, which were in this Island, with infinite many Wolves as, by reason of the great woods and fastnesses,° there are yet in Ireland.

BAILEY This our discourse is somewhat from our matter, yet not altogether impertinent. For if this lie hidden and men be ignorant of the state of former times, our present swelling and ambitious conceits may seem to assume more commendation, for present art and industry in reforming the earth, than ages of old. Wherein I perceive, and by your discourse collect, that our fathers did more in ten years than we in forty.

SURVEYOR It is true. Because we saw not the earth's former deformities, we dreamt it was then as now it is, from the beginning. Whereas indeed our forefathers, by their diligence and travail, left unto our forefathers, and they, by increasing experience and endeavour, left unto us [this land]

° **desert**: uninhabited place.   ° **Dorps**: small villages.   ° **champaign**: open grounds.
° ***Forestae***: Latin term for legally designated forests or hunting grounds.
° **fastnesses**: refuges.

fair and fruitful, free from briars, bushes, and thorns, whereof they found
it full.

[225] And this field wherein now we are may be an instance: for you see
by the ancient ridges or lands, though now overgrown with bushes, it hath
been arable land, and now become fit for no use, unless it be reformed.
And the bushes that are in this field, you see, are such shrubs, and dwarf
bushes, and fruitless briars, as are never like to prove good underwood,
nor good haying or hedging stuff. If it were fit for either, and the country
scant of such provision, it might be preserved. But since they have been
so cropped and bruised with cattle, and since this country is full and most
inclinable by nature to this kind of stuff, more than sufficient for fencing
and fuel, and corn ground and good pasture nothing plentiful, if the ten-
ant were a good husband, he would stock it up and plough it.

※ ※ ※

THOMAS TRAHERNE
"Dumbness" (*c.* 1660)

While most early moderns imagined the Golden Age existing only in remote prehistory, Traherne's poetry portrays it as the lot of every infant. The purity (or
instinctive megalomania) of childhood dissolves all boundaries between mine and
thine, sense and spirit, humanity and nature. In "Dumbness" Traherne laments
the fall from this Edenic state of bliss due to the acquisition of language, which
drives a wedge between the child and the natural world (Watson 2006, 307).
Paradoxically, language both alienates humans from the environment and expresses our intimacy with it. Traherne elsewhere reflects on the "ecstasy of innocence"
in his *Centuries of Meditation* (3.2–3.3), which offers a prose companion to this
poem. While Traherne should be seen in the context of the religious culture of the
late seventeenth century, his portrait of the child as nature-mystic also makes him
a precursor of Wordsworth and Blake.
Source: Bodleian MS Eng. poet c.42, 6ʳ⁻ᵛ. With emendations from BL Burney
MS 392.

> Sure Man was born to meditate on Things,
> And to Contemplate the Eternal Springs
> Of God and Nature, Glory, Bliss, and Pleasure,
> That Life and Love might be his Heav'nly Treasure;
> And therefore Speechless made at first that he
> Might in himself profoundly busied be,
> And not vent out° before he hath ta'en in
> Those° Antidotes that° guard his Soul from Sin.
>   Wise Nature made him Deaf, too, that he might
> Not be disturbed, while he doth take Delight
> In inward Things, nor be depraved with Tongues,

10

° **vent out**: giving] BL.   ° **Those**: Such] BL.   ° **that**: as] BL.

Nor injured by the Errors and the Wrongs
That Mortal Words convey; for Sin and Death
Are most infusèd by accursèd Breath
That, flowing from Corrupted Entrails, bear
Those hidden Plagues which Souls may justly° fear.
　　This, my Dear Friends, this was my Blessèd Case;
For nothing spoke to me but the fair Face
Of Heav'n and Earth, before myself could° speak.
I then my Bliss did, when my Silence, break.°   20
My Non-Intelligence of Human Words
Ten thousand Pleasures unto me affords;
For while I knew not what they to me said,
Before their Souls were into mine conveyed,
Before that Living Vehicle of Wind
Could breathe into me their infected Mind,
Before my Thoughts were leavened with theirs, before
There any Mixture was; the Holy Door,°
Or Gate of Souls was closed,° and mine being One
Within itself to me alone was Known.   30
Then did I dwell within a World of Light,
Distinct and Separate from all Men's Sight,
Where I did feel strange Thoughts and such Things° see
That were, or seemed, only revealed to Me.
There I saw all the World Enjoyed by one;
There I was in the World myself alone.°
No Business Serious seemed but one; no Work°
But one was found; and that did in me lurk.°
　　D'ye ask me What? It was with Clearer Eyes
To see all Creatures full of Deities,   40
Especially Oneself;° and to Admire
The Satisfaction of all True Desire;
'Twas to be Pleased with all that God hath done;
'Twas to Enjoy e'en° All beneath the Sun;
'Twas with a Steady and immediate° Sense
To feel and measure all° the Excellence
Of Things;° 'twas to inherit Endless Treasure,
And to be filled with Everlasting Pleasure;
To reign in Silence and to Sing alone;
To see, love, Covet, have, Enjoy and Praise, in one;   50

° **may justly**: "alone" crossed out and "justly" written in superscript in Bodleian.
° **before ... could**: when I could not] BL.
° **I ... break**: I did my Bliss, when I did Silence break] BL. Underlined in Bodleian.
° **Holy Door**: sacred door in the Vatican opened only during Jubilee Years, during which pilgrims who passed through would be cleansed of sin.
° **closed**: as yet not opened] BL; both imply a state before religious understanding or indoctrination.
° **Things**: "Secrets" struck through in Bod.; Secrets] BL.
° **There ... alone**: There All Things seemed to end in Me alone] BL.
° **seemed ... Work**: deemed, but that which is] BL.
° **But ... lurk**: Designed to perfect my Eternal Bliss] BL.
° **with Clearer ... Oneself**: these lines are omitted in BL, presumably for their scandalous pantheism.
° **even**: omitted from BL; "even All" underlined in Bodleian.
° **and immediate**: quick and lively] BL.　　° **feel ... all**: duly to estimate] BL.
° **Things**: all God's Works] BL.

To Prize and to be ravished; to be true,
Sincere and Single in a blessèd View
Of all his Gifts.° Thus was I pent° within
A Fort, Impregnable to any Sin,
Until the Avenues being Open laid,
Whole Legions Entered and the Forts Betrayed.
Before which time a Pulpit in my Mind,°
A Temple and a Teacher I did° find,
With a large Text to comment on. No Ear
60   But Eyes themselves were all the Hearers there,
And every Stone and every Star a Tongue,
And every Gale of Wind a Curious° Song.
The Heavens were an Oracle, and spake
Divinity; the Earth did undertake°
The office of a Priest; and I, being Dumb
(Nothing besides was dumb), all things did come
With Voices and Instructions. But when I
Had gained a Tongue,° their Power began to die.
Mine Ears let other Noises in, not theirs:
70   A Noise disturbing all my Songs° and Prayers.
My Foes pulled down the° Temple to the Ground.
They my Adoring° Soul did deeply Wound
And, casting that into a Swoon,° destroyed
The Oracle, and all I there enjoyed.
And having once inspired me with a Sense
Of foreign Vanities, they march out thence
In Troops that Cover and despoil my Coasts,
Being, though Invisible, most Hurtful Hosts.°
Yet the first Words mine Infancy did hear,°
80   The Things which in my Dumbness did appear,°
Preventing° all the rest, got such a root
Within my Heart, and stick so close unto't,
It may be Trampled on, but still will grow;
And Nutriment to Soil itself will owe.
The first Impressions are Immortal all;
And let mine Enemies hoop, Cry, roar, or Call,°
Yet these will° whisper if I will but hear,
And penetrate the Heart, if not the Ear.

                            ❧ ❧ ❧

° **Of ... Gifts**: struck through and "To prize and praise" written in superscript in Bodleian.
° **To reign ... pent**: omitted from BL.
° **Before ... Mind**: Ere which unhappy time, within my Mind] BL.
° **did**: could] BL.   ° **Curious**: Psalm or] BL.
° **Divinity ... undertake**: in Bodleian, "to me" crossed out after Divinity, and "itself" after Earth.
° **gained ... Tongue**: learnt to speak] BL.   ° **Songs**: Hymns] BL.   ° **the**: my] BL.
° **They ... Adoring**: And my untainted] BL.
° **And .. Swoon**: Marred all my inward Faculties] BL.   ° **And having ... Hosts**: omitted in BL.
° **Yet ... hear**: Yet to mine Infancy what first appeared] BL.
° **The Things ... appear**: The Truths which (being Speechless) I had heard] BL.
° **Preventing**: preceding.
° **mine Enemies ... Call**: my Foes cry ne'er so loud or call] BL.   ° **will**: still] BL.

LUCY HUTCHINSON
[The Third Day] and [The Naming of the Animals]
(*c.* 1670*s*)

In 1679, an anonymous poem was published entitled *Order and Disorder*. It was misattributed to Sir Allen Apsley until 2001, when David Norbrook outlined a compelling case that Apsley's sister, Lucy Hutchinson, is the likelier author. As an epic based on the Book of Genesis, the poem has obvious parallels with Milton's *Paradise Lost*. The first selection below describes the literal greening of the earth on the third day of creation. Like *Paradise Lost*, this poem admires the verdant world as an ideal habitat for humans, both physically and spiritually/intellectually. The second excerpt celebrates the transparent understanding of the nature of other animals which Adam enjoyed but which postlapsarian humans have lost. While Hutchinson asserts that humans are "King" over all other creatures, this "sovereign power" (24) is elsewhere tempered by the poem's anti-monarchical views (she defended her husband's decision to sign the warrant for Charles I's execution), and its Calvinist pessimism about the lowliness of the human condition.
Source: *Order and Disorder* (1679), 14–15, 28, 30–1 (Cantos 2 and 3).

[The Third Day]

Now the great fabric in all parts complete,
Beauty was called forth to adorn the seat;
Where Earth, fixed in the centre, was the ground,
A mantle of light air compassed it round.
Then first the wat'ry, then the fi'ry wall,
And glitt'ring heaven last involving° all.
Earth's fair green robe vied with the azure skies,
Here proud Woods near the flaming Towers did rise.
The valleys' Trees, though less in breadth than height,
Yet hung with various fruit, as much delight.
Beneath these, little shrubs and bushes sprung,   80
With fair flowers clothed and with rich berries hung,
Whose more delightful fruits seemed to upbraid
The tall trees yielding only barren shade.
Then sprouted Grass and Herbs and Plants,
Prepared to feed the earth's inhabitants,
To glad their nostrils and delight their eyes,
Revive their spirits, cure their maladies.
Nor by these are the senses only fed,
But th'understanding too, while we may read
In every leaf,° lectures of Providence,   90
Eternal Wisdom, Love, Omnipotence:
Which th'eye that sees not, with hell's mists is blind;
That which regards not, is of brutish kind.

° **involving**: enveloping.   ° **leaf**: foliage, but with wordplay on page.

The various colours, figures, powers of these
Are their Creator's growing witnesses,
Their glories emblems are, wherein we see
How frail our human lives and beauties be:°
E'en like those flowers which at the sunrise spread
Their gaudy leaves, and are at evening dead,
100   Yet while they in their native lustre shine,
The Eastern Monarchs are not half so fine.°
In richer robes God clothes the dirty soil
Than men can purchase by their sin and toil.
Then rather fields than painted courts admire,
Yet seeing both, think both must feed the fire.
Only God's works have roots and seeds, from whence
They spring again in grace and excellence,
But men's have none: like hasty lightning they
Flash out, and so forever pass away …

[The Naming of the Animals]

The whole Earth was one large delightful Field,
That till man sinned no hurtful briars did yield,
But God enclosing one part from the rest,
A Paradise in the rich spicy East
Had stored with Nature's wealthy Magazine,°
140   Where every plant did in its lustre shine …
           And now did God the new created King
190   Into the pleasures of his earthly palace bring:
The air, spice, balm, and amber did respire;
His ears were feasted with the Sylvan Choir;
Like country girls, grass flowers did dispute
Their humble beauties with the high-born fruit …
Striving which of them should yield most delight,
And stand the finest in their Sovereign's sight …
           A shady Eminence there was, whereon
The noble Creature° sat, as on his throne,
When God brought every Fowl and every Brute,
That he might Names unto their natures suit,°
Whose comprehensive understanding knew
How to distinguish them at their first view;
And they retaining those names ever since,
Are monuments of his first excellence,
And the Creator's providential grace,
220   Who in those names left us some prints to trace;

° **How frail … be**: marginal note cites Job 14:2 and Ezekiel 40:6–8.
° **Eastern … fine**: marginal note cites Matthew 6:28–30.
° **Magazine**: storehouse.   ° **noble Creature**: Adam.
° **Names … suit**: Isidore of Seville's *Etymologies* (c. 630) and medieval bestiaries popularized the
belief that the Hebrew names Adam gave the animals captured something of their innate essence
or divinely appointed niche.

Nature, mysterious grown, since we grew blind,
Whose Labyrinths we should less easily find
If those first appellations, as a clew,°
Did not in some sort serve to lead us through,
And rectify that frequent gross mistake,
Which our weak judgements and sick senses make,
Since man, ambitious to know more, that sin
Brought dullness, ignorance, and error in.

° **clew**: ball of yarn that could be unwound and followed to navigate a labyrinth, but with wordplay on clue.

Natural Theologies
Psalm 104
(*c.* 900–400 *BCE*)

The German scholar Johann Herder once claimed it was worth studying Hebrew for a decade simply to read Psalm 104 in its original language. With its evident similarities to the opening book of Genesis, it belongs to a group known as the Creation Psalms (which includes 8, 19, 25, 64, 139). But whereas Genesis presents an orderly, sober account of creation, Psalm 104 is rhapsodic and exuberant. Everything in nature revels in the pleasure of simply being alive, and its mere existence is apprehended as poetic. In a world of such extravagant splendour, song (or poetry) becomes a sacred duty, an outpouring of gratitude for the beauty of the earth and the numerous resources it provides to sustain and enrich life. Inspired by Psalm 148, the Jacobean preacher Godfrey Goodman would imagine every creature joined in an inaudible refrain of "We sing the praise of our Maker," and assert that other animals are capable of prayer and even salvation (*The Creatures Praising God*, 1622, 22–8).

Traditionally, most of the Psalms, including 104, were attributed to King David. Biblical scholars today are dubious of Davidic authorship, and estimates of their provenance range from roughly 900 to 400 BCE. Some parts of the Psalms may be even older, with roots in the "praise poetry" of ancient Egypt and Mesopotamia. The Creation Psalms, in other words, represent some of the oldest written records of eco-spirituality in world literature. Psalm translations were popular throughout early modern Europe, although many sacrificed literary merit to make them easier to sing. In the 1580s, Philip Sidney undertook to translate them into more sophisticated English verse. He completed the first forty-three before his untimely death in 1586. His sister Mary took up the project and finished it thirteen years later. Far from a slavish literal rendering, her *Psalter* is remarkable for its metrical ingenuity, and for the liveliness of its imagery that delights in the confusion of nature and culture. Its popularity is attested by eighteen extant manuscripts, and 104 seems to have been particularly admired, as it was one of three psalms transcribed in two different manuscripts (All Souls College, Oxford MS 155, 123^r–7^r; Inner Temple Library, Petyt MS 538, vol. 43, l284^r–6^r). Source: Bodleian MS Rawl. Poet. 24, with annotations from Penshurst MS.

> Make, O my soul, the subject of thy song,
> Th'eternal Lord. O Lord, O God of might,
> To thee, to thee, all royal pomps belong.
> Clothèd art thou in state and glory bright;
> For what is else this eye-delighting light,
> But unto thee a garment wide and long?
> The vaulted heaven, but a curtain right,
> A canopy, thou over thee hast hung?

The rafters that his parlour's roof sustain,
In chevron° he on crystal waters binds. 10
He on the winds, he on the clouds doth reign:
Riding on clouds, and walking on the winds,
Whose wingèd blasts his word as ready finds
To post for him as Angels of his train,°
As to effect the purposes he minds,
He makes no less the flamy fire fain.°

By him the Earth a steadfast base doth bear,
And steadfast so as time nor force can shake,
Which once round waters garment-like did wear,
And hills in seas did lowly lodging take. 20
But seas from hills a swift descent did make,
When swelling high by thee they chidden° were;
Thy thunder's roar did cause their conduits° quake,
Hast'ning their haste with spur of hasty fear.

So waters fled, so mountains high did rise,
So humble valleys deeply did descend,
All to the place thou didst for them devise:
Where bounding Seas with unremovèd end,
Thou badst they should themselves no more extend
To hide the Earth, which now unhidden lies, 30
Yet from the Mountains' rocky sides didst send
Springs' whisp'ring murmurs, Rivers' roaring cries.

Of these the beasts which on the plains do feed
All drink their fill; with these their thirst allay
The Asses wild, and all that wildly breed;
By these in their self-chosen mansions stay
The free-born Fowls, which through the empty way
Of yielding air, wafted with wingèd speed,
To art-like notes of nature-tunèd lay,°
Make earless bushes give attentive heed. 40

Thou, thou of heav'n the windows dost unclose,
Dewing the mountains with thy bounty's rain.
Earth, great with young, her longing doth not lose,°
The hopeful ploughman hopeth not in vain.
The vulgar° grass, whereof the beast is fain,°
The rarer herb man for himself hath chose.
All things, in brief, that life in life maintain,
From Earth's old bowels fresh and youngly grows.

° **chevron**: an inverted V-shape.   ° **train**: retinue.   ° **fain**: eager.   ° **chidden**: scolded.
° **conduits**: channels.   ° **lay**: song.
° **Dewing . . . lose**: cf. Carew's translation, "when on her Womb thy Dew is shed / The pregnant Earth is brought to bed"(4).
° **vulgar**: common.   ° **fain**: pleased (to eat).

Thence wine, the counter-poison unto care;
50   Thence oil, whose juice unpleats° the folded brow;
Thence bread, our best, I say not daintiest fare,
Prop yet of hearts, which else would weakly bow.
Thence, Lord, thy leavèd people bud and blow,
Whose princes thou, thy Cedars, dost not spare
A fuller draught of thy cup to allow,
That highly raised above the rest they are.

Yet highly raised they do not proudly scorn
To give small birds an humble entertain,
Whose brickle° nests are on their branches born,
60   While in the Firs the Storks a lodging gain.
So highest hills rock-loving Goats sustain,
And have their heads with climbing traces° worn,
That safe in Rocks the Conies may remain;
To yield them caves, their rocky ribs are torn.

Thou mak'st the Moon, the Empress of the night,
Hold constant course with most inconstant face;
Thou mak'st the Sun, the chariot-man of light,
Well know the start and stop of daily race.
When he doth set, and night his beams deface,
70   To roam abroad wood-burgesses° delight:
Lions, I mean, who, roaring all that space,
Seem then of thee to crave their food by right.°

When he returns they all from field retire,
And lay them down in cave, their home, to rest.
They rest; man stirs to win a workman's hire,°
And works till sun have wrought his way to west.
Eternal Lord, who greatest art and best,
How I amazed thy mighty works admire!
Wisdom in them hath every part possessed,
80   Whereto in me no wisdom can aspire.

Behold the Earth, how there thy bounties flow!
Look on the sea, extended hugely wide:
What wat'ry troops swim, creep, and crawl and go,
Of great, of small, on this, that, ev'ry side!
There the sail-wingèd ships on waves do glide;
Sea monsters° there their plays and pastimes show,
And all at once in seasonable tide
Their hungry eyes on thee their feeder throw.

° **unpleats**: smooths.   ° **brickle**: brittle.   ° **traces**: tracks made by animals.
° **burgesses**: citizens.
° **Lions ... right**: the annotation of this verse in the Geneva Bible reads, "they only find meat according to God's providence, who careth even for the brute beasts."
° **hire**: wages.   ° **Sea monsters**: cf. Geneva's "Leviathan" and Carew's "huge Whales with finny feet" (5).

Thou giv'st, they take; thy hand itself displays.
They, fillèd, feel the plenties of thy hand: 90
All darkened lie deprivèd of thy rays.
Thou tak'st their breath,° not one can longer stand;
They die, they turn to former dust and sand,
Till thy life-giving Spirit do must'ring raise
New companies to reinforce each band,
Which, still supplièd, never whole decays.°

So may it, O, so may it ever go!
Jehovah's works his glorious gladness be,
Who touching Mountains, Mountains smoking grow;
Who eyeing Earth, Earth quakes with quiv'ring knee.   100
As for myself, my silly° self, in me
While life shall last, his worth in praise° to show
I framèd have a resolute decree,
And thankful be, till being I forgo.

O, that my song might good acceptance find:
How should my heart in great Jehovah joy!
O, that some plague this irreligious kind,
Ingrate to God, would from the earth destroy!
Meanwhile my Soul, incessantly employ
To high Jehovah's praise my mouth and mind: 110
Nay, all, since all his benefits enjoy,
Praise him whom bands of time nor age° can bind.

⧰ ⧰ ⧰

° **breath**: Carew daringly translates this as "Soul" (5).
° **New … decays**: these lines suggest that God does not permit a species to die out, a doctrine that
  was still widely accepted until Georges Cuvier presented conclusive proof of extinction in 1796.
° **silly**: feeble, insignificant.   ° **praise**: Rawl.; song] Penshurst.
° **whom … age**: Penshurst; whose bands of time no age] Rawl.

GUILLAUME DE SALLUSTE DU BARTAS
"The World's a Book in Folio" (1578)

The Book of Nature is a common trope in Renaissance theology and natural history. In addition to fostering a holistic view of the earth as a literary creation, the
metaphor can also be regarded as (in the words of Michel Foucault) "the reverse
and visible side of another transference, and a much deeper one, which forces
language to reside in the world, among the plants, the herbs, the stones, and the
animals" (35). At a time when Protestant Reformers were seeking to scrape away
received tradition in favour of a direct encounter with Holy Writ, this analogy would have promoted a corresponding hermeneutics of nature that encouraged closer observation of the biophysical world. The author of this example,

Du Bartas, was a French Huguenot, admired by English Protestant poets such as
Spenser and Milton.
Source: *Divine Weeks*, trans. Joshua Sylvester (1605), 7–8.

> The World's a Book in Folio,° printed all
> With God's great Works in Letters Capital;
> Each Creature is a Page, and each effect,
> A fair Character,° void of all defect.
>   But as young Truants, toying in the Schools,
> Instead of Learning, learn to play the fools,
> We gaze but on the Babies° and the Cover,
> The gaudy Flowers° and Edges gilded-over;
> And never farther for our Lesson look
> Within the Volume of this various Book,
> Where learnèd Nature rudest ones instructs,
> That by his wisdom God the World conducts.
>   To read this Book we need not understand
> Each stranger's gibb'rish, neither take in hand
> Turks' Characters, nor Hebrew Points° to seek,
> Nile's Hieroglyphics, nor the Notes of Greek.
> The wand'ring Tartars,° the Antarctics wild,
> Th'Alarbies° fierce, the Scythians° fell, the Child
> Scarce seven-year old, the ble*è*d, agèd eye,
> Though void of Art, read here indifferently.°
> But he that wears the spectacles of Faith
> Sees through the Spheres, above their highest height;
> He comprehends th'Arch-mover of all Motions,
> And reads (though running) all these needful Notions.
> Therefore, by Faith's pure rays illuminèd,
> These sacred Pandects° I desire to read,
> And, God the better to behold, behold
> Th'Orb° from his Birth, in's Ages manifold.

10

20

৯৫ ৯৫ ৯৫

° **Folio**: a large-format book, whose printed sheets had been folded once.
° **Character**: letter.
° **Babies**: title-pages or frontispieces, so named because they often depicted cherubs.
° **Flowers**: decorative floral-shaped motifs in the margins of Renaissance books.
° **Points**: diacritic marks in Hebrew that aid in pronunciation.
° **Tartars**: nomadic tribes of Central Asia.   ° **Alarbies**: Arabs.
° **Scythians**: inhabitants of Asiatic Russia.   ° **indifferently**: equally.
° **Pandects**: compendia of laws.   ° **Orb**: universe.

GIORDANO BRUNO
"The World Soul" (1584)

Burned at the stake for heresy in 1600, Bruno has long been hailed as a martyr of modern science; he may also come to be canonized as a prophet of ecological philosophy. Between 1583 and 1585, the Italian philosopher travelled through England, debating his controversial teachings with members of the English intelligentsia. If the Oxford dons dismissed him as an arrogant eccentric, Bruno's defence of Copernicus and the *anima mundi* made an indelible impression on the likes of Samuel Daniel, Philip Sidney, John Florio, Walter Ralegh, and Christopher Marlowe. The Copernican theory of a heliocentric universe was first imported to England by Thomas Digges in 1576, but Bruno was among the first to champion it in public. By displacing humans from the epicentre of creation, the new cosmology signals the start of a gradual shift away from an anthropocentric worldview. As for his belief in the infinite universe and the plurality of worlds (recently confirmed by the discovery of exo-planets), their ecocritical implications were made clear by the seventeenth-century polymath Robert Burton: if the universe is infinite and possibly inhabited by other beings, then "how are all things made for man?" (55).

Rather than reproduce Bruno's notorious case for a sun-centred solar system, the excerpt below highlights his revival of Pythagorean, Stoic, Lucretian, and Hermetic cosmology to propose that the universe is animate and sentient. Advancing one of the first philosophical arguments for pan-psychism – the notion that all matter is endowed with some residue of mind – Bruno, like the contemporary theorists of the New Materialism, boldly redefines the parameters of life and agency.

Source: *Cause, Principle, Unity*, trans. Robert de Lucca (1998), 37–8, 42–4, 49–50.

TEOFILO° The universal intellect is the innermost, most real and proper faculty or potential part of the World Soul. It is that one and same thing that fills everything, illuminates the universe, and directs Nature to produce her various species suitably. It is to the production of natural [38] things what our intellect is to the production of the representation of things. The Pythagoreans call it the "mover" and "agitator of the universe." As the poet has expressed,

> Pervading its members, mind stirs the whole mass
> And mingles with its body.°

The Platonists call it "world-artificer."° They believe it proceeds from the higher world, which is indeed one, to this sensible world, which is divided into many, and where, because of the separation of its parts, both harmony and discord reign. This intellect, infusing and instilling something of its own into matter, while itself remaining immobile and undisturbed,

---

° **Teofilo**: a self-portrait of Bruno; the name suggests "beloved of God" in Latin.
° **Pervading ... body**: from Virgil, *Aeneid*, 6.726–7. See Ralegh's translation below (p. 64).
° **world-artificer**: see Plato's *Timaeus* (1578 Stephanus edition, pp. 27–31).

produces all things. The Hermeticists° say that it is "most fecund in seeds," or yet that it is the "seed sower" because it impregnates matter with all forms, which … succeed in shaping, forming, and weaving matter in ways that are so remarkable and numerous that they cannot be ascribed to chance. Orpheus° calls it "the eye of the world" because it sees both the inside and outside of all natural things … Empedocles° calls it "the differentiator," since it never tires of distinguishing the forms confused within Nature's bosom … Plotinus° says it is "the father" and "progenitor" because it distributes seeds in Nature's fields and is the proximate dispenser of forms. As for us, we call it "the internal artificer," because it shapes matter, forming it from inside like a seed or root shooting forth and unfolding the trunk …

[42] DICSONO° I seem to be hearing something very novel. Are you claiming perhaps that not only the form of the universe, but also the forms of natural things are souls?

TEOFILO Yes.

DICSONO But who will agree with you there?

TEOFILO But who could reasonably refute it?

DICSONO Common sense tells us that not everything is alive.

TEOFILO The most common sense is not the truest sense.

DICSONO I can readily believe that that last point is defensible. But it is not enough for one to be able to defend a thing to render it true: we must be able to provide a proof …

TEOFILO So which do you think are not true parts of the world?

DICSONO Those which are not primary bodies, as the Peripatetics° call them: the Earth, with the waters and other parts that, as you say, constitute the entire creature …

[43] TEOFILO But what are these things that are not animated, or that are not parts of animated things?

DICSONO Do you not think a few of them are right before our eyes? All lifeless things.

TEOFILO And which things do not possess life? Or at least the vital principle?

DICSONO So, in short, you hold that there is nothing that does not possess a soul and that has no vital principle.

° **Hermeticists**: followers of Hermes Trismegistus, an ancient Egyptian sage believed to be a contemporary of Moses. The Hermetic text *Poemander* imagines a divine spirit descending upon and impregnating the universe.
° **Orpheus**: mythic bard in Greek legend; eighty-seven hymns (some dating back to perhaps the third century BCE) were dubiously attributed to him in antiquity.
° **Empedocles**: pre-Socratic philosopher, credited with popularizing the theory of the four elements as the "roots" of the material world.
° **Plotinus**: neo-Platonic philosopher, who believed in the mystical "one-ness" of creation. See his *Enneads* (IV.8–9).
° **Dicsono**: alias for Alexander Dickson, who became Bruno's most outspoken English disciple.
° **Peripatetics**: followers of Aristotle. Bruno is here challenging Aristotelian orthodoxy.

TEOFILO Yes, exactly.

POLIINNIO Then a dead body has a soul? So my clogs, my slippers, my boots, my spurs, as well as my ring and my gauntlets are supposedly animated? ...

[44] TEOFILO I will say, then, that the table is not animated as a table, nor are the clothes as clothes, nor the leather as leather, nor the glass as glass, but as natural things and composites they have within them matter and form. All things, no matter how small, have in them part of that spiritual substance ... for in all things there is spirit and there is not the least corpuscle that does not contain within itself some portion that may animate it.

POLIINNIO *Ergo quidquid est, animum est.*°

TEOFILO Not all things that have a soul are called animate.

DICSONO Then at least all things have life?

TEOFILO All things that have a soul are animated in terms of substance, but their life is not recognizable to the Peripatetics, who define life too strictly and grossly, using the extrinsic and sensible act and not the substance ... If, then, spirit, soul, life is found in all things and in varying degrees fills all matter, it can assuredly be deduced that it is the true act and true form of all things. The World Soul, then, is the formal constitutive principle of the universe and all it contains. I say that life is found in all things; the soul is necessarily the form of all things; that form presides everywhere over matter and governs the composites, determines the composition and cohesion of the parts ...

[49] POLIINNIO I would like very much to know how the World Soul is a form which is present everywhere in its totality, if it is indivisible. It must, then, be very large, even of infinite dimension, since you say the world is infinite.

GERVASIO Here is good reason, indeed, for it being so large. It is like what a preacher in Grandazzo in Sicily said of our Lord: to signify that he is present everywhere he ordered a crucifix as large as the church in the image of God the Father ... who possesses such long legs that they stretch down to earth, which he uses as a footstool. To this preacher came a certain peasant, saying, "Reverend father, how many ells° of cloth would it take to make his hose?" Another said that all Milazzo's and Nicosia's° chickpeas, haricots, and broad beans would not suffice to fill his belly. Be careful, then, that this World Soul is not cut out in the same way ...

TEOFILO In short, you must know, then, that the World Soul and divinity are not entirely present everywhere and through every part in the same way as some material thing could be ... If we say the World Soul and universal form are everywhere, we do not mean in some corporeal or dimensional sense ... They are everywhere present in their entirety in a spiritual way. To take an example (crude as it is), you might imagine a voice which is entire

---

° *Ergo ... est*: Therefore whatever is, is animate (ensouled).
° **ells**: yards.   ° **Milazzo ... Nicosia**: two Sicilian towns.

and inside the whole room and in every part of it; in effect, one hears [50]
it everywhere entirely there ... Divinity is entire in any part whatsoever,
just as my voice is heard entirely from all sides of the room.

⁂ ⁂ ⁂

RICHARD HOOKER

"The Law Which Natural Agents Have Given Them to Observe, and Their Necessary Manner of Keeping It" (1593)

Richard Hooker was one of the champions of the Elizabethan Settlement, de-
voting his considerable intellectual energies to carving out a *via media* between
Catholicism and Puritanism. This yearning for balance and moderation also
shapes his cosmology. Following E. M. W. Tillyard, most historians have tended
to point to *Laws of Ecclesiastical Polity* as the last systematic defence of the sacred,
medieval image of the universe. More recently, Hooker's work has been read as "an
inevitably disfiguring attempt to give that image some major features of modern
secularism" (McGrade xiv). This tension plays out in the sections reprinted below.
In the midst of his eloquent paeans to natural law and order, Hooker recognizes
that the world suffers periodic outbursts of disorder or "swervings" – a term that
may owe something to Lucretian atomism. Hooker's homily is famously echoed in
Ulysses's monologue on "degree" in Shakespeare's *Troilus and Cressida*.
Source: *Of the Laws of Ecclesiastical Polity* (1593), 52–5.

To come to the law of nature: albeit thereby we sometimes mean that
manner of working which God hath set for each created thing to keep,
yet forasmuch as those things are termed most properly natural agents
which keep the law of their kind unwittingly, as the heavens and elements
of the world, which can do no otherwise than they do; and forasmuch as
we give unto intellectual natures the name of voluntary agents that so we
may distinguish them from the other, expedient it will be that we sever the
law of nature observed by the one from that which the other is tied unto.
Touching the former, their strict keeping of one tenure, statute, and law
is spoken of by all, but hath in it more than men have as yet attained to
know, or perhaps ever shall attain, seeing the travail of wading herein is
given of God to the sons of men, that perceiving how much the least thing
in the world hath in it more than the wisest are able to reach unto, they
may by this means learn humility.

Moses° in describing the work of creation attributeth speech unto God:
God said, "Let there be light; Let there be a firmament; Let the waters
under the heaven be gathered together into one place; Let the earth bring
forth; Let there be light in the firmament of heaven." Was this only the
intent of Moses, to signify the infinite greatness of God's power by the

---

° **Moses**: believed to be the author of Genesis.

easiness of his accomplishing such effects without travail, pain, or labour? Surely, it seemeth that Moses had herein besides this a further purpose: namely, first to teach that God did not work as a necessary but a voluntary agent ... Secondly, to show that God did then institute a law natural to be observed by creatures ... by a solemn injunction. His commanding those things to be which are and to be in such sort as they are, to keep that tenure and course which they do, importeth the establishment of nature's law. This world's first creation and the preservation since of things created, what is it but only so far forth a manifestation by execution what the eternal law of God is concerning things natural? And as it cometh to pass in a kingdom rightly ordered that after a law is once published it presently takes effect far and wide, all states framing themselves thereunto, even so let us think it fareth in the natural course of the world. Since the time that God did first proclaim the edicts of his law upon it, heaven and earth have hearkened unto his voice and their labour hath been to do his will. He "made a law for the rain"; He gave his "decree unto the sea, that the waters should not pass [53] his commandment."°

Now if nature should intermit her course and leave altogether, though it were but for a while, the observation of her own laws; if those principal and mother elements of the world, whereof all things in this lower world are made, should lose the qualities which now they have; if the frame of that heavenly arch erected over our heads should loosen and dissolve itself; if the celestial spheres should forget their wonted motions and by irregular volubility° turn themselves any way as it might happen; if the prince of lights of heaven, which now as a Giant doth run his unwearied course, should, as it were, through a languishing faintness begin to stand and to rest himself; if the Moon should wander from her beaten way; the times and seasons of the year blend themselves by disordered and confused mixture; the winds breathe out their last gasp; the clouds yield no rain; the earth be defeated of heavenly influence; the fruits of the earth pine away as children at the withered breasts of their mother no longer able to yield them relief; what would become of man himself, whom these things now do all serve? See we not plainly that obedience of creatures unto the law of nature is the stay° of the whole world?

Notwithstanding with nature it cometh sometimes to pass as with art. Let Phidias° have rude and obstinate stuff to carve, though his art do that it should, his work will lack that beauty which otherwise in fitter matter it might have had. He that striketh an instrument with skill may cause notwithstanding a very unpleasant sound if the string whereon he striketh chance to be incapable of harmony ...[This] defect in the matter

---

° **He ... commandment**: Job 28:26 (see Caryl's commentary) and Proverbs 8:29.
° **volubility**: rotation.   ° **stay**: support, prop.
° **Phidias**: Greek sculptor (c. 480–430 BCE). His statue of Zeus at Olympia was hailed as one of the Seven Wonders of the ancient world.

of things natural they who gave themselves unto the contemplation of nature amongst the heathen observed often. But the true original cause thereof, divine malediction, laid for the sin of man upon these creatures which God had made for the use of man, this being an article of that saving truth which God hath revealed unto his Church, was above the reach of their merely natural capacity and understanding. But howsoever these swervings° are now and then incident into the course of nature, nevertheless so constantly the laws of nature are by natural agents observed, that no man denieth but those things which nature worketh are wrought either always or for the most part after one and the same manner ...

Although we are not of opinion therefore, as some are, that nature in working hath before her certain exemplary draughts or patterns, which subsisting in the bosom of the Highest, and being thence discovered, she fixeth her eye upon them as travellers by sea upon the pole-star of the world, and that according thereunto she guideth her hand to work by imitation ... We rather embrace the oracle of Hippocrates: ... "Each thing both in small and in great fulfilleth the task which destiny hath set down." And concerning the manner of executing and fulfilling of the same: "What they do they know not, yet is it in show and appearance as though they did know what they do, and the truth is they do not discern [54] the things which they look on."°

Nevertheless, forasmuch as the works of nature are no less exact than if she did both behold and study how to express some absolute shape or mirror always present before her – yea, such her dexterity and skill that no intellectual creature in the world were able by capacity to do that which nature does without capacity and knowledge—it cannot be but nature hath some director of infinite knowledge to guide her in all her ways. Who the guide of nature but only the God of nature? ... Those things which nature is said to do are by divine art performed, using nature as an instrument. Nor is there any such art or knowledge divine in nature herself working, but in the guide of nature's work ... This workman, whose servitor nature is, being in truth only one, the heathens imagining to be more, gave him in the sky the name of Jupiter; in the air the name of Juno; in the water the name of Neptune; in the earth the name of Vesta and sometimes Ceres; the name of Apollo in the sun; in the moon the name of Diana; the name of Aeolus and diverse others in the winds; and, to conclude, even so many guides of nature they dreamed of as they saw were kinds of things natural in the world. These they honoured, as having [55] power to work or cease accordingly as men deserved of them. But unto us there is one only guide of all agents natural, and he both the creator and the worker of all in all, alone to be blessed, adored, and honoured by all forever.

❧ ❧ ❧

° **swervings**: a concept Hooker seems to have borrowed from Lucretius. See Feerick and Nardizzi.
° **Each ... on**: from Hippocrates, *Regimen*, 4.236–7.

JOHN DONNE
"Why are we by all Creatures waited on?" (*c.* 1609)

Numbered among Donne's "Holy Sonnets," this poem dares to question whether the bestial condition might be superior to the human, and urges humans to see their privileged niche in the universe as an inscrutable miracle. Does it foreshadow or attempt to stave off the pessimism of Donne's *Anatomy* in Part VI?
Source: *Poems* (1633), 37; with capitalization and emendations from Westmoreland MS, 1ʳ.

> Why are we° by all Creatures waited on?
> Why do the prod'gal elements supply
> Life and food to me, being more pure than I,
> Simple, and farther from corruption?
> Why brook'st thou, ignorant horse, subjection?
> Why dost thou, Bull and boar, so sillily°
> Dissemble weakness, and by one Man's stroke die,
> Whose whole kind you might swallow and feed upon?
> Weaker I am,° woe is me, and worse than you:
> You have not sinned, nor need be timorous.°   10
> But wonder at a greater wonder: for to us
> Created Nature° doth these things subdue;
> But their Creator, whom sin nor Nature tied,
> For us, his creatures and his foes, hath died.

⅏ ⅏ ⅏

° **are we**: am I] Westmoreland.   ° **sillily**: meekly, naïvely.
° **Weaker I am**: Alas, I'm weaker] Westmoreland.
° **timorous**: fearful (of damnation). Cf. Donne's Holy Sonnet 5.
° **Created Nature**: a translation of the theological phrase *Natura naturata*, emphasizing its passive
   dependence upon God, in contrast to *Natura naturans*, Nature naturing, or Creative Nature.

WALTER RALEGH
"How It Is To Be Understood That the Spirit of God Moved Upon the Waters" and "That Nature Is No Principium Per Se*"*° (1614)

In these extracts from his monumental *History of the World,* Ralegh crosses lances with neo-Stoic thinkers such as Bruno and Lipsus, who had effectively deified nature. Yet Ralegh also reveals himself to be a careful student of these heterodox authors, and denouncing their "impiety monstrous" actually enables the public dissemination of a radical materialist or at least a Deist philosophy that he and his

° ***Principium per se***: origin in itself.

intellectual circle were suspected of secretly believing. While denying that Nature is God, does Ralegh insinuate that God is nature?
Source: *The History of the World* (1617), 7, 13.

"How It Is To Be Understood That the Spirit of God Moved Upon the Waters"

The Spirit of God which moved upon the waters° cannot be taken for a breath or wind, nor for any other creature separate from the infinite active power of God, which then formed and distinguished, and which now sustaineth and giveth continuance, to the Universal.° "For the Spirit of the Lord filleth all the world, and the same is it which maintaineth all things," saith Solomon° ... And this working of God's Spirit in all things, Virgil hath expressed excellently:

> The Heav'n, the Earth, and all the liquid Main,°
> The Moon's bright globe and Stars titanian,°
> A Spirit within maintains, and their whole mass,
> A Mind, which through each part infused doth pass,
> Fashions and works, and wholly doth transpierce
> All this great Body of the Universe ...°

[13] "That Nature is No *Principium Per Se*"

And for this working power which we call Nature, the beginning of motion and rest according to Aristotle, the same is and nothing else but the strength and faculty which God hath infused into every creature, having no other self-ability than a clock° after it is wound up by a man's hand hath. These therefore that attribute unto this faculty any first or sole power have therein no other understanding than such a one hath who looking into the stern of a ship, and finding it guided by the helm and rudder, doth ascribe some absolute virtue to the piece of wood, without all consideration of the hand that guides it, or the judgement which also directeth and commandeth that hand.

⁂ ⁂ ⁂

° **moved ... waters**: Genesis 1:2.   ° **Universal**: universe.
° **For ... Solomon**: from the apocryphal Wisdom of Solomon 1:7.   ° **Main**: ocean.
° **titanian**: titanic, but also sun-like, alluding to heliocentric theory.
° **The Heaven ... Universe**: *Aeneid*, 6.724–9. A famous passage spoken by Aeneas's father in the underworld, and hence possessing an oracular authority in Virgil's epic. Bruno also cites it in his defence of the *anima mundi*. This is believed to be Ralegh's own translation.
° **clock**: an early vision of a mechanistic universe, later popularized by Descartes.

GEORGE WITHER
"Song for Rogation Week" (1623)

Every spring, parishes throughout early modern England would gather to process around their fields while reciting psalms and beseeching God to bless their crops and cattle. This holiday, known as Rogation, had roots in pagan ceremonies to expel the spirits of winter. During the Reformation, zealous Puritans denounced such prayers as magical thinking, and sought to strip the perambulations of their sacramental character. In his 1563 "Homily for the Days of Rogation Week," Bishop John Jewel defends the custom in the conviction that God "is invisible everywhere and in every creature, and fulfilleth both heaven and earth with his presence" (443). These processions were an important occasion for reaffirming communal bonds by dispensing charity and, through a kind of experiential cartography, settling boundary disputes; significantly, Jewel urges parishes to use the holiday to oppose enclosures. It was also a time for reaffirming humanity's bond with the earth through fasting and prayer. George Wither's versifying of the Rogation liturgy neatly illustrates the correspondence between prayer, poetry, and eco-piety. Like Jewel, Wither defends this embattled holiday on the grounds that by "viewing God's yearly blessing upon the grass, the corn, and other fruits of the earth, we might be the more provoked to praise him" (191). Wither also specifies that his verses should be sung to the tune of *Veni Creator* (Come, Creator), reinforcing the notion of God's immanence in the natural world.
Source: *The Hymns and Songs of the Church* (1623), 191–3.

> Let not the Seasons of this year,
> As they their courses do observe, 10
> Engender those Contagions here,
> Which our transgressions do deserve.
> Let not the Summer worms impair
> Those bloomings of the Earth we see,
> Nor Blastings or distempered Air
> Destroy those Fruits that hopeful be …
>
> And as we heedfully observe
> The certain limit of our Grounds,
> And outward quiet to preserve,
> About them walk our yearly Rounds,
> So let us also have a care,
> Our soul's possession, LORD, to know; 30
> That no encroachments on us there
> Be gainèd by our subtle Foe.
>
> What pleasant Groves, what goodly Fields!
> How fruitful Hills and Dales have we!
> How sweet an Air our Climate yields!
> How stored with Flocks and Herds are we!
> How Milk and Honey doth o'erflow!
> How clear and wholesome are our Springs!
> How safe from rav'nous Beasts we go!
> And, oh, how free from poisonous things! 40

For these and for our Grass, our Corn,
For all that springs from Blade or Bough,
For all those blessings that adorn
Or Wood or Field this kingdom through,
For all of these, thy praise we sing,
And humbly, LORD, entreat thee, too,
That Fruit to thee we forth may bring,
As unto us thy Creatures do.

50

So in the sweet refreshing shade
Of thy Protection sitting down,
Those gracious Favours we have had,
Relate we will to thy renown;
Yea, other men, when we are gone,
Shall for thy mercies honour Thee,
And famous make what thou hast done,
To such as after them shall be.°

꙳ ꙳ ꙳

° **after ... be**: for more on Wither's concern for posterity, see his poem in Part VI.

JOHN MILTON
"On the Morning of Christ's Nativity" (1629)

This work by arguably England's greatest religious poet dramatizes a pivotal moment in the history of Western culture and consciousness: the incarnation of Christ and the downfall of pagan animism. As it surveys the sacred sites of the ancient world, the ode begins to resemble an exorcism: the oracles fall mute and the *genii loci* (spirits of place) flee before the son of God like nocturnal creatures before the rising sun (a fortuitous pun in which the poem delights). As Milton would have known, the early Church had decided to celebrate Christmas on 25 December to replace the Roman holidays of Saturnalia and *Sol Invictus* (Feast of the Unconquered Sun). While the former honoured the god Saturn, the latter celebrated the lengthening of daylight after the winter solstice. The poem thus sets up an opposition between Christianity and solar monotheism while unwittingly exposing how much the two have in common.

Composed when Milton was a student at Cambridge, the poem was probably inspired by Joseph Mede, a tutor at Milton's college who had written a commentary on Plutarch's essay "On the Cessation of Oracles." And yet for all its piety, the "Nativity Ode" is a text of beguiling complexity. It betrays an elegiac fondness for the pagan tradition it maligns, like the heroic grandeur bestowed on Satan in *Paradise Lost*. In confusing the *Pax Romana* with the *Pax Christiana*, Milton smudges the line he draws between BC and AD, as the surprising conflation of

Christ with Pan suggests. Does he spit on the graves of the ancient fertility gods or rob them? Is it permissible to wield animistic language to combat animism? Can you fight Ovid with Ovid?

Source: *Poems Upon Several Occasions* (1673), 2–12.

The Hymn

1

It was the Winter wild,
While the Heav'n-born child
All meanly wrapt in the rude manger lies;
Nature in awe to him
Had doffed her gaudy trim,°
With her great Master so to sympathize:
It was no season then for her
To wanton with the Sun, her lusty Paramour.

30

2

Only with speeches fair
She woos the gentle Air
To hide her guilty front with innocent Snow,
And on her naked shame,
Pollute with sinful blame,
The Saintly Veil of Maiden White to throw,
Confounded that her Maker's eyes
Should look so near upon her foul deformities.

40

3

But he her fears to cease,
Sent down the meek-eyed Peace;
She crowned with Olive green, came softly sliding
Down through the turning sphere,
His ready Harbinger,
With Turtle° wing the amorous clouds dividing,
And waving wide her myrtle wand,
She strikes a universal Peace through Sea and Land …

50

7

And though the shady gloom
Had given day her room,
The Sun himself withheld his wonted speed,
And hid his head for shame,
As his inferior flame,
The new-enlightened world no more should need;
He saw a greater Sun appear
Than his bright Throne or burning Axletree could bear …

80

° **trim**: apparel.   ° **Turtle**: turtle-dove.

19

The Oracles are dumb,
No voice or hideous hum
Runs through the archèd roof in words deceiving.
Apollo from his shrine
Can no more divine,
With hollow shriek the steep of Delphos° leaving.
No nightly trance, or breathèd spell,
180   Inspires the pale-eyed Priest from the prophetic cell.

20

The lonely mountains o'er,
And the resounding shore,
A voice of weeping heard, and loud lament;
From haunted spring and dale,
Edged with poplar pale,
The parting Genius° is with sighing sent;
With flower-enwoven tresses torn
The Nymphs in twilight shade of tangled thickets mourn.

21

In consecrated Earth,
190   And on the holy Hearth,
The Lars° and Lemures° moan with midnight plaint;
In Urns and Altars round,
A drear and dying sound
Affrights the Flamens° at their service quaint;
And the chill Marble seems to sweat,
While each peculiar power forgoes his wonted seat.

22

Peor° and Baalim,°
Forsake their Temples dim,
With that twice-battered god of Palestine,°
200   And moonèd Ashtoreth,°
Heav'n's Queen and Mother both,

° **Delphos**: site of a famous oracle consecrated to Apollo.
° **Genius**: spirit, derived from the Latin verb meaning to create or produce. In the Greco-Roman world, sacred springs, groves, and mountains were inhabited by *genii loci* – spirits of place.
° **Lars**: the tutelary deities of a house, city, or field in Roman religion.
° **Lemures**: Latin for spirits or ghosts, later applied to the nocturnal primates of Madagascar.
° **Flamens**: ancient Roman priests.
° **Peor**: a mountain god worshipped by Moabites, as described in Chapter 25 of the Book of Numbers.
° **Baalim**: Ba'al was an honorific, equivalent to "Lord," and applied by many ancient Semitic peoples to their local deities. Several of those named here in the "Nativity Ode" reappear as rebel angels in *Paradise Lost*.
° **god of Palestine**: Dagon, a Mesopotamian fertility god associated with both grain and fish (see 1 Samuel 5:2–7).
° **Ashtoreth**: Astarte or Ishtar, a prominent goddess in the ancient Middle East associated with fertility and sexuality.

Now sits not girt with Tapers' holy shine;
The Libyan Hammon° shrinks his horn,
In vain the Tyrian Maids their wounded Thammuz° mourn.

23

And sullen Moloch° fled,
Hath left in shadows dread,
His burning Idol all of blackest hue;
In vain with Cymbals' ring,
They call the grisly King,
In dismal dance about the furnace blue;   210
The brutish gods of Nile as fast,
Isis° and Horus° and the Dog Anubis,° haste.

24

Nor is Osiris° seen
In Memphian Grove or Green,
Trampling the unshowered Grass with lowings loud.
Nor can he be at rest
Within his sacred chest,
Naught but profoundest Hell can be his shroud;
In vain with Timbreled° Anthems dark
The sable-stoled° Sorcerers bear his worshipped Ark.   220

25

He feels from Judah's Land
The dreaded Infant's hand,
The rays of Bethlehem blind his dusky eyne;°
Nor all the Gods beside,
Longer dare abide,
Nor Typhon° huge, ending in snaky twine:
Our Babe, to show his Godhead true,
Can in his swaddling bands control the damnèd crew.

26

So when the Sun in bed,
Curtained with cloudy red,   230
Pillows his chin upon an Orient wave.

° **Hammon**: a Carthaginian god of weather and agriculture.
° **Thammuz**: ancient Near Eastern god of vegetation, whom the Greeks identified with Adonis.
° **Moloch**: ancient Phoenician god whose followers performed child sacrifice.
° **Isis**: Egyptian goddess whose cult was associated with nature, maternity, and magical healing. Her tears for Osiris were said to make the Nile flood.
° **Horus**: the falcon-headed Egyptian god, who presided over the sky and hunting.
° **Anubis** : the dog-headed Egyptian god, who oversaw the embalming and burial of the dead.
° **Osiris**: the Egyptian god of both the underworld and fertility, who was sometimes depicted as a bull (Osiris-Apis).
° **Timbrel**: an ancient tambourine.
° **sable-stoled**: black-shawled. Stole is a liturgical vestment draped over a priest's shoulders.
° **eyne**: eyes (archaic plural).
° **Typhon**: snake-like god and son of Gaia, later identified with the Egyptian god Set.

The flocking shadows pale
Troop to th'infernal Jail,
Each fettered Ghost slips to his several grave,
And the yellow-skirted Fays°
Fly after the Night-steeds, leaving their Moon-loved maze.

27

But see the Virgin blest,
Hath laid her Babe to rest.
Time is our tedious song should here have ending;
240   Heav'ns youngest-teemèd Star°
Hath fixed her polished Car,
Her sleeping Lord with Handmaid Lamp attending;
And all about the Courtly Stable,
Bright-harnessed° Angels sit in order serviceable.

≈ ≈ ≈

° **Fays**: fairies.   ° **Star**: the Star of Bethlehem.   ° **harnessed**: armoured.

GEORGE HERBERT
"Man" and "Providence" (1633)

While Renaissance sceptics like Giambattista Gelli portray humans as maladapted
to the wild, the devotional poetry of Anglican priest George Herbert radiates a
sense of being miraculously at home in a bespoke world where everything has
been designed especially for human comfort and delight. A chief reason why is
that Herbert views the body as a microcosm perfectly attuned to the universe
or macrocosm, which it both encapsulates and symbolizes. In its love of human
symmetry and proportion, the first poem is a literary equivalent of Da Vinci's
famous "Vitruvian Man." Despite its outrageous anthropocentrism, "Man" is cited approvingly in Emerson's 1836 essay "Nature," a manifesto of the American
Transcendentalist movement and a touchstone for ecocriticism. The second poem
(drawing on the rhapsodic Creation Psalm tradition) sees all organic life as living
poetry and as interconnected in a holy rapport that Nicholas Johnson equates
with "ecological justness" (161), while reading the poet's inconsistencies as a kind
of integrity. How does Herbert's "Providence" both endorse and subvert human
exceptionalism?
Source: *The Temple* (1633), 83–5, 109–13.

"Man"

My God, I heard this day
That none doth build a stately habitation,
But he that means to dwell therein.
What house more stately hath there been,

Or can be, than is Man, to whose creation
All things are in decay?

For Man is ev'ry thing
And more: he is a tree, yet bears more° fruit;
A beast, yet is, or should be more.
Reason and speech we only bring: 10
Parrots may thank us if they are not mute;
They go upon the score.°

Man is all symmetry,
Full of proportions, one limb to another,
And all to all the world besides:
Each part may call the farthest brother;
For head with foot hath private amity,
And both with moons and tides.

Nothing hath got so far,
But Man hath caught and kept it as his prey. 20
His eyes dismount the highest star:
He is in little all the sphere.°
Herbs gladly cure our flesh because that they
Find their acquaintance there.

For us the winds do blow,
The earth doth rest, heav'n move, and fountains flow.
Nothing we see but means our good,
As our delight, or as our treasure:
The whole is either our cupboard of food
Or cabinet of pleasure. 30

The stars have° us to bed;
Night draws the curtain, which the sun withdraws:
Music and light attend our head.
All things unto our flesh are kind
In their descent and being; to our mind
In their ascent and cause.

Each thing is full of duty:
Waters united are our navigation;
Distinguishèd, our habitation;°
Below, our drink; above, our meat;° 40
Both are our cleanliness. Hath one such beauty?
Then how are all things neat?

More servants wait on Man
Than he'll take notice of: in ev'ry path

° **more**: an emendation from the Williams manuscript; the 1633 text reads "no."
° **go ... score**: are in our debt (for teaching them to speak).   ° **sphere**: the universe.
° **have**: guide.   ° **habitation**: firm land created by separation of earth and seas.
° **meat**: food (since crops are nourished by rain).

He treads down that which doth befriend him,
When sickness makes him pale and wan.
Oh mighty love! Man is one world, and hath
Another to attend° him.

Since then, my God, thou hast
So brave a palace built, O dwell in it,
That it may dwell with thee at last!
Till then, afford us so much wit
That, as the world serves us, we may serve thee,
And both thy servants be.

50

"Providence"

Of all the creatures both in sea and land
Only to Man thou hast made known thy ways,
And put the pen alone into his hand,
And made him Secretary of thy praise.

Beasts fain° would sing; birds ditty to their notes;
Trees would be tuning on their native lute
To thy renown: but all their hands and throats
Are brought to Man, while they are lame and mute.

10

Man is the world's high Priest: he doth present
The sacrifice for all, while they below
Unto the service mutter an assent,
Such as springs use that fall and winds that blow.

He that to praise and laud thee doth refrain,
Doth not refrain unto himself alone,
But robs a thousand who would praise thee fain,
And doth commit a world of sin in one.

20

The beasts say, Eat me: but, if beasts must teach,
The tongue is yours to eat but mine to praise.
The trees say, Pull me: but the hand you stretch
Is mine to write, as it is yours to raise.

Wherefore, most sacred Spirit, I here present
For me and all my fellows praise to thee;
And just it is that I should pay the rent,
Because the benefit accrues to me ...

Thy cupboard serves the world; the meat is set,
Where all may reach: no beast but knows his feed.

50

° **attend**: serve.   ° **fain**: eagerly.

Birds teach us hawking; fishes have their net:
The great prey on the less, they on some weed.

Nothing engendered doth prevent his meat:°
Flies have their table spread ere they appear.
Some creatures have in winter what to eat;
Others do sleep, and envy not their cheer.°

How finely dost thou times and seasons spin,
And make a twist° chequered with night and day!
Which as it lengthens winds and winds us in,
As bowls go on, but turning all the way.   60

Each creature hath a wisdom for his good.
The pigeons feed their tender offspring, crying,
When they are callow; but withdraw their food
When they are fledge, that need may teach them flying.

Bees work for man; and yet they never bruise
Their master's flower, but leave it, having done,
As fair as ever and as fit to use:
So both the flower doth stay and honey run.

Sheep eat the grass, and dung the ground for more;
Trees after bearing drop their leaves for soil;   70
Springs vent their streams, and by expense get store;
Clouds cool by heat and baths by cooling boil.

Who hath the virtue to express the rare
And curious virtues both of herbs and stones?
Is there an herb for that? O that thy care
Would show a root that gives expressions!° …

Thou hast hid metals. Man may take them thence,
But at his peril. When he digs the place
He makes a grave, as if the thing had sense,
And threatened man that he should fill the space.

E'en poisons praise thee. Should a thing be lost?
Should creatures want for want of heed their due?
Since where are poisons, antidotes are most:
The help stands close, and keeps the fear in view.

The sea, which seems to stop the traveller,
Is by a ship the speedier passage made.   90
The winds, who think they rule the mariner,
Are ruled by him and taught to serve his trade.

° **prevent … meat**: precede its food supply.   ° **cheer**: feeding.   ° **twist**: fabric.
° **root … expressions**: aids eloquence.

And as thy house is full, so I adore
Thy curious art in marshalling thy goods.
The hills with health abound; the vales with store;
The South with marble; North with furs and woods …

Light without wind is glass; warm without weight
Is wool and furs; cool without closeness, shade;
Speed without pains, a horse; tall without height,
A servile hawk; low without loss, a spade.

All countries have enough to serve their need:
If they seek fine things, thou dost make them run
For their offence, and then dost turn their speed
To be commerce and trade from sun to sun.

Nothing wears clothes but Man; nothing doth need
But he to wear them. Nothing useth fire
But Man alone, to show his heav'nly breed,
And only he hath fuèl in desire.

When th'earth was dry, thou mad'st a sea of wet;
When that lay gathered, thou didst broach the mountains;
When yet some places could no moisture get,
The winds grew gard'ners, and the clouds good fountains.

Rain, do not hurt my flowers, but gently spend
Your honey drops; press not to smell them here.
When they are ripe, their odour will ascend,
And at your lodging with their thanks appear …

Most herbs that grow in brooks are hot and dry.
Cold fruits warm kernels help against the wind.
The lemon's juice and rind cure mutually.
The whey of milk doth loose,° the milk doth bind.°

Thy creatures leap not,° but express a feast
Where all the guests sit close and nothing wants.
Frogs marry fish and flesh; bats, bird and beast;
Sponges, nonsense and sense; mines, th'earth and plants.

To show thou art not bound, as if thy lot
Were worse than ours, sometimes thou shiftest hands.
Most things move th'under-jaw: the crocodile not.
Most things sleep lying: th'elephant leans or stands.

But who hath praise enough? Nay, who hath any?
None can express thy works but he that knows them,

110

120

130

140

° **loose**: as a laxative.   ° **bind**: cure diarrhoea.
° **Thy … not**: i.e. there are no gaps in nature.

And none can know thy works, which are so many
And so complete, but only he that owns them.°

All things that are, though they have sev'ral ways,
Yet in their being join with one advice°
To honour thee: and so I give thee praise
In all my other hymns, but in this twice.

🙌 🙌 🙌

° **But who … owns them**: Izaak Walton quotes this stanza, along with lines 24–8, in *The Compleat Angler.*
° **advice**: opinion.

THOMAS BROWNE
"Nature is the Art of God" (*c.* 1635)

The Latin title of Browne's most famous work translates as "A Physician's Religion." While the book predates Robert Hooke's and Anton van Leeuwenhoek's publications on microscopy, Browne's writing manifests the same fascination with insects and minutiae that drove their research. Nothing in nature should be disregarded as puny, useless, disgusting, or ugly. The human body is not an entity unto itself but a host to hundreds of minuscule creatures. In contrast to Milton's "Nativity Ode", he even praises the polytheistic religions of the Greco-Romans and Egyptians for their willingness to read the Book of Nature, that "universal and public manuscript." Such principles inspired Browne to amass one of the greatest seventeenth-century collections of scientific specimens, including a caged curlew, two whale skulls, several dozen bird eggs, aquariums full of fish, and hundreds of insects.
Source: *Religio Medici* (1642), 30–6.

Natura nihil agit frustra° is the only indisputable axiom in Philosophy.° There are no Grotesques° in nature, nor any thing framed to fill up empty cantons° and unnecessary spaces. In the most imperfect creatures,° and such as were not preserved in the Ark (but having their seeds and principles in the womb of nature are everywhere where the power of the Sun is): in these is the wisdom of his hand discovered. Out of this rank, Solomon

° ***Natura … frustra***: "Nature does nothing in vain." This formula goes back to Aristotle (*On the Heavens*, 271a; *On the Generation of Animals*, 744a).
° **Philosophy**: natural philosophy.
° **Grotesques**: early editions use the Italian "grottesco," a word that originally refers to chimerical depictions of humans and animals, "fantastically combined and interwoven with foliage and flowers" (*OED* 1).
° **cantons**: nooks.
° **imperfect creatures**: insects purportedly born from spontaneous generation.

chose the object of his admiration. Indeed, what reason may not go to school to the wisdom of Bees, Ants, and Spiders?° What wise hand teacheth them to do what reason cannot teach us? Ruder heads stand amazed at those prodigious pieces of nature: Whales, Elephants, Dromedaries, and [31] Camels; these, I confess, are the colossus and majestic pieces of her hand. But in these narrow Engines there is more curious Mathematics, and the civility of these little Citizens more neatly set forth the wisdom of their Maker. Who admires not Regiomontanus° his Fly beyond his Eagle, or wonders not more at the operation of two souls in those little bodies than but one in the trunk of a Cedar?° I could never content my contemplation with those general pieces of wonders (the flux and reflux of the sea, the increase° of Nile, the conversion of the Needle to the North), and have studied to match and parallel those in the more obvious and neglected pieces of Nature, which without further travel I can do in the Cosmography° of myself. We carry with us the wonders we seek without us. There is all Africa and her prodigies in us. We are that bold and [32] adventurous piece of nature which he that studies wisely learns in a compendium what others labour at in a divided piece and endless volume.

Thus there are two books from whence I collect my Divinity: besides that written one of God, another of his servant Nature: that universal and public Manuscript that lies expansed unto the eyes of all. Those that never saw him in the one have discovered him in the other. This was the Scripture and Theology of the Heathens. The natural motion of the Sun made them more admire him than its supernatural station did the children of Israel.° The ordinary effect of nature wrought more admiration in them than in the other all his miracles. Surely the Heathens knew better how to join and read these mystical letters than we Christians, who cast a more careless eye on these common Hieroglyphics, and disdain to suck Divinity from the [33] flowers of nature. Nor do I so forget God as to adore the name of Nature, which I define not with the schools, the principle of motion and rest, but that straight and regular line, that settled and constant course the wisdom of God hath ordained to guide the actions of his creatures, according to their several kinds. To make a revolution every day is the nature of the sun because that necessary course which God hath ordained it, from which it cannot swerve, by a faculty from that voice which first did give it motion. Now this course of Nature God seldom alters or perverts, but like an excellent Artist hath so contrived his work that with the self-same instrument, without a new creation, he may effect his obscurest designs.

° **Solomon**: ... **spiders**: see Proverbs 6:6.
° **Regiomontanus**: the Latin name of Johannes of Königsberg (1436–76), a German mathematician-engineer renowned for his animal automatons.
° **two souls ... Cedar**: According to Aristotle, plants possess only a nutritive soul, while animals possess both a nutritive and a sensitive soul.
° **increase**: annual flooding or perhaps its supposed spontaneous generation of life.
° **Cosmography**: description of the universe.
° **supernatural station ... Israel**: see Joshua 10:12–15.

Thus he sweeteneth the water with a wood,° preserveth the creatures in the Ark, which the blast of his mouth might have as easily created. For God is like a skilful Geometrician, [34] who, when more easily and with one stroke of his Compass he might describe or divide a right line, had yet rather do this in a circle or longer way, according to the constituted and forelaid principles of his art. Yet this rule of his he doth sometimes pervert, to acquaint the world with his prerogative, lest the arrogance of our reason should question his power, and conclude he could not. And thus I call the effects of Nature the works of God, whose hand and instrument she only is. And therefore to ascribe his actions unto her is to devolve the honour of God, the principal agent, upon the instrument: which if with reason we may do, then let our hammers rise up and boast they have built our houses, and our pens receive the honour of our writings.

I hold there is a general beauty in the works of God, and therefore no deformity in any kind or species of creature whatsoever. [35] I cannot tell by what logic we call a Toad, a Bear, or an Elephant, ugly, they being created in those outward shapes and figures which best express the actions of their inward forms. And having passed that general visitation of God, who saw that all that he had made was good, that is, conformable to his will, which abhors deformity, and is the rule of order and beauty; there is no deformity but in monstrosity, wherein notwithstanding there is a kind of beauty, Nature so ingeniously contriving the irregular parts, as they become sometimes more remarkable than the principal fabric. To speak yet more narrowly, there was never anything ugly or misshapen but the Chaos, wherein notwithstanding, to speak strictly, there was no deformity because no form. Nor was it yet impregnate by the voice of God. Now nature is not at variance with art, nor art with nature: they being both the servants of his providence. [36] Art is the perfection of Nature. Were the world now as it was the sixth day, there were yet a Chaos. Nature hath made one world and Art another. In brief, all things are artificial,° for nature is the Art of God.

ᎧᎧ ᎧᎧ ᎧᎧ

° **sweeteneth ... wood**: Exodus 15:25.   ° **artificial**: artfully made.

THOMASINE PENDARVES
[Embracing the Creatures] (1649)

The following dream vision was recounted in a letter sent to the Ranter Abiezer Coppe. The author, identified only by her initials, T. P, is probably Thomasine Pendarves (née Newcomen), who came from a Devonshire tin-mining family. Married to a Baptist minister from Abingdon, she began to preach herself and became affiliated with the Ranters – a name assigned to a disorganized cult of religious dissenters that sprang up during the English Civil War. The sect attracted notoriety (and persecution) for their heretical beliefs that drinking, swearing, and sex were not sinful. Although she invites Coppe to interpret the dream, Pendarves manages a respectable exegesis of her own. The vision suggests why Pendarves would have been attracted to the teaching of Ranters like Coppe and Lawrence Clarkson that God resides in the creation (including other animals). Such pantheistic beliefs encouraged some Dissenters to advocate vegetarianism and even nudism in the hope that such practices could restore humans to an Edenic state of harmony with the environment.

Source: *Sweet Sips of Some Spiritual Wine* (1649), 41–3.

I was in a place where I saw all kind of Beasts of the field, wild and tame together, and all kinds of creeping Worms and all kind of Fishes—in a pleasant river, where the water was exceeding clear—not very deep—but very pure—and no mud or settling at the bottom, as ordinarily is in ponds or rivers. And all these Beasts, Worms, and Fishes, living and recreating themselves together, and myself with them. Yea, we had so free a correspondence together as I oft-times would take the wildest of them and put them in my bosom,° especially such (which afore) I had exceedingly feared, such as I would not have touched or come nigh, as the Snake and Toad, etc.—and the wildest kind as ever I saw, and the strangest appearances as ever I saw in my life.

At last I took one of the wildest, as a tiger or such like, and brought it in my bosom away from all the rest, and put a collar about him for mine own. And when I had thus done, it grew wild again, and strove to get from me. And I had great trouble about it. As first [42] because I had it so near me, yet it should strive to get from me. But notwithstanding all my care, it ran away. If you could tell me the interpretation of it, it might be of great use to the whole body.°

Now I must acquaint you I am not altogether without teaching in it. For when I awoke, the vision still remained with me. And I looked up to the Father to know what it should be. And it was shown me that my having so free a commerce with all sorts of appearances was my spiritual liberty ... There is another scripture which hath much followed me. And that is, "God beheld all things that he made, and lo, they were very good."° Now concerning my taking one of them from all the rest (as distinct) and setting a collar about it—this was my weakness. And here comes in all our bondage and death, by appropriating of things to ourselves and for ourselves.° For could I have been contented to have enjoyed this little, this one thing in the liberty of the Spirit—I had never [43] been brought to that tedious care in keeping, nor that exceeding grief in losing.

᠅ ᠅ ᠅

° **bosom**: embrace, although a more literal reading is possible. The passage invites comparison with Eve before the fall, and the millenarian prophecy of the lion snuggling with the lamb in Isaiah 11:6.
° **body**: metaphor for the Ranter community.   ° **God ... good**: Genesis 1:31.
° **appropriating ... ourselves**: The Ranters renounced private property.

JOSEPH CARYL
"To cause it to rain on the earth where no man is" (1653)

To an ecocritic, Job 38 presents one of the most profound episodes in the entire Bible. Speaking from within a whirlwind, God poses a flurry of rhetorical questions for which the beleaguered Job has no answer: "Where wast thou when I laid the foundations of the earth?" (38:4) Although the voice was usually understood literally, some seventeenth-century Protestants began to interpret it in a metaphorical sense. Like the storm that humbles the homeless King Lear, the whirlwind's ferocity confronts Job with a world whose phenomena remain stubbornly opaque to the human intellect – a world not devised for humans. Such an interpretation can be found in this commentary on Job by the non-conformist divine Joseph Caryl, which seeks to fathom why God would create and nourish wilderness. In his equally voluminous commentary on Job, the famed French theologian Jean Calvin can only throw up his hands at this passage and declare "God's wisdom is hidden from us" (771). In *Mosaical Philosophy* (written 1638, translated 1659), the theosophist Robert Fludd cites extensively from Job 38 as a rebuke to the hubris of Aristotelian science (38–40). Caryl's reading inches further towards a non-anthropocentric view of creation. No wonder the environmentalist Bill McKibben praises this particular verse in *The End of Nature* (75–6).
Source: *An Exposition ... Upon the ... Five Last Chapters of the Book of Job* (1653), 206–9.

> "To cause it to rain on the earth where no man is, on the wilderness where there is no man" (Job 38:26).

The Lord speaks here of a special place to which he designs the Rain. Where should that be? Surely the pastures, and tilled grounds, gardens, and vineyards, places cultivated and inhabited by men; the Lord hath Rain for them, yet not all for them, or not for them all. Here the Cargo or lading of the clouds is consigned to places uninhabited by man. He causeth it to rain on the earth where no man is ... Travellers and navigators have found some parts of the earth which were counted uninhabitable,° not only habitable, but actually inhabited by many people. Yet there may be some parts of the earth habitable in their own nature, wherein no man dwells, or in which (as the text speaks) no man is. Yea, possibly there are some parts of the earth uninhabitable, or wherein no man can dwell. Now is it not strange that the Lord should carry his rain to such parts of the earth, to places where no man is? Where there are neither Cities, nor Towns, nor Villages—no, nor the meanest Cottages—nor a man breathing on the face of that earth? ... If we would know what the Lord intends by earth where no man is, the Text answers, "the Wilderness where there is no man," or "where none of Adam dwelleth," as Mr. Broughton° translates. So then this latter clause of the verse is but a repetition of the same thing, yet a repetition made not only

---

° **counted uninhabitable**: ancient geographers such as Aristotle had supposed the Arctic and equatorial regions could not sustain human life.
° **Broughton**: Hugh Broughton, an English scholar of Hebrew, who published a translation of Job in 1610.

for variety and elegancy but also to [207] signify the certainty of the thing: that God gives rain even to such places where no man is ...

[208] But from the wilderness and from heaths and deserts, which are dry places, how should vapours rise? Yet, saith God, though there is no rain begotten there, yet I will send rain thither. I will cause the wind to rise and carry the clouds, and the thunder shall break the clouds, and they shall pour down waters upon the wilderness. Did not the Lord cause the winds to drive the clouds over wildernesses and desert places and there to unburden themselves, they would be altogether without rain. Hence note: where Nature denies or natural causes produce no rain, God can give it. The clouds may deny rain to the wilderness because the wilderness yields no moisture to make clouds, yet the Lord sends rain thither.

Again, consider the wilderness and desert places as they are here held forth, together with the providence of God concerning them, and so note: the care and providence of God extends itself to all places, even to places uninhabited. It is no wonder that God should provide rain to places that are inhabited; but where no man is, there to water the earth, to what purpose is that? Yet the Lord will water such places (as it were) by his own hand, and (as 'tis said) "Turn the wilderness into standing water, and dry ground into Water-springs."° Though there be no man to eat the fruit which the rain produceth from the earth (of which the text speaks afterward), yet God will send rain to make that land fruitful for the beasts' sake, that they may have grass and green things to feed upon. God will provide for the beasts of the earth, where there are no men to provide for them, nor to be provided for. God is a great Housekeeper. He nourisheth all living creatures as well as men. As he preserves, so he feeds the beasts of the [209] Earth and the fishes of the Sea as well as men. "These all wait upon thee, O Lord, that thou mayest give them their meat in due season."° ... And that he may do so, he gives them rain in due season: "He causeth it to rain on the Earth where no man is, and upon the wilderness where there is no man." God hath beasts to provide for where men are not, and he will not let a beast that he hath made want food; the very worms shall have a support of life.

ॐ ॐ ॐ

° **Turn ... springs**: Psalms 107:35.   ° **These ... season**: Psalms 104:27.

JOHN RAY

from The Wisdom of God Manifested in the Works of
Creation (1691)

In the work of John Ray (or Wray), early modern natural theology arrives at the
doorstep of modern biology. For Ray, however, the two were not so much neighbours as housemates. Growing up in an Essex village, Ray developed a fascination
with nature at an early age. His mother reportedly practised herbal medicine and
may have passed on her knowledge of plants to her son. Ray went on to pursue
botanical studies at Cambridge, becoming a fellow of Trinity College and, eventually, the Royal Society. He is one of the first English naturalists to advocate the
formation of a more complex taxonomy for classifying living things, anticipating
the work of Linnaeus. In the process, he outlined an early definition of the species
concept. Ray was no armchair naturalist; he travelled widely throughout Britain
and Europe collecting specimens and even conducted innovative experiments on
plant physiology, discovering how xylem transports water within trees and forms
rings in the trunk. Although he underestimates the number of species by several
orders of magnitude (the Catalogue of Life database currently lists 1.74 million
known species), his work exudes a profound appreciation of biodiversity, valuing all
organic life in and of itself rather than for its utility to humans. His treatise is a stun-
ning example of how religious and scientific mentalities could co-exist in the early
modern period, even as Ray redefines the scriptural warrant for human dominion.
Source: *The Wisdom of God Manifested in the Works of Creation* (1691), 1–2, 5–9,
113–14, 117–18, 127–30.

"How manifold are thy Works, O Lord? In wisdom hast thou made
them all" (Psalm 104:24).

That the number of corporeal Creatures is immeasurably great, and known
only to the Creator himself may thus probably be collected: first of all, the
number of fixed Stars is on all hands acknowledged to be next to infinite;
secondly, every fixed Star in the now [2] received hypothesis is a Sun or
Sun-like body, and in like manner encircled with a chorus of Planets moving about it; thirdly, each of these Planets is in all likelihood furnished
with as great variety of corporeal Creatures, animate and inanimate, as the
Earth is, and all as different in Nature as they in place from the terrestrial,
and from each other. Whence it will follow that these must be much more
infinite than the stars; I do not mean absolutely ... infinite, but only infinite or innumerable as to us, or their number prodigiously great ...

[4] But leaving now the celestial bodies, I come now to the terrestrial,
which are either inanimate or animate. The inanimate are the Elements,
Meteors, Fossils of all sorts, at the number of which last I cannot give any
probable guess. But if the rule ... holds good (viz. how much more imperfect any genus or order of beings is, so much more numerous are the
species contained under it) ... then should there be more species of Fossils
or generally of inanimate bodies than of Vegetables, of which there is some
reason to doubt ...

[5] Animate bodies are divided into four great Genera or Orders: Beasts, Birds, Fishes, and Insects. The Species of Beasts, including also Serpents, are not very numerous. Of such as are certainly known and described I dare say not above 150 … The number of Birds known and described may be near 500, and the number of Fishes … more than double the number. How many of each genus remain yet undiscovered one cannot certainly nor very nearly conjecture. But we may suppose the whole sum of Beasts and Birds to exceed by a third part, and Fishes by one half, those known … The Insects, … [6] I conjecture, cannot be fewer than 1,800 or 2,000 species, perhaps many more … The Butterflies and Beetles are such numerous tribes that I believe in our own native country alone the species of each kind may amount to 150 or more … [7] The number of Plants contained in C. Bauhin's *Pinax*° is about 6,000 … [8] [Yet] I cannot think but that there are in the World more than double that number, there being in the vast continent of America as great a variety of species as with us … And if on the other side of the Equator there be much land still remaining undiscovered, as probably there may, we must suppose the number of Plants to be far greater.

What can we infer from all this? If the number of Creatures be so exceeding great, how great—nay, immense— must needs be the power and wisdom of him who formed them all! For (that I may borrow the words of a noble and excellent author°) as it argues and manifests more skill by far in an Artificer to be able to frame both Clocks and Watches, Pumps and Mills, Grenades and Rockets, than he could display in making but one of those sorts of engines; so the Almighty discovers more of his wisdom in forming such a vast multitude of different sorts of Creatures, and all with admirable and irreprovable° Art, [9] than if he had created but a few …

[113] Methinks by all this provision for the use and service of Man, the Almighty interpretatively speaks to him in this manner: "I have placed thee in a spacious and well-furnished World. I have endued thee with an ability of understanding what is beautiful and proportionable, and have made that [114] which is so agreeable and delightful to thee. I have provided thee with materials whereon to exercise and employ thy art and strength; I have given thee an excellent instrument,° the hand, accommodated to make use of them all; I have distinguished the Earth into Hills, and Valleys, and Plains, and Meadows, and Woods; all these parts capable of culture and improvement by industry." …

[117] I persuade myself that the bountiful and gracious Author of Man's being and faculties and all things else, delights in the beauty of his Creation, and is well pleased with the industry of Man in adorning the Earth with beautiful Cities and Castles, with pleasant Villages and Country Houses,

---

° **Pinax**: *Pinax theatri botanici* (1623), by the Swiss botanist Caspar or Gaspard Bauhin.
° **author**: Robert Boyle. See *A Disquisition about the final causes of natural things* (1688 66).
° **irreprovable**: unreproachable.
° **instrument**: the definition of the hand as "the tool of tools" goes back to Aristotle (*On the Soul*, Book 3).

with regular Gardens and Orchards and Plantations of all sorts of Shrubs and Herbs and Fruits for Meat, Medicine, or moderate Delight, with shady Woods and Groves, and Walks set with rows of elegant Trees, with Pastures clothed with Flocks, and Valleys covered over with Corn, and Meadows burdened with Grass, and whatever else [118] differenceth a civil and well-cultivated Region from a barren and desolate Wilderness ...

[127] It is a generally received opinion that all this visible World was created for Man; that Man is the end of Creation, as if there were no other end of any Creature but some way or other serviceable to Man. This opinion is as old as Tully, for saith he in his second book of *De natura deorum,* "*Principio ipse mundus deorum hominum[que] causa factus est; quae[que] in eo sunt Omnia ea parata ad fructum hominum & inventa sunt.*"° But though this be vulgarly received, yet wise men nowadays [128] think otherwise. Dr. More° affirms,

> That Creatures are made to enjoy themselves, as well as to serve us, and that it's a gross piece of ignorance and rusticity to think otherwise.°

And in another place,

> This comes only out of pride and ignorance or a haughty presumption, because we are encouraged to believe, that in some sense, all things are made for Man, therefore to think that they are not at all made for themselves. But he that pronounceth this is ignorant of the nature of Man, and the knowledge of Things. For if a good Man be merciful to his Beast, then surely, a good God is bountiful and benign, and takes pleasure that all his Creatures enjoy themselves that have life and sense, and are capable of enjoyment.°

For my part, I cannot believe that all things in the world were so made for Man that they have no other use.

For it's highly absurd and unreasonable to think that bodies of such vast magnitude as the fixed Stars were only made to twinkle to us ... [129] And I believe there are many species in Nature which were never yet taken notice of by Man, and consequently of no use to him, which yet we are not to think were created in vain, but are likely (as the Doctor saith) to partake of the overflowing goodness of the Creator, and enjoy their own beings. But though in this sense it be not true that all things were made for Man, yet thus far it is: that all Creatures in the world may be some way or other useful to us, at least in the exercise of our wits and understandings in considering and contemplating of them, and so afford us subjects of

---

° ***Principio ... sunt***: In the 1683 translation of Marcus Tullius Cicero's *On the Nature of the Gods* this passage reads, "In the first place, then, the whole universe itself was created for the sake of the gods and of men, and whatever therein is prepared and invented for the behoof [benefit] of man" (178).

° **Dr. More**: Henry More (1614–87), one of the leading Cambridge Platonists, and the teacher of Ann Conway.

° **That ... otherwise**: from More's *Antidote Against Atheism* (1655), 92.

° **This ... enjoyment**: ibid., 81.

admiring and glorifying their and our Maker. Seeing, then, we do believe and assert that all things were in some sense made for us, we are thereby obliged to make use of them for those purposes for which they serve us: else we frustrate this end of the Creation. Now some of them serve only to exercise our minds; many others there be, which might probably serve us to good purpose, whose uses are not discovered … [130] Some reproach methinks it is to learned men that there should be so many Animals still in the World whose outward shape is not yet taken notice of or described, much less their way of generation, food, manners, uses, observed. If Man ought to reflect upon his Creator the glory of all his Works, then ought he to take notice of them all and not to think anything unworthy of his cognizance. And truly the wisdom, art, and power of Almighty God shines forth as visibly in the structures of the body of the minutest Insect as in that of a Horse or Elephant.

PART II

The Tangled Chain

Hierarchy and the Human Animal
AMBROISE PARÉ
"Of Monsters by the Confusion of Seed of Diverse Kinds"
(1572)

"Monstrous" births are splayed across dozens of early modern broadsides and were even exhibited to a prurient public at markets and fairs. Most commentators agreed they were portents from an angry God; when an unwed woman in Kent gave birth in 1568 to a child described as leopard-mouthed it was deemed a stern warning against premarital sex. Various theories circulated as to how these anatomical anomalies were engendered. Some attributed it to witchcraft, as in the 1640 case of the *Hog's-faced Gentlewoman Called Tannakin Skinker*. Others held that the imagination of the parents during conception or pregnancy could produce defects, as exemplified by a fashion-obsessed mother who gave birth to a child with skinfolds around its neck resembling a ruff. Another common theory, outlined below by a renowned French physician, proposed that monstrous births were the result of bestiality. A 1533 Parliamentary Act declared bestiality (along with sodomy) a capital offence, and Assize Records document thirty cases from the Elizabethan period alone in which people were indicted for "buggery" with horses, cows, dogs, and sheep (Thomas 119). Few offenders, however, were prosecuted to the full extent of the law, which, in accordance with the Book of Leviticus, held the animal equally culpable. Since so many of the prodigious birth texts emphasize the bestial characteristics of the unfortunate child's appearance, the phenomenon was also a disturbing reminder of the precariousness of the animal/human boundary, undercutting the conviction that humans were made in God's image.
Source: *The Works of that Famous Surgeon Ambroise Paré, trans.* Thomas Johnson (1634), 982–5.

That which followeth is a horrid thing to be spoken. But the chaste mind of the Reader will give me pardon and conceive that which not only the Stoics but all Philosophers who are busied about the search of the causes of things must hold: that there is nothing obscene or filthy to be spoken. Those things that are accounted obscene may be spoken without blame, but they cannot be acted or perpetrated without great wickedness, fury, and madness. Therefore, that ill which is in obscenity consists not in word but wholly in the act. Therefore in times past there have been some, who nothing fearing the Deity, neither Law, nor themselves (that is, their soul), have so abjected and prostrated themselves that they have thought themselves nothing different from beasts. Wherefore Atheists, Sodomites,° Outlaws, forgetful of their own excellency and divinity and transformed by filthy lust,

---

° **Sodomites**: deviants.

have not doubted° to have filthy and abominable° copulation with beasts. This so great, so horrid a crime (for whose expiation all the fires in the world are not sufficient), though they, too maliciously crafty, have concealed and the conscious beasts could not utter, yet the generated misshapen issue hath abundantly spoken and declared by the unspeakable power of God, the revenger and punisher of such impious and horrible actions. For of this various and promiscuous confusion of seeds of a different kind, monsters have been generated and born, who have been partly men and partly beasts.

The like deformity of issue is produced if beasts of a different species do copulate together, nature always affecting° to generate something which may be like itself. For wheat grows not but by sowing of wheat, nor an apricot but by the setting or grafting of an apricot; for nature is a most diligent preserver of the species of things …

Anno Dom. 1493 there was generated of a woman and a dog an issue which from the navel upwards perfectly resembled the shape of the mother, but therehence downwards the sire; that is, the dog …

[983] Coelius Rhodiginus writes that at Sibaris° a herdsman called Chrathis fell in love with a goat and accompanied with her. And of this detestable and brutish copulation an infant was born, which in legs resembled the dam but the face was like the father's.

Anno Dom. 1110 in a certain town of Liège° … a sow farrowed a pig with the head, face, hands, and feet of a man, but in the rest of the body resembling a swine.

Anno Dom. 1564 at Brussels, at the house of one Joest Dictzpeert … a sow farrowed six pigs, the first whereof was a monster representing a man in the head, face, forefeet and shoulders, but in the rest of the body another pig. For it had the genitals of a sow pig, and it sucked like the other pigs. But the second day after it was farrowed it was killed of the people, together with the sow, by reason of the monstrousness of the thing …

[984] Anno Dom. 1571 at Antwerp, the wife of one Michael, a Printer, … brought forth a monster wholly like a dog, but that it had a shorter neck, and the head of a bird, but without any feathers on it. This monster was not alive, for that the mother was delivered before her time; but she giving a great screech in the instant of her deliverance, the chimney of the house fell down …

[985] There are some monsters in whose generation by this there may seem to be some divine cause, for that their beginnings cannot be derived or drawn from the general cause of monsters; that is, nature, or the errors thereof.

❦ ❦ ❦

° **doubted**: scrupled.   ° **abominable**: spelled "abhominable," following the Renaissance
  derivation of the word from *ab homine* (outside the human).
° **affecting**: intending.   ° **Sibaris**: ancient city in southern Italy.
° **Liège**: in Belgium.

REGINALD SCOT
"That the Body of a Man Cannot Be Turned into the Body of a Beast By a Witch" (1584)

The Elizabethan lawyer Reginald Scot published a scathing exposé on witchcraft as a mass delusion perpetrated by charlatans, gullible simpletons, pagan poetry, and Popish superstition. His attitude reflects a growing scepticism towards magic in the wake of the Protestant Reformation. Although his *Discovery* seeks to debunk witchcraft, writers such as Shakespeare and Jonson would, ironically, ransack it as a treasure trove of folk beliefs and authentic lore on the occult. The following tale of a man transformed into an ass is an important inter-text for *A Midsummer Night's Dream.*
Source: *The Discovery of Witchcraft* (1584), 53, 55–7.

It happened in the city of Salamis in the kingdom of Cyprus … that a ship laden with merchandise stayed there for a short space. In the meantime, many of the soldiers and mariners went to shore to provide fresh victuals; among which number, a certain Englishman … went to a woman's house a little way out of the city … to see whether she had any eggs to sell: who, perceiving him to be a lusty young fellow, a stranger and far from his country (so as upon the loss of him there would be the less miss or inquiry), she considered with herself how to destroy him, and willed him to stay there … while she went to fetch a few eggs for him … After some detracting° of time, she brought him a few eggs, willing him to return to her if [his] ship were gone when he came. The young fellow returned towards the ship, but before he went aboard he would needs eat an egg or twain to satisfy his hunger. And within short space he became dumb and out of his wits, as he afterwards said. When he would have entered into the ship, the mariners beat him back with a cudgel, saying, "What a murrain° lacks the ass? Whither the devil will this ass?"

The ass, or young man (I cannot tell by which name I should term him) being many times repelled, and understanding their words that called him ass, considering that he could speak never a word and yet could understand everybody, he thought that he was bewitched by the woman at whose house he was. And therefore when by no means he could get into the boat, but was driven to tarry and see her departure … he remembered the witch's words and the words of his own fellows that called him ass, and returned to the witch's house, in whose service he remained by the space of three years, doing nothing with his hands all that while, but carried such burdens as she laid on his back, having only this comfort: that although he were reputed an ass among strangers and beasts, yet that both this witch and all other witches knew him to be a man …

° **detracting**: interval.   ° **murrain**: disease (a curse).

[55] But was this man an ass all this while? Or was this ass a man? Bodin°
saith (his reason only reserved) he was truly transubstantiated into an ass,
so as there must be no part of a man but reason remaining in this ass. And
yet Hermes Trismegistus° thinketh he hath good authority and reason to
say … "A human soul cannot receive any other than a human body, nor yet
can light° into a body that wanteth reason of mind" … [56] The body of
man is subject to diverse kinds of agues, sicknesses, and infirmities, whereunto an ass's body is not inclined. And man's body must be fed with bread,
etc. and not with hay. Bodin's ass-headed man must either eat hay or nothing, as appeareth in the story. Man's body also is subject unto death, and
hath his days numbered. If this fellow had died [while still transformed]
… I marvel then what would have become of this ass … [and] whether he
should have risen at the Day of Judgement in an ass's body and shape; for
Paul saith that that very body which is sown and buried a natural body is
raised a spiritual body.° The life of Jesus is made manifest in our mortal
flesh, and not in the flesh of an ass.

God hath endued every man and every thing with his proper nature,
substance, form, qualities, and gifts, and directeth their ways. As for the
ways of an ass, he taketh no such care; howbeit, they have also their properties and substance several to themselves. For there is one flesh (saith Paul)
of men, another flesh of beasts, another of fishes, another of birds.° And
therefore it is absolutely against the ordinance of God (who hath made
me a man) that I should fly like a bird, or swim like a fish, or creep like a
worm, or become an ass in shape; insomuch as if God would give me leave,
I cannot do it: for it were contrary to his own order and decree, and to the
constitution of any body which he hath made …

What a beastly assertion is it that a man, whom God hath made according to his own similitude and likeness,° should be by a witch turned into a
beast? What an impiety is it to affirm that an ass's body is the temple of the
Holy Ghost? Or an ass to be the child of God, and God to be his Father, as
it is said of man? … Bodin may go hide him for shame, especially when he
shall understand that even into these our bodies which God hath framed
after his own likeness he hath also breathed that spirit, which Bodin saith
is now remaining within an ass's body: which God hath so subjected in
such servility under the foot of man, of whom God is so mindful that he
hath made him little lower than angels—yea, than himself—and crowned
him with glory and worship, and made him to have dominion over the
works of his hands, as having put all things under his feet, all sheep and

---

° **Bodin**: Jean Bodin, French philosopher, legal scholar, and author of *On the Demon-Mania of the
  Sorcerers* (1580).
° **Trismegistus**: supposed author of ancient Egyptian texts, regarded as a contemporary of Moses.
  The quotation is from the hermetic text "Poimandres."
° **light**: descend.   ° **that … body**: 1 Corinthians 15:44.   ° **For … birds**: 1 Corinthians 15:39.
° **likeness**: see Genesis 1:26 (p. 29).

oxen—yea, wolves, asses, and all other beasts of the field, the fowls of the air, the fishes of the sea, etc.° Bodin's poet, Ovid, whose *Metamorphoses* makes so much for him, saith, to the overthrow of this fantastical imagination ...

> [57] The Lord did set man's face so high,
> That he the heavens might behold,
> And look up to the starry sky,
> To see his wonders manifold.°

Now if a witch or a devil can so alter the shape of a man as contrarily to make him look down to hell like a beast, God's works should not only be defaced and disgraced, but his ordinance should be wonderfully altered, and thereby confounded.

❦ ❦ ❦

° **subjected ... etc.**: Psalms 8:5–8.   ° **The Lord ... manifold**: *Metamorphoses*, 1.85–86.

MICHEL DE MONTAIGNE
"Apology for Raymond Sebond" (*c.* 1580)

Sebond was the author of a theological treatise that sought to reconcile natural philosophy and divinity by arguing that God could be apprehended through studying the Book of Nature (*liber naturae*). Montaigne's title, however, is misleading. Rather than defend Sebond, he wages a blistering assault on the vanity and fallibility of the human intellect, exposing how very little of that infinite book we can decipher with certainty. In this famous extract, he questions the presumption of human superiority over other animals. Montaigne's scepticism had an electrifying influence on Shakespearean tragedy, Bacon's essays, and Donne's poetry. In puncturing Renaissance humanism's inflated self-conception, it ranks among the most caustic indictments of anthropocentrism ever penned.
Source: *The Essays*, 2.12, trans. John Florio (1603), 258–66, 269, 279–81.

Let us now but consider man alone, without other help armed, but with his own weapons, and unprovided of the grace and knowledge of God ... Let us see what holdfast° or freehold° he hath in this gorgeous and goodly equipage.° Let him with the utmost powers of his discourse make me understand upon what foundation he hath built those great advantages and odds he supposeth to have over other creatures. Who hath persuaded him that this admirable moving of heaven's vault, that the eternal lights of these

---

° **holdfast**: security.   ° **freehold**: absolute possession (of land).
° **equipage**: equipment for an expedition, i.e. human endowments.

lamps, so fiercely rolling, that the horror-moving and continual motion of this infinite vast Ocean were established and continue so many ages for his commodity and service?

Is it possible to imagine anything so ridiculous as this miserable and wretched creature, which is not so much as master of himself, exposed and subject to the offenses of all things, and yet dareth call himself Master and Emperor of this Universe? In whose power it is not to know the least part of it, much less to command the same. And the privilege, which he so fondly challengeth, to be the only absolute creature in this huge world's frame, perfectly able to know the absolute beauty and several parts thereof, and that he is only of power to yield the great Architect thereof due thanks for it, and to keep account both of the receipts and layings out of the world, who hath sealed him this patent? Let us show him his letters of privilege for so noble and so great a charge. Have they been granted only in favour of the wise? Then concern they but a few. Are the foolish and wicked worthy of so extraordinary a favour? … Being the worst part of the world, should they be preferred before the rest? Shall we believe [this man]? "For whose cause shall a man say the world was made? In sooth, for those creatures' sake which have the use of reason; those are Gods and men, than whom assuredly nothing is better."° We shall never sufficiently baffle the impudence of this conjoining. But, silly wretch, what hath he in him worthy of such an advantage? …

[259] Consider the power and domination these [celestial] bodies have not only upon our lives and condition of our fortune … but also over our dispositions and inclinations, our discourses and wills, which they rule, provoke, and move at the pleasure of their influences … Why do we then deprive them of soul, of life, of discourse? … Shall we say we have seen the use of a reasonable soul in no other creature but man? What? Have we seen anything comparable to the Sun? Leaveth he to be because we have seen nothing semblable unto it? And doth he [260] leave his moving because his equal is nowhere to be found? If that which we have not seen is not, our knowledge is wonderfully° abridged …

Presumption is our natural and original infirmity. "Of all creatures man is the most miserable and frail, and therefore the proudest and disdainfulest."° Who perceiveth and seeth himself placed here, amid the filth and mire of the world, fast tied and nailed to the worst, most senseless and drooping part of the world, in the vilest corner of the house and farthest from heaven's cope,° with those creatures that are the worst of the three conditions, and yet dareth imaginarily place himself above the circle of the

---

° **For … better**: Cicero, *On the Nature of the Gods*, Book 2.   ° **wonderfully**: astonishingly.

° **Of … disdainfulest**: Pliny, *Natural History*, 7.

° **cope**: cloak, i.e. canopy. This passage interprets a geocentric universe as evidence of humanity's distance from the divine.

Moon and reduce heaven under his feet. It is through the vanity of the same imagination that he dare equal himself to God; that he ascribe divine conditions unto himself; that he selecteth and separateth himself from out of the rank of other creatures, to which his fellow creatures and compeers he cuts out and shareth their parts and alloteth them what portion of means or forces he thinks good. How knoweth he by virtue of this understanding the inward and secret motions° of beasts? By what comparison from them to us doth he conclude the brutishness he ascribeth unto them? When I am playing with my Cat, who knows whether she have more sport in dallying with me than I have in gaming with her? We entertain one another with mutual apish tricks. If I have my hour to begin or refuse, so hath she hers.

Plato, in setting forth the Golden Age under Saturn, among the chiefest advantages that men had then reporteth the communication he had with beasts: of whom, inquiring and taking instruction, he knew the true qualities and differences of every one of them; by and from whom he got an absolute understanding and perfect wisdom, whereby he led a happier life than we do. Can we have a better proof to judge of man's impudence, touching beasts? This notable author was of opinion that in the greatest part of the corporal form which Nature hath bestowed on them she hath only respected the use of the prognostications° which in his days were thereby gathered. The defect that hindereth communication between them and us, why may it not as well be in us as in them? It is a matter of divination to guess in whom the fault is that we understand not one another. For we understand them no more than they us. By the same reason may they as well esteem us beasts as we them. It is no great marvel if we understand them not. No more do we the Cornish, the Welsh, or Irish ... We must note the parity that is between us. We have some mean understanding of their senses; so have beasts of ours, about the same measure. They flatter and fawn upon us, they threat and entreat us; so do we them. Touching other matters we manifestly perceive there is a full and perfect communication amongst them, and that not only those of the same kind understand one another but even such as are of different kinds ... [261] There is no motion nor gesture that doth not speak, and speaks in a language very easy, without any teaching to be understood ...

Is it without judgement [that Swallows] ... choose from out a thousand places that which is fittest for them to build their nests? ... [262] We perceive by the greater part of their works what excellence beasts have over us, and how weak our art and short our cunning is if we go about to imitate them. We see, notwithstanding even in our grossest works, what faculties we employ in them, and how our mind employeth the uttermost of her skill

---

° **motions**: impulses.   ° **prognostications**: predictions. See Plato, *Timaeus*, 72b–d.

and forces in them. Why should we not think as much of them? Wherefore do we attribute [their] works ... unto a kind of unknown, natural and servile inclination? Wherein, unawares, we give them great advantage over us to infer that nature, led by a certain loving kindness, leadeth and accompanieth them (as it were by the hand) unto all the actions and commodities of their life, and that she forsaketh and leaveth us to the hazards of fortune, and by art to quest and find out those things that are behooveful and necessary for our preservation ... So that their brutish stupidity doth in all commodities exceed whatsoever our divine intelligence can effect.

Verily, by this account we might have just cause and great reason to term her a most unjust and partial stepdame. But there is no such thing; our polity is not so deformed and disordered. Nature hath generally embraced all her creatures, and there is not any but she hath amply stored with all the necessary means for the preservation of their being. For the daily complaints which I often hear men make ... exclaiming that man is the only forsaken and outcast creature naked on the bare earth, fast-bound and swathed, having nothing to cover and arm himself withal but the spoil of others, whereas Nature hath clad and mantled all other creatures, some with shells, some with husks, some with rinds, with hair, with wool, with stings, with bristles, hides, and moss, with feathers, with scales, with fleeces, and with silk, according as their qualities might need or their conditions require; and hath fenced and armed them with claws, with nails, with talons, with hooves, with teeth, with stings, and with horns, both to assail others and to defend themselves; and hath moreover instructed them in everything fit and requisite for them, as to swim, to run, to creep, to fly, to roar, to bellow, and to sing, whereas man only (oh silly, wretched man) can neither go, nor speak, nor shift, nor feed himself unless it be to whine and weep only, except he be taught:

> An infant, like a shipwrecked ship-boy cast from seas,
> Lies naked on the ground, and speechless, wanting all
> The helps of vital spirit, when nature with small ease
> [263] Of throes, to see first light, from her womb lets him fall,
> Then, as is meet, with mournful cries he fills the place,
> For whom so many ills remain in his life's race.
> But diverse herds of tame and wild beasts forward spring.
> Nor need they rattles, nor of nurses cock'ring kind,°
> The flatt'ring broken speech, their lullaby need sing.
> Nor seek they diverse coats as diverse seasons bind.
> Lastly, no armour need they, nor high-rearèd wall,
> Whereby to guard their own, since all things unto all
> Work-master° Nature doth produce,
> And the earth largely to their use.°

° **cock'ring kind**: pampering care.   ° **Work-master**: Work-mistress] 1613.
° **An infant ... use**: Lucretius, *On the Nature of Things*, 5.223–36.

Such complaints are false. There is greater equality and more uniform relation in the policy of the world. Our skin is as sufficiently provided with hardiness against the injuries of the weather as theirs; witness diverse nations which yet never knew the use of clothes … Our whining, our puling,° our weeping is common to most creatures … As for our use of eating and feeding, it is in us, as in them, natural and without teaching … The nations that have so lately been discovered so plenteously stored with all manner of natural meat and drink (without care or labour) teach us that bread is not our only food, and (without toiling) our common mother Nature hath with great plenty stored us with whatsoever should be needful for us—yea, as it is most likely, more richly and amply than nowadays she doth, as we have added so much art unto it.

> The earth itself at first of own accord,
> Did rich men's vineyards and clean fruit afford.
> It gave sweet offsprings food from sweeter soil,
> Which yet scarce greater grow, for all our toil,
> Yet tire therein we do
> Both ploughmen's strength and Oxen too …°

[264] And the industry to enable, the skill to fortify, and the wit to shelter and cover our body by artificial means, we have it by a kind of natural instinct and teaching. Which to prove: the Elephant doth whet and sharpen his teeth he useth in war, … the wild Boar whets his tusks. When the Ichneumon is to grapple with the Crocodile he walloweth his body in the mire, then lets the same dry and harden upon him … Why shall we not say it is as natural for us to arm ourselves with wood and iron?

As for speech, sure it is that if it be not natural it is not necessary. I believe, nevertheless, that if a child [were] bred in some uncouth solitariness, far from haunt of people, … [he] would no doubt have some kind of words to express, and speech to utter his conceits. And it is not to be imagined, that Nature hath refused us that mean and barred us that help which she hath bestowed upon many and diverse other creatures. For what is that faculty we see in them when they seem to complain, to rejoice, to call one unto another for help, and bid one another to loving copulation (as commonly they do) by the use of their voice, but a kind of speech? And shall not they speak among themselves that speak and utter their mind unto us, and we to them? How many ways speak we unto our Dogs, and they seem to understand and answer us? With another language, and with other names speak we unto and call them than we do our Birds, our Hogs, our Oxen, our Horses, and such like. And according to their different kinds we change our idiom.

° **puling**: crying.　　° **The earth … too**: Lucretius, *On the Nature of Things*, 2.1157–63.

> So Ants amid their sable-coloured band
> One with another, mouth to mouth confer,
> Hap'ly their way or state to understand.°

Me seemeth that Lactantius doth not only attribute speech unto beasts, but also laughing.° And the same difference of tongues, which according to the diversity of countries is found amongst us, is also found amongst beasts of one same kind ...

We are neither above nor under the rest: whatever is under the cope of heaven (saith the wise man°) runneth one law and followeth one fortune.

> All things enfolded are,
> In fatal bonds as fits their share.°

[265] Some difference there is; there are orders and degrees, but all is under the visage of one same nature.

> All things proceed in their course, natures all
> Keep difference, as in their league doth fall.°

Man must be forced and marshalled within the lists of this policy. Miserable man, with all his wit, cannot in effect go beyond it. He is embarred and engaged, and, as other creatures of his rank are, he is subjected in like bonds and without any prerogative or essential pre-excellency. Whatever Privilege he assume unto himself, he is of very mean condition. That which is given by opinion or fantasy hath neither body nor taste. And if it be so that he alone, above all other Creatures, hath this liberty of imagination and this licence of thoughts, which represent unto him both what is and what is not, and what him pleaseth, falsehood and truth, it is an advantage bought at a very high rate, and whereof he hath little reason to glory. For thence springs the chiefest source of all the mischiefs that oppress him: as sin, sickness, irresolution, trouble, and despair.

But to come to my purpose: I say, therefore, there is no likelihood we should imagine the beasts do the very same things by a natural inclination and forced ingenuity which we do of our own free will and industry. Of the very same effects we must conclude alike faculties, and by the richest effects infer the noblest faculties, and consequently acknowledge that the same discourse and way we hold in working, the very same, or perhaps some other better, do beasts hold ...

By that reason, the Fox, which the inhabitants of Thrace use when they will attempt to march upon the ice of some frozen river, and to that end let her go loose afore them, should we see her running along the riverside,

---

° **So Ants ... understand**: Dante, *Purgatorio*, 26.34–6.
° **Lactantius ... laughing**: see *Treatise on the Anger of God*, 7.
° **wise man**: Solomon, supposed author of Ecclesiastes. The remainder of the sentence paraphrases 9:2.
° **All things ... share**: Lucretius, *On the Nature of Things*, 5.874.
° **All things ... fall**: ibid., 5.921–2.

approach her ear close to the ice to listen whether by any far or near distance she may hear the noise or roaring of the water running under the same, and, according as she perceiveth the ice thereby to be thick or thin, to go either forward or backward; might not we lawfully judge that the same discourse possesseth her head as in like case it would ours? And that it is a kind of debating, reason, and consequence, drawn from natural sense? Whatsoever maketh a noise moveth; whatsoever moveth is not frozen; whatsoever is not frozen is liquid; whatsoever is liquid yields under any weight. For to impute that only to a quickness of the sense of hearing, without discourse or consequence, is but a fond conceit and cannot enter into my imagination. The like must be judged of so many wiles and inventions wherewith beasts save themselves from the snares and escape the baits we lay to entrap them. And if we will take hold of any advantage tending to that purpose, that it is in our power to seize upon them, to employ them to our service, and to use them at our pleasure, it is but the same odds we have one upon another. To which purpose we have our slaves or bondmen …

[266] Touching strength, there is no creature in the world open to so many wrongs and injuries as man. He need not a Whale, an Elephant, nor a Crocodile, nor any such other wild beast, of which one alone is of power to defeat a great number of men; silly° lice are able to make Sulla give over his dictatorship. The heart and life of a mighty and triumphant Emperor is but the breakfast of a silly little Worm° …

[269] It is one same nature, which still doth keep her course … I have seen amongst us men brought by sea from distant countries, whose language, because we could in no wise° understand, and that their fashions, their countenance, and their clothes did altogether differ from ours; who of us did not deem them brutish and savage? Who did not impute their muteness unto stupidity or beastliness, and to see them ignorant of the French tongue, of our kissing the hands, of our low-louting° courtesies, of our behaviour and carriage, by which, without contradiction, human nature ought to take her pattern? Whatsoever seemeth strange unto us and we understand not, we blame and condemn. The like befalleth us in our judging of beasts …

[279] Touching corporal beauty, before I go any further, it were necessary I knew whether we are yet agreed about her description. It is very likely that we know not well what [is] beauty, either in nature or in general, since we give so many and attribute so diverse forms to human beauty … And if we impartially enter into judgement with ourselves, we shall find that if there be any creature or beast less favoured in that than we,

---

° **silly**: puny. On Sulla's death from lice, see Plutarch's *Lives*.
° **The heart … worm**: these lines have fed speculation that Shakespeare had read Montaigne when he wrote or revised *Hamlet*.
° **wise**: way.   ° **louting**: bowing.

there are others (and that in great numbers) to whom nature hath been more favourable than to us. "We are excelled in comeliness by many living creatures."° ... And that prerogative which poets yield unto our upright stature, looking towards heaven whence her beginning is—

Where other creatures on earth look and lie,
A lofty look God gave man, bade him pry
On heav'n, raised his high count'nance to the sky—°

is merely poetical. For there are many little beasts that have their sight directly fixed towards heaven. I find the Camel's and the Ostrich's neck much more raised and upright than ours. What beasts have not their face aloft and before, and look not directly opposite as we, and in their natural posture descry not as much of heaven and earth as man doth? ... As for [our] outward appearance and true shape of the visage, it is the Monkey or Ape ... [280] As for inward and vital parts, it is the Hog. Truly, when I consider man all naked—yea, be it in that sex which seemeth to have and challenge the greatest share of eye-pleasing beauty—and view his defects, his natural subjection, and manifold imperfections, I find we have had much more reason to hide and cover our nakedness than any creature else. We may be excused for borrowing those which nature had therein favoured more than us, with their beauties to adorn us, and under their spoils of wool, of hair, of feathers, and of silk to shroud us ...

They say that if Circe had presented Ulysses with two kinds of drink, the one to turn a wise man into a fool, the other to change a fool into a wise man, he would rather have accepted that of folly than have been pleased that Circe should transform his human shape into a beast's. And they say that wisdom herself would thus have spoken unto him: "Meddle not with me, but leave me rather than thou shouldest place me under the shape and body of an Ass."° What? This great and heavenly wisdom? Are philosophers contented, then, to quit it for a corporal and earthly veil? Why, then, it is not for reason's sake, nor by discourse and for the soul, we so much excel beasts. It is for the love we bear unto our beauty, unto our fair hue, and goodly disposition of limbs [281] that we reject and set our understanding at nought, our wisdom and what else we have. Well, I allow of this ingenious and voluntary confession. Surely they knew those parts we so much labour to pamper to be mere fantasies. Suppose beasts had all the virtue, the knowledge, the wisdom and sufficiency of the Stoics, they should still be beasts. Nor might they ever be compared unto a miserable, wretched, and senseless man. For, when all is done, whatsoever is not as we are is not of any worth. And God, to be esteemed of us, must

---

° **We ... creatures**: Seneca, *Epistles*, 124.22.   ° **Where ... sky**: Ovid, *Metamorphoses*, 1.84–85.
° **Circe ... Ass**: Montaigne here engages with Plutarch's "Common Conceptions Against the Stoics," but see Giambattista Gelli's *Circe* (1549), in which Ulysses's men prefer the bestial condition.

... draw somewhat near it. Whereby it appeareth that it is not long° of a true discourse, but of a foolish hardiness and self-presuming obstinacy we prefer ourselves before other creatures, and sequester ourselves from their condition and society.

ᘻ ᘻ ᘻ

° **long**: because.

FRANCIS BACON

"Prometheus, or the State of Man" (1609)

In *The Wisdom of the Ancients*, Bacon decodes thirty-one Greek myths as allegorical premonitions of his own philosophical beliefs, thereby coating his revolutionary agenda for scientific progress with a patina of antiquity. While Bacon has been justly accused of equipping modern science with a chauvinistic epistemology bent on interrogating and torturing a female Nature, his figurations are more varied and complex. In "Pan," for instance, nature is gendered male and depicted as half-animal, and consists of fluid hybrids rather than being sharply divided into discrete ranks or steps, albeit Bacon still imagines this continuum as a vertical hierarchy with humans (synonymous with order) at the top. In "Proteus," wrestling with an androgynous shape-shifter provides a licence for the aggressive manipulation of the material world via scientific experimentation. In the extract below, the myth of Prometheus confirms Bacon's sense of humankind as *Homo faber* (man the maker) and the apex of creation. Yet Bacon also shrewdly appropriates Montaigne's scepticism, fearing that too high an opinion of the human condition might sap the will to innovate and forge new technologies that will further extend human empire over the earth.
Source: *The Wisdom of the Ancients*, trans. Sir Arthur Gorges (1619), 119–20, 124–31.

The Ancients deliver that Prometheus made a man of Clay, mixed with certain parcels° taken from diverse animals, [and] studying to maintain this his work by Art [120] ... stole up to heaven with a bundle of twigs, which he, kindling at the Chariot of the Sun, came down again and communicated it with men. And yet they say that (notwithstanding this excellent work of his) he was requited with ingratitude in a treacherous conspiracy. For they accused both him and his invention to Jupiter, ... [who], in a merry mood, granted unto men not only the use of fire, but perpetual youth ...

[124] This fable demonstrates and presseth° many true and grave speculations ... Prometheus doth clearly and elegantly signify Providence.° For in the universality of nature, the fabric and constitution of Man only was by the Ancients picked out and chosen and attributed unto Providence

° **parcels**: parts. ° **presseth**: advances.
° **Providence**: divine omniscience but also human foresight. The name Prometheus in Greek means "forethinker."

as a peculiar° work. The reason of it seems to be not only in that the nature of man is capable of a mind and understanding, which is the seat of Providence, and therefore it would seem strange and incredible that the reason [125] and mind should so proceed and flow from dumb and deaf principles, as that it should necessarily be concluded the soul of man to be endued with providence, not without the example, intention, and stamp of a greater providence.

But this also is chiefly propounded:° that man is, as it were, the centre of the world in respect of final causes; so that if man were not in nature all things would seem to stray and wander without purpose, and like scattered branches (as they say) without inclination to their end. For all things attend on man, and he makes use of and gathers fruit from all creatures. For the revolutions and periods of Stars make both for the distinctions of times and the distribution of the world's site. Meteors also are referred to the presages of tempests, and winds are ordained as well for navigation as for turning of Mills and other engines. And plants and animals, of what kind so ever, are useful either [126] for men's houses and places of shelter, or for raiment, or food, or medicine, or for ease of labour, or … for delight and solace; so that all things seem to work not for themselves, but for man.

Neither is it added without consideration that certain particles° were taken from diverse living creatures and mixed and tempered with that clayey mass, because it is most true that, of all things comprehended within the compass of the universe, Man is a thing most mixed and compounded. Insomuch that he was well termed by the Ancients a "little world." For although the Chemics° do with too much curiosity take and wrest the elegancy of this word, Microcosm, to the letter, contending to find in man all minerals, all vegetables and the rest, or anything that holds proportion with them, yet this proposition remains sound and whole: that the body of man, of all material beings, is found to be most compounded [127] and most organical,° whereby it is endued and furnished with most admirable virtues and faculties. And as for simple bodies, their powers are not many, though certain and violent, as existing without being weakened, diminished, or stinted by mixture. For the multiplicity and excellency of operation have their residence in mixture and composition. And yet, nevertheless, man in his originals seems to be a thing unarmed, and naked, and unable to help itself, as needing the aid of many things. Therefore Prometheus made haste to find out fire, which suppeditates° and yields comfort and help in a manner to all human° wants and necessities. So that if the soul be the "form of forms" and if the hand be "the instrument

---

° **peculiar**: special.   ° **propounded**: proposed.   ° **particles**: parts or organs.
° **Chemics**: chemists or alchemists; see Paracelsus, *Nine Books of Archidoxes*.
° **most organical**: furnished with most organs.
° **suppeditates**: supplies.   ° **human**: spelled "humane" throughout the essay.

of instruments,"° fire deserves well to be called the succour of succours, or the help of helps, which infinite ways affords aid and assistance to all labours and mechanical arts, and to the sciences themselves ...

[128] There follows next a remarkable part of the parable: that men, instead of gratulation° and thanksgiving, were angry, and expostulated the matter with Prometheus, insomuch that they accused both him and his invention unto Jupiter, which was so acceptable unto him that he augmented their former commodities with a new bounty.

[129] Seems it not strange that ingratitude towards the author of a benefit ... should find such approbation and reward? No, it seems to be otherwise. For the meaning of the allegory is this: that men's outcries upon the defects of nature and Art proceed from an excellent disposition of the mind and turn to their good, whereas the silencing of them is hateful to the gods and redounds not so much to their profit. For they that infinitely extol human nature, or the knowledge they possess, breaking out into a prodigal admiration of that they have and enjoy, adoring also those sciences they profess, would have them be accounted perfect ... [130] On the contrary, such as bring nature and Art to the bar with accusations and bills of complaint against them are indeed of more true and moderate judgements, for they are ever in action, seeking always to find out new inventions. Which makes me much to wonder at the foolish and inconsiderate dispositions of some men, who (making themselves bondslaves to the arrogance of a few) have the philosophy of the Peripatetics° ... in so great esteem that they hold it not only an unprofitable, but a suspicious and almost heinous thing to lay any imputation of imperfection upon it. I approve rather of Empedocles his opinion ... and of Democritus° his judgement (who with great moderation complained how that all things were involved° [131] in a mist) that we knew nothing; that we discerned nothing; that truth was drowned in the depths of obscurity; and that false things were wonderfully joined and intermixed with true ... Let men therefore be admonished that by acknowledging the imperfections of Nature and Art they are grateful to the Gods, and shall thereby obtain new benefits and greater favours at their bountiful hands. And the accusation of Prometheus their Author and Master (though bitter and vehement) will conduce more to their profit than to be effuse in the congratulation of his invention. For, in a word, the opinion of having enough is to be accounted one of the greatest causes of having too little.

᠀ ᠀ ᠀

° **form .... instruments**: from Aristotle, *On the Soul*, 3.8.   ° **gratulation**: rejoicing.
° **Peripatetics**: Aristotelians.   ° **Empedocles ... Democritus**: pre-Socratic philosophers.
° **involved**: enveloped.

RENÉ DESCARTES
"The Animal Machine" (1637)

Descartes is often credited with ushering in a mechanistic worldview in seventeenth-century Europe. In the following selection from his landmark *Discourse*, he notoriously proposes that other animals are mere machines, and thus incapable of experiencing pain in any meaningful sense. It is no surprise that Descartes performed vivisections, and his theory of the "bête-machine" helped underwrite animal experimentation in England, such as Robert Hooke's 1667 attempt to prolong the life of a vivisected dog by pumping air into its lungs with bellows. In addition to articulating a split between the mind and body, his philosophy marks a widening of the ontological chasm between humans and other animals in early modern culture.
Source: *A Discourse of a Method*, anonymous translation (1649), 91–5.

And herein I particularly insisted ... that if there were such Machines°
which had organs and the exterior figure of an Ape, or of any other unreasonable creature, we should find no means of knowing them not to be
altogether of the same nature as those Animals: whereas if there were any
which resembled our bodies and imitated our actions as much as morally it
were possible, we should always have two most certain ways to know that,
for all that, they were not real men. The first of which is that they could
never have the use of speech, nor of other signs in framing it, as we have,
to declare our thoughts to others. For we may well conceive that a machine
may be so made that it may utter words, and even some proper to the
[92] corporal actions, which may cause some change in its organs (as if we
touch it in some part and it should ask what we would say, or so as it might
cry out that one hurts it and the like), but not that they can diversify them
to answer sensibly to all what shall be spoken in its presence, as the dullest
men may do. And the second is that although they did diverse things as
well (or perhaps better) than any of us, they must infallibly fail in some
others, whereby we might discover that they act not with knowledge, but
only by the disposition of their organs. For whereas reason is a universal
instrument which may serve in all kind of encounters, these organs have
need of some particular disposition for every particular action. Whence
it is that it is morally impossible for one Machine to have several organs
enough to make it move in all the occurrences of this life in the same manner as our reason makes us move.

Now by these two means [93] we may also know the difference which
is between Men and Beasts. For 'tis a very remarkable thing that there are
no men so dull and so stupid, without excepting those who are out of
their wits, but are capable to rank several words together, and of them to
compose a discourse by which they make known their thoughts. And that,

---

° **machines**: automatons.

on the contrary, there is no other creature, how perfect or happily soever brought forth, which can do the like: the which happens not because they want° organs. For we know that Pies and Parrots can utter words even as we can, and yet cannot speak like us: that is to say, with evidence that they think what they say; whereas Men being born deaf and dumb ... usually invent of themselves to be understood by those who (commonly being with them) have the leisure to learn their expressions.

[94] And this not only witnesseth that Beasts have less reason than men, but that they have none at all. For we see there needs not much to learn to speak. And forasmuch as we observe inequality amongst beasts of the same kind as well as amongst men, and that some are more easily managed than others, 'tis not to be believed but that an Ape or a Parrot which were the most perfect of its kind should therein equal the most stupid child (or at least a child of a distracted brain), if their souls were not of a nature wholly different from ours. And we ought not to confound words with natural motions which witness passions, and may be imitated by Machines as well as by Animals; nor think (as some of the ancients) that beasts speak, although we do not understand their language. For if it were true, since they have diverse organs which relate to ours, they could as well make themselves understood by us as by their like.

It is likewise very [95] remarkable that although there are diverse creatures which express more industry than we in some one of their actions, yet we may well perceive that the same show none at all in many others: so that what they do better than we proves not at all that they have reason (for by that reckoning they would have more than any of us, and would do better in all other things), but rather that they have none at all; and that it is Nature only which works in them according to the disposition of their organs, as we see a Clock, which is only composed of wheels and springs, can reckon the hours and measure the times more exactly than we can with all our prudence.

⁂ ⁂ ⁂

° **want**: lack.

MARGARET CAVENDISH
[Animal Intelligence] (1664)

Once dismissed as an eccentric, Margaret Cavendish has garnered serious attention in recent years as an iconoclastic thinker and poet who challenged the orthodoxies of the male-dominated scientific community. In the two extracts below from her *Philosophical Letters* (1.10, 2.5), Cavendish attacks Thomas Hobbes and Henry More (and indirectly Descartes) for their hubris and ignorant contempt of non-humans. Interestingly, Cavendish first voiced these epistemological theories on animal cognition in a series of poems ("A Discourse of Beasts," "Of Fishes," and "Of Birds," 105–6), and dramatized them again in her anti-Baconian utopia *The Blazing World*.

Source: *Philosophical Letters* (1664), 38, 40–1, 146–7.

Madam,

"Understanding," says your author, "is nothing else but conception caused by speech; and, therefore, if speech be peculiar to man (as, for ought I know, it is), then is understanding peculiar to him also."° Where[by] he confineth understanding only to speech and to mankind. But, by his leave madam, I surely believe that there is more understanding in Nature than that which is in speech. For if there were not, I cannot conceive how all the exact forms in generations could be produced, or how there could be such distinct degrees of several sorts and kinds of creatures, or distinctions of times and seasons, and so many exact motions and figures in Nature …

[40] Again, your author says, "That Man doth excel all other Animals in this faculty: that when he conceives anything whatsoever, he is apt to inquire the consequences of it, and what effects he can do with it." Besides this, says he, Man hath "another degree of excellence: that he can by words reduce the consequences he finds to general rules called theorems or aphorisms; that is, he can reason or reckon not only in number, but in all other things, whereof one may be added unto or subtracted from another."°

To which I answer that, according to my reason, I cannot perceive but that all creatures may do as much, but by reason they do it not after the same manner or way as Man. Man denies they can do it at all, which is very hard. For what man knows whether Fish do not know more of the nature of Water, and ebbing and flowing, and the saltiness of the Sea? Or whether Birds do not know more of the nature and degrees of Air, or the cause of Tempests? Or whether Worms do not know more of the nature of Earth, and how Plants are produced? Or Bees of the several sorts of juices of Flowers than Men? And whether they do not make their aphorisms and theorems by their manner of intelligence? For though they have not the speech of Man, yet thence doth not [41] follow that they have no intelligence at all. But the ignorance of Men concerning other creatures is the cause of despising other creatures, imagining themselves as petty Gods in Nature, when as Nature is not capable to make one God, much less so many as Mankind; and were it not for Man's supernatural soul, Man would not be more supreme than other creatures in Nature …

° **"Understanding … also"**: Hobbes, *Leviathan*, 1.4. Hobbes then describes a bird that has flown into a house and is unable to find the way out as an illustration of animal stupidity.
° **"That man … another"**: ibid., 1.5.

[146] Madam,

I cannot well conceive what your author means by the "common laws of Nature."° But if you desire my opinion how many laws Nature hath and what they are, I say Nature hath but one law (which is a wise law): viz. to keep infinite matter in order, and to keep so much peace as not to disturb the foundation of her government. For though Nature's actions are various and so many times opposite, which would seem to make wars between several parts, yet those active parts, being united into one infinite body, cannot break Nature's general peace ...

[147] Concerning the pre-eminence and prerogative of Man, whom your author calls "the flower and chief of all the products of nature upon this globe of the earth,"° I answer that Man cannot well be judged of himself because he is a party, and so may be partial. But if we observe well we shall find that the elemental Creatures are as excellent as Man, and as able to be a friend or foe to Man as Man to them ... I cannot perceive more abilities in Man than in the rest of natural Creatures: for though he can build a stately house, yet he cannot make a honey-comb; and though he can plant a slip, yet he cannot make a tree; though he can make a sword or knife, yet he cannot make the metal. And as Man makes use of other Creatures, so other Creatures make use of Man, as far as he is good for anything. But Man is not so useful to his neighbour or fellow-creatures as his neighbour or fellow-creatures to him, being not so profitable for use as apt to make spoil.

꙰ ꙰ ꙰

° **common laws ... nature**: marginal note cites Henry More, *Antidote Against Atheism*, 2.2.
° **"the flower ... earth"**: ibid., 3.

JOHN BULWER
"Man was at first but a kind of Ape" (1650)

The theory that humans descended from apes was entertained long before Darwin. No doubt it provoked outrage and censure (as it does here in a treatise denouncing cosmetics, bizarre hair styles, and other forms of body modification), and would have been whispered in private more often than defended in print. Although the author – interestingly, one of the first advocates of educating the deaf through sign language – appeals to "Nature's Book" and the "Great Chain of Being" to defend the traditional model of a static universe of creatures unchanged since the sixth day, he nevertheless bewails the possibility humans might move along or even down this scale.

Source: *Anthropometamorphosis* (1653), B3ʳ–B4ᵛ.

Insomuch as considering these injurious neglects and the tampering that hath been used among all Nations to alter the mould of their Bodies, we may say, as Plato° in effect affirms, that only the first men which the world possessed were made by God, but the rest were made and born answerable to the discourse of Man's invention. The just contemplation of which vanity made that sound more strangely in my ears that in discourse I have heard to fall, somewhat in earnest, from the mouth of a philosopher (one in points of common belief indeed too sceptical): that man was a mere Artificial creature, and was at first but a kind of Ape or Baboon, who, through his industry (by degrees), in time had improved his Figure and his Reason up to the perfection of man. It is indeed an old Observation of Pliny° that all the Race and kind of Apes resemble the proportion of men perfectly in the Face, Nose, Ears, and Eyelids, which eyelids these Creatures alone of all four-footed have under their eyes as well as above. Nay, they have paps and nipples in their breasts as Women; arms and legs bending contrary ways, even as ours do; nails they have likewise and fingers like to us, with the middle finger longer than the rest as ours be; thumbs and great toes they have, moreover, with joints like (in all the world) to a man; [B3ᵛ] and all the inward parts are the very same [as] ours, as if they were made just by one pattern. Yet they a little differ from us in the Feet, for … the sole of their foot is answerable to the palm of their hand. Their nails are channelled half-round like a gutter tile, whereas in man they be flat and broad. And Galen,° who was a great dissecter of Apes and therein acknowledged the resemblance to man, yet observes that the Thumb of an Ape differs much from that of a man. But by this new History of abused Nature it will appear a sad truth that man's endeavours have run the clean contrary course, and he hath been so far from raising himself above the pitch of his original endowments that he is much fallen below himself. And in many parts of the world is practically degenerated into the similitude of a Beast …

[B4ʳ] This whole world is one book; and is it not a barbarous thing, when all the whole book besides remains entire, to [B4ᵛ] deface that leaf in which the Author's picture, the image of God, is expressed, as in man? All other creatures keep their ranks, their places and natures in the world; only man himself disorders all, and that by displacing himself, by losing his place. While we dispute in Schools whether, if it were possible for Man to do so, it were lawful for him to destroy any one species of God's creatures, though it were but the species of Toads and Spiders (because this were a

° **Plato**: see his *Timaeus*, 91–2, which proposes that men were created first and that the intellectually deficient were reborn as women and animals.
° **Pliny**: Roman naturalist; see his *Natural History*, 11.44.
° **Galen**: ancient Greek physician. In England, comparative primate anatomy first developed in the late seventeenth century (see the introduction to Heyrick's poem, p. 117 below).

taking away one link of God's chain, one note of his harmony), we have taken away that which is the jewel at that chain, that which is the burden of the song, insomuch that we are not only inferior to the beasts, but we are ourselves become beasts, a most lamentable descent.

⁊ᵛ ⁊ᵛ ⁊ᵛ

ANN CONWAY
"This Transmutation of Things out of one Species into another" (c. 1675)

Affiliated with the Cambridge Platonists, Lady Ann Conway (née Finch) was an exceptionally gifted thinker, deeply read in ancient philosophy, and influenced by popular religious movements like Quakerism. Like Cavendish, she boldly challenged the male scientific authorities of her day and the emergent mechanistic worldview. Although she sought to refute the pantheism of Spinoza and would be more accurately characterized as a Pythagorean than a proto-Darwinian, her philosophical monism advances a holistic vision of nature as a vast, complexly interlinked continuum. In the excerpt below, she ponders a universe of infinite creatures, considers the mutability of species, and even speculates that humans possess a sense of environmental justice. How do her metaphysics and Ladder of Being model compare with the natural history of John Ray (see Part 1) and his understanding of biodiversity?
Source: *Principles of the Most Ancient and Modern Philosophy* (1692), 18–19, 21, 28–9, 49, 63–70.

Seeing God is infinitely powerful there can be no Number of Creatures so great that he cannot always make more. And because, as is already proved, he doth whatsoever he can do, certainly his Will, Goodness, and Bounty, is as large and extensive as his Power; whence it manifestly follows that Creatures are infinite and created in infinite manners, so that they cannot be limited or bounded with any Number or Measure. For example, let us suppose the whole Universality of Creatures to be a Circle whose Semi-diameter shall contain so many Diameters of the Earth as there are Grains of Dust or Sand in the whole Globe of the Earth. And if the same should be divided into Atoms so small that 100,000 of them could be contained in one Grain of Poppy seed, now who can deny but the infinite Power of God could have made this Number greater, and yet still greater, even to an infinite Multiplication? ...

[19] Also by the like Reason is proved that not only the whole Body or System of Creatures considered together is infinite, or contains in itself a kind of Infinity, but also that every Creature, even the least that we can discern with our Eyes or conceive in our Minds, hath therein such an Infinity of Parts, or rather entire Creatures, that they cannot be numbered ...

Therefore those who teach that the whole number of Creatures is Finite, and consists of so many Individuals as may be numbered ... consider so great Majesty with too low and unbeseeming a Conception, ... whom they confine to so narrow an Habitation, as a few little Bees shut up within the limits of an Hive, containing the measure of a few Inches ...

[28] Moreover, the consideration of this infinite Divisibility of everything into Parts always less is no unnecessary [29] or unprofitable Theory, but a thing of very great moment: viz. that thereby may be understood the Reasons and Causes of Things, and how all Creatures from the highest to the lowest are inseparably united one with another by means of subtler Parts interceding or coming in between, which are the Emanations of one Creature into another, by which also they act one upon another at the greatest distance. And this is the Foundation of all Sympathy and Antipathy which happens in Creatures. And if these things be well understood ... [one] may easily see into the most secret and hidden Causes of Things, which ignorant men call occult Qualities ...

[49] That all Creatures in their own Nature are changeable, the distinction between God and Creatures, duly considered, evidently evinces ... For if any Creature were of itself and in its own Nature unchangeable that Creature would be God, because Immutability is one of his incommunicable Attributes.

Now let us consider how far this Mutability may reach or be extended and, first, whether one Individual can be changed into another of the same or a different Species. This, I say, is impossible. For then the very Essences of Things would be changed, which would make a great confusion, not only in the Creatures, but in the Wisdom of God, which made all Things ...

[63] Yet the Individuals of Creatures are always but finitely good and finitely distant, *quod* Species, or as to Species, and only potentially Infinite: that is, always capable of further perfection without end. As if there should be supposed a certain Ladder, which should be infinitely long, containing infinite Steps, [64] yet those Steps are not infinitely distant one from another; otherwise there could be no ascension nor descension made thereon. For Steps (in this example) signify the various Species of Things, which cannot be infinitely distant one from another or from those which are next unto them. Yea, daily experience teaches us that the Species of diverse Things are changed, one into another, as Earth into Water, and Water into Air, and Air into Fire or Ether ... And so also Stones are changed into Metals, and one Metal into another. But lest some should say these are only naked Bodies and have no Spirit, we shall observe the same not only in Vegetables, but also in Animals, like as Barley and Wheat are convertible the one into the other ... which is well enough known to House-keepers in many Provinces, and especially in Hungary, where if Barley be sown Wheat springs up instead thereof ... [65] And in Animals, Worms are changed into Flies, and Beasts and Fishes that Feed on Beasts and Fishes

of a different kind do change them into their own Nature and Species ...
And did not the Earth also at the same Command° bring forth Beasts and
creeping Things, which for that Cause were real and proper Parts of the
Earth and Waters? And as they had their Bodies from the Earth, so likewise
they had their Spirits or Souls from the same ... [66] And the Spirit of
Man ought to have Dominion over these Spirits ... so as to subdue them
to himself, and exalt them to a higher degree, (viz.) into his own proper
Nature ... [But] he suffered the Earthly Spirits existing within him to get
Dominion over him, and so became like them; wherefore it is said, "Earth
thou art, and unto Earth thou shalt return,"° which hath no less a spiritual
than a literal Signification.

Now we see how gloriously the Justice of God appears in this
Transmutation of Things out of one Species into another. And that there
is a certain Justice which operates not only in Men and Angels [67] but in
all Creatures is most certain. And he that doth not observe the same may
be said to be utterly blind. For this Justice appears as well in the Ascension
of Creatures as in their Descension; that is, when they are changed into
the better and when into the worse. When into the better, this Justice distributes to them the Reward and Fruit of their good Deeds; when into the
worse, the same punishes them with due Punishments, according to the
Nature and Degree of the Transgression. And the same Justice hath given a
Law to all Creatures, and written the same on their Natures ...

[68] God hath also put the same instinct of Justice in Man towards
Beasts and Trees of the field. For whosoever he be that is a good and just
Man, the same loves his Beasts that serve him, and taketh care of them
that they have their Food and Rest, and what else is wanting to them. And
this he doth not do only for his own profit, but out of a Principle of true
Justice. For should he be so cruel to them as to require their Labour and
yet deny them their necessary Food, then certainly he transgresseth that
Law which God hath written on his Heart. And if he kills any of them only
to fulfil his own pleasure, he acts unjustly, and the same measure will again
be measured unto him. So likewise a Man that hath a certain fruitful Tree
in his Orchard that prospereth well, he dungs and cleanses the same that it
may wax better and better. But if it be barren and encumbers the Ground,
then he heweth it down with an Axe and burns it with fire ...

[69] If a Man hath neither lived an angelical nor diabolical but a brutish
... Life on Earth ... shall not the same Justice most justly cause that ... he
also (at least, as to his external Form, in bodily Figure) should be changed
into that Species [70] of Beasts to whom he was inwardly most like in
Qualities and Conditions of Mind? And seeing this brutal Spirit is now
become superior and predominant in him, and holds the other captive,
is it not very probable when such a Man dies that the very same brutish

° **Command**: Genesis 1:24.
° **Earth ... return**: Genesis 3:19.

Spirit shall still have Dominion in him, and carry the human Soul with
it whithersoever it pleaseth and compel it to be subservient unto it? And
when the said brutish Spirit returns again into some Body and hath now
Dominion over that Body, so that its Plastic° faculty hath the Liberty of
forming a Body after its own Idea and Inclination (which before in the
human Body it had not), it necessarily follows that the Body which this
vital Spirit forms will be brutal and not human.° For the brutal Spirit
cannot produce and form any other Figure because its plastic Faculty is
governed of its Imagination, which it doth most strongly imagine to itself,
or conceive its own proper Image, which therefore the external Body is
necessarily forced to assume.

༄ ༄ ༄

° **Plastic**: creative, malleable.
° **the Body ... not human**: human is spelled humane. These lines present a shocking defence of
   Pythagorean metempsychosis (see Part I). For another contemporary rehabilitation of this theory,
   see Whitelocke Bulstrode's *Essay of Transmigration* (1692).

ANONYMOUS

from Scala Naturæ (1695)

Before Carl Linnaeus unveiled his taxonomic system in 1735, Renaissance naturalists mainly relied on the Aristotelian method of classifying organisms based
on their habitat (land, water, air) and their supposed faculties (nutritive, sensitive, ratiocinative). For theologians, biological diversity was regarded as a sign of
God's grandeur and sometimes imagined as a chain or ladder descending from
God to angels to humans to animals to plants to metals to minerals to soil. This
analogical worldview informs and was arguably reinforced by the prominent use
of cross-species metaphors in literature. For simplicity's sake, this schema can be
pictured as a Venn diagram consisting of three partially overlapping circles: (1)
Greco-Roman natural philosophy – particularly the works of Aristotle and Pliny,
(2) Judeo-Christian doctrine and scriptural commentaries on the creation story
in Genesis, and (3) empirical observation by contemporary naturalists. Although
the influential literary historian E. M. W. Tillyard famously proclaimed this the
"Elizabethan World Picture," it was rarely set forth in a sustained, systematic
fashion prior to the eighteenth century, as the late date of this text (occasioned
by Deist scepticism about the existence of angels) indicates. Moreover, writers as
sophisticated as Marlowe, Shakespeare, and Donne never simply subscribe to received dogma; they also question or subvert it. Rather than a static and monolithic
belief system, the "World Picture" would have experienced spikes and dips in
popularity dependent on prevailing political (and meteorological) conditions. By
1600, these three circles were already drifting apart (see Part VI) due to the centrif-
ugal force exerted by the Little Ice Age, Copernican cosmology, and newly rediscovered philosophies such as atomism. Increased social mobility would have also

contributed to its decline, as critics have rightly exposed the ideological valence of this infatuation with order and rank as a means of naturalizing the inequalities of feudalism. But does that negate the potential of texts like the following, with their acute sense of the congruence or interdependence of various species, to promote a proto-ecological sensibility, as Gabriel Egan has argued? Or, as Simon Estok contends, is the ladder metaphor (with its emphasis on ascending to the spiritual realms) too hierarchical and thus decidedly inferior to the web model preferred by ecologists today?

Source: *Scala Natura* (1695), 6, 8–17.

The lowest order of beings is that of the inanimate, in which we look upon the Earth as most inferior, both in place and esteem. The Water is more lively and moving; the Air still exceeding the watery element, yielding breath for the support of all living things. But the fiery nature exceeds all the former, not only by reason of its exquisite agility, but because 'tis the very fund and source of Vegetation. I make no doubt to say that Fire is the very Vegetative Soul of all Animate Nature° ...

[8] 'Twould be endless to pursue all these steps of Nature, even in the lowest rank of inanimate beings, as to show amongst the Stones how one excelleth another, from the Pebble to the Topaz; or to set forth the degrees which are in Metals, from Iron to the purest Gold ...

[10] Now of animate things there are three distinct specific natures: the one still exceeding the other, not only in degree but in the perfection of its rank and order. Thus Vegetables, who have simply life with those operations which are suitable to it in a low degree, are excelled by Sensibles, which enjoy not only growth, but a proper life of sense, with faculties and operations corresponding thereunto. This is also exceeded by the Rational Nature, which surmounts Vegetation and Sense by the addition of intellectual capacity ...

[11] And now if we survey the Vegetable order, who can enumerate all the various species of beings contained within that sphere? It has been the work of ages to compose an herbal, every succeeding age having added something to the labours of the former, but still leaving the work to be consummated by future generations ... [12] I make no doubt to say that the surface of the Earth is of a Vegetable nature, and that the Grass and some common excrescences are no more the productions of seed sown than the feathers upon Birds, or hair upon Beasts, or on the heads of Men ... [13] But who is able to go step by step through all the various degrees of perfection which are in Vegetables, from the cortex° of the Earth, which is the lowest, to the sensitive and humble Plants,° which are the highest rank of vegetables at present known to us?

And now as it is but one step from the inanimate to the lowest animate nature, viz. the Vegetable; so is it but one remove from Vegetable to

---

° **Fire ... Nature**: a view attributed to the Greek philosopher Heraclitus.
° **cortex**: literally bark, but here probably referring to lichen.
° **sensitive ... Plants**: such as the Touch-me-not, which droops when handled.

Sensitive Beings. For as the surface of the Earth producing plants was the *Nexus utriusque Naturae,* the very link which chained the Inanimate and Vegetable natures together, [14] so shall we find some Vegetables which in a manner partake of Sensible Nature, and are productive of the lowest size of animals, as the mere earth produceth the meanest vegetables. Witness those small Insects which are bred in Flowers and Herbs; the Flies which are lodged in Oak and Elm leaves, being bred in small cavities thereupon; and those Grubs to which the Oak-apple and Hazelnut are as a matrix. So that here you have the *Nexus Naturae vegetabilis et sensitivae,* the link which unites the Vegetable and Sensitive Natures together, and thereby makes all the steps in this *Scala Naturae,* this Ascent of Nature, to be even and of equal distance from each other, and suffers no chasm or gap in the climax° of Nature. In short, Insects [15] are … the very flour, yeast, and highest working of Vegetable Nature …

[16] To reckon up the several sorts of perfect Animals, either Birds, Beasts, or Fish, has been attempted by many naturalists, though as yet not brought to perfection by reason of the great variety which is observed in each of their classes. My business is from hence to arise to the third step of animate nature, viz. the Rational or Intellectual. Now as the regular steps and degrees of perfection have been observed through the Inanimate, Vegetative, and Sensitive beings (as from the Pebble to the Diamond, [17] Iron to Gold, from the Shrub to the Cedar, and from the Bat to the Eagle), so may a parallel difference be seen amongst Men, with respect to stupidity and acuteness, barbarity and civility, cowardice and courage, and with regard to virtuous or vicious inclinations. So that although logic will not give us leave to say that there are different species of Men, yet our experience will tell us that there are several sorts of Men distinguished from each other, as Metals, Minerals, Stones, Birds, Fish, and Beasts differ amongst themselves in their respective classes.

ᐛ ᐛ ᐛ

° **climax**: "ascending series or scale" (*OED* 2).

Beasts

EDWARD TOPSELL

from A History of Four-Footed Beasts (1607)

The first major work of English zoology was by and large a translation of a text compiled by the Swiss naturalist Conrad Gesner (1516–65). For modern readers, it is a book of perplexing contradictions. It rejects many of the superstitions recorded by Pliny, yet includes ambivalent entries for the unicorn (excerpted below) and lamia (a woman with a cat-like body covered in scales whose shapely breasts lure men to their doom). It stresses the authority of eyewitness accounts, yet recycles dozens of fabulous anecdotes from poets, classical historians, and especially the Bible as admissible evidence. It tries to pry off the theological goggles through which the medieval bestiary tradition had viewed non-humans, while still promoting zoology as a sacred science. Readers of Topsell's epistle will not be surprised to learn that the author himself was, like most Renaissance naturalists, a clergyman. With its startling mixture of lore and fact, superstition and scepticism, Topsell's bestiary is a representative specimen of its time.

Source: *History of Four-Footed Beasts* (1607), A4ʳ–A6ʳ, 712–13, 716, 719.

[Dedicatory Epistle°]

When I affirm that the knowledge of Beasts is Divine, I do mean no other thing than the right and perfect description of their names, figures, and natures, and this is in the Creator himself most Divine; and therefore such as is the fountain, such are the streams issuing from the same into the minds of men. Now it is most clear in Genesis how the Holy Ghost remembereth the creation of all living creatures, and the Four-footed next before the creation of man, as though they alone were appointed the Ushers, going immediately before the race of men ...

The old Manichees° among other blasphemies accused the creation of hurtful, venomous, ravening, and destroying Beasts, affirming them to be made by an evil God; and also they accused the creation of Mice and other unprofitable creatures, because their dullness was no kinder to the Lord (but like cruel and covetous misers, made no account of those Beasts which brought not profit to their purse). You know ... how that grave Father Augustine° answereth that calumny: first, affirming that the same

---

° **Dedicatory Epistle**: addressed to Richard Neile, Dean of Westminster.

° **Manichees**: a religious sect that believed in cosmological dualism: that the material world was essentially evil and at war with the spiritual or good.

° **Augustine**: see *City of God*, 12.5, in which Augustine contends that animals are most divine when they remain in their "true posture of nature," or wild state.

thing which seemed idle to men was profitable to God; and the same that appeared ugly to them was beautiful to him … He therefore wisely compareth a fool that knows not the use of the creatures in this world to one ignorant that cometh into the workhouse of a cunning man, viewing a number of strange tools and having no cunning but in an axe or a rake, thinketh that all those rare inventions of a wise workman are idle toys. And whilst thus he thinketh, wandering to and fro, not looking to his feet, suddenly falleth into some furnace in the same workhouse, or chance to take up some sharp tool whereby he is wounded; then he also thinketh that the same are hurtful and dangerous. But we that are ashamed to deny the use of instruments in the shops of rare Artisans, but rather admire their invention … concludeth that all Beasts are either *utilia*,° and against them we dare not speak; or *pernitiosa*,° whereby we are terrified, that we should not love this perilous life; or else they are *superflua*,° which to affirm were most ridiculous. For as in a great house all things are not for use, but some for ornament, so is it in this world, the inferior palace of God.° Thus far Augustine …

These things have I principally laboured in this Treatise to show unto men what Beasts are their friends and what their Enemies, which to trust and which avoid, in which to find nourishment and which to shun as poison … Surely, it was for that a man might gain out of them much divine knowledge, such as is imprinted in them by nature, as a type or spark of that great wisdom whereby they were created: in Mice and Serpents, a foreknowledge of things to come; in the Ant … a providence against old age; in the Bear, the love of young: in the Lion, his stately pace; in the Cock and Sheep, change of weather … [Thus] every beast is a natural vision, which we ought to see and understand, for the more clear apprehension of the invisible majesty of God …

[A5ʳ] How great is the love and faithfulness of Dogs; the meekness of Elephants; the modesty or shamefastness of the adulterous Lioness; the neatness and politure° of the Cat and Peacock; the justice of the Bee, which gathereth from all flowers that which serveth their turn, and yet destroyeth not the flower; the care of the Nightingale to make her voice pleasant; the chastity of a Turtle;° the canonical° voice and watchfulness° of a Cock; and, to conclude, the utility of a Sheep. All these and ten thousand more I could recite to show what the knowledge of the nature of brutish creatures doth work or teach the minds of men …

° *utilia*: useful.   ° *pernitiosa*: harmful.   ° *superflua*: superfluous.
° **For … God**: Gesner's preface also scorns a merely utilitarian appraisal of animals: "Aristotle maketh it a true property of a noble, liberal, and well-governed mind, to be more delighted with the rare, pleasant, and admirable qualities of a beast, than with the lucre and gain that cometh thereby" (¶2v).   ° **politure**: elegance.   ° **Turtle**: turtle-dove.
° **canonical**: authoritative (literally, in conformity with church law dictating times of day designated for religious devotions).   ° **watchfulness**: vigilance.

Now again the necessity of this History is to be preferred before the Chronicles and records [A5ᵛ] of all ages made by men, because the events and accidents of the time past are peradventure such things as shall never again come in use. But this showeth that Chronicle which was made by God himself: every living beast being a word; every kind being a sentence; and all of them together a large history, containing admirable knowledge and learning, which was, which is, which shall continue (if not forever) yet to the world's end.

The second thing in this discourse which I have promised to affirm is the truth of the History of Creatures; for the mark of a good writer is to follow truth and not deceivable fables. And in this kind I have passed the straitest passage, because the relation of most things in this book are taken out of heathen writers, such as peradventure are many times superstitiously credulous, and have added of their own very many rash inventions, without reason, authority, or probability, as if they had been hired to sell such fables. For ... I would not have the reader of these Histories to imagine that I have inserted or related all that ever is said of these Beasts, but only so much as is said by many ... If at any time [Gesner] seemed obscure, I turned to the Books which I had at hand to guess their meaning, putting in that which he had left out of many good Authors, and leaving out many magical devices. Now although I have used no small diligence or care in collecting those things which were most essential to every Beast, most true without exception and most evident by the testimony of many good authors, yet I have delivered in this treatise many strange and rare things, not as fictions, but miracles of nature for wise men to behold and observe to their singular comfort ... not withholding their consent to the things expressed, because they entreat of living things made by God himself ... [A6ʳ] And although I do not challenge° a power of not erring, yet because I speak of the power of God, that is unlimitable, I will be bold to aver that for truth in the Book of creatures (although first observed by Heathen men) which is not contrary to the book of Scriptures ... For how shall we be able to speak the whole counsel of God unto his people, if we read unto them but one of his books, when he hath another in the world, which we never study past the title or outside, although the great God have made them an Epistle Dedicatory to the whole race of mankind?

"Of the Unicorn"

[712] That there is such a beast, the Scripture itself witnesseth. For David thus speaketh in the ninety-second Psalm: ... "my horn shall be lifted up like the horn of a Unicorn," whereupon all Divines that ever wrote have

---

° **challenge**: claim.

not only collected° that there is a Unicorn, but also affirm the similitude to be betwixt the Kingdom of David and the horn of the Unicorn ... Good men which worship God and follow his laws are compared to Unicorns, whose greater parts as their whole bodies are unprofitable and untamable, yet their horn maketh them excellent; so in good men, although their fleshy parts be good for nothing and fall down to the earth, yet their grace and piety exalteth their souls to the heavens ... [There be some that have taken this Rhinoceros for the Monoceros, the Unicorn, because of this one horn, but they are deceived]° ... for the Rhinoceros hath not one horn, but two ... [Unicorns also appear in] the prophecy of Isaiah 34, and in many other places of Scripture, whereby God himself must needs be traduced if there be no Unicorn in the world ...

[713] [Various reports seem to describe] but one and the same beast ... Whereby I gather that it is no other beast than the wild Ass, or at the least the wild Ass cometh nearest to the Unicorn of all others. For they agree in these things: first, in that both of them have one horn° in the middle of the forehead; secondly, in that both of them are bred in India; thirdly, in that they are both about the bigness of a Horse; fourthly, in their celerity and solitary life; fifthly and lastly, in their exceeding strength and untamable natures. But herein they differ both in their feet and colours: for the feet of the wild Asses are whole and not cloven like the Unicorn's, and their colour white in their body, and purple on their head ...

[716] The horn of this Beast being put upon the Table of Kings and set amongst their junkets° and banquets doth bewray the venom if there be any such therein by a certain sweat which cometh over it ... It cannot be denied that this our Unicorn's horn was taken from some living wild Beast;° for there are found in Europe to the number of twenty of these horns pure,° and so many broken ... I do also know that which the King of England° possesseth to be wreathed in spires, even as that accounted in the Church of St. Denis, than which they suppose none greater in the world, and I never saw anything in any creatures more worthy praise than this horn. The substance is made by nature, not Art, wherein all the marks are found which the true horn requireth ...

[719] These Beasts are very swift, and their legs have no Articles.° They keep for the most part in the deserts, and live solitary in the tops of the Mountains. There was nothing more horrible than the voice or braying of it; for the voice is strained above measure. It fighteth both with the mouth

---

° **collected**: concluded.   ° **There ... deceived**: interpolated from p. 596.
° **horn**: the Indian wild ass does not have a horn. It seems likely that Gesner's sources confused it with the Indian rhinoceros.   ° **junkets**: delicacies.
° **Beast**: most "unicorn" horns were actually taken from narwhals.   ° **pure**: intact.
° **King of England**: Henry VIII ingested medicines made from ground unicorn horn; Queen Elizabeth was presented with one (actually a narwhal horn) in 1577 by Martin Frobisher, who found it on a beach in northern Canada.   ° **Articles**: joints.

and with the heels: with the mouth biting like a Lion, and with the heels kicking like a Horse. It is a beast of an untamable nature, and therefore the Lord himself in Job° saith that he cannot be tied with any halter, nor yet accustomed to any cratch° or stable. He feareth not Iron or any iron Instrument …

It is said that Unicorns, above all other creatures, do reverence Virgins and young Maids, and that many times at the sight of them they grow tame, and come and sleep beside them; for there is in their nature a certain savour wherewithal the Unicorns are allured and delighted. For which occasion the Indian and Ethiopian Hunters use this stratagem to take the beast: they take a goodly strong and beautiful young man, whom they dress in the apparel of a woman, besetting him with diverse odoriferous flowers and spices … The Unicorn, deceived with the outward shape of a woman and sweet smells, cometh unto the young man without fear, and so suffereth his head to be covered and wrapped within his large sleeves, never stirring but lying still and asleep, as in his most acceptable repose. Then, when the Hunters by the sign of the young man perceive him fast and secure, they come upon him and by force cut off his horn and send him away alive. But concerning this opinion we have no elder authority than Tzetzes,° who did not live above five hundred years ago; therefore I leave the Reader to the freedom of his own judgement to believe or refuse this relation.

ᴥ ᴥ ᴥ

° **Job**: 39:12.　　° **cratch**: cowshed.
° **Tzetzes**: a twelfth-century Byzantine poet, who relates this story in his *Chiliades.*

THOMAS HEYRICK
"On an Ape" (1691)

While a trained ape was exhibited in Southwark around 1600 (see Dugan *et al.*) and Kenelm Digby wrote of a baboon that could play guitar (320), displays of primate intelligence in Renaissance England usually provoked scoffing laughter rather than respect. The following poem, however, worries that apes are much closer to us than we to angels. Heyrick's suspicions were apparently confirmed seven years later when the pioneering comparative anatomist Edward Tyson dissected an infant chimpanzee (now on display at the London Natural History Museum). Discovering forty-eight anatomical similarities between it and a human (including the morphology of the brain and larynx) and thirty-four differences, Tyson hailed this "pygmy" in his *Orang-outang, sive Homo sylvestris* as a "nexus between the animal and the rational" (¶2ʳ).
Source: *Miscellany Poems* (1691), 16–17.

This Creature, that our scorn doth grow,
Whose actions we with laughter see,
Of reason doth resemblance show,
And follows us with pleasing mimicry.
It aims at wit, a Man would grow,
And would be rational, if it knew how.

'Tis more than we to Angels can;
Their deeds we cannot imitate.
We're after all endeavours, Man.
10   Nor can we e'en in shadow change our state;
Nor what they are, or what they do,
Can we but e'en in show attain unto.

Trifles our anxious heads do fill,
Which this blessed Creature trouble not;
Quarrels thence flow, the cause of ill,
While unconcern'dness is his happy lot.
He is our scorn, and much more we
The scorn or pity may of Angels be.

Like Man ambitiously he acts,
20   While we in paths of Beasts do tread;
Follow vain fools in vicious tracks,
And e'en to hell are by example led.
Great aims his mind doth upward call,
While basely we to what's below us crawl.

᪥ ᪥ ᪥

WILLIAM SHAKESPEARE
[The Courser and the Jennet]

Shakespeare's first published poem includes a masterfully etched portrait of a
pair of horses. Lines 295–300 present an equine blazon, describing the physical
features regarded as most desirable by early modern horse-breeders (cf. Conrad
Heresbach's *Four Books of Husbandry*, 114ᵛ–16ʳ). Since horses served as both trans-
port and status symbols (with rare imports fetching high prices), it is tempting to
liken them to automobiles. The analogy is an imperfect one. Unlike cars, tractors,
or tanks, horses are sentient creatures, who have to be "broken" and trained by
their riders – a process that could foster either domineering attitudes (see Gervase
Markham's disturbing account in his 1607 *Cavelarice* of the torture inflicted on
colts [49–53, 96–97]) or cross-species friendship (as attested by Nicholas Morgan's
"Of Lovingness to Man"). In Renaissance literature, the horse and the centaur
often symbolize the unruly passion of the animal body. In Shakespeare's poem,
Venus urges the courser's behaviour as proof that heterosexual desire (and male
pursuit of the female) is natural, but the coy Adonis subverts the attempt to draw
heteronormative analogies between other animals and humans.
Source: *Venus and Adonis* (1593), C2ᵛ–C3ᵛ.

But lo, from forth a copse° that neighbours by,
A breeding Jennet,° lusty, young, and proud,   260
Adonis' trampling Courser° doth espy,
And forth she rushes, snorts, and neighs aloud.
The strong-necked steed, being tied unto a tree,
Breaketh his rein, and to her straight goes he.

Imperiously he leaps, he neighs, he bounds,
And now his woven girths° he breaks asunder,
The bearing earth with his hard hoof he wounds,
Whose hollow womb resounds like heaven's thunder.
The iron bit he crusheth 'tween his teeth,
Controlling what he was controllèd with.   270

His ears up-pricked, his braided hanging mane
Upon his compassed crest° now stand on end;
His nostrils drink the air, and forth again
As from a furnace, vapours doth he send.
His eye, which scornfully glisters like fire,
Shows his hot courage° and his high desire.

Sometime he trots, as if he told° the steps
With gentle majesty and modest pride.
Anon he rears upright, curvets,° and leaps,
As who should say, "Lo, thus my strength is tried.   280
And this I do, to captivate the eye
Of the fair breeder that is standing by."

What recketh° he his rider's angry stir,°
His flattering "Holla,"° or his "Stand, I say"?
What cares he now for curb° or pricking spur,
For rich caparisons° or trappings gay?
He sees his love, and nothing else he sees,
For nothing else with his proud sight agrees.

Look when° a painter would surpass the life
In limning out a well-proportioned steed,   290
His Art with Nature's workmanship at strife,
As if the dead the living should exceed:
So did this Horse excel a common one
In shape, in courage, colour, pace, and bone.°

° **copse**: a managed woodland, periodically cut for timber.
° **Jennet**: small Spanish horse. "Breeding" implies a mare in heat.
° **Courser**: large, strong horse used in war and hunting; its name derived from the French "to run."
° **girths**: bands.   ° **compassed crest**: curved neck.   ° **courage**: lust.
° **told**: counted.   ° **curvets**: leaps on hind legs with forelegs raised.   ° **recketh**: cares for.
° **stir**: fuss.   ° **Holla**: halt.   ° **curb**: bit.   ° **caparisons**: ornamental saddle-cloth.
° **Look when**: Consider how.   ° **bone**: build.

Round hoof, short-jointed,° fetlocks° shag and long,
Broad breast, full eye, small head, and nostril wide,
High crest, short ears, straight legs, and passing strong,
Thin mane, thick tail, broad buttock, tender hide:
Look what a horse should have, he did not lack,
300 Save a proud rider on so proud a back.

Sometime he scuds° far off, and there he stares;
Anon he starts at stirring of a feather.
To bid the wind a base° he now prepares,
And whe'er° he run or fly, they know not whether;°
For through his mane and tail the high wind sings,
Fanning the hairs, who wave like feathered wings.

He looks upon his love, and neighs unto her;
She answers him, as if she knew his mind,
Being proud, as females are, to see him woo her,
310 She puts on outward strangeness, seems unkind,
Spurns at his love, and scorns the heat he feels,
Beating his kind° embracements with her heels.

Then, like a melancholy malcontent,
He vails° his tail that, like a falling plume,
Cool shadow to his melting° buttock lent.
He stamps, and bites the poor flies in his fume.°
His love, perceiving how he was enraged,
Grew kinder, and his fury was assuaged.

His testy° master goth about to take him,
320 When lo, the unbacked° breeder, full of fear,
Jealous° of catching, swiftly doth forsake him,
With her the horse, and left Adonis there.
As they were mad unto the wood they hie° them,
Outstripping crows that strive to overfly them.

&ewc; &ewc; &ewc;

° **short-jointed**: shorter pastern bones, believed to make the horse sturdier.
° **fetlocks**: hair-covered joints above the hooves.   ° **scuds**: darts.
° **base**: to play the game of prisoner's base (team tag).   ° **whe'er**: whether.
° **whether**: which, but also suggesting whither.   ° **kind**: natural.   ° **vails**: lowers.
° **melting**: sweaty.   ° **fume**: tantrum.   ° **testy**: ill-tempered.   ° **unbacked**: unmounted.
° **Jealous**: mistrustful.   ° **hie**: hasten.

JOHN HARINGTON
"My Dog Bungay" (1608)

In 1570, the Cambridge physician John Caius (or Keys) published a learned monograph *Of English Dogs*, a work that attests both to a growing urge to systematize knowledge of other species and to the affective bond between humans and canines in the sixteenth century (see Part IV). Many Renaissance gentlemen kept dogs for practical purposes such as hunting, yet John Harington seems to have valued his liver-spotted water spaniel for his intelligence and loyalty rather than his swiftness in the chase. In this letter to Prince Henry, whose father was a notorious cynophile, Harington pays tribute to the dog's "strange feats" that call into question the human monopoly on reason. Although he once beat his wife's lapdog (and then wrote an apologetic poem, featured in Part IV), his evident grief at Bungay's death and the fact he even had the dog's portrait painted suggest an extension of kinship to a "companion species" (Haraway). How does this eulogy compare with Launce's rebuke of his hapless dog Crab in Shakespeare's *Two Gentlemen of Verona*?
Source: *Nugae Antiquae* (1804), 380–4.

Having good reason to think your Highness had good will and liking to read what others have told of my rare dog, I will even give a brief history of his good deeds and strange feats. And herein will I not play the cur° myself, but in good sooth relate what is no more nor less than bare verity. Although I mean not to disparage the deeds of Alexander's horse,° I will match my dog against him for good carriage; for if he did not bear a great Prince on his back, I am bold to say he did often bear the sweet words of a greater Princess° on his neck.

I did once relate to your Highness after what sort his tackling° was wherewith he did [381] sojourn from my house at the Bath to Greenwich Palace,° and deliver up to the court there such matters as were entrusted to his care. This he hath often done and came safe to the Bath, or my house here at Kelston, with goodly returns from such nobility as were pleased to employ him. Nor was it ever told our Lady Queen that this messenger did ever blab ought concerning his high trust, as other have done in more special matters. Neither must it be forgotten … how he once was sent with two charges of sack wine from the Bath to my house by my man Combe, and on his way the cordage did slacken. But my trusty bearer did now bear himself so wisely as to covertly hide one flasket in the rushes and take the other in his teeth to the house. After which he went forth and returned with other part of his burden to dinner. Hereat your Highness may perchance marvel and doubt. But we have living testimony of those who wrought in the fields, and espied his work, and now live to tell they did

---

° **play the cur**: misbehave like a stupid or ill-bred dog (see *Two Gentlemen of Verona*, 4.4.1, and "play the dog" in the ensuing paragraph).
° **Alexander's horse**: Bucephalus, famous for his strength and grace.   ° **Princess**: Elizabeth.
° **tackling**: equipment or bag.   ° **Bath … Greenwich**: a distance of over 120 miles.

much long to play the dog, and give stowage to the wine themselves. But they did refrain, and watched the passing of this whole business.

I need not say how much I did once grieve [382] at missing this dog. For on my journey towards London some idle pastimers did divert themselves with hunting mallards in a pond, and conveyed him to the Spanish Ambassador's, where (in a happy hour) after six weeks I did hear of him. But such was the court he did pay to the Don that he was no less in good liking there than at home. Nor did the household listen to my claim or challenge till I rested my suit on the dog's own proofs, and made him perform such feats before the nobles assembled as put it past doubt that I was his master. I did send him to the hall in the time of dinner and made him bring thence a pheasant out of the dish, which created much mirth. But much more when he returned at my commandment to the table and put it again in the same cover. Herewith the company was well content to allow me my claim, and we both were well content to accept it, and came homewards. I could dwell more on this matter but *jubes renovare dolorem.*°

I will now say in what manner he died. As we travelled toward the Bath, he leaped on my horse's neck, and was more earnest in fawning and courting my notice than what I had observed for time back. And after my chiding his disturbing my passing forward, he gave me some [383] glances of such affection as moved me to cajole him. But, alas, he crept suddenly into a thorny brake, and died in a short time ...

Now let Ulysses praise his dog Argus, or Tobit be led by that dog° whose name doth not appear. Yet could I say such things of my Bungay° (for so was he styled) as might shame them both, either for good faith, clear wit, or wonderful deeds. To say no more than I have said, of his bearing letters to London and Greenwich, more than a hundred miles. As I doubt not but your Highness would love my dog, if not myself, I have been thus tedious in his story, and again say that of all the dogs in your father's court, not one hath more love, more diligence to please, or less pay for pleasing than him I write of. For verily a bone would content my servant when some expect of [384] greater matters or will knavishly find out a bone of contention ...

P. S. I have an excellent picture [of Bungay], curiously limned, to remain in my posterity.

⅌ ⅌ ⅌

° *jubes ... dolorem*: "You bid me to revive griefs," from *Aeneid*, 2.3.
° **Tobit ... dog**: a seeing-eye dog mentioned in the apocryphal Book of Tobit (5, 11).
° **Bungay**: As Harington was an avid theatre-goer, it seems likely that he named the dog after the magician in a popular play by Robert Greene, perhaps in recognition of the similarities between interspecies communication and conjuring.

WILLIAM BALDWIN
from Beware the Cat (*c.* 1553)

Beware the Cat is sometimes hailed as the first English novel. The accolade is misleading, as it lacks the fidelity to "realism" that came to define the genre in the eighteenth century. Nevertheless, the book unquestionably ranks among the most resplendent gems of Renaissance prose fiction. It was composed around 1553, but Baldwin had to tuck it away during the reign of Queen Mary because of its mordant anti-Catholic satire. In Part 1, the narrator is sitting beside a fire at an inn and overhears two eerie tales about talking cats. Overcome with curiosity to understand the caterwauling of the cats outside his window at night, he ingests a magical confection made from gobbets of a cat's liver, brain, hair, and dung, as well as a fox's heart, a kite's stomach, and a hedgehog's kidneys. The potion works and the narrator can now comprehend the cacophonous non-human soundscape of Tudor London. Concealed in an alley in Aldgate, he eavesdrops on a gathering of cats and, in the selection below, overhears the testimony of one named Mouse-slayer. The domestic freedom and nocturnal habits of the cats make them privy to all the clandestine misdoings going on behind closed doors and in the dark, particularly the persistence of taboo Catholic practices and superstitions. While the cats might be regarded as a fanciful metaphor for a Tudor intelligence ser-vice, their meaning scratches much deeper; they can be seen to possess a "feline empire" (Shannon 184), and an alternative epistemology that undercuts human and authorial omniscience. In *The Animal That Therefore I Am*, the philosopher Jacques Derrida describes the uncanny feeling he experiences when he notices his cat staring at him naked in his bathroom. Although mingled with scatological humour, this same uncanny quality pervades Baldwin's book, as we see human foibles reflected through an animal gaze.
Source: A *Marvellous History Entitled Beware the Cat* (1584), E5^v–E8^r.

"My Master also made much of me because I would take meat in my foot, and therewith put it to my mouth and feed. In this house dwelt an ungra-cious fellow, who, delighting much in unhappy turns, on a time took four walnut shells and filled them full of soft pitch and put them upon my feet. And then [he] put my feet into cold water till the pitch was hardened and then he let me go. But Lord how strange it was to me to go in shoes! And how they vexed me! For when I ran upon any steep thing they made me slide and fall down. Wherefore all that afternoon, for anger that I could not get off my shoes, I hid me in a corner of the garret which was boarded, under which my Master and Mistress lay. And at night when they were all in bed, I spied a Mouse playing in the floor. And when I ran at her to catch her, my shoes made such a noise upon the boards that it waked my master, who was a man very fearful of sprites. And when he with his servants hearkened well to the noise, which went pit-pat, pit-pat, as it had been the trampling of a horse, they waxed all afraid and said surely it was the devil. And as [E6^r] one of them, a hardy fellow, even he that had shoed me, came upstairs to see what it was, I went downward to meet him and made such a rattling, that when he saw my glistering eyes, he fell down backward, and broke his head, crying out, 'The devil! The devil! The devil!' Which his Master and all the rest hearing, ran naked as they were into the street and cried the same cry.

Whereupon the neighbours arose and called up among other an old Priest, who lamented much the lack of holy water, which they were forbidden to make.° Howbeit, he went to church and took out of the Font some of the Christening water, and took his Chalice and a wafer unconsecrated, and put on a Surplice and his stole about his neck, and fetched out of his chamber a piece of holy Candle, which he had kept two year, and herewith he came to the house. And with his Candlelight in the one hand and a holy-water sprinkle° in the other hand, and his Chalice and wafer in sight in his bosom and a pot of Font-water at his girdle, up he came praying toward the garret, and all the people after him. And when I saw this, and thinking I should have seen some mass that night, as many nights before in other places I [E6ᵛ] had, I ran towards them thinking to meet them. But when the Priest heard me come, and by a glimpsing had seen me, down he fell upon them that were behind him, [and] with his chalice hurt one, with his water pot another, and his holy candle fell into another Priest's breech beneath, who (while the rest were hawsoning° me) was conjuring our maid at the stair-foot and all to-besinged him, for he was so afraid with the noise of the rest which fell that he had not the power to put it out. When I saw all this business, down I ran among them where they lay on heaps, but such a fear as they were all in then I think was never seen afore. For the old priest which was so tumbled among them that his face lay upon a boy's bare arse,° which belike was fallen headlong under him, was so astonished [that] when the boy (which for fear beshit himself) had all to-rayed° his face, he neither felt nor smelt it nor removed from him.

Then went I to my dame, which lay among the rest, God knoweth, very madly, and so mewed and curled about her that at last she said, 'I ween° it be my Cat.' That hearing, the knave that had shoed me, and calling to mind that erst he had forgot, said it [E7ʳ] was so indeed and nothing else.

That hearing, the priest, in whose holy breech the holy candle all this while lay burning, he took heart of grace,° and before he was spied rose up and took the candle in his hand and looked upon me and all the rest of the company, and fell a-laughing at the handsome lying of his fellow's face. The rest hearing him, came every man to himself and arose and looked upon me and cursed the knave which had shoed me, who would in no case be aknown of it. This done, they got hot water and dissolved the pitch and plucked off my shoes. And then every man, after they desired each other not to be aknown of this night's work for shame, departed to their lodgings, and all our household went to bed again."

° **holy water ... make:** As per Thomas Cranmer's 1549 Book of Common Prayer. The religious paraphernalia brought by the priest were traditionally used in the then forbidden ritual of exorcism.   ° **sprinkle:** an aspergillum or brush.   ° **hawsoning:** exorcizing.
° **arse:** a marginal note reads "A meet pillow for a Magician."   ° **to-rayed:** befouled.
° **ween:** believe.   ° **heart ... grace:** courage.

When all the Cats, and I, too, for company, had laughed° at this apace, Mouse-slayer proceeded and said:

"After this about three-quarters of a year, which was at Whitsuntide° last, I played another prank and that was this. The Gentleman who ... was accepted and retained of my mistress came often home to our house, and always in my Master's absence was doing with my Dame. [E7ᵛ] Wherefore desirous that my Master might know it, for they spent his goods so lavishly between them that, notwithstanding his great trade of Merchandise, they had unweeting° to him almost undone him already, I sought how I might bewray° them: which ... came to pass thus. While this Gentleman was doing with my dame, my Master came in so suddenly that he had no leisure to pluck up his hose, but with them about his legs ran into a corner behind the painted cloth,° and there stood, I warrant you, as still as a mouse. As soon as my master came in, his wife, according to her old wont, caught him about the neck and kissed him and devised many means to have got him forth again. But he being weary sat down and called for his dinner. And when she saw there was none other remedy she brought it him, which was a mess of pottage and a piece of Beef, whereas she and her franion° had broke their fast with Capons, hot Venison, marrow-bones, and all other kind of dainties. I seeing this, and minding to show my Master how he was ordered, got behind the cloth, and to make the man speak I all to-pawed him with my claws upon [E8ʳ] his bare legs and buttocks: and for all this he stood still and never moved. But my Master heard me and, thinking I was catching a mouse, bade my dame go help me, who, knowing what beast was there, came to the cloth and called me away, saying, 'Come Puss, come Puss,' and cast me meat onto the floor. But I, minding another thing and seeing that scratching could not move him, suddenly I leapt up and caught him by the genitals with my teeth, and bit so hard that, when he had restrained more than I thought any man could, at last he cried out and caught me by the neck, thinking to have strangled me. My Master, not smelling but hearing such a Rat as was not wont to be about such walls, came to the cloth and lifted it up and there he found this bare-arsed Gentleman strangling me, who had his stones° in my mouth. And when I saw my Master I let go my hold, and the Gentleman his, and away I ran immediately to the place where I now dwell, and never came there since, so that how they agreed among them I cannot tell, nor never durst go see, for fear of my life."

❧ ❧ ❧

° **laughed**: a marginal note reads "The Author laughed in [a] cat's voice."
° **Whitsuntide**: Pentecost, the eighth Sunday after Easter.
° **unweeting**: unbeknownst.   ° **bewray**: expose.   ° **painted cloth**: wall-hanging decorated with images.
° **franion**: lover.   ° **stones**: testicles.

KENELM DIGBY

"Concerning the Invention of Foxes and Other Beasts" and "Of the Several Cryings and Tones of Beasts" (1644)

Whereas philosophers like Plutarch, Montaigne, and Thomas Browne were willing to grant other species a modest portion of reason and at least a gestural language, the courtier-physician Digby here dismisses the clever feats attributed to foxes as random luck, and animal cries as mere pneumatics. This verdict contrasts starkly with the celebration of the fox's shrewdness in medieval fables, and two poems featuring a talking fox by the Welsh herbalist and hunter, Huw Llwyd (c. 1568–1630). Revealingly, Digby was an admirer of Descartes, and actually visited him in Holland in 1640. Published five years before the first English translation of Descartes, Digby's *Two Treatises* present "the earliest fully worked out system of mechanical philosophy in English" (Henry 225). Although he believed in the magical weapon-salve, Digby's viewpoint is representative of the mid-seventeenth century in its appeal to physiology and personal experience, and its refusal to glean moral lessons from animal behaviour.

Source: *Two Treatises* (1644), 307–9, 313, 316–18.

But now to speak of their invention,° I must confess that among several of them there appeareth so much cunning in laying of their plots ... [308] that one might think they wrought by design, and had a distinct view of an end, for the effecting of which they used discourse to choose the likeliest means.

To this purpose, the subtleties of the fox are of most note. They say he useth to lie as if he were dead, thereby to make hens and ducks come boldly to him; that in the night, when his body is unseen, he will fix his eyes upon poultry and so make them come down to him from their roost; that to rid himself of the fleas that afflict him in the summer, he will sink his body by little and little into the water, while the fleas creep up to his head (to save themselves from drowning) and from thence to a bough he holdeth in his mouth, and will then swim away, leaving them there; that to cozen° the badger of his earth,° he will piss in it, as knowing that the rank smell of his urine will drive the other cleanlier beast to quit it; that when dogs are close upon him and catching at him, he will piss upon his tail and, by firking° that up and down, will endeavour (you may believe) to make their eyes smart, and so retard their pursuit that he may escape from them ...

[309] Now to penetrate into the causes of these and of such like actions, we may remember how we showed in the last chapter that the beating of the heart worketh two things: the one is that it turneth about the species,° or little corporeities° (streaming from outward objects) which remain in the memory; the other is that it is always pressing on to some motion or other, out of which it happeneth that when the ordinary ways of getting

---

° **invention**: intelligence.   ° **cozen**: cheat.   ° **earth**: sett or den.   ° **firking**: flicking.
° **species**: "emanations from outward things, forming the direct object of cognition" (*OED* 5). A common theory in ancient texts on optics.   ° **corporeities**: bodies.

victuals or of escaping from enemies do fail a creature whose constitution is active, it lighteth sometimes (though peradventure very seldom) upon doing something out of which the desired effect followeth, as it cannot choose but fall out now and then, although chance only do govern their actions. And when their action proveth successful, it leaveth such an impression in the memory that whensoever the like occasion occurreth that animal will follow the same method. For the same species do come together from the memory into the fantasy.° But the many attempts that miscarry, and the ineffectual motions which straits° do cast beasts upon, are never observed. Nor are there any stories recorded of them: no more than in the temple of Neptune were kept upon the registers the relations of those unfortunate wretches, who, making vows unto that god in their distress, were nevertheless drowned ...

[313] But how many foxes do there perish in attempts which, if they had succeeded, would have been accounted by slight judgers to be notable subtleties, but miscarrying are esteemed tumultuary° motions without design, caused by that animal's fantasy and spirits when he is in extremity? I remember how upon a time when I was hunting one, he (being hard set and but little before the dogs and the hunters) caught in his mouth the bough of a crooked ash tree he [had] run up a pretty way; which, being in a hedge, he thereby hung down along the side of the hedge. And when we struck him over the ribs with our poles, he would not quit his hold (so strongly the fear of the dogs wrought in his fantasy) till greater blows knocked him on the head; which showeth evidently that this action was the effect of chance pressing his fantasy to do something, and not any reason or discourse providing for his safety ...

[316] Of that of the fox's weighing his goose before he would venture to carry it over the river, were it plainly true as it is set down I avow I should be hard set to find the principles from whence that discretion in him proceeded. But I conceive this tale may be paired with that which telleth us of another fox, who, having his prey taken from him by an eagle, brought the next day a new prize into the same place, having first rolled it in the fire so that some burning coals stuck upon it; which the eagle coming again and snatching from him, carried to her nest, which was thereby set on fire, and the young ones falling down became the fox's share instead of what their dam° had robbed him of. Such stories, so quaintly contrived, are fitter for a moral than for a natural philosopher. Aesop may entertain himself and his disciples with them, while all the reflection I shall make upon them is that when I hear any such finely ordered tales, I cannot doubt but they are well amended in the relation by those that tell them ...

[317] But before we go to the next point, we cannot forbear mentioning their vanity as well as ignorance, who, to purchase the estimation of deeper knowers of nature, would have it believed that beasts have complete languages

---

° **fantasy**: imagination.   ° **straits**: difficulties.   ° **tumultuary**: disorderly.   ° **dam**: mother.

as men have to discourse with one another in; which they vaunted they had the intelligence of ... But it was because they had more pride than knowledge. Of which rank, one of the chief was Apollonius,° surnamed from Tyana. For if he had known how to look into the nature of beasts, he would have perceived the reason of the diverse voices which the same beast in diverse occasions formeth.

This is evident: that an animal's lungs and chest, lying so near as they do unto his heart, and all voice being made by the breaths coming out of his mouth and through his windpipe, it must necessarily follow that by the diverse ordering of these instruments his voice will become diverse. And these instruments will be diversely ordered in him according to the diverse motions of his heart: that is, by diverse passions in him (for so we may observe in ourselves that our breath is much changed by our being in passion) ... Consequently, as a beast is agitated by various passions, he must needs utter variety of voices, which cannot choose but make diverse impressions in other beasts that have commerce with him, whether they be of the same kind as he is or of a different. And so we see that if a dog setteth upon a hog, the bitten hog's cry maketh an impression in the other hogs to come to their fellow's rescue, and in other dogs to run after the crying hog. In like manner, anger in a dog maketh snarling or barking; pain, whining; [318] desire, another kind of barking; and his joy of seeing a person that he useth° to receive good by will break out in another kind of whining. So in a hen, her diverse passions work diverse kinds of clucking: as when she seeth a kite, she hath one voice; when she meeteth with meat, another; when she desireth to gather her chickens under her wings, a third ... So that who would look curiously into the motions of the dispositions of a beast's vocal instruments and into the motions of the spirits about his heart (which motion we have showed is passion) would be able to give account, why every voice of that beast was such a one, and what motion about the heart it were that caused it ...

Out of this discourse also reason may be given why birds are more musical than other creatures: to wit, because they are of a hotter complexion, and therefore to their bigness do require more breath and air to cool them; and consequently do make more noise and more variety of it. Likewise among beasts, dogs are the most vocal of any that converse with us, who, by their ready anger, appear to be the hottest ...

And thus it is evident that there is no true language among beasts: their voices not being tokens of diverse things or conceptions, but merely the effects of diverse breathings, caused by diverse passions. Wherefore, since both breathing and passion are easily reduced to the common principles of rarity° and density, we need not trouble ourselves any further to seek into the origin of this vocal faculty of beasts.

※ ※ ※

° **Apollonius**: a Pythagorean sage (first century CE), reputed to have the power to speak to animals (Philostratus, *Life of Apollonius*, 1.20).   ° **useth**: is accustomed.   ° **rarity**: thinness.

THOMAS TRYON
"Of the Language of Sheep" (1684)

Born in the Cotswolds, Tryon worked as a shepherd in his youth, so his keen observations of sheep behaviour and his veterinary advice are based on personal experience. Among the most jaw-dropping conjectures of this seventeenth-century vegetarian is that a non-meat diet could permit early humans to understand the language of animals. Although it is easy to scoff at Tryon's nature mysticism, the denial of language to other species is a recurrent gripe among ecocritics, and some of his arguments accord with the contemporary theory of zoosemiotics.
Source: *Countryman's Companion* (1684), 59–63.

Although Sheep have by Nature but one only Tone or Bleat, yet they can communicate their Minds to each other by varying and altering the same, according to the respective states of their Minds and Spirits, and suitable to the occasion, no less readily than Mankind do convey [60] their conceptions by articulate words; for when such a Centre is awakened, then presently such a sound is predominant in the bleat. The like is to be understood in all other Creatures, even in Men; for every word does vary in its sound, according to what property is awakened in the sevenfold Nature.° And look whatever property carries the upper Dominion, such a Sound or Tone is chief in the word, and carries along with it the power of that Property or Principle, and by way of spirits it incorporates with its similes in those to whom such words are directed. And according to the Radix° of each word, so do they kindle either Love or Anger; for every Word does sound forth the state and nature of that Centre, whence they proceed.

Which the great Prophet Moses seems to intimate, where he saith that God brought all Creatures to Adam, and he gave them Names expressing their Natures, or according to their Natures.° That is, the very Word in itself did comprehend and sound forth the genuine Nature, Complexion, Disposition, Inclination, and what Form and Property did predominate, so that to hear any Creature named was (then) to have a complete Definition, or at least Description of the true internal [61] Nature, Virtues, and Vices of that Creature: which was the true Language of Nature and the Original, which Man hath fooled away by suffering his mind and desires to enter into the evil, unclean, violent, savage, wrathful Nature of Bears, Tigers, etc. But the Beasts and Birds do still retain that first natural Mother Tongue, which the Creator endowed them with in the beginning, and are not deprived of it because they have firmly and constantly kept and observed the pure Law of Nature;° and therefore can understand by one single Bleat,

---

° **sevenfold Nature**: Tryon makes several references to seven properties or animating spirits in nature that trigger various psychophysiological effects (perhaps derived from Jakob Böhme's *Quellgeister*).   ° **Radix**: root.
° **God ... Natures**: Genesis 2:20; see the excerpt from Hutchinson in Part 1, pp. 50–51 above.
° **Law of Nature**: i.e. vegetarianism (see Genesis 1:29).

Sound, or Tone the various States, Inclinations, and Dispositions of each other, as also express Fullness, Hunger, Love, Hate, Joy, Sorrow … which no mortal man can do by any one Word, Sound, or Tone.

As, for example, a Flock of Sheep of 400 or 500 are slaiting° and grazing by a Cornfield or inviting Pasture: if any one of them sees any pass in the Hedge, that Sheep shall slip in and fall afeeding with silence, and not so much as Bleat or hardly look up, except for fear, knowing she is where she ought not to be. But observe the next Sheep that sees this that is got into the Corn: no sooner does she give a Bleat or two, but it does as sensibly [62] call or alarm the whole Flock, as particular Words do men, or the sounds of Trumpets and Drums do Soldiers; and then presently they all fall to running into the Corn, making a noise, and Bleating till the whole Field ring of them. But at other times particular Sheep in the Flock will bleat for sundry occasions: as when they want their Lambs or Fellows; as also when they are otherwise discomposed with Hunger, Cold, or the like. But then none of the rest will so much as look up, except their Lambs, which (if they are within hearing) will run through the whole Flock and quickly find their proper Dams° by their Calls. Also, they can distinguish the Shepherd's Whistle … from all other Whistles, and will turn at the hearing of it; and many other things of the like nature, which experienced and observing Shepherds know to be true. So true it is that the Creator hath endowed all the inferior Creatures with admirable Natural Gifts of Self-preservation and distinguishing Senses amongst themselves, far exceeding Man, who yet was made a thousand degrees more sublime; but he wandered out of the Path of that pure Law and Way he was ordained to walk in, whereas those [63] other inferior Creatures have not, and therefore they all retain those Original Gifts bestowed upon them in their Creation.

⁂

° **slaiting**: pasturing   ° **proper Dams**: own mothers.

JACQUES DU FOUILLOUX
"The Badger" (1561)

Due to their fondness for barnyard poultry, badgers were classified as vermin by a 1566 Act of Parliament, and a shilling bounty placed on their head. When not killed outright, they were often baited with dogs. Shakespeare's comparison of the hounded Malvolio to a baited badger (*Twelfth Night*, 2.5.102) suggests that only the more Puritan-minded would have found the "good pastime" objectionable. That the most detailed Elizabethan portrait of the reclusive badger comes from a French hunting manual and was later incorporated into Topsell's *Four-Footed Beasts* demonstrates the alliance in the Renaissance between venery and natural

history (and that the latter was very much a pan-European enterprise), and helps explain the co-existence of loving scrutiny and flippant cruelty in contemporary writings about wild animals. While translating Fouilloux, Gascoigne inserted several empathetic poems from the point of view of the quarry (see Part IV, p. 337), but the badger is not among them. Even John Clare's 1830 poem voices little moral outrage at the practice, focusing more on the badger's admirable tenacity. To discourage the sport, the 1973 Badger Bill made hunting them illegal, to the chagrin of many farmers. Badger culls were permitted again in 2013, allegedly due to fears of tuberculosis, and have since become a cause célèbre of animal rights activists.
Source: *The Noble Art of Venery* (1575), 184–6, 190–1, 196.

The Badger maketh his hole commonly in sand or light earth, which is easy to dig, and in open places, to have the comfort of the Sun; for they sleep incessantly and are much fatter than Fox cubs be. As touching their hair, they have a grey coat, and [young badgers] are somewhat whiter than the old, waxing greyer and greyer the elder that they be ... [They] live upon all flesh, and will hunt after carrion. They do great hurt in Warrens and Cunnigars,° especially when they be full of little rabbits, for they make a hole right above the nest and go straight to them, whereas the fox followeth the hole's mouth until he come at the nest. I have seen a Badger take a sucking Pig in my presence, and carried him clean away unto his earth. It is sure that they desire Hog's flesh more than any other, for if you train [185] a piece of pork ... upon their burrow they will sure come out unto it. They prey also upon all Poultry: as Geese, Ducks, Hens, and such like.

I can speak by experience, for I have brought up some tame until they were four years old ... Being so brought up, they are very gentle, and will play with young whelps and never hurt them. And the rest of the day that they neither feed nor play, they bestow in sleeping. Those which I have brought up would come to me at a call, and follow me like whelps of hounds. They are very chill of cold, and if you let them lie in a chamber where there is any fire, they will creep so near it that they will burn their coats and their feet also many times. And then are they very hard to be healed. They will be fed with anything: bread, cheese, fruits, birds, or anything that you will give them.

When it snoweth or is hard weather, then they come not out of their holes sometimes in two or three days together, the which I have observed at their hole's mouth when it hath snowed and lied there so thick that they could not have stirred out, but that I might have perceived them. As I have seen that after three days they have come out for pure hunger and gone to prey for meat. It is a pleasure to behold them when they gather stuff for their nest or for their couch: as straw, leaves, moss, and such other things. And with their forefeet and their head, they will wrap up as much together as a man would carry under one arm, and will make shift to get

° **Cunnigars**: rabbit burrows.

it into their holes and couches. This subtlety they have: that when they perceive the Terriers begin to yearn° them and to bay at them, they will stop the hole between the Terriers and them, lest the Terriers should follow them any further. And then, if the Terriers bay still, they will remove their baggage with them and go into another chamber or angle of their Burrow. They live long, and when they wear old, then some of them fall blind, and cannot come forth of their holes. Then, if they be the Badgers°, the Sows feed them; and, if it be the Sow, the Badger feedeth her likewise …

[186] All these things I have seen by experience: they are long-lived, and hard to kill. For I have seen a well-biting Greyhound take a Badger and tear his guts out of his belly, and yet the Badger hath fought still, and would not yield to death. True it is that they are very tender upon the snout, and you cannot give them so little a blow upon the snout with a stick, but that they will die immediately …

[190] He that would hunt a Badger must seek the earths and burrows where they lie, and in a fair moonshine night, let him go unto them upon a clear wind° and stop all the holes but one or two. And in those let him set sacks or pokes° fastened with [191] some drawing string which may shut him in soon as he straineth the bag … If the hounds chance to encounter him, or to undertake the chase before he be gotten into his earth, or re-covered near unto it, then will he stand at bay like a boar,° and make you good pastime … [196] Being thus taken, put them into a sack or poke, to hunt with your Terriers in your gardens or close courts, at your pleasure. He that will be present at such pastimes may do well to be booted. For I have lent a Fox or a Badger ere now a piece of my hose, and the skin and flesh for company, which he never restored again.

⁂ ⁂ ⁂

° **yearn**: bark (at a scent).   ° **Badgers**: males, also called boars.   ° **clear wind**: upwind.
° **pokes**: bags.
° **boar**: wild boar were either locally extinct or critically endangered in southern England by the fourteenth century.

RICHARD BRATHWAITE
"The Squirrel" and "The Hedgehog" (1634)

Brathwaite was born in Kendall, near the Lake District, which helps explain his fondness for nature imagery. However, "the first Lakeland poet" was also an ur-bane Oxbridge-educated wit, and his *Strange Metamorphosis* is a prime example of the Renaissance tendency to view landscape through an Ovidian prism. To understand man, the preface declares, we must "seek him in the wilderness … [where] we find him, not in his own similitude, but like Ulysses' crew, trans-formed into every shape we meet with" (A3ʳ⁻ᵛ). The text thus presents a series of self-consciously anthropomorphic depictions of various fauna and flora, such as a bear, bat, peacock, moss, and even a coalmine. The first extract below has an added poignancy today due to the fact that Britain's indigenous red squirrel has almost vanished since the American grey squirrel was introduced in the 1870s. The second comprises one of the best early modern descriptions of the hedgehog, a species classified as vermin in Tudor statutes but which in 2013 received the most votes in a contest to name the natural emblem of Britain. Sadly, their population has plummeted nearly 40 per cent in the UK since the year 2000, and conservationists now regard them as a barometer for the ecological health of the British countryside.

Source: *A Strange Metamorphosis of Man, Transformed into a Wilderness* (1634), B3ᵛ–5ᵛ, B8ʳ–C2ᵛ.

The Squirrel is that nimble Reveller of the Forest who is always set upon a merry pin.° It is the innocence of his gentle breast that makes his heart so light and the body so naturally active. He keeps Holiday every day, and is never without his pumps° on, to be ready to dance; for he will dance you beyond measure, and yet be never out of his dance. He is very desperate° in his tricks, so that if he chance to fall he ventures his neck, life, and all. He is no Carpet-knight° [B4ʳ] that danceth on strewed tapestries; for he will dance upon a tree without any music: but this in the Forest only; for in the City he hath another manner with him, where it is ridiculous to dance without music, and therefore gets him a dancing school with a chime of little Bells at least. He is a four-footed bird that is kept in a cage:° not to sing, for he hath no voice that is worth the hearing, but to dance only. One would wonder to see him so well breathed, who will hold out so long and yet not be tired, especially [B4ᵛ] considering the diet he uses being commonly nuts, so apt with us to breed obstructions and the phthisic.° With an apple and a nut or two he will make himself not only an handsome collation° but a royal feast. It is very strange what teeth the thief hath; for he will pare you a walnut as big as his head much sooner than we an apple—yea, and devour the kernel, and all ere you would imagine. He hath a good face, and he knows it well, and some beauty withal, whereof he is exceeding choice and tender; [for] he never [B5ʳ] goes especially in the Sun but he carries his Umbrella about him, which serves him likewise for a cloak in a shower of rain. He that should mark him well would think him a puppet made in fashion of a Squirrel, that by engines were made so to mount up and down, and that either he had no joint at all, or all were nothing else but joints; for he moves not his head so much as his whole body when he moves. He is very neat, for he washes his face at every bit he eats; and should be a Jew° in that, but in other things hath no Religion [B5ᵛ] in him at all. In a word, I hold him to have a good nature with him,

---

° **merry pin**: cheerful mood.   ° **pumps**: dancing shoes.   ° **desperate**: reckless.
° **Carpet-knight**: a knight whose rank was due to social prestige rather than military valour.
° **cage**: squirrels were sometimes kept as pets, as shown in a famous portrait by Hans Holbein.
° **phthisic**: cough.   ° **collation**: light meal.
° **Jew**: because of ritual ablutions practised in Judaism.

and a pretty wit; and though he seem to have a cunning head, yet stayed enough from any debauchments ...

[B8ʳ] The Hedgehog is a right Urchin° and a peevish Elf that cannot be meddled with at no hand. He is a whole fort in himself: he, the Governor; his skin, the walls; his prickles, the Corps de garde.° He is very jealous and suspicious by nature, so that he never takes his [B8ᵛ] rest till he have set the watch. He hath a drawbridge to collect himself with at his pleasure, especially when he stands upon his guard, so as it were impossible to make any breach into him. He is a great enemy to the winds, principally the North and South, and, therefore, having but two gates to the City where he keeps his hold, he hath barricades for them both to shut them out.° There are two sorts of them: one for land, who never put to sea; the other seafaring men° that never come to land—who as they differ [C1ʳ] in trade of life so do their manners. Yet both are weather-wise alike, and both crafty enough it seems to provide for themselves; for if the one have his fort, the other his ship to trust to. And if the one keep out the wind at his doors, the other in a storm will stick to his tackling and take in stones for his Ballast, or, if need be, cleave to an anchor ... He is all comb, though not to comb with, which hath no teeth but to [do] mischief with, and therefore [C1ᵛ] is no friend from the teeth outward, while every tooth is a very sting. He is but a milksop° yet, and a very suckling, who will hang on the speens° of every Cow, which therefore makes him cry so like a child. He cannot brag much of his gentry whose father was a Boar, his mother a Sow, himself a Pig, and all begot under a hedge. If there be any such place as Hogs Norton° is, where Pigs play on the organs, it is surely with them, who have such a squeaking cry with their wind instruments. What [C2ʳ] his flesh is to eat I know not, but I should think he should eat him whole were as good have a burr in his throat. They say his flesh is as good and as tender as a Rabbit, but this I am sure: their fur is nothing near so gentle. As the Fox hath his hole, so hath he his bush, from whence there is no getting him forth till he be fired out. He is no great meddler himself, nor loves to be meddled with; nor any that is wise, I think, will tease° with him, who knows how touchy he is. For my part, if I stumble [C2ᵛ] not on him I will have nothing to do with him.

⁂ ⁂ ⁂

° **Urchin**: another name for the hedgehog, but also slang for a brat or hunchback.
° **Corps de garde**: sentinels.
° **enemy ... out**: a legend derived from Aristotle and Pliny, and repeated in Topsell.
° **seafaring men**: i.e. sea urchins, according to the belief that every land animal had an equivalent in the water.   ° **milksop**: timid weakling.
° **speens**: teats. Another erroneous folk belief that may have encouraged the killing of hedgehogs (worth 2 pence a head according to the 1566 Vermin Act).
° **Hogs Norton**: legendary village inhabited by boorish yokels and organ-playing pigs.
° **tease**: annoy, with pun on comb.

EDWARD MAY
"On a Toad" (1633)

The belief that humans had been created in God's image promoted an anthropocentric narcissism among many early moderns. The following poem is a memorable
example of how this doctrine could foster contempt towards species regarded as rad-
ically Other, such as amphibians and insects. It thus offers a revealing counterpoint
to the excerpts by Montaigne, Browne, and Cavendish, which recognize the fallacy
of humans judging themselves the most exquisite creatures on the planet.
Source: *Epigrams Divine and Moral* (1633), B4ᵛ.

> One that was walking in a sunshine day,
> Seeing an ugly Toad lie in the way,
> Fell passionately aweeping; his friend by
> Inquired the cause, he sadly made reply:
> How that the sight of that same loathsome thing,
> Did to his conscience the remembrance bring
> Of his ingratitude to God; that he
> Had never given thanks for th'exellency
> Of his creation, being made and framed
> Like his own image, by his breath enflamed,   10
> When he being in the Potter's hands as clay
> Within his power inscrutable° it lay
> To fashion and bestow on him the feature
> Of that same Toad, e'en the most deformedst creature.
> Thus basest things heav'n makes an instrument,
> To humble those are willing to repent.

ᵉ❧ ❧ ❧

° **inscrutable**: the 1633 reading "instructable" is likely a misprint.

JOHN DERRICKE
"[Why] the Irish ground ... neither breedeth nor fostereth up any venomous beast or worm" (1581)

Fear of zoological Other and the cultural Other are strangely entwined in this
poem written to celebrate the 1578 victory of English forces led by Henry Sidney
over the Irish resistance. In the extract below, Derricke (who served under Sidney)
spins an etiological fable to account both for the ferocity of the Irish opposition
and for the peculiar fact that the island does not have any snakes. In contrast to
the legend that St Patrick expelled them, Derricke imagines them as banished
by the Roman gods. Following Apollo's advice, Jove creates wood-kerns (Irish
soldiers, who often engaged in guerrilla warfare) to occupy hills where the snakes

had lived to prevent an evil race from building Babel-like towers (fortresses) that would challenge the authority of the gods. The fable reveals a troubling correspondence between colonial occupation and the destruction of biodiversity, even if Derricke imagines the Irish as the instigators of this destruction as a precedent to justify English schemes to "improve" Ireland by clearing forests and draining bogs. Does extermination function here as a metaphor for genocide?
Source: *Image of Ireland* (1581), C2ᵛ–D2ᵛ.

	For where time past it did possess each hurtful wicked beast,
	The hissing serpent with her mate, and worm of poison least,
	Yet now no such it will retain, it voucheth not to see:
300	The Frog, the Toad, nor Viper vile, within her bounds to be.
	If time have changèd thus the ground, I stand therein in doubt,
	Or whether that the Gods themselves have driv'n those Serpents out …
	I think when as such brutes were made then gods both great and small,
	Consulted with th'infernal ghosts and mountain Sprites withal,
	How and what sort they might repulse, or bring to small effect,
	The world's intent that would so vile Dame Nature's laws reject.
	In which consult° one steppèd forth (as far as I can guess),
320	Apollo was that reverend sire, chief in this business …
340	"There be a Crew of mountain gods, possessing earth below;
	Pray that their godheads would a few of Martial men bestow,
	To keep (say ye) a little plat,° in which is most mistrust,
	And through which the foreign foe perforce there travel must" …
	Though God Apollo spoke full wise, Mars 'gan again reply: …
	"How may the Gods that hills possess grant this unjust request?
350	Or who would deem Apollo sage had folly in his breast?
	Know ye not in that savage soil the Adder there to dwell?
	And see you not the Cockatrice° and slaying Serpent fell?
	Behold you not the Slow-worm° there, with Viper's generation?
	May ye not see the Frog and Toad there have their procreation?
	Cannot each wight (except the blind) the savage beasts perceive?
	As Lion,° Wolf,° and rav'ning Bear,° whose herds they oft deceive?
	The tameless Panther them amongst, with Tigers' cruèl kind?
	The Leopard, with a thousand more, as Nature hath assigned?
	How then may man have comp'ny with this hurtful generation?
360	Or sons of men with noisome worms enjoy their consolation?"
	"Why," said Apollo, "angry Mars, each part may well agree,
	When as by Jove each slaying beast abstracted° thence shall be.
	Jove first shall banish quite the beasts—yea, he shall clean destroy
	The thing that might in any wise° the soldiers ought annoy.

° **consult**: council.   ° **plat**: outpost.
° **Cockatrice**: mythical serpent whose gaze could blind.
° **Slow-worm**: legless lizard *Anguis fragilis* (now a protected species in the UK). It is not believed to be native to Ireland.   ° **Lion**: not native to Ireland (neither are the tiger or panther).
° **Wolf**: although they survived much longer in Ireland than in England, the last Irish wolf was reported killed in 1786.
° **bear**: the Irish brown bear is thought to have been hunted to extinction in the Paleolithic period.
° **abstracted**: removed.   ° **wise**: ways.

And they debarrèd once from thence, in safe Security,
The Soldiers then in open field by day and night may lie,
To watch and ward lest ireful foes, through Pilgrim's sly pretence,°
Should unawares against the Gods their warlike suit commence …"
"Indeed," said Mars, "it may be so, if Jove thereto agree.
But first 'tis meet that every hill in level sort should be."
"Be whist,° O Mars!" said thund'ring Jove …
"Each hurtful beast that noisome is I will command away;   380
Not one shall rest° the Mountain men by any kind to fray.
The croaking Toad that ugly seems, with Snakes and Adders fell,
Shall be dismissed and sent forthwith to Pluto's ghosts in hell,
To feed thereon, themselves to glut, sufficing hungry maw.
Yea, they themselves, without constraint, themselves shall thither draw.
Let therefore little Mountain Gods a troupe (as they may spare)
Of breechless men, at all assays,° both levy and prepare,
With mantles down unto the shoe, to lap° them in by night,
With spears and swords and little darts to shield them from despite.
And let some have their breeches close,° to nimble things annexed,   390
With safer means to dance the bogs, when they by foes are vexed.
With glibbèd° heads like Mars himself, their malice to express,
With ireful hearts and bloody hands, soon prone to wickedness."
Jove spake, 'twas done, and I suppose then Serpents were dismissed,
And sent away: which to be true, now credit if you list.°
Again,° the Irish, young and old, presumeth for to say,
Their saint (Saint Patrick) was the man that banished them away.
And therefore is Saint Patrick held in passing admiration:
Still worshippèd of all that stock with holy veneration.
No beast that noyeth° mortal man is procreated there.   400
It bringeth forth no Lion fierce, nor yet the rav'ning Bear.
No beasts (I say) which do possess one jot of cruèl kind,
Except the Wolf that noisome is, in Irish soil I find.
But as for other sorts of beasts,° delighting mortal eye,
Therein consists her chiefest praise: who may it here deny?

২৳ ২৳ ২৳

° **Pilgrim's sly pretence**: English Protestants saw Irish pilgrimage as a pretext for mobilizing against
  the occupation.   ° **whist**: quiet.   ° **rest**: remain.   ° **at all assays**: in every crisis.
° **lap**: enfold, coil.
° **close**: short. Irish foot-soldiers wore short trousers (trews) that allowed them to wade and move
  more nimbly ("dance") through the bogs.
° **glibbed**: many Irish wore a large fringe over their forehead.   ° **list**: like.
° **Again**: alternatively.   ° **noyeth**: annoys.
° **beasts**: Derricke goes on to name horses, goats, several species of hawk, and eagles.

Birds

JOHN SKELTON
from "Speak, Parrot" (c. 1521)

While beasts talk in many early modern stories, "Speak, Parrot" is one of
the few in which this Aesopian fantasy has a shred of credibility. Henry VIII
reportedly owned an African grey parrot (some of which possess thousand-word
vocabularies), although Skelton's poem describes the rose-ringed parakeet – a species now naturalized in and around London. Besides taking satiric pecks at the
greed, vanity, and political squabbling of Henry's courtiers, the bird also lampoons Renaissance humanists and their educational reforms, including education
for women. Humanist pedagogues expected their pupils to learn several languages
by rote (Skelton's parrot speaks no fewer than nine). In other words, students
would often have to parrot back, as it were, the words of their lesson without
comprehending them. While some critics suspect the text to be corrupt, the apparent non sequiturs may be Skelton's attempt to mimic the bird's squawking out
phrases at random. However, the poet also identifies with the bird in demanding
liberty to speak freely, and the poem's levity belies the profundity of the questions
it raises about animal intelligence (Boehrer 2002, 99–132). The same can be said
of Skelton's "Philip Sparrow," which both commemorates and spoofs the emotional bond between a young woman and her avian companion, and even features a mock-requiem mass for the dead bird. How does the parrot challenge not
only the human monopoly on reason and language but also the exclusive claim
to an immortal soul? The beautiful, rational, musical, over-educated, polyglot
parrot seems a parodic embodiment of Renaissance humanism's exalted view of
humanity.
Source: *Certain Books Compiled by Master Skelton* (1545), A2ʳ–A2ᵛ, A5ᵛ.

My name is Parrot, a bird of paradise,
By Nature devisèd of a wonderous kind,
Daintily dieted with diverse delicate spice,
Till Euphrates,° that flood, driveth me into Ind,°
Where men of that country by fortune me find,
And send me to great Ladies of estate.
Then Parrot must have an almond or a date,

A cage curiously carven with silver pin,°
Properly painted to be my coverture,
10   A mirror of glass, that I may toot° therein.
These maidens full meekly with many a diverse flower,
Freshly they dress and make sweet my bower,
With "Speak, Parrot, I pray you," full courteously they say:
"Parrot is a goodly bird, a pretty Popinjay."°

° **Euphrates**: river in present-day Iraq once regarded as a boundary of Eden.
° **Ind**: India or, more broadly, the East.   ° **pin**: bars.   ° **toot**: peep.
° **Popinjay**: parrot.

With my beak bent, my little wanton eye,
My feathers fresh as is the Emerald green,
About my neck a circlet like the rich ruby,
My little legs, my feet both feat° and clean,
I am a minion to wait upon the queen.
"My proper Parrot, my little pretty fool."°   20
With ladies I learn, and go with them to school.

"Ha, ha, ha, Parrot, ye can laugh prettily!"
Parrot hath not dined of all this long day.
Like your puss-cat, Parrot can mew and cry;
In Latin, in Hebrew, Arabic and Chaldee,°
In Greek tongue Parrot can both speak and say,
As Persius, that poet, doth report of me,
Quis expedivit psittaco suum chaire?°

Douce° French of Paris, Parrot can learn,
Pronouncing my purpose after my property,°   30
With "*Parlez bien Parrot, ou parlez rien.*"°
With Dutch, with Spanish, my tongue can agree.
In English to God Parrot can supply:
"Christ save King Henry the VIII, our Royal King,
The red rose° in honour to flourish and spring!" ...

For Parrot is no churlish chough, nor no fleckèd pie;°
Parrot is no pendugum that men call a carling;°
Parrot is no woodcock, nor no butterfly;
Parrot is no stammering stare that men call a starling;   210
But Parrot is my own dear heart and my dear darling.
Melpomene,° the fair maid, she burnished his beak.
I pray you let Parrot have liberty to speak.

Parrot is a fair bird for a Lady;
God of his goodness him framèd and wrought.
When Parrot is dead, she doth not putrefy.°
Yea, all things mortal shall turn unto nought,
Except man's soul, that Christ so dear bought:
That never may die, nor never die shall.
Make much of Parrot, the popinjay royal.   220

° **feat**: neat, elegant.   ° **fool**: jester, but here a term of endearment.
° **Chaldee**: Ancient Aramaic, spoken in the Babylon of biblical times.
° *Quis ... chaire*: "Who taught the parrot to say hello?" From Persius, *Satires*, Prologue, 8.
° **Douce**: sweet, soft.   ° **property**: quality.
° *Parlez ... rien*: Speak well parrot or speak nothing.
° **red rose**: the Tudor rose conjoins the red and white, although the former is larger.   ° **pie**: magpie.
° **pendugum ... carling**: pendugum can mean a garrulous person and carling can be a term of
   contempt for an old woman, sometimes applied to a witch. However, pendugum here almost
   certainly also refers not to the penguin but to the now-extinct great auk.
° **Melpomene**: Muse of Song and Tragedy.
° **she ... putrefy**: due to its plumage, the parrot does not immediately show signs of post-mortem
   decay.

For that peerless prince that Parrot did create,
He made you of nothing by his majesty.
Point° well this problem that Parrot doth prate,
And remember among how Parrot and ye
Shall leap from this life, as merry as we be.
Pomp, pride, honour, riches, and worldly lust,
Parrot saith plainly shall turn all to dust.

꒰ ꒰ ꒰

° **Point**: consider.

HENRY VAUGHAN
"The Eagle" (1655)

Early modern Britain was home to two species of eagle: the golden and the white-tailed. Due to habitat loss and hunting, they were locally extinct in England and Wales by the early twentieth century. A small number of golden eagles survived in the Scottish Highlands, while the white-tailed (probably the one described below) was completely exterminated; it has since been reintroduced in western Scotland. Its disappearance would doubtless have saddened Henry Vaughan, who finds in its soaring a symbol of spiritual exaltation. Does the religious symbolism eclipse the bird's "material dress" or illuminate it? How does this poem compare with Hopkins's "Windhover"?
Source: *Thalia Redivia* (1678), 3–4.

'Tis madness sure, and I am in the Fit,
To dare an Eagle with my unfledged wit.
For what did ever Rome or Athens sing,
In all their Lines, as lofty as his wing?
He that an Eagle's Powers would rehearse
Should with his plumes first feather all his Verse.
    I know not, when into thee I would pry,
Which to admire: thy Wing first, or thine Eye;
Or whether Nature at thy birth designed
10   More of her Fire for thee, or of her Wind.
When thou in the clear Heights and upmost Air
Dost face the Sun and his dispersèd Hair,°
Ev'n from that distance thou the Sea dost spy,
And sporting in its deep, wide Lap the Fry.
Not the least Minnow there, but thou canst see:
Whole Seas are narrow spectacles to thee …
Then with such fury he begins his flight,

° **Hair**: sunbeams.

As if his Wings contended with his sight.
Leaving the Moon, whose humble light doth trade
With Spots, and deals most in the dark and shade,   30
To the day's Royal Planet he doth pass,
With daring Eyes, and makes the Sun his glass.°
Here doth he plume and dress himself, the Beams
Rushing upon him like so many Streams,
While with direct looks he doth entertain
The thronging flames, and shoots them back again.°
And thus from star to star he doth repair,
And wantons in that pure and peaceful air.
Sometimes he frights the starry Swan, and now
Orion's fearful Hare, and then the Crow.°   40
Then with the Orb itself he moves, to see
Which is more swift: th'Intelligence° or He.
Thus with his wings his body he hath brought,
Where man can travel only in a thought.
   I will not seek, rare bird, what Spirit 'tis
That mounts thee thus; I'll be content with this:
To think that Nature made thee to express
Our soul's bold Heights in a material dress.

❧ ❧ ❧

° **glass**: mirror. The Roman naturalist Pliny reported that eagles could stare directly at the sun.
° **shoots ... again**: According to ancient emission theory, sight results from eye-beams emanating from the eye.
° **Swan ... Hare ... Crow**: the constellations of Cygnus, Lepus, and Corvus.
° **Intelligence**: angelic power believed to propel planetary rotation.

GEORGE MORLEY

"The Nightingale" (*c.* 1633)

Long before the nightingale enchanted Coleridge, Wordsworth, and Keats, dozens of Renaissance writers – such as Philip Sidney, John Davies, Richard Barnfield, Thomas Middleton, Patrick Hannay, Martin Parker, Richard Brathwaite, and John Milton – composed tributes to this same bird. Whereas the Romantics present the bird's singing as a metaphor for their own supposedly spontaneous artistry, Renaissance writers, informed by their classical education, tend to imagine it as the lament of the transformed Athenian princess, Philomela, who had her tongue cut out by her rapist (see Shakespeare's *Titus Andronicus* and Mary Wroth's "Come merry Spring, delight us"). Perhaps the most remarkable Elizabethan nightingale poem is George Gascoigne's "Complaint of Philomene," which he began composing in April 1562 after hearing the bird sing while riding on the highway between Chelmsford and London. After yearning to understand what its song means, the poet dreams that the bird undergoes a reverse metamorphosis back into human form. A key reason for the enduring popularity of the myth is that Renaissance writers (in an inverse onomatopoeia) heard the rapist's name in one of the nightingale's cries (their repertoire includes over 140 different calls). The same urge to anthropomorphize the nightingale is present in George Morley's poem, which circulated widely in manuscript. The transcription below records several significant variants, and those involving gendered pronouns are particularly noteworthy given the ironic discovery that only male nightingales sing.

Source: Bradford, Hopkins MS 32D86/34 f.43, with emendations from St John's College, Cambridge MS S.32 6v, BL MS 47111, and *Muses' Recreation* (1655).

My limbs were weary and my head oppressed
With drowsiness, and yet I could not rest.
My bed was such nor down nor feathers° can
Make one more soft, though Jove himself turn Swan.°
No fear-distracted thought my slumber broke:
I heard no Screech-Owl shriek,° no Raven croak.
Sleep for the Flea I might, for that proud elf°
Had taken leave and was asleep itself.°
But 'twas night's darling and the wood's best° jewel,
10   The Nightingale, that was so sweetly cruel.
She° wooed mine ears to rob mine eyes of sleep,
That whilst she sang of Tereus° they might weep,
And yet rejoice, the tyrant did her wrong.
Her cause of woe was burden° of her song,
Which whilst I listened to and strove to hear,
'Twas such I could have wished myself all ear.
'Tis false the poets feign of Orpheus:° he
Could neither move a stone nor draw a tree°
To follow him, but wheresoe'er she flies
20   The grovy Satyr and the Fairy hies°
About° her perch to dance her° roundelays;
For she sings ditties° to them whilst Pan plays.
Yet she sung better now, as if in me°
She meant with sleep to try the mastery.
But whilst she chanted thus the Cock° for spite,
Day's hoarser herald, chid away the night.
Thus robbed of sleep, my eyelids' nightly guest,°
Methought I lay content, though not at rest.

⁂

° **feathers**: pillow] MS 47111.
° **Make … Swan**: Jove transformed himself into a swan to seduce the Spartan princess Leda. MS 47111 reads "Or the white feathers of the snowy Swan."   ° **shriek**: *MR*; squeak] Hopkins.
° **Sleep … elf**: Cam; Sleep for the Flea, that proud insulting elf] Hopkins and *MR*.
° **itself**: herself] Cam.   ° **wood's best**: world's chief] *MR*.   ° **She**: Cam; It] Hopkins.
° **Tereus**: Philomela's rapist; sorrows] Cam.
° **burden**: refrain. Several early modern writers claim to hear the sound "Tereu" in the nightingale's song (e.g. Gascoigne's "Complaint of Philomene," Lyly's *Campaspe*).
° **Orpheus**: see Ovid's *Metamorphoses*, 10.
° **tree**: tear] Cam.; could neither move a beast, a stone, or tree] *MR*.
° **The … hies**: *MR*; She makes a grove: Satyrs and Fairies hies] Hopkins.   ° **About**: Afore] *MR*.
° **her**: their] Cam.   ° **sings ditties**: doth ditty] Cam; sings distichs] *MR*.
° **Yet … me**: line missing from Cam.   ° **Cock**: Lark] Cam.   ° **guest**: quest] Cam.

WILLIAM TURNER

[The Kite] (1555) *and [The Robin and Redstart]* (1544)

Red kites are aggressive scavengers, and were once a common sight in early modern towns, where they functioned like a sanitation crew in disposing of waste and carrion. As the following account suggests, however, most people regarded them as thieving vermin, and by the mid-twentieth century they were extirpated from England, with only a few breeding pairs left in Wales. Their reintroduction and recovery over the past few decades is one of the success stories of avian conservation in the UK.

The father of English ornithology, Turner published the first serious work on birds in English in 1544. His unflattering picture of the kite is characteristic of Tudor natural history in its tendency to moralize animal behaviour. The second extract adopts a more scientific tone. It features a meticulous observation of a robin building its nest and demonstrates how Renaissance naturalists were beginning to insist on first-hand experience of natural phenomena rather than place absolute faith in classical authorities.

Source: *A New Book of Spiritual Physic* (1555), 54ʳ–5ᵛ, and *Avium Praceipuarum* (1544), 127; *Turner on Birds*, trans. A. H. Evans (Cambridge University Press, 1903), 157–9.

[The Kite]

A covetous gentleman is like a greedy glede. A glede, otherwise called a puttock or a kite, hath the form and fashion of a hawk, and afar off looketh very like a hawk (which is a noble bird), but if ye come nearhand him ye shall know him by his whining and lamentable pewing,° as though he could never get enough. Ye shall also see him do other things than a right° hawk doth, which, for the most part, feedeth upon his own prey that he hath gotten himself. The kite resteth but little, and is almost always flying. And ever he looketh downward to the earth after one prey or other. In the time that he buildeth his nest he carrieth all that he can catch and snatch unto it: rags, clothes, napkins, kerchiefs, boys' caps, and sometimes purses, as I have heard say. And all the whole year through there is no prey that cometh amiss unto him; he eateth upon all kind of carrion. He thinketh no shame to eat worms; [54ᵛ] he cleeketh° away goslings, ducklings, chickens, and all kinds of young birds that cannot fly or otherwise provide for themselves. He is so bold sometimes in England (I never saw it so, neither in Italy [nor] in any part of Germany where I have been) that he dare take butter and bread out of boys' hands in the streets of towns, cities, and villages. He is more unshamefaced than ever any begging friar was. For he

---

° **pewing**: crying.   ° **right**: true.   ° **cleeketh**: snatches

will, without any asking or begging, take away tripes° and puddings from wives, whilst they are in washing of them. And this doth he most earnestly and unshamefastly, when as he hath young. But what profit cometh unto him and all his for his manifold robbery and ravin?° Very little. For he abideth still a foul kite.

[The Robin and Redstart]

All that Aristotle° has written of these two birds Pliny° has copied from him into his own work. But in this matter each of them, relying on the tales of fowlers more than on his own experience, has wandered greatly from the path of truth. For both the birds are seen at the same time. Moreover, tame Rubeculae,° when fed in cages, constantly retain the same appearance. Moreover, I have very often seen the birds in England nesting at the same time, though in very different ways. The Rubecula, which has a ruddy breast no less in summer than in winter, nests as far as possible from towns and cities in the thickest briars and shrubs after this fashion. Where it finds oak leaves in plenty, or leaves like the oak, it builds its nest among the leaves themselves close to the roots of briars or the thicker shrubs: and when completed, covers it with leaves as if with topiary work. Nor does access lie open to the nest on every side, but by one way alone is entrance gained. And at that place where it enters the nest the bird builds a long porch of leaves before the doorway: and on going forth to feed, closes the end with leaves. [Although] what I now describe I first observed when quite a boy, nevertheless, I am not going to deny that it may build otherwise. If any have observed another way of [their] nesting, let them tell it, and they certainly will not a little gratify the students of such things, myself among the first. I have imparted truthfully to others what I saw …

The Ruticilla° nests in hollow trees and (as I often have had experience) in chinks and cracks of walls and outhouses in the midst of our towns, though where the throng of men is not so great. The male has a black head, a red tail, but otherwise is like the female, save that he repeatedly utters a little song. Either sex flirts° the tail continually. The female Phoenicurus° and its brood are so much like young of Rubeculae that they can scarcely be distinguished by the sharpest eye. But by the motion of the tail they may be recognised. For the Rubeculae, although they move the tail, yet after they have lowered it, at once raise it again; nor does it quiver twice or

---

° **tripes**: dish made of animal innards.   ° **ravin**: thieving, predation.

° **Aristotle**: the Greek philosopher-naturalist proposed that the Robin and Redstart were the same species, and that the two names merely distinguish their summer and winter plumage (*History of Animals*, 8.9, 49b, 632b14–633a28).   ° **Pliny**: see *Natural History*, 10.29.

° **Rubeculae**: European robins.

° **Ruticilla**: Redstart, though this Latin name is now applied to the American variety.

° **flirts**: flicks.   ° **Phoenicurus**: Latin name for the European Redstart.

thrice as does that of the Ruticillae. For no sooner have the Ruticillae once begun to move the tail than they go on till they have lightly moved it three or four times altogether, [159] just as young small birds flutter their wings soliciting meat from their mothers. In summer, when there is enough and more of food found in the woods, and they are not troubled by any cold (a thing which forces them in winter to resort to cities, towns, and villages), Rubeculae retire to the most solitary places with their young. And so it is no marvel that Rubeculae do not occur in summer everywhere. And what wonder is it that Ruticillae are not met with in winter, since throughout the whole of winter they are hidden?° And further, when the young Rubeculae, having almost assumed the full red on their breasts at the end of autumn, come nearer to towns and villages, the Ruticillae, which were hitherto seen during the whole summer, disappear and then are no more noticed till the following spring. Wherefore, things being thus, anyone may easily perceive what gave a handle to Aristotle or to those who reported this error to him.

❧ ❧ ❧

° **hidden**: Redstarts winter in central Africa. Turner's denial that the bird metamorphoses was a stepping-stone towards the theory of migration.

HENRY CHILLESTER
"A Commendation of the Robin Redbreast" (1579)

This ode captures the peculiar tendency of Renaissance nature poetry to exalt its subject through negative allusions to classical mythology, as the poet (probably Henry Chillester, whose 1581 verses sing the praises of the skylark and nightingale) struggles to glimpse the robin through a thicket of Ovidian figures. Its setting is thus both an actual woodland and a literary *locus amoenus*, a duality betrayed by the title of the book in which it appears, *The Forest of Fancy*. Although its tone is often didactic, the collection also features joyous paeans to the rooster, rose, and hazel nut.
Source: *The Forest of Fancy* (1579), J3ᵛ–K1ᵛ.

When Hiems° with his hoary frosts and blust'ring Boreas° blast
Had run his race, and Lady Ver° her pleasant course had passed,
Then Aestas° entered in by course, and Phoebus'° golden rays,
Whose scorching heat mild Zephyrus° assuaged at all assays,
Were spread abroad through every coast, which caused each thing to joy,
Then was it pleasure great to see the little Fishes play,

° **Hiems**: winter.   ° **Boreas**: north wind.
° **Ver**: spring. The 1579 text confusingly applies the masculine pronoun "his" to Lady Ver.
° **Aestas**: Summer.   ° **Phoebus**: Roman god of the sun.   ° **Zephyrus**: west wind.

And friscoes° fetch about the banks to find some pleasant bait,
While they un'wares entangled are by Fishers' foul deceit.
Then every tree is fresh and green, then Flora° on the ground
10   Her mantle spreads, and fertile fields with pleasant Flowers abound;
The dainty Dames from every place do thither fast resort,
And Garlands make of croppèd flowers, of sundry scent and sort.
In every street great stirring is, some quaff and make good cheer;
Some leap, some dance, some sing, some play, some chase the light-foot Deer.
Here Orpheus° with his pleasant Harp, there Amphion° with his Lute,
Do make most pleasant melody and carping cares confute.
The am'rous youths do stray the streets and with their Ladies walk,
And some again do pass the day with passing pleasant talk;
So every man to please his mind some pastime doth frequent,
20   To drive away all drowsy dumps and sluggish sloth prevent.
It chancèd so this time, that as in bed I lay,
Oppressèd sore with painful pangs, about the break of day,
I started up and forth I walked into the fields so fair,
Myself to solace there at will and take the pleasant air.
The ground that garnished was with flowers did yield so sweet a smell,
That noisome savours none were felt, it did them all repel;
Then passed I forth with stealing steps and looked about me round,
To take a view of everything wherein I pleasure found;
And by and by from far methought I seemed a sound to hear,
30   Which still the further that I passed more pleasant did appear.
It was so sweet a melody that sure I thought some muse,
Or else some other heav'nly wight,° did there frequent and use.
But as I cast mine eye aside on branch of willow tree,
A little Robin redbreast then there sitting did I see;
And he it was, and none but he, that did so sweetly sing.
But sure in all my life before I never heard the thing
That did so much delight my heart, or caused me so to joy,
As did that little Robin's song that there I heard that day.
The Poets feign that Orpheus made both stones and trees to dance,
40   When he upon his Harp did play; they also do advance°
So much Arion° for his skill, that when into the seas
He should be cast they said that he a Dolphin so did please,
That safe she brought him unto shore when death he did aspect,°
And from all perils perilous did him right well protect;
Mercurius made the hundred eyes of Argos° all to sleep,
With playing on an Oaten pipe, his knowledge was so deep;
Yet sure I think their harmony might not co-equal be,
With that this little Robin made, it so delighted me.
Nay, sure I think the Muses nine may not with him compare,
50   Nor yet Apollo for his skill, whose music was so rare.

° **friscoes**: leaps.   ° **Flora**: Roman goddess of flowers.
° **Orpheus**: legendary poet who could charms beasts and trees with his music.
° **Amphion**: mythological figure whose music magically raised the walls of ancient Thebes.
° **wight**: being.   ° **advance**: praise.
° **Arion**: legendary bard whose singing summoned a dolphin to rescue him from pirates.
° **aspect**: expect.   ° **Argos**: hundred-eyed monster charmed by Mercury.

Full oftentimes my heart doth wish this pretty bird to have,
For more than any worldly thing the same I still do crave.
And if my luck might be so good this Robin once to gain,
 Then greatly would my joys abound and heart should feel no pain.
For never did I see the thing that I so well could like;
Therefore above all other things to have the same I seek.
For colour and for comeliness all birds he doth surmount;
His flesh is very delicate, full many men account.
God grant, therefore, that I may gain this Robin at my will,
Then do I hope to use him so that he shall tarry still.   60
For rather would I lose my life, and all things else beside,
Than from my Robin I would part, at any time or tide.

2& 2& 2&

RICHARD BRATHWAITE
"The Lapwing" and "The Swallow" (1621)

The theory that swallows migrated during winter was not recorded in print until
1667. Most naturalists believed that they hibernated, a view expressed in a poem
translated by Abraham Cowley in 1656. Brathwaite, however, apparently recognized
them as seasonal visitors much earlier. If the poem moralizes animal behaviour, it
also indicates how literature could be a forum for natural history. This is evident
in "The Lapwing" as well, as Brathwaite describes the habits of the ground-nesting
bird and replicates its call (which earned it the nickname "peewit") in the refrain
that concludes each stanza. Due to its loss of habitat, it is now a "Red List" species.
Source: *Nature's Embassy* (1621), 245–7, 251–3.

"The Lapwing"

Unhappy I to change my airy nest,
For this same marshy dwelling where I rest,
Wherefore my song while I repeat,
I'll close it up:
Rue yet, rue yet.

Every Cowherd driving his beasts to graze,
Disturbs my rest, me from my nest doth raise,
Which makes my young take up this song,
To wreak my wrong:
Rue yet, rue yet.   10

Thou subtle Stock Dove° that hast cheated me,
By taking up thy nest where I should be,

° **Stock Dove**: a type of wild pigeon that sometimes shares the lapwing's farmland habitat.

Hast me and mine in peril set,
Whose song is fit:
Rue yet, rue yet.

Solely retirèd, see I live alone,
Far from recourse or sight of anyone,
And well that life would suit with me,
Were I but free:
20 Rue yet, rue yet.

Young ones I have, that thinking I am fled,
Do leave their nest and run with shell on head,
And having found me out we cry,
Both they and I:
Rue yet, rue yet.

Crest-curlèd mates, why do you bear so long
The Stock Dove's pride, that triumphs in your wrong?
Let us our signals once display,
And make him say:
30 Rue yet, rue yet.

Too tedious hath our bondage been iwis,°
And only patience was the cause of this,
Where if we would contract our power,
We'd sing no more:
Rue yet, rue yet.

March on then bravely, as if Mars were here,
And hate no guest so much as slavish fear,
Let the proud Stock Dove feel your wing,
That he may sing:
40 Rue yet, rue yet.

Let none escape, though they submissive seem,
Till you have spoiled and quite unfeathered them,
So you shall make them vail the wing,
And henceforth sing:
Rue yet, rue yet.

"The Swallow"

You chatt'ring Fleer, you Fawn,° you summer friend, °
Not following us, but our success,
Will this your flatt'ring humour ne'er have end?

° **iwis**: truly. ° **Fawn**: flatterer, also young animal; spelled "faun."
° **summer friend**: fair-weather friend. Swallows now arrive in England on average fifteen days earlier than they did in the 1960s (Hayhow *et al.* 2017, 16), and so may have migrated much later in the cooler seventeenth century.

Of all other meritless?
Fly, I say, fly, be gone;
Haunt not here to Albion:°
She should be spotless, as imports her name,
But such as you are born to do her shame.

How many fair protests and solemn vows,
Can your hateful consorts make,   10
Whereas (heav'n knows) these are but only shows
Which you do for profit's sake?
O then leave our coast and us,
Blemished by your foul abuse;
Virtue can have no being, nor could ever,
Where th'Parasite is deemed a happy liver …

Springtime when flowers adorn the cheerful mead,
And each bird sings on her spray,
When flow'ry groves with blossoms chequerèd,
And each day seems a marriage day,
Chatt'ring Swallow thou canst chose
Then a time to visit us;   30
Such are these feignèd friends: make much upon us
When we are rich, but being poor they shun us.

The stormy winter with his hoary locks,
When each branch hangs down his head,
And icy flaw° candies the ragged rocks,
Making fields discolourèd,
Drives thee from us and our coast,
Where in springtime thou repost;°
Thus thou remains with us in our delight,
But in our discontent th'art out of sight.   40

᪥ ᪥ ᪥

° **Albion**: ancient name for Britain, from the Latin *alba* (white) for the white chalk cliffs.
° **flaw**: flakes of frost.   ° **repost**: return, reposed.

ANONYMOUS
A Battle of Birds (1621)

Few sights in nature are as breathtaking as a murmuration of starlings performing their aerial acrobatics in the autumn twilight. Ornithologists now speculate the phenomenon is a way for the birds to deter predators, share body heat before roosting, or exchange information on food sources. In this Renaissance broadside, however, the collision of two flocks apparently resulted in a territorial battle. While many ballads traffic in the fabulous, there is no reason to doubt the report. The Roman naturalist Pliny described avian warfare back in the first century (10.26), and starlings do fight over nesting grounds. Nevertheless, the ballad's narration of this battle which took place outside of Cork may be affected by tensions between Irish Catholics and incoming English Protestant settlers. That premoderns viewed massive swarms of birds with dread is well attested in Renaissance literature (see the "flight of ravens" in *Edward III*, scene 13, and *Julius Caesar*, 5.1.80–8). When Cork burned down in 1622, this starling murmuration was seen in retrospect as an omen of the city's doom. This ballad is a prime example of the early modern tendency to ascribe supernatural significance to rare or complex animal behaviour that seemingly defied the assumption that non-humans were irrational. Such murmurations are even rarer today, as the UK starling population has declined 66 per cent since the 1970s. Incidentally, any American who witnesses a murmuration can thank (or blame) William Shakespeare, as the non-native was imported to the US in 1890 by a naturalist who wanted his country to possess every species of bird mentioned by Shakespeare.

Source: *A Battle of Birds* (1621).

> Mark well God's wondrous works and see
> What things therein declarèd be,
> Such things as may with trembling fear,
> Fright all the world the same to hear;
> For like to these which here I tell,
> No man alive remembreth well.
>
> The eighth day of September last,
> Which made all Ireland much aghast,
> Were seen (near Cork) such flights of Birds
> Whose numbers cannot well by words
> Accounted be; for greater store
> Was never seen nor known before.
>
> The flights so many legions seemed,
> As thousand thousands° they were deemed,
> All soaring up, along the sky,
> As if the battle were on high,
> In multitudes without compare,
> Which like black clouds made dim the air.
>
> First from the eastern skies appeared
> A flight of Stares,° which greatly feared
> The people there the same to see,
> As like could not remembered be;
> For they in warlike squadrons flew,
> As if they others would pursue.
>
> And as this flight thus hov'ring lay,
> Preparèd all in battle ray,°

10

20

° **thousand thousands**: murmurations can in fact contain a million birds.   ° **Stares**: starlings.
° **ray**: lined in formation.

From out the west, another came,
As great in number as the same,
And there opposed in warlike might
Themselves against the other flight.   30

Whereas these Stares, or Starling Birds,
For want of helmets, glaves, and swords,
They used their talons, bills, and beaks,
And such a battle undertakes,
That trembling fear and terror brought
To all which saw this battle fought.

For first, the eastern flight sat down,
With chatt'ring noise upon the ground,
As if they challenged all the rest
To meet and fight, e'en breast to breast,   40
Where presently was heard from far
The same like chatt'ring sound of war.

And thereupon the western flight
Down by the eastern Birds did light,
Where after they a while had sat,
Together in their Birdlike chat,
They all upon a sudden rose,
And each the other did oppose.

The Second Part

And filling thus the azure sky
With these their troops up mounted high,   50
They seemed more thick than motes i'th sun,
A dreadful battle there begun;
And in their kind° more strongly fought,
Than can imagined be by thought.

Thousands of thousands, on a heap,
Upon the others' backs did leap,
With all their forcèd strengths and might
To put their Bird-like foes to flight;
And as it were in battle ray,
Long time they kept them thus in play.   60

To fight this battle in the air,
Their bills and beaks their weapons were,
Which they performed in such a sort,
As makes me doubtful to report,
That silly° Birds should thus arise,
And fight so fiercely in the skies.

° **kind**: nature.   ° **silly**: lowly.

But so it was and strange withal
That Birds should thus at discord fall,
And never cease till they had slain
70   Thousands stark dead upon the plain,
Where people took them up in fear:
A thing most strange to see and hear.

With broken wings, some fell to ground,
And some poor silly° Birds were found
With eyes picked out, struck down half-dead,
And some no brains left in their head,
But battered forth and killed outright,
Most strangely in this airy fight.

Yet long with loud and chatt'ring cries,
80   Each company 'gainst other flies,
With bloody beaks, remorseless still,
Their feathered foes to maim or kill,
Where, whilst this battle did remain,
Their bodies fell like drops of rain.

Thousands were to the City borne,
With wounded limbs and bodies torn,
For all the fields were overspread
With mangled starlings that lay dead
In blood and feathers, strange to see,
90   Which men took up abundantly.

It was a wonder to explain
The number of them hurt and slain.
And, being a wonder, let it rest.
The Lord above, he knoweth best
What these poor creatures did intend,
When thus to battle they did bend.

But such a battle ne'er was fought
By silly° Birds, which have no thought
In doing ill, nor any mind
100   To work contrary to their kind:
But yet as nature gave them life,
So here they strangely fell at strife.

What now for truth is published forth,
Esteem it as a news of worth,
And by the wonder of these days,
Learn to leave off all wicked ways;
For sure it is that God it sent
That of our sins we should repent.

☙ ☙ ☙

° **silly**: piteous.
° **silly**: innocent.

HESTER PULTER
"The Lark" (c. 1655)

Pulter lived in Broadfield in rural Hertfordshire, where "shut up in a country grange" (79ʳ) she composed over a hundred poems (only rediscovered in 1996) under the pseudonym Hadassas. Some voice her bitterness at the royalist defeat, while others, including "The Lark," depict the tribulations of motherhood in an age of high infant mortality. The poem is notably more empathetic than Marvell's account of the slain rail in "Appleton House," but still betrays a leisure-class viewpoint in its scorn for the rural labourer who carelessly destroys a lark's nest. Similar tensions exist today between farmers and conservationists in the UK, as autumn sowing and insecticide use are blamed for a 60 per cent drop in skylark numbers since the 1970s (Hayhow *et al.* 2017, 7).
Source: Brotherton MS Lt q 32, 68ᵛ–70ᵛ.

See how Arachne° doth her Hours Pass,
In weaving Tinsel on the verdant Grass;
Look how it glitters now the sun doth Rise,
The Bane of Harmless sheep and death of flies,
And over it the slow and Unctuous Snail
In winding knots doth draw a slimy Trail.
The cheerful Lark as in the Air she Flies,
And on this Gossamer casts down her eyes,
Takes it for Mirrors Laid by Rural Swains,
And therefore fears to Light upon the plains;   10
But with alacrity aloft she Flies,
And early sings her Morning sacrifice,
And in her Language magnifies his Name,
From whose immensity all creatures came.
Do thou, my Soul, sing too: let none on Earth
Or Air beyond thee go; think on thy Birth.
For though my Body's dust, thou art a spark
Celestial; for shame outsing the Lark.
She hath but one life that she spends in praise;   20
Thou hast and shalt have two, yet wastes thy days
In Bleeding sighs and Fruitless briny tears,
In Melancholy thoughts, vain causeless Fears.
Learn thou of this sweet Airy Chorister;
Do thou her cheerful Actions Register.
For I have seen Walking one summer's day,
To take the Air when Flora° did display
Her youthful Pride, as she did smiling Pass,
She threw her Flowered Mantle on the Grass,
Which straight allured a Sunburnt Rural Clown°
To come and Mow these Fading Beauties Down.   30
Unbraced, unblessed, he doth with haste repair°
This valley to deflower, than Temp'° more fair,

° **Arachne**: the spider in classical mythology.   ° **Flora**: Roman goddess of flowers.
° **Clown**: peasant.   ° **repair**: go.   ° **Temp'**: Tempe, valley beloved by the Greek Muses.

Thus stewed in sweat this Gripple, hidebound° slave
Cuts near the Ground, the greater Crop to have,
Greedy of gain and swelt'ring him he hied,
Mowing by chance near where a spring did Glide,
That in her Purling Language seemed to chide,
Because he Robbed her of her chiefest pride;
But he Regardless of her murmuring Woe,
40   Still nearer to the Rill did straddling Go.
In this sweet place the Lark took such delight,
Because it shady was and out of sight;
By this cool Rivulet she took such Pleasure
That here she placed her Young: e'en all her treasure
Was here enclosed, in one round little nest,
Which this indulgent Bird warmed with her breast,
And by the Echo of this Bubbling Spring,
She meant to teach her Airy Young to sing.
But in a Moment all her Joys were Quashed,
50   In twinkling of an eye her hopes were Dashed;
For this bold scoundrel without Fear or wit,
Her Pretty Globe-like Nest in Sunder split.
Some are in Middle Cut, some of their Head;
Thus all her Young are either Maimed or Dead.
One not quite killed doth weakly Fly about,
Which soon perceivèd is by this Rude Lout,°
Who Throws his Scythe away, to it doth run,
Meaning to carry it to his Young° Son,
Which having caught and it in's Pocket put,
60   With sweaty Glove he doth't in prison shut.
Next day he Gives it to his crying squall,°
Who in a thread this pretty Bird doth Haul
Hither and thither, as his fond desire
Him Leads; but ere't be Night it doth expire.
The poor old Dam, seeing this sad Massacre,
With heavy Heart to her light Wings betakes her,
Yet Hovering below in hope to find
Some of her Brood, according to their kind,
To Follow her; but seeing at Last there's none
70   That doth survive, she sadly makes her moan;
Yet mounts and sings, though in a sadder Tone.
Thus as thou art afflicted here below,
My troubled soul, still nearer to Heaven go.
Let every troublesome Heart-breaking Cross
Like Surly Billows to thy Hav'n thee Toss,
And as thy Friends and Lovely Children Die,
So thou, my soul, to Heav'n for Comfort Fly.

❦ ❦ ❦

° **Gripple, hidebound**: greedy, stingy.
° **Lout**: drudge.   ° **Young**: struck through in MS and replaced with "little."
° **squall**: contemptuous term for a little person, but also suggesting shriek.

JOHN CAIUS
"Of the Puffin" (1570)

Best known for his pioneering work on English dogs, Caius also authored a zoological treatise on rare animals. In an age before nature documentaries and seaside holidays, even English seabirds like the puffin and brent goose would have been exotic beasts to many people. Caius also describes species from farther afield, such as a polar bear and silver fox, brought to London by Russian merchants. In 1548 he saw two white ravens in Cumberland, and his report that "nothing unlucky followed them" (211) is characteristic of the fitful campaign by Tudor naturalists to sift legend from fact. Likewise, that Caius kept a puffin for research purposes attests to a methodological shift in Renaissance natural history towards personal observation. Source: *De rariorum animalium atque stirpium [Of Rare Animals and Plants]* in *Turner on Birds*, trans. A. H. Evans (1903), 205, 207.

There is a certain seabird of our country, in size and form of body like a little duck ... with webbed and reddish feet, placed nearer to the hinder parts than in other web-footed kinds except the Pygosceles;° with a somewhat thin beak, rather more extended in breadth vertically than stretching laterally to a very great length, furrowed by four red grooves above, and two below, pale ochre in colour. The part lying between these and the head is bluish, and of such a shape as is the moon when ten days have elapsed from conjunction.° The bird is black on the upper surface of the whole body, save where the eyes are set, which are enclosed in white: but it is wholly white below, save on the upper breast, where it is black. It gets its living from the sea. This bird our people call the Puffin; we say Pupin from its ordinary cry of "pupin." It hides in holes, as the Charadrius° does. And so it is driven out from a rabbit's burrow by a ferret turned in by any hunter in a place situated not far from the sea. It is used as fish among us during the solemn fast of Lent:° being in substance and taste not unlike a seal. It is a gregarious animal, and has its proper time for lying hidden,° as the cuckoo and swallow. [207] It lays for the most part two eggs in rabbit burrows in the earth. It does not trust to its wings save in sight of the sea. It seems a lazy animal, but patient of injury. It eats flesh more readily than fish, and that of a rabbit in preference to that of any other animal, but in either case raw; it throws up what is boiled or roasted. Other human victuals it does not touch. In summer it washes itself but never drinks, so far as can be ascertained by observation: whether this was because salt water was wanting, I know not. The droppings are like those of an Accipiter.° When

---

° **Pygosceles**: now a scientific name for the brush-tailed penguin, but Caius is probably thinking of the now-extinct great auk.　　° **conjunction**: new moon.　　° **Charadrius**: the plover.
° **Lent**: when beef and chicken were forbidden (see Part IV).
° **lying hidden**: hibernating. In fact, puffins, like cuckoos and swallows, migrate during winter.
° **Accipiter**: hawk.

there was nothing to eat it begged for food with its ordinary cry repeated and lowered, by calling out "pupin, pupin." I kept one at my house for eight months. It bit with right good will those who supplied it with food or touched it, but in a mild and harmless way. It was satisfied with little food; for it is not a voracious bird, as our cormorant is.

⁂

WILLIAM HARVEY AND FRANCIS WILLOUGHBY
[Gannets at Bass Rock] (1633, 1661)

Bass Rock in the Firth of Forth is home to the largest colony of northern gannets in the world, and has been hailed as one of the natural wonders of Britain. The island's natural history attracted attention in the early sixteenth century in John Mair's *Deeds of the Scots* and Hector Boece's 1527 *Description of Albion*. Its scenic beauty so impressed King James VI during a 1581 visit that he offered to buy it from its owner at any price, and later issued legislation to protect its seabirds from hunters (Nelson 283). Harvey visited in 1633, while accompanying King Charles I on his coronation trip to Scotland. Best known for his discovery of the circulation of the blood, Harvey was also fascinated by bird eggs. In 1661, the naturalists Francis Willoughby and John Ray visited the island, and Willoughby incorporated Harvey's observations into his book.
Source: *The Ornithology* (1678), 18–19.

"There is a little Island, the Scots call it Bass, standing very high, environed with steep and craggy Cliffs (one might more truly and properly call it a huge Rock than an Island), not much more than a mile in compass. In the months of May and June the surface of this island is almost wholly covered with Nests, Eggs, and young Birds, so that for the multitude of them one can scarce anywhere freely set one's foot. And such a number of Birds there is flying over one's head that like Clouds they cover the Sky and take away the sight of the Sun, making such a noise and din with their cries that people talking together nearhand can scarce hear one another. If from thence as from a lofty Tower or high Precipice you look down upon the Sea underneath, you shall see it every way covered with an infinite number of Birds of diverse sorts, swimming up and down, intent upon their prey: in like manner as Pools of water in some places in the Springtime are seen overspread with Frogs, or the open hills and steep mountains are beheld at a distance thick-set and, as it were, clothed with flocks of Sheep and Goats. If you list to sail about the Island and from below look up [at] the Cliffs, as it were, overhanging your head, you might see on all the shelves and ledges of the Rocks and craggy Cliffs innumerable rows of birds of all sorts and magnitudes, more in number than the Stars that appear in a clear and Moonless night. If you look at them that are coming to the Island or flying

away at a distance, you would take them to be huge swarms of Bees." Thus
far Dr. Harvey ...

[19] The Birds that chiefly frequent this Island that they may breed there
are 1. Solan Geese,° which are proper° to the Bass, not breeding elsewhere
about Britain that we know of. When we were there near mid-August, all
the other Birds were departed, only the Solan Geese remained upon the
Island, their young being not yet fully grown and fledged. The manner of
getting them is by letting down a man in a basket by a rope from the top
of the Cliff, who gathers the young off the ledges of the Rocks as they let
him down or draw him up. 2. The Turtle-Dove, or Sea-Turtle, so called
here (as I suppose) from some similitude it hath to the Turtle-Dove. It
is a whole-footed bird and, I suspect, the same that we have described
under the title of the Greenland-Dove. This also is a bird peculiar to this
Island. 3. The Scout, which is either the Lomwia, or the Alka,° ... though
we believe that both these Species breed here. These are found also in
many other places about England. 4. The Scarf, which ... I take to be the
Cormorant. 5. The Kittiwake, a sort of small Seagull, besides many other
Species of Gulls.

※ ※ ※

° **Solan Geese**: old name for the northern gannet.   ° **proper**: unique.
° **Alka**: great auk, now extinct.

Fish

EDMUND SPENSER
"Huge Sea monsters" (1590)

When a 1617 pamphlet speaks of "a mighty sea monster or whale" (10) discovered upon a beach near Harwich, such confusion is representative of early modern attitudes towards marine life, especially creatures of greater-than-human proportions (see Brayton). This same ambivalence can be found in Book 2, Canto 12 of *The Faerie Queene*, when Sir Guyon voyages across the ocean to the Bower of Bliss and encounters an armada of sea monsters resembling those that slither along the margins of Renaissance maps, such as the 1539 *Carta Marina* of Olaus Magnus. In stanza 26, however, the Palmer informs Guyon that these fabulous chimeras are simply marine fauna, distorted and transfigured by fear and the poetic imagination. The consequences of such dread or lurid wonder could be severe; how does the Palmer's reaction compare with that of the inhabitants of Ipswich and Bermuda (see Part IV) when confronted with exotic sea creatures? The passage thus pivots from an enchanted medieval vision of the ocean towards the proto-scientific mentality of Protestant naturalists who were attempting to disentangle fact from legend. While the poet equates the physical otherness of marine life with monstrosity, representing the ocean as "beyond human knowledge and control" (Brayton 26), the Palmer's acceptance of the ocean's inhuman ecology might reflect the greater confidence of Renaissance sailors to venture upon it in the Age of Exploration and Conquest. Underneath the allegory we might discern some of Spenser's own trepidations during his crossing of the Irish Sea. The seagull- and cormorant-haunted "Rock of Vile Reproach" is almost certainly modelled on the island known as Ireland's Eye, which Spenser sailed past in 1580. Source: *The Faerie Queene* (1590), 369.

21

Sudden they see from midst of all the Main,
The surging waters like a mountain rise,
And the great sea puffed up with proud disdain,
To swell above the measure of his guise,
As threat'ning to devour all that his power despise.

22

The waves came rolling, and the billows roar
Outrageously, as they enragèd were,
Or wrathful Neptune did them drive before
His whirling chariot, for exceeding fear:
For not one puff of wind there did appear,
That all the three° thereat waxed much afraid,
Unweeting° what such horror strange did rear.
Eftsoons° they saw a hideous host arrayed
Of huge Sea monsters, such as living sense dismayed.

° **three**: Guyon, the Palmer, and the Ferryman.   ° **Unweeting**: ignorant.   ° **Eftsoons**: next.

23

Most ugly shapes and horrible aspects,
Such as Dame Nature's self might fear to see,
Or shame, that ever should so foul defects
From her most cunning hand escapèd be,
All dreadful portraits of deformity:
Spring-headed Hydras;° and sea-shouldering Whales,
Great Whirlpools,° which all fishes make to flee;
Bright Scolopendraes,° armed with silver scales;
Mighty Monoceroses,° with immeasured tails.

24

The dreadful fish that hath deserved the name
Of death,° and like him looks in dreadful hue;
The grisly Wasserman,° that makes his game
The flying ships with swiftness to pursue;
The horrible Sea-satyr,° that doth show
His fearful face in time of greatest storm;
Huge Xiphias,° whom mariners eschew
No less than rocks (as travellers inform);
And greedy Rosmarines° with visages deform.

25

All these and thousand thousands many more,
And more deformèd Monsters thousandfold,
With dreadful noise and hollow rumbling roar,
Came rushing in the foamy waves enrolled,
Which seemed to fly for fear them to behold.
No wonder if these did the knight appal:
For all that here on earth we dreadful hold,
Be but as bugs° to fearen babes withal,
Comparèd to the creatures in the sea's entrails.

26

"Fear nought," then said the Palmer, well advised,
"For these same Monsters are not these indeed,
But are into these fearful shapes disguised
By that same wicked witch,° to work us dread,
And draw from on this journey to proceed."
Then lifting up his virtuous staff on high,

° **Hydras**: many-headed serpent defeated by Hercules, but also recorded as a name for sea snakes.
° **Whirlpools**: spouting whales.
° **Scolopendraes**: fabulous sea-centipedes, described by the Greek naturalist Aelian.
° **Monoceroses**: narwhals.
° **dreadful ... death**: walrus, also known as the morse, which resembles the Latin for death (*mors*).
° **Wasserman**: merman, but also the dolphin, which often swims in a ship's wake.
° **Sea-satyr**: mythical beast, but possibly the seal, which was reported to surface before storms.
° **Xiphias**: swordfish.   ° **Rosmarines**: another name for the walrus.   ° **bugs**: bogeys.
° **witch**: Acrasia, the enchantress of the Bower of Bliss.

He smote the sea, which calmèd was with speed,
And all that dreadful Army fast gan fly
Into great Tethys'° bosom, where they hidden lie.

❦ ❦ ❦

° **Tethys**: primeval titaness of the ocean.

TOMOS PRYS
"The Porpoise" (c. 1594–1600)

Tomos Prys (or Thomas Price) was an Elizabethan Welsh poet and privateer, although by the time he composed these lines he had evidently grown disenchanted with the sailor's life. While the speaker's tone veers towards the wistful, the propulsive rhythm of the traditional Welsh verse form known as *cywydd*, consisting of seven-syllable lines in alliterative rhymed couplets (later imitated by the Victorian poet Gerard Manley Hopkins), helps relay the porpoise's joyous vitality. How does Prys make the porpoise seem far more at home in the oceanic environment than humans, lured by wealth and glory?
Source: *The Burning Tree*, trans. Gwyn Williams (1956), 207–11.

Porpoise, swift, trim, and handsome,
Finely leaping the fair waves,
Colourful, sharp-browed sea-calf,
Make smooth the course of one who weeps.
You are happy when you can be seen,
Merry in the wave-top where land ends.
Of fierce look on cold-rimmed face,
A bear's face in the cold flood,
You frisk and shiver like a fever
10   And then you heave away.
You strive with water, dark toadstool,
You look at it and snort;
It's as though you plough straight through
The foam of brittle waves;
You cut the salt sea open,
You must have the wave's heart.
Swift, lovely one, brave shadow,
Skull of the sea, pillion° to the strand,
A water-viper hoeing the wave,
20   With a look that frightens the heart.
White-bellied and good-natured
Wanderer of the captive deep,
Wild boar of the brine, in urgent mastery
He crosses the sea in a fine great sweep.
Throughout summer, when the weather changes,
He comes rocking along before the storm;
Fierce boar, churn of hell-fury,

° **pillion**: messenger.

Cross and greedy before the wild tide,
Strapping with gold-crested breastplate,
A fish with a closed tunic;   30
Sea's burden, two-breasted Leviathan,
He slips and catches along the wave's slope.
Saddle of the sea, take a bearing,
Steer a course to the loud water,
Choose a fathom, go on my behalf,
A messenger from a remembering man;
Take your way from your bunk at Menai°
Unswervingly to Lisbon;
Swim along there awhile
To the edge of Spain, heart of the world.   40
You are a heavenly swimmer,
Swim to the chase, you lively one.
Ask at the water's limit
(Let us give praise!) for a soldier,
Pirs Gruffudd,° who saddened all breasts,
Pearl of true faith, pure heart,
The honour of Penrhyn, its fine son,
Gentle lord, lustiest of men.
It is six weary years
Since he took ship abroad,   50
To the seas beyond the estuary,
Over the bar across the world …
Now give a grunt and tell him,
Beseech him to evade this fate
And soon to leave the sea
To others from now on.
There's little profit to be gained
Waiting at dusk on the cold waters,
And much shame and evil comes
Easily from sea-faring today.
It's good for a brisk man to leave the shore,
To sail the sea far over the world   80
To gain, though a cold captive,
True knowledge of this world.
But it's not good or godly
To keep on in this way …
Let him come home, devotedly
To lead his men to fine land,
Captain of the azure *Grace*,
And a clean-handed captain.
God in his grace will grant him
The treasure of giving up the sea.

  ❧ ❧ ❧

° **Menai**: strait that separates mainland Wales from the Isle of Anglesey.
° **Pirs Gruffudd**: Piers Griffith (1568–1628), a Welsh privateer. If reports can be trusted that Griffith left in
1588 to fight against the Spanish Armada, this would date the poem to 1594. He returned to Wales with
a captured Spanish ship in 1600, which thus provides a likely endpoint for the poem's composition.

MICHAEL DRAYTON
[Fish in the River Trent] (1622)

In this extract from *Poly-Olbion* Drayton praises the Trent's cleanliness, and seizes on the legend that its name derives from the thirty species of fish found in its waters to insert one of the numerous catalogues of creatures that adorn his epic. Although Drayton's tally only reaches twenty-four, it reveals an unmistakable admiration for what we now call biodiversity. Since the seventeenth century some species, like the sturgeon, have vanished from the Trent, while a few non-natives have been introduced.
Source: *Poly-Olbion* (1622), 2.120–1 (Song 26).

Through my perspicuous° Breast the pearly Pebbles shine.
I throw my Crystal Arms along the Flow'ry Valleys,
Which lying sleek and smooth, as any Garden Alleys,
Do give me leave to play whilst they do Court my Stream,
220 And crown my winding banks with many an Anadem.°
My Silver-scalèd Schools about my Streams do sweep,
Now in the shallow Fords, now in the falling Deep,
So that of every kind, the new-spawned num'rous Fry
Seem in me as the Sands that on my Shore do lie:
The Barbel, than which Fish a braver doth not swim,
Nor greater for the Ford within my spacious brim,
Nor (newly taken) more the curious taste doth please;
The Grayling, whose great Spawn is big as any Peas;
The Perch with pricking Fins, against the Pike prepared,
230 As Nature had thereon bestowed this stronger guard,
His daintiness to keep (each curious palate's proof)
From his vile rav'nous foe; next him I name the Ruff,
His very near Ally, and both for Scale and Fin,
In taste and for his bait (indeed) his next of kin;
The pretty slender Dare, of many called the Dace,
Within my liquid glass, when Phoebus looks his face,
Oft swiftly as he swims his silver belly shows,
But with such nimble slight that ere you can disclose
240 His shape, out of your sight like lightning he is shot;
The Trout by Nature marked with many a Crimson spot,
As though she curious were in him above the rest,
And of freshwater Fish, did note him for the best;
The Roche, whose common kind to every Flood doth fall;
The Chub, (whose neater name) which some a Chevin call,
Food to the Tyrant Pike (most being in his power)
Who, for their num'rous store, he most doth them devour;
The lusty Salmon then, from Neptune's wat'ry Realm,

° **perspicuous**: clear.   ° **Anadem**: garland.

When as his season serves, stemming my tideful Stream,
Then being in his kind, in me his pleasure takes
(For whom the Fisher then all other Game forsakes),   250
Which bending of himself to th'fashion of a Ring,
Above the forcèd Weirs, himself doth nimbly fling,
And often when the Net hath dragged him safe to land,
Is seen by natural force to scape his murd'rer's hand,
Whose grain doth rise in flakes, with fatness interlarded,
Of many a liquorish lip, that highly is regarded.
And Humber, to whose waste° I pay my wat'ry store,
Me of her Sturgeons° sends, that I thereby the more
Should have my beauties graced, with something from him sent.
Not Ancum's° silvered Eel exceedeth that of Trent,   260
Though the sweet-smelling Smelt be more in Thames than me,
The Lamprey and his Less° in Severn gen'ral be,
The Flounder, smooth and flat, in other Rivers caught,
Perhaps in greater store, yet better are not thought.
The dainty Gudgeon, Loche, the Minnow, and the Bleak,
Since they but little are, I little need to speak
Of them, nor doth it fit me much of those to reck,°
Which everywhere are found in every little Beck;°
Nor of the Crayfish here, which creeps amongst my stones,
From all the rest alone, whose shell is all his bones: 270
For Carp, the Tench, and Bream, my other store among,
To Lakes and standing Pools that chiefly do belong,
Here scouring° in my Fords, feed in my waters clear,
Are muddy Fish in Ponds to that which they are here.

❧ ❧ ❧

° **waste**: expanse.
° **Sturgeons**: according to UK law (still in effect), sturgeons and whales legally belong to the Crown, and it was customary in the Renaissance to send pieces of them to the monarch.
° **Ancum**: a Scottish loch renowned for eels.
° **Less**: smaller variety, known as the lampern or river lamprey.   ° **reck**: reckon.
° **Beck**: brook.   ° **scouring**: scurrying.

IZAAK WALTON
"Observations of the Salmon" and "Observations of the Eel" (1655)

Just as early modern hunters were often accidental zoologists, many anglers were de facto ichthyologists. There is no better example of this than Izaak Walton. As his recent editor observes, Walton's intimate knowledge of each particular species' habits, habitats, life cycle, and food – and the interconnections between

them – "promotes a keen appreciation of what we would now term ecology," albeit this knowledge is ultimately marshalled for the purpose of killing the fish, and thus grates against the pastoral mentality of live-and-let-live (Swann 2014, xviii). Critics have seen his piscatorial pursuits as a retreat from politics in the aftermath of the Civil War, or an attempt to reassert royalist control over the realm through mastery of the countryside and its natural history. While there is much truth in those views, it is the author's fascination with fish and his delineation of the skill required to catch them (which means knowing the fish better than it knows itself) that best explains the *Angler's* enduring popularity as one of the most beloved sporting books in the English language. Among the fourteen fish profiled by Walton, the salmon and eel have been chosen because of their historic importance in the British diet, their distance on the Chain of Being, and the fact that both have experienced worrisome population declines over the past century (eel numbers are down 90 per cent since the 1970s).
Source: *The Compleat Angler* (1655), 181–2, 184–6, 188, 259–62, 266–7.

"Observations of the Salmon"

The Salmon is accounted the King of freshwater fish, and is ever bred in Rivers relating to the Sea, yet so high or far from it as admits of no tincture of salt or brackishness. He is said to breed or cast his spawn in most Rivers in the month of August. Some say that then they dig a hole or grave in a safe place in the gravel and there place their eggs of spawn (after the Melter has done his natural office), and then hide it most cunningly, and cover it over with gravel and stones, and then leave it to their Creator's protection, by whose power the Spawn becomes [182] Samlets the next Spring following.

The Salmon, having spent their appointed time and done this natural duty in the fresh water, they then haste to the Sea before Winter, both the Melter and Spawner.° But if they be stopped by Floodgate or Weirs, or lost in the fresh water, then those so left behind by degrees grow sick and lean and unseasonable and kipper;° that is to say, they have bony gristles grow out of their lower chaps … which hinders their feeding. And in time such fish so left behind pine away and die …

[184] Though they make very hard shift to get out of the fresh Rivers into the Sea, yet they will make harder shift to get out of the salt into the fresh Rivers to spawn, or to possess the pleasures that they formerly found in them. To which end they will force themselves through Floodgates or over Weirs or hedges, or stops in the water, even beyond common belief. Gesner° speaks of such places as are known to be eight foot high above water. And our Camden° mentions … the like wonder to be in Pembrokeshire, where the River Tivy falls into the sea: that the fall is so downright and so high that the people stand in wonder at the strength and flight that they see the Salmon use to get out of the Sea into the said River. And the manner and height of

° **Melter and Spawner**: male and female.   ° **kipper**: spawning salmon.
° **Gesner**: Conrad Gesner, Swiss naturalist.   ° **Camden**: William Camden, *Britannia*, 654–5.

the place is so notable that it is known far by the name of the Salmon-leap, concerning which take this also out of honest Michael Drayton:°

> [185] And when the Salmon seeks a fresher stream to find
> (Which hither from the Sea comes yearly by his kind),
> As he towards season grows, and stems the wat'ry tract
> Where Tivy, falling down, makes a high cataract,
> Forced by the rising Rocks that there her course oppose,
> As though within her bound they meant her to enclose:
> Here, when the labouring fish does at the foot arrive,
> And finds that by his strength he does but vainly strive,
> His tail takes in his mouth,° and bending like a bow
> That's to full compass drawn, aloft himself doth throw:
> Then springing at this height, as doth a little wand,
> That bended end to end, and started° from man's hand,
> Far off itself doth cast; so does the Salmon vault.
> And if at first he fail, his second Somersault°
> He instantly assays, and from his nimble ring
> Still yerking,° never leaves until himself he fling
> Above the opposing stream.°

And next I shall tell you that it is observed by Gesner and others that there is no better Salmon than in England, and that though some of our northern countries have as fat and as large as the River Thames, none are of so excellent a taste ...

The age of a Salmon exceeds not ten years, so let me tell you his growth is very sudden. It is said after he has got into the Sea he becomes from [186] a Samlet ... to be a Salmon in as short a time as a Gosling to become a Goose. Much of this has been observed by tying a ribbon, or some known tape or thread, in the tail of some young Salmons, which have been taken in Weirs as they swum towards the salt water, and then by taking a part of them again with the known mark, at the same place at their return from the Sea, which is usually about six months after. And the like experiment hath been tried upon young Swallows, who have, after six months absence, been observed to return to the same chimney, there to make their nests and their habitations for the Summer following; which hath inclined many to think that every Salmon usually returns to the same River in which it was bred, as young Pigeons taken out of the same Dovecote have also been observed to do ...

[188] You shall observe ... he does not (as the Trout and many other fish) lie near the waterside or bank or roots of trees, but swims in the deep and broad parts of the water, and usually in the middle, and near the ground,

° **Drayton**: From *Poly-Olbion* (1612), 88, with several variants or miscopyings by Walton. This quotation does not appear in the 1653 edition of the *Angler*. Walton may have added it to shift responsibility onto the "honest" poet for the myth that leaping salmon bite their tails.
° **mouth**: teeth] 1612.   ° **started**: flirted (i.e. sprung)] 1612.
° **Somersault**: 1612; Summer sought,] Walton.   ° **yerking**: twitching.
° **opposing stream**: streamful top] 1612. In *Poly-Olbion*, the salmon-leap in the Tivy is followed by a description of the "now-perished" beaver, which once inhabited this river.

and that there you are to fish for him; and that he is to be caught as the Trout is, with a Worm, a Minnow ... or with a Fly ...

[259] "Observations of The Eel"

It is agreed by most men that the Eel is a most dainty fish. The Romans have esteemed her the Helena° of their feasts, and some the Queen of palate pleasure. But most men differ about their breeding. Some say they breed by generation as other fish do, and others that they breed (as some worms do) of mud ... or out of the putrefaction of the earth. Others say that ... eels are bred of a particular dew falling in the months of May or June ...

[260] I have seen in a river in July, in a river not far from Canterbury, some parts of it covered over with young Eels about the thickness of a straw; and these Eels did lie on the top of that water, as thick as motes are said to be in the Sun ... And Gesner quotes Venerable Bede to say that in England there is an island called Ely, by reason of the innumerable [261] numbers of Eels that breed in it. But that Eels may be bred ... either of dew or out of the corruption of the earth seems to be made probable by the barnacles and young goslings bred by the sun's heat and the rotten planks of an old ship° ...

[262] It is granted by all or most men that Eels for ... the six cold months of the year stir not up and down, ... but get into the soft earth or mud, and there many of them together bed themselves and live without feeding upon anything (as I have told you some Swallows have been observed to do in hollow trees for those six cold months). And this the Eel and Swallow do, as not being able to endure winter weather° ... [As] he is impatient of cold, so it hath been observed that in warm weather an Eel has been known to live five days out of the water ...

[266] Eels do not usually stir in the daytime, for then they hide themselves under some covert, or under boards or planks about Flood-gates, or Weirs, or Mills, or in holes in the Riverbanks; so that you, observing your time in a warm day when the water is lowest, may take a strong small hook tied to strong line ... [267] and it is scarce to be doubted but that if there be an eel within sight of it, the eel will bite instantly ...

When I go to dress an Eel ... I wish he were as long and big as that which was caught in the Peterborough River in the year 1667, which was a yard and three quarters long. If you will not believe me, then go and see at one of the Coffeehouses in King Street in Westminster.°

⁊ ⁊ ⁊

° **Helena**: after Helen of Troy because its phallic shape earned it a reputation as an aphrodisiac; the Mediterranean moray is known as the *Muraena helena*.
° **barnacles ... ship**: many Renaissance naturalists still subscribed to Aristotle's theory of spontaneous generation and medieval legends that barnacle geese hatched from rotting wood.
° **winter weather:** scientists now believe that eels, like swallows, migrate.
° **When ... Westminster**: This paragraph was added to the 1676 edition.

Insects

THOMAS MOFFETT

The Theatre of Insects (1589)

One might assume that most early modern Europeans would have regarded the diminutive world of creepy-crawly things with contempt or disgust, if not fear and loathing. In sixteenth-century English the word "bug" signified something like bogeyman and would revealingly come to be used as a generic word for beetles. Yet many Elizabethans also took delight in the miniature, and the correspondence between the microcosm and macrocosm in neo-Platonic cosmology may have helped pique interest in these seemingly lowly or "lesser creatures." The first great English entomologist, Thomas Penny (c. 1530–89), travelled all over England and Europe collecting specimens, and corresponded with many leading naturalists on the Continent. After his death, Penny's notes and sketches were compiled and given a literary polish by Thomas Moffett, a physician and author of a poem about silkworms (which features Pyramus and Thisbe and may have influenced Shakespeare's burlesque of that tale in A *Midsummer Night's Dream*). Although Moffett completed the book in 1589, his publishers balked at the cost of printing such a massive tome (which ran to 1,200 folio pages). *The Theatre of Insects* was finally published in 1634 in Latin and in English fourteen years later. While unfurling the medicinal use, moral significance, and alien beauty of insects, Moffett undercuts the anthropocentric prejudice that size is a true measure of importance.
Source: *The Theatre of Insects* (1658), Ggggɪ^v–Gggg2^v.

I shall add this concerning the dignity of this History of Insects (lest we should think God made them in vain, or we describe them): that in the universal world there is nothing more divine than these except Man. For however in show they are most abject and sordid, yet if we look more nicely° into them, they will appear far otherwise than they promise on the bare outside.

"It oft times comes into my mind," saith Gallisardus,° "to think of our Italians, who commonly admire vehemently things notable for magnitude, or new and unusual, but things obvious in all places, and that are very small they despise. Yet if they look exactly to the matter it will be easy to observe that the divine force and power show themselves more effectually in mean things, and they are far more miraculous than those things the world with open mouth respects so much and admires. If any man bring from far the wonderful Bittern,° Elephant, Crocodile, there is no man but runs quickly to see that because it is new and unusual ... But no man regards Hand-worms,° Worms-in-wine,° Earwigs, Fleas, because they are obvious to all men and very small, as if they were but the pastimes of a lascivious and drunken Nature, and that she had been sober only in making

° **nicely**: closely.   ° **Gallisardus**: Pierre Gallisard, sixteenth-century French theologian.
° **Bittern**: heron-like wader now rare in Britain due to the draining of the fens.
° **Hand-worms**: mites.   ° **Worms-in-wine**: fruit fly larva.

those huge and terrible beasts." Nor is this vice peculiar to the Italians only, but it is common to the English and all mankind, who—that they may see those large beasts that carry towers, the African Lion, the huge Whale, the Rhinoceros, the Bear and Bull—take sometimes a long journey to London, and pay money for their places on the scaffold to behold them brought upon the stage.°

Yet where is Nature more to be seen than in the smallest matters, where she is entirely all? "For in great bodies the workmanship is easy, the matter being ductile; but in these that are that are so small and despicable, and almost nothing, what care? How great is the effect of it? How unspeakable the perfection?" as Pliny° saith. Do you require Prudence? Regard the Ant. Do you desire Justice? Regard the Bee. Do you commend Temperance? Take advice of them both. Do you praise Valour? See the whole generation of Grasshoppers. Also look upon the Gnat (a little Insect not worth speaking of) that with her slender hollow nose will penetrate so far into the thick skin of the Lion that thou canst hardly or not at all thrust a sword or javelin in so far. A man hath need of steel to bore into oaks, which the Wood-worm eats hollow with her teeth, as the sound can testify … But if I would relate the skill of some of them in building, fighting, playing, working, perhaps I might be thought overcurious in these small things (of which the Law takes no notice) and [Gggg2ʳ] more negligent in greater matters.

Now I come to their use: and that manifold, and in respect unto God, to Nature, or to Man, very great. For if the Gentiles, according to the saying of the Apostle Paul, know God by the creatures,° truly they may hence as from a higher watchtower behold his Omnipotence, Majesty, Providence … Would you have a Musician? Hearken to the Grasshopper, which is always filled with singing, and lives without meat, and by her most pleasant melody challengeth the Nightingale. Would you hear a Trumpeter? Hold your ear to the Beehive; hear the humming noise. Hearken a little to the Gnat, in whose small beak the great Master workman hath formed that horrid and clanging sound of the Trumpet … For you must not think that in Man only the Art of the great Artificer is so great … but what creature so ever you would dissect you shall find the like art and wisdom to appear in it. And such creatures as you cannot possibly dissect will make you to admire the more, the smaller they are … Farewell then all those that so much esteem of creatures that are very large. I acknowledge that God appears in their magnitude, yet I see more of God in the History of lesser Creatures. For here is more of prudence, sagacity, art, ingenuity, and of certain evident divine being. Wouldst thou praise Nature, God's ordinary hand? From whence wouldst thou take thy beginning better than from Insects? … [Gggg2ᵛ] I let pass that admirable variety, comeliness,

---

° **stage**: Moffett versified much of this passage in *The Silkworms and Their Flies* (1599 34–35).
° **Pliny**: see *Natural History*, 11.2.   ° **know … creatures**: Romans 1:20.

and fecundity that is in Insects, which commend the riches of quickening Nature in greater multitude, and sets forth the greater plenty of it, which cannot be exhausted.

If you consider men, as [insects] cure almost all the diseases of men's bodies (as I shall declare more at large in their History), so they furnish their minds with variety of examples of virtues, whereby they may instruct their souls and teach them that otherwise would be very wicked. Wherefore Solomon, the principal master of true wisdom amongst men, sends sluggards to the Ants' hill, and tumultuous people to the bands of Locusts, and incites mortal men to the contemplation of the Spiders in their houses,° that from the School of Insects we may learn virtue and lift up our eyes unto the power of God, which are too much turned away from him. "Go to," saith Tertullian, "O Man, thou reliest upon thy own strength, and distrustest God, yet consider that there is so great strength in the smallest creature he hath made that thou canst not endure it, nor ever be able to do as much. Imitate if thou canst the Spider's curiosity; endure the sting of the Spider phalangium;° avoid the nastiness of Lice; take a Gnat out of thy throat; sleep when Fleas or Wiglice° bite fiercely; keep thy trees safe from Caterpillars; drive away Weevils, Tree-worms, Vine-worms, and Timber-worms."° Wherefore, as God shows his power more in this more notable Artifice of Insects, so his great mercy is more apparent because there is hardly any disease of the mind or body but a remedy may be fetched from this storehouse to cure them both. If men should deny that they contribute very much to feed and fat and cure many other creatures, Birds and Fishes would plead for them, and the brute beasts that feed on grass would speak in their behalf.

⁂

° **Wherefore Solomon … houses**: Proverbs 6:6, and 30:27–8, formerly attributed to Solomon.
° **phalangium**: venomous.   ° **Wiglice**: bedbugs.
° **Tertullian … timber-worms**: adapted from *Against Marcion*, 1.14.

CHARLES BUTLER

The Feminine Monarchy, or a Treatise Concerning Bees (1609)

While Renaissance writers often present bees as a "pattern" of feudal society, the first work of melittology in English shockingly established (although too late for Queen Elizabeth's courtier-poets to exploit the fact) that the leader of the hive was female. Attempting to frame this as the exception that proves the rule of patriarchy, Butler dwells on the moral, political, and spiritual lessons to be learned from bees. Astute scientific observation drawn "out of experience" is thus mingled with poetry and lore (as when Butler cites Virgil or reports the tale of a woman who cured an infected hive with a consecrated wafer) and warped by wishful thinking (as in his claim that bees sing to each other, prefiguring the discovery that they communicate through dance).

Source: *The Feminine Monarchy, or a Treatise Concerning Bees* (1609), A1^r–A3^r, A7^v–A8^r, B2^v, E2^v–F1^r.

Among all the creatures which our bountiful God hath made for the use and service of man, in respect of (1) great profit with small cost, (2) of their ubiquity or being in all countries, (3) of their continual labour and consenting order, the Bees are most to be admired. For first, with provision of a hive and some little care and attendance, which need be no hindrance to other business, but rather a delightful recreation amid the same, they bring in store of sweet delicates, most wholesome both for meat and medicine … [A1^v] Secondly … there is no ground of what nature so ever it be, whether it be hot or cold, wet or dry, hill or dale, woodland or champaign, meadow, pasture or arable, in a word whether it be battle° or barren, which yieldeth not matter for the Bee to work upon. And thirdly, in their labour and order, at home and abroad, they are so admirable that they may be a pattern unto men, both of the one and of the other. For unless they be let° by weather, weakness, or waste of matter to work on, their labour never ceaseth … For their order, it is such that they may well be said to have a commonwealth, since all they do is in common, without any private respect … They work for all; they watch for all; they fight for all … [A2^r] Their dwelling and diet are common to all alike. They have like common care both of their wealth and young ones … and all this under the government of one Monarch, of whom above all things they have principal care and respect, loving, reverencing, and obeying her in all things° …

If she go forth to solace herself (as sometime she will) many of them attend upon her, guarding her person before and behind: they which come before her every now and then returning and looking back, and making withal an extraordinary noise, as if they spoke the language of the Knight Marshal's men.° And so away they fly together, and anon in like [A2^v] manner they attend her back again. This I may say because I have seen it, although the Philosopher° be of another mind … But if they have many Princes, as when two fly away with one swarm, or when two swarms are hived together, they strike one of them presently … The next day they carry her forth either dead or deadly wounded … [A3^r] for the Bees abhor as well polyarchy° as anarchy, God having showed in them unto men an express pattern of a perfect monarchy, the most natural and absolute form of government …

° **battle**: nourishing.   ° **let**: hindered.
° **all things**: here follows a passage from Virgil's *Georgics*, 4.   ° **Knight Marshal's men**: royal bailiffs.
° **Philosopher**: Aristotle.   ° **polyarchy**: government with multiple rulers.

[A7ᵛ] But if thou wilt have the favour of thy Bees that they sting thee not, thou must avoid such things as offend them. Thou must not be (1) unchaste; (2) uncleanly, for impurity and sluttishness° (themselves being most chaste and neat) they utterly abhor; thou must not come amongst them (3) smelling of sweat or having a stinking breath caused either through eating of leeks, onions, garlic, and the like; ... thou must not be given to (4) surfeiting or drunkenness; thou must not come (5) puffing and blowing or sweating unto them, neither hastily stir among them nor violently defend thyself [A8ʳ] when they seem to threaten thee, but softly moving thy hand before thy face, gently put them by; and lastly, thou must be (6) no stranger unto them. In a word thou must be chaste, cleanly, sweet, sober, quiet, and familiar. So they will love thee and know thee from all other ...

[B2ᵛ] A certain simple woman, having some stalls of Bees which yielded not unto her her desired profit, but did consume and die of the murrain,° made her moan to another woman more simple than herself, who counselled her to get a consecrated host or round godamighty° and put it among them. According to whose advice, she went to the priest to receive the host, which when she had done, she kept it in her mouth. And being come home again she took it out, and [B3ʳ] put it into one of her hives. Whereupon the murrain ceased and the honey abounded. The woman therefore lifting up the hive at the due time to take out the honey saw there (most strange to be seen) a chapel° built by the Bees with an altar in it, the walls adorned by most marvellous skill of architecture with windows conveniently set in their places; also a door and a steeple with bells, and the host being laid upon the altar, the bees making a sweet noise round about it.

But whether this more do argue the supernatural knowledge and skill of the Bees, or the miraculous power of the host, or the spiritual craftiness of him whose coming is by the working of Satan with all power and signs and lying wonders, it may be some will make a question ...

[E2ᵛ] Albeit generally among creatures the males, as more worthy, do master the females, yet in these the females have the pre-eminence ... But let no nimble-tongued Sophisters° gather a false conclusion from these true premises, that they by the example of these may arrogate to themselves the like superiority ... [For] he that made these to command their males, commanded them to be commanded° ...

[E3ʳ] Yet this they may note by the way: that albeit the females in this kind have the sovereignty, yet have the males the louder voice, as it is in other living things: doves, owls, thrushes, etc., the males being known by their sounding and shrill notes from the silent females° ...

° **sluttishness**: slovenliness.   ° **murrain**: infectious disease.   ° **round godamighty**: communion wafer.
° **chapel**: for another vision of the hive as a chapel, see Tailboys Dymoke's *The Bumble Bee* (1599 c4ʳ–4ᵛ).
° **Sophisters**: specious reasoners.
° **commanded**: several scriptural passages by the Apostle Paul (e.g. Ephesians 5:22) enjoin wives to submit to their husbands.
° **silent females**: although this is generally true in England, many female birds sing in tropical regions.

The bees breeding or laying of seeds begin to cease in some by Leo, in some not before Virgo.° After which time these Amazonian° Dames, having conceived for the next year, send away their mates, and kill those that afterwards force in among them …

[E4ᵛ] The next prince, when she perceiveth a competent number to be fledge and ready, beginneth the music in a begging tune, as if she did pray her queen-mother to let them go. Whereunto if she yield consent by her answering … then look for a swarm … [F1ʳ] They sing both in triple time: the princess thus° … but the Queen in a deeper voice … so that when they sing together sometime they agree in a perfect third, sometimes in a Diapenthe … sometimes in a Diapason.° With these tunes answering one another, and some [F1ᵛ] pauses between, they go solemnly round about the hive, so to give warning unto all the company … You may hear them best in the evenings and mornings. If there be many of the Queen's breed that are ripe, they join with her in her tune, the more to incite the swarm to go that their tune may come the sooner. I have heard three of them together. But none dare counterfeit the voice of the Prince; for that were treason to her person.

❧ ❧ ❧

° **Leo … Virgo**: by 22 July or just after 22 August.
° **Amazonian**: Butler quotes a famous passage from Herodotus on the Scythian warrior-women.
° **thus**: Butler prints a musical transcription of notes in the key of C-flat major.
° **Diapenthe … Diapason**: seventh; octave.

RICHARD LOVELACE
"The Ant" (c. 1655)

Lovelace composed several lyrics about microfauna, including "The Snail," "A Fly Caught in a Cobweb," "The Toad and the Spider," and "The Grasshopper." Many of them voice the poet's royalist convictions and "The Ant" is no exception. It satirizes the Puritan ethic of the Cromwell era, which drives the agrarian capitalist to overexploit the land and its resources for profit. Grain-hoarding was a much-lamented problem in early modern England (Shakespeare himself has been accused of it) because it created artificial shortages that drove up food prices. Whereas Aesop's fable commends the industrious ant and condemns the indolent grasshopper, the Cavalier Lovelace reverses this polarity, insisting on the former's lowly place in both the food chain and the Chain of Being.
Source: *Lucasta Posthume* (1659), 13–14.

> Forbear, thou great good husband,° little Ant,
> A little respite from thy flood of sweat.
> Thou thine own horse and cart under this Plant,

° **good husband**: thrifty farmer.

Thy spacious tent, fan thy prodigious heat.
Down with thy double load of that one grain!
It is a granary for all thy train.

Cease large example of wise thrift awhile
(For thy example is become our Law),
And teach thy frowns a seasonable smile.
So Cato sometimes the naked Florals° saw.   10
And thou, almighty foe, lay by thy sting,
Whilst thy unpaid musicians, Crickets, sing.

Lucasta,° she that holy makes the day,
And 'stills° new Life in fields of Feuillemort,°
Hath back restored their verdure with one ray,
And with her eye bid all to play and sport.
Ant, to work still Age will thee truant call,
And to save now th'art worse than prodigal.

Austere and Cynic!° Not one hour t'allow,   20
To lose with pleasure what thou got'st with pain,
But drive on sacred festivals thy plough,
Tearing highways with thy o'er-chargèd wain.°
Not all thy lifetime one poor minute live,
And thy o'er-laboured bulk with mirth relieve?

Look up then miserable Ant, and spy
Thy fatal foes, for breaking of her law,
Hov'ring above thee: Madam Margaret Pie,°
And her fierce servant, meagre Sir John Daw.°
Thyself and storehouse now they do store up,
And thy whole harvest, too, within their crop.   30

Thus we unthrifty thrive within Earth's tomb,
For some more rav'nous and ambitious jaw:
The grain in th'Ant's, the Ant's in the Pie's womb,°
The Pie in th'Hawk's, the Hawk's i'th' Eagle's maw.
So scattering to hoard 'gainst a long day,
Thinking to save all, we cast all away.

⁂ ⁂ ⁂

° **Cato ... Florals** : Cato (the Younger), a Roman stoic who once attended the *Floralia* – a spring festival dedicated to the goddess Flora in which actresses performed nude. Lovelace's example is undercut by the fact Cato walked out in protest.
° **Lucasta**: the poet's beloved (supposedly based on Lucy Sacheverell); her name puns on the Latin for "pure light."
° **'stills**: instills.   ° **Feuillemort**: dead leaves.
° **Cynic**: philosophical sect of ancient Greece known for its asceticism.
° **o'erchargèd wain**: overladen wagon.   ° **Margaret Pie**: magpie.   ° **John Daw**: jackdaw.
° **womb**: stomach.

MARGARET CAVENDISH
"Of the Spider"° (1653)

This chilling poem plays on the analogy between the web-making of the spider, the sewing of Renaissance women, and Cavendish's transgressive act of writing (Bowerbank). While the Duchess, who loved designing stately homes, clearly identifies with the spider, the poem also darkly hints that the domestic world can be a place of entrapment and predation.
Source: *Poems and Fancies* (1653), 151.

> The Spider's Housewif'ry no Webs doth spin
> To make her Cloth, but Ropes to hang Flies in.
> Her Bowels are the Shop where Flax is found,
> Her Body is the Wheel that goeth round,
> A Wall her Distaff, where she sticks thread on,°
> The Fingers are the Feet that pull it long.°
> And wheresoever she goes ne'er idle sits,°
> Nor wants a House, builds one with Ropes and Nets:°
> Though it be not so strong as Brick and Stone,
> Yet strong enough to bear light Bodies on.
> Within this House the Female Spider lies,
> The whilst the Male doth hunt abroad for Flies,
> Ne'er leaves° till he the Flies gets in, and there°
> Entangles him° within his subtle Snare:
> Like Treacherous Host, which doth° much welcome make,
> Yet watches how his Guest's Life he° may take.

10

🙣 🙣 🙣

° **Of the Spider**: Of a Spider's Web] 1664.
° **A … on**: Her Distaff, where she sticks the Thread's a Wall] 1664.
° **The … long**: Her Feet the Fingers are she pulls withal] 1664.
° **And … sits**: She's Busy at all times, not Idle lies] 1664.
° **Nor … nets**: A House she Builds with Nets to catch the Flies] 1664.   ° **leaves**: leaving] 1664.
° **and there**: which are] 1664.   ° **Entangles him**: Entangled soon] 1664.
° **Host … doth**: Hosts, which do] 1664.
° **Yet … he**: Their Guests, yet watch how they their Lives] 1664.

ANONYMOUS
"Upon the biting of Fleas" (c. 1650)

As people rarely bathed in early modern England, fleas were endemic. No doubt many travellers in roadside inns, like the carriers in *1 Henry* IV, experienced the agony of a sleepless night tormented by fleabites. The following work appears in an unpublished poetry miscellany from the time of Charles I, and was later printed in *The Muses' Recreation* (1655), compiled by John Mennis and James Smith. Although

Donne's "Flea" is far more artful, this poem is perhaps more representative in its frustrated sense of human subjection to a tiny insect.

Source: BL MS 3398, 70^{r–v}.

Summon up all the terrifying pains
That ever were invented by the brains
Of earthly Tyrants; then descend to Hell
And count the horrid tortures that do dwell
In the dark Dungeon, where the horrid stone
Makes Sisyphus° his panting entrails groan,
Where Tantalus° (in midst of plenty cursed)
Is doomed to famine and eternal thirst,
Where the pale Ghosts are lashed with whips of steel:
Yet these are gentle to the pangs I feel,   10
Vexed with a Thousand Pygmy fiends, and such
As dare not stand the onset° of a touch.
Strange kind of Combatants, whose Conquest lies
In nimbly skipping from their Enemies,
While they with eager fierceness lay about
To catch the thing they fain° would be without!
The sable furies bravely venture on,
But when I 'gin t'oppose them, whip,° they're gone.
Doubtless I think each is a Magic Dancer,
Bred up by some infernal Necromancer,   20
But that I do believe they scarce ere knew
'Mong all their Spirits such a damnèd crew.
Some, when they would express the gentle sting
Of a slight pain, call it a Flea-biting:
But were they in my place they soon would find
A cause sufficient for to change their mind.
Some, telling how they vexed another, say
I sent him with a Flea in's ear away:
Only to show what trouble hath possessed
Him whom this little creature doth molest.   30
It is reported that a Mouse can daunt
The courage of a mighty Elephant;
Compare my bigness and the Flea's to theirs,
And I have smaller reason for my fears.
And yet I tremble when I feel them bite:
Oh how they sting my flesh! Was black-browed night
And the whist° stillness of it made by Fate
To make man happy or unfortunate?
If there be any happiness or rest
In pangs of torture, I am fully blest.   40
All my five senses are combined in one:

° **Sisyphus**: figure from Greek mythology, punished with having to roll a stone uphill for eternity.
° **Tantalus**: Greek mythological figure, punished with eternal hunger.   ° **onset**: onslaught.
° **fain**: gladly.   ° **whip**: instantly (an expression like presto!)   ° **whist**: hushed.

For, but my sense of feeling, I have none,
And that is left me to increase my smart.
Blood-sucking Tyrants, will you ne'er depart?
Why do you hang in Clusters on my skin?
Come one-to-one and try what you can win.
You coward Ethiop° Vermin! O, you Gods,
You are unjust to load me with such odds.
If Jove-born Hercules can't deal with° two,
50   Then what can I against a Legion do?
Their number frights me, not their strength. I'll dare
The Lion, Panther, Tiger, or the Bear
To an encounter to be freed from these
Relentless demi-Devils, cursèd Fleas.

※ ※ ※

° **Ethiop**: a racist jibe at the flea's blackness.
° **deal with**: overcome (a proverbial expression).

Plants

EDMUND SPENSER
[The Oak and the Briar] (1579)

The following Aesopian fable concludes the "February" eclogue of Spenser's
Shepheardes Calender. While New Historicist scholars have decoded it as an allegory about political rivalries and generational conflict at the Elizabethan court,
the poem has an urgent environmental message as well; oaks were vital to ship-
building, and their disappearance was becoming an alarming concern in the late
sixteenth century (see Part V). In fact, this poem may be one of the first works
of English literature composed in response to an actual tree-felling: in May 1579
Bishop Aylmer – whom Spenser criticizes in "July" as Morrel or "Mar-Elm" – was
summoned before the Privy Council and accused of having chopped down 400
trees at Fulham Palace (Long 732). While Spenser notoriously advocated destroying the woodland hideouts of Irish guerrilla fighters, a letter survives in his own
hand entrusting one of his Irish neighbours with "the keeping of all the woods
which I have in Ballygannon [now a nature reserve] … without making any spoil
thereof" (BL Add. MS 19869). Rather than treat the political and ecological as
distinct, Spenser entwines the two, as Thenot's elegy for the fallen dotard is simultaneously a plea to respect the elderly, and is thus typical of Spenser grafting the
human and arboreal in a kind of ecological uncanny (cf. Fradubio in Book 1 of
The Faerie Queene). "February" also glances at the controversial felling of "gospel
oaks," trees endowed with sacred status in Catholic Rogation ceremonies (Borlik
2011, 109–18). Considering he was a Protestant who frowned on such superstitions, it is notable that Spenser named his son Sylvanus (after the pagan god of the
woods). Although the Great Chain of Being divides plants into a hierarchy – with
oaks and cedars at the top, moss at the bottom, and the briar in between – *The
Shepheardes Calender* (the structure of which mimics husbandry manuals and almanacs) here imparts a fundamental lesson in ecology: that different life-forms are
interconnected, and harming one can inadvertently harm another.
Source: *The Shepheardes Calender* (1579), 5^r–7^r.

> THENOT   There grew an aged Tree on the green,
> A goodly Oak° sometime had it been,
> With arms full strong and largely displayed,
> But of their leaves they were disarrayed:°
> The body big, and mightily pight,°
> Thoroughly rooted, and of wondrous height:
> Whilom had been the King of the field,
> And mochel mast° to the husband° did yield,
> And with his nuts larded many swine.   110
> But now the grey moss marred his rine,°

° **Oak**: a symbol of monarchy, lineage, the English nation, and Druidic religion.
° **disarrayed**: despoiled, naked.   ° **pight**: pitched.   ° **mochel mast**: many acorns.
° **husband**: farmer.   ° **rine**: rind, bark.

His bared boughs were beaten with storms,
His top was bald, and wasted with worms,
His honour decayed, his branches sere.
    Hard by his side grew a bragging briar,°
Which proudly thrust into th'Element,°
And seemed to threat the Firmament.
It was embellished with blossoms fair,
And thereto ay woned to repair°

120   The shepherds' daughters, to gather flowers,
To paint their garlands with his colours.
And in his small bushes used to shroud°
The sweet Nightingale, singing so loud:
Which made this foolish Briar wax so bold,
That on a time he cast° him to scold,
And snub the good Oak, for he was old.
    "Why standst there," quoth he, "thou brutish block?
Nor for fruit, nor for shadow serves thy stock.°
Seest how fresh my flowers been spread,

130   Dyed in lily white and crimson red,
With leaves engrained in lusty green,
Colours meet° to clothe a maiden Queen.
Thy waste° bigness but cumbers the ground,
And darks the beauty of my blossoms round.
The mouldy moss, which thee accloyeth,
My cinnamon smell too much annoyeth.
Wherefore soon I rede° thee, hence remove,
Lest thou the price of my displeasure prove."°
So spake this bold Briar with great disdain.

140   Little him answered the Oak again,
But yielded, with shame and grief adawed,°
That of a weed he was overawed.°
    It chanced after upon a day,
The Husbandman self to come that way,
Of custom for to survey his ground,
And his trees of state° encompass° round.
Him when the spiteful briar had espied,

° **Briar**: although it can refer to any thorny plant, Spenser has in mind the sweet briar or eglantine, which does not tolerate shade. Spenser's contemporaries associated it with not only beauty but also ambition because of its upward climbing. In Australia, it is now classed as an invasive species.   ° **Element**: air.   ° **woned to repair**: frequented.
° **used … shroud**: habitually sheltered.   ° **cast**: resolved.
° **stock**: tree-trunk (but also applied to Catholic idols).   ° **meet**: fit.
° **waste**: superfluous.
° **rede**: advise, with pun on rede or rid (to clear land).   ° **prove**: suffer.   ° **adawed**: daunted.
° **overawed**: overcrawed] 1586.
° **trees of state**: according to Spenser's mysterious commentator, E. K., the "taller trees fit for timber wood."   ° **encompass**: perambulate, as was customary in early modern property surveys.

Causeless complained, and loudly cried
Unto his Lord, stirring up stern strife:
"O my liege Lord, the God of my life,   150
Pleaseth you ponder your Suppliant's plaint,°
Caused of wrong and cruel constraint,
Which I your poor Vassal daily endure:
And, but your goodness the same recure,
Am like for desperate dole° to die,
Through felonious force of mine enemy."
   Greatly aghast with this piteous plea,
Him rested the goodman° on the lea,
And bade the Briar in his plaint proceed.
With painted words then 'gan this proud weed   160
(As most usen ambitious folk)
His coloured crime with craft to cloak.
   "O my sovereign, Lord of creatures all,
Thou placer of plants both humble and tall,
Was not I planted of thine own hand,
To be the primrose° of all thy land,
With flow'ring blossoms to furnish the prime,°
And scarlet berries in Summertime?
How falls it then, that this faded Oak,
Whose body is sere, whose branches broke,   170
Whose naked Arms stretch unto the fire,
Unto such tyranny doth aspire,
Hindering with his shade my lovely light,
And robbing me of the sweet sun's sight?
So beat his old boughs my tender side,
That oft the blood springeth from wounds wide:
Untimely my flowers forced to fall,
That been the honour of your coronal.°
And oft he lets his cankerworms° light
Upon my branches, to work me more spite: 180
And oft his hoary locks down doth cast,
Wherewith my fresh flowerets° been defaced.
For this, and many more such outrage,
Craving your goodlihead° to assuage
The rancorous rigour of his might,
Nought ask I, but only to hold my right:
Submitting me to your good sufferance,°
And praying to be guarded from grievance."
   To this the Oak cast him to reply
Well as he couth,° but his enemy   190
Had kindled such coals of displeasure,

° **plaint**: complaint.   ° **dole**: distress.   ° **goodman**: male head of household or farm.
° **primrose**: the first or best (rather than the flower so-named).   ° **prime**: spring.
° **coronal**: garland or crown.   ° **cankerworms**: caterpillars.   ° **flowerets**: blossoms.
° **goodlihead**: graciousness.   ° **sufferance**: sanction.   ° **couth**: could.

That the goodman nould° stay his leisure,
But home him hasted with furious heat,
Increasing his wrath with many a threat.
His harmful Hatchet he hent° in hand
(Alas, that it so ready should stand)
And to the field alone he speedeth
(Ay little help to harm there needeth).
Anger nould let him speak to the tree,
E'naunter° his rage might cooled be,
But to the root bent his sturdy stroke,
And made many wounds in the waste° oak.
The Axe's edge did oft turn again,
As half unwilling to cut the grain:
Seemed the senseless iron did fear,
Or to wrong holy eld did forbear.
For it had been an ancient tree,
Sacred with many a mystery,°
And often crossed with the priest's crue,°
And often hallowed with holy water dew.
But such fancies were foolery,
And broughten this Oak to this misery.
 For nought might they quitten° him from decay:
For fiercely the goodman at him did lay.
The block oft groaned° under the blow,
And sighed to see his near overthrow.
In fine,° the steel had pierced his pith,
Then down to the earth he fell forthwith:
His wondrous weight made the ground to quake,
Th'earth shrunk under him, and seemed to shake.
There lieth the Oak, pitied of none.
     Now stands the Briar like a Lord alone,
Puffed up with pride and vain pleasance:
But all this glee had no continuance.
For eftsoons Winter 'gan to approach,
The blust'ring Boreas° did encroach,
And beat upon the solitary Briar:
For now no succour was seen him near.
Now 'gan he repent his pride too late:

200

210

220

° **nould**: wouldn't.   ° **hent**: seized.   ° **E'naunter**: Lest that.
° **waste**: ruinous, but also suggesting barren.
° **Sacred ... mystery**: the following lines describe then-forbidden Catholic rites performed before
  "gospel oaks," which were blessed during Rogation-tide, and carved with crosses signifying they
  should not be felled. In the woodcut, Thenot the older shepherd appears to have a cross in his
  palm.
° **crue**: cruet. According to E. K., a "holy water pot, wherewith the popish priest used to sprinkle
  and hallow the trees from mischance. Such blindness was in those times, which the poet supposeth
  to have been the final decay of that ancient Oak."
° **quitten**: save.
° **block oft groaned**: E. K. commends this paradox as "a lively figure, which giveth sense and feeling
  to insensible creatures," and cites a precedent from Virgil.
° **In fine**: at last.   ° **Boreas**: north wind.

For naked left and disconsolate, 230
The biting frost nipped his stalk dead,
The watery wet weighed down his head,
And heaped snow burdened him so sore,
That now upright he can stand no more:
And being down, is trod in the dirt
Of cattle, and browsed,° and sorely hurt.
Such was th'end of this ambitious Briar,
For scorning Eld –
CUDDY Now I pray thee shepherd, tell it not forth.
Here is a long tale, and little worth. 240
So long have I listened to thy speech,
That grafted to the ground is my breech,
My heart-blood is well-nigh frorne° I feel,
And my galosh grown fast to my heel.
But little ease of thy lewd° tale I tasted.
Hie thee home shepherd, the day is nigh wasted.

ᚵ ᚵ ᚵ

° **browsed**: implying that the Briar will not be able to regenerate. Tudor timber laws forbid cattle
from entering recently felled copses, but the practice was not always enforced, and a cow is
depicted munching the Briar in the "February" woodcut.   ° **frorne**: frozen.   ° **lewd**:
crude.

WILLIAM LAWSON
[The Size and Age of Trees] (1618)

This arboricultural treatise appeared at a time of mounting concern about deforestation following the sale of Crown woods, and was reprinted several times
throughout the seventeenth century. Lawson offers a wealth of practical advice
on how to plant, graft, and extend the life of trees both for "use and adornment."
In the excerpt below he marvels at the greater-than-human size and longevity
of trees, encouraging readers to think about stewardship as a long-term enterprise. His seeking to ascertain the facts about a tree's biology through direct observation, local knowledge networks, and quantitative comparison demonstrates
how Renaissance gardening manuals, as Rebecca Bushnell has argued, often make
forays into natural history.
Source: *A New Orchard and Garden* (1618), 42–3, 49–50, 52.

What living body have you greater than of trees? The great Sea monsters
(whereof one came aland at Teesmouth in Yorkshire, hard by us, eighteen
yards in length and near as much in compass) seem hideous, huge, strange,
and monstrous because they be indeed great: but especially because they
are seldom seen. But a Tree living, come to his growth and age, twice that
length and of a bulk never so great ... is not admired because he is so commonly seen. And I doubt not but if he were well regarded from his kernel,

by succeeding ages, to his full strength, the most of them would double their measure. About fifty years ago I heard by credible and constant report that in Brougham Park° ... there lay a blown Oak whose trunk was so big that two horsemen, being the one on the one side and the other on the other side, they could not one see another. To which if you add his arms, boughs, and roots, and consider of his bigness, what would he have been if preserved to the vantage?° Also I read in *The History of the West Indians*, out of Peter Martyr,° that sixteen men taking hands one with another, were not able to fathom one of those trees about.

Now Nature having given to such a faculty by large and infinite roots, taws,° and tangles, to draw immediately his sustenance from our common mother the Earth (which is like in this point to all other mothers that bear) hath also ordained that the tree overloaded with fruit and wanting sap to feed all she hath brought forth, will wean all she cannot feed, like a woman bringing forth more children at once than she hath teats. See you not how trees especially, by kind being great, standing so thick and close that they cannot get plenty of sap, pine away all the grass, weeds, lesser shrubs and trees – yea, and themselves also for want of vigour of sap? ...

[43] This is one of the chief causes why so many of our Orchards in England are so evil-thriving when they come to growth, and our fruit so bad. Men are loath to bestow much ground and desire much fruit, and will neither set their trees in sufficient compass, nor yet feed them with manure. Therefore of necessity Orchards must be foiled° ...

[49] All this Treatise of Trees tends to this end: that men may love and plant Orchards, whereunto there cannot be a better inducement than that they know ... that all that benefit they shall reap thereby, whether of pleasure or profit, shall not be for a day or a month, or one, or many, but many hundred years ...

I have apple trees standing in my little Orchard ... whose age ... I have inquired of diverse aged men eighty years and upwards ... [50] I assure myself they are not come to their growth by more than two parts of three, which I discern not only by their own growth but also by comparing them with the bulk of other trees ... If my trees be 100 years old, and yet want 200 of their growth before they leave increasing, which makes 300, then we must needs resolve that these 300 years are but the third part of a tree's life: because (as all things living besides) trees must have allowed them for their increase one third, another third for their stand, and a third part of time also for their decay.° All which time of a tree amounts to 900 years ...

° **Broughham Park**: possibly one of the "Three Brethern" – large oaks trees in Whinfell Forest, one of which still stood in 1698 when Celia Fiennes visited and noted its thirteen-yard circumference.
° **to ... vantage**: i.e. longer.
° **Peter Martyr**: Italian historian of Spanish exploration in South America. See his *Decades of the New World* (1555), 194.   ° **taws**: root-fibres.   ° **foiled**: fertilized.
° **one third ... decay**: a common belief in early modern biology derived from Aristotle. Lawson overestimates the apple tree's life-span, which is typically closer to 100 years.

[52] And if fruit-trees last to this age, how many ages is it to be supposed strong and huge timber-trees will last, whose huge bodies require the years of diverse Methuselahs° before they end their days?

❧ ❧ ❧

° **Methuselah**: biblical patriarch reported to have lived 969 years.

WILLIAM STRODE
"On a Great Hollow Tree"° (*c.* 1634)

The fact that early modern England experienced such rapid historical change helps explain why old trees, survivors of a bygone era and symbols of decayed nobility, attracted poets like they did wood-boring pests. Fascinated by its greater-than-human life-span, Strode views the tree as a repository of cultural memory, a portal to the mythological past and a Merry Old England under threat in the run-up to the Civil War. In its veneration for the elm's size and antiquity, the poem anticipates Cowper's "Yardley Oak." Sadly, the elm trees that towered over the early modern English landscape are now almost gone. In the 1970s, Dutch elm disease wiped out an estimated 25 million of them. Although the English elm was itself likely imported by the Romans, Strode's tribute now seems both a meditation on ecological continuity and a reminder of its fragility.
Source: British Library, Sloane MS 1792, 89ᵛ–91ʳ, with emendations from Corpus Christi College, Oxford, MS 325, 60ᵛ–1ᵛ and Rosenbach 243/4 136–39.

> Prithee stand still awhile and view this Tree,
> Renowned and honoured for antiquity°
> By all the neighbour twigs; for such are all
> The Trees adjoining, be they ne'er so tall,
> Compared to this. If here Jack° Maypole stood,
> All men would swear 'twere but a fishing rod.
> Mark but the giant trunk, which when you see,
> Then think° how many woods and groves there be
> Comprised within one Elm. The hardy stock
> Is knotted like a Club: and who dares mock   10
> His strength by shaking it? Each brawny limb
> Could° pose° the Centaur Monychus,° or him

° **Tree**: MS 325 (CC) includes a subtitle, "Westwell Elm." Bodleian MS Eng. Poet e. 97 gives the title as "On An Old Decayed Vast Hollow Tree," while Rosenbach MS 243/4 is even more precise: "Upon Westwell great-Elm, standing at good-man Berry's gate, at the Farm; within two miles of Burford in Oxfordshire; being the drinking-Tree at Whitsuntide."
° **antiquity**: in CC struck through and replaced with "majority."
° **Jack**: in CC struck through and replaced with "the."   ° **Then think**: CC; Look but] Sloane.
° **Could**: Sloane; Would] CC.   ° **pose**: confound.
° **Monychus**: See Ovid, *Metamorphoses*, 12.499.

That waved a hundred hands,° ere he could wield
That sturdy weight, whose large extent can shield°
A poor man's tenement. Great Ceres' Oak,
Which Erysichthon° felled, could not provoke
Half so much hunger for his punishment
As hewing this would do by consequent.
    Nothing but Age could tame it; Age came on,
20   And lo, a lingering consumption
Devoured the entrails, where a hollow cave
Without the workman's help began to have
The figure of a Tent, a pretty Cell,
Where grand Silenus° might not scorn to dwell,
And Owls might fear to harbour, though they brought
Minerva's° warrant so to bear them out
In this their bold attempt. Look down into
The twisted curls, the wreathing to and fro
Contrived by nature, where you may descry
30   How Hall and Parlour, how the Chambers lie.
And wer't not strange to see men stand alone
On legs of skin without the flesh or bone?
Or that the selfsame creature should survive
After the heart° is dead? This tree can thrive
Thus maimed and thus impaired;° no other prop
But only bark remains to keep it up.
Yet thus supported it doth firmly stand,
Scorning the sawpit, though so near at hand.
No yawning grave this grandsire Elm can fright,
40   Whilst youngling Trees are martyred in his sight.
O, learn from nature such thrift that maintains,°
With needy mire° stol'n up in hidden veins,
So main° a bulk of wood. Three columns rest
Upon that rotten trunk, whereof the least
Were mast for Argo.° Th'open bark below
And three long legs alone do make it show
Like a huge Trivet° or a monstrous chair,
With th'heels turned upward. How proper, oh how fair°
A seat were this for old Diogenes°
50   To grumble in and bark out oracles!
There might a Druid harp his prophecy,
And answer to the Raven's augury

° **him … hands**: the titan Briareus.
° **shield**: CC; shade] Sloane.
° **Erysichthon**: Thessalonian king who cut down a grove of oaks sacred to Ceres and was punished
  with insatiable hunger. See selections from Lyly, Drayton, and Aubrey in Part v.
° **Silenus**: forest spirit, usually portrayed as a drunken old man with the legs and ears of a horse.
° **Minerva**: Roman goddess of learning, to whom owls were sacred.
° **heart**: with wordplay on heartwood.   ° **impaired**: Rosenbach; marred] Sloane, CC.
° **O … maintains**: Sloane; O learn the thrift of nature as maintains] CC.
° **mire**: Sloane; juice] CC.   ° **main**: mighty.
° **Argo**: legendary ship of Jason and the Argonauts.   ° **Trivet**: tripod.
° **fair**: Sloane; rare] CC.   ° **Diogenes**: Cynic philosopher who lived in a wooden tub.

That builds above. Why grew not this strange tree
Near Delphos?° Had his wooden Majesty
Stood in Dodona° forest, then would Jove
Forgo his Oak and only this approve.
Had those old Germans° who did once admire
Deformèd groves and (worshipping with fire)
Burnt Men unto their Gods,° had they but seen
These hornèd stumps, they° canonized had been,   60
And highly too. This Tree would calve° more Gods
Than they had men to sacrifice by odds.°
You Hamadryads,° that wood-born be,
Tell me the causes how this portly tree
Grew to this haughty stature: was it then
Because the mummies° of new-buried° men
Fattened the ground? Or 'cause the neighbour spring
Conduits of moisture to the root did bring?   70
Was it with Whitsun sweat° or ample snuffs°
Of my Lord's beer that such a bigness stuffs
And breaks the bark? O this is it no doubt!
This Tree I warrant you can number out
Your Westwell Annals and distinctly tell
The progress of these hundred years as well
By Lords and Ladies as ere Rome could do
By Consulships. These boughs can witness too
How Goodman Berry tripped it in his youth,
And how his daughter Joan of late, forsooth,
Became her place. It° might as well have grown,   80
If Pan had pleased, atop of Westwell Down
Instead of that proud Ash, and easily
Have given aim to travellers° passing by
With wider arms. But see it more desired
Here to be loved at home than there admired;°
And here it porter-like defends the gate,
As if it once had been great Ascapate.°
Had war-like Arthur's days enjoyed this Elm,
Sir Tristram's blade and good Sir Lancelot's helm
Had then bedecked his locks with fertile store   90
Of votive relics which those Champions wore,
Until perhaps (as 'tis with great men found)
Those burd'nous honours crushed it to the ground.
But in these merry times 'twere far more trim°

° **Delphos**: site of temple and oracle dedicated to Apollo.   ° **Dodona**: grove of oaks sacred to Jove.
° **Germans**: the Roman historian Tacitus reports that Germanic tribes worshiped in groves and
  practised human sacrifice.   ° **Burnt ... Gods**: The manuscripts read "Gods unto their gods".
° **These ... they**: Sloane; This horned stump, it] Rosenbach.
° **calve**: CC, Rosenbach; claim] Sloane.   ° **by odds**: by far.
° **Hamadryads**: forest spirits who dwelt inside trees.   ° **mummies**: Sloane; mummy] CC.
° **new-buried**: CC; so many] Sloane.
° **Whitsun sweat**: dancing under trees was a custom during Church ales on Whitsunday.
° **snuffs**: gulps.   ° **It**: CC; That] Sloane.   ° **travellers**: CC; strangers] Rosenbach.
° **admired**: CC ends here.
° **Ascapate**: giant defeated by the legendary Sir Bevis of Southampton.   ° **trim**: apt.

If pipes and citterns hung on every limb;
And since the fiddlers it hath heard so long,
I'm sure by this time it deserves my song.

꙾ ꙾ ꙾

ROBERT HERRICK

"The Willow Tree," "The Vine," "Parliament of Roses to Julia," and "Divination by a Daffodil" (1648)

Renaissance culture invested plants with symbolic properties based on their biological characteristics. Since the willow's branches hang downward, the sympathetic imagination saw it as weeping, and rejected or grieving lovers sought refuge in its shade or wore its leaves as a badge (cf. Ophelia's death, and the "Willow Song" in *Othello*). Although indebted to Ovid, "The Vine" presents an original and highly disturbing dream vision of the sexual assault of a woman by a plant. The next poem hinges upon the associations of the rose (a symbol of the Tudors) with both royalty and femininity. In contrast, "Divination by a Daffodil" strikes a more sombre tone. As one of the first plants to sprout in late winter, the daffodil offered a symbol for the soul's resurrection, but Herrick's later poem "To Daffodils" concludes that everything in nature dies (humans included) "ne'er to be found again" (144).
Source: *Hesperides* (1648), 120, 14, 4–5, 40.

"The Willow Tree"

Thou art to all lost love the best,
The only true plant found,
Wherewith young men and maids distressed
And left of love are crowned.

When once the Lover's Rose is dead,
Or laid aside forlorn,
Then Willow-garlands 'bout the head
Bedewed with tears are worn.

10 When with Neglect (the Lover's bane)
Poor Maids rewarded be,
For their love lost, their only gain
Is but a Wreath from thee.

And underneath thy cooling shade,
When weary of the light,
The love-spent Youth and love-sick Maid
Come to weep out the night.

"The Vine"

I dreamt this mortal part of mine
Was Metamorphosed to a Vine,
Which crawling one and every way,
Enthralled my dainty Lucia.
Methought her long small legs and thighs
I with my Tendrils did surprise;
Her Belly, Buttocks, and her Waist
By my soft Nervelets were embraced.
About her head I writhing hung,
And with rich clusters (hid among   10
The leaves) her temples I behung,
So that my Lucia seemed to me
Young Bacchus° ravished by his tree.
My curls about her neck did crawl,
And arms and hands they did enthral,
So that she could not freely stir
(All parts there made one prisoner).
But when I crept with leaves to hide
Those parts, which maids keep unespied,
Such fleeting pleasures there I took   20
That with the fancy I awoke,
And found (Ah me!) this flesh of mine
More like a Stock° than like a Vine.

"Parliament of Roses to Julia"

I dreamt the Roses one time went
To meet and sit in Parliament:
The place for these and for the rest
Of flowers, was thy spotless breast:
Over the which a State° was drawn
Of Tiffany, or Cobweb Lawn;°
Then in that Parly, all those powers
Voted the Rose the Queen of flowers.
But so, as that herself should be
The maid of Honour unto thee.

"Divination by a Daffodil"

When a Daffodil I see,
Hanging down his head towards me,
Guess I may what I must be:

° **Bacchus**: god of wine, enamoured with the nymphs Syke and Staphilis, who were transformed
into the fig tree and vine, respectively.   ° **Stock**: tree-trunk or wooden log.
° **State**: canopy.   ° **Tiffany … Cobweb Lawn**: fine, transparent linens.

First, I shall decline my head;
Secondly, I shall be dead;
Lastly, safely burièd.

⁂

ANONYMOUS

[The Crab-tree's Lament] (1558)

This poem appears in a manuscript that may have belonged to the Tudor minstrel,
Richard Sheale of Tamworth. Read allegorically, it could be a lament for the plight
of poor vagrants, with whom a wandering harper like Sheale would have sympathized. On a literal level, however, the poem conducts a quaint dispute between a
talking tree and nature, in which the former ironically articulates an anthropocentric opinion: if the crab-tree, which imagines its trunk as a disabled arboreal body
(like Richard III), has no purpose, why was it created? This anxiety lingers, despite
the tree's attempt to soften the charge by demonstrating the use of crab-apples to
make verjuice, a common vinegar-like ingredient in Renaissance cookery.
Source: MS Ashmole 48, 102ᵛ–103ʳ.

First when thou, nature, all things brought to pass,
To every herb and tree thou granted virtue and courage:°
What did I offend, poor crab-tree, alas,
Crooked and deformed, to be set in every hedge?

Not only I am depraved° of my shape,
But nature also my fruit hath so soured,
That I am disdained for mine unhap,°
And here set in the way of beasts to be devoured.

Where other pleasant trees bearing fruit do abide,
10   With the olive, cypress, juniper or bay,
For my crooked shape in the hedge I me hide,
My fruit blown down and trodden in the way.

Crooked I am, not fair, large, nor straight,
And ever excluded where other do remain.
To beasts wild, most common food and bait;
I, disfigured tree, whom all men do disdain.

The orange, the lemon, the grenade° also,
The damson, the pear, and eke the cherry round,
Endowed be with virtue, so be other mo;°
20   Only I am barren, wherein no goodness does abound.°

° **courage**: vitality.   ° **depraved**: degenerate, but spelling "depreved" could imply deprived.
° **unhap**: misfortune.   ° **grenade**: pomegranate.   ° **mo**: more.
° **abound**: on the bottom of 102v, the scribe began a new stanza with the words "But in me, poor
crab-tree."

On me there hangs neither pleasant leaf nor bark,
Nor fruit, also greatly to be desired;
Save my crooked knobs to sustain age old and stark,
My fruit to make verjuice, and my body to be fired.

Birds in me to breed they do me clean° refuse,
By the way I stand most commonly on the plain.
No man of me is glad but such as cannot choose,
When greedy hunger to eat dost them constrain.

If any man in an unhappy hour
Does again of my fruit unwarily to assay,   30
What a frowning face on me does he lour,
And in hasty rage and fume does cast me way!

Since that to profit of nothing I serve,
For mine unsavoury taste no man does me desire,
Mine unpleasant fruit, even as it does deserve,
I bequeath to the mortar and my body to the fire.

Thus I, Jack Sauce, do make my last will,
Poor Crabtree, I mean, by interpretation;
When the tanner° hath ground my fruit in his mill,
I bequeath my liquor to the whole congregation.   40

When my body is dead and laid in grave,
I desire all cooks for me to pray,
For in their custody my liquor they have,
For to serve their turn both night and day.

ॐ ॐ ॐ

° **clean**: entirely.
° **tanner**: tanners ground tree bark to tan leather, and their mills could also be used to grind apples.

WILLIAM TURNER
"Orobanche" (1568)

The first illustrated English herbal, the self-titled *Great Herbal* of 1526, was actually a translation of a French text from 1498. This work, in turn, was the product of a long medieval tradition mingling Greco-Roman science, Arab medicine, and occult lore. Whereas the Tudor scholars who could read learned works on botany had little first-hand experience with plants, the herb-women and apothecaries who did possess practical knowledge were not fluent in Greek or Latin. The first great English botanist to bridge these camps was William Turner, whose 1551 *New Herbal* pioneered a more empirical approach. As he writes in the preface to the 1568 edition, because I would not be like unto a crier that cryeth a lost horse in the market and telleth all the marks and tokens that he hath and yet never saw the horse, nether could know the horse if he saw him, I went into Italy and into diverse parts of Germany to know and see the herbs myself, and to know by practise their powers and working: not trusting only to the old herb wives and apothecaries (as many physicians have done of late years) but, in the matter of simples, mine own eyes and knowledge (3v).

As a result of his travels, reading, and tireless fieldwork, Turner identified nearly 300 species of plant not previously known. His zeal for fact can be gauged from his courageously digging up mandrakes to test the legend that they emitted a fatal shriek when uprooted. The extract below is a description of a parasitic plant now known as broomrape. It is noteworthy for its subtle assault on pre-Reformation folklore about plants, its methodical observation, and for its unflinching depiction of the plant world as a realm of strife.
Source: *Herbal* (1568), 71ᵛ, with emendations from 1551 (P5ʳ) to showcase Turner's self-revision.

I have no common English name for this herb, neither any French or Dutch name. Howbeit, it may be called in English Chokefitch or Chokeweed. Orobanche hath the name in Greek of strangling or choking of bitter fitches, which are called in Greek "*Oroboy*." This herb is called about Morpeth° in Northumberland New Chapel Flower, because it grew in a chapel there in a place called Bottlebanks,° where the unlearned people did worship the image of Saint Mary and reckoned that the herb grew in that place by virtue of that image.°

Orobanche, as Dioscorides° writeth, is a reddish stalk two spans high and sometimes higher; tender, rough, without any leaf, [yet] with a flower something whitish but turning toward yellow. The root is a finger thick. And when the stalk shrinketh for dryness it is like a hollow pipe. It is plain that this herb groweth among certain pulses, and that it choketh and strangleth them, whereof it hath the name of Orobanche, that is Chokefitch or Strangletare. Thus far Dioscorides … The herb which I have taken and taught fifteen years ago° to be Orobanche, which also now of late years Matthiolus° hath set out for Orobanche, groweth in many places of England, both in the north country beside Morpeth, where it is called Our Lady of New Chapel's Flower, and also in the south country a little from sheaves in the broom closes. But it hath no name there. I have seen it in diverse places of Germany, and first of all between Cologne and

---

° **Morpeth**: Turner's hometown.   ° **Bottlebanks**: present-day Bothal.
° **I have … image**: This paragraph is from the 1551 edition. As a zealous Protestant, Turner was eager to squash out such superstitions and replace Catholic-tainted nomenclature. See also John Parkinson's commentary on and illustrations of the passion fruit in *Paradisi in Sole* (1629, 394–6).
° **Dioscorides**: Ancient Greek naturalist.
° **fifteen years ago**: in the 1551 edition (actually seventeen by the time of publication).
° **Mattholius**: Matthias de L'Obel, Flemish botanist-physician who settled in England.

Rodenkirchen. The herb is commonly a foot long and oft longer. I have marked it many years but I could never see any leaf upon it. But I have seen the flowers in diverse places of diverse colours, and for the most part wheresoever I saw them they were reddish or turning to a purple colour in some places. But in figure they were like unto the flowers of Clary,° with a thing in them representing a cock's head. The root is round and much after the fashion of a great leek's head, and there grow out of it certain long things like strings which have in them in certain places sharp things like teeth,° wherewith it claspeth and holdeth the root that it strangleth. I have found it oft-times clasping and holding marvellously soft the roots of broom, so that they looked as they had been bound folded oft about with small wire. And once I found this herb growing beside the common clover or meadow trefoil, which was all withered; and when I had dug up the root of the trefoil to see what should be the cause that all other clovers or trefoils about were green and fresh [while] that trefoil should be dead, I found the roots of Orobanche fast clasped about the roots of the clover, which as I did plainly perceive drew out all the natural moisture from the herb that it should have lived withal and so killed it.

ᴥ ᴥ ᴥ

° **Clary**: also known as wild sage, or *Salvia verbenaca*. Its name is a contraction of "clear-eye," revealing its medicinal use.
° **like teeth**: 1568; like a dog holding a bone in his mouth. Notwithstanding, I have not seen any broom choked with this herb] 1551.

JOHN GERARD
The Herbal (1597)

The literally ground-breaking monograph of William Turner would at the century's end be displaced by the encyclopaedic tome of John Gerard. Although it is often called "Gerard's Herbal," that title is misleading: much of its content was in fact "gathered" (i.e. copied without attribution, mainly from Matthias de L'Obel and Rembert Dodoens). Nevertheless, Gerard was an experienced gardener, having worked for twenty years in the extensive show-gardens of William Cecil, the Lord Treasurer (to whom he dedicates the book). Gerard's unscrupulous borrowings are understandable if not forgivable, given the superhuman scope of the undertaking. He includes entries for thirty varieties of tulip alone (introduced to Europe in the 1570s), twelve kinds of daffodil, ten irises, sixteen roses, and fifteen cherries. He was also interested in transplanting exotics to England, and his book includes some of the earliest references to hyacinths, sunflowers, and the potato (recently imported from America). Gerard's preface lays greater stress on the aesthetic beauty of plants in comparison to earlier herbals, but still maintains

a religious sensibility that regards the medicinal properties of plants as a sign of the benevolence of a divinely created nature.
Source: *Herbal* (1597), A2^{r-v}, B3^{r}.

Among the manifold creatures of God … that have all in all ages diversely entertained many excellent wits and drawn them to the contemplation of the divine wisdom, none have provoked men's studies more or satisfied their desires so much as plants have done: and that upon just and worthy causes. For if delight may provoke men's labour, what greater delight is there than to behold the earth apparelled with plants, as with a robe of embroidered work, set with orient pearls, and garnished with great diversity of rare and costly jewels? If this variety and perfection of colours may affect the eye, it is such in herbs and flowers that no Apelles nor Zeuxis° ever could by any art express the like. If odours or if taste may work satisfaction, they are both so sovereign in plants (and so comfortable) that no confection of the apothecaries can equal their excellent virtue. But these delights are in the outward senses. The principal delight is in the mind, singularly enriched with the knowledge of these visible things setting forth to us the invisible wisdom and admirable workmanship of almighty God. The delight is great, but the use greater, and joined often with necessity. In the first ages of the world they were the ordinary meat° of men, and have continued ever since of necessary use both for meats to maintain life and for medicine to recover health. The hidden virtue of them is such that (as Pliny° noteth) [A2^{v}] the very brute beasts have found it out, and (which is another use that he observes) from thence the dyers took the beginning of their art.

Furthermore, the necessary use of these fruits of the earth doth plainly appear by the great charge and care of almost all men in planting and maintaining of gardens, not as ornaments only but as a necessary provision also to their houses. And here beside the fruit, to speak again in a word of delight, gardens (especially such as your Honour° hath) furnished with many rare simples do singularly delight when in them a man doth behold a flourishing show of summer beauties in the midst of winter's force, and a goodly spring of flowers when abroad a leaf is not to be seen.

Besides these and other causes there are many examples of those that have honoured this science. For to pass by a multitude of the philosophers, it may please your Honour to call to remembrance that which you know of some noble princes that have joined this study with their most important matters of state: Mithridates° … Evax° … and Diocletian° … The example of

---

° **Apelles … Zeuxis**: Famous painters in ancient Greece.
° **meat**: food.   ° **Pliny**: Roman naturalist (see *Natural History*, 8.27, 22.2).
° **Honour**: William Cecil, Lord Burghley, who employed Gerard as a gardener on his country estates, and to whom the dedicatory epistle is addressed.
° **Mithridates (VI)**: Pontian emperor, famed for concocting a herbal antidote for poison.
° **Evax**: legendary Arabian king credited with writing a book on the magical properties of stones.
° **Diocletian**: Roman emperor, who cultivated large gardens after his abdication.

Solomon° is before the rest and greater, whose wisdom and knowledge was such that he was able to set out the nature of all plants from the highest Cedar to the lowest Moss ...

To the large and singular furniture° of this noble Island I have added from foreign places all the variety of herbs and flowers that I might any way obtain; I have laboured with the soil to make it fit for plants, and with the plants, that they might delight in the soil, that so they might live and prosper under our climate, as in their native and proper country. What my success hath been, and what my furniture° is, I leave to the report of them that have seen your Lordship's gardens, and the little plot of mine own especial care and husbandry. But because gardens are private and (many times finding an ignorant or a negligent successor) come soon to ruin, there be that have solicited me ... to make my labours common,° and to free them from the danger whereunto a garden is subject ...

"In commendation of John Gerard, for his diligence in simpling,°by W. Westerman"°

Our mother Earth possessed with woman's pride,
Perceiving Gerard to be beauty's judge,
And that her treasure is not unespied,
Of her fair flowering brats she is no snudge:°
But here and there where Gerard loves to trudge,
Her verdant mantle spreading round about,
She boasts the pleasance of her goodly rout.°

They all take Gerard for chief friend of theirs,
To whom they frame a garland for a sign
Of that pure love, which each to other bears.
O, let the red Rose and the Eglantine,°
Vouchsafe their presence in his garland twine;
Let those fair flowers of our English field,
Unwithered long their fragrant odours yield.

☙ ☙ ☙

° **Solomon**: ancient Jewish king, reputed to have written a book describing every variety of plant.
° **furniture**: provision (i.e. native plants).   ° **furniture**: accomplishment.
° **common**: public.   ° **simpling**: gathering herbs.
° **Westerman**: William Westerman, vicar of Sandridge. The first three stanzas, insisting on the superiority of botany to astronomy, have been omitted.   ° **snudge**: miser.
° **rout**: assembly.
° **Rose ... Eglantine**: flowers associated with Queen Elizabeth, worn on her Accession Day.

JOHN DONNE
[The Mandrake] (1601)

Donne's *Progress of the Soul* seizes on the Pythagorean theory of transmigration or metempsychosis to imagine the journey of a single soul as it passes through a sparrow, a fish, a whale, a mouse, a wolf, a wolf-dog mix, an ape, and Cain's wife. In his preface, Donne reminds the reader that the soul might be reborn not only in an animal body but also in a plant. Did Donne write it merely as a youthful exercise in Ovidianism gone wild? Or does its joco-serious tone disguise its sobering message about ecological reciprocity among various organisms that feed upon or breed with one other? The Chain of Being proves to be not a tidy hierarchy but a hopeless tangle. In the following extract, the soul passes from the apple that tempted Eve into a mandrake. Due to the uncanny resemblance between its bifurcated root and human anatomy, this plant was a magnet for superstitions: that they sprouted from the sperm or menstrual blood of hanged criminals, and shrieked when uprooted. The herbalist William Turner reports in the 1560s that mandrake roots resembling "puppets" (with faces and hair) were sold in England at fairs, but dismisses them as "feigned trifles and not natural," carved by "crafty thieves to mock the poor people withal, and to rob them both of their wit and their money" (46ʳ) (see Figure 3). Whereas Gerard, too, debunks these "ridiculous tales," Donne revives them and finds the mandrake a fascinating nexus between humans and plants.
Source: *Poems* (1633), 8–9.

> The plant thus abled to itself did force
> A place, where no place was; by nature's course,
> As air from water, water fleets° away
> From thicker bodies, by this root thronged° so,
> His spongy confines gave him place to grow;
> Just as in our streets when the people stay
> To see the Prince, and so fill up the way
> That weasels scarce could pass, when she comes near
> They throng and cleave up,° and a passage clear,
140   As if for that time their round bodies flattened were.
>
> His right arm he thrust out towards the East,
> Westward his left; th'ends did themselves digest°
> Into ten lesser strings: these fingers were;
> And as a slumb'rer stretching on his bed,
> This way he this, and that way scatterèd
> His other leg, which feet with toes upbear;
> Grew on his middle parts,° the first day, hair,
> To show that in love's business he should still
> A dealer be, and be used well or ill:
150   His apples kindle,° his leaves force of conception kill.°

° **fleets**: evaporates.   ° **thronged**: squeezed.   ° **cleave up**: cling together.
° **digest**: divide.   ° **parts**: part] 1635.   ° **kindle**: 1635; kind] 1633.
° **His apples ... kill**: while the fruit was believed to be an aphrodisiac, the leaves were rumoured to induce miscarriage. All parts of the mandrake are in fact toxic in large doses, which explains their reputed power to cause madness.

A mouth, but dumb, he hath: blind eyes, deaf ears;
And to his shoulders dangle subtle hairs;
A young Colossus° there he stands upright;
And as that ground by him were conquerèd,
A leafy garland wears he on his head,
Enchased with little fruits, so red and bright
That for them you would call your love's lips white;
So, of a lone unhaunted place possessed,
Did this soul's second inn, built by the guest,
This living buried man, this quiet mandrake, rest.   160

No lustful woman came this plant to grieve,
But 'twas because there was not yet but Eve;
And she (with other purpose) killed it quite.
Her sin had now brought in infirmities,
And so her cradled child the moist-red eyes
Had never shut, nor slept since it saw light.
Poppy she knew, she knew the mandrake's might,
And tore up both, and so cooled her child's blood.°
Unvirtuous weeds might long unvexed have stood,
But he's short-lived that with his death can do most good.   170

❧ ❧ ❧

° **Colossus**: giant statue at Rhodes, one of the Seven Wonders of the ancient world.
° **Poppy ... blood**: poppy and mandrake are soporifics and were used to alleviate fevers.

JOHN HEYWOOD
"A Rose and A Nettle" (1550)

The Aesopian fable should not be categorized as Renaissance nature writing but is chiefly a form of moral philosophy for the masses. The following example by Heywood proffers a typical warning about social upstarts and the dangers of low company. Nevertheless, its curiosity about whether plants might alter the nature of their neighbours attests to Renaissance interest in plant "sympathy," or what we would now call biodynamics. In fact, the rhizomatic nettle forages on a coarse scale while the rose's taproot draws nutrients intensively from a smaller area, allowing the two species to co-exist. If Heywood's poem is primarily a satire on social climbers at the Tudor court, it also registers anxiety about the slipperiness of the Chain of Being, and the tendency of so-called weeds to outcompete flowers and herbs.
Source: *A Hundred Epigrams* (1550), B4^{r-v}.

What time herbs and weeds and such things could talk,
A man in his garden one day did walk,
Spying a nettle green as th'Emerald spread,
In a bed of roses like the Ruby red.°
Between which two colours, he thought by his eye,
The green nettle did the red rose beautify.
Howbeit, he asked the nettle what thing
Made him so pert,° so nigh the rose to spring.
"I plant me with these roses," said the nettle,
"Their mild properties in me to settle;
And you, in laying unto me your nose,
Shall smell how a nettle may change to a rose."

He did so: which done, his nostrils so pritched°
That rashly he rubbed, where it no whit itched;
To which smart° mock and wily beguiling,
He the same smelling, said smoothly smiling:
"Roses convert nettles? Nay, they be too fell;°
Nettles will pervert roses rather, I smell."

10

꩜ ꩜ ꩜

° **red**: a small white rose superimposed upon a large red one (with green petals around the edges)
   was a symbol of the Tudor dynasty.
° **pert**: impertinent, presumptuous.   ° **pritched**: prickled.   ° **smart**: painful, clever.
° **fell**: vigorous, savage.

FRANCIS BACON
"Sympathy and Antipathy of Plants" (*c.* 1625)

Experienced gardeners observed that the growth of plants could be affected by
their proximity to other species. Bacon's denial that this amounts to "sympathy"
or "antipathy" is in keeping with his assault on animism as magical thinking.
However, his analysis does suggest a rudimentary understanding of ecological dynamics, and botanists today are again studying how plants "communicate" with
each other via chemicals.
Source: *Sylva Sylvarum* (1627), 123–4.

There are many ancient and received traditions and observations touching
the Sympathy and Antipathy of Plants: [124] ... that some will thrive best
growing near others, which they impute to Sympathy, and some worse,
which they impute to Antipathy. But these are idle and ignorant conceits,
and forsake the true indication of the causes, as the most part of experiments that concern Sympathies and Antipathies do. For as to Plants, neither is there any such secret friendship or hatred as they imagine. And if we
should be content to call it Sympathy and Antipathy, it is utterly mistaken;
for their Sympathy is an Antipathy, and their Antipathy is a Sympathy. For

it is thus: wheresoever one Plant draweth such a particular juice out of the Earth, as it qualifieth the Earth, so as that juice which remaineth is fit for the other Plant, there the neighbourhood doth good because the nourishments are contrary or several. But where two Plants draw much the same juice, there the neighbourhood hurteth. For the one deceiveth the other ...

Where Plants are of several natures and draw several juices out of the Earth, there (as hath been said) the one set by the other helpeth. As it is set down by diverse of the Ancients that rue doth prosper much and becometh stronger if it be set by a Fig tree, which, we conceive, is caused not by reason of friendship, but by extraction of a contrary juice: the one drawing juice fit to result sweet, the other bitter. So they have set down likewise that a Rose set by Garlic is sweeter, which likewise may be because the more fetid juice of the Earth goeth into the Garlic and the more odorate into the Rose.

ૐ ૐ ૐ

Gems, Metals, Elements, Atoms
JOHN MAPLET
"Sovereign Virtues in Stones" (1567)

Despite being the first work in English to label itself "natural history," Maplet's *Green Forest* is a fantastic compendium of residual medieval beliefs in the occult qualities of metals, stones, plants, and animals. Like many Tudor texts that seek to impose order on the natural world, it adheres to a taxonomy based on human-centred valuations of degree or rank. In the section devoted to minerals and stones, Maplet divides them into three varieties: base, common, and precious. The last of these three were known as gems and endowed with magical properties. The nickname he gives to even the base variety, "hurtfoot," hints at the fact that Elizabethans did not regard stones and minerals as entirely inert, but as living creatures with a "vegetable soul," although this was already being denied in France when Maplet's book appeared.

Source: *A Green Forest* (1567) 1ᵛ–2ʳ, 4ᵛ–5ᵛ, 8ʳ, 9ᵛ–10ʳ, 16ʳ, 18ʳ–19ʳ.

Of Amethyst

The Amethyst also groweth in India. It is Prince among those Gems that be Purple-coloured ... His force [2ʳ] or virtue availeth against drunkenness. It keepeth a man waking, and driveth away ill cogitations and thoughts, [and] sharpeneth the understanding ...

[4ᵛ] Of Coral

The Coral groweth in the Red Sea, and so long as it is and hath his being in the waters, it is a kind of Wood. But by and by after that it is taken forth of the water and cometh into the air ... it hardeneth and becometh a stone. ... Isidore ... reports that it resisteth lightnings° ... [5ʳ] They say that it is of power to rid us from all devilish dreams and peevish fantasies ...

[5ᵛ] Of the Diamond

The Diamond is one of those that be counted something precious. It is in colour almost Crystal-like, but somewhat more resplendishing, and is as good (if it be of any bigness) as a looking glass. Jorach° calleth it another eye, such certainty and truth giveth it in things done in his presence ...

° **Isidore ... lightnings**: see Isidore of Seville's *Etymologies*, 16.
° **Jorach**: ancient author of works (now lost) on natural history.

[6ᵛ] Of Echites°

Echites is a stone both of India and Persia ... It is in colour violet-like. And there is a pair of them, male and female, and be most commonly found both together in the Eagle's nest, without the which the Eagle cannot bring forth her young ... These stones, bound to a woman's body, being with child, do hasten childbirth.° And Jorach saith that if any man have ... one of these and put it under that man's meat or trencher° that he suspecteth to be in fault of anything, if that he be guilty, he shall not be able through this to swallow down his meat ...

[8ʳ] Of Gagates°

It being left in the place where Serpents breed driveth them clean away. And Dioscorides° saith that this being put into the drink of a Maid or Virgin will easily give you judgement whether that she be a true and right Maid, yea or no. For, saith he, after that she hath drunk of this and doth not anon after make water° ... then take her and esteem her a pure Virgin. And, contrariwise, if she do not continue and stay herein some season, judge of her otherwise ...

[9ᵛ] Of Gold

Gold is the head of all other Metals, and is in the chiefest degree that Nature instituted Metals by ripeness and perfection at the last to come unto. But even as by stops and lets, partly by such imbecility as is within us and about us, partly by envious and clean contrary disposition of the Air and Planets in their Orbs ... we be many of us cut off before we come to old age, the last degree of Nature ... so there is order and ways to order in all Metals: from the first to the last, from the most vile and base to the most precious and richest. Which kind of order and degree every Metal, although it were of the rawest and basest sort, should attain to in his due time were it not for impediments and hindrances, either of cold and barren ground, or for lack of the Sun his purifying and ripening, or for infection of rusty and copperous Minerals being nigh neighbour to them ... [10ʳ] There is nothing to look to so beautiful as this, neither is there anything so pure. The Physicians say that it comforteth and expelleth all superfluities in the body, and is effectual against the Leprosy. Likewise his leaf° buried in wine maketh it available° against diseases and consumption of the Spleen, and other perturbations Melancholic.

° **Echites**: aetites, also know as eaglestones.
° **childbirth**: aetite has a hollow cavity with a loose pebble inside, and so was considered analogous to the womb.
° **trencher**: plate.   ° **Gagates**: jet.   ° **Dioscorides**: ancient Greek botanist and physician.
° **make water**: urinate.   ° **leaf**: gold leaf.   ° **available**: effective.

[16ʳ] Of Nesorpora or Toadstone

Nesorpora is a stone of Pontus,° very precious, marvellous white, and as they say, it is found in a Toad's head, out of the which it is plucked and taken forth, and is purified by lying a certain space steeping in strong wines and running water, as Dioscorides beareth witness. In this stone is apparently seen very often the very form of a Toad, with bespotted and coloured feet, but those ugly and diffusedly. It is available against envenoming …

[18ʳ] Of the Ruby

The Ruby is a stone which of some is supposed to be found in the Crab's head, most commonly red, yet notwithstanding sometimes found in yellow colour. It availeth against the biting of the Scorpion and Weasel if it be applied thereto plaster-like …

[18ᵛ] Of the Sapphire

The Sapphire is Sky-coloured or blue … It is one of the noblest and royal sorts amongst all Gems, and most meet to be worn only upon King's and Prince's fingers. This, for his sovereignty of the *Lapidare*,° is called the Gem of Gems … Cardan° saith it is good … to the eyesight, and that nothing in the whole world doth more recreate or delight the eyes than the Smaragd° and Sapphire do. Albertus Magnus° saith that he [19ʳ] hath proved it twice that with the only touching of this precious stone, the party so diseased hath been rid of the grievous sore the Carbuncle.° It is marvellously efficacious against all venom. Wherefore, if thou put a Spider into a box, and upon the mouth of the box, being shut, thou layest the true Sapphire and keep the Spider but a very short time within the same, the Spider being vanquished and overcome by such mean of close virtue dieth suddenly.

❦ ❦ ❦

° **Pontus**: region along the southern coast of the Black Sea.   ° *Lapidare*: precious stones.
° **Cardan**: Girolamo Cardano, author of Latin treatise *On Subtlety* (1550).   ° **Smaragd**: emerald.
° **Albertus Magnus**: medieval German theologian and naturalist, author of the magical *Book of Secrets*.   ° **Carbuncle**: boil.

ANNE BRADSTREET
"The Four Elements" (1650)

Before the modern periodic table of 118 elements, natural philosophers divided the stuff of the universe into four basic units: Fire, Air, Water, and Earth. In pre-Newtonian physics the elements possess tremendous agency (each striving to be with its kind and in its assigned place), prompting many early modern writers to personify them. While some saw their relationship as harmonious, Bradstreet's female-gendered elements contend for mastery, recalling a famous speech in Marlowe's *Tamburlaine*: "Nature, that framed us of four elements, / Warring within our breasts for regiment, / Doth teach us all to have aspiring minds" (2.7.18–20). Such views of nature as a battleground became common in the aftermath of the English Civil War.
Source: *The Tenth Muse* (1650), 5.

> Fire, Air, Earth, and Water did all contest
> Which was the strongest, noblest, and the best,
> Who the most good could show, and who most rage,
> For to declare themselves they all engage;°
> And in due order each her turn should speak,
> But enmity this amity did break:
> All would be chief, and all scorned to be under,
> Whence issued rains and winds, lightning and thunder;
> The quaking Earth did groan, the sky looked black;
> The Fire, the forcèd Air, in sunder crack;   10
> The sea did threat the heavens, the heavens the earth;
> All lookèd like a Chaos or new birth;
> Fire broiled Earth, and scorchèd Earth it choked;
> Both by their darings Water so provoked
> That roaring in it came, and with its source
> Soon made the combatants abate their force;
> The rumbling, hissing, puffing was so great,
> The world's confusion it did seem to threat;
> But Air at length° contention so abated,
> That betwixt hot and cold she arbitrated   20
> The other's enmity: being less, did cease;
> All storms now laid, and they in perfect peace,
> That Fire should first begin, the rest consent,
> Being the most impatient Element.°

❧ ❧ ❧

° **who … engage**: who was of greatest use and might'est force / In placid Terms they thought now to
 discourse] 1678.
° **But … length**: Till gentle Air] 1678.
° **Being … Element**: The noblest and most active Element] 1678.

MARGARET CAVENDISH
"Motion directs, while Atoms dance" and
"A World in an Earring" (1653)

Two developments in early modern Europe unveiled new orders of being too
small to be perceptible to the human eye. The first was the invention of the
compound microscope (c. 1590), which enabled Robert Hooke to discern life in
mould and Anton van Leeuwenhoek to detect a teeming world of "animalcules"
(little animals), which we now call protozoa and bacteria. The second was the
rediscovery of Lucretian atomism, which assigned the most fundamental elements of life a remarkable agency in shaping and directing natural phenomena
(see Part 1). Both developments fascinated Margaret Cavendish, the Duchess of
Newcastle, who conducted experiments with microscopes (although she eventually grew disillusioned with them) and composed poems personifying atoms. As
an aspiring scientist and poet at a time when women were deterred from both
fields, Cavendish notably grants a female Nature an imposing authority, and here
imagines a female fashion accessory as a kind of microverse unknown to male
scientists. While her contemporaries, such as Robert Boyle and Thomas Hobbes,
increasingly sought to purge scientific writing of what they saw as the *ignis fatuus*
of metaphor, Cavendish seems to use poetry as a laboratory for testing the plausi-
bility of a scientific theory by the power of the art it generates.
Source: *Poems and Fancies* (1653), 17, 45–6; with annotations from the 1664 edition.

"Motion directs, while Atoms dance"

Atoms will dance, and measures keep just time,°
And one by one will hold° round circle line,
Run in and out, as we do dance the Hay,°
Crossing about, yet keep just time and way,
While Motion, as Music, directs the Time:°
Thus by consent they altogether join.°
This Harmony is Health, makes Life live long,°
  But when they're° out, 'tis death, so dancing's done.

"A World in an Earring"

An Earring round° may well a Zodiac be,
Wherein a Sun goeth round, and° we not see;
And Planets seven about that Sun may move,

° **Atoms ... time**: Atoms will in just Measures dance, and join] 1664.
° **And ... hold**: All one by one in a] 1664.
° **Hay**: a country dance that involved winding in between and around the other dancers.
° **While ... Time**: Whilst Motion doth direct; and thus they dance] 1664.
° **Thus ... join**: And meet all by consent, not by mere chance] 1664.
° **This ... long**: This Consort's Health, which Life depends upon] 1664.
° **they're**: 'tis] 1664.   ° **round**: omitted in 1664.   ° **and**: which] 1664.

And He stand still, as some wise° men would prove;
And fixèd Stars, like twinkling Diamonds, placed
About this Earring, which a World is vast.
That same which doth the Earring hold, the hole,
Is that which we do call the Pole.°
There nipping Frosts may be, and Winter° cold,
Yet never on the Lady's Ear take hold.   10
And Lightnings, Thunder, and great Winds may blow
Within this Earring, yet the Ear not know.
There Seas may ebb and flow where Fishes swim,°
And Islands be, where Spices grow therein.°
There crystal Rocks hang dangling at each Ear,
And Golden Mines as Jewels may they wear.
There Earthquakes be, which Mountains vast down fling,
And yet ne'er stir the Lady's Ear nor Ring.
There Meadows be, and Pastures fresh and green,
And Cattle feed, and yet be never seen;   20
And Gardens fresh,° and Birds which sweetly sing,
Although we hear them not, in an Earring.
There Night and Day, and Heat and Cold, and so°
May Life and Death, and Young and Old, still grow.°
Thus Youth may spring and several Ages die,
Great Plagues may be, and no Infections nigh.
There Cities be, and stately Houses built,°
Their inside gay and finely may be gilt.
There Churches be, and Priests to teach therein,°
And Steeple too, yet hear the Bells not ring.   30
From thence may pious Tears to Heaven run,
And yet the Ear not know which way they're gone.
There Markets be, and things both° bought and sold,
Know not the price, nor how the° Markets hold.
There Governors do rule and Kings do° reign,
And Battles fought, where many may be slain,°
And all within the compass of this Ring,
And yet not° tidings to the Wearer bring.   40
Within the Ring wise Counsellors may sit,
And yet the Ear not one wise word may get.
There may be dancing all Night at a Ball,

° **some wise**: learned] 1664.   ° **Which ... Pole**: we call the North and Southern-pole] 1664.
° **Winter**: Winter's] 1664.
° **There ... swim**: Fish there may swim in Seas, which ebb and flow] 1664.
° **And ... therein**: And Islands be wherein do Spices grow] 1664.   ° **fresh**: fine] 1664.
° **There ... so**: There may be Night and Day, and Heat and Cold] 1664.
° **May ... grow**: As also Life and Death, and Young and Old] 1664.
° **There ... built**: Great Cities there may be, and Houses built] 1664.
° **There ... therein**: Churches may they've, wherein Priests teach and sing] 1664.
° **and things both**: where things are] 1664.
° **Know ... the**: Though th'Ear not knows the price their] 1664.
° **do ... do**: may ... may] 1664.
° **fought ... slain**: may be fought, and many slain] 1664.
° **And yet not**: Whence they no] 1664.

And yet the Ear be not disturbed at all.
There Rivals° Duels fight, where some are slain;
There Lovers mourn, yet hear them not complain.
And Death may dig a Lover's grave: thus were
A Lover dead in a fair Lady's Ear.
But when the Ring is broke, the World is done,
Then Lovers they into Elysium run.°

° **There Rivals**: Rivals may] 1664.
° **they … run**: are into Elysium gone] 1664. Elysium is the abode of blessed spirits in Greek
mythology.

PART III

Time and Place

Seasons

HENRY HOWARD

"Description of Spring, Where Each Thing Renews, Save Only the Lover" (c. 1535)

When the Italian Renaissance arrived in England in the 1530s via the works of Sir Thomas Wyatt and Henry Howard, the Earl of Surrey, it encouraged a newfound appreciation of nature as a storehouse of imagery. Nevertheless, readers should not presume Howard's sonnet records a first-hand encounter with the environment; a translation of Petrarch's Rime 310, it presents, like much Renaissance pastoral, a mediated literary landscape. Moreover, as in Shakespeare's Sonnets 98 and 99 and Thomas Lodge's "The earth late choked with showers," the closing couplet registers an intensification of inwardness that alienates the human subject from the rhythms of the seasons (it may even have been written while Howard was in prison). Significantly, however, Howard replaces several of Petrarch's classical allusions with English fauna, thus imbuing the poem with an earthier feel and adapting it to match the local environment. In this regard it is noteworthy that the title (following Petrarch) names the season as spring while the poem identifies it as summer. This confusion reflects the looser usage of the two terms in early modern England, when summer officially began not on the solstice (then called Midsummer) but on 1 May. Rather than hail spring or summer, English poets often praise May as the ideal compound of both, so it was in effect a season of its own, while the annual tradition (which came under assault after the Reformation) of gathering greenery and dancing round the maypole on May Day encouraged human communities to participate in the drama of biological renewal (see Dekker's "Merry Month of May" and Herrick's "Corinna's Going A-Maying").
Source: *Songs and Sonnets* (1557), A2^v.

> The soot° season that bud and bloom forth brings,
> With green hath clad the hill and eke the vale.
> The nightingale with feathers new she sings,
> The turtle° to her mate hath told her tale.
> Summer is come, for every spray now springs.
> The hart hath hung his old head° on the pale,
> The buck in brake his winter coat he flings,
> The fishes fleet with new-repairèd scale,
> The adder all her slough° away she slings,
> The swift swallow pursueth the flies small,   10
> The busy bee her honey now she mings.°

° **soot**: sweet.   ° **turtle**: turtle-dove.   ° **old head**: antlers.
° **slough**: skin.   ° **ming**: mingles.

Winter is worn that was the flowers' bale.
And thus I see among these pleasant things,
Each care decays, and yet my sorrow springs.

⁂

ALEXANDER HUME
"Of the Day Estival" (1599)

The title of the poem reprinted below derives from the Latin word for summer,
aestas, and should not be confused with festival. Nevertheless, a holiday spirit pervades this ballad verse (which opens at dawn – perhaps on the summer solstice –
and concludes at dusk) and the landscape it depicts. Influenced by the Psalm
tradition, which exalts nature as the ultimate instantiation of God's benevolence,
the poem is notable for the vibrancy and naturalism of its pastoral imagery. After
enduring a long, dark Scottish winter, Hume would be particularly appreciative
of the comforts of summer. Although Hume's spelling has been modernized, the
transcription aims to preserve some of the Scots in recognition that a regional
dialect can help capture a sense of place.
Source: *Hymns or Sacred Songs* (1599), 13–20.

O perfect light, quhilk shed° away,
The darkness from the light,°
And set a ruler o'er the day,
Another o'er the night.

Thy glory when the day forth flies,
More vively° does appear,
Than at midday unto our eyes,
The shining Sun is clear.

The shadow of the earth anon,
Removes and drawės by,
Since in the east, when it is gone,
Appears a clearer sky.°

Quhilk Sun perceive the little larks,
The lapwing and the snipe,
And tune their songs like nature's clarks,°
O'er meadow, moor, and stripe.°

But every bazed° nocturnal beast,
No longer may abide,

10

° **quhilk shed**: which divided. The verb was often used in Scots for separating livestock.
° **darkness ... light**: see Genesis 1:4.   ° **vively**: vividly.
° **sky**: a marginal note here reads "The crepuscule matutine" or morning twilight.
° **clarks**: clerks, here suggesting choristers.   ° **stripe**: small stream.   ° **bazed**: startled.

They hie away both most and least,°
Themselves in house to hide ...   20

For joy the birds with bolden° throats,
Against his visage sheen,
Take up their kindly music notes,
In woods and gardens green.   40

Up braids° the careful husbandman,
His corns and vines to see,
And every timous° artisan
In booth works busily.

The pastor° quits the slothful sleep,
And passes forth with speed,
His little camow-nosèd° sheep
And routing kine° to feed.

The passenger from perils sure
Gangs° gladly forth the way.   50
Brief, every living creature
Takes comfort of the day ...

The time so tranquil is and still,
That nowhere shall ye find,
Save on any high and barren hill,
An air of peeping wind.

All trees and simples great and small,
That balmy leaves do bear,
As they were painted on a wall,
No more they move or steir.°   80

Calm is the deep and purple sea,
Yea, smoother not the sand,
The waves that welt'ring wont to be,
Are stable like the land.

So silent is the cessile° air,
That every cry and call,
The hills and dales and forest fair
Again repeat them all.

The rivers fresh, the caller° streams,
O'er rocks can softly rin,°   90

° **hie ... least**: haste away, both the biggest and smallest.   ° **bolden**: swollen.
° **braids**: rises.   ° **timous**: early-rising.   ° **pastor**: shepherd.
° **camow-nosed**: flat-nosed.   ° **routing kine**: bellowing cattle.   ° **Gangs**: goes.
° **steir**: stir.   ° **cessile**: yielding.   ° **caller**: cool.   ° **rin**: run.

The water clear like crystal seems,
And makes a pleasant din.

The fields and earthly superfice,°
With verdure green is spread,
And naturally but° artifice,
In parti-colours cled.°

The flourishes° and fragrant flowers,
Through Phoebus° fost'ring heat,
Refreshed with dew and silver showers,
Cast up an odour sweet.

The cloggèd° busy humming bees,
That never think to drown,
On flowers and flourishes of trees,
Collect their liquor brown.

The Sun most like a speedy post,
With ardent course ascends,
The beauty of the heavenly host,
Up to our Zenith tends ...

The breathless flocks draw to the shade,°
And fraischeur° of their fold,
The startling nolt,° as they were mad,
Run to the rivers cold.

The herds beneath some leafy tree,
Amidst the flowers they lie,
The stable ships upon the sea,
Tend up their sails to dry.

The hart, the hind, and fallow deer,
Are tapished° at their rest,
The fowls and birds that made the beir,°
Prepare their pretty nest ...

Forth of their skeps° some raging bees,
Lie out and will not cast,°
Some other swarms hive on the trees,
In knots together fast.

The corbies° and the cackling kaes°
May scarce the heat abide,

° **superfice**: surface.   ° **but**: without.   ° **cled**: clad.
° **flourishes**: blossoms.   ° **Phoebus**: the sun.   ° **clogged**: laden.
° **shade**: a marginal note here reads "A description of midday."
° **fraischeur**: freshness.   ° **nolt**: oxen.   ° **tapished**: retired.   ° **beir**: clamour.
° **skeps**: hives.   ° **cast**: swarm.   ° **corbies**: ravens.   ° **kaes**: jackdaws.

Hawks preen on the sunny breeze,
And wedder° back and side.

With gilded eyes and open wings,
The cock his courage shows,
With claps of joy his breast he dings,°
And twenty times he crows.   160

The dove with whistling wings so blue,
The winds can fast collect,
Her purple pins° turn many hue,
Against the sun direct.

Now noon is went, gone is midday,
The heat does slake at last,
The sun descends down west away,
Fra° three of clock be past.

A little cool of braithing wind,
Now softly can arise,   170
The works through heat that lay behind,
Now men may enterprise.

Forth fares the flocks to seek their food,
On every hill and plain,
Quhilk labourer as he thinks good,
Steps to his turn again.

The rayons of the Sun we see,
Diminish in their strength,
The shade of every tower and tree,
Extended is in length.   180

Great is the calm for everyquhair,
The wind is sitten down,
The reek thraws° right up in the air,
From every tower and town.

Their firdoning° the bonny birds,
In banks they do begin,
With pipes of reeds the jolly herds,°
Hold up the merry din.

The Mavis° and the Philomeen,°
The Starling whistle loud,   190

° **wedder**: weather (air themselves).   ° **dings**: beats.   ° **pins**: pinions.
° **Fra**: As soon as (northern). A marginal note here reads "A description of the evening."
° **reek thraws**: smoke curls.   ° **firdoning**: warbling.   ° **herds**: herdsmen.
° **Mavis**: thrush.   ° **Philomeen**: nightingale.

The Cushats° on the branches green,
Full quietly they crowd.

The gloaming comes, the day is spent,°
The Sun goes out of sight,
And painted is the occident,
With purple sanguine bright.

The scarlet nor the golden thread,
Who would their beauty try,
Are nothing like the colour red,
And beauty of the sky.

Our west horizon circular,
Fra time the Sun be set,
Is all with rubies, as it were,
Or Roses red o'er-fret.

What pleasure were to walk and see,
Endlang° a river clear,
The perfect form of every tree,
Within the deep appear?

The Salmon out of cruives° and creils,°
Up haulèd into scouts,°
The bells and circles on the weels,°
Through leapings of the trouts.

Oh, then it were a seemly thing,
While all is still and calm,
The praise of God to play and sing,
With cornett and with shalm.°

But now the herds° with many shout,
Call others by their name,
"Ga, Billie,° turn our gude° about!
Now time is to go home."

With belly full the beasts belive,°
Are turnèd from the corn,
Quhilk soberly they homeward drive,
With pipe and lilting horn.

200

210

220

° **Cushats**: wood pigeons.   ° **spent**: a marginal note reads "The crepuscule vespertine."
° **Endlang**: along.   ° **cruives**: weirs.   ° **creils**: baskets.
° **scouts**: small boats.   ° **bells … weels**: bubbles and ripples in the pools.
° **cornett … shalm**: a cornett is a Renaissance wind instrument made from wood and horn; a shalm is an oboe-like woodwind.
° **herds**: herdsmen.   ° **Ga, Billie**: Go, Billy (possibly a first name but also Scots for "buddy").
° **gude**: cattle.   ° **belive**: remaining.

Through all the land great is the gild,°
Of rustic folk that cry,
Of bleating sheep fra° they be filled,
Of calves and routing ky.°

All labourers draw home at even,
And can till° other say,   230
Thanks to the gracious God of heaven,
Quhilk send this summer day.

ﻌ ﻌ ﻌ

° **gild**: throng.   ° **fra**: when.   ° **ky**: cows.   ° **till**: to.

NICHOLAS BRETON
"Harvest" and "October" (1626)

The almanac was an important genre of agrarian writing that contributed greatly
to the narrativizing of the seasons and months. Following the lead of Spenser's
Shepheardes Calender, poets composed their own literary almanacs to cater to
this yearning for predictable weather during the volatile Little Ice Age (see Part
VI). Breton's description of harvest has neither the poignancy of Shakespeare's
autumnal sonnet 73 nor the exuberance of Herrick's "Hock-Cart," which celebrates humans becoming "Lords of Wine and Oil," but compensates with an
acute sense of how all living things (humans included) must adapt their regimen
to seasonal change. Incidentally, harvest, the original Anglo-Saxon term for the
third season, was commonly used in Renaissance England, perhaps more than the
Latinate autumn or "fall of the leaf" (the abbreviated version of which is now an
Americanism). The finely etched vignette of October, meanwhile, illustrates how
the second half of the season evokes a very different reaction than the first.
Source: *Fantastics Serving for Prognostications* (1626), B2ᵛ–B3ʳ, C4ᵛ.

"Harvest"

It is now Harvest and the Lark must lead her young out of the nest, for the
Scythe and the Sickle will down with the grass and the corn. Now are the
hedges full of Berries and the highways full of Rogues, and the lazy Limbs
must sleep out their dinner. The Ant and the Bee work for their winter
provision and, after a frost, the Grasshopper is not seen. Butter, milk, and
[B3ʳ] cheese are the Labourer's diet, and a pot of good Beer quickens his
spirit. If there be no plague the people are healthy, for continuance of motion is a preservation of nature. The fresh of the morning and the cool of
the Evening are the times of Court walks, but the poor traveller treads out
the whole day. Malt is now above wheat with a number of mad people, and

a fine shirt is better than a Frieze Jerkin.° Pears and Plums now ripen apace and, being of a watery substance, are cause of much sickness. The pipe and the tabor now follow the Fairs, and they that have any money make a gain of their markets. Bucks now are in season and Partridges are rowen-tailed,° and a good Retriever is a Spaniel worth the keeping. In sum, it is a time of much worth, when, if God be well pleased, the world will thrive the better. And, to conclude, this is all that I will say of it: I hold it the Heaven's Bounty, the Earth's Beauty, and the World's Benefit

[C4ᵛ] "October"

It is now October, and the lofty winds make bare the trees of their leaves, while the hogs in the Woods grow fat with the fallen Acorns. The forward Deer begin to go to rut, and the barren Doe groweth good meat. The Basket-makers now gather their rods, and the fishers lay their leaps° in the deep. The load-horses go apace to the Mill, and the Meal-market is seldom without people. The Hare on the hill makes the Greyhound a fair course,° and the Fox in the woods calls the Hounds to a full cry. The multitude of people raiseth the price of wares, and the smooth tongue will sell much. The Sailor now bestirreth his stumps,° while the Merchant liveth in fear of the weather. The great feasts are now at hand for the City, but the poor must not beg for fear of the stocks. A fire and a pack of Cards keep the guests in the Ordinary° ... and kind hearts and true Lovers lie close to keep off cold. The Titmouse now keeps in the hollow tree, and the Blackbird sits close in the bottom of a hedge. In brief, for the little pleasure I find in it I thus conclude of it: I hold it a Messenger of ill news, and a second service° to a cold dinner.

҂ ҂ ҂

° **Frieze Jerkin**: woollen jacket, with pun on freeze.
° **rowen-tailed**: full grown. Rowen was a term for a mature partridge.
° **leaps**: baskets for catching fish.   ° **course**: race.   ° **bestirreth … stumps**: exerts himself.
° **Ordinary**: tavern.   ° **service**: course.

ALEXANDER BARCLAY

"The winter snows, all covered is the ground" (*c.* 1518)

Although loosely based on an eclogue debating the merits of the city versus the countryside by the Italian poet Mantuan, this poem sketches a vibrant picture of winter in Tudor Britain. Dating texts on the basis of weather events can be problematic, but it seems a plausible conjecture that Barclay drew upon memories of the bitterly cold winter of 1515–16, when the Thames froze over. The poem recognizes the hardships of the season ("For costly was fire in hardest of the year"), especially for the rural poor, and the shepherds envy the fur-clad Londoners, whose urban economy is not so dependent upon the rhythms of nature. Yet Barclay tries to make winter seem festive and cosy, and the "uplandishman" or country-dweller Faustus observes that winter scarcity used to encourage the pastoral virtues of thrift and hospitality, while the younger generation drawn to the city now spend improvidently. If Faustus seems to the win the debate, much of the English public voted with its feet, as London tripled in size during the sixteenth century. Did the Little Ice Age drive urbanization?

Source: *Fifth Eclogue* (1518), A2ᵛ–A4ʳ.

> AMYNTAS The winter snows, all covered is the ground,
> The north wind blows all with a fearful sound,
> The long icicles at the eaves hang,
> The streams frozen, the night is cold and long.
> Where boats rowed, now carts have passage,
> From yoke the oxen be loosed and bondage.
> The ploughman resteth, avoid° of all business,
> Save when he tendeth his harness for to dress.
> Mabley his wife sitteth before the fire,
> All black and smoky, clothed in rude attire,   10
> Seething° some gruel and stirring the pulment°
> Of peas or frument,° a noble meat for Lent.°
> The summer season men counteth now laudable,
> Whose fervour before they thought intolerable.
> The frosty winter and weather temperate,
> Which men then praised, they now dispraise and hate:
> Cold they desired, but now it is present
> They brawl° and grutch,° their minds not content.
> Thus mutable men them pleased cannot hold:
> At great heat grutching, and grutching when it is cold …   20
>   Each time and season hath his delight and joys.
> Look in the streets, behold the little boys:
> How in fruit season for joy they sing and hope,
> In Lent each one full busy is with his top,
> And now in winter, for all the grievous cold,
> All rent and ragged a man may them behold.   30
> They have great pleasure supposing well to dine;
> When men be busied in killing of fat swine,
> They get the bladder and blow it great and thin,
> With many beans or peas bound within,
> It rattleth, soundeth, and shineth clear and fair,
> While it is thrown and cast up in the air,
> Each one contendeth and hath a great delight
> With foot or with hand the bladder for to smite …
> Running and leaping they drive away the cold.
> The sturdy ploughmen, lusty, strong, and bold,
> Overcometh the winter with driving the football,

° **avoid**: free.   ° Seething: simmering.   ° **pulment**: pottage.

° **frument**: frumenty, wheat boiled in seasoned milk.

° **Lent**: meat here means food, as flesh was forbidden during Lent. In Mantuan, the shepherd exclaims, "Give me Pythagoras's homely fare" (i.e. a vegetarian meal).

° **brawl**: squabble.   ° **grutch**: grumble.

Forgetting labour and many a grievous fall …
Here may we wallow while milk is on the fire;
If it be curdled, of bread we need no crumb.
If thou bide, Faustus, thereof thou shalt have some.
FAUSTUS Winter declareth hard need and poverty,
Then men it feeleth which have necessity.
Truly, Amyntas, I tell thee mine intent:
70   We fond young people be much improvident.
We stray in summer without thought, care, or heed
Of such thing as we in winter shall have need.
As soon as we hear a bagpipe or a drone,
Then leave we labour; there is our money gone.
But when the north wind with storms violent
Hath brought cold winter, poor wretches to torment,
And void of leaves is every bough and tree,
That one may clearly the empty nests see,
Then is all our wool and lambs gone and sold,
80   We tremble naked and die almost for cold,
Our shoulders all bare, our hose and shoes rent,
By reckless youth thus all is gone and spent.
This cometh for wanting of good provision;
Youth daineth° counsel, scorning discretion.
When poverty thus hath caught us in his snare,
Then doth the winter our mad folly declare.

❧ ❧ ❧

° **daineth**: disdains.

Country Houses

GEORGE GASCOIGNE
[The Wild Man of Kenilworth] (1575)

In July 1575, the Earl of Leicester hosted one of the most famous royal entertainments of Elizabeth's reign at his Warwickshire estate. In addition to a bear-baiting (see Part IV), he hired the poet George Gascoigne to prepare a series of al fresco interludes. In this scene depicting a wild man kneeling before the queen, Gascoigne performs the subjection of the landscape and its resources to the monarch on her progress through the realm (Montrose, Yoch). Unlike Spenser's "April" eclogue and the other country-house poems in this section, a live open-air performance can be an unpredictable affair. Constant rain cancelled many of the pageants. When the wild man uprooted a sapling as a club and threw it down as a token of submission, it landed near the queen's horse, causing it to buck and bolt. While some found this mishap the best part of the show, the moment also undercuts the text's proclamation of royal authority, revealing the unruly agency of the non-human environment in outdoor performances.

Source: *Whole Works* (1587), A6ᵛ–A7ʳ.

Herewith he fell on his knees and spoke as followeth:

O Queen, I must confess it is not without cause,
These civil people so rejoice that you should give them laws.°
Since I, which live at large, a wild and savage man,
And have run out a wilful race since first my life began,
Do here submit myself, beseeching you to serve,
And that you take in worth my will, which can but well deserve.
Had I the learnèd skill which in your head is found,
My tale had flowed in eloquence where now my words are drowned.
Had I the beauty's blaze which shines in you so bright,
Then might I seem a Falcon fair, which now am but a Kite.   10
Could I but touch the strings which you so heav'nly handle
I would confess that fortune then full friendly did me dandle.
O Queen without compare, you must not think it strange,
That here amid this wilderness your glory so doth range;
The winds resound your worth, the rocks record your name.
These hills, these dales, these woods, these waves,
These fields pronounce your fame.

ﻪ ﻪ ﻪ

° **laws:** Elizabeth was reasserting control over Crown forests, and Parliament had passed a Vagabonds Act in 1572 (strengthened in 1575) that called for unlicensed vagrants (many of whom squatted in the woods) to be whipped and branded in the ear.

AEMELIA LANYER
"The Description of Cookham" (1610)

This poem commemorates Lanyer's sojourn at the Berkshire estate of her patron
Margaret Clifford, the Countess of Cumberland. It fondly recalls the community
of women who gathered there, united by their shared intellectual and religious
sympathies. Lanyer's pleasure in the company and support of her patron is projected onto the landscape, which shares in her ecstatic gratitude. If the pastoral
imagery is stylized, the poem evinces a genuine love of the local topography. The
lease on the property having expired, Lanyer mourns the breaking up of this sis-
terly community as a second exile from Eden. As the Countess was residing there
while separated from her philandering husband with whom she was involved in
a legal dispute, the estate must have seemed a refuge from a male-dominated
society. No wonder recent commentaries discern in Lanyer's verse a "poetics
of ecological awareness deeply critical of hierarchical systems that exploit both
people and the environment" (Noble 99).
Source: *Salve Deus Rex Judaeorum* (1611), H2ʳ–I1ʳ.

> Farewell sweet Cookham, where I first obtained
> Grace from that Grace where perfect Grace remained;°
> And where the Muses gave their full consent,
> I should have power the virtuous to content;
> Where princely Palace willed me to indite,°
> The sacred Story° of the Soul's delight.
> Farewell sweet Place, where virtue then did rest,
> And all delights did harbour in her breast;
> Never shall my sad eyes again behold
> Those pleasures which my thoughts did then unfold.
> Yet you, great Lady, Mistress of that Place,
> From whose desires did spring this work of Grace,
> Vouchsafe to think upon those pleasures past,
> As fleeting worldly joys that could not last,
> Or as dim shadows of celestial pleasures,
> Which are desired above all earthly treasures.
> Oh how methought against you thither came,
> Each part did seem some new delight to frame!
> The House received all ornaments to grace it,
> And would endure no foulness to deface it.
> And Walks put on their summer liveries,
> And all things else did hold like similes:
> The Trees with leaves, with fruits, with flowers clad,
> Embraced each other, seeming to be glad,
> Turning themselves to beauteous Canopies,
> To shade the bright Sun from your brighter eyes;
> The crystal Streams with silver spangles graced,
> While by the glorious Sun they were embraced;

10

20

° **Grace … remained**: favour from her illustrious patroness, a model of righteousness.
° **indite**: compose.   ° **Story**: Lanyer's religious poem *Salve Deus Rex Judaeorum*.

The little Birds in chirping notes did sing,
To entertain both You and that sweet Spring; 30
And Philomela° with her sundry lays,
Both You and that delightful Place did praise.
Oh how methought each plant, each flower, each tree,
Set forth their beauties then to welcome thee!
The very Hills right humbly did descend
When you to tread upon them did intend;
And as you set your feet, they still did rise,
Glad that they could receive so rich a prize.
The gentle Winds did take delight to be
Among those woods that were so graced by thee; 40
And in sad murmur uttered pleasing sound,
That Pleasure in that place might more abound.
The swelling Banks delivered all their pride,
When such a Phoenix once they had espied.
Each Arbour, Bank, each Seat, each stately Tree,
Thought themselves honoured in supporting thee.
The pretty Birds would oft come to attend thee,
Yet fly away for fear they should offend thee.
The little creatures° in the Burrow by
Would come abroad to sport them in your eye; 50
Yet fearful of the bow in your fair hand,
Would run away when you did make a stand.
Now let me come unto that stately Tree,
Wherein such goodly Prospects you did see:
That Oak that did in height his fellows pass,
As much as lofty trees, low-growing grass,
Much like a comely Cedar, straight and tall,
Whose beauteous stature far exceeded all.
How often did you visit this fair tree,
Which seeming joyful in receiving thee, 60
Would like a Palm tree spread his arms abroad,
Desirous that you there should make abode;
Whose fair green leaves, much like a comely veil,
Defended Phoebus when he would assail;
Whose pleasing boughs did yield a cool fresh air,
Joying his happiness when you were there;
Where, being seated, you might plainly see
Hills, vales, and woods, as if on bended knee
They had appeared, your honour to salute,
Or to prefer some strange unlooked-for suit: 70
All interlaced with brooks and crystal springs,
A Prospect fit to please the eyes of Kings.
And thirteen shires appeared all in your sight;°
Europe could not afford much more delight.
What was there then but gave you all content,

° **Philomela**: the nightingale, supposedly an Athenian princess transformed following her rape.
° **creatures**: rabbits.
° **thirteen ... sight**: although the vista is far-reaching, this claim exaggerates the distance.

While you the time in meditation spent
Of their Creator's power, which there you saw,
In all his Creatures held a perfect Law;
And in their beauties did you plain descry,
His beauty, wisdom, grace, love, majesty.
In these sweet woods how often did you walk
With Christ and his Apostles there to talk;
Placing his holy Writ in some fair tree,
To meditate what you therein did see.
With Moses you did mount his holy Hill,
To know his pleasure and perform his Will.
With lowly David you did often sing
His holy Hymns° to Heaven's Eternal King.
And in sweet music did your soul delight,
To sound his praises, morning, noon, and night.
With blessèd Joseph you did often feed
Your pinèd° brethren, when they stood in need …
And you, sweet Cookham, whom these Ladies leave,
I now must tell the grief you did conceive
At their departure; when they went away,
How everything retained a sad dismay.
Nay, long before, when once an inkling came,
Methought each thing did unto sorrow frame:
The trees that were so glorious in our view,
Forsook both flowers and fruit when once they knew
Of your depart; their very leaves did wither,
Changing their colours as they grew together.
But when they saw this had no power to stay you,
They often wept, though speechless, could not pray° you;
Letting their tears in your fair bosoms fall,
As if they said, "Why will ye leave us all?"
This being vain, they cast their leaves away,
Hoping that pity would have made you stay.
Their frozen tops, like Age's hoary hairs,
Show their disasters, languishing in fears.
A swarthy rivelled° rind all overspread,
Their dying bodies half-alive, half-dead.
But your occasions called you so away,
That nothing there had power to make you stay.
Yet did I see a noble grateful mind
Requiting each according to their kind,
Forgetting not to turn and take your leave
Of these sad creatures, powerless to receive
Your favour, when with grief you did depart,
Placing their former pleasures in your heart,
Giving great charge to noble Memory,

° **Hymns**: Psalms.
° **pined**: starved. During a seven-year famine in Egypt, Joseph gave grain to his starving brothers who had betrayed him. It is a pastoral convention to praise the patron's hospitality.
° **pray**: entreat.
° **rivelled**: shrivelled.

There to preserve their love continually;
But specially the love of that fair tree,
That first and last you did vouchsafe to see,
In which it pleased you oft to take the air
With noble Dorset,° then a virgin fair,   160
Where many a learned Book was read and scanned.
To this fair tree, taking me by the hand,
You did repeat the pleasures which had passed,
Seeming to grieve they could no longer last;
And with a chaste, yet loving kiss took leave;
Of which sweet kiss I did it soon bereave,°
Scorning a senseless creature should possess
So rare a favour, so great happiness.
No other kiss it could receive from me,
For fear to give back what it took of thee.   170
So I, ingrateful Creature, did deceive it
Of that which you in love vouchsafed to leave it.
And though it oft had given me much content,
Yet this great wrong I never could repent;
But of the happiest made it most forlorn,
To show that nothing's free from Fortune's scorn,
While all the rest with this most beauteous tree,
Made their sad consort Sorrow's harmony.
The Flowers that on the banks and walks did grow,   180
Crept in the ground; the Grass did weep for woe.
The Winds and Waters seemed to chide together,
Because you went away, they knew not whither;
And those sweet Brooks that ran so fair and clear,
With grief and trouble wrinkled did appear.
Those pretty Birds that wonted were to sing,
Now neither sing, nor chirp, nor use their wing,
But with their tender feet on some bare spray,
Warble forth sorrow and their own dismay.
Fair Philomela leaves her mournful ditty,
Drowned in deep sleep, yet can procure no pity.   190
Each arbour, bank, each seat, each stately tree,
Looks bare and desolate now for want of thee,
Turning green tresses into frosty grey,
While in cold grief they wither all away.
The Sun grew weak, his beams no comfort gave,
While all green things did make the earth their grave.
Each briar, each bramble, when you went away,
Caught fast your clothes, thinking to make you stay.
Delightful Echo, wonted to reply
To our last words, did now for sorrow die.   200
The house cast off each garment that might grace it,
Putting on Dust and Cobwebs to deface it.

° **Dorset**: Lady Anne Clifford.
° **bereave**: deprive; that is, Lanyer kisses the tree on the spot where Margaret Clifford had kissed it.

All desolation then there did appear,
When you were going whom they held so dear.
This last farewell to Cookham here I give,
When I am dead thy name in this may live;
Wherein I have performed her noble hest,°
Whose virtues lodge in my unworthy breast,
And ever shall, so long as life remains,
210   Tying my life to her by those rich chains.

⁊ ⁊ ⁊

° **hest**: bidding.

BEN JONSON

"To Penshurst" (*c.* 1611)

In 1611, Jonson stayed with Robert Sidney, the Viscount Lisle and brother of cour-
tier-poet Philip, at his Kentish country estate, where he composed the following
tribute to his host's hospitality – a hospitality made possible by the stewardship of
natural resources. The poem deftly blends together classical approaches to nature
in Roman literature: the pastoral odes of Horace, the georgics of Virgil, and the
mythological confections of Ovid. Jonson's vision of the estate as a remnant of
the Golden Age, however, obscures the arduous labours of the rural poor (as
Raymond Williams noted) and mystifies the violence by which humans transform the environment – including other animals – into agricultural commodities
(Remien). More positively, Leah Marcus has linked the country-house genre to
a series of "Jacobean and Caroline initiatives for reversing the growth of London
and increasing the prosperity of the countryside" (142) (see Appendix A). By reading the poem as a bid to stem urban sprawl (Hiltner) or tout the symbiotic benefits of sustainable food production (Tigner 2015), ecocritics continue to uphold
"Penshurst" as a manifesto on ethical dwelling.
Source: *Works* (1616), 819–21.

Thou art not, Penshurst, built to envious show,
Of touch° or marble, nor can boast a row
Of polished pillars or a roof of gold;
Thou hast no lantern,° whereof tales are told,
Or stairs or courts, but stand'st an ancient pile,
And, these grudged at, art reverenced the while.
Thou joy'st in better marks, of soil, of air,
Of wood, of water; therein thou art fair.
Thou hast thy walks for health as well as sport;
10   Thy Mount, to which the Dryads do resort,
Where Pan and Bacchus their high feasts have made
Beneath the broad beech, and the chestnut shade;
That taller tree, which of a nut was set
At his great birth,° where all the Muses met.

° **touch**: touchstone.   ° **lantern**: a small glass dome.
° **birth**: Philip Sidney's, born in 1554. In fact, the Sidney Oak was already several hundred years old
when Jonson saw it, it died in 2016.

There in the withèd bark are cut the names
Of many a Sylvan, taken with his flames.°
And thence the ruddy Satyrs oft provoke
The lighter Fauns to reach thy Lady's oak.
Thy copse too, named of Gamage,° thou hast there,
That never fails to serve thee seasoned deer,   20
When thou wouldst feast or exercise thy friends.
The lower land, that to the river bends,
Thy sheep, thy bullocks, kine, and calves do feed;
The middle grounds thy mares and horses breed.
Each bank doth yield thee conies, and the tops,
Fertile of wood, of Ashore and Sidney's copses,°
To crown thy open table doth provide
The purple pheasant with the speckled side;
The painted partridge lies in every field,
And for thy mess° is willing to be killed.   30
And if the high swollen Medway fail thy dish,
Thou hast thy ponds° that pay thee tribute fish:
Fat, agèd carps that run into thy net;
And pikes, now weary their own kind to eat,
As loath the second draught or cast to stay,°
Officiously at first themselves betray;
Bright eels that emulate them and leap on land,
Before the fisher or into his hand.
Then hath thy orchard fruit, thy garden flowers,
Fresh as the air, and new as are the hours.   40
The early cherry, with the later plum,
Fig, grape, and quince, each in his time doth come;
The blushing apricot and woolly peach
Hang on thy walls,° that every child may reach.
And though thy walls be of the country stone,
They're reared with no man's ruin, no man's groan;
There's none that dwell about them wish them down,
But all come in, the farmer and the clown,°
And no one empty-handed, to salute
Thy lord and lady, though they have no suit.   50
Some bring a capon,° some a rural cake,
Some nuts, some apples; some that think they make
The better cheeses bring 'em, or else send
By their ripe daughters, whom they would commend
This way to husbands, and whose baskets bear

° **Sylvan ... flames**: lovestruck rustic or forest spirit.
° **Gamage**: Robert Sidney's wife, Barbara Gamage, who fed deer in a stand of woods. A family
  tradition reports that she went into labour underneath a tree there that was subsequently known as
  the "Lady's Oak."
° **copses**: small woodlands periodically felled or pollarded and allowed to regenerate, which may
  have provided fuel for the Sidneys' ironworks.
° **ponds**: a fishpond was dug on the estate and stocked with carp in 1567.   ° **mess**: meal.
° **draught ... stay**: to await the second cast of net or fishing-line.
° **Hang ... walls**: fruit trees were often espaliered.
° **clown**: peasant.   ° **capon**: castrated chicken.

An emblem of themselves in plum or pear.
But what can this (more than express their love)
Add to thy free provisions far above
The need of such? Whose liberal board doth flow
60   With all that hospitality doth know!
Where comes no guest but is allowed to eat,
Without his fear, and of thy lord's own meat;
Where the same beer and bread and self-same wine
That is his Lordship's shall be also mine;
And I not fain to sit (as some this day
At great men's tables) and yet dine away.
Here no man tells° my cups nor, standing by,
A waiter doth my gluttony envy,
But gives me what I call and lets me eat;
70   He knows below he shall find plenty of meat;
Thy tables hoard not up for the next day;
Nor, when I take my lodgings, need I pray
For fire or lights or livery; all is there,
As if thou, then, wert mine, and I reigned here:
There's nothing I can wish for which I stay.°
That found King James, when hunting late this way,
With his brave son, the Prince, they saw thy fires
Shine bright on every hearth, as the desires
Of thy Penates° had been set on flame
80   To entertain them, or the country came
With all their zeal to warm their welcome here.
What (great I will not say, but) sudden cheer
Didst thou then make 'em! And what praise was heaped
On thy good lady then! Who therein reaped
The just reward of her high housewifery;
To have her linen, plate, and all things nigh
When she was far; and not a room but dressed,
As if it had expected such a guest!
These, Penshurst, are thy praise, and yet not all.
90   Thy lady's noble, fruitful, chaste withal.
His children thy great lord may call his own:
A fortune in this age but rarely known.
They are and have been taught religion; thence
Their gentler spirits have sucked innocence.
Each morn and even they are taught to pray,
With the whole household, and may every day
Read in their virtuous parents' noble parts,
The mysteries of manners, arms, and arts.
Now, Penshurst, they that will proportion thee
100   With other edifices, when they see
Those proud ambitious heaps, and nothing else,
May say, their lords have built, but thy lord dwells.

⁂

° **tells**: counts.   ° **stay**: wait.   ° **Penates**: Roman household gods, displayed near the hearth.

THOMAS CAREW
"To Saxham" (*c.* 1635)

Saxham was the country estate of Sir Henry Crofts near Bury St Edmunds. While indebted to "Penshurst," Carew's poem responds to a natural disaster, an extreme cold spell – quite possibly the Great Frost of 1634–5 (see Cartwright's poem in Part VI, p. 524). Consequently, it is not simply about place but the interactions between place, climate, and social class. Despite – or rather because of – the inclement weather, the house remains a pastoral *locus amoenus*, one to which both the poor and the animals flee like environmental refugees. Although the perspective remains anthropocentric (animals and resources exist primarily to sustain human life), Carew praises the stewardship of the estate that makes such hospitality possible, as the Crofts family has the foresight (and wealth) to plan for the vagaries of the climate during the Little Ice Age.
Source: *Poems* (1640), 45–7.

> Though frost and snow locked from mine eyes
> That beauty which without door lies,
> Thy gardens, orchards, walks, that so
> I might not all thy pleasures know,
> Yet, Saxham, thou within thy gate
> Art of thyself so delicate,°
> So full of native sweets that bless
> Thy roof with inward happiness,
> As neither from nor to thy store
> Winter takes aught, or Spring adds more.   10
> The cold and frozen air had starved
> Much poor, if not by thee preserved,
> Whose prayers have made thy Table blest
> With plenty, far above the rest.
> The season hardly did afford
> Coarse cates° unto thy neighbour's board,
> Yet thou hadst dainties, as the sky
> Had only been thy Volary;°
> Or else the birds, fearing the snow
> Might to another deluge grow,   20
> The Pheasant, Partridge, and the Lark,
> Flew to thy house as to the Ark.
> The willing Ox of himself came
> Home to the slaughter with the Lamb,
> And every beast did thither bring
> Himself, to be an offering.°
> The scaly herd more pleasure took,
> Bathed in thy dish than in the brook;
> Water, Earth, Air, did all conspire
> To pay their tributes to thy fire,   30
> Whose cherishing flames themselves divide

° **delicate**: charming.   ° **cates**: victuals.   ° **Volary**: aviary.
° **offering**: the *sua sponte* fantasy (McRae 1990, 232) of animals willingly sacrificing themselves for human consumption, imitating Jonson's "Penshurst."

Through every room, where they deride
The night and cold abroad; whilst they,
Like suns within, keep endless day.
Those cheerful beams send forth their light
To all that wander in the night,
And seem to beckon from aloof
The weary Pilgrim to thy roof,
Where, if refreshed, he will away,
40   He's fairly welcome; or, if stay,
Far more; which he shall hearty find
Both from the Master and the Hind.°
The stranger's welcome each man there
Stamped on his cheerful brow doth wear.
Nor doth this welcome or his cheer
Grow less 'cause he stays longer here.
There's none observes, much less repines,°
How often this man sups or dines.
Thou hast no Porter at thy door
50   T'examine or keep back the poor,
Nor locks nor bolts: thy gates have been
Made only to let strangers in.
Untaught to shut, they do not fear
To stand wide open all the year,
Careless who enters, for they know
Thou never didst deserve a foe.
And as for thieves, thy bounty's such,
They cannot steal, thou giv'st so much.

૨૪ ૨૪ ૨૪

° **Hind**: servant.   ° **repines**: grumbles.

ANDREW MARVELL
"Upon Appleton House" (*c.* 1651)

Refusing orders to invade Scotland, Lord Thomas Fairfax resigned as the head of
parliamentary forces in the north and retired in disgrace to his country estate Nun
Appleton in Yorkshire. As the tutor of Fairfax's daughter, Andrew Marvell resided
there in the summer of 1651, and composed this ode to their bucolic haven. The
poem's complexity results from its surveying a range of environs – house, garden,
meadow, and woods – through a variety of genres and attitudes. It not only praises
the psychological benefits of pastoral retreat but also calls for the regeneration of
the war-ravaged land through georgic stewardship and ecological dwelling that
"tempers human mastery over nature" (McColley 2007, 16).
Source: *Miscellaneous Poems* (1681), 76–8, 87–90, 93, 95–9.

1

Within this sober Frame expect
Work of no foreign Architect;
That unto Caves the Quarries drew
And Forests did to Pastures hew;
Who of his great Design in pain
Did for a Model vault his Brain,
Whose Columns should so high be raised
To arch the Brows that on them gazed.

2

Why should of all things Man unruled
Such unproportioned dwellings build?
The Beasts are by their Dens expressed,
And Birds contrive an equal Nest;
The low-roofed Tortoises do dwell
In cases fit of Tortoise-shell.
No Creature loves an empty space;
Their Bodies measure out their Place.

3

But He, superfluously spread,
Demands more room alive than dead.
And in his hollow Palace goes
Where Winds as he themselves may lose.
What need of all this Marble Crust
T'impark the wanton Mote of Dust,
That thinks by Breadth the World t'unite
Though the first Builders° failed in Height?

4

But all things are composèd here
Like Nature, orderly and near;
In which we the Dimensions find
Of that more sober Age and Mind,
When larger-sizèd Men did stoop
To enter at a narrow loop;
As practising, in doors so strait,°
To strain themselves through Heaven's Gate …

9

A Stately Frontispiece of Poor°
Adorns without the open Door:
Nor less the Rooms within commends
Daily new Furniture of Friends.

° **Builders**: of the Tower of Babel (Genesis 11:1–9).
° **strait**: narrow (see Matthew 7:14).   ° **Poor**: porphyry.

The House was built upon the Place
Only as for a Mark of Grace;
And for an Inn to entertain
Its Lord awhile, but not remain.

10

Him Bishop-Hill or Denton may,
Or Bilbrough,° better hold than they:
But Nature here hath been so free
As if she said leave this to me.
Art would more neatly have defaced
What she had laid so sweetly waste:°
In fragrant Gardens, shady Woods,
Deep Meadows, and transparent Floods …

41

O Thou, that dear and happy Isle,
The Garden of the World erewhile,
Thou Paradise of four Seas,
Which Heaven planted us to please,
But to exclude the World did guard
With wat'ry if not flaming Sword;°
What luckless Apple did we taste,
To make us Mortal, and thee Waste?°

42

Unhappy! shall we never more
That sweet Militia restore,
When Gardens only had their Towers,
And all the Garrisons were Flowers,
When Roses only Arms might bear,
And Men did rosy Garlands wear?
Tulips, in several Colours barred,
Were then the Switzers° of our Guard.

43

The Gardener had the Soldier's place,
And his more gentle Forts did trace.
The nursery of all things green
Was then the only Magazine.°
The Winter Quarters were the Stoves,°
Where he the tender Plants removes.
But War all this doth overgrow:
We Ord'nance plant and Powder sow …

° **Bishop-Hill … Bilbrough**: estates belonging to the Fairfax family.
° **waste**: wild.   ° **flaming Sword**: see Genesis 3:24.   ° **Waste**: devastated (by war).
° **Switzers**: Swiss guards, whose red- and yellow-striped uniforms recall the streakings of the tulip
  petal.
° **Magazine**: storehouse, arsenal.   ° **Stoves**: hothouses.

47

And now to the Abyss I pass
Of that unfathomable Grass,
Where Men like Grasshoppers appear,
But Grasshoppers are Giants there:
They, in their squeaking Laugh, condemn
Us as we walk more low than them;
And from the Precipices tall
Of the green spires to us do call.

48

To see Men through this Meadow dive,
We wonder how they rise alive:
As, under Water, none does know
Whether he fall through it or go.
But as the Mariners that sound
And show upon their Lead the Ground,
They bring up Flowers so to be seen,
And prove they've at the Bottom been.

49

No Scene that turns with Engines strange
Does oft'ner than these Meadows change;
For when the Sun the Grass hath vexed,
The tawny Mowers enter next,
Who seem like Israelites° to be,
Walking on foot through a green Sea.
To them the Grassy Deeps divide,
And crowd a Lane to either Side.

50

With whistling Scythe and Elbow strong,
These Massacre the Grass along:
While one, unknowing, carves the Rail,°
Whose yet unfeathered Quills her fail.
The Edge all bloody from its Breast
He draws, and does his stroke detest;
Fearing the Flesh untimely mowed
To him a Fate as black forebode …

61

But I, retiring from the Flood,
Take Sanctuary in the Wood;
And, while it lasts, myself embark°
In this yet green, yet growing Ark;

° **Israelites**: an allusion to Moses parting the Red Sea (Exodus 14).
° **Rail**: a family of birds that includes moorhens, coots, and crakes. Marvell probably refers to the landrail or corncrake, a reclusive species (now endangered) which nests in tall grass.
° **embark**: with wordplay on tree-bark.

Where the first Carpenter° might best
Fit Timber for his Keel have Pressed;
And where all Creatures might have shares,
Although in Armies, not in Pairs.

62

The double Wood of ancient Stocks°
Linked in so thick a Union° locks,
It like two Pedigrees° appears:
On one hand Fairfax, th'other Veres;
Of whom though many fell in war,
Yet more to Heaven shooting are;
And as they Nature's Cradle decked,
Will in green Age her Hearse expect …

67

Then as I careless on the Bed
Of gelid° Strawberries do tread,
And through the Hazels thick espy
The hatching Thrastle's° shining Eye,
The Heron from the Ash's top,
The eldest of its young lets drop,
As if it Stork-like did pretend
That Tribute to its Lord to send.

68

But most the Hewel's° wonders are,
Who here has the Holt-felster's° care.
He walks still upright from the Root,
Meas'ring the Timber with his Foot;
And all the way, to keep it clean,
Doth from the Bark the Wood-moths glean.
He with his Beak examines well
Which fit to stand and which to fell.

69

The good he numbers up and hacks,
As if he marked them with the Axe.
But where he, tinkling with his Beak,
Does find the hollow Oak to speak,
That for his building he designs,
And through the tainted Side he mines.
Who could have thought the tallest Oak
Should fall by such a feeble Stroke!°

° **first Carpenter**: Noah.   ° **Stocks**: trunks, but with pun on lineage.
° **Union**: with wordplay on marriage.
° **Pedigrees**: a play on the conceit of the "family tree."   ° **gelid**: icy.
° **Thrastle**: thrush.   ° **Hewel**: woodpecker.   ° **Holt-felster**: woodcutter.
° **Who could … stroke**: a possible allusion to the execution of Charles I and defeat of Charles II.
  On tree-felling in the poem, see Theis, 2015.

70

Nor would it, had the Tree not fed
A Traitor-Worm, within it bred
(As first our Flesh corrupt within
Tempts impotent and bashful Sin).
And yet that Worm triumphs not long,
But serves to feed the Hewel's young:
While the Oak seems to fall content,
Viewing the Treason's Punishment.

71

Thus I, easy Philosopher,
Among the Birds and Trees confer;
And little now to make me wants,°
Or° of the Fowls or of the Plants.
Give me but Wings as they and I
Straight floating on the Air shall fly;
Or turn me but and you shall see
I was but an inverted Tree.°

72

Already I begin to call
In their most-learned Original;
And where I Language want, my Signs
The Bird upon the Bough divines;
And more attentive there doth sit
Than if She were with Lime-twigs knit.
No Leaf does tremble in the Wind
Which I returning cannot find.

73

Out of these scattered Sibyl's Leaves°
Strange Prophecies my Fancy weaves,
And in one History consumes,
Like Mexique-Paintings, all the Plumes.°
What Rome, Greece, Palestine ere said,
I in this light Mosaic read.
Thrice happy he who, not mistook,
Hath read in Nature's mystic Book.

☙ ☙ ☙

° **wants**: lacks.　　° **Or**: either.
° **inverted Tree**: This trope goes back to Plato and was a commonplace in Renaissance emblem
　books.
° **Sibyl's leaves**: the priestesses at the Delphic oracle divined by reading scattered laurel leaves.
° **Mexique … plumes**: Aztec mosaics made from feathers.

Gardens

THOMAS HILL

"Rare inventions and defences for most seeds" (1577)

A garden is always a battleground, an attempt by humans to stake out a plot of land for their exclusive use. Naturally, other species do not acknowledge our right to monopolize vast patches of the earth, provoking humans to devise a number of strategies for deterring or destroying perceived invaders. In the first English gardening manual, Thomas Hill shares dozens of recipes for protecting crops, some involving sympathetic magic and others deploying what we would now call biological pest control, such as training cats and tame weasels to catch moles. In the mid-twentieth century this traditional lore gave way to synthetic pesticides like DDT, which prompted Rachel Carson to write her landmark exposé *Silent Spring*, kick-starting the modern environmental movement.
Source: *The Gardener's Labyrinth* (1577), 30–3, 66, 69, 71.

All worthy Writers agree that in vain the husbandly Gardener shall travail … if the Seeds bestowed in the earth [31] happen after to be endamaged, either of Worms and other creeping things, or otherwise scraped up and wasted by Birds … [So] that the owner or Gardener may avoid these injuries, it is high time that he employ a care and diligence in the conceiving of these remedies and secrets following. If Seeds to be committed to the Earth are a little time before the bestowing steeped in the juice of Houseleek or Sengreen, they shall not only be without harm preserved from Birds, Ants, Field Mice, and other spoilers of the garden herbs, but what plants shoot up of these shall after prove the better and worthier …

And for lack of this herb altogether, [Columella°] reporteth that the Gardener may use instead of it the Soot cleaving on the chimney, which gathered a day before the bestowing of the seeds in the earth and mixed for a night with them, doth the like defend the seeds in safety.

The Greek writers of husbandry … report that those seeds may be preserved in safety from all evil and garden monsters if the bare head, without flesh, of either Mare or She-ass (having been covered of the male) be buried in the Garden, or that the middest° of the same fixed on a stake set into the earth be erected.

The worthy Pliny° further reporteth that there is a Garlic growing in the fallow field (named Allium) which, on such wise boiled that the same will not grow again and strewn on the Beds sown, doth in such manner avail that Birds after will not scrape up the earth, nor spoil the seeds [32]

° **Columella**: Roman agricultural writer, author of *De re rustica*.
° **middest**: torso.   ° **Pliny**: Roman author of *Natural History* (see 17.28, 19.10).

bestowed in them. And such which have eaten of this are taken (as being astonished°) with the hand. The well-practised Africanus° unto the same matter instructeth that if a quantity of Wheat or Barley be boiled or infused in wine and mixed with Sneezewort … and the same sprinkled abroad by the paths of the beds round about, it doth on such wise defend the seeds sown from the injury of Birds. But those being in a manner dead by eating of this, or at the least stark drunk, he willeth then to hang up by the legs on a long rod stuck in the earth, to the terror and fearing away of all other Birds coming to the place.

Nor [does] this worthy Author omitteth the rare practice of the decoction of river Crayfish: with which if the Gardener shall sprinkle his seeds before the sowing, Birds will never after (a matter to be marvelled at) approach to the Garden Beds. Yea, the plants beside which are sprung or shot out of these shall endure and continue safe and free from all the injuries of creeping things. There are certain skilful practitioners which affirm to have availed mightily in driving away Birds by the only sprinkling of this decoction above taught on the plants come up, which matter hath of many been experienced above a hundred times, so that the same were wrought at a certain period and time of the Moon …

[33] [Apuleius°] further willeth that, for a safety of the seeds bestowed, a speckled Toad … be drawn by a line in the night-time, round about the Garden or field afore the earth be laboured or diligently digged and dressed of the Gardener: and the same after enclosed in an earthen pot to be buried in the midst of the Garden or fallow Field, which, at the present sowing time approached, shall then be digged forth and thrown or carried from that place a great distance off …

The Egyptian and Greek instructors of husbandry report that the seeds … will remain ungnawed or bitten and free of harm by creeping things in the Garden if the seeds shall be committed to the earth when the Moon possesseth her half-light, or is quarter old° …

[61] That worthy Pliny in his *Book of Histories* writeth that … the pure mother° of the Oil Olive, without any salt in it, doth also drive the worms away and defend the Plants and Herbs from being after gnawed of them. And if they shall cleave to the roots of the plants, through malice or breeding of the dung, yet this weedeth them clean away. The Plants or Herbs will not after be gnawed or harmed by Garden fleas if with the natural

---

° **astonished**: stupefied.
° **Africanus**: Sextus Julius Africanus, an early Christian writer and supposed author of the encyclopaedic *Kestoi*; he advocated the use of biological and chemical weapons against Rome's enemies.
° **Apuleius**: Roman author, best known for *The Golden Ass*, who is credited with several passages in the *Geoponica*, a tenth-century compendium of ancient agricultural texts from which Hill derives much esoteric lore.
° **moon … old**: this superstition may have been motivated by an observed correlation between insect activity and lunar cycles.   ° **mother**: dregs.

remedy, as with the Herb Rocket, the Gardener shall bestow his beds in many places ...

[66] Many there be which to drive away these harmful Moles do bring up young Cats in their Garden ground and make tame Weasels to the end that either of these ... may so drive away this pestiferous annoyance, being taught to watch at their strait passages and mouths of the holes coming forth. Others there be also which diligently fill and stop up their holes with the red Ochre or Ruddle and juice of the wild Cucumber ... But some exercise this easy practice: taking a live Mole and burning the powder of Brimstone about him, being in a deep Earthen pot through which he is procured to cry, all others in the meantime, as they report, are moved to resort thither ...

[69] The learned Democritus° affirmeth that the serpents assuredly do die if the gardener strew or throw oaken leaves on them, or if any spitteth fasting into their mouth gaping or wide open ...

[71] But in this place is not to be omitted that serpents greatly hate the fire, not for the same cause that this dulleth their sight, but because the nature of fire is to resist poison. These also hate the strong savoury° far flying which the garlic and red onions procure ... But they are mightily displeased [by] and sorest hate the ash tree, insomuch that the serpents neither to the morning nor longest evening shadows of it will draw near, but rather shun the same and fly far off. As a like matter Pliny° reporteth was on a time proved by enclosing a serpent within a large circle made of green ash tree leaves, in the middle of which a quick fire made ... At the last, [the serpent] rather crept to the fire, where he perished, than by any means would draw near to the circle of the ash tree leaves. Yet here learn the marvellous benignity of nature, which permitteth not the serpents to come forth of the earth before the ash tree buddeth forth, nor to hide them again before the leaves fall off.

⁂ ⁂ ⁂

° **Democritus**: Greek philosopher, whose lost work "On Agriculture" is excerpted in the *Geoponica*.
° **savoury**: odour.   ° **Pliny**: *Natural History*, 16.13.

ANONYMOUS

"The Mole-catcher's Speech" (1591)

The following is an extract from "A Speech Made Before the Queen at Theobalds," the Hertfordshire estate of Lord Burghley, Elizabeth's most trusted advisor. It has been credited to George Peele, John Lyly, and even Burghley's son, Robert Cecil, but these attributions are all conjectural. Like the garden scene in Shakespeare's *Richard II* (p. 236), it hinges on the analogy between horticulture and statecraft,

inviting the audience to read the large show-gardens the Burghleys created as advertisements of their fitness to govern. In this speech, the quarrel between the mole-catcher and the gardener represents the differences between soldiers and politicians, while the moles signify traitors.
Source: Egerton MS 2623, 18ʳ–18ᵛ.

Good Lady ... I cannot discourse of knots and mazes; sure I am that the ground was so knotty° that the gardener was amazed to see it, and as easy had it been, if I had not been, to make a shaft of a cammock° as a garden of that croft.° I came not to claim any right for myself, but to give you yours. For that had the bickering been between us there should have needed no other justice of peace than this° to have made him a mittimus° to the first gardener that ever was, Adam ...

Now for this gardener twitteth° me with my vocation, I could prove it a mystery° not mechanical and tell the tale of the giant's daughter which was turned to a mole because she would eat fairer bread than is made of wheat, wear finer cloth than is made of wool, drink neater wine than is made of grapes; why she was blind and light of hearing; and how good clerks told me that moles in fields were like ill subjects in commonwealths, which are always turning up the place in which they are bred. But I will not trouble your Majesty, but every day pray on my knees that all those that [18ᵛ] be heavers at your state may come to a mole's blessing: a knock on the pate and a swing on a tree. Now madam for this gardener, command him to tend his garden. And till his melancholy be past let him walk in the alleys and pick up worms like a lapwing.

২৳ ২৳ ২৳

° **knotty**: rugged, but punning on "knots" or patterns popular in Tudor garden designs.
° **cammock**: crooked staff.   ° **croft**: enclosed ground.
° **this**: marginal note here reads "his molespade."   ° **mittimus**: legal writ transferring custody.
° **twitteth**: teases.   ° **mystery**: profession.

WILLIAM SHAKESPEARE
[The Duke of York's Garden] from Richard II *(c. 1595)*

At this juncture of the play, Richard has been deposed by Bolingbroke (the future Henry IV), and Shakespeare traces an elaborate comparison between governing and gardening, one already foreshadowed in John of Gaunt's famed hymn to England as "this blessed plot" (2.1.50). In an agrarian society, this was not simply a trite analogy: the economy and hence political stability were tied to crop yields. In a preceding scene, Shakespeare glances at contemporary environmental degradation when Bolingbroke condemns Richard's minions, significantly named Bushy and Green, for having "disparked [his] parks and felled [his] forest woods" (3.1.23). Such failures of stewardship would have had a disturbing topicality in the midst of the "disordered spring" and dearth of the mid-1590s (see Bruckner 2013, and

Part VI). The scene thus offers a precedent for grounding political authority in sound environmental policy.

Source: *Mr. William Shakespeare's Comedies, Histories, and Tragedies* (1623), G3ʳ–G3ᵛ, with emendations from the 1597 Quarto.

3.4

Enter a Gardener *and two* Servants.
[*The* Queen *and two* Ladies *hide.*]

GARDENER Go, bind thou up yond° dangling Apricots,°
Which, like unruly Children, make their Sire
Stoop with oppression of their prodigal weight.
Give some supportance to the bending twigs.
Go thou, and like an Executioner,
Cut off the heads of too° fast growing sprays,
That look too lofty in our Commonwealth:
All must be even in our Government.
You thus employed, I will go root away
The noisome Weeds that without profit suck
40   The Soil's fertility from wholesome flowers.
SERVANT° Why should we, in the compass of a Pale,°
Keep Law and Form and due Proportion,
Showing as in a Model our firm Estate,
When our Sea-walled Garden, the whole Land,
Is full of Weeds, her fairest Flowers choked up,
Her Fruit trees all unpruned, her Hedges ruined,
Her Knots disordered, and her wholesome Herbs
Swarming with Caterpillars?
GARDENER   Hold thy peace.
He that hath suffered this disordered Spring
50   Hath now himself met with the Fall of Leaf.
The Weeds that his broad-spreading Leaves did shelter,
That seemed, in eating him, to hold him up,
Are pulled° up, Root and all, by Bolingbroke°—
I mean the Earl of Wiltshire, Bushy, Green.
SERVANT   What, are they dead?
GARDENER   They are; and Bolingbroke
Hath seized° the wasteful King. Oh, what pity is it
That he had not so trimmed and dressed his Land
As we this Garden! We at time of year,°
Do wound the Bark, the skin of our Fruit-trees,
60   Lest being overproud in Sap and Blood,
With too much riches it confound itself.

° **yond**: young] Q1.   ° **Apricots**: The original spelling, Apricocks, brings out a bawdy innuendo.
° **too**: two] Q1. The Quarto reading more directly evokes the execution of Bushy and Green.
° **Servant**: Man] Q1.   ° **Pale**: enclosure.   ° **pulled**: plucked] Q1.
° **Bolingbroke**: spelled Bullingbrooke in Q1 and F.
° **seized**: ceased] Q1.
° **and … year**: The text is mislineated here in both Q and F; I have followed Capell's emendation.

Had he done so to great and growing men,
They might have lived to bear and he to taste
Their fruits of duty. Superfluous branches
We lop away that bearing boughs may live.
Had he done so, himself had borne the Crown,
Which waste and idle hours hath quite thrown down ...
QUEEN [*Aside*] Oh, I am pressed to death through want of speaking!
Thou, old Adam's likeness, set to dress this Garden:
How dares thy harsh rude tongue sound this unpleasing news?
What Eve, what Serpent hath suggested thee
To make a second fall of cursèd man?
Why dost thou say King Richard is deposed?
Dar'st thou, thou little better thing than earth,
Divine his downfall? ...   80
GARDENER Pardon me, Madam. Little joy have I
To breath these news; yet what I say is true ...
Post you to London and you'll find it so;
I speak no more than everyone doth know.
QUEEN ... Gard'ner, for telling me this news of woe,   101
I would° the Plants thou graft'st may never grow.   *Exit* [*with* Ladies].
GARDENER Poor Queen, so that thy State might be no worse,
I would my skill were subject to thy curse.
Here did she drop a tear; here in this place
I'll set a Bank of Rue,° sour Herb of Grace:
Rue, e'en for ruth, here shortly shall be seen
In the remembrance of a weeping Queen.

❧ ❧ ❧

° **I would**: Pray God] Q1. Compare the queen's curse with Isabella's destruction of the arbour and
  "garden plot" where her son was murdered in Kyd's *Spanish Tragedy* (4.2).
° **Rue**: associated with repentance, pity (ruth), and memory.

FRANCIS BACON
"Of Gardens" (1625)

Renaissance gardens were not monolithic, but varied widely in dimensions, contents, style, and purpose. While the middling classes had practical kitchen gardens (tended mainly by women), the affluent also devised lavish show gardens on
their country estates. In his classic study on the topic, Roy Strong identifies four
major varieties predominant during the reigns of successive monarchs: (1) the
Heraldic (1509–58), epitomized by the knot-covered square plots adorned with
heraldic beasts found in Henry's Hampton Court gardens; (2) the Emblematic
(1558–1603), featuring fountains and topiary art advertising moral lessons and the
prestige of Elizabethan nobles; (3) the Mannerist (1603–25), marked by highly
contrived designs and gimmicks like hydraulic statuary and mechanical birds;
and (4) the Eclectic (1625–42), which mingles the previous three and is represented by the Earl of Pembroke's estate at Wilton. Broadly speaking, however, most

Renaissance gardens tended to feature ornate patterns and geometrical designs. Gardens are of course living expressions of cultural ideals about the natural world. The taste for such emphatically orderly gardens can be perceived as a compensatory fantasy of imposing order on the unruliness of the early modern environment – a backlash against the chronic insecurity felt by an agrarian society, or even a reaction against environmental degradation (Tigner 2012, 6–10). By Bacon's time, however, landscape architects were introducing grottos, heaths carefully cultivated to look uncultivated, or – in the paradoxical phrase of Henry Wotton – "wild regularity" in garden design (109). These developments already foretoken the English landscape garden of the eighteenth century, which broke with the rigid *jardin à la française* and capitalism's aggressively utilitarian view of nature, seeking instead to create picturesque vistas of what Bacon terms "Natural wildness."
Source: *The Essays* (1625), 266, 270–9.

God Almighty first planted a Garden. And indeed, it is the Purest of Human° pleasure. It is the Greatest Refreshment to the Spirits of Man, without which Buildings and Palaces are but Gross Handiworks. And a Man shall ever see that when Ages grow to Civility and Elegancy Men come to Build Stately sooner than to Garden Finely, as if Gardening were the Greater Perfection. I do hold it in the Royal Ordering of Gardens there ought to be Gardens for all the Months in the Year, in which severally° Things of Beauty may be then in Season … [270] that you may have *Ver Perpetuum*° as the place affords …

And because the Breath of Flowers is far sweeter in the Air (where it comes and goes, like the warbling of Music) than in the hand, therefore nothing is more fit for that delight than to know what be the Flowers and Plants that do best perfume the Air. Roses, Damask and Red, are fast° Flowers of their Smells, so that you may walk by a whole Row of them and find nothing of their Sweetness—yea, though it be in a Morning's Dew. Bays likewise yield no Smell as they grow; Rosemary little; nor Sweet Marjoram. That which above all others yields the sweetest Smell in the Air is the Violet, especially the White-double-Violet, which comes twice a Year: about the middle of April and about Bartholomew-tide.° Next to that is the Musk-rose; then the Strawberry Leaves dying, which [is] a most [270] excellent Cordial Smell; then the Flower of the Vines …

For Gardens (speaking of those which are indeed Prince-like …), the Contents ought not well to be under Thirty Acres of Ground, and to be divided into three [271] Parts: a Green in the entrance; a Heath or Desert in the going forth; and the Garden in the midst, besides Alleys on both Sides. And I like well that four Acres of Ground be assigned to the Green, six to the Heath, four and four to either side, and twelve to the Main Garden. The Green hath two pleasures: the one, because nothing is more pleasant to the Eye than Green Grass kept finely shorn; the other, because it will give you a

---

° **human**: spelled humane.   ° **severally**: successively.
° ***Ver Perpetuum***: eternal summer. In the omitted passage, Bacon lists a staggering ninety-five
  varieties of plants and the month in which they flower or bear fruit.
° **fast**: stingy.   ° **Bartholomew-tide**: 24 August.

fair Alley in the midst by which you may go in front upon a Stately Hedge, which is to enclose the Garden ... As for the making of Knots or Figures with Diverse-Coloured Earths, that they may [272] lie under the Windows of the House ... they be but Toys. You may see as good Sights many times in Tarts.

The Garden is best to be Square, encompassed on all the four sides with a Stately Arched Hedge ... Over the Arches let there be an entire Hedge, of some four Foot High, framed also upon Carpenter's Work; and upon the Upper Hedge, over every Arch, a little Turret, with a Belly,° enough to receive a Cage of Birds ... [273] For the ordering of the Ground within the great Hedge, I leave it to Variety of Device, advising, nevertheless, that whatsoever form you cast it into, first it be not too busy or full of Work. Wherein I for my part do not like Images cut out in Juniper or other Garden stuff. They be for Children. Little low Hedges, Round like Welts, with some Pretty Pyramids, I like well; and in some places fair Columns upon Frames of Carpenter's Work. I would also have the Alleys spacious and fair ... [274] I wish also in the very Middle a Fair Mount, with three Ascents, and Alleys, [wide] enough for four to walk abreast, which I would have to be perfect Circles, without any Bulwarks or Embossments; and the whole Mount to be thirty Foot high; and some fine Banqueting House, with some Chimneys neatly cast, and without too much Glass.°

For Fountains, they are a great Beauty and Refreshment. But Pools mar all, and make the Garden unwholesome and full of Flies and Frogs ... And for fine Devices of arching Water without spilling and making it rise in several Forms (of Feathers, Drinking Glasses, Canopies, and the like), they be pretty things to [276] look on, but nothing to Health and Sweetness.

For the Heath, which was the Third Part of our Plot, I wish it to be framed, as much as may be, to a Natural wildness. Trees I would have none in it, but some Thickets, made only of Sweetbriar and Honeysuckle, and some Wild Vine amongst; and the Ground set with Violets, Strawberries, and Primroses, for these are sweet and prosper in the Shade; and these to be in the Heath, here and there, not in any order. I like also little Heaps, in the nature of Mole-hills (such as are in Wild Heaths), to be set, some with Wild Thyme; some with Pinks; some with Germander, that gives a good Flower to the Eye: ... part of which Heaps to be [277] with Standards of little Bushes, pricked upon their top, ... [but] kept with Cutting that they grow not out of course ...

[278] For the Main Garden, I do not deny but there should be some fair Alleys ranged on both sides with Fruit Trees, and ... Arbours with Seats, set in some decent Order; but these to be by no means set too thick, but to leave the Main Garden so as it be not close, but the Air open and free ...

For Aviaries, I like them not, except they be of that largeness as they may be [279] turfed and have living Plants and Bushes set in them, that the

---

° **Belly**: cavity.
° **Glass**: a luxury item in early modern building, as glass-making consumed loads of expensive wood.

Birds may have more Scope and Natural Nestling, and that no Foulness appear in the Floor of the Aviary. So I have made a Platform° of a Princely Garden, partly by Precept, partly by Drawing: not a Model, but some general Lines of it. And in this I have spared for no Cost. But it is nothing for Great Princes that, for the most part, taking Advice with Workmen, with no less Cost, set their Things together, and sometimes add Statues and such Things for State and Magnificence, but nothing to the true Pleasure of a Garden.

؏ ؏ ؏

° **Platform**: foundation.

ANDREW MARVELL
"The Garden" and "The Mower against Gardens" (c. 1651)

Gardens are often sites of contemplation and psychological refuge – particularly for the leisure classes who do not labour in them. The speaker in Marvell's first poem regresses back to an Adam-like innocence, while redirecting his erotic energy from the opposite sex onto plants. Stanza 6 famously lauds the power of the human imagination to both transform and merge with the non-human environment. But are these two feats in some ways contradictory? While Marvell strives to abolish the distinction between the poet and nature through a "sensuous reciprocity" (McColley 2007, 13), Robert Watson (2006, 118) contends that language (especially literary language) only charts the gulf between humans and their surroundings, even when it seeks to recuperate an Edenic epistemology.

Similar ironies haunt the second poem, in which a mower condemns grafting and defends the uncultivated wild in artful verses composed in couplets of alternating pentameter and tetrameter. Several Renaissance agricultural writers shared Marvell's disapproval of grafting as a "presumptuous and almost blasphemous" (Bushnell 146) interference in the natural order, an opinion voiced by Shakespeare's Perdita, who nonetheless wishes to violate the social order by marrying a prince. How does the mower's rhetoric compare with that deployed today against genetically modified organisms?
Source: *Miscellaneous Poems* (1681), 48–51, 40–1.

"The Garden"

I
How vainly men themselves amaze
To win the Palm, the Oak, or Bays;°
And their incessant Labours see
Crowned from some single Herb or Tree,

° **Bays**: laurel garlands worn by victors of poetry competitions in antiquity.

Whose short and narrow-vergèd Shade
Does prudently their Toils upbraid;
While all Flowers and all Trees do close
To weave the Garlands of repose.

2

Fair Quiet, have I found thee here,
And Innocence, thy Sister dear!
Mistaken long, I sought you then
In busy Companies of Men.
Your sacred Plants, if here below,
Only among the Plants will grow;
Society is all but rude,
To this delicious Solitude.

3

No white nor red was ever seen
So am'rous as this lovely green.
Fond Lovers, cruèl as their Flame,
Cut in these Trees their Mistress' name:
Little, alas, they know or heed,
How far these Beauties Hers exceed!
Fair Trees! wheresoe'er your barks I wound,
No Name shall but your own be found.

4

When we have run our Passions' heat,
Love hither makes his best retreat.
The Gods that mortal Beauty chase
Still in a Tree did end their race:
Apollo hunted Daphne so,
Only that She might Laurel grow;
And Pan did after Syrinx speed,
Not as a Nymph, but for a Reed.°

5

What wondrous Life in this I lead!
Ripe Apples drop about my head;
The Luscious Clusters of the Vine
Upon my Mouth do crush their Wine;
The Nectarine and curious Peach,
Into my hands themselves do reach;
Stumbling on Melons as I pass,
Ensnared with Flowers, I fall on Grass.

6

Meanwhile the Mind, from pleasures less,
Withdraws into its happiness;

° **Apollo … reed**: See Ovid's *Metamorphoses*, 1.639–700, 858–87.

The Mind, that Ocean where each kind
Does straight its own resemblance find;
Yet it creates, transcending these,
Far other Worlds, and other Seas;
Annihilating all that's made
To a green Thought in a green Shade.

7

Here at the Fountain's sliding foot,
Or at some Fruit-tree's mossy root,
Casting the Body's Vest aside,
My Soul into the boughs does glide:
There like a Bird it sits and sings,
Then whets and combs its silver Wings;
And, till prepared for longer flight,
Waves in its Plumes the various Light.

8

Such was that happy Garden-state,
While Man there walked without a Mate.
After a Place so pure and sweet,
What other Help could yet be meet!°
But 'twas beyond a Mortal's share
To wander solitary there:
Two Paradises 'twere in one
To live in Paradise alone.

9

How well the skilful Gard'ner drew
Of flowers and herbs this Dial new;
Where from above the milder Sun
Does through a fragrant Zodiac run;
And, as it works, th'industrious Bee
Computes its time as well as we.
How could such sweet and wholesome Hours
Be reckoned but with herbs and flowers?

"The Mower against Gardens"

Luxurious° Man, to bring his Vice in use,
Did after him the World seduce,
And from the fields the Flowers and Plants allure,
Where Nature was most plain and pure.
He first enclosed within the Garden's square
A dead and standing pool of Air,
And a more luscious Earth for them did knead,

° **meet**: apt, punning on the Bible's description of Eve as Adam's "helpmeet."
° **Luxurious**: extravagant, but also lecherous.

Which stupefied them while it fed.
The Pink grew then as double as his Mind;
The nutriment did change the kind.   10
With strange perfumes he did the Roses taint,
And Flowers themselves were taught to paint.°
The Tulip white did for complexion seek,
And learned to interline its cheek;
Its Onion root they then so high did hold,
That one was for a Meadow sold.°
Another World was searched, through Oceans new,
To find the Marvel of Peru.°
And yet these Rarities might be allowed,
To Man, that sov'reign thing and proud,   20
Had he not dealt between the Bark and Tree,
Forbidden mixtures there to see.
No Plant now knew the Stock from which it came;
He grafts upon the Wild the Tame,
That the uncertain and adult'rate fruit
Might put the Palate in dispute.
His green Seraglio° has its Eunuchs too,
Lest any Tyrant him outdo;
And in the Cherry he does Nature vex,
To procreate without a Sex.   30
'Tis all enforced, the Fountain and the Grot,
While the sweet Fields do lie forgot,
Where willing Nature does to all dispense
A wild and fragrant Innocence;
And Fauns and Fairies do the Meadows till,
More by their presence than their skill.
Their Statues, polished by some ancient hand,
May to adorn the Gardens stand;
But howsoe'er the Figures do excel,
The Gods themselves with us do dwell.

ༀ ༀ ༀ

° **paint**: wear cosmetics.   ° **Meadow sold**: during the peak of Dutch Tulipomania in the mid-1630s.
° **Marvel of Peru**: *Mirabilis jalapa* or the four o'clock flower.   ° **Seraglio**: harem.

ABRAHAM COWLEY
"The Garden" (1667)

Like Marvell, Cowley celebrates the garden as a place of physico-psychological re-
juvenation and spiritual meditation. Unlike Marvell's mower, however, Cowley defends grafting as an improving of nature that makes the gardener feel "almost a god."
In the final stanza, the relationship between gardener and plant is likened to that
of Apollo and Daphne, drawing a problematic analogy between grafting and rape.
Source: *Essays of Abraham Cowley* (1869), 74–5.

9

Where does the wisdom and the power divine
In a more bright and sweet reflection shine?
Where do we finer strokes and colours see
Of the Creator's real poetry,
Than when we with attention look
Upon the third day's volume of the book?°
If we could open and intend° our eye,
We all like Moses should espy
E'en in a bush the radiant Deity.°
But we despise these his inferior ways
(Though no less full of miracle and praise):
Upon the flowers of heaven we gaze;
The stars of earth no wonder in us raise,
Though these perhaps do more than they
The life of mankind sway.
Although no part of mighty nature be
More stored with beauty, power, and mystery,
Yet to encourage human industry,
God has so ordered that no other part
Such space and such dominion leaves for art.

10

We nowhere art do so triumphant see,
As when it grafts or buds the tree;
In other things we count it to excel,
If it a docile scholar can appear
To Nature, and but imitate her well.
It overrules and is her master here.
It imitates her Maker's power divine,
And changes her sometimes, and sometimes does refine.
It does, like grace, the fallen tree restore
To its blest state of Paradise before.
Who would not joy to see his conquering hand
O'er all the vegetable world command,
And the wild giants of the wood receive
What laws he's pleased to give?
He bids the ill-natured crab produce
The gentler apple's winy juice,
The golden fruit that worthy is,
Of Galatea's° purple kiss;
He does the savage hawthorn teach
To bear the medlar and the pear;
He bids the rustic plum to rear

° **third … book**: in Genesis, God creates plants on the third day.
° **intend**: dilate.   ° **Moses … Deity**: see Genesis 3:2.
° **Galatea**: sea-nymph, given golden and purple grapes in Ovid (*Metamorphoses*, 13.956–7).

A noble trunk, and be a peach.
E'en Daphne's° coyness he does mock,
And weds the cherry to her stock,
Though she refused Apollo's suit,
E'en she, that chaste and virgin tree,
Now wonders at herself to see
That she's a mother made, and blushes in her fruit.

2♦ 2♦ 2♦

° **Daphne**: nymph transformed into a laurel tree (*Metamorphoses*, 1.671–6).

Pastoral: Pastures, Meadows, Plains, Downs

PHILIP SIDNEY

from The Arcadia (*c.* 1585)

Ostensibly set in ancient Greece and inspired by the work of the Italian Jacopo Sannazaro, Sidney's pastoral romance also depicts an idealized Elizabethan countryside, modelled on the Wiltshire estate of his sister, the Countess of Pembroke. Notoriously, much of the Earl of Pembroke's manorial lands had been enclosed in the mid-sixteenth century, and Sidney's dismissive account of the Helot uprising can be viewed as a condemnation of anti-enclosure riots (see Part v). Whereas the previous open-field system allowed commons to be divided into strips and used for multiple purposes, enclosed lands could be made more uniform to maximize profits or impose upon them a consistent landscape design. Achieving "order in confusion," Kalander's garden rejects both the disorder of the commons and the monoculture of agrarian capitalists, exhibiting a horticultural *sprezzatura* that disguises the nobility's management of the land as natural. Rather than an escape from history, the *Arcadia* here foresees the environmental degradation caused by the English Civil War, and its "golden world" reflects a feudal land ethic in which the beauty and ecological stability of the countryside result from aristocratic stewardship.
Source: *The Countess of Pembroke's Arcadia* (1593), 3^v–5^v.

In the time that the morning did strew roses and violets in the heavenly floor against the coming of the Sun, the nightingales (striving one with the other which could in most dainty variety recount their wrong-caused sorrow°) made them put off their sleep, and rising from under a tree (which had that night been their pavilion) they went on their journey, which by and by welcomed Musidorus' eyes, wearied with the wasted soil of Laconia, with delightful prospects.

There were hills which garnished their proud heights with stately trees; humble valleys whose base estate seemed comforted with refreshing of silver rivers; meadows enamelled with all sorts of eye-pleasing flowers; thickets which, being lined with most pleasant shade, were witnessed so to by the cheerful disposition of many well-tuned birds; each pasture stored with sheep feeding with sober security, while the pretty lambs with bleating oratory craved the dams' comfort; here a shepherd boy piping as though he should never be old; there a young shepherdess knitting and withal singing, and it seemed that her voice comforted her hands to work and her hands kept time to her voice's music. As for the houses of the country (for many houses came under their eye), they were all scattered, no two being one by the other, and yet not so far off that it barred mutual succour: a show, as it were, of an accompanionable solitariness and of a civil wildness.

° **sorrow**: alluding to the myth of Philomela, the ravished princess who was transformed into the nightingale.

"I pray you," said Musidorus, then first unsealing his long silent lips, "what countries be these we pass through which are so diverse in show: the one wanting no store, the other having no store but of want?"

"The country," answered Claius, "where you were cast ashore and are now passed through is Laconia: not so poor by the barrenness of the soil (though in itself not passing fertile) as by a civil war, which being these two years within the bowels of that estate between the gentlemen and the peasants (by them named Helots) hath in this sort as it were disfigured the face of nature, and made it so inhospitable as now you have found it ...

"But this country where now you set your foot is Arcadia, and even hard by is the house of Kalander, whither we lead you: this country being thus decked with peace and (the child of peace) good husbandry. These houses you see so scattered are of men as we two are that live upon the commodity of their sheep, and therefore in the division of the Arcadian estate are termed shepherds: a happy people, wanting little [4ʳ] because they desire not much" ...

[4ᵛ] Kalander one afternoon led him abroad to a well-arrayed ground he had behind his house, which he thought to show him before his going, as the place himself more than in any other delighted. The backside of the house was neither field, garden, nor orchard, or rather it was both field, garden, and orchard; for as soon as the descending of the stairs had delivered them down, they came into a place cunningly set with trees of the most taste-pleasing fruits; but scarcely they had taken that into their consideration but that they were suddenly stepped into a delicate green; of each side of the green a thicket, and behind the thickets again new beds of flowers, which being under the trees, the trees were to them a pavilion and they to the trees a mosaical floor, so that it seemed that Art therein would needs be delightful by counterfeiting his enemy Error and making order in confusion.

In the midst of all the place was a fair pond whose shaking crystal was a perfect mirror to all the other beauties, so that it bare show of two gardens: one in deed, the other in shadows. And in one of the thickets was a fine fountain made thus: a naked Venus of white marble, wherein the graver had used such cunning that the natural blue veins of the marble were framed in fit places to set forth the beautiful veins of her body ...

[5ʳ] This country Arcadia, among all the provinces of Greece, hath ever been had in singular reputation, partly for the sweetness of the air and other natural benefits, but principally for the well-tempered minds of the people, who (finding that the shining title of glory so much affected by other nations doth indeed help little to the happiness of life) are the only people which, as by their justice and providence, give neither cause nor hope to their neighbours to annoy them, so are they not stirred with false praise to trouble others' quiet, thinking it a small reward for the wasting of their own lives in ravening, that their posterity should long after say they had done so. Even the Muses seem to approve their good determination by choosing this country for their chief repairing place, and by bestowing their perfections [5ᵛ] so largely here that the very shepherds have their fancies lifted to so high conceits, as the learned of other nations are content both to borrow their names and imitate their cunning.

❧ ❧ ❧

RICHARD BARNFIELD

from The Affectionate Shepherd (1594)

Since its inception in ancient Greece, the pastoral has been a favoured literary mode for expressing both biophilia – the "urge to affiliate with other forms of life" (Wilson) – and homoerotic desire. Both of these are on display in an uneasy tension in this poem, alternatively entitled "The Complaint of Daphnis for the Love of Ganymede." An elaborate riff on Marlowe's famous lyric "Come live with me and be my love," and a possible influence on Shakespeare's *As You Like It*, Barnfield's pastoral suggests how male delight in the great outdoors might foster homosexual attachment, subverting the coding of such passions as unnatural. Source: *The Affectionate Shepherd* (1594), B1ᵛ–B3ʳ.

> And when it pleaseth thee to walk abroad,
> Abroad into the fields to take fresh air,
> The Meads with Flora's treasure should be strawed,°
> The mantled meadows and the fields so fair.
> And by a silver well (with golden sands)
> 120 I'll sit me down and wash thine ivory hands.
>
> And in the swelt'ring heat of summer time,
> I would make Cabinets° for thee, my Love;
> Sweet-smelling Arbours made of Eglantine
> Should be thy shrine, and I would be thy dove.
> Cool Cabinets of fresh green Laurel° boughs
> Should shadow us, o'er-set with thick-set Yews.
>
> Or if thou list° to bathe thy naked limbs,
> Within the Crystal of a Pearl-bright brook,
> Pavèd with dainty pebbles to the brims,
> 130 Or clear, wherein thyself thyself mayest look,
> We'll go to Ladon,° whose still trickling noise
> Will lull thee fast asleep amidst thy joys.

° **strawed**: sprinkled (with flowers).   ° **Cabinets**: bowers.
° **Laurel**: the name of the speaker, Daphnis, means laurel in Greek.   ° **list**: wish.
° **Ladon**: river in Greece, with possible wordplay on lad.

Or if thou'lt go unto the Riverside,
To angle for the sweet freshwater fish,
Armed with thy implements that will abide°
(Thy rod, hook, line) to take a dainty dish;
Thy rods shall be of cane, thy lines of silk,
Thy hooks of silver, and thy baits of milk …

Or if thou dar'st to climb the highest Trees
For Apples, Cherries, Medlars, Pears, or Plums,
Nuts, Walnuts, Filberts,° Chestnuts, Services,°
The hoary Peach, when snowy winter comes;
I have fine Orchards full of mellowed fruit,
Which I will give thee to obtain my suit …　　　　　　　　150

If thou wilt come and dwell with me at home,
My sheepcote shall be strewn with new green rushes;
We'll haunt the trembling Prickets° as they roam
About the fields, along the hawthorne bushes;
I have a piebald Cur° to hunt the Hare:
So we will live with dainty forest fare.

Nay, more than this, I have a Garden-plot,
Wherein there wants nor herbs, nor roots, nor flowers　　　170
(Flowers to smell, roots to eat, herbs for the pot),
And dainty Shelters when the Welkin° lours;
Sweet-smelling Beds of Lilies and of Roses,
Which Rosemary banks and Lavender encloses.

There grows the Gillyflower, the Mint, the Daisy
(Both red and white), the blue-veined Violet,
The purple Hyacinth, the Spike° to please thee,
The scarlet-dyed Carnation bleeding yet;
The Sage, the Savoury, and sweet Marjoram,
Hyssop, Thyme, and Eyebright,° good for the blind and dumb.　　180

The Pink, the Primrose, Cowslip and Daffadilly,
The Harebell blue,° the crimson Columbine,
Sage, Lettuce, Parsley, and the milk-white Lily,
The Rose, and speckled flower called Sops-in-wine,°
Fine pretty Kingcups, and the yellow Boots,°
That grows by Rivers and by shallow Brooks.

And many thousand more I cannot name,
Of herbs and flowers that in gardens grow,

° **abide**: serve, wait patiently.　　° **Filberts**: hazelnuts.　　° **Services**: wild sorb-apples.
° **Prickets**: young male deer (with innuendo).　　° **piebald Cur**: dog with light and dark-coloured patches.　　° **Welkin**: sky.　　° **Spike**: French lavender.
° **Eyebright**: plants in the genus Euphrasia, used to treat eye ailments because their streaked petals resemble a bloodshot eye.　　° **Harebell blue**: bluebell (now used for the bluebell bellflower).
° **Sops-in-wine**: a kind of red dianthus with a white spot.
° **Kingcups … Boots**: two names for the marsh-marigold.

190
> I have for thee; and Conies that be tame,
> Young Rabbits, white as swan and black as crow,
> Some speckled here and there with dainty spots;
> And more I have two milch° and milk-white Goats.
>
> All these and more I'll give thee for thy love,
> If these and more may 'ticeth love away;
> I have a Pigeon-house, in it a Dove,
> Which I love more than mortal tongue can say.
> And last of all, I'll give thee a little Lamb
> To play withal, new weanèd from her Dam.

⁊ℰ ⁊ℰ ⁊ℰ

° **milch**: milk-producing.

MICHAEL DRAYTON
"A Nice Description of Cotswold" (1612)

By the late Middle Ages, the Cotswolds region had become a hub of England's thriving wool trade. Drayton here imagines a mutual attraction between its rolling hills and the nearby fertile vales as a metaphor for the sustainability of a bioregional, mixed economy of pastoral and arable farming. In other words, the poem recognizes the ecological reasons why sheep-farming flourished here. Drayton also captures why this particular breed was so highly valued and its "golden fleece" exported abroad. Although Drayton praises this managed and manicured landscape, the environmental impact of intensive sheep-grazing can be gauged from the fact that the word "wold" in Anglo-Saxon meant a wooded upland but by the thirteenth century had come to signify an open elevated plain.
Source: *Poly-Olbion* (1612), 1.232–3 (Song 14).

> But, noble Muse, proceed immediately to tell
> How Evesham's fertile Vale at first in liking fell
> With Cotswold, that great King of Shepherds, whose proud site
220
> When that fair Vale first saw, so nourished her delight,
> That him she only loved; for wisely she beheld
> The beauties clean° throughout that on his surface dwelled:
> Of just and equal height, two banks arising which
> Grew poor (as it should seem) to make some Valley rich;
> Betwixt them thrusting out an Elbow of such height,
> As shrouds the lower soil, which shadowed from the light,
> Shoots forth a little Grove that in the Summer's day
> Invites the Flocks for shade that to the Covert stray;
> A Hill there holds his head, as though it told a tale,
230
> Or stoopèd to look down or whisper with a Vale,
> Where little purling winds like wantons seem to dally,

° **clean**: completely.

And skip from Bank to Bank, from Valley trip to Valley;
Such sundry shapes of soil where Nature doth devise,
That she may rather seem fantastical than wise.
    T'whom Sarum's Plain gives place: though famous for her Flocks,
Yet hardly doth she tithe° our Cotswolds' wealthy locks.
Though Lemster° him exceed for fineness of her ore,°
Yet quite he puts her down for his abundant store.
A match so fit as he, contenting to her mind,
Few Vales (as I suppose) like Evesham hapt° to find.   240
Nor any other Wold like Cotswold ever sped,
So fair and rich a Vale by fortuning to wed.
He hath the goodly Wool, and she the wealthy Grain:
Through which they wisely seem their household to maintain.
He hath pure wholesome Air and dainty crystal Springs;
To those delights of his, she daily profit brings.
As to his large expense, she multiplies her heaps;
Nor can his Flocks devour th'abundance that she reaps:
As th'one with what it hath the other strove to grace.
    And now that everything may in the proper place   250
Most aptly be contrived, the Sheep our Wold doth breed
(The simplest though it seem) shall our description need,
And Shepherd-like the Muse thus of that kind doth speak:
No brown nor sullied black the face or legs doth streak,
Like those of Moorland, Chalk,° or of the Cambrian hills
That lightly laden are, but Cotswold wisely fills
Her with the whitest kind, whose brows so woolly be,
As men in her fair Sheep no emptiness should see.
The Staple° deep and thick, through to the very grain,°
Most strongly keepeth out the violentest rain;   260
A body long and large, the buttocks equal broad,
As fit to undergo the full and weighty load;
And of the fleecy face, the flank doth nothing lack,
But everywhere is stored, the belly as the back.
The fair and goodly Flock, the Shepherd's only pride,
As white as Winter's snow, when from the River's side
He drives his new-washed Sheep; or, on the Shearing day,
When as the lusty Ram, with those rich spoils of May,
His crooked horns hath crowned, the Bellwether° so brave,
As none in all the Flock they like themselves would have.   270

              ❧ ❧ ❧

° **tithe**: furnish a tenth.   ° **Lemster**: Leominster, known for its fine wool.   ° **ore**: fine wool.
° **hapt**: chanced.   ° **Chalk**: Cank] 1612. Presumably a misprint for cauk, an archaic spelling.
° **Staple**: wool.   ° **grain**: skin.   ° **Bellwether**: lead sheep of the flock.

WILLIAM BROWNE
"The Swineherd" (1614)

Although seldom read today, William Browne was admired by Romantics such as Keats, Clare, and fellow Devonshire native Coleridge. Among his contemporaries, Browne was a well-regarded pastoral poet who moved in a literary circle that included Michael Drayton, John Davies, and George Wither. His second eclogue can be decoded as a satire on a would-be poetaster who sought to ingratiate himself into this group. On a literal level, however, it documents the misuse of commons due to a growing individualism and materialism that the poet views as inimical to the pastoral values of community and simplicity.
Source: *The Shepherd's Pipe* (1614), C4^{r-v}, D1^{v}–D2^{r}.

The Argument
Two shepherds here complain the wrong
Done by a swinish Lout,
That brings his Hogs their Sheep among,
And spoils the Plain throughout. …

	WILLY Harm take the Swine! What makes he here?
	What luckless planet's frowns
	Have drawn him and his Hogs in fere°
20	To root our daisied downs?
	Ill might he thrive! And may his Hogs
	And all that ere they breed
	Be ever worried° by our Dogs,
	For so presumptuous deed.
	Why kept he not among the Fens?
	Or in the Copses by?
	Or in the Woods and braky° glens,
	Where Haws and Acorns lie?
	About the Ditches of the Town,
30	Or Hedgerows he might bring them.
	JOCKY But then some pence° 'twould cost the Clown°
	To yoke and eke to ring° them.
	And well I ween° he loves no cost
	But what is for his back:
	To go full gay him pleaseth most,
	And lets his belly lack.
	Two suits he hath: the one of blue,
	The other homespun grey;
	And yet he means to make a new
40	Against next revel day …
	WILLY But if I fail not in mine Art,

° **fere**: company.   ° **worried**: snapped at, harassed.   ° **braky**: overgrown.
° **pence**: fees for pannage (grazing rights for swine) increased during the seventeenth century due to enclosure.
° **Clown**: yokel.   ° **ring**: fit with nose rings to keep them from digging.   ° **ween**: know.

I'll send him to his yard,
And make him from our plains depart
With all his dirty herd.
I wonder he hath suffered been
Upon our Common here;
His Hogs do root our younger treen°
And spoil the smelling briar.
Our purest wells they wallow in,
All overspread with dirt,   130
Nor will they from our arbours lin,°
But all our pleasures hurt.
Our curious° benches that we build
Beneath a shady tree,
Shall be o'erthrown, or so defiled
As we would loathe to see.
Then join we Jocky; for the rest
Of all our fellow Swains,
I am assured will do their best
To rid him from our plains.   140

❧ ❧ ❧

° **treen**: trees.   ° **lin**: leave.   ° **curious**: carefully made.

WILLIAM STRODE
"On Westwell Downs" (c. 1640)

The word *down* can be used loosely as a synonym for hill, but more specifically it refers to the "treeless, undulating chalk uplands of the south and southeast of England" (*OED* 2). There is a Westwell in the Kent Downs, but this poem is set near Westwell in Oxfordshire on the eastern edge of the Cotswolds. Strode's imagery captures how this quintessentially English landscape owes its garden-like appearance to centuries of intensive management and sheep-farming.
Source: Corpus Christi College, Oxford MS 325, 59ᵛ–60ʳ.

When Westwell Downs I 'gan to tread,
Where cleanly winds the Green do sweep,
Methought a Landscape° there was spread,
Here a bush and there a sheep.
The pleated wrinkles on the face
Of wave-swol'n° Earth did lend such grace
As shadowings in Imagery,
Which both deceive and please the Eye.

The Sheep sometimes do tread the Maze,
By often winding in and in,   10
And sometimes round about they trace,
Which Milkmaids call a Fairy ring;
Such Semicircles have they run,

° **Landscape**: the term originally signifies a painting of scenery rather than the scenery itself.
° **wave-swol'n**: hilly.

Such lines across so trimly spun,
That Shepherds learn whene'er they please
A new Geometry with Ease.

The slender food upon the Down
Is always even, always bare,
Which neither Spring nor Winter's frown
20   Can aught improve or aught impair.
Such is the barren Eunuch's chin,
Which thus doth evermore begin
With tender down° to be o'ercast,
Which never comes to hair at last.

Here and there two hilly Crests,
Amidst them hug a pleasant Green,
And these are like two swelling breasts,
That close a tender Vale between.
Here could I read or sleep or play,
30   From early morn till flight of Day,
But hark! A Sheep-bell calls me up,
Like Oxford College bells, to sup.

ᗖ ᗖ ᗖ

° **down**: fuzz (with quibble).

ROBERT HERRICK
"To Meadows" (1648)

In this pastoral elegy, Herrick links the failure to observe the rites of May with the
sterility of the earth. While it may hint that profit-conscious farmers were putting
more land under the plough, it also seems to be a variation of the anthropocentric
tree-falling-in-a-forest conundrum: the meadows are desolate without the presence of humans.
Source: *Hesperides* (1648), 125.

You have been fresh and green,
You have been filled with flowers:
And you the Walks have been
Where Maids have spent their hours.

You have beheld how they
With Wicker Arks° did come
To kiss, and bear away
The richer Cowslips home.

You've heard them sweetly sing,
10   And seen them in a Round:
Each Virgin like a Spring,
With Honeysuckles crowned.

° **Arks**: baskets.

But now we see none here,
Whose silv'ry feet did tread,
And with dishevelled Hair,
Adorned this smoother Mead.

Like Unthrifts, having spent
Your stock and needy grown,
You're left here to lament
Your poor estates, alone.   20

᙭ ᙭ ᙭

JOHN AUBREY
[Salisbury Plains and the Downs] (c. 1656–1685)

Best known as a celebrity biographer and folklorist, John Aubrey had a keen interest in natural history and was a regular at the Royal Society. The selection below
contains one of the first formulations of the phenomenon known as tree succession
later studied by Thoreau. It is remarkable for its insight that the supposedly
"natural" beauty of the English landscape was largely the result of human intervention. Significantly, however, this recognition does not diminish Aubrey's admiration for the sheep-shaped terrain of the downs, or for the pastoral literature,
such as Sidney's *Arcadia*, that sings its praises.
Source: *Natural History of Wiltshire*, Bodleian MS Aubrey, 1:18ᵛ–19ʳ, 2:111ʳ–12ʳ.

Edmund Waller Esq. (Poet) made a query I remember at the Royal Society
about 1666, whether Salisbury Plains were always plains? He said then that
he did cut down a beech-wood at Beconsfield, and afterwards there came
up a birch-wood. In the county of Wiltshire are no beeches, except in the
southeast, and at the Forest of Grovely, belonging to the Earl of Pembroke:
disafforested 1683, to be converted to pasture for profit's sake. In time of
old, when the whole nation was but a great forest, and encumbered with
trees, why might not the Romans burn down the beeches, etc. on our
downs, to turn them to pasturage and corn ground? Which was the best
improvement for this tract of ground.

[18ᵛᵒ] In Jamaica and in other plantations° of America (e.g. in Virginia)
the natives did burn down great quantities of woods to cultivate the soil
with maize and potato roots, which plains were there made by firing the
woods to sow corn. They do call these plains savannahs (from Mr. Watson
of Yarmouth in Norfolk, who lived several years in those parts). Who
knows but that Salisbury plains, etc., might be made long time ago after
this manner and for the same reason? ...

° **18v**: this paragraph appears on the preceding verso, but was intended to be inserted here in support
of Waller's theory.   ° **plantations**: colonies.

[19ʳ] I have oftentimes wished for a map of England coloured according to the colours of the earth, with marks of the fossils and minerals …

[111ʳ] We now make our ascent to the second elevation or the hill-country, known by the name of the Downs, or Salisbury Plains; and they are the most spacious plains in Europe, and the greatest remains (that I can hear of) of the smooth, primitive world when it lay all under water° … The turf is a short, sweet grass, good for sheep, and delightful to the eye, for its smoothness like a bowling green, and pleasant to the traveller, who wants here only variety of objects to make his journey less tedious: for here is *nil nisi campus et aer,*° not a tree, or rarely a bush, to shelter one from a shower … At Everleigh is a large oaken-copse, but not thriving, but very dwarfish. Neither do the few thorns that are here flourish … The first wood that salutes your eyes is Grovely Forest, in the midst whereof was a stately high oak which appeared above all the rest, called Starton's Hat,° which was felled down about 1652.

[112ʳ] The soil of the downs I take (generally) to be a white earth or malm.° More south, sc. about Wilton and Chalk, the downs are inter-mixed with boscages that nothing can be more pleasant, and in the sum-mertime does excel Arcadia in verdant and rich turf and moderate air, but in winter indeed our air is cold and raw. The innocent lives here of the shepherds do give us a resemblance of the golden age° …

And, to speak from the very bottom of my heart, not to mention the integrity and innocence of shepherds, upon which so many have insisted and copiously declaimed, methinks he is much more happy in a wood that at ease contemplates the universe as his own, and in it the sun and stars, the pleasing meadows, shades, groves, green banks, stately trees, flowing springs, and the wanton windings of a river, fit objects for quiet innocence, than he that with fire and sword disturbs the world, and measures his pos-sessions by the waste that lies about him.

These plains do abound with hares, fallow deer, partridges, and bustards.° In this tract is the Earl of Pembroke's noble seat at Wilton …

° **water**: Renaissance geology mainly consisted of attempts to identify evidence of Noah's Flood. This passage appears to have been written earlier, between 1652 and 1666, before Waller proposed that the Downs resulted from deforestation, and Robert Hooke began his lectures refuting Flood geology.   ° *nil … aer*: nothing but plains and sky.

° **Starton's Hat**: hat was slang in southern England for a clump of trees on a hilltop.

° **malm**: chalky sandstone, or soil containing it. In accordance with geohumoralism, Aubrey proposes that the soil quality and climate of different regions affect the temperament of the inhabitants.

° **golden age**: in the MS, Aubrey cites verses from Lucretius's *On the Nature of Things* (5.1385–410), prefixed with the heading "Divinity in a Shepherd's Life," but the excerpt is pasted over with a small square of paper containing the next paragraph's summary.

° **These … bustards**: Aubrey's Victorian editor notes that the fallow deer and bustards "have long since disappeared."

[111ᵛ] and these romancy plains and boscages did no doubt conduce to the heightening of Sir Philip Sidney's fancy. He lived much in these parts, and his most masterly touches of his pastorals he wrote here upon the spot, where they were conceived. [112ʳ] 'Twas about these purlieus° that the Muses were wont to appear to Sir Philip Sidney, and where he wrote down their dictates in his tablebook,° though on horseback.

ॐ ॐ ॐ

° **purlieus**: disafforested land adjacent to a designated forest.   ° **tablebook**: notebook.

Georgic: Fields, Farms
VIRGIL
Georgics (*c.* 29 *BCE*)

In the early sixteenth century, most Tudor gentlemen would have scoffed at farm-work as drudgery. That such attitudes changed is due in no small part to the re-discovery of this text by the Roman poet Virgil, who knew first-hand the joys and frustrations of farming. His husbandry manual in verse was so influential that the term georgic became shorthand for all writing about agriculture. In contrast to pastoral, which adopts the contemplative perspective of the leisure-loving shep-herd, georgic celebrates the farmer's more aggressive intervention in the natural world. Rather than bemoan the loss of the Golden Age as Ovid does, Virgil cele-brates labour as a cure for idleness (which would have appealed to the Puritan work ethic of many English readers) and perhaps also urban overpopulation, which was worrying Emperor Augustus and had become a glaring problem in Stuart London. English translations of Virgil by Abraham Fleming in 1589 and this one by Thomas May, a friend of Ben Jonson's, contributed to the growing mania for agricultur-al "improvement." The ecocritical merit of the georgic mode is ambiguous, as it could encourage more efficient farming methods (manuring, fallowing, tree care, and rotating crops), but also enclosing commons or putting more meadows, wood-lands, and heath under the plough to boost profits (see McRae 1990).
Source: *Virgil's Georgics*, trans. Thomas May (1628), 3–5, 7–9.

> When first the spring dissolves the mountain snow,
> When th'earth grows soft again and west winds blow,
> Then let your Oxen toil in furrows deep,
> Let use from rusting your bright ploughshares keep.
> Those crops which twice have felt the sun and twice
> The cold will Ploughmen's greediest wish suffice.
> Harvests from thence the crowded barns will fill.
> But lest the fields we ignorantly till,
> To know how different lands and climates are,
> All winds and seasons, let it be our care,
> What every Region can or cannot bear:
> Here corn thrives best; vines best do prosper there;
> Some Lands are best for fruit, for pasture some …
> These several virtues on each land and clime
> Nature bestowed, even from the point of time
> When stones in th'emptied world Deucalion° threw,
> From whence th'hard-hearted race of mankind grew.
> Therefore when first the year begins do thou
> Thy richest grounds most deep and strongly plough,
> That Summer's piercing Sun may ripen more,
> And well digest the fallow glebe. But poor

50

60

° **Deucalion**: survivor of a global deluge in classical mythology. An oracle instructs him and his wife to cast stones over their shoulders in order to repopulate the earth. See Ovid, *Metamorphoses*, 1.

And barren grounds about October plough:
Not deep in one, lest weeds that rankly grow
Spoil the rich crop; in th'other, lest the dry   70
And sandy grounds quite without moisture lie.
And let thy field each other year remain
Fallow and eared, to gather heart again ...
                 But best it is to keep
The ground one year at rest; forget not then   80
With richest dung to hearten it again,
Or with unsifted ashes; so 'tis plain
That changing seeds gives rest unto a field;
And 'tis no loss to let it lie untilled …
For Jove himself, loathe that our lives should prove
Too easy, first caused men the ground to move,
Filled mortal hearts with cares, nor suffered he
The world to fall into a lethargy.
Before Jove's reign no Ploughmen tilled the ground,
Nor was it lawful then their Lands to bound.
They lived in common all, and everything
Did without labour from earth's bosom spring.
Jove venom first infused in Serpents fell,
Taught Wolves to prey and stormy Seas to swell,   130
Robbed leaves of honey and hid fire from men,
And banished wine, which ran in rivers then,
That th'arts by need might so in time be found;
Corn might be sought by tilling of the ground,
And hidden fire from flint's hard veins be drawn.
Then Aldern° boats first ploughed the Ocean,
The Sailors numbered then and named each star:
The Pleiades, Hyades, and the Northern Car.°   150
Deceiving birdlime then they learned to make,
And beasts by hunting or by toils to take;   140
Dragnets were made to fish within the deep,
And casting nets did rivers' bottoms sweep.
Then iron first and saws were understood,
For men before with wedges cleft their wood.
Then th'arts were found; for all things conquered be°
By restless toil and hard necessity.
First yellow Ceres taught the world to plough,
When woods no longer could afford enough
Wild crabs° and acorns, and Dodona° lent
Her mast° no more. Then miseries were sent   150
To vex the art of tillage: blastings killed
The stalks; and fruitless thistles in the field
Prevailing spoiled the corn; rough weeds did grow,
Of burs and brambles troubling it; and now

° **Aldern**: made from alder trees.   ° **Northern Car**: the Big Dipper, then commonly known as
Charles's Wain or Wagon.   ° **all things conquered be**: Virgil's original Latin phrase *Laboria*
omnia vi(n)cit, usually translated "Work conquers all," would become a well-known adage.
° **crabs**: crab-apples.   ° **Dodona**: the oak, alluding to a sacred grove in ancient Greece.
° **mast**: acorns (see Lilliat's poem in Part VI).

Within the fields among the harvest grain
Corn-vexing darnel and wild oats did reign:
That now, unless thou exercise the soil,
Fright birds away, and with continual toil
Lop off the shadowing boughs, and pray for rain
160   Devoutly still, thou mayst behold in vain
Thy neighbour's heap of corn with envious eyes,
Labouring with mast thy hunger to suffice.

ﷺ ﷺ ﷺ

THOMAS TUSSER
"The Praise of Husbandry" (1570)

Tusser's agricultural treatise first appeared in 1557 and was reprinted fourteen times over the next century, as the author expanded it from 100 to 500 useful "points" or tips. Along with Conrad Heresbach's *Four Books of Husbandry* (which enjoyed seven English editions between 1577 and 1631), it was one of the top-selling books in early modern England, a kind of bible for the back-to-the-land movement. Although the title of this riddling poem is something of a spoiler, its personi-fication of Good Husbandry establishes its vital importance for economic and political stability. The verses bespeak a newfound sense of the dignity of labour among the middling classes, and an increasingly proprietary attitude towards the earth's resources.
Source: *Five Hundred Points of Good Husbandry, United to as Many of Good Housewifery* (1570), A2ᵛ, with emendations from 1573.

I seem but a drudge, yet I pass any king;
To such as can use me, great wealth I do bring.
Since Adam first lived, I never did die;
When Noah was a shipman, there also was I.
The earth is my storehouse, the sea my fishpond;
What they have to pleasure with, is in my hand.°
What hath any life but I help to preserve?
What thing° without me but is ready to starve?
In Woodland, in Champaign, City or Town,
10   If I long be absent, what falleth not down?
If I long be present, what goodness can want,
Though things at my coming were never so scant?
Of such as do love me (what need to recite,
Yea, though of the poorest), whom make I not knight?°
Great Kings I do succour, else wrong would it go,
The King of all kings hath appointed it so.

ﷺ ﷺ ﷺ

° **What … hand**: What good is in either, by me it is found.] 1573.   ° **thing**: wight] 1573.
° **Of … knight**: So many as love me and use me aright, / With treasure and pleasure I richly requite.] 1573.

HUGH PLAT

"A Philosophical Garden,"
"Gillyflowers," and "Grafting" (1608)

Although it looks like a compendium of gardening tips, *Flora's Paradise* aspires
to be something much grander. It dreams of a revolutionary soil science that
could someday make England rival Spain, Italy, or even the Garden of Eden
in its output of fruits and vegetables. Plat insists that his knowledge has been
"wrung out of the earth by the painful hand of experience" (A8ʳ), and his modest success with cultivating grapes in London only inflamed his ambitions. In
prescribing the chemical transformation of soil to enhance its fertility, his astro-
alchemical georgic looks forward to the modern agrochemical industry. Indeed,
Plat's formula is virtually identical to a nitrogen-based fertilizer later described
by Johannes Glauber (*Prosperity of Germany*, 396-7), whose work was steeped
in the alchemical theories of Paracelsus. *Flora's Paradise* thus supports Rebecca
Bushnell's claim that gardens and orchards are not only material but also ideological spaces for redefining the parameters of the natural. The extracts peddling
advice on gillyflowers, grafting, and defying seasonal change may very well have
prompted Shakespeare's renegotiation of the domains of nature and art in *The
Winter's Tale.*
Source: *Flora's Paradise* (1608), 1–10, 78–9, 82, 92–3, 120–1, 124, 140, 143–4.

A Philosophical Garden

First, pave a square plot with brick ... [2] Fill it with the best vegetable
[Saturn]° you can get [and] ... make contrition° of the same ... Imbibe°
it with *Aqua-coelestis*° ... [and after it is] dry, let it stand two or three days
without any imbibition that it may the better attract from all heavenly
influence° ... [3] Then plant what rare flowers, fruits, or seeds you please
therein. And if my Theory of Nature deceive me not, this [Saturn] so enriched from the heavens, without the help of any manner of soil, marl, or
compost ... will make the same to flourish and fructify in a strange and
admirable manner. Yea, and I am persuaded that it will receive any Indian°
plant, and [4] make all vegetables to prosper in the highest degree, and
to bear their fruits in England as naturally as they do in Spain, Italy, or

---

° **vegetable Saturn**: probably soil mingled with dung, urine, and lime, and thus rich in saltpetre
  or potassium nitrate. Plat recounts his experiments with various fertilizers in *Diverse New Sorts
  of Soil* (1594), but the cornucopian vision of *Flora's Paradise* seems inspired by the promises of
  alchemical theory (see Edward Kelley's *Discourse on the Vegetable Menstruum of Saturn*). Plat here
  uses only the planet's astrological sigil, and probably felt this discovery was too innovatory to share
  with the general public, as the Crown's authority to commandeer grounds laden with saltpetre (a
  vital ingredient in gunpowder) was already controversial. For more on saltpetre, see Martin and
  Goldstein, 2017.   ° **contrition**: ground powder.
° **Imbibe**: moisten.   ° ***Aqua-coelestis***: a spiced cordial, here used as an alchemical fertilizer.
° **influence**: astrological energies.   ° **Indian**: exotic.

elsewhere ... [5] I could remember more philosophical plants in England, were it not that the loss of Ripley's° life, that [6] renowned Alchemist, who suffered death (as the secret report goeth) for making a Pear-tree to fructify in Winter, did command an *altum silentium*° in these matters ...

Nay, if the earth itself, after it hath thus conceived from the clouds, were then left to bring forth her own fruits and flowers in her own time, and no seeds or plants placed therein by the hand of Man, [7] it is held very probable (unless for the sin of our first parents, begun in them and mightily increased in us, the great God of Nature, even *Natura naturans,*° should recall or suspend those fructifying blessings which at the first he conferred upon his celestial Creatures) that this heavenly earth, so manured° with the stars, would bring forth such strange and glorious plants, fruits, and flowers, as none of all the Herbalists that ever wrote till this day, nor any other, unless Adam himself were alive again, could either know, [8] or give true and proper names unto these most admirable simples.

Also, in the work of fructification, I think that Corn itself may be so philosophically° prepared, only by imbibition in the philosopher's aqua-vitae,° that any barren ground, so as it be in nature kindly for Corn, shall bring forth a rich crop without any matter added to the ground. And so with a small or no charge a man may sow yearly upon the same ground. And he that knoweth how to lay his fallows truly, [9] whereby they may become pregnant from the heavens and draw abundantly that celestial and generative virtue into the Matrix of the Earth, this man no doubt will prove the true and philosophical Husbandman, and go beyond all the country Corydons° of the Land, though never so well acquainted with Virgil's *Georgics,* or with Master Bernard Palissy° his congelative part of rainwater ... Though he observed more than either Varro, Columella,° [10] or any of the ancient writers in this kind did ever dream of, yet doth he come many degrees short of this heavenly mystery ...

° **Ripley**: George Ripley (1415–90), cleric and alchemist. Plat goes on to deny that his grafting was a "conjuration" and claims Ripley was executed for the "denial of his medicine."
° ***altum silentium***: perpetual silence.
° ***Natura naturans***: creating Nature. As opposed to *Natura naturata*, created nature.
° **manured**: fertilized. In astrological botany, the light of various celestial bodies radiated different sorts of energy into plants.
° **philosophically**: scientifically.
° **aqua-vitae**: some kind of distilled alcohol, in which the seeds could be steeped prior to sowing. The philosopher may refer to Aristotle, to whom the occult *Secret of Secrets* was erroneously attributed.
° **Corydon**: literary term for a farmer, from Virgil's *Georgics*.
° **Palissy**: French alchemist and potter who developed the first theory of the water cycle. Congelative (or generative) water was his term for groundwater rich in minerals.
° **Varo, Columella**: Roman agricultural writers.

"Gillyflowers"

[78] Remove a plant of stock gillyflowers° when it is a little wooded and not too green, and water it presently. Do this three days after the full [moon],° and remove it twice more before the change.° Do this in barren ground; and likewise [79] three days after the next full moon, remove again and remove once more before the change. Then at the third full moon, viz. eight days after, remove again and set it in very rich ground, and this will make it bring forth a double flower ...

[82] Remove both double and single-stock gillyflowers when they are half a foot high, and then they will stand six or seven years, whereas otherwise they will decay very speedily ...

[92] Towards winter, new earth° you gillyflowers, carnations, and other such flowers as you would defend from the violence of winter. Then whelm° carnation pots that are bottomless upon them ... And by this means neither the sharp winds nor the frost can easily pierce to [93] their roots ...

"Grafting"

[120] You may graft upon the bearing bough of an apple tree a contrary apple. And when that scion° is grown great enough to receive another graft, you may graft a contrary fruit thereon. But an apple scion doth not agree with a pear [121] stock (nor *è contra*°), nor a plum upon an apple or a pear stock ...

[124] A peach may well be grafted or inoculated in a plum stock, and will thrive better than upon his own stock ...

[140] A scion of a pippin° grafted upon a crab° stock is more kindly and keepeth better, without touch of canker, than being grafted upon a pippin. Per Parson Simson° ...

[143] *Quere:*° what herbs, flowers, or branches of trees may be grafted upon the bay or holly tree, or any such tree as keepeth green in winter, to make them also carry [144] green leaves in Winter?

❧ ❧ ❧

° **stock gillyflowers**: variety now known as stock or *Matthiola incana*. For more on grafting gillyflowers, see Parkinson, *Paradisi in Sole* (1629, 17–22).
° **Do this ... moon**: in the belief that lunar phases affected sap flow as they do the tides.
° **earth**: replant or heap more soil over the roots.   ° **change**: new moon.
° **whelm**: overturn to use as a covering.   ° **scion**: the twig or shoot grafted to the stock.
° *è contra*: vice-versa.   ° **pippin**: variety of sweet apple.
° **crab**: the crab-apple.
° **Parson Simson**: one of several unknown gardeners whose experiments and advice Plat shares.
° *Quere:* Question.

MARGARET CAVENDISH

"Earth's Complaint" (1653)

In contrast to Tusser's praise of husbandry, Cavendish here denounces the environmental impact of intensive agriculture. Only the heavens seem exempt from human rapacity.
Source: *Poems and Fancies* (1653), 106.

O Nature, Nature, hearken to my Cry,
Each minute wounded am, but cannot die.°
My Children, which I from my Womb did bear,
Do dig my Sides and all my Bowels tear,
Do° plough deep Furrows in my very Face;
From Torment I have neither time nor place.
No other Element is so abused,
Nor by Mankind so cruèlly is used.
Man cannot reach the Skies to plough and sow,
Nor can they set or make the Stars to grow;
But they are still as Nature first did° plant,
Neither Maturity nor Growth they want.
They never die, nor do they yield their place
To younger Stars, but still run their own Race.
The Sun doth never groan young Suns to bear,
For he himself is his own Son and Heir.
The Sun just in the centre sits as King,°
The Planets round about encircle him.°
The slowest° Orbs over his Head turn slow,
And underneath, the swiftest Planets go.
Each° several Planet several measures take,
And with their motions they° sweet music make.
Thus all the Planets round about him move,
And he returns them Light for their kind Love.

10

20

❧ ❧ ❧

° **Each ... die**: I'm Wounded sore, but yet I cannot Die] 1664.   ° **Do:** They] 1664.
° **first did**: did them] 1664.
° **The ... King**: He in the Centre sits just like a King] 1664. The poem makes an implicit contrast between the heavens and England's recently overthrown monarchy.
° **The ... him**: Round him the Planets are as in a Ring] 1664.   ° **slowest**: largest] 1664.
° **Each**: All] 1664.   ° **they**: do] 1664.

Forests, Woods, Parks

WILLIAM HARRISON
"Of Parks and Warrens" (1577)

Unlike parks today, Tudor parks were restricted spaces – owned by the king, nobles, or gentry – and reserved for keeping deer and other game. As England's population exploded in the sixteenth century, some persons began to feel that too much of the nation's land was set aside by the wealthy for private hunting grounds. In his *Perambulation of Kent* (1576), William Lambarde estimated that half of the county's parks had been disparked "within memory." The high point probably occurred in the 1540s. Disparking slowed considerably during Elizabeth's reign (Pitmann), a trend that Harrison here seeks to reverse.
Source: *Holinshed's Chronicles* (1587), 204–5.

In every shire of England there is great plenty of parks, whereof some … (well near to the number of two hundred) [are] for [the] daily provision of that flesh appertaining to the prince; the rest to such of the nobility and gentlemen as have their lands and patrimonies lying in or near unto the same. I would gladly have set down the just number of these enclosures to be found in every county. But since I cannot so do, it shall suffice to say that in Kent and Essex only are to the number of one hundred, and twenty in the bishopric of Durham, wherein great plenty of fallow deer is cherished and kept. As for warrens of conies, I judge them almost innumerable, and daily like to increase by reason that the black skins of those beasts are thought to countervail the prices of their naked carcases, and this is the only cause why the grey are less esteemed …

Our parks are generally enclosed with [a] strong pale made of oak, of which kind of wood there is great store cherished in the woodland countries from time to time in each of them, only for the maintenance of the said defence and safekeeping of the fallow deer from ranging about the country. Howbeit, in times past diverse have been fenced in with stone wall, especially in the times of the Romans, who first brought fallow deer into this land (as some conjecture), albeit those enclosures were overthrown again by the Saxons and Danes …

I find also the circuit of these enclosures in like manner contain often times a walk of four or five miles, and sometimes more or less. Whereby it is to be seen what store of ground is employed upon that vain commodity, which bringeth no manner of gain or profit to the owner, since they commonly give away their flesh, never taking penny for the same, except the ordinary fee and parts of the deer given unto the keeper by a custom.

[205] Wherein times past many large and wealthy occupiers were dwelling within the compass of some one park, and thereby great plenty of corn and cattle seen and to be had among them, beside a more copious procreation of human issue, whereby the realm was always better furnished with able men to serve the prince in his affairs, now there is almost nothing kept but a sort of wild and savage beasts, cherished for pleasure and delight.° And yet some owners still desirous to enlarge those grounds, as either for the breed and feeding of cattle, do not let° daily to take in more, not sparing the very commons whereupon many townships now and then do live, affirming that we have already too great store of people in England; and that youth by marrying too soon do nothing profit the country, but fill it full of beggars, to the hurt and utter undoing (they say) of the commonwealth.

Certes° if it be not one curse of the Lord to have our country converted in such sort from the furniture° of mankind into the walks and shrouds of wild beasts, I know not what is any.° How many families also these great and small games (for so most keepers call them) have eaten up and are likely hereafter to devour, some men may conjecture, but many more lament, since there is no hope of restraint to be looked for in this behalf, because the corruption is so general. But if a man may presently give a guess at the universality of this evil by contemplation of the circumstance, he shall say at the last that the twentieth part of the realm is employed upon deer and conies already, which seemeth very much.

❧ ❧ ❧

° **delight**: marginal note here reads, "Tillage and mankind diminished by parks."
° **let**: cease.   ° **furniture**: provisions.   ° **Certes**: certainly.
° **any**: "The decay of the people [population decline] is the destruction of a kingdom" (marginal note).

PHILIP SIDNEY

"O sweet woods" (c. 1580)

The following lyric consists of three fourteen-line stanzas written in asclepiadics, an ornate classical meter that scans -- -uu- -uu- u- (where - represents a long syllable and u a short one). The highly artificial rhythm is consistent with the fact that the Arcadian woods are very much a literary place. The focus is more on the subjective workings of the mind in nature rather than on the woods themselves,

which are defined negatively as the opposite of the city and court. The speaker
is a prince disguised as a shepherd Dorus, but his sentiments can be assumed to
echo those of Sidney, who had fled the court for his sister's Wiltshire estate. This
pastoral rhapsody thus suggests how the vexations of life at court or in increasingly
crowded London intensified fondness for the countryside.
Source: *Countess of Pembroke's Arcadia* (1593), 120ʳ⁻ᵛ.

> O sweet woods, the delight of solitariness!
> O how much I do like your solitariness!
> Where man's mind hath a freed consideration
> Of goodness to receive lovely direction;
> Where senses do behold th'order of heav'nly host,
> And wise thoughts do behold what the creator is.
> Contemplation here holdeth his only seat,
> Bounded with no limits, borne with a wing of hope,
> Climbs even unto the stars; Nature is under it.°
> Naught disturbs thy quiet, all to thy service yields,   10
> Each sight draws on a thought (thought, mother of science);
> Sweet birds kindly do grant harmony unto thee,
> Fair trees' shade is enough fortification,
> No danger to thyself, if 't be not in thyself.
>
> O sweet woods, the delight of solitariness!
> O how much I do like your solitariness!
> Here no treason is hid, veilèd in innocence,
> Nor envy's snaky eye finds any harbour here,
> Nor flatterers' venomous insinuations,
> Nor cunning humorists'° puddled opinions,   20
> Nor courteous ruin of proffered usury,
> Nor time prattled away, cradle of ignorance,
> Nor causeless duty, nor cumber of arrogance,
> Nor trifling title of vanity dazzleth us,
> Nor golden manacles stand for a paradise;
> Here wrong's name is unheard, slander a monster is.
> Keep thy sprite from abuse; here no abuse doth haunt.
> What man grafts in a tree dissimulation?
>
> O sweet woods, the delight of solitariness!
> O how well I do like your solitariness!   30
> Yet, dear soil, if a soul closed in a mansion
> As sweet as violets, fair as lily is,

° **Nature … it**: echoing Sidney's claim in the *Apology* that natural and moral philosophers must
  follow nature, whereas "the Poet … lifted up with the vigour of his own invention, doth grow
  in effect another nature … He goeth hand in hand with Nature, not enclosed within the narrow
  warrant of her gifts, but freely ranging only within the Zodiac of his own wit" (C1ᵛ).
° **cunning**: 1622; coming] 1593. Humorist signifies a person whose imbalance of bodily humours
  makes them prone to strange obsessions or quirks.

Straight as Cedar, a voice stains° the Canary birds,
Whose shade safety doth hold, danger avoideth her;
Such wisdom that in her lives speculation;
Such goodness that in her simplicity triumphs;
Where envy's snaky eye winketh or else dieth,
Slander wants a pretext, flattery gone beyond:
O! If such a one have bent to a lonely life,
40   Her steps glad we receive, glad we receive her eyes,
And think not she doth hurt our solitariness,
For such company decks such solitariness.

᛭ ᛭ ᛭

° **stains**: surpasses.

NICHOLAS BRETON
"Now lies this walk along a wilderness" (1592)

Early modern literature often portrays landscape in allegorical terms. In this example, a master dispatches five servants on a journey through a wilderness, which the poem equates with spiritual perdition. Along the way the good servant passes through a gauntlet of Roman goddesses – Venus, Diana, Flora, Ceres – personifying the sensual beauty and pleasures of the material world. After shunning these temptations, the pilgrim comes to a wood inhabited by an Ovidian menagerie of humanoid animals. Rather than a place of solace and innocence described by Sidney, the wilderness here resembles the "wandering wood" of Spenser's *Faerie Queene*, a place of savagery and unreason.
Source: *The Pilgrimage to Paradise* (1592), 1, 4–5, 8–13.

Now lies this walk along a wilderness,
20   A forest full of wild and cruèl beasts,
The earth untilled, the fruit unhappiness,
The trees all hollow, full of owlets' nests,
The air unwholesome, or so foul infected,
As hardly rests,° that may not be rejected …

Along the walk, the walk, alas, too long,
Amid the hapless hills and doleful dales,
Where sighs and sobs do sound but sorrow's song,
100   While sweetest truths are crossed by sorry tales,
And darkest clouds are clapped° before the sun,
These wary creatures have their way begun …

° **rests**: resides (anything).   ° **clapped**: thrust.

When passing on they fell into a wood,
A thicket full of brambles, thorns, and briars,
A graceless grove that never did man good,
But wretched sendings of the world's desires,
 Where Snakes and Adders and such venomed things,
 Had slain a number with their cruêl stings.

Some metamorphosed like Actaeon° were,   260
Diana smiling at their lewd desires;
Some Semitaurs° and some more half a Bear;
Other half Swine, deep wallowing in the mires:
 All beastly minds, that could not be reformed,
 Were to the shapes of their own shame transformed.

There might he see a Monkey with an Ape,
Climbing a tree and cracking of a nut;
One sparrow teach another how to gape,
But not a tame one, taught to keep the cut;°
 And many a jackdaw in his foolish chat,
 While parrots prated of they knew not what.   270

There might he see Bears baited all with dogs,
Till they were forced to fly into their dens;
And wild Boars beating of the lesser hogs,
While cocks of game were fighting for their hens;
 A little ferret, hunting of a Cony;
 And how the old Bees sucked the young Bees honey.

There might he hear the Lions in their roaring,
While lesser beasts did tremble at the sound.
There might he see Bulls one another goring,
And many a hart sore hunted with a hound,   280
 While Philomene,° amid the queachy° spring,
 Would cease her note, to hear the Cuckoo sing.

There might he see a falcon beaten down
By carrion crows that crossed her in her flight;
A russet Jerkin face a velvet gown,°
While base companions braved a noble Knight;
 And crafty foxes creep into their holes,
 While little hops° were climbing lofty poles.

There might he see the Satyrs in their dances,
Half-men, half-beasts, or devils in their kinds.   290
There might he see the Muses in their trances
Lie down as dead, as if they had no minds.

° **Actaeon**: Greek hunter transformed into a stag after he spied Diana bathing.
° **Semitaurs**: half-bull, half-man.   ° **taught ... cut**: trained to behave.
° **Philomene**: the nightingale.   ° **queachy**: boggy.
° **russet .. gown**: a commoner oppose an aristocrat.   ° **hops**: grasshoppers.

There might he see, in all, so little good,
As made him wish he had been through the wood.

Yet in the path wherein he sweetly passed,
No evil thing had power to take a place.
No venomed serpent might his poison cast,
No filthy monster nor ill-favoured face,
No lion, Bear, dog, Monkey, fox, nor Crow,
300   Could stop the way where virtue was to go.

ॐ ॐ ॐ

JOHN MANWOOD
"The Definition of a Forest" (1598)

The word forest in early modern English was a legal term designating land set aside as a royal game preserve. The practice spread with the Normans, who placed large tracts of land – such as the "New Forest" in Hampshire – under the jurisdiction of the Crown, often to the chagrin of the local peasantry. Royal forests were scaled back under the Forest Charter of 1217, but by the Elizabethan period the dire environmental consequences of disafforestation had become glaringly apparent. Clearly, not everyone agreed with Harrison that England had too many parks. In 1592 John Manwood published a commentary on these ancient forestry laws, which he expanded and revised six years later into a polemic urging the monarch to "afforest" more land and properly staff the nation's forestry service. As gamekeeper of Waltham Forest, Manwood had a first-hand glimpse of the decimation of the deer and trees. In the dedication, Manwood praises the "great and provident care" of the queen, who had supported the timber laws (see Appendix A), and Charles Howard, who, as Lord High Admiral of the navy, had particular reason to be concerned about the rising price of wood. Yet Manwood's treatise is also a sobering reminder that early modern attitudes towards environmental protection do not square neatly with the eco-sensibilities of today; he advocates preserving woodlands in order to ensure that the monarch has a steady population of animals to kill for sport. Considering that the forests were, like national parks, highly managed places, it would be inaccurate to think of them as pristine wilderness. Source: *Treatise of Forest Laws* (1598), A1ʳ–D3ᵛ.

A Forest is a certain Territory of woody grounds and fruitful pastures, privileged for wild beasts and fowls of Forest, Chase,° and Warren° to rest and abide in, in the safe protection of the King, for his princely delight and pleasure; which ... is bounded with unremovable marks, meres,° and boundaries, known by matter of record or else by prescription; [A1ᵛ] and also replenished with wild beasts of venery or Chase, and with great coverts of vert, for the succour of the said wild beasts to have their abode in ...

° **Chase**: an unenclosed park, belonging to a private subject rather than the Crown.
° **Warren**: enclosed park, belonging to a private subject rather than the Crown.
° **mere**: strip between forest and adjacent land.

And therefore a forest doth chiefly consist of these four things: ... of vert, venison, particular laws and privileges, and of certain meet officers appointed for that purpose, to the end that the same may the better be preserved and kept for a place of recreation and pastime meet for the royal dignity of a Prince ...

[A2ᵛ] There be diverse Lordships, liberties, and precincts that are full of woods, coverts, and fruitful pastures – yea, and perhaps of wild beasts also. And yet the same is no forest, forasmuch as the place is not privileged for those wild beasts to have a firm peace in from the hurt of any other person more than the proper owner of the soil ... A Forest is not a privileged place generally, for all manner of beasts, but only for those that are of Forest, Chase, and Warren. The wild beasts of the Forest are five and no more: ... the Hart, the Hind, the Hare, the Boar, the Wolf. The beasts of Chase are also five: the Buck, the Doe, the Fox, the Marten, and the Roe ... The beasts and fowls of the Warren are these: the Hare, the Cony, the Pheasant, the Partridge ... All these have Privilege within the Forest ...

[A3ʳ] And by the words following, "For his princely delight and pleasure," is showed the final cause, to what end and purpose the wild beasts and fowls are so protected: ... which is for the delight and pleasure of the King only, and his nobles, and for no other end nor purpose ...

[B1ᵛ] A Forest must always have beasts of venery or chase abiding in it, for otherwise the same is no forest. For if there be neither, ... men may fell their woods that they have within the Forest and destroy their Coverts ... and in like manner convert their pastures and meadows that they have within the Forest into arable land ... [B2ʳ] And by these words, "great Coverts of vert for the succour of wild beasts to have their abode in," is showed the necessity of the preservation of the coverts of the Forest ... [for] the destruction of the coverts doth banish the wild beasts ... Wherefore men may not fell or cut down their own woods that are coverts, being within the forest, without a licence of the Lord Chief Justice in Eyre° of the Forest. And a licence from him to cut down their woods ... is not to be granted unless there be sufficient coverts for the wild beasts besides left, remaining unfelled. And those woods of covert that are felled by licence, yet the sprigs thereof must be carefully preserved° that they may grow to be coverts again in short time ...

[B2ᵛ] The Officers that a Forest must of necessity have are these: a Steward, Verderers, Foresters, Regarders, Agisters, and Woodwards,° which

---

° **Eyre**: itinerant judge who presided over forestry courts in different locations.
° **sprigs ... preserved**: first stipulated in a 1483 Act, and mandated in subsequent Elizabethan Timber Acts (see Appendix A).
° **Steward ... Woodwards**: a verderer oversees cases of "trespass against the vert and venison"; a forester is "sworn to protect the vert and venison ... and apprehend all offenders"; a regarder monitors the amount of vert and venison; an agister collects fees from farmers who graze animals on forest land; and a woodward manages the timber.

officers are they that do hold the court of the Forest for the due execution of the Forest Laws ...

[B4ʳ] The laws do allow unto the king ... this prerogative: to have his places of recreation and pastime wheresoever he will appoint ... For the king may by the Law make a Forest even at his will [B4ᵛ] and pleasure for them to rest and abide in, even as by Law he may enter into the ground of any of his subjects wheresoever there are any mines of gold or silver ... [C1ʳ] And although men may kill such wild beasts in their wildness, when they are found wandering, being found out of any Forest, Park, Chase or Warren, yet no man hath any property in them until they have killed them. For during the time of their wildness they are *nullis in rebus*° and must needs be said to be ... in the king's possession ...

[C3ᵛ] As I do take it, a great part of our most ancient forests in England had their first beginning in this manner: when this realm, at the first being a wilderness full of huge great woods because it was not inhabited with people, the same was also full of wild beasts ... [C4ʳ] and after the same began to be inhabited with people, they did daily more and more destroy the woods and great thickets that were near unto the places where they did inhabit, so that still as the land increased and flourished with people, whose nature could not endure the abundance of savage beasts so cruelly to annoy them as they then did, they sought by all means possible how to destroy such great woods and coverts ... and so by that means the wild beasts were all driven to resort to those places where the woods were left remaining ... In the Saxon's time, they called those places *Paldy* or *Walds*, that is to say, forests or woods ... [After King Edgar] did greatly destroy the wolves° and foxes ... the residue that were then remaining being beasts of great pleasure ... to hunt and chase ... the king began to grow careful for the preservation of them, and therefore they began to privilege those woods and places where those wild beats were remaining ... [C4ᵛ] until that King Canute the Dane ... in 1018 did appoint such Forests and Chases as then were their limits and bounds: ... "where I will that my beasts shall have firm peace and quietness, upon pain to forfeit as much as a man may forfeit" ...

[D2ᵛ] And hereupon the Latinists have framed this Latin word *Foresta* ... being compounded of those two words *fera* and *statio* ... and [D3ʳ] so have we framed this English word, a forest,° being compounded of these two words: "For" and "Rest" ...

[D3ᵛ] There doth grow unto the King by a Forest especially these two benefits: ... first, the plenty and increase of Deer; ... secondly, the great woods and timber trees, as well as of his subjects as of his own demesne woods ... are most especially preserved thereby, to be in readiness when

° ***nullis in rebus***: no one's property.
° **wolves**: see Caius, "Why there are no wolves" (Part IV, p. 336).
° **forest**: Manwood consistently spells the word with two r's.

the King shall have need of them, which otherwise would be cut down and destroyed ... The slender and negligent execution of the forest laws hath not only been the decay and destruction of the Deer almost in all places within this Realm in Forests, but also of Wood and Timber, the want thereof, as well as at this present time as in time to come, shall appear in the Navy of this Realm.

꙳ ꙳ ꙳

ANTHONY BRADSHAW
"A Friend's Due Commendation of Duffield Frith"
(*c.* 1588–1608)

The following poem is a defiant tribute to the medieval system of forest government, which, like a hollow oak, slowly decayed throughout the early modern period. Declared a royal forest in 1285, Duffield Frith comprised a large section of what is now south-central Derbyshire, and once abounded with trees, deer, wild boar, and wolves. The author of this poem praises the natural bounty of this region and the forestry service that helps sustain it, while also hinting that the lax enforcement of forest law has led to the denuding of the woodlands. A 1560 survey recorded 59,412 large oaks in the forest; by 1587 the number had dropped to 2,764 (see Falvey). The Oxford-educated Bradshaw was appointed the deputy steward of the forest in 1595, and, like John Manwood, promoted the maintenance of royal control over the land to prevent its resources from being overconsumed. Although the poem is dated 1588 and appears after an entry from December 1598, the references to King James indicate that it was revised (if not rewritten) between 1604 and 1608 – when Bradshaw was removed from his post by the Earl of Shrewsbury, who promptly felled much of the remaining woodlands to fuel his ironworks. When Charles I disafforested Duffield in 1633, few trees would have been left standing.
Source: Derbyshire Records Office D2402 A/PZ 2/1.

6

Whoso with me will take sweet air on top of Chevin Hill,
  Most bounds and grounds of Duffield Fee° may view and take his fill.
From Alderwasley to Burley, so North and South it bendeth,
From Collins Clark to Hough Park side, it East to West extendeth ...

9

Duffield Forest yet heads its name, though now not stored with game,
Nor ven'ry° hath for princely sport, which want there none doth blame;
Saving some parks replenished are, disparked though others be,
And vert and woods and officers stand, as I shall show to thee.

° **Fee**: territory or estate.   ° **ven'ry**: hunting.

10

This Forest hath it four brave woods in midst of it that lie:
Hulland, Duffield, Colebrook, Belper,° the same castle fast by;
Fine thicks° and lands that do contain and herbage good that yield,
40   And skirted with so sweet assart° as ever man beheld.

11

All which in order good to keep, such forest laws as need
Are executed duly there at woodmote courts° with speed.
The pawnage,° tack,° rents, and duties thereof, with customs raised,
Collectors four receive and pay at th'audit times always.

12

This Forest small environed is with six parks yet remaining:
Morley, Belper, Postern, Shottle, and Ravensdale appertaining;
All which are farmèd at this time, and yield no deer at all,
Save only Mansell Park hath game, and yet but very small.

13

Wherefore those Keepers' names shall pass, their offices and fees,
50   Though heretofore they were esteemed, each one [of] their degrees.
In Shottle and Postern tenants had herbage° at easy rates,
Of which they are now quite debarred, and shut out of those gates …

16

The High Steward hath his bobbers° to walk and mark such trees
As bondhold tenants° are allowed, for which they have some fees.
Verderers,° Rangers,° and Knaves° of Forest, and off'cers have been moe,
Which now are discontinued place and ease: I let them go …

20

And as the off'cers for their pains allowèd are some fees,
So tenants which such duties pay in wood have liberties.
But if [the] wood without warrant and livery be felled,
80   Such trespasser a fine° therefore to pay shall be compelled …

° **Belper**: from the French, *beau repair*, "beautiful resort."   ° **thicks**: thickets.
° **assart**: fields that replaced cleared woodlands.
° **woodmote courts**: responsible for enforcing forest law. Bradshaw presided over woodmotes in
  1598, 1600, and 1604, and imposed stiff fines on people illegally cutting trees.
° **pawnage**: money paid to permit hogs to feed on mast in the king's forest.
° **tack**: payment due to one's feudal superior.
° **herbage**: permission to graze cattle.
° **bobbers**: an unusual term, presumably derived from the verb bob, meaning "to strike."
° **bondhold tenants**: feudal servants granted parcels of manorial lands.
° **Verderers**: officers in charge of the beasts and vegetation in the forest.
° **Rangers**: gamekeepers.   ° **Knaves**: young servants?
° **fine**: in 1598, Bradshaw fined 123 people for stealing wood.

23

The soil all kinds of corn it yields, and eke° good cattle breeds,
And wool and lead, and iron and coal, and most things that men needs.　　90
On healthy hills and valleys warm men there have habitation,
And food and raiment to suffice men's corps° and recreations …

33

Such healthy pleasant hills, and valleys warm and sound,
Sweet water springs, fruit trees, and store of wooded ground,　　130
And mines for iron, slate, coal, and stone, and other profits many,
As Duffield's manors yield to thee, I know not like or any.

34

What more than this can reason wish t'expect in Duffield Fee?
Who this dislikes deserveth less, and worser plant° may he.
And touching customs laudable, freedoms and liberties,°
Their Charter good and Custom book the same right well descries.

35

Which if they keep inviolate and well together hold,
A mighty man cannot them wrest with silver nor with gold.
But if the faggot° bond once break, and sticks fly to and fro,
Then Duffield Frith° turns upside down, their wealth is overthrown.　　140

36

If any man object and say Duffield leas° should be enlarged,
No, no, in truth, say I, in fact Duffield is overcharged.
Their commons and their fuel draw more people there to dwell
Than all their said commodities are able to keep well …

51

The better sort of Duffield men, their customs understands,
And how they do concern themselves, their houses and their lands.
The poorer sort and ignorant, which custom books have none,
By song may learn some customs now, and memory° alone.

52

Then since this Frith doth yield all things aforerecited,
To plant themselves therein, who would not be delighted?
And thus I have thee told the reasons of my royse,°
And why for pleasant dwelling Duffield shall have my voice.

° **eke**: also.　　° **corps**: body.　　° **plant**: settle.
° **freedoms and liberties**: Bradshaw here acknowledges ancient rights of common in the forest,
　while a subsequent stanza insists that they cannot be extended.
° **faggot**: bundle of wood.
° **Frith**: originally a wooded area but by the mid-seventeenth century the word had come to
　designate pastureland or gaps between woodlands.
° **leas**: spelled "lays," i.e. fallow or uncultivated lands, often signifying commons.　　° **royse**: boasting.
° **memory**: memorize.

53

God save King James, our noble prince, and prosper his long Reign
210   Over this Frith and manors all, our lord for to remain.
God bless his council courts, and all th'off'cers of the Duchy,°
The noble Earl of Shrewsbury,° and of Duffield Frith and Fee.

54

Farewell sweet Chevin Hill, with all thy brave prospects,°
Which temptest me one May morning to write this crude effect,
Which rashly done, if taken well and censured as I meant,
I shall rest loving to this Frith, and think my time well spent.

※ ※ ※

° **Duchy**: Duffield Frith was part of the Duchy of Lancaster.
° **Earl of Shrewsbury**: the 7th Earl, Gilbert Talbot (father of Aletheia). Although Talbot was the
   High Steward of the royal forests in the north (and Bradshaw technically worked for him), his
   ironworks at Hopping-Mill were a major culprit in the deforestation of Duffield.
° **prospects**: vistas.

MICHAEL DRAYTON
"The Forest of Arden" (1612)

Poly-Olbion is an ambitious survey of the topography, history, and natural history of each of England's thirty-nine historic counties. Like Shakespeare, Drayton hailed from Warwickshire, and it may not be a coincidence that the section devoted to his native county features some of his best poetry. Although *As You Like It* was based on Thomas Lodge's *Rosalynde* and ostensibly set in the Forest of Ardennes along the borders of Belgium, France, and Germany, *Poly-Olbion* offers a more detailed sketch of the environmental context of Shakespeare's great pastoral comedy. Drayton here laments the grubbing up of the woodlands, drawing upon the antiquarian perspective of deep time to convey how severely they have been depleted. Skirted by the Roman roads, the area was sparsely populated and still heavily wooded at the time of the Norman Conquest. Much of the deforestation censured here took place between 1100 and 1350, and again during a second population boom beginning around 1550 (Skipp). Arden was never under royal jurisdiction and hence not technically a forest, but the labelling of it as such indicates that the word was beginning to acquire its modern meaning. Drayton does not focus purely on the trees alone, however; he also valued the woodlands as a bio-diverse habitat for medicinal plants, birds (he catalogues fourteen species native to England), and deer. The hunting episode is rife with tensions: its celebration of the sport elicits sympathy for the stag whilst also perhaps promoting the campaign of people like Manwood to cordon off more woodlands as game preserves.
Source: *Poly-Olbion* (1612), 1.213–17 (Song 13).

Muse, first of Arden tell, whose footsteps yet are found
In her rough woodlands more than any other ground
That mighty Arden held, e'en in her height of pride:
Her one hand touching Trent, the other Severn's side.
The very sound of these the Wood-nymphs doth awake,
When thus of her own self the ancient Forest° spake:
   "My many goodly sites, when first I came to show,
Here opened I the way to mine own overthrow.   20
For when the world found out the fitness of my soil,
The gripple° wretch began immediately to spoil
My tall and goodly woods, and did my grounds enclose:
By which in little time my bounds I came to lose.°
When Britain first her fields with Villages had filled,
Her people waxing still, and wanting where to build,
They oft dislodged the Hart, and set their houses where
He in the Broom and Brakes° had long time made his lair.
Of all the Forests here within this mighty Isle,
If those old Britons then me Sovereign did enstyle,   30
I needs must be the great'st; for greatness 'tis alone
That gives our kind the place: else were there many a one
For pleasantness of shade that far doth me excel.
But of our Forest's kind the quality to tell,
We equally partake with Woodland as with Plain,
Alike with Hill and Dale, and every day maintain
The sundry kinds of beasts upon our copious wastes,°
That me for profit breed, as well as those of chase."
   Here Arden of herself ceased any more to show,
And with her sylvan joys the Muse along doth go.   40
   When Phoebus lifts his head out of the Winter's wave,
No sooner doth the Earth her flowery bosom brave,°
At such time as the Year brings on the pleasant Spring,
But Hunts-up to the Morn the feathered Sylvans° sing.
And in the lower Grove, as on the rising Knoll,
Upon the highest spray of every mounting pole,
Those Choristers are perched, with many a speckled breast.
Then from her burnished gate, the goodly glittering East
Gilds every lofty top, which late the humorous° Night
Bespangled had with pearl to please the Morning's sight;   50
On which the mirthful Choirs, with their clear open throats,
Unto the joyful Morn so strain their warbling notes,
That Hills and Valleys ring, and e'en the echoing Air
Seems all composed of sounds, about them everywhere:
The Throstle° with shrill Sharps, as purposely he sung
T'awake the lustless° Sun, or chiding that so long

° **Forest**: consistently spelled with two r's.   ° **gripple**: greedy.
° **my bounds ... lose**: No evidence indicates that Arden was ever a royal forest with official bounds.
° **Broom and Brakes**: gorse and thickets.   ° **wastes**: uncultivated land.   ° **brave**: display.
° **Sylvans**: woodland creatures, but also mythical forest spirits.   ° **humorous**: damp.
° **Throstle**: song-thrush.   ° **lustless**: lethargic.

He was in coming forth that should the thickets thrill;°
The Ouzel° near at hand, that hath a golden bill,
As Nature him had marked of purpose t'let us see
60   That from all other Birds his tunes should different be:
For with their vocal sounds they sing to pleasant May;
Upon his dulcet pipe the Merle° doth only play.
When in the lower Brake, the Nightingale hard by,
In such lamenting strains the joyful hours doth ply,
As though the other Birds she to her tunes would draw:
And but that Nature (by her all-constraining law)
Each Bird to her own kind this season doth invite,
They else, alone to hear that Charmer of the Night
(The more to use their ears), their voices sure would spare,
70   That moduleth her tunes so admirably rare,
As man to set in Parts, at first had learned of her.
To Philomel° the next, the Linnet we prefer;
And by that warbling bird, the Woodlark place we then;
The Red-sparrow;° the Nope;° the Redbreast; and the Wren;
The Yellow-pate,° which though she hurt the blooming tree,
Yet scarce hath any bird a finer pipe than she;
And of these chanting Fowls, the Goldfinch not behind,
That hath so many sorts descending from her kind;
The Tydie,° for her notes as delicate as they;
80   The laughing Hecco;° then the counterfeiting Jay;
The softer with the shrill (some hid among the leaves,
Some in the taller trees, some in the lower greaves°)
Thus sing away the Morn, until the mounting Sun,
Through thick exhalèd fogs, his golden head hath run,
And through the twisted tops of our close Covert creeps
To kiss the gentle Shade, this while that sweetly sleeps.
        And near to these our Thicks, the wild and frightful Herds,
Not hearing other noise but this of chatt'ring Birds,
Feed fairly on the Lands, both sorts of seasoned Deer:
90   Here walk the stately Red, the freckled Fallow there;
The Bucks and lusty Stags amongst the Rascals° strewed,
As sometimes gallant spirits amongst the multitude.
Of all the Beasts which we for our venerial° name,
The Hart amongst the rest, the Hunter's noblest game:
Of which most Princely Chase, since none did ere report,
Or by description touch, t'express that wondrous sport
(Yet might have well beseemed the ancients' nobler Songs)
To our old Arden here, most fitly it belongs …
                    Now when the Hart doth hear

° **thrill**: pierce (with sound).   ° **Ouzel**: blackbird.
° **Merle**: another name for the blackbird. A marginal note here reads "Of all Birds, only the
    Blackbird whistleth."
° **Philomel**: nightingale.   ° **Red-sparrow**: chaffinch?   ° **Nope**: bullfinch.
° **Yellow-pate**: yellow-hammer.   ° **Tydie**: blue titmouse? twite?
° **Hecco**: woodpecker.   ° **greaves**: twigs.   ° **Rascal**: "young, lean, or inferior deer" (*OED* 5).
° **venerial**: belonging to the chase.

The often-bellowing hounds to vent° his secret lair,
He rousing rusheth out, and through the Brakes doth drive,
As though up by the roots the bushes he would rive.   120
And through the cumbrous thicks, as fearfully he makes,
He with his branchèd head the tender Saplings shakes,
That sprinkling their moist pearl do seem for him to weep;
When after goes the Cry,° with yellings loud and deep,
That all the Forest rings, and every neighbouring place,
And there is not a hound but falleth to the Chase.
Recheating° with his horn, which then the Hunter cheers,
Whilst still the lusty Stag his high-palmed° head upbears,
His body showing state,° with unbent knees upright,
Expressing (from all beasts) his courage in his flight.   130
But when th'approaching foes still following he perceives,
That he his speed must trust, his usual walk he leaves,
And o'er the Champaign flies, which when th'assembly find,
Each follows as his horse were footed with the wind.
But being then embossed,° the noble stately Deer,
When he hath gotten ground (the kennel cast arear),
Doth beat the Brooks and Ponds for sweet refreshing soil:
That serving not, then proves° if he his scent can foil,
And makes amongst the herds and flocks of shag-woolled Sheep,
Them frighting from the guard of those who had their keep.   140
But when as all his shifts his safety still denies,
Put quite out of his walk, the ways and fallows tries,
Whom when the Ploughman meets, his team he letteth stand
T'assail him with his goad; so with his hook in hand,
The Shepherd him pursues, and to his dog doth hallow,
When with tempestuous speed the hounds and Huntsmen follow;
Until the noble Deer through toil bereaved of strength,
His long and sinewy legs then failing him at length,
The Villages attempts, enraged, not giving way
To anything he meets, now at his sad decay.   150
The cruél rav'nous hounds and bloody Hunters near,
This noblest beast of Chase, that vainly doth but fear,
Some bank or quickset° finds, to which his haunch opposed,
He turns upon his foes that soon have him enclosed.
The churlish-throated hounds then holding him at bay,
And as their cruél fangs on his harsh skin they lay,
With his sharp-pointed head he dealeth deadly wounds.
The Hunter coming in to help his wearied hounds,
He desperately assails, until oppressed by force
He, who the Mourner is to his own dying Corpse,   160
Upon the ruthless earth his precious tears° lets fall.

⁊ ⁊ ⁊

° **vent**: reveal.   ° **Cry**: pack of hounds.   ° **Recheating … horn**: returning at the sound of the horn.
° **palmed**: antlered.   ° **state**: stout.   ° **embossed**: foaming at the mouth from exhaustion.
° **proves**: tries.   ° **quickset**: hedge.
° **tears**: "his tears are held to be precious in medicine" (marginal note).

EDWARD HERBERT

"Made upon the Groves near Merlow Castle" (1620)

In a famous miniature painted by Isaac Oliver, a debonair courtier reclines against a tree beside a flowing brook (Figure 6). His posture, expression, and the landscape all connote melancholy, a fashionable disease among the affluent in Renaissance England. As Sidney's "O sweet woods" (p. 267) suggests, the melancholic's sense of social alienation could foster an attachment to the natural world. Fittingly, the man portrayed in this portrait, Edward Herbert, also composed an ode to woodlands. A friend of Ben Jonson, John Donne, and Mary Wroth, Herbert (later Baron Herbert of Cherbury) served as English ambassador to Paris, and wrote the following Petrarchan sonnet while staying at the Châteaux de Mello, thirty miles north of the city. Whereas Renaissance writers often portray the wildwood as a gloomy place, visited only by the dejected or lovelorn, this poem views the groves as a temple of moderation, felicity, and love, where plants reproduce without the heartaches attendant on human coupling.

Source: *Occasional Verses* (1664), 54, with emendations from BL Add. MS 37157, 10ᵛ.

> You well-compacted° Groves, whose light and shade
> Mixed equally produce nor heat nor cold,
> Either to burn the young or freeze the old,
> But to one even temper being made,
> Upon a Green° embroidering through each Glade
> An Airy Silver and a Sunny Gold,
> So clothe the poorest that they do behold
> Themselves in riches which can never fade,
> While the wind whistles and the birds do sing,
> While your twigs clip,° and while the leaves do frizz,°
> While the fruit ripens which those trunks do bring:
> Senseless to all but love, do you not spring
> Pleasure of such a kind as truly is
> A self-renewing vegetable bliss?

10

᠅ ᠅ ᠅

° **well-compacted**: this compound adjective suggests the groves were managed or perhaps even planted.
° **Green**: Grave] BL.   ° **clip**: embrace   ° **frizz**: curl, from the French *friser*.

FIGURE 6 Isaac Oliver, "Edward Herbert" (c. 1610). National Trust. Todd White Art Photography.

MARY WROTH
[Pamphilia's Tree-Carving] (1621)

Wroth's *Urania* is a pastoral romance inspired by her uncle Philip Sidney's *Arcadia*. Like Sidney and Herbert, Wroth's heroine is a melancholic who finds solace in the solitude of a garden wood. Pamphilia's melancholy, however, is compounded by her status as a woman in a patriarchal culture. Rather than a place of danger, the forest affords a refuge from her male-dominated society, and her portrayal of it may be modelled on the managed woodlands surrounding her husband's estate at Loughton in Essex. In the episode below, she carves a poem in tree-bark, a common pastoral topos (see Knight 2014, 81–108). The gesture can be seen as an attempt to literalize Wroth's "pathetic stylistics" (Bowerbank 35) – to make the ash tree share the feelings inscribed in it. Yet the blessing she carves in the tree ironically also harms it, offering an object lesson that the "sympathy, caretaking, and compassion between 'woman' and 'nature' are not givens, as more essentialist strands of ecofeminism have imagined them to be" (Nardizzi and Jacobson 189). Source: *Urania* (1621), 74–6.

Then opened she a door into a fine wood, delicately contrived into strange and delightful walks; for although they were framed by Art, nevertheless they were so curiously counterfeited as they appeared natural.° These

---

° **framed … natural**: another example of horticultural *sprezzatura*, anticipating the English landscape garden. See Bacon's essay "Of Gardens" (p. 237).

pleased her only to pass through into a little Grove, or rather a pretty tuft
of Ashes, being environed with such unusual variety of excellent pleasures
as, had she had a heart to receive delight from anything but Love, she
might have taken pleasure in that place; for there was a purling, murmuring, sad Brook, weeping away her sorrows, desiring the banks to ease her,
even with tears; but, cruel, they would not so much as stay them to comfort, but let them slip away with as little care as great ones do the humble
Petitions of poor suitors. Here was a fine grove of Bushes, their roots made
rich with the sweetest flowers for smell and colour; there a Plain; here a
Wood; fine hills to behold, as placed that her sight need not for natural
content stray further than due bounds; at their bottoms, delicate Valleys
adorned with several delightful objects. But what were all these to a loving
heart? Alas, merely occasions to increase sorrow: Love being so cruel as to
turn pleasures in this nature to the contrary course, making the knowledge
of their delights but serve to set forth the perfecter mourning, triumphing
in such glory where his power rules not only over minds but on the best
of minds. And this felt the perplexed Pamphilia, who, with a Book in her
hand (not that she troubled it with reading, but for a colour of her solitariness), walked beholding these pleasures till grief brought this issue. Seeing
this place delicate without as she was fair, and dark within as her sorrows,
she went into the thickest part of it, being such as if Phoebus° durst not
there show his face for fear of offending the sad Princess, but a little glim-
meringly (as desirous to see and fearing to be seen) stole here and there a
little sight of that all-deserving Lady … The tops of the trees joining so
close, as if in love with each other, could not but affectionately embrace.
The ground in this place where she stayed was plain, covered with green
grass, which, being low and thick, looked as if of purpose it had been covered with a green velvet carpet to entertain this melancholy Lady for her
the softer to tread, loth to hurt her feet lest that might make her leave it.
This care proved so happy, as here she took what delight it was possible
for her to take in such kind of pleasures: walking up and down a pretty
space, blaming her fortune, but more accusing her love who had the heart
to grieve her, while she might more justly have chid herself, whose fear had
forced her to too curious° a secrecy …

[75] In this estate she stayed a while in the wood, gathering sometimes
flowers which there grew, the names of which began with the letters of his
name,° and so placing them about her. "Well Pamphilia," said she, "for all
these disorderly passions, keep still thy soul from thought of change; and
if thou blame anything, let it be absence, since his presence will give thee
again thy fill of delight … And now poor grass," said she, "thou shalt suffer
for my pain, my love-smarting body thus pressing thee."

° **Phoebus**: the sun.   ° **curious**: anxious.
° **his name**: Pamphilia is enamoured with Amphilanthus, and their relationship is based on Wroth's
  affair with her cousin, William Herbert, with whom she had two children out of wedlock.

Then laid she her excelling self upon that then most blessed ground. "And in compassion, give me some rest," said she, "on you, which well you may do, being honoured with the weight of the loyalest, but most afflicted princess that ever this kingdom knew. Joy in this and flourish still, in hope to bear this virtuous affliction. O Morea,° a place accounted full of Love, why is Love in thee thus terribly oppressed and cruelly rewarded? … Sweet Land, and thou more sweet Love, pardon me, hear me, and commiserate my woe." Then hastily rising from her low green bed, "nay," said she, "since I find no redress, I will make others in part taste my pain, and make them dumb partakers of my grief." Then taking a knife, she finished a Sonnet, which at other times she had begun to engrave in the bark of one of those fair and straight Ashes, causing that sap to accompany her tears for love, that for unkindness:

> Bear part with me, most straight and pleasant Tree,
> And imitate the Torments of my smart,
> Which cruél Love doth send into my heart.
> Keep in thy skin this testament of me,
> [66] Which Love engraven hath with misery,
> Cutting with grief the unresisting part,
> Which would with pleasure soon have learned love's art,
> But wounds still cureless must my rulers be.
> Thy sap doth weepingly bewray thy pain,
> My heart-blood drops with storms it doth sustain;
> Love, senseless, neither good nor mercy knows.
> Pitiless I do wound thee, while that I,
> Unpitied and unthought on, wounded cry;
> Then outlive me and testify my woes.

And on the roots whereon she had laid her head, serving (though hard) for a pillow at that time to uphold the richest World of wisdom in her sex, she wrote this:

> My thoughts thou hast supported without rest,
> My tired body here hath lain oppresst
> With love and fear. Yet be thou ever blest:
> Spring, prosper, last; I am alone unblest …

[Then] rising and giving as kind a farewell-look to the tree as one would do to a trusty friend, she went to the brook, upon the bank whereof were some fine shady trees and choice thorn bushes which might, as they were mixed, obtain the name of a pretty Grove; whereinto she went and, sitting down under a Willow,° there anew began her complaints, pulling off those branches, sometimes putting them on her head.

᙭ ᙭ ᙭

° **Morea**: Peloponnesian peninsula in southern Greece (the ostensible setting of *Urania*).
° **Willow**: symbol of unhappiness in love.

WILLIAM HABINGTON
"To Castara, venturing to walk too far in the neighbouring wood" (1633)

While courting Lucy Herbert, the daughter of the 1st Baron of Powis, Habington addressed a series of poems to her under the name Castara. This sonnet is likely set around the Anglo-Welsh border, and showcases the fear that wilderness could evoke in the early modern era. Since the wolf is thought to have vanished from England and Wales by the fifteenth century, Habington's resuscitating it seems like a joco-serious ploy to exert control over his new wife and discourage her from seeking the freedom and solace that Mary Wroth finds in the forest-scape. By ordering her not to wander into the woods, Habington genders the wild a masculine space. Source: *Castara* (1640), 46.

> Dare not too far Castara, for the shade
> This courteous thicket yields hath man betrayed
> A prey to wolves; to the wild powers o'th' wood,
> Oft travellers pay tribute with their blood.
> If careless of thyself, of me take care,
> For like a ship where all the fortunes are
> Of an advent'rous merchant, I must be,
> If thou should'st perish, banquerout° in thee.
> My fears have mocked me. Tigers when they shall
> Behold so bright a face will humbly fall
> In adoration of thee. Fierce they are
> To the deformed, obsequious to the fair.
> Yet venture not; 'tis nobler far to sway
> The heart of man than beasts, whom man obey.

10

❧ ❧ ❧

° **banquerout**: bankrupt.

KATHERINE PHILIPS
"Upon the graving of her Name upon a Tree in Barn Elms' Walks" (1669)

Barn Elms was a large park and manor house on the western outskirts of London in the borough of Richmond-on-Thames. Although now a wetlands and recreation grounds, it became a fashionable picnic spot during the Restoration. Samuel Pepys visited in 1667 and enjoyed strolling through the alley of elms for which it was named. Philips may have gone there to call on Abraham Cowley, a royalist poet who lived in the area and whose pastoral verse she deeply admired. How do her views on tree-carving compare with Wroth's? Source: *Poems* (1669), 137.

Alas, how barbarous are we,
Thus to reward the courteous Tree,
Who its broad shade affording us,
Deserves not to be wounded thus!
See how the Yielding Bark complies
With our ungrateful injuries.
And seeing this, say how much then
Trees are more generous than Men,
Who by a Nobleness so pure
Can first oblige, and then endure.   10

ક ક ક

Heaths, Moors

JOHN NORDEN
"Heathy Ground" (1607)

The British landscape is chequered with heath: open shrubland with acidic soil that is not conducive to farming. At high elevations, heaths are known as moors, and the UK contains roughly 10–15 per cent of the moors in the world, mainly in Devonshire, Staffordshire, Yorkshire, and Scotland. Although not nearly as biodiverse as wetlands, heaths provide a vital habitat for several rare and endangered species. In the following dialogue, the surveyor John Norden (an advocate of agrarian improvement and what we would now call sustainable growth) recognizes that heaths vary from place to place, and proposes methods by which some of them might be converted into arable land to help feed England's growing population. The campaign met with some success, as the heaths are much smaller today than they were in Tudor times.
Source: *The Surveyor's Dialogue* (1607), 234–7.

BAILEY But what say you to this heathy ground? [235] I think of all other grounds, this is the most unprofitable.

SURVEYOR Indeed, naturally all heathy grounds are barren, and that comes by the saltiness of the soil ... for salt is hot, and heat drieth, and too much drought breeds barrenness and leanness ... Therefore, though heathy grounds be commonly in the highest degree of barrenness, yet are some more ... tractable and more easily reduced to some use than others, and therefore hath sundry names. Heath is the general or common name, whereof there is one kind called Heather, the other Ling. And of these particulars, there are also sundry kinds distinguished by their several growth, leaves, stalks, and flowers: as not far from Gravesend there is a kind of Heather that beareth a white flower and is not so common as the rest, and the ground is not so exceeding barren as some other, but by manurance would be brought to profitable tillage. Some (and the most) doth bear a purple or reddish flower, as in the Forest of Windsor and in Suffolk and sundry other places: and this kind is most common, and groweth commonly in the worst ground. In the North parts, upon the Mountains and Fells, there is a kind of Ling that bears a berry. Every of these hath his peculiar earth wherein it delighteth: some in sandy and hot grounds, as between Wilford Bridge and Snape Bridge in Suffolk (and that is bettered especially and the heath killed best and soonest by [236] good fat marle); some in gravelly and cold earth, and that is hard to be cured, but with good stable dung. But there is a kind of heathy ground that seemeth altogether unprofitable for tillage because that the gravel and clay together retaineth a kind of black water, which so drencheth the earth and causeth so much cold as no husbandry can relieve it. Yet if there be chalk-hills near this kind of earth, there may be some good done upon it; for that only or lime will comfort the earth, dry up the super-fluous water, and kill the heath. But the sandy heathy ground is contrarily amended ... with fat marle, and that is commonly found near these heathy grounds, if men were provident and forward to seek for it ... But if men will not endeavour to search for the hidden blessings of God, which he hath laid up in store in the bowels of the earth for their use ... they may make a kind of idle and vain show of good husbandry, when indeed they only plough and sow, and charge the earth to bring forth fruit of its own accord, when we know it was cursed for our sakes and commanded to deny us increase without labour, sweat, and charge°...

BAILEY I think there is no disease in the body of man, but nature hath given virtue to some other [237] creatures, as to herbs, plants, and other things to be medicines for the same: so is there no kind of ground so mean, barren, and defective, but God hath provided some means to better it, if man, to whom he hath given all, will search for it, and use the same to that end it was provided for.

꒰ꕤ ꒰ꕤ ꒰ꕤ

° **cursed ... charge**: as a result of original sin (Genesis 3:17–20).

JOHN SPEED
[Norfolk Heaths and Yorkshire Dales] (1612)

Although many early moderns took a grim view of heaths, Speed highlights their fertility and bounty. Enterprising farmers often burned them to sow crops and improve the grazing, prompting Parliament to pass an act in 1609 restricting the practice. Today many heaths and scenic uplands, such as the Yorkshire Dales, are protected national parks. Much of their rugged beauty, however, is the result of deforestation by prehistoric humans. Those ecologists who favour re-wilding over conservation have called for the reintroduction of trees, sniffing at heath as a burnt and desolate land with the "ambience of a nuclear winter" (Monbiot 215), in language that echoes Macbeth's reference to the "blasted heath."
Source: *The Theatre of Empire* (1612), 35, 79.

[Norfolk Heaths]

The Champaign aboundeth with Corn, Sheep, and Conies, and herein the barren Heaths (as the providence of our Ancestors hath of old disposed them) are very profitable. For on them principally lie our Fold-courses, called of the Saxons (whose institution they therefore seem to be) *Faldsocun*, that is, Liberty of fold or faldage.° These Heaths by the

° **faldage**: right to pasture sheep in movable folds to manure the land.

Composture° of the sheep (which we call Tathe°) are made so rich with Corn that, when they fall to be sown, they commonly match the fruitfullest grounds in other Countries; and laid° again, do long after yield a sweeter and more plentiful feed for sheep; so that each of them maintain other, and are the chiefest wealth of our Country …

[Yorkshire Dales]

[79] Although the Soil in the generality be not fruitful, as lying very high and full of ragged rocks and swelling mountains, yet the sides thereof stooping in some places do bear good grass, and the bottoms and valleys are not altogether unfertile. That part that borders upon Lancashire is so mountainous and waste, so unsightly and full of solitariness, that the bordering neighbours call certain little rivers that creep along this way by a contemptible name, Hellbecks. That part again where the River Ure cutteth through the vale called Wensleydale is very good ground, where great flocks of sheep do pasture, and which in some places do naturally yield great plenty of Lead-stones. In other places where the Hills are barren and bare of Corn and Cattle, they make a recompense of those wants by the store of Copper, Lead, and stone, or Pit-coal, with the which they are abundantly furnished. That part where the River Swale running down Eastward, out of the West Mountains (with a violent and swift stream) to unlade herself into the River Ure, and passing along a large and open vale which derives the name from her, and is called Swaledale, hath a neighbouring place full of Lead-Ore. And for the lack of woods which doth here much pinch the People, they are requited again with plenty of grass, which this place yields them in great abundance. Thus hath provident nature for every discommodity made amends with a contrariety, and furnished the defects of one place with sufficient supply from another.

❧ ❧ ❧

° **Composture**: Speed's spelling "compasture" fuses compost and pasture.
° **Tathe**: dung.   ° **laid**: left fallow.

TRISTRAM RISDON
[Dartmoor and the Devonshire Countryside] (c. 1633)

The early seventeenth century witnessed a vogue for chorography: the survey of the topographical features, natural resources, and history of a particular county or region. A Devonshire antiquary embarked on a study of his native county in 1605, labouring over it for nearly thirty years. Risdon's "peritinerary" circulated in manuscript (BL Add. MS 36748, Stowe MS 819), but was not published until 1714. In the extract below, he describes what is now Dartmoor National Park, famous in literary history as the setting of *The Hound of the Baskervilles*, a legend based on the fate of Richard Cabell (d. 1677), who would have been a near contemporary of Risdon. Risdon's account, however, reveals that Dartmoor was not entirely a howling wilderness, and the Devon countryside was subject to industry and agrarian "improvement" schemes.

Source: *Chorographical Description or Survey of the County of Devon* (1811), 6–9.

Between the North and South Hams° (for that is the ancient name) there lieth a chain of hills, consisting of a blackish earth, both rocky and heathy, called by a borrowed name of its barrenness Dartmoor;° richer in its bowels than in the face thereof, yielding tin and turf, which, to save for fuel, you would wonder to see how busy the by-dwellers be at some seasons of the year; whose tops and tors° are in the winter often covered with a white cap, but in the summer the bordering neighbours bring great herds of cattle and flocks of sheep to pasture there. From these hills, or rather mountains, the mother of many rivers, the land declineth either way. Witness their diverse courses: some of which disburden themselves into the British ocean, others by long wandering seek the Severn sea.

This waste° King John assigned to be a forest,° and King Henry III did not only confirm his father's grant for Dartmoor and Exmoor ... but for avoiding sundry inconveniences did set down the certain bounds of Dartmoor ...

Albeit the greatest part of this county is of its own nature barren and full of brakes° and briars, nevertheless, by the industry of man and God's blessing withal, it yieldeth plenty and variety of all things for the use of man: as cattle and such beasts, both of profit and pleasure, as are found in other places of this realm. Howbeit, those of pleasure are much diminished, for many parks are disparked and converted from pleasure to profit: from pasturing wild [7] beasts to breeding and feeding of cattle, sheep, and tillage.

Our flocks of sheep make not that show as elsewhere because the enclosures bereave the eye of its knowledge. But yet the trade of clothing is as much used in this county as in any other of the realm. The feeding of beefs is not so much discerned as in other shires, where great droves are driven to London, for the great navigation in these western parts requireth store of victuals, which is fully supplied by our own breed ... Corn we have plentiful of all sorts: as wheat, rye, barley, oats, pulse, vetches, as well as for navigation as for the sustenance of the inhabitants.

For trees, it hath the like variety as are found in other places of this kingdom, with which in former times it hath more abounded. For now, what with good husbandry and cleansing of the ground, and what by ill husbandry in felling and selling, the trees and timber are well shortened; which we in part feel and future times will find wanting ...

[8] Likewise, out of the bowels of the earth are found and digged sundry rich mines and minerals: some of tin and lead, some of iron and other

---

° **Hams**: pasturelands.　° **called ... Dartmoor**: implying its name derives from dearth, whereas it and the River Dart probably come from the Celtic word for oaks (Mills).
° **tors**: hills, rocky peaks. ° **waste**: uncultivated land. ° **forest**: royal hunting grounds.
° **brakes**: thickets.

metals, and, in following those veins of tin, some have lighted on silver ... And there is not the barrenest place but yieldeth some commodity: as stones of sundry sorts, and of late days quarries of slate are found out, wherewith they cover houses. Coals also are of late digged up for the supply of fuel, and burning of limestones, whereof it is not destitute ...

Well-watered is this province with clear rivers, as no one shire doth exceed it ... Havens we have, with convenient harbours and safe ports, passing well-stored with fish of all sorts, whose names I am not able to express; among which the herring and the pilchard are the most beneficial ... for by traffic of them, commodities are transported into this land from foreign nations. In a word, so convenient is this shire seated that from sea nor land is any commodity wanting to [9] these people for substance or safety. I speak not this upon a vain ostentation of my country, but to admonish every man in particular and all our nation in general to be thankful to God for the great blessings he hath bestowed upon them, and to consider the more they have received the more will be required at their hands. Therefore they are in all thankfulness to be used, according to God's will, to the good of his church, and especially employed by each one to behalf and good of another, and not any way to be abused, lest this talent° of the good creatures of God be taken from us, and given to another nation, more worthy thereof.

⁊⊱ ⁊⊱ ⁊⊱

° **talent**: coin, an allusion to Christ's Parable of the Talents (Matthew 25:14–30).

RICHARD JAMES

[Pendle Hill and the Wild Moorlands] (1636)

As attested by *Macbeth* (and possibly *King Lear*), many early moderns regarded heaths as places of deprivation, savagery, and witchcraft. Such impressions would have been bolstered by a notorious 1612 witchcraft trial in Lancashire in which the accused confessed to meeting in secret near Pendle Hill, a desolate landscape surrounded by the Bowland Fells and West Pennine Moors. The description of it below appears in a 400-line poem by Richard James – a friend of Ben Jonson and Robert Cotton – recounting a trip through Lancashire and Cheshire. Although James also finds the scenery inspiring, his text reveals why the word heathen is etymologically related to heath.
Source: *Iter Lancastrense* (1636) repr. in *Remains Historical and Literary Connected with the Palatine Counties of Lancaster and Chester* (1845), 10.

> "Penigent, Pendle Hill, Ingleborough:
> Three such hills be not all England thorough."
> I long to climb up Pendle; Pendle stands
> Round cop,° surveying all the wild moorlands,

280

° **cop**: summit.

And Malkin's Tower,° a little cottage, where
Report makes caitiff° witches meet to swear
Their homage to the devil, and contrive
The deaths of men and beasts …
                              I wonder much
If judges sentence with belief on such ….
                              Yet I do confess,   290
Needs must strange fancies poor old wives possess,
Who in these desert, misty moors do live,
Hungry and cold, and scarce see priest to give
Them ghostly° counsel. Churches far do stand
In laymen's hands, and chapels have no land
To cherish learned Curates.

🙥 🙥 🙥

° **Malkin's Tower**: alleged meeting place of the Lancashire witches.   ° **caitiff**: wretched.
° **ghostly**: spiritual.

GERRARD WINSTANLEY
"The barren land shall be made fruitful" (1649)

In the early modern era, most heaths were commons used by the rural poor for grazing and turf-cutting. Winstanley's vision of the miraculous transformation of the heaths was part of the Levellers' campaign to protect them from enclosure (see Winstanley's diatribe in Part v, p. 409). While his desire to cultivate it aligns with the georgic mentality of Norden, it also springs from his radical belief that the new English Commonwealth might restore Eden on earth.
Source: A *New Law of Righteousness Budding Forth* (1649), 60.

At this time "the barren land shall be made fruitful,"° for the Lord will take off the curse.° And if any grumble and say, "the Heaths and Commons are barren, and the like," and so draw against the work [and] all that I say, let them go their way. Their portion is not here; they live in the low flesh, not in the height of the spirit. And they know not the mystery of the Lord, who is now restoring Israel from bondage, and fetching them out of all lands where they were scattered into one place, where they shall live and feed together in peace. And then there shall be no more pricking briar in all the holy Mountain.

🙥 🙥 🙥

° **barren … fruitful**: Zachariah 8:11–13.
° **curse**: Genesis 3:17 encouraged the belief that heaths only appeared after humans sinned.

Mountains, Hills, Vales

ROBERT SOUTHWELL
"A Vale of Tears" (*c.* 1578)

The sublime is generally regarded as an eighteenth-century concept, formulated by the philosophers Immanuel Kant and Edmund Burke. Nevertheless, early modern writers and painters such as Roelant Savery had intimations of the "pleasing horror" that dramatic landscapes could inspire. The following poem appears within a collection of religious verse, which might invite an allegorical reading of the wilderness it depicts. As a Jesuit priest who travelled widely throughout the Continent and England, Southwell may have been better acquainted with actual wilderness than many of his contemporaries. In 1578, he walked from Paris to Rome and this poem is likely based on his crossing of the Alps.
Source: British Library Add MS 10422, 26ᵛ–28ᵛ; with emendations from *Moenie* (1595), 27–30.

A Vale there is enwrapped with dreadful shades,
Which thick° of mourning pines shrouds from the sun,
Where hanging cliffs yield short and dumpish° glades,
And snowy floods with broken streams do run;

Where eye-room° is from rock to cloudy sky,
From thence to dales with stony ruins strawed,°
Then to the crushèd water's frothy fry,
Which tumbleth from the tops where snow is thawed;

10   Where ears of other sound can have no choice,
But various blust'ring of the stubborn wind
In trees, in caves, in straits with diverse noise,
Which now doth hiss, now howl, now roar by kind;

Where waters wrestle with encount'ring stones,
That break their streams and turn them into foam,
The hollow clouds full fraught with thund'ring groans,
With hideous thumps discharge their pregnant womb.

And in the horror of this fearful° choir
Consists the music of this doleful place;
All pleasant birds their tunes from thence retire,
20   Where none but heavy notes have any grace.

° **thick:** grove.   ° **dumpish:** melancholy.   ° **eye-room:** vista.
° **strawed:** strewn or sprinkled; shroud] 1595.   ° **fearful:** frightening.

Resort there is of none but pilgrim wights,°
That pass with trembling foot and panting heart;
With terror cast in cold and shudd'ring frights,
They judge° the place to terror framed by art.

Yet nature's work it is, of art untouched,
So strait indeed, so vast unto the eye,
With such disordered order strangely couched,
And so with pleasing horror low and high,

That who it views must needs remain aghast,
Much at the work, more at the maker's might;   30
And muse how Nature such a plot could cast,
Where nothing seemeth wrong, yet nothing right:

A place for mated° minds, an only bower
Where every thing doth soothe° a dumpish mood;
Earth lies forlorn, the cloudy sky doth lour,
The wind here weeps, here sighs, here cries aloud.

The struggling flood between the marble groans,
Then roaring beats upon the craggy sides;
A little off, amidst the pebble stones,
With bubbling streams and purling noise it glides.   40

The pines thick set, high grown and ever green,
Still clothe the place with shade° and mourning veil;
Here gaping cliff, there mossy plain is seen,
Here hope doth spring, and there again doth quail.

Huge massy stones that hang by tickle° stays,
Still threaten fall,° and seem to hang in fear;
Some withered trees, ashamed of their decays,
Beset with green are forced grey coats to wear.

Here crystal springs crept out of secret vein,
Straight find some envious hole that hides their grace;   50
Here searèd tufts lament the want of rain,
There thunder-wrack gives terror to the place.

All pangs and heavy passions here may find
A thousand motives suitly° to their griefs,
To feed the sorrows of their troubled mind,
And chase away Dame Pleasure's vain reliefs.

To plaining° thoughts this vale a rest may be,
To which from worldly joys° they may retire;

° **wights:** persons.   ° **They judge:** And all] 1595.   ° **mated:** amazed.   ° **soothe:** declare, encourage.   ° **shade:** 1595; sad] BL.
° **tickle:** precarious.   ° **suitly:** suiting.   ° **plaining:** complaining.   ° **joys:** toys] 1595   ° **fall;** foul] 1595.

Where sorrow springs from water, stone, and tree;
60   Where every thing with mourners doth conspire.

Sit here, my soul, mayne° streams of tears afloat,
Here all thy sinful foils° alone recount;
Of solemn tunes make thou the doleful note,
That to thy ditties dolour may amount.

When Echo doth repeat thy painful cries,
Think that the very stones thy sins bewray,
And now accuse thee with their sad replies,
As heaven and earth shall in the latter day.

70   Let former faults be fuėl of thy fire,
For grief in limbeck° of thy heart to still°
Thy pensive thoughts and dumps of thy desire,
And vapour tears up to thy eyes at will.

Let tears to tunes, and pains to plaints be pressed,
And let this be the burden° of thy song,
"Come, deep remorse, possess my sinful breast;
Delights, adieu! I harboured you too long."

❦ ❦ ❦

° **mayne:** guide; mourn] 1595.   ° **foils:** disgraces.   ° **limbeck:** alembic (glass distilling
vessel).   ° **still:** distil.   ° **burden:** refrain.

THOMAS CHURCHYARD
"A Discourse of Mountains" (1587)

While it has been argued that mountains were transformed from gloomy protu-
berances to glorious heights only in the late seventeenth century (Nicolson), glim-
mers of the latter attitude can be found much earlier. Thomas Churchyard was a
grizzled ex-soldier who had seen action in Ireland and Flanders, so his survey of
Wales could be regarded as an extension of his military activities on behalf of the
budding English empire – the mountains offering the queen a "panoptic vision"
of her Welsh domains (Oakley-Brown). Yet Churchyard also praises mountains as
refuge for both wilderness and the spartan virtues, touting the moral and phys-
iological benefits of dwelling amid such rugged terrain, which gives the Welsh a
distinct identity and hence troubles the assumption they can be easily assimilated.
Source: *The Worthiness of Wales* (1587), M1ʳ–M3ʳ.

Dame Nature drew these Mountains in such sort,
As though the one should yield the other grace,
Or as each Hill itself were such a Fort,
They scorned to stoop to give the Cannon place.
If all were plain and smooth like garden ground

Where should high woods and goodly groves be found?
The eyes' delight, that looks on every coast
With pleasures great and fair prospect, were lost.

On Hill we view far off both field and flood,
Feel heat or cold, and so suck up sweet air,   10
Behold beneath great wealth and worldly good,
See wallèd Towns and look on Countries fair.
And who so sits or stands on Mountain high,
Hath half a world in compass of his eye:
A platform° made of Nature for the nonce,°
Where man may look on all the earth at once.

These ragged Rocks bring plainest people forth.
On Mountain wild the hardest Horse is bred.
Though grass thereon be gross and little worth,
Sweet is the food where hunger so is fed.   20
On roots and herbs our fathers long did feed,°
And near the Sky grows sweetest fruit indeed.
On marshy meres° and wat'ry mossy ground,
Are rotten weeds and rubbish dross unsound.

The fogs and mists that rise from vale below,
A reason makes that highest Hills are best;
And when such fogs doth o'er the Mountain go
In foulest days, fair weather may be guessed.°
As bitter blasts on Mountains big doth blow,
So noisome smells and savours breed below.   30
The Hill stands clear and clean from filthy smell;
They find not so that doth in Valley dwell.

The Mountain men live longer many a year
Than those in Vale, in plain, or marshy soil;
A lusty heart, a clean complexion clear,
They have on Hill that for hard living toil.
With Ewe and Lamb, with Goats and Kids they play,
In greatest toils to rub out weary day;
And when to house and home good fellows draw,
The lads can laugh at turning of a straw.°   40

No air so pure and wholesome as the Hill,
Both man and beast delights to be thereon;
In heat or cold it keeps one nature still,
Trim, neat, and dry, and gay to go upon.
A place most fit for pastime and good sport,
To which wild Stag and Buck doth still resort.
To cry of Hounds, the Mountain echo yields,
A grace to Vale, a beauty to the fields.

° **platform**: terrace or rampart (for mounting artillery).   ° **nonce**: purpose.   ° **roots … feed**: alluding to the belief that early humans were vegetarians.   ° **guessed**: original spelling "gest" might also signify guest.   ° **meres**: ponds.   ° **turning … straw**: trifles.

It stands for world, as though a watch° it were,
A stately guard to keep green meadow mild.
The Poets feign on shoulders it doth bear
The heavens high, but there they are beguiled.
The maker first of Mountain and of Vale,
Made Hill a wall to clip° about the Dale:
A strong defence for needful fruit and corn,
That else by blast might quickly be forlorn.

If boisterous winds were not withstood by strength,
Repulsed by force and driven backward too,
They would destroy our earthly joys at length,
And through their rage they would much mischief do.
God saw what smart and grief the earth would bide°
By sturdy storms and piercing tempests' pride,
So Mountains made to save the lower soil,
For fear the earth should suffer shameful spoil …

You may compare a King to Mountain high,
Whose princely power can bide both brunt and shock
Of bitter blast or thunderbolt from Sky;
His Fortress stands upon so firm a Rock.
A Prince helps all, and doth so strongly sit,
That none can harm by fraud, by force, nor wit.
The weak must lean where strength doth most remain;
The Mountain great commands the little Plain.

As Mountain is a noble, stately thing,
Thrust full of stones and Rocks as hard as steel,
A peerless piece, compared unto a King,
Who sits full fast on top of Fortune's wheel;
So is the Dale a place of subtle air,
A den of dross, oft times more foul than fair,
A dirty Soil, where water long doth bide,
Yet rich withal, it cannot be denied …

Wealth fosters pride and heaves up haughty heart,
Makes wit o'erween and man believe too far,
Infects the mind with vice in every part,
That quickly sets the senses all at war.
In Valley rich these mischiefs nourished are;
God planted peace on Mountain poor and bare.
By sweat of brows the people live on Hill,
Not sleight of brain, not craft nor cunning skill …

Who sleeps so sound as he that hath no Sheep,
Nor herd of Beasts to pasture and to feed?
Who fears the Wolf, but he who Lambs doth keep,
And many an hour is forced to watch indeed?

° **watch**: watchtower.   ° **clip**: embrace, encircle.   ° **bide**: suffer, endure.

Though gold be gay and cordial in his kind,
The loss of wealth gripes° long a greedy mind.
Poor Mountain folk possess not such great store,
But when it's gone, they care not much therefore.

જ્જ જ્જ જ્જ

° **gripes**: afflicts.

WILLIAM BROWNE
"A Landscape" and "Description of a Solitary Vale" (1613)

The word landscape derives from the Dutch *landschap* and originally signified a painting of natural scenery, not the scenery per se. Its first recorded appearance in English dates from 1605, and through its figurative usage by poets such as Milton it gradually came to mean the prospect or vista itself. The first passage below represents the first example in English literature of a sustained comparison of actual topography to a painting, anticipating the notion of the picturesque popularized by William Gilpin in 1768. It appears in *Britannia's Pastorals*, a work teeming with images of English rural life. Browne's poem has received scant critical attention due to its rambling, disjointed narrative, but an ecocritic might be inclined to see this "less as a fault than as a function of the poem's decentralizing vision of the national landscape" (O'Callaghan). In contrast to the idyllic pastoral setting of the first extract, the second passage depicts a rugged wilderness, which the Proem identifies as an allegorical "Vale of Woe." Yet Browne's verse mingles delight with the melancholy, and may be modelled on the terrain of his native Devon, as his hometown of Tavistock stands next to scenic Dartmoor.
Source: *Britannia's Pastorals* (1613), 1.42 (Song 2), 78 (Song 4).

"A Landscape"

And as within a Landscape that doth stand,
Wrought by the Pencil of some curious° hand,
We may descry, here meadow, there a wood;
Here standing ponds, and there a running flood;
Here on some mount a house of pleasure vanted,°
Where once the roaring Cannon had been planted;   830
There on a hill a Swain pipes out the day,
Outbraving all the Choristers of May.
A Huntsman here follows his cry of hounds,
Driving the Hare along the fallow grounds,
Whilst one at hand, seeming the sport t'allow,
Follows the hounds, and careless leaves the Plough.
There in another place some high-raised land,
In pride bears out her breasts unto the strand.

° **curious**: skilful.   ° **vanted**: displayed, with suggestion of vantage-ground.

840

Here stands a bridge, and there a conduit-head;°
Here round a Maypole some the measures tread;
There boys the truant play and leave their book;°
Here stands an Angler with a baited hook.°
There for a Stag one lurks within a bough;
Here sits a Maiden milking of her Cow.
There on a goodly plain (by time thrown down)
Lies buried in his dust some ancient Town,
Who, now invillaged,° there's only seen
In his vast ruins what his state had been:
And all of these in shadows° so expressed

850

Make the beholder's eye to take no rest.

"Description of a Solitary Vale"

580

Between two hills, the highest Phoebus° sees,
Gallantly crowned with large Sky-kissing trees,
Under whose shade the humble valleys lay,
And Wild Boars° from their dens their gambols play,
There lay a gravelled walk o'er-grown with green,
Where neither track of man nor beast was seen.
And as the Ploughman when the land he tills,
Throws up the fruitful earth in ridgèd hills,
Between whose Chevron° form he leaves a balk,°
So 'twixt those hills had Nature framed this walk:
Not over dark nor light, in angles bending,

590

And like the gliding of a Snake descending;
All hushed and silent as the mid of night,
No chatt'ring Pie nor Crow appeared in sight,
Yet further in I heard the Turtle-dove,
Singing sad dirges of her lifeless Love;
Birds that compassion from the rocks could bring
Had only licence in that place to sing,
Whose doleful notes the melancholy Cat°
Close in a hollow tree sat wondering at.

° **conduit-head**: reservoir.
° **boys … book**: Browne later describes in greater detail the joy of children who prefer playing outdoors to studying (1.87) .
° **angler … hook**: *Britannia's Pastorals* also includes a memorable depiction of fishing (1.102–3)
° **invillaged**: reduced to a village (Browne's coinage).
° **shadows**: images.   ° **Phoebus**: the sun.
° **Wild Boars**: believed to be locally extinct or critically endangered in England; King James had just imported some from France in 1608 and 1611.
° **Chevron**: pointed.
° **balk**: ridge of unploughed land.
° **Cat**: presumably the European wildcat, a species once common in wooded districts of England but now critically endangered and found only in the Scottish Highlands. In the early modern period they were hunted as vermin; between 1590 and 1610, one Devonshire town paid bounties for eighteen slain wildcats (Lovegrove 225).

And Trees that on the hillside comely grew,
When any little blast of Aeol° blew,   600
Did nod their curlèd heads, as they would be
The Judges to approve their melody.

᠅ ᠅ ᠅

° **Aeol**: wind.

THOMAS HOBBES
from The Wonders of the Peak (c. 1627)

In 1627, while working as a tutor for the Cavendish family at Chatsworth in Derbyshire, Thomas Hobbes toured the Peak District. A decade he later published Latin verses recounting his adventures. Although the poem veers into hyperbole when it dubs the Peaks "the English Alps," it reveals how this foreboding landscape had become a tourist destination and a site of literary inspiration by the mid-seventeenth century (see works by Drayton, John Taylor, and Charles Cotton). Hobbes's account also captures the early modern tendency to perceive landscape in terms of the female body, and to superimpose on wild or subterranean places the infernal topography of the classical underworld.
Source: *De mirabilis pecci; The Wonders of the Peak*, anonymous translation (1678), 16–18, 30–2, 40–4, 50–4.

From thence our horse with weary feet and slow,
Towards a steep Hill's high top, do climbing go,
And after many a tug and weary Strain,   120
Half breathless, they the Summit do gain.
Turning about with wonder we espy
The birds now lazily to creep, not fly;
And that the Pico° of the Mountain's brow
Had pierced the body of the Clouds quite through.
Derwent° appears but as a crooked line,
And Chatsworth as a point it doth entwine.
W'had gone but little further when we found
The Hill's soft back, cut deep with many a wound;
And did the earth in whitish ranks° espy   130
Cast up in heaps, upon the surface lie …
For man (wealth's great invader, wheresoe'er
It hidden lies) with fire and Steel does tear
The bowels of the earth, and rends in twain
The Stony cover of the leaden vein;°
And boldly dares, if poverty compel,

° **Pico**: peak.   ° **Derwent**: a tributary of the Trent that flows through the Peak District.
° **ranks**: rows (spoil tips).
° **leaden vein**: lead was mined in the Peaks as far back as Roman times, although operations
   expanded in the late sixteenth century with improved mining technology. The Derwent catchment
   area and Peak District peatlands consequently have some the highest levels of residual lead
   contamination in Europe, which may be remobilized by flooding (Kossoff *et al.*).

To rob th'Exchequer° of the Prince of Hell.
Not always without danger: two° were caught,
As in their Mother's womb they deeply wrought,
160   By death, who suddenly o'erwhelmed them there,
Where they themselves had digged a Sepulchre …
230   Behind a ruined mountain does appear
Swelling into two parts, which turgent° are
As when we bend our bodies to the ground,
The buttocks amply sticking out are found …
And now we're come (I blushing must rehearse),
As most do style it, to the Devil's Arse° …
250   But we with wonder and amaze admire
The tall prodigious Rocky Hemisphere,°
How without prop 'tis capable to bear
So vast a weight, how it the mountain stays,
And the eternal Geometrician praise …
Turned to the left a thousand pace or so,
To the Peak Forest without Tree we go;
320   Hemmed in with Stony fence, the naked Deer
Cold Winter pinches, not a leaf does here
To shelter them upon these hills appear.
Summer's fierce heat does scorch them, not a shade
From the Sun's ray to cover them is had.
Many the bloody wantonness of man
Destroys with Dog, his loved companion.
Many the changes when the Heavens frown,
Some Eldon° with wide jaws does swallow down.
Of the torn earth a dire hiatus 'tis,
330   Which should I labour truly to express,
The Ancients I to council call in vain,
For no such thing the Poets ere could feign …
She's dumb,° as conscious of the form obscene:°
340   Upon the side of a fair hill that's green,
Its rim descending with the mountain's scene,
Driving off herds that graze around it far,
And sucking with dark lungs the pliant air;
While from the edge we prostrate view't, the sight
O'th' vast abyss does each of us affright.
With fear and dread the bold spectator spies,
No bounds to stop the progress of his eyes.
And though the stony battlements assure,
Whos'e'er leans on them may have sight secure,
350   Yet still distrust our fearful minds invades,

° **Exchequer**: treasury.
° **two**: in a marginal note, Hobbes reports witnessing the rescue of one of the two miners.
° **turgent**: swollen.   ° **Devil's Arse**: Peak Cavern, near Castleton, one of the "Seven Wonders" of the Peaks.   ° **Hemisphere**: cavern.
° **Eldon**: Eldon Hole, a deep chasm, another of the "Seven Wonders" of the Peaks.
° **She's dumb**: quiet. Hobbes assumes that modesty prevents his female guide from pointing out the anatomical resemblance he spies in the terrain.
° **obscene**: a footnote in the text reads, "The mouth of the hole is of a cunnoid form or like the privities of a woman" (cf. Cotton's reference in his *Wonders of the Peak* to "Nature's pudenda," 1).

And we retire from the dreadful shades …
'Tis said great Dudley° to this Cave came down
In famed Eliza's Reign, a Peer well known.
He a poor Peasant for a petty price,
With Rope around his middle, does entice, 420
And pole in hand like to Sarissa° tight,
And basket full of Stones, down to be let,
And pendulous to hang i'th' midst o'th' Cave;
Thence casting stones, intelligence to have
By list'ning of the depth of this vast hole.
The trembling wretch descending with his pole
Puts by the Stones, that else might on him roll;
By their rebounds casts up a space immense,
Where every stroke does death to him dispense,
Fearing the thread on which his life depends, 430
Chance might cut off ere Fate should give commands.
After a hundred yards he had below
I'th' earth been drowned, far as the Rope would go,
And long enough hung by't within the Cave;
To th'Earl (who now impatient was to have
His answer) He's drawn up; but whether fear
Immoderate distracted him, or 'twere
From the swift motion as the Rope might wreath,
Or Spectrums° from his fear, or Hell beneath
Frighted the wretch, or the Soul's citadel 440
Were stormed or taken by some Imp of Hell,
For certain 'twas he raved: this his wild eyes,
His paleness, trembling, all things verifies.
Where venting something none could understand,
Enthusiastic° hints ne'er to be scanned,
He ceasing dies after eight days were gone.
But th'Earl informed how far the Cave went down,
He trembling from it hastes, not willing now,
Nor yet this way, down to the shades to go.

❧ ❧ ❧

° **Dudley**: Earl of Leicester, who visited the Peaks during one of his trips to the spa at Buxton in the 1570s.
° **Sarissa**: long spear.   ° **Spectrums**: spectres.   ° **Enthusiastic**: frenzied (as if possessed).

ANNE KEMP
"A Contemplation on Basset's Down Hill" (*c.* 1658)

The following text is the only surviving work attributed to Anne Kemp. Virtually nothing is known of her apart from what can be inferred from the poem itself. It is not even certain if she resided near Meysey Hampton in Gloucestershire, where Basset's Hill is located, as she speaks of it as an outsider. As McRae and Bending observe, the poem appears to be modelled on John Denham's *Cooper's Hill*, but offers a more personal rather than political view of landscape (43), valuing Basset's Down precisely because of its remoteness from the filth and hubbub of the city. Source: *A Contemplation on Basset's Down Hill* (1658).

> If that exact Appelles° now did live,
> And would a picture of Elysium° give,
> He might portray the prospect which this Hill
> Doth show, and make the eye command at will.
> Here's many a shire whose pleasantness for sight
> Doth yield to the Spectators great delight.
> There's a large Field gilded with Ceres' gold;°
> Here a green mead doth many Heifers hold;
> There's pasture grown with verdant grass, whose store
> Of Argent° sheep shows th'owner is not poor.
> Here springs do intimate Meanders make,
> Excelling far Oblivion's Lethe° Lake.
> There Woods and Copses harbour as many
> And sweet melodious Choristers as any
> Elysium yields, whose Philomelan° lays
> Merit the highest of the Lyric's praise.
> Here's Flora decked with robes of Or and Azure,
> Fragrantly smelling, yields two senses pleasure.
> Hence Zephyrus doth breathe his gentle gales
> Cool on the Hills, and sweet throughout the Vales.
> How happy are they that in this Climate dwell?
> Alas! They can't their own sweet welfare tell.
> Scarce I myself whilst I am here do know it
> Till I see its Antithesis to show it.
> Here are no smoking streets, nor howling cries,
> Deaf'ning the ears, nor blinding of the eyes;
> No noisome smells t'infect and choke the air,
> Breeding diseases envious to the Fair.
> Deceit is here exiled from Flesh and Blood
> (Strife only reigns, for all strive to be good).
> With Will° his verse I here will make an end,
> And as the Crab doth always backward bend,°
> So, though from this sweet place I go away,
> My loyal heart will in this Climate stay.
> Thus heartless doth my worthless body rest,
> Whilst my heart liveth with the ever-blest.

Line numbers: 10, 20, 30

❧ ❧ ❧

° **Apelles**: ancient Greek painter, famed for his realism.
° **Elysium**: abode of the blessed in Greek mythology; an ideal state of happiness.
° **Ceres' gold**: wheat.   ° **Argent**: silver.
° **Lethe**: river of forgetfulness in the classical underworld.
° **Philomelan**: nightingale-like. See the poem by Morley in Part II, p. 141.
° **Will**: possibly an allusion to William Shakespeare (Evans). If so, it would be the earliest known reference to reading Shakespeare outdoors.
° **bend**: walk.

THOMAS BURNET
"Concerning the Mountains of the Earth" (1684)

Burnet's book provoked controversy in its own day for suggesting that the antediluvian earth was smooth and uniform, and the mountains only cropped up after Noah's Flood. Rather than lament this transformation, however, Burnet finds in mountains a reminder of the mind-bending antiquity of the earth, and imagines them as geological ruins worthy of even more admiration than the historical ruins of Rome. His sense of the overwhelming grandeur of mountains makes him an important prophet of the sublime.
Source: *Sacred Theory of Earth* (1684), 139–44.

The greatest objects of Nature are, methinks, the most pleasing to behold; and, next to the great Concave of the Heavens and those boundless Regions where the Stars inhabit, there is nothing that I look upon with more pleasure than the wide Sea and the [140] Mountains of the Earth. There is something august and stately in the Air of these things that inspires the mind with great thoughts and passions. We do naturally upon such occasions think of God and his greatness. And whatsoever hath but the shadow and appearance of [the] INFINITE, as all things have that are too big for our comprehension, they fill and overbear the mind with their Excess, and cast it into a pleasing kind of stupor and admiration.

And yet these Mountains we are speaking of, to confess the truth, are nothing but great ruins, but such as show a certain magnificence in Nature, as from old Temples and broken Amphitheatres of the Romans we collect the greatness of that people. But the grandeur of a Nation is less sensible to those that never see the remains and monuments they have left, and those who never see the mountainous parts of the Earth scarce ever reflect upon the causes of them, or what power in Nature could be sufficient to produce them. The truth is the generality of people have not sense and curiosity enough to raise a question concerning these things, or concerning the Original of them. You may tell them that Mountains grow out of the Earth like Fuzz-balls, or that there are Monsters underground that throw up Mountains as Moles do Mole-hills; they will scarce raise one objection against your doctrine. Or if you would appear more Learned, tell them that the Earth is a great Animal and these are Wens that grow upon its body. This would pass current for Philosophy, so much is the World drowned in stupidity and sensual pleasures, and so little inquisitive into the works of God and Nature.

There is nothing doth more awaken our thoughts or excite our minds to inquire into the causes of such things than the actual view of them, as I have had experience myself when it was my fortune to cross the Alps and Appennine Mountains; for the sight of those wild, vast, and indigested heaps of Stones and Earth did so deeply strike my fancy that I was not easy till I could give myself some tolerable account how that confusion came in Nature. 'Tis true the [141] height of Mountains compared with the Diameter of the Earth is not considerable, but the extent of them and the ground they stand upon bears a considerable proportion to the surface of the Earth; and if from Europe we may take our measures for the rest, I easily believe that the Mountains do at least take up the tenth part° of the dry land.

The Geographers are not very careful to describe or note in their Charts the multitude or situation of Mountains. They mark the bounds of Countries, the site of Cities and Towns, and the course of Rivers, because these are things of chief use to civil affairs and commerce, and that they design to serve, and not Philosophy or Natural History. But Cluverius° in his description of ancient Germany, Switzerland and Italy, hath given Maps of those Countries more approaching to the natural face of them, and we have drawn (at the end of this chapter) such a Map of either Hemisphere without marking Countries or Towns, or any such artificial things, distinguishing only Land and Sea, Islands and Continents, Mountains and not Mountains; and 'tis very useful to imagine the Earth in this manner, and to look often upon such bare draughts as show us Nature undressed, for then we are best able to judge what her true shapes and proportions are …

Suppose a man were carried asleep out of a Plain Country, amongst the Alps, and left there upon the top of one of the highest Mountains: when he waked and looked about him, he would think himself in an enchanted Country, or carried into another World … to see on every hand of him a multitude of vast bodies thrown together in confusion, [142] … Rocks standing naked round about him, and the Valleys gaping under him, and at his feet, it may be, a heap of frozen Snow in the midst of Summer. He would hear the thunder come from below, and see the black Clouds hanging beneath him …

[143] If one could at once have a prospect of all [the world's mountain ranges] together, one would be easily satisfied that the Globe of the Earth is a more rude and indigested Body than 'tis commonly imagined. If one could see all the Kingdoms of the earth at one view, [one could perceive] how they lie in broken heaps; the Sea hath overwhelmed one half of them, and what remains are but the taller parts of a ruin. Look upon those great ranges of Mountains in Europe or in Asia whereof we have given a short survey: in what confusion [144] do they lie? They have neither form nor beauty, nor shape nor order, no more than the Clouds in the Air. Then how barren, how desolate, how naked are they? How they stand neglected by Nature? Neither the Rains can soften them, nor the Dews from Heaven make them fruitful.

I have given this short account of the Mountains of the Earth to help to remove that prejudice we are apt to have or that conceit that the present

° **tenth part**: the actual figure is over 20 per cent.
° **Cluverius**: Philip Clüver, a German geographer.

Earth is regularly formed. And to this purpose I do not doubt but that it would be of very good use to have natural Maps of the Earth, as we noted before, as well as civil, and done with the same care and judgement. Our common Maps I call civil, which note the distinction of Countries and of Cities, and represent the Artificial Earth as inhabited and cultivated. But natural Maps leave out all that, and represent the Earth as it would be if there was not an Inhabitant upon it, nor ever had been: the Skeleton of the Earth, as I may so say.

ਟੱ ਟੱ ਟੱ

JANE BARKER
"The Prospect of a Landscape, Beginning with a Grove" (1688)

Barker grew up near the fen region of rural Lincolnshire, studying Latin and medicine with the aid of her brother. She befriended a group of poets at St John's College, Cambridge, and her poems circulated amongst this coterie before they were finally published in 1688, after her move to London and conversion to Catholicism. Influenced by Cowley and Restoration pastoral, her verses revel in the blurring of nature and culture while expressing a genuine attachment to the English landscape.
Source: *Poetical Recreations* (1688), 20–3.

> Well might the Ancients deem a Grove to be
> The Sacred Mansion of some Deity;
> For it our Souls insensibly does move
> At once to humble Piety and Love …
> By these our rationality is shown,
> The cognisance by which from Brutes were known …
> But those whom gentle Laws of Love can't bind,
> Are Savages of the most sordid kind.
> But none like these do in our Shades obtrude,
> Though scornfully some needs will call them rude,
> Yet Nature's culture is so well expressed,
> That Art herself would wish to be so dressed;
> For here the Sun conspires with ev'ry Tree
> To deck the Earth with Landscape-Tapestry;   20
> Then through some space his brightest Beams appear,
> Which does erect a Golden Pillar there.
> Here a close Canopy of Boughs is made;
> There a soft, grassy Cloth of State is spread,
> With Gems and gayest Flowers embroidered o'er,
> Fresh as those Beauties honest Swains adore.
> Here Plants for health and for delight are met:

The Cephalic° Cowslip, Cordial Violet;
Under the Diuretic° Woodbine grows
30   The Splenetic° Columbine, Scorbutic° Rose;
The best of which, some gentle Nymph doth take
For faithful Corydon° a Crown to make …
And Birds around, through their extended throats,
40   In careless Consort chant their pleasing Notes …
Ah silly Town! Wilt thou ne'er learn to know
What happiness in Solitude does grow? …
Fly to some calm retreat, where you may spend
Your life in quietude with some kind Friend,
In some small Village and adjacent Grove,
70   At once your Friendship and your Wit improve …
And if thy mind to Contemplation leads,
80   Who God and Nature's Books has surely needs
No other Object to employ his thought,
Since in each leaf such Mysteries are wrought,
That who so studies most shall never know
Why the straight Elm's so tall, the Moss so low.
Oh, now I could enlarge upon this Theme,
But that I'm unawares come to the stream,
Which at the bottom of this Grove does glide;
And here I'll rest me by its flow'ry side.

° **Cephalic**: cowslip was used to alleviate headache.
° **Diuretic**: provoking urination.   ° **Splenetic**: used to treat spleen or melancholy.
° **Scorbutic**: scurvy-curing.
° **Corydon**: conventional name for a shepherd in pastoral literature.

Lakes, Rivers, Oceans

RICHARD BRATHWAITE
"The Lake" (1634)

It is fitting that England's first Lakeland poet wrote a proem personifying a lake. Brathwaite's relentless anthropomorphising captures the Renaissance tendency to comprehend nature by seeing ourselves reflected in it, while water's fluidity makes it the ultimate shape-shifter.
Source: *A Strange Metamorphosis of Man, Transformed into a Wilderness* (1634), C8ʳ–D3ʳ.

The Lake is Diana's glass, or common mirror of the rest of Nymphs, wherewith they dress themselves. It is a liquid crystal, whose Ice thereof make the perfect Crystal, while [C8ᵛ] the Sands in the bottom as the black of the mirror makes the foil that causeth the reflection. It is more properly a sea than the sea itself, because indeed a true congregation of waters so gathered into the stony cistern of the Rocks. He is no flatterer, but a true tell-troth,° for he will show the Stag his branchy horns, the Ass his prodigious ears, and discover the Satyr to be a beast as he is by his attire. He is very liberal of his liquids to all the Forest, for let them provide meat elsewhere, and he will find them drink enough: [D1ʳ] exceedingly blessed of God for this his hospitality, for though he have given drink to all our Desert° from the time of Noah, his store is never a whit the less. He is very patient, who will suffer any reasonable burden to be laid on his back and bear it willingly, if it sink not of itself, or be not perhaps stirred up and set on by the malicious blasts of the calumnious winds; for then he will so lash forth with his waves like so many kicks of the heel that twenty-to-one he unhorseth whatsoever is on his back … [D1ᵛ] He is not hot, but yet of that quality that he will bear no coals,° especially if active and lively. As great as he is, there is no Snake shall creep in at a lesser hole than he; and like him where he gets but his head in once, with time enough he will draw his whole body after him. He is free to lend what he hath, as appears by the Sun, who is always borrowing of his store, which he fetches and draws with [D2ʳ] his exhalation, but looks to be repaid again with interest. He loves to keep company with the nobler sort, who are truly generous and

---

° **tell-troth**: truth-teller.
° **Desert**: wilderness.
° **bear … coals**: to carry coals was proverbial for bearing insults or submitting to something shameful. The idiom here may glance at the presence of charcoal works in the Lake District.

better than himself, and will bear with them, especially the more airy they be, as come from a higher family. But for the ignobler multitude, as the earth and earthly things, he condemns them and sets them at his foot. He is so pitiful° that he will communicate himself to any that stands in need of him, and will even spend and exhaust himself to do them good, being never more troubled than [D2ᵛ] when he finds himself so limited that he cannot go forth to help his neighbour. He is cold of constitution, and will congeal through fear with the least frost, and then the very boys may triumph over him, and even ride upon him at their pleasure. He is stable and constant, and not so fleeting as the Sea which hath his ebbs and flows; while being contented with his own estate, he lives most happy in his solitude, remaining so private in the Wilderness, where, like a true Hermit, he keeps an exact and endless silence in [D3ʳ] his cell assigned him by nature.

❧ ❧ ❧

° **pitiful**: compassionate.

WILLIAM BROWNE
[Marina and the River-God] (1613)

When a heartsick shepherdess named Marina hurls herself into a spring, a river god rescues her and offers to share with her the bounty of his waters. Although based on an incident in John Fletcher's *Faithful Shepherdess*, Browne's version brims with a genuine love for the River Tavy that flowed through his hometown of Tavistock in Devon. He does not name the river god explicitly, but frequently references the Tavy elsewhere, including the poem's opening line, and in Song 3, when he portrays its marriage to its tributary the Wallabrook in a scene modelled on Spenser's marriage of the Thames and Medway. In comparison to Fletcher and Spenser, Browne was more of an outdoorsman; he seems to have enjoyed fishing (his pastoral epic includes a meticulous description of the angler's craft), and is accordingly far more attentive to the river as not simply a mythological but an ecological space. He even voices a concern for the cleanliness of the water (although this prompts Marina to wish away amphibians whose spawn was thought to contaminate it), and this episode captures Browne's tendency to subordinate human-centred plots to natural processes like the water cycle.
Source: *Britannia's Pastorals* (1613), 19–24, 28 (Songs 1 and 2).

700
The fall of her did make the God below,
Starting, to wonder whence that noise should grow;
Whether some ruder Clown in spite did fling
A Lamb, untimely fall'n, into his Spring;
And if it were, he solemnly then swore
His Spring should flow some other way; no more
Should it in wanton manner ere be seen
To writhe in knots, nor give a gown of green
Unto the Meadows, nor be seen to play,

Nor drive the Rushy mills that in his way
The Shepherds made; but rather for their lot,
Send them red waters that their sheep should rot. 710
And with such Moorish Springs embrace their field
That it should nought but Moss and Rushes yield …
He'd show his anger by some flood at hand,
And turn the same into a running sand …
        But when as in his water
The corpse came sinking down, he spied the matter,
And catching softly in his arms the Maid
He brought her up …
"The best of Fishes in my flood
Shall give themselves to be her food:
The Trout, the Dace, the Pike, the Bream,
The Eel that loves the troubled stream,
The Miller's-thumb,° the hiding Loach,
The Perch, the ever-nibbling Roach,
The Shoats° with whom is Tavy fraught,
The foolish Gudgeon, quickly caught, 60
And last the little Minnow fish,
Whose chief delight in gravel is.
In right she cannot me despise
Because so low mine Empire lies;
For I could tell how Nature's store
Of Majesty appeareth more
In waters than in all the rest
Of Elements. It seemed her best
To give the waves most strength and power,
For they do swallow and devour 70
The earth; the waters quench and kill
The flames of fire, and mounting still
Up in the air are seen to be,
As challenging a seignory
Within the Heavens, and to be one
That should have like dominion.
They be a ceiling and a floor
Of clouds, caused by the vapour's store
Arising from them, vital spirit,
By which all things their life inherit, 80
From them is stopped, kept asunder.
And what's the reason else of Thunder? …
And can there anything appear
More wonderful than in the air
Congealèd waters oft to spy
Continuing pendant in the Sky? … 90
Or falling down oft time in rain
Doth give green liv'ries to the plain,
Make Shepherds' Lambs fit for the dish,

° **Miller's-thumb**: bullhead.
° **Shoats**: a smaller trout, peculiar to Devon and Cornwall.

100   And giveth nutriment to fish;
       Which nourisheth all things of worth
       The earth produces and brings forth …
       To Trees and Plants I comfort give,
       By me they fructify and live …
       Who seeth this can do no less
       Than of his own accord confess,
       That notwithstanding all the strength
       The earth enjoys in breadth and length,
       She is beholding to each stream,
       And hath receivèd all from them.
       Her love to him she must then give
       By whom herself doth chiefly live …
       Thou shalt acknowledge springs have done
       As much for thee as anyone" …
                                    "May first,"
       Quoth Marina, "Swains give Lambs to thee;
280   And may thy Flood have seignory
       Of all Floods else, and to thy fame
       Meet greater Springs,° yet keep thy name.
       May never Ewet° nor the Toad
       Within thy Banks make their abode.
       Taking thy journey from the Sea,
       Mayest thou ne'er happen in thy way
       On Nitre° or on Brimstone Mine
       To spoil thy taste. This Spring of thine
       Let it of nothing taste but earth
290   And salt conceivèd in their birth.
       Be ever fresh! Let no man dare
       To spoil thy Fish, make lock or weir,
       But on thy Margent still let dwell
       Those flowers which have the sweetest smell …
       Let as much good betide to thee,
       As thou hast favour showed to me.

                        ❧ ❧ ❧

° **greater Springs**: the Tavy has several tributaries, including the rivers Lumburn and Walkham.
° **Ewet**: eft, or river newt.   ° **Nitre**: saltpetre.

JOHN TAYLOR

from Taylor on Thame Isis (1632)

Justly dubbed the "water poet," John Taylor was one of the most prolific travel writers in early modern England. In 1623 he journeyed up the River Avon in Hampshire (not to be confused with the Avon that flows through Warwickshire) to Salisbury. Nine years later he voyaged up the Thames, and was appalled by the misuse and obstruction of the river by private individuals valuing profit over the public good. As a waterman who ferried passengers across the Thames for a living,

Taylor had a professional interest in improving the nation's waterways. In 1664, Parliament passed an act to make the river navigable just as Taylor had proposed. Source: *Taylor on Thame Isis* (1632), A2^r–A3^v, B1^r–B2^v, C1^r–C3^r.

Our patron Phoebus,° whose sweet influence
Doth quicken all our reason, life, and sense,
'Tis he that makes grass grow and Rivers spring,
He makes both my song's subject and me sing;
His beams the water do extenuate
To vapours, and those vapours elevate
Into the middle Region, where they tumble
And melt, and then descend and are made humble,
Moist'ning the face of many a spacious hill,
Where soaking deep the hollow vaults they fill,   10
Where into Rivers they again break out:
So nature in a circle runs about.
Large Downs do treasure up great store of rain,
Whose bowels vent it in the vales again …
The famous river Isis hath her spring
Near Tetbury, and down along doth bring,
As handmaids to attend her progress, Churn,
Coln, Windrush, Evenlode, Leach, whose windings turn,
And Meads and Pastures trims, bedecks, and dresses,
Like an invaluable chain of S's …
These fountains and fish-breeding rivulets
(The Country's nurses, nourishers, and teats)   50
Attend Dame Isis down to Dorchester,
Near which her lovely Tame doth meet with her;
There Tame his Isis doth embrace and kiss,
Both joined in one, called Tame or Tame Isis.
Isis like Salmacis° becomes with Tame
Hermaphrodite in nature and in name° …
Through many Countries as these waters pass,
They make the Pastures fructify in grass:
Cattle grow fat, and cheese and butter cheap,
Hay in abundance, Corn by strick° and heap,   170
Beasts breed, and Fish increase, Fowls multiply;
It brings Wood, Coal, and Timber plenteously.
It bears the lame and weak, makes fat the lean,
And keeps whole towns and countries sweet and clean.
Wer't not for Thames, as Heaven's high hand doth bless it,
We neither could have fish nor fire to dress it;
The very Brewers would be at a fault,
And buy their water dearer than their malt;
And had they malt and water at desire,

° **Phoebus**: the sun.
° **Salmacis**: river in Turkey whose waters supposedly would make men who bathed in it effeminate; it acquired this power when its naiad attempted to rape the bathing Hermaphroditus (See Ovid's *Metamorphoses*, 4.352–481).
° **Hermaphrodite … name**: because of the confluence of rivers gendered female and male.
° **strick**: unit of measurement for grain.

180   What shift° (a God's name) would they make for fire?
        There's many a Seaman, many a Navigator,
        Watermen, fishers, bargemen on this water,
        Themselves and families beyond compare,
        In number more than hundred thousands are,
        Who do their Prince and Country often serve,
        And wer't not for this river might go starve;
        And for the good to England it hath done,
        Shall it to spoil and ruin be let run?
        Shall private persons for their gainful use,
190   Engross the water and the land abuse?
        Shall that which God and nature gives us free,
        For use and profit in community,
        Be barred from men, and dammed up as in Thames?
        A shameless avarice surpassing shames …
        Shall Thames be barred its course with stops and locks,
        With Mills and hills, with gravel beds and rocks,
        With weirs and weeds, and forcèd Islands made,
        To spoil a public for a private Trade?
        Shame fall° the doers, and Almighty's blessing
440   Be heaped upon their heads that seek redressing.
        Were such a business to be done in Flanders,
        Or Holland 'mongst the industrious Netherlanders,°
        They to deep passages would turn our hills,
        To Windmills they would change our watermills;
        All helps unto this river they would aid,
        And all impediments should be destroyed …
        In common reason, all men must agree
        That if the river were made clean and free,
        One Barge, with eight poor men's industrious pains,
        Would carry more than forty carts or wains …
        Thus men would be employed, and horse preserved,
460   And all the country at cheap rates be served …
        Then should this worthy work be soon begun,
        And with successful expedition done:
        Which I despair not of, but humbly plead,
        That God his blessings will increase and spread
        On them that love this work, and on their heirs,
470   Their goods and chattels, and on all that's theirs.

                          ❧ ❧ ❧

° **shift**: expedient.   ° **fall**: befall.
° **Netherlanders**: Dutch engineers were currently overseeing the drainage of the fens.

HENRY VAUGHAN
"To the River Usk" (1651)

In his Sonnets, Shakespeare boasts that his poetry can preserve the beauty of his
beloved for all eternity. In contrast, Vaughan composed a poetry collection (whose

Latin title translates as "The Swan of Usk" – a more fitting moniker for Vaughan than Swan-of-Avon is for Shakespeare) extolling the commemorative power of verse to bestow quasi-immortality on rivers and groves. A native of Wales, Vaughan spent the bulk of his life in scenic Breconshire, and his poetry often struggles to express a spiritual transcendence of the material world precisely because of his profound love for his earthly place. Composed in the immediate aftermath of the Civil War, this poem wishes the Usk might be forever untainted by pollution and the ravages of battle, a fate Vaughan laments in "The Bird," in which "The pleasant Land to brimstone turns / And all her streams grow foul." Vaughan may have been concerned about charcoal-manufacturing and silver-mining in the region, particularly after Thomas Bushell, a protégé of Francis Bacon, took control of mining operations in 1637 and swiftly deforested much of the Talybont Valley. Today, the Usk (which derives from the Welsh for "fish") is protected as a Site of Special Scientific Interest because of the variety of wildlife it supports, and Vaughan would no doubt be pleased to learn that there is a hiking trail dedicated to him along its banks.

Source: *Olor Iscanus* (1651), 1–3.

> Thus Poets (like the Nymphs, their pleasing themes)
> Haunted the bubbling Springs and gliding streams,
> And happy banks, whence such fair flowers have sprung,
> But happier those where they have sat° and sung!
> Poets (like Angels) where they once appear
> Hallow the place, and each succeeding year
> Adds rev'rence to't, such as at length doth give
> This agèd faith: that there their Genii° live.
> Hence th'Ancients say that from this sickly air,
> They pass to Regions more refined and fair,   20
> To Meadows strewed with Lilies and the Rose,
> And shades whose youthful green no old age knows,
> Where all in white they walk, discourse, and sing,
> Like Bees' soft murmurs, or a chiding Spring.
> But Isca,° whensoe'er those shades I see,
> And thy loved Arbours must no more know me,
> When I am laid to rest hard by thy streams,
> And my Sun sets, where first it sprang in beams,
> I'll leave behind me such a large, kind light,
> As shall redeem thee from oblivious night,   30
> And in these vows, which (living yet) I pay,
> Shed such a Precious and Enduring Ray,
> As shall from age to age thy fair name lead
> Till Rivers leave to run, and men to read.
> First, may all Bards born after me
> (When I am ashes) sing of thee!
> May thy green banks and streams (or none)
> Be both their Hill and Helicon;
> May Vocal Groves grow there, and all
> The shades in them Prophetical,   40

° **sat**: the original spelling "sate" also suggests fed.   ° **Genii**: spirits.
° **Isca**: A Latinization of Usk.

Where laid° men shall more fair truths see
Than fictions were of Thessaly;°
May thy gentle Swains (like flowers)
Sweetly spend their youthful hours,
And thy beauteous Nymphs (like Doves)
Be kind and faithful to their Loves.
Garlands and Songs and Roundelays,
Mild, dewy nights and Sunshine days,
The Turtle's° voice, joy without fear,
50   Dwell on thy bosom all the year!
May the Ewet° and the Toad
Within thy Banks have no abode,
Nor the wily, winding Snake
Her voyage through thy waters make.
In all thy Journey to the Main
No nitrous Clay nor Brimstone-vein
Mix with thy streams, but may they pass
Fresh as the air and clear as Glass,
And where the wand'ring Crystal treads,
60   Roses shall kiss and couple heads.
The factor°-wind from far shall bring
The Odours of the scattered Spring,
And laden with so rich a ware,
Spend it in spicy whispers there.
No sullen heats, nor flames that are
Offensive and Canicular,°
Shine on thy Sands, nor pry to see
Thy scaly, shading family,
But Noons as mild as Jasper's rays,°
70   Or the first blushes of fair days.
What gifts more Heav'n or Earth can add
With all those blessings be thou clad!
Honour, Beauty,
Faith and Duty,
Delight and Truth,
With Love and Youth,
Crown all about thee! And whatever Fate
Impose elsewhere, whether the graver state,
Or some toy else, may those loud, anxious Cares
80   For dead and dying things (the Common Wears
And shows of time) ne'er break thy Peace, nor make
Thy reposed Arms to a new war awake!

° **laid**: reclining.
° **Thessaly**: region of Greece and setting of many episodes in classical mythology.
° **Turtle's**: turtle-dove's.
° **Ewet**: eft, or greater water-newt. These verses echo Browne's tribute to the Tavy (itself based on Fletcher's *Faithful Shepherdess*), p. 310.
° **factor**: trader's agent.
° **Canicular**: referring to the hot days around the rising of the Dog star on 11 August.
° **Jasper's rays**: green chalcedony, believed to radiate medicinal powers.

But Freedom, Safety, Joy and Bliss,
United in one loving kiss,
Surround thee quite, and stile° thy borders,
The Land redeemed from all disorders!

⁂

° **stile**: protect.

JOHN DONNE

"The Storm" and "The Calm" (1597)

In July 1597, Donne joined an expedition to the Azores to raid Spanish treasure-ships. On the way, the fleet encountered a powerful gale, and Donne composed a verse letter to his friend Christopher Brooke, likening the traumatic ordeal to war and the apocalypse. After refitting their ships, the flotilla set out again only to find itself becalmed off the island of St George. The irony of this reversal was not lost on Donne. The second letter has been compared to a "photographic double exposure" (Carey 54) in that it superimposes images from Elizabethan London upon the Azores' seascape. Yet the confusion of nature and culture is also a compensatory fantasy that only heightens the sense of human helplessness in the grip of oceanic forces.
Source: *Poems* (1633), 57–61.

"The Storm"

Then like two mighty Kings, which dwelling far
Asunder, meet against a third to war,
The South and West winds joined, and as they blew,
Waves like a rolling trench before them threw.   30
Sooner than you read this line did the gale,
Like shot, not feared till felt, our sails assail;
And what at first was called a gust, the same
Hath now a storm's, anon a tempest's name.
Jonah,° I pity thee, and curse those men,
Who when the storm raged most did wake thee then …
But when I waked, I saw that I saw not.
I and the Sun, which should teach me, had forgot
East, West, day, night; and I could but say,
If th'world had lasted, now it had been day.   40
Thousand our noises were, yet we 'mongst all
Could none by his right name, but thunder call.
Lightning was all our light, and it rained more
Than if the Sun had drunk the sea before.
Some coffined in their cabins lie, equally
Grieved that they are not dead, and yet must die.

° **Jonah**: see Jonah 1:6.

And as sin-burdened souls from graves will creep
At the last day, some forth their cabins peep,
And trembling ask, "What news?" and do hear so,
50   Like jealous husbands, what they would not know.
Some sitting on the hatches would seem there
With hideous gazing to fear away fear.
Then note they the ship's sicknesses, the Mast
Shaked with an ague,° and the Hold and Waist°
With a salt dropsy° clogged, and all our tacklings
Snapping, like too high-stretched treble strings.
And from our tattered sails rags drop down so,
As from one hanged in chains a year ago.
Even our Ordnance placed for our defence,
60   Strive to break loose and 'scape away from thence.
Pumping hath tired our men, and what's the gain?
Seas into seas thrown, we suck in again;
Hearing hath deafed our sailors, and if they
Knew how to hear, there's none knows what to say.
Compared to these storms, death is but a qualm,°
Hell somewhat lightsome,° and the Bermudas calm.
Darkness, light's elder brother, his birthright
Claims o'er this world, and to heav'n hath chased light.
All things are one, and that one none can be,
70   Since all forms uniform deformity
Doth cover; so that we, except God say
Another Fiat,° shall have no more day.
So violent, yet long, these furies be,
That though thine absence starve me, I wish not thee.

"The Calm"

Our storm is past, and that storm's tyrannous rage,
A stupid calm, but nothing it doth 'suage.
The fable° is inverted, and far more
A block afflicts now than a stork before.
Storms chafe and soon wear out themselves or us;
In calms, heav'n laughs to see us languish thus.
As steady as I can wish my thoughts were,
Smooth as thy mistress' glass, or what shines there,
The sea is now. And, as these Isles° which we

° **ague**: fever.   ° **Waist**: mid-section of a ship's upper deck.
° **dropsy**: disease causing the body to swell with fluid.   ° **qualm**: pang of faintness or nausea.
° **lightsome**: luminous. Hell was supposedly dark.
° **Fiat**: let there be, the Latin word used for God's creation of light in Genesis.
° **fable**: Aesop's fable of the frogs that demanded a king. At first they were given a log or block.
   When they continued to complain, Jove appointed a stork to rule over them, who promptly
   devoured them.
° **Isles**: the Azores.

Seek, when we can move, our ships rooted be.   10
As water did in storms, now pitch runs out
As lead, when a fired Church becomes one spout.
And all our beauty and our trim decays,
Like courts removing, or like ended plays …
Earth's hollownesses, which the world's lungs are,
Have no more wind than th'upper vault of air.   20
We can nor left friends° nor sought foes recover,
But meteor-like, save that we move not, hover.
Only the Calenture° together draws
Dear friends, which meet dead in great fishes' jaws …
He that at sea prays for more wind, as well
Under the poles may beg cold, heat in hell.   50
What are we then? How little more, alas,
Is man now than before he was? He was
Nothing; for us, we are for nothing fit;
Chance or ourselves still disproportion it.
We have no power, no will, no sense. I lie:
I should not then thus feel this misery.

ঽ ঽ ঽ

° **friends**: the becalmed ships under the command of Ralegh had become separated from those led
by Essex.
° **Calenture**: a tropical fever that purportedly caused delirious sailors to leap overboard.

SAMUEL DANIEL

[Milford Haven] (1610)

To celebrate Henry Stuart's investiture as the Prince of Wales, the Lord Mayor
of London and several livery companies prepared a river pageant at Chelsea not
unlike the one Shakespeare describes in *Antony and Cleopatra*. Riding in a barge
festooned with streamers and accompanied by musicians, the Prince and his party were greeted by "two artificial sea-monsters, one in fashion of a whale, the
other like a dolphin, with persons richly apparelled sitting upon them, who at
the meeting and parting of the Lord Mayor and his company, with the Prince,
were to deliver certain speeches unto him" (A4ᵛ). The festivities continued in a
masque (excerpted below) entitled *Tethys' Festival*, performed before the court at
Whitehall on 5 June 1610, but with an elaborate scenic backdrop depicting the
strategic Welsh port of Milford Haven. Queen Anne assumed the role of the goddess of fresh water, Princess Elizabeth played the Thames, and countesses and
ladies in waiting performed the parts of the English rivers in their respective home
counties. Literary critics have not failed to note the blatant similarities with the
procession of the rivers at the marriage of the Thames and Medway in Spenser's
Faerie Queene, and with the wedding masque in Shakespeare's *Tempest*. Even
more so than these texts, *Tethys' Festival* foresees that the mightiness of the British
Empire will result from its status as a maritime nation, and its mastery of the sea
and its resources. The masque thus wades into the debate sparked by the Dutch
lawyer Grotius's *Mare Liberum, or Freedom of the Seas* (1609); three years after

its performance, the Scottish lawyer William Welwood would publish a heated rebuttal that the ocean is not an aquatic commons but that nations like England can assert territorial rights to the waters around their shores.
Source: *The Order and Solemnity of the Creation of the High and Mighty Prince Henry* (1610), E2ᵛ–F3ᵛ.

On the Traverse° which served as a curtain for the first Scene was figured a dark cloud, interspersed with certain sparkling stars, which, at the sound of a loud music, being instantly drawn, the Scene was discovered with these adornments. First, on either side stood a great statue of twelve foot high representing Neptune and Nereus: Neptune holding a Trident with an Anchor made to it, and this Motto, *Hic artibus*, that is, *Regendo & retinendo*,° alluding to [E3ʳ] this verse of Virgil, *Hae tibi erunt artes, etc*;° Nereus holding out a golden fish in a net, with this word *Industria* …

The Scene itself was a Port or Haven with Bulwarks at the entrance, and the figure of a Castle commanding a fortified town. Within this Port were many Ships, small and great, seeming to lie at anchor, some nearer and some farther off, according to perspective. Beyond all appeared the Horizon or termination of the Sea, which seemed to move with a gentle gale, and many Sails, lying some to come into the Port, and others passing out. From this Scene issued Zephyrus with eight Naiads, Nymphs of fountains, and two Tritons sent from Tethys to give notice of her intendment, which was the Antimasque or first show. The Duke of York presented Zephyrus, in a short robe of green satin embroidered with golden flowers [E3ᵛ] with a round wing made of lawns° on wires, and hung down in labels; behind his shoulders two silver wings; on his head a Garland of flowers consisting of all colours; and on one Arm, which was out bare, he wore a bracelet of gold set with rich stones. Eight little ladies near of his stature represented the Naiads, and were attired in light robes adorned with flowers, their hair hanging down and waving with Garlands of water ornaments on their heads.

The Tritons wore skin-coats of watchet° Taffeta (lightened with silver) to show the Muscles of their bodies. From the waist almost to the knee were fins of silver in the manner of basses; a mantle of Sea-green, laced and fringed with gold, tied with a knot upon one shoulder, and falling down in folds behind, was fastened to the contrary side; on their heads garlands of Sedge, with trumpets of writhen shells in their hand; Buskins° of Sea-green laid with silver lace. These persons thus attired, entered with this song of four parts, and a music of twelve lutes …

[E4ʳ] The song ended, Triton in the behalf of Zephyrus delivers Tethys' message with her presents (which was a trident to the king, and a rich sword and scarf to the Prince of Wales) in these words:

° **Traverse**: screen.   ° *Hic .. retinendo*: these arts, reigning and retaining.
° *Hae .. artes*: And these will be your arts, [to impose the ways of peace]. From Virgil, *Aeneid*, 6.852.
° **lawns**: fine linens.   ° **watchet**: a light blue fabric.   ° **Buskins**: knee-high boots.

From that intelligence which moves the Sphere
Of circling waves (the mighty Tethys, Queen
Of Nymphs and rivers, who will straight appear,
And in a human Character be seen)
We have in charge to say, that even as Seas
And lands are graced by men of worth and might,
So they return their favours; and in these
Exalting of the good seem to delight,
Which she, in glory lately visiting
The sweet and pleasant Shores of Cambria,° found
By an unusual and most forward Spring
Of comfort, wherewith all things did abound,
For joy of the Investiture at hand
Of their new Prince, whose Rites with acts renowned
Were here to be solemnised on this Strand;
And therefore straight resolves t'adorn the day
With her all-gracing presence, and the train
Of some choice Nymphs she pleased to call away
From several Rivers which they entertain.
And first the lovely Nymph of stately Thames,°
(The darling of the Ocean) summoned is;
Then those of Trent° and Arun's° graceful streams;
Then Derwent° next, with clear-waved worthiness;
The beauteous Nymph of crystal-streaming Lee°
Gives next attendance; then the Nymph of Aire,°
With modest motion makes her sweet repair;°
The Nymph of Severn° follows in degree,
With ample streams of grace; and next to her
The cheerful Nymph of Rother° doth appear
With comely Medway,° th'ornament of Kent;
And then four goodly Nymphs that beautify
Camber's fair shores, and all that continent:
The graces of clear Usk, Olwy, Dulesse, Wye.°
All these within the goodly spacious Bay
Of manifold inharbouring Milford meet,
The happy Port of Union, which gave way
To that great hero Henry,° and his fleet,
To make the blest conjunction that begat
A greater, and more glorious far than that.
From hence she sends her dear loved Zephyrus,
To breath out her affection and her zeal

° **Cambria**: Wales.   ° **Thames**: played by Princess Elizabeth.
° **Trent**: played by Arabella Stuart.
° **Arun**: played by Aletheia Talbot, the Countess of Arundel (see Part IV, p. 385).
° **Derwent**: played by the Countess of Derby.   ° **Lee**: played by the Countess of Essex.
° **Aire**: played by the Countess Anne Clifford, owner of Skipton Castle.
° **repair**: visit.   ° **Severn**: performed by the Countess of Montgomery, Susan Herbert.
° **Rother**: performed by Viscountess Haddington.
° **Medway**: performed by Lady Elizabeth Gray.
° **Usk ... Wye**: Four rivers in Wales, played by, respectively, Lady Windsor, Lady Katherine Peter,
Lady Elizabeth Guilford, and Lady Winter.
° **Henry**: Henry VII landed at Milford to fight Richard III and establish the Tudor dynasty.

To you, great Monarch° of Oceanus,
And to present this Trident as the seal
And ensign of her love and of your right.
And therewithal she wills him, greet the Lord
And Prince of th'Isles (the hope and the delight,
Of all the Northern Nations) with this sword,
Which she unto Astraea° sacred found,
And not to be unsheathed but on just ground.
Herewith, says she, deliver him from me
This scarf, the zone of love and Amity,
T'engird the same; wherein he may survey,
Infigured all the spacious Empery
That he is born unto another day;
Which, tell him, will be world enough to yield
All works of glory ever can be wrought.
Let him not pass the circle of that field,
But think Alcides' pillars° are the knot,
For there will be within the large extent
Of these my waves, and wat'ry Government
More treasure, and more certain riches got
Than all the Indies to Iberus° brought,
For Nereus will by industry unfold
A chemic° secret, and turn fish to gold.
This charge she gave, and looks with such a cheer
As did her comfort and delight bewray,°
Like clear Aurora when she doth appear
In brightest robes to make a glorious day.

❧ ❧ ❧

° **Monarch**: King James.
° **Astraea**: goddess of justice. The Crown Jewels included a sword of justice.
° **Alcides' pillars**: Strait of Gibraltar.
° **Iberus**: Spain. These lines urge Henry to look west to the Atlantic rather than compete with Spain
　　for control of the Mediterranean or West Indies.　　° **chemic**: alchemical.
° **bewray**: reveal.

ANONYMOUS
A Poetical Sea-Piece (1633)

The following poem illustrates Steve Mentz's sobering observation that "the Age
of Discovery was an Age of Disaster" (2015 xxvii). Its title-page makes the dubious claim that it was transcribed "out of an elderly manuscript." It also offers a
clue on how to read it: as an intervention in the *paragone* debate that attempts to
exalt poetry as the supreme art form. To settle the dispute, the author appeals to
Endymion Porter, who was a well-known art collector at the court of Charles I
and had himself narrowly survived a shipwreck off the Dorset coast in 1629. As an
example of *ekphrasis*, it can be usefully compared to a seascape such as Brueghel
the Elder's *A Sea Storm*. What features of the ocean does the poem capture that a
painting could not (and vice versa)?
Source: *A Poetical Sea-Piece* (1633).

So spake the stormy fiend, whose work it was
To vex the air and seas as smooth as glass,
To roll on heaps till they on end do stand,
Where they against the winds do breaking band,
And lift at heaven, and in their ranging race
'Twixt ridge and ridge, the deep engulfing space
Appears like jaws infernal, mouths of hell,
To swallow whole Fleets whole, none left to tell
The losses happening in those liquid graves.
Thus while the winds do tyrannize the waves,   10
Great claps of thunder break from thickened sky,
And shafts of lightning through the region fly ...
The wild seas madded thus, in their affray
Do threaten with their dash to put out day.
The rocks in sight would fain have shrunk the head,
The hidden to be seen in vain do dread.
The battered shores had almost yielded back,
The waves so little of their wills did lack;   20
And but for bounds the world's creator fixed,
All th'elements had once again been mixed ...
Like chorus between acts so came the rain,
Peal after peal, then tragic storms again ...
The ship's sides crack, the tackle tears like thread:
Some ply the pump; some cry, "We all are dead!"
Here climbs a nimble boy unto the top,
When him now halfway or not halfway up,
A gust prevents, which ducks into the deep
The shrouds° themselves, and from the ropes doth sweep
The venturous climber, darting him as far,
As globe of stone from instrument of war ...
The planks start out, the ribs in pieces crack,
No timber is so strong, but yieldeth back,
And as the waves rush in, forth shoots the ware,
Such as remained t'accompany despair.
With them the deeps are spread: here barrels float,
There packs not yet through-wet, and chests of note,   150
And men and boys ride on them while they may,
Then shriek out last farewells and fall away.
The wine with brine doth mix; and mingled so,
The curlèd foam doth no pure whiteness show,
But dipped in claret dye pretends to blush.
One swallowing surge the Merchants' hopes doth crush ...
And though the Ocean opens to the sky,
Where none alive is near to bid or buy,   160
A world of scattered goods on billows green,
As at a mart, yet they in vain are seen ...
The rav'nous fish (those wolves of Neptune's field),
A passage short to quick and dead do yield

° **shrouds**: sails.

Through greedy maws; but corpses thrown on shore
Find burial there, and people to deplore.
The coward under hatches feels the fall,
Not daring sight to use, nor speech at all,
And stops his ears just as his breath is stopped ...
[But] the valiant man against despair cries "No."
And though of all things else bereft and left,
190   Himself he leaves not. God no greater gift
Hath given unto man than such a mind,
Beneath the which are fortune, seas, and wind:
Above it nothing else but God alone,
And to him knit is always so his own.

❧ ❧ ❧

MARGARET CAVENDISH
"Similarizing the Sea to Meadows and Pastures" (1653)

The following poem is another example of the versatility of the sea as a literary
symbol. It is preceded by verses comparing its saltiness to a desert and followed
by ones likening waves to rebels. Since England was a maritime nation renowned
for its wool, its poets may have been especially drawn to the oceanic pastoral, and
Cavendish's version can proudly stand beside Ralegh's epic simile of the sea as
pasture in Spenser's *Colin Clout Comes Home Again* (237–63).
Source: *Poems and Fancies* (1653), 146–7. With emendations from 1664.

The Waves like Ridges of Ploughed land are° high,
Whereat the Ship doth stumble,° down doth lie;°
But in a Calm, level Meadows seem,°
And by° its Saltness makes it look as green.
When Ships thereon a slow, soft pace they° walk,
Then Mariners, as Shepherds, sing and talk.
Some whistle, and some on their Pipes do play,
Thus merrily° will pass their time away.
And every Mast is like a Maypole high,
10   Round which they dance, though not so merrily
As Shepherds do when they their Lasses bring,
Whereon are Garlands tied with Silken string.°
But on their Mast, instead of Garlands, hung°
Huge Sails and Ropes to tie those Garlands on.°

° **are:** 1664; lies] 1653.   ° **doth stumble:** oft stumbling] 1664.
° **lie:** a marginal note reads "Here the ship is taken for a horse."
° **level ... seem:** like Meadows seen] 1664.   ° **And by:** Level] 1664.
° **they:** do] 1664.   ° **Thus merrily:** And thus with Mirth] 1664.
° **Whereon ... string:** Garlands to Maypoles tied with a Silk-string] 1664.
° **But ... hung:** Instead of Garlands they hang on their Mast] 1664.
° **on:** fast] 1664.

Instead of Lasses they do dance with Death,
And for their Music they have Boreas'° breath;
Instead of Wine and Wassails, drink salt Tears,
And for their Meat they feed on nought but Fears.
For Flocks of Sheep, great shoals of Herrings swim,
As rav'nous Wolves the Whales° do feed on them.   20
As sportful Kids skip over Hillocks green,
So dancing Dolphins on the Waves are seen.
The Porpoise, like their watchful Dog espies,
And gives them warning when great Winds will rise.
Instead of Barking, he his Head will° show
Above the waters, where they roughly flow.°
When show'ring Rains pour° down and Winds do blow,°
Then fast Men° run for Shelter to a Tree:
So Ships at Anchor lie upon the Sea.

ﻢ ﻢ ﻢ

° **Boreas**: the north wind.   ° **As ... Whales**: The Whales as Ravenous Wolves] 1664.
° **will**: doth] 1664.
° **roughly flow**: 1664; rough do flow] 1653. An ancient meteorological belief held that leaping
   dolphins signalled an approaching storm.
° **pour**: spelled "power."
° **When ... blow**: And like as Men in time of showering Rain / And Wind do not in open Fields
   remain] 1664.
° **Then ... Men**: But quickly run] 1664.

THOMAS HEYRICK
"The Submarine Voyage" (1691)

In 1620, the Dutch engineer Cornelius Drebbel descended into the Thames in
a submersible and reportedly remained underwater for three hours. This experiment signals a growing interest not only in naval warfare but also in marine
biology. Naturalists and writers have long been fascinated by the inaccessible spectacle of the ocean floor. While Clarence's dream in *Richard III* is the best-known
example, Thomas Heyrick, the grand-nephew of the poet Robert Herrick and a
passionate angler, composed an elaborate and fanciful meditation of a dolphin's-
eye-view of the sea (cf. Prys's "The Porpoise," p. 160), toggling between a sense of
the underwater world as both profoundly inhuman and uncannily familiar. The
poem thus presents equivocal evidence for the claim that "between 1660 and 1675
the mysteries of the ocean began to fade with the progress made in England by
oceanography" (Corbin 18).
Source: *Miscellany Poems* (1691), 5–7, 14–15.

7

But who of Thee, false Element, can speak,
   Thou treach'rous Sea, that smil'st to wreck?
That dost new Faces every day put on,
   As variable as thy Guide, the Moon?
What boundless Mind can fathom Thee,

That by thy Changing shun'st Discovery?
And why, just Heav'n, dost thou long Life bestow
O'th senseless Hart and stupid Crow,
O'th' Serpent that her Skin can cast,
And th'Eagle that doth many Ages last,
To whom it nothing doth Import,
That can't to Noble Speculations rise,
Nor Nature's secrets view with sharp sagacious Eyes?
Why should swift Change snatch man's short Thread away,
That only can due Homage pay,
The great Attendant on thy Court?
And why should Art be long, and Life be short?
Why should Amphibious Creatures see
What doth to Man a Secret lie,
Into the Depth of the Abyss go down,
And in two Empires live, while Man's confined to one?

8

May some kind Genius° gratify
My daring Curiosity,
That would the Sea's surprising Bottom see,
The wonders Nature secret keeps
In her vast Storehouse of the Deeps:
The various Plants that deck the wat'ry plain,
The Trees and Shrubs that it adorn,
And precious Products that on them are born,
The massy Heaps of Pearl and Golden Ore,
The working Sea hath driven up in store,
With all the scattered Riches of the Main,
The num'rous subjects of the Realm of Waves,
The Fountains of the Deep and Subterranean Caves!

9

———————————— Scarce had I spoke,
When Neptune chanced my wish to hear,
That's often Deaf to shipwrecked Wretch's Prayer,
And liked my bold Ambition well.
A sudden Numbness all my Members stroke;°
The cheerful Light that welcome Comfort gives
And th'wearied Mind with Joy relieves,
With an unpleasing force my Eyes did strike,
And the Sun's heat I did dislike.
Weary o'th' too-thin piercing Air,
Another Element my thoughts employs.
The wat'ry Plains I view with pleasèd Eyes.
Fearless the noise of Storms I hear,
The foaming Surges bring no cause of fear,
And Hurricanes become familiar.

° **Genius**: spirit.   ° **stroke**: struck.

I longed to visit Neptune's court,
And see the Tritons' and the Sea-Nymphs' sport.
Meanwhile within a Change I found,
Nature was working some new feat,
And summoned all her Powers to meet:
Armour of scales enclosed me round;
My Hands and Legs did nimble Fins display,
That could through yielding Water cut their way.
And from the Cliff, whose Downfall stemmed the Eye,
And made e'en starting Nature fly,
Fearless I cast myself into the Sea.
A Dolphin now I sport and play i'th' Main;
Do unto Man my Ancient Love retain,
And Reason still and Curiosity remain.

10

But oh, what Language doth suffice to tell
The Rapine and Oppression,
The armèd Force and Violence,
That in those liquid Regions dwell?
Justice and Equity were flown,
And Right and Property not known.
No Laws to be the Poor's defence,
No Tenderness to Innocence.
The Less became the Greater's Prey,
Only because they could not fight;
And while these others swallow, They,
And what they had devoured, became another's Right.
No one by Might or Subtlety's secured;
The Greater still commands the Lesser's fate.
Now this devours, and now he is devoured;
All on unruly Appetite doth wait:
So cursèd is an Anarchy,
So insupportable Democracy.
Insatiate Element! How well with Thee
Do thy Inhabitants agree!
Pity from both of you is banishèd,
Justice from both of you is fled;
And when you do devour,
You both are hungry still and gape for more …

23

There One, new-dead, becomes the Fish's prey,
And jostling Crowds his Members gnaw;
His mangled Limbs around do draw.
Haddocks and Cods make him their meat;
Lobsters and Crabs his Entrails eat,
And in his hollow Trunk their Eggs do lay;
And these by the next Fisher took,

By pleasing Bait and deadly Hook,
Become to Men luxurious food.
Men do Mankind in Fishes eat, and they
On Men revenge their near Relations' blood.
A Mixture in our Nature is,
And the next step's a Metempsychosis.°

° **Metempsychosis**: the transmigration of the soul between different species, as proposed by the Greek philosopher Pythagoras.

PART IV

Interactions

Animal-Baiting

ROBERT LANEHAM |

[Bear-Baiting at Kenilworth°] (1575)

When Queen Elizabeth visited Kenilworth Castle in 1575, her host, Robert Dudley, the Earl of Leicester, arranged a hunt and a bear-baiting as part of the entertainments. Laneham's jocular letter describing the festivities conveys the untroubled delight some early moderns took in blood sport. However, the allegorical portrayal of the baiting as a litigious trial reflects a tendency to impose human meanings on non-humans (and vice versa), blurring the species divide on which the cruelty is predicated.

Source: *A Letter Wherein Part of the Entertainment unto the Queen's Majesty at Kenilworth Castle in Warwickshire in this Summer's Progress, is Signified* (1575), 21–4.

Wednesday, her Majesty rode into the Chase,° a-hunting again of the hart of force.° The Deer, after his property, for refuge took the soil, but so mastered by hot pursuit on all parts that he was taken quick° in the pool. The watermen held him up hard by the head while, at her Highness's commandment, he lost his ears° for a ransom, and so had pardon of his life.

Thursday, the fourteenth of this July and the sixth day of her Majesty's coming, a great sort of ban-dogs° were there tied in the outer Court and thirteen bears in the inner. Whosoever made the panel, there were enough for a Quest° and [22] one for a challenge,° and need were. A wight° of great wisdom and gravity seemed their foreman to be, had it come to a Jury. But it fell out that they were caused to appear there upon no such matter, but only to answer to an ancient quarrel between them and the ban-dogs in a cause of controversy that hath long depended,° been obstinately full often debated with sharp and biting arguments on both sides, and could never be decided, grown now to so marvellous a malice that with spiteful upbraids and uncharitable chafings always they fret, as far as anywhere the one can hear, see, smell the other, and indeed at utter deadly foehood. Many a maimed member (God wot), bloody face, and a torn coat hath the quarrel cost between them, so far likely the less yet now to be appeased as there wants not partakers to back them on both sides.

Well, sir, the Bears were brought forth into the Court, the Dogs set to them to argue the points even face to face. They had learned counsel also

---

° **Kenilworth**: Laneham's use of the variant spelling "Killingworth" seems apposite given the frequent descriptions of blood sport. ° **Chase**: unenclosed park.
° **of force**: the aristocratic form of hunting, in which the deer is chased with hounds until too exhausted to flee further. ° **quick**: alive.
° **ears**: a punishment, known as cropping, meted out in Tudor England to vagrants and dissidents.
° **ban-dogs**: mastiffs. ° **Quest**: inquest.
° **challenge**: additional juror in case one was deemed objectionable. ° **wight**: person.
° **depended**: awaited settlement.

on both parts. What? May they be counted partial that are retained but on the one side? I ween° no. Very fierce both the one and the other eager [23] in argument: if the dog in pleading would pluck the bear by the throat, the bear with traverse° would claw him again by the scalp; confess [if he] list, but avoid he could not that was bound to the bar;° and his counsel told him that it could be to him no policy in pleading.

Therefore, thus with fending and proving,° with plucking and tugging, scratching and biting, by plain tooth and nail on the one side and the other, such expense of blood and leather was there between them as a month's licking, I ween, will not recover: and yet [they]remain as far out as ever they were.

It was a sport very pleasant of these beasts to see the bear with his pink eyes leering after his enemy's approach, the nimbleness and wait° of the dog to take his advantage, and the force and experience of the bear again to avoid the assaults. If he were bitten in one place, how he would pinch in another to get free: that if he were taken once, then what shift (with biting, with clawing, with roaring, tossing, and tumbling) he would work to wind himself from them; and when he was loose, to shake his ears twice or thrice with the blood and the slaver about his physiognomy, was [24] a matter of a goodly relief.

ᘍ ᘍ ᘍ

° **ween**: think.   ° **traverse**: legal term for denial of plea.   ° **bar**: where criminals stand during their trial (i.e. tied to the stake).
° **fending … proving**: wrangling.   ° **wait**: patience.

PHILIP STUBBES

"Bear-baiting and other Exercises Used Unlawfully in Ailgna" (1583)

Theatre historians have long painted Philip Stubbes in the sombre colours of a Puritan killjoy. His *Anatomy of Abuses* ranks among the most infamous anti-theatrical screeds of the Elizabethan era. From an ecocritical perspective, however, Stubbes had some valid objections to the entertainment industry of his day. While he does voice compassion for animal suffering, Stubbes is motivated more by disgust with baiting's aggravation of human animality, since "to watch a baiting, to enact anthropocentrism, is to reveal not the stability of species status, but the animal that lurks within" (Fudge 2002, 15). His jeremiad points to a disconcerting affinity between animal torture and theatre in early modern England (Höfele). Source: *The Anatomy of Abuses* (1583), P1ᵛ–P5ʳ.

These Heathenical exercises upon the Sabbath day,° which the Lord hath
consecrate to holy uses for the glory of his Name and our spiritual comfort,
are not in any respect tolerable or to be suffered. For is not the baiting of
a Bear (besides that it is a filthy, stinking, [P2ʳ] and loathsome game) a
dangerous and perilous exercise, wherein a man is in danger of his life every
minute of an hour? Which thing, though it were not so, yet what exercise
is this meet° for any Christian? What Christian heart can take pleasure to
see one poor beast to rend, tear, and kill another, and all for his foolish
pleasure? And although they be bloody beasts to mankind and seek his
destruction, yet we are not to abuse them, for his sake who made them and
whose creatures they are. For notwithstanding that they be evil to us and
thirst after our blood, yet are they good creatures in their own nature and
kind, and made to set forth the glory and magnificence of the great God,
and for our use: and therefore for his sake not to be abused. It is a common
saying amongst all men, borrowed from the French: *Qui aime Jean, aime
son chien* (love me, love my dog); so love God, love his creatures.

If any should abuse but the dog of another man, would not he who
owneth the dog think that the abuse thereof resulteth to himself? And shall
we abuse the creatures of God—yea, take pleasure in abusing them—and
yet think that the contumely done to them redoundeth not to him who
made them? But admit it were granted that it were lawful to abuse the
good Creatures of God, yet is it not lawful for us to spend our golden years
in such idle and vain exercises, daily and hourly, as we do.

[P2ᵛ] And some who take themselves for no small fools are so far assot-
ted° that they will not stick to keep a dozen or a score of great mastiffs and
ban-dogs, to their no small charges, for the maintenance of this goodly
game (forsooth), and will not make any bones° of 20, 30, 40, 100 pounds
at once to hazard at a bait with "Fight dog, fight bear," say they, "the devil
part all." And to be plain, I think the Devil is the Master of the Game,°
bearward, and all. A goodly pastime, forsooth, worthy of commendation,
and well-fitting these Gentlemen of such reputation. But how much the
Lord is offended for the profanation of his Sabbath by such unsavoury exercises, his Heavenly Majesty of late hath revealed, pouring forth his heavy
wrath, his fearful judgements, and dreadful vengeance upon the Beholders
of these vanities …°

[P3ᵛ] Besides these exercises, they flock thick and threefold to the cockfights, an exercise nothing inferior to the rest … [P4ʳ] They have houses
erected to the purpose, flags, and ensigns hanged out to give notice of it to
others, and proclamation goes out to proclaim the same, to the end that
many may come to the dedication of this solemn feast of mischief. The

---

° **Sabbath**: King James' 1617 "Declaration of Sport" would ban baiting on Sundays.   ° **meet**: fit.
° **assotted**: infatuated.   ° **not … bones**: raise no objections.
° **Master of the Game**: appointed keeper of the monarch's bears, bulls, and dogs.
° **But … vanities**: the omitted section describes how an earthquake (probably the 1580 Dover Straits
quake) killed seven spectators at a baiting.

Lord supplant them. And as for hawking and hunting upon the Sabbath day,° it is an exercise upon that day no less unlawful than the other. For no man ought to spend any day of his life, much less every day in his life, as many do, in such vain and idle pastimes. Wherefore let gentlemen take heed; for be sure accounts must be given at the Day of Judgement for every minute of time, both how they have spent it and in what exercises …

I never read of any in the volume of the sacred scripture that was a good man and a hunter: Esau was a great hunter but a reprobate; Ishmael [P4ᵛ] a great hunter but a miscreant; Nimrod° a great hunter but yet a reprobate and a vessel of wrath. Thus I speak not to condemn hawking and hunting altogether, being used for recreation now and then, but against the continual use thereof daily, hourly, weekly, yearly—yea, all the time of their life, without intermission. And such a felicity have some in it, as they make it all their joy, bestowing more upon hawks and hounds, and a sort of idle lubbers to follow them, in one year than they will impart to the poor members of Christ Jesus in seven years, peradventure in all the days of their life.

So long as man in Paradise persisted in innocence, all beasts whatsoever were obedient to him, and came and prostrated themselves before him. But ever since his fall, they have fled from him and disobeyed him because of his sin: that seeing he disobeyed the Lord, they again disobeyed him. For so long as man obeyed God, so long they obeyed him. But so soon as man disobeyed God, they disobeyed him, and became enemies to him,° as it were, seeking to revenge the injury which man had done unto God in disobeying his laws. Wherefore, the cause why all beasts do fly from us and are become Enemies to us is our disobedience to the Lord, which we are rather to sorrow for than to hunt after their deaths by the shedding of their blood.

[P5ʳ] If necessity or want of other meats enforceth us to seek after their lives, it is lawful to use them in the fear of God, with thanks to his name. But for our pastimes and vain pleasure's sake, we are not in any wise° to spoil or hurt them. Is he a Christian man, or rather a pseudo-Christian, that delighteth in blood? Is he a Christian that spendeth all his life in wanton pleasures and pleasant delights? Is he a Christian that buyeth up the corn of the poor, turning it into bread (as many do) to feed dogs for his pleasure? Is he a Christian that liveth to the hurt of his Neighbour in treading and breaking down his hedges, in casting open his gates, in trampling of his corn, and otherwise in prejudicing him as hunters do? Wherefore God give them grace to see to it and to mend it betimes ere it be too late … Let us not defer to leave the evil and to do good, lest the wrath of the Lord be kindled against us, and consume us from off the upper face of the earth.

❧ ❧ ❧

° **Sabbath day**: James's 1617 "Declaration" did not prohibit hunting and hawking on Sundays, infuriating the Puritans.   ° **Esau … Ishmael … Nimrod**: See Genesis 25:27, 21:20, 10:8–9.
° **enemies to him**: a common interpretation of the scriptures, although Genesis 3:15 only speaks of enmity between serpents and humans.
° **wise**: way.

ROBERT WILD
"The Combat of the Cocks" (1637)

Cockfights were popular sporting events in early modern England prior to the passage of the 1835 Cruelty to Animals Act. In addition to the lives of the creatures, at stake was money and (as in football derbies today) bragging rights between neighbouring towns. As the anthropologist Clifford Geertz demonstrated in his piercing study of Balinese cockfights, however, these brutal spectacles could also reflect or excite political conflicts, and the Puritans suppressed them in 1654 as disturbances of the peace. This poem was apparently based on true events, as several manuscript witnesses give its title as "A terrible true troublesome tragical relation of a duel fought at Wisbech June 17 1637." The poem has been misattributed to Thomas Randolph, who died in 1635, but some manuscripts (Folger MS V.a. 148, Rosenbach MS 239/18) credit it more plausibly to Robert Wild, a student at nearby Cambridge, later ordained a deacon at Peterborough. Mingling droll wit with pathos, the poem both endorses and mocks the presumption that such violence bestows a vicarious masculinity on the male spectators.
Source: *The High and Mighty Commendation of a Pot of Good Ale* (1642), A3ᵛ–A4ᵛ, with emendations from Sloane MS 1925, 24ᵛ–7ᵛ, and Cambridge MS 79, 2ʳ–8ʳ.

> Go you tame Gallants, you that have the name,
> And would accounted be Cocks of the Game;
> That have brave spurs° to show for't and can crow,
> And count all dunghill breed that cannot show
> Such painted plumes as yours; that think't no vice,
> With Cock-like lust to tread your Cockatrice;°
> Though Peacocks, Woodcocks,° Weathercocks you be,
> If you're no fighting Cocks, you're not for me.
> I of two feathered Combatants will write;   10
> He that to th'life means to express the fight
> Must make his ink o'th' blood which they did spill,
> And from their dying wings borrow his quill.
>   No sooner were the doubtful people set,
> The matches made, and all that would had bet,
> But straight the skilful Judges of the play,
> Bring forth their sharp-heeled Warriors, and they
> Were both in linen bags, as if 'twere meet
> Before they died to have their winding-sheet.
> With that in th'pit they are put, and when they were
> Both on their feet, the Norfolk Chanticleer   20
> Looks stoutly at his ne'er before seen foe,
> And like a Challenger begins to crow,
> And shakes his wings, as if he would display
> His warlike colours, which were black and grey.
> Meantime the wary Wisbech° walks and breathes

° **brave spurs**: the horseman's ornate spiked heel and the rooster's back-claw.
° **Cockatrice**: slang for whore; in Renaissance zoology more often applied to the mythical basilisk rather than the hen.   ° **Woodcocks**: snipe-like bird, a byword for stupidity.
° **Wisbech**: town on the northeastern border of Cambridgeshire and Norfolk.

His active body, and in fury wreathes
His comely crest, and often looking down,
He whets his angry beak upon the ground.
With that they meet, not like that Coward breed
30   Of Aesop:° these can better fight than feed;
They scorn the dunghill, 'tis their only prize
To dig for pearl within each other's eyes.
They fought° so long that it was hard to know
To the skilful whether they did fight or no,
Had not the blood which dyed the fatal floor
Borne witness of it; yet they fight the more,
As if each wound were but a spur to prick
Their fury forward: lightning's not more quick
Nor red than were their eyes; 'twas hard to know
40   Whether 'twas blood or anger made them so.
And sure they had been out had they not stood
More safe by being fencèd in with° blood.
Yet still they fight; but now, alas, at length,
Although their courage be full tried, their strength
And blood began to ebb. You that have seen
A water-combat on the Sea between
Two roaring, angry, boiling billows, how
They march and meet and dash their curlèd brows,
Swelling like graves, as if they did intend
50   T'entomb each other ere the quarrel end;
But when the wind is down, and blust'ring weather,
They are made friends and sweetly run together,
May think these Champions such. Their combs grow low,
And they that leapt even now, now scarce can go.
Their wings, which lately at each blow they clapped
(As if they did applaud themselves), they flapped.°
And having lost the advantage of the heel,
Drunk with each other's blood, they only reel.
From both their° eyes such drops of blood did fall,
60   As if they wept them for their funeral.
And yet they would fain fight; they come so near,
As if they meant into each other's ear
To whisper death; and when they cannot rise,
They lie and look blows in each other's eyes.
        But now the Tragic part after the fight,
When Norfolk Cock had got the best of it,
And Wisbech lay a-dying, so that none,
Though sober, but might venture seven-to-one;
Contracting (like a dying Taper) all
70   His force, as meaning with that blow to fall,
He struggles up, and having taken wind,

° **Aesop**: presumably an allusion to the hungry roosters in "The Cock and the Jewel" rather than
   "The Fighting Cocks and the Eagle."
° **fought**: Sloane; fight] HMC.   ° **with**: Sloane; by] HMC.
° **they flapped**: Sloane; how slapped] HMC.   ° **both their**: Sloane; either] HMC.

Ventures a blow, and strikes the other blind.
And now poor Norfolk having lost his eyes,
Fights only guided by the Antipathies.°
With him, alas, the Proverb holds too° true:
The blows his eyes ne'er saw his heart must° rue.
At length by chance he stumbling on his foe,
Not having any strength to deal° a blow,
He falls upon him with a wounded head,
And made the conqueror's° wings his feather-bed;   80
Where lying sick, his friends were very chary
Of him, and fetched in haste an Apothecary.
But all in vain, his body did so blister,
That it was incapable of any clyster;°
Wherefore at length op'ning his fainting bill,
He called a Scrivener, and thus made his will.
   "*In primis*: Let it never be forgot,
My body freely I bequeath to th'pot,
Decently to be boiled; and for its tomb,
Let it be buried in some hungry womb.   90
Item: Executors I will have none,
But he that on my side laid seven-to-one;
And like a Gentleman that he may live,
To him and to his heirs my comb I give,
Together with my brains, that all may know,
That often times his brains did use to crow.
Item: It is my will, to th'weaker ones,
Whose wives complain of them, I give my stones.°
To him that's dull I do my spurs impart;
And to the Coward I bequeath my heart.   100
To Ladies that are light,° it is my will
My feathers should be giv'n; and for my bill,
I'd give't a Tailor, but it is so short
That I'm afraid he'll rather curse me for't.
And for the Apothecary's fee, who meant
To give me a clyster, let my rump be sent.
Lastly, because I feel my life decay,
I yield, and give to Wisbech Cock the day."

            ❧ ❧ ❧

° **Antipathies**: instinctive hostility. In his 1630 meditation "Upon the Sight of a Cockfight," Joseph
   Hall, the Bishop of Exeter, concludes, "Since Man's sin brought Debate into the World, Nature is
   become a great quarreller" (61).   ° **too**: Sloane; not] HMC.
° **saw ... must**: Sloane; see ... most] HMC.
° **strength ... deal**: Sloane; power ... strike] HMC.
° **made the conqueror's**: Sloane; makes his conquered] HMC.   ° **clyster**: enema.
° **stones**: testicles.   ° **light**: promiscuous.

Hunting, Hawking

JOHN CAIUS
"Why there are no wolves in England" (1570)

The wolf was once common throughout Anglo-Saxon England, as the name of the first warrior-hero in English literature (Beowulf) hints. As the medieval economy came increasingly to depend on the wool trade, however, the wolf posed an obvious financial liability. Despite Caius's claim here, evidence indicates that small populations may have survived in northern England and Wales up until the late fifteenth century. Edward I (r. 1272–1307) commissioned a professional wolf-trapper to exterminate them, and a wolf-hunter was employed in Sherwood Forest as late as 1432. While these campaigns took a toll, no doubt it was the steady diminishing of its woodland habitat that brought about the wolf's demise. The wolf proved harder to eradicate in Scotland, where King James VI ordered wolf-hunts three times per year and placed a bounty on them of six shillings per head. Legend has it that Sir Ewen Cameron slew the last wolf in 1680 in the Scottish Highlands, where proposals now are being considered to reintroduce the species to help keep the deer population under control.
Source: *Of English Dogs,* trans. Abraham Fleming (1576), 23–4.

Our shepherd's dog is not huge, vast, and big, but of an indifferent stature and growth, because it hath not to deal with the bloodthirsty wolf, since there be none in England, which happy and fortunate benefit is to be ascribed to the puissant Prince Edgar,° who, to the intent that the whole country might be evacuated and quite cleared from wolves, charged and commanded the Welshmen (who were pestered with these butcherly beasts above measure) to pay him yearly tribute: which was … 300 Wolves. Some there be which write that Ludwall, Prince of Wales, paid yearly to King Edgar 300 wolves in the name of an exaction (as we have said before). And that by the means hereof within the compass and term of [24] four years, none of those noisome and pestilent Beasts were left in the coasts of England and Wales. This Edgar wore the Crown royal and bore the Sceptre imperial of this kingdom about the year of our Lord 959, since which time we read that no Wolf hath been seen in England, bred within the bounds and borders of this country. Marry,° there have been diverse brought over from beyond the seas for greediness of gain and to make money, for gazing and gaping, staring and standing to see them, being a strange beast, rare, and seldom seen in England.

⚹ ⚹ ⚹

° **Prince Edgar**: ironically, known as Edgar the Peaceful (r. 959–75). This story derives from William of Malmesbury's *Chronicle* (1125).   ° **Marry:** indeed.

GEORGE GASCOIGNE
"The Woeful Words of the Hart to the Hunter" and
"The Otter's Oration" (1575)

Modern readers might find it odd that the author of a French hunting manual, Jacques du Fouilloux, would include several verses from the perspective of bayed animals. However, many early conservationists up to the time of Theodore Roosevelt and Aldo Leopold were originally hunters, and some of the most meticulous observations about beasts in the Renaissance were written by people who also enjoyed killing them (see Fouilloux's entry on the badger in Part II, p. 130). Gascoigne, who two years previously had sketched a self-deprecating portrait of himself as an inept hunter, not only translated all of Fouilloux's poems, including the "Complaint du Cerf" (excerpted here below), but also added three more of his own devising, one of which is "The Otter's Oration." The otter was particularly loathed by fishermen, as attested by Walton's *Compleat Angler*, in which Piscator wishes to "destroy the very breed of them" (4), and the slaughter of a mother and her pups prompts this cheery quip: "God keep you all, gentlemen, and send you meet this day with another bitch-otter, and kill her merrily, and all her young ones" (45). Walton's wish almost came true in the twentieth century, when the combination of hunting and pesticides pushed the otter to the brink of extinction in England (from which it has since bounced back after it was protected in 1977). In *The Noble Art of Venery*, the "ironic juxtaposition" (Bates 142) of the hunter's prose and quarry's verse creates some disturbing tensions. Are the poems cynical advertisements of the efficacy of the manual's advice? Reminders that the hunt should be conducted with a humane or ethical respect for its victims? Or a kind of editorial sabotage, exposing the hypocrisy and savagery of humans? Arguably, Gascoigne's talking animals elicit such pity as to undercut the supposed nobility of the sport.

Source: *The Noble Art of Venery* (1575), 136–40, 359, 358, 363 (The "Otter" is mispaginated, presumably because it was a late addition).

"The Woeful Words of the Hart to the Hunter"

Methinks I hear the Horn, which rends the restless air,
With shrillest sound of bloody blast and makes me to despair.
Methinks I see the Toil,° the tanglings and the stall,°
Which are prepared and set full sure to compass me withal.
Methinks the For'ster stands full close in bush or Tree,
And takes his level° straight and true; methinks he shoots at me: 70
And hits the harmless Heart° of me unhappy Hart,
Which must needs please him by my death, I may it not astart° ...
Perchance with sickness he hath troubled been of late,
And with my marrow thinketh to restore his former state.

° **Toil**: net.   ° **stall**: decoy.   ° **level**: aim.
° **Heart**: spelled "Harte." The hart was becoming scarce in Elizabethan England, and by the nineteenth century survived only in the Scottish Highlands.   ° **astart**: escape.

Maybe his heart° doth quake, and therefore seeks the bone,°
Which Huntsmen find within my heart when I, poor Hart, am gone …
Yea, more than this, maybe he thinks such nouriture°
Will still prolong men's days on earth since mine so long endure.°
But O, mischievous man, although I thee outlive,
By due degrees of age unseen, which Nature doth me give,
Must thou therefore procure my death for to prolong
Thy ling'ring life in lusty wise?° Alas, thou dost me wrong.
Must I with mine own flesh, his hateful flesh so feed,
Which me disdains one bite of grass or corn in time of need?
Alas, Man, do not so; some other beasts go kill,
Which work thy harm by sundry means (and so content thy will),
110　Which yield thee no such gains in life as I renew,
When from my head my stately horns (to thy behoof) I mew.°
But since thou art unkind, ungracious, and unjust,
Lo, here I crave of mighty Gods, which are both good and just,
That Mars may reign with Man; that strife and cruël war
May set man's murd'ring mind on work, with many a bloody jar;°
That drums with deadly dub may countervail the blast,
Which they with horns have blown full loud, to make my mind aghast;
That shot as thick as hail may stand for Crossbow shoots;
120　That Cuisses,° Greves,° and such may serve instead of Hunter's boots;
That girt with siege full sure, they may their toils repent;
That Ambuscados stand for nets, which they against me bent;
That when they see a spy, which watcheth them to trap,
They may remember ring-walks° made in arbour me to hap;°
That when their busy brains are exercisèd so,
Harts may lie safe within their lair and never fear their foe.
But if so chance there be some dastard dreadful mome,°
Whom Trumpets cannot well entice, nor call him once from home,
And yet will play the man in killing harmless Deer,
130　I crave of God that such a ghost° and such a fearful phere°
May see Diana naked;° and she (to venge her scorns)
May soon transform his harmful head into my harmless horns,
Until his hounds may tear that heart of his in twain,
Which thus torments us harmless Harts, and puts our hearts to pain.

° **heart**: spelled "Hart."
° **bone**: the *os cordis*, actually mineralized tissue, was thought to cure heart ailments.
° **nouriture**: food (i.e. venison).
° **endure**: reports by Greek and Roman naturalists that stags could live thirty times longer than
　humans encouraged consumption of their body parts (like rhino horn today) for their supposed
　rejuvenating powers; their actual life span is closer to 15–18 years.
° **wise**: style.
° **mew**: shed. Ground antler was believed to confer numerous health benefits, and is still prescribed
　today in traditional Chinese medicine.
° **jar**: discord.
° **Cuisses**: thigh armour. The stag's curse both affirms and undercuts Gascoigne's claims that
　hunting is an ideal pastime for soldiers.
° **Greves**: shin armour.
° **ring-walks**: scouting the perimeter of hunting grounds for quarry.　° **hap**: capture.
° **mome**: fool.　° **ghost**: soul.　° **phere**: fellow.
° **Diana naked**: an allusion to the Actaeon myth (see Ovid, *Metamorphoses*, 3.160–304).

"The Otter's Oration"

Why stand we beasts abashed or spare to speak?
Why make we not a virtue of our need?
We know by proof in wit we are too weak,
And weaker much because all Adam's seed°
(Which bear away the weight of wit indeed)
Do daily seek our names for to disdain
With slanderous blot, for which we Beasts be slain.

First, of myself before the rest to treat,
Most men cry out that fish I do devour;°
Yea, some will say that Lambs with me be meat:°   10
I grant to both; and he that hath the power
To feed on fish that sweeter were than sour,
And had young flesh to banquet at his fill,
Were fond to franch° on garbage, grains, or swill.

But master Man, which findeth all this fault,
And strains device° for many a dainty dish,
Which suff'reth not that hunger him assault,
But feeds his fill on every flesh and fish,
Which must have all, as much as wit can wish,
Us silly° Beasts, devouring Beasts do call;   20
And he himself, most bloody beast of all.

Well yet methinks I hear him preach this Text:
"How all that is, was made for use of man."°
So was it sure, but therewith follows next
This heavy place, expound it who so can:
"The very Scourge and Plague of God his ban,°
Will light on such as quaintly can devise
To eat more meat than may their mouths suffice."°

Now master Man, stand forth and here declare,
Who ever yet could see an Otter eat   30
More meat at once than servèd for his share?
Who sees us beasts sit bibbing° in our seat,
With sundry wines and sundry kinds of meat,

° **seed**: progeny.
° **fish ... devour**: the description of the otter preceding the poem notes, "even as a fox, polecat, wildcat, or badger will destroy a warren, so will the otter destroy all the fish in your ponds, if she once have found the way to them" (200).
° **Lambs ... meat**: for an otter to kill a lamb is extremely rare, and only happens when the otter's regular food supply fails.
° **fond to franch**: foolish to feast.   ° **device**: ingenuity.   ° **silly**: harmless, innocent.
° **How all ... man**: a paraphrase of Genesis 1:26, the dominion mandate.   ° **ban**: curse.
° **The very scourge ... suffice**: Probably an allusion to Numbers 11:13–20, where the Israelites complain of eating manna and demand meat, and God makes them eat quail for a month "until it comes out at [their] nostrils," and then slays them with a plague.
° **bibbing**: binge-drinking.

Which breed disease, yfostered in such feasts?
If men do so, be they not worse than beasts?

The beastly man must sit all day and quaff;
The Beast indeed doth drink but twice a day.
The beastly man must stuff his monstrous maw
With secret cause of surfeiting always,
40   Where beasts be glad to feed when they get prey,
And never eat more than may do them good,
Where men be sick and surfeit thorough° food.

Who sees a Beast for savoury sauces long?
Who sees a Beast or° Chick or Capon cram?°
Who sees a Beast once lulled on sleep with song?
Who sees a Beast make ven'son of a Ram?°
Who sees a Beast destroy both whelp and dam?
Who sees a Beast use beastly Gluttony?
Which man doth use for great Civility.

50   I know not, I, if diving be my fault;
Methinks most men can dive as well as I.
Some men can dive in Cellar and in Vault,
In Parlour, Hall, Kitchen, and Buttery,°
To smell the roast, whereof the fume doth flee.
And as for gains, men dive in every stream;
All frauds be fish,° their stomachs never squeam.°

So to conclude, when men their faults can mend,
And shun the shame wherewith they beasts do blot;
When men their time and treasure not mispend,
60   But follow grace, which is with pains ygot;
When men can vice rebuke and use it not;
Then shall they shine like men of worthy fame:
And else they be but Beasts well worthy blame.

૨૬ ૨૬ ૨૬

° **thorough**: by means of.   ° **or**: either.
° **cram**: force-feed. Capons are castrated roosters, and were often fattened so (see the excerpt from
   Moffett, p. 377).   ° **Ram**: meat from an adult male sheep is tough and gamey compared to lamb.
° **Buttery**: cellar or pantry for alcohol.   ° **fish**: easy victims (of fraud).
° **squeam**: squeamish.

HENRY PORTER
[Lady Smith's Denunciation of the Hunt] (1597)

Porter's play is undoubtedly written in cross-repertorial dialogue with Shakespeare's *Merry Wives of Windsor*, in which Falstaff, who had earlier poached a deer, receives his come-uppance while in the cuckold-like guise of the antlered forest spir- it "Herne the Hunter." While the eponymous women in Porter's comedy are primarily angry with each other, in this scene Lady Smith's temper is enflamed against her hunter husband. Some Renaissance women, most notably Queen Elizabeth, did joyfully participate in blood sport, while others began to question the masculine ethos of the hunt. In branding the would-be deer-slayer a tyrant, her speech anticipates Jaques's rant in *As You Like It* and Margaret Cavendish's anti-hunting poetry.
Source: *Two Angry Women of Abingdon* (1599), E4^{r-v}.

> SIR RALPH Come on my hearts.° I'faith, it is ill luck,
> To hunt all day and not kill anything.
> What sayest thou Lady? Art thou weary yet?
> LADY I must not say so sir.
> RALPH   Although thou art.
> WILL And can you blame her to be forth so long,
> And see no better sport?
> RALPH Good faith, 'twas very hard.
> LADY   No, 'twas not ill.
> Because you know it is not good to kill.
> RALPH Yes, venison, Lady.
> LADY   No, indeed, nor them;
> Life is as dear in Deer° as 'tis in men.   10
> RALPH But they are killed for sport.
> LADY   But that's bad play,
> When they are made to sport their lives away.
> RALPH 'Tis fine to see them run.
> LADY   What out of breath?
> They run but ill that run themselves to death.
> RALPH They might make then less haste and keep their wind.
> LADY Why then they see the hounds bring death behind.
> RALPH Then 'twere as good for them at first to stay,
> As to run long and run their lives away.
> LADY Ay, but the stoutest of you all that's here
> Would run from death, and nimbly scud° for fear.   20
> Now, by my troth, I pity those poor elves.°
> RALPH Well, they have made us but bad sport today.
> LADY Yes, 'twas my sport to see them 'scape away.
> WILL I wish that I had been at one Buck's fall.
> LADY Out thou wood-tyrant! Thou art worst of all.

° **hearts**: the original spelling "harts" plays on another name for mature male deer.
° **dear in Deer**: spelled "deere in Deare."   ° **scud**: scurry.   ° **elves**: creatures.

WILL A woodman,° Lady, but no tyrant I.
LADY Yes, tyrant-like thou lov'st to see lives die.
RALPH Lady, no more. I do not like this luck,
To hunt all day and yet not kill a Buck.
30   Well, it is late, but yet I swear I will
Stay here all night, but I a Buck will kill.
LADY All night? Nay, good Sir Ralph Smith, do not so.
RALPH Content ye, Lady. Will, go fetch my bow.
A bevy of fair Roes° I saw today
Down by the groves, and there I'll take my stand
And shoot at one: God send a lucky hand.
LADY Will ye not then, Sir Ralph, go home with me?
RALPH No, but my men shall bear thee company.
Sirs, man her home. Will, bid the Huntsmen couple,°
40   And bid them well reward their hounds tonight.
Lady, farewell. Will, haste ye with the Bow;
I'll stay for thee here by the grove below.
WILL I will, but 'twill be dark, I shall not see.
How shall I see ye then?
RALPH Why hollo to me, and I will answer thee.
WILL Enough, I will.
RALPH   Farewell.   *Exit.*
LADY How willingly dost thou consent to go,
To fetch thy master that same killing bow.
WILL Guilty of death I willing am in this,
50   Because 'twas our ill haps today to miss:
To hunt and not to kill is hunter's sorrow.
Come Lady, we'll have ven'son ere tomorrow.

ᘒᘒ ᘒᘒ ᘒᘒ

° **woodman**: hunter.
° **Roes**: one of two deer species native to Britain. They were already scarce in Tudor times, and
   extirpated from England around the early nineteenth century, until they were reintroduced.
° **couple**: fasten the hounds together in pairs.

JONAS POOLE

[*Killing Polar Bears and Walrus in the Arctic*] (1606, 1609)

In the early seventeenth century, the Muscovy Company sponsored numerous expeditions to the Arctic to hunt walruses and whales (for ivory and oil), and to trade with Russian merchants for timber, fish, and fur. A favourite destination was the aptly named Bear Island in the Barents Sea, where English sailors massacred a variety of wildlife, including polar bears, seals, seabirds, and Arctic foxes. These excerpts from the fifth and seventh voyages provide eye-witness testimony not only of pre-industrial sea-ice levels but also of thriving ecosystems, brutally pillaged by the incursions of global capitalism. Incidentally, the two bear cubs they orphaned and brought back to London as exotic curiosities may have been marshalled onto the Jacobean stage in Jonson's *Oberon* and Shakespeare's *Winter's Tale* (Duckert 2013). Although early modern romances depict human terror of man-eating bears, Poole's account makes it clear that bears had as much to fear from bear-eating men.

Source: *Purchas His Pilgrims* (1625), 3:559–64, 66.

[Fifth Voyage, 1606]

The four and twentieth [of June] we put off again, and being five and forty leagues from the Cape° we met with Ice; and upon a piece of Ice we saw a Bear. The Ship being on ahead of us bore close to the Ice, and Master [Thomas] Weldon shot the said Bear dead at the first shot. This Bear was from the nearest land above seven and twenty leagues, and lived off Seals or other fish that he could prey upon …

The fifth and sixth days [of July] we were troubled with much Ice; but, it being broken, we brought the ends of our cables to our mainmasts and, having a good tide, we did sheer, as we term it, clear of the Ice. We rode thus in Ice … until the thirteenth [of July], at what time the Ice° began to go away and the Morses° came on shore. For their nature is such that they will not come on land as long as any Ice is about the land.

The fourteenth, we went on land: Master Weldon and Master [Stephen] Bennett with the Ship's company, and I with the company of the Pinnace. And being altogether on shore, and seeing of the beasts sufficient to make our voyage, we prepared to go to killing. Master Weldon and Master Bennett appointed me to take eleven men with me and to go beyond the beasts where they lay that they and we might meet at the midst of them, and so enclose them that none of them should get into the Sea.

° **Cape**: North Cape, the northern tip of Norway. A marginal note reads "Ice within forty-five leagues of the North Cape."

° **Ice**: this melt occurs much earlier now, as the Barents has experienced some of the most dramatic reductions of sea-ice anywhere on the planet; whereas it only averaged one ice-free month each year as recently as the 1980s, it is now ice-free for six (Onarheim and Arthun 8390).

° **Morses**: walruses.

[560] As I fetched a compass about, before we were aware, rose a great white Bear within a Pike's length of us. Whereupon we made a stand, and myself, having both a Musket and a Lance, thought to have shot him. But remembering myself that the report of my Piece might make all the Morses go into the Sea, and so hazard our Voyage, I went to him with my Lance. All this while he sat foaming at the mouth and would not stir, but gaped and roared as though he would have eaten us all. But presently we pricked him in the snout, and then with an easy pace we proceeded on with our business. And before six hours were ended, we had slain about 700 or 800 Beasts. And after that Master Weldon slew the Bear. For ten days space we plied our business very hard, and brought it almost to an end. [But] the four and twentieth of July, we had the wind at North-east, and it froze so hard that the Ice did hang on our Clothes ...

[Seventh Voyage, 1609]

[561] We were furnished with two ships, determining to go to Tipany in Lapland° to buy fish of the Laps and Russians, and afterward to go to Cherry Island:° the one was called *The Lioness*, in which I went for Master; the other *The Paul*, which was there the last year, 1608 ...

The ninth day [of May] I prepared to go over Land to the North side ... with three men in my company. I myself had a Musket and about a quarter of a pound of Powder and six Bullets, a Half-pike in mine hand, and a Hatchet at my back. One of the men had a birding Piece;° the other two had each of them a Javelin. We went over the Snow and Ice apace° outward, but came wearily homeward, by reason we rested not anywhere. And when we were within a mile of the other side, one of my company said he saw a Bear. Whereupon we looked up and saw three great ones. Whereupon I made a stand, and gave each of my company some Aqua vitae,° and a little Bread, and told them that we must not in any case seem fearful because the nature of them is such that whosoever seemeth fearful or offereth to run away they will seize upon him. In this time I made my Musket ready. And the Bears, seeing us to come toward them, stood upon their feet; and two of them went toward the Sea. The third stood still, champing and foaming as though he would have eaten us. When I was within shot of him, he began to follow his fellows, still looking behind him with his former gesture. In the meanwhile, I got ground of him, the three men following me with their weapons. In the end the angry devil turned back and came directly toward me. I let him come within two long Pike's-lengths and

---

° **Lapland**: homeland of the Sami people, stretching from Norway to northwest Russia. Tipany was likely near the Rybachy peninsula or Pechenga in Murmansk Oblast.
° **Cherry Island**: the former English name of Bear Island (after Sir Francis Cherry, an investor in the Muscovy Company).
° **Piece**: gun.   ° **apace**: quickly.   ° **Aqua vitae**: probably brandy.

gave him such a welcome that he fell down stone dead. The company that were with me were glad as well as I. Yet I had been at the killing of Bears before. After this Bear was slain, we told° seventeen more, whereof three were young ones. This done, we went on to the seaside, where we found the Shallop° which we left the year before. We were no sooner set to eat a little food, but there came a Bear with two young ones as big as Lambs of a month old. They skipped about their dam's neck, and played with one another very wantonly.° The dam came so near that I shot at her. And being loath to hurt the young ones, being playing about her foreparts, I shot her through the top of the shoulder. Then she went away. Immediately we saw another Bear coming toward us, which ... stood upon his hinder feet twice or thrice, using the same countenance that the first did ... I let him come very near ... thinking to give him his passport.° [But] the flint of my Musket was broken, which made him come very near us. Then the fellow that had the birding piece shot him in the foot, whereupon he ran away faster than we could follow him. We seeing so many Bears, and having no store of Powder nor Shot, bent our journey toward our ship again. We had not come a quarter of a mile, but we saw a huge Bear fast asleep on the Snow. I went softly toward him, and gave him such a fillip° that he never rose out of the place where he lay. His skin when he was flayed was thirteen foot long. A near neighbour of his, hearing the report of my Piece, came toward me, and him I slew also ...

By three of the clock the next morning, we came to the Northeast point with the ship. There we manned our [562] Shallop, and Master Thomas Weldon and I went on shore, where he slew five Bears and I one (and I wounded two more very sore). And before a North Sun, our men had flayed them all: both them that I slew the day before, and them that we slew this last time, for they were all together ...

The thirteenth [of May], we saw very much Ice to the Southwards and Westwards, which came driving so fast toward the shore where we rode that we were forced to weigh,° and stood to the North side of the Island. The Ice followed us still. Then we stood to the East side of the Island, and there we found both the Island and ourselves encompassed round with Ice. But the wind being Westerly, and a good stiff gale, it blew the Ice about a mile and a half from the Eastern side. By which means, we got betwixt the Ice and the Island, and stood to the Southward, but saw not anything in all the Sea save Ice ... [We] could not see open Sea till the fifteenth of the same month. At a Northwest Sun, we saw the open Sea; only a ledge of Ice which began to part asunder was betwixt us and it. Toward that place we stood; and intending by God's help to get through, we made provision to defend the ship from the Ice by hanging Cables' ends, Planks, and Capstan

---

° **told**: counted.   ° **Shallop**: small sailing boat.   ° **wantonly**: frolicsomely.
° **give ... passport**: to the next world.   ° **fillip**: blow.   ° **weigh**: hoist anchor.

bars° about the bows of our ship. But for all our fenders, our ship had a great knock upon a piece of Ice. About a North Sun, we got out into the open Sea, with humble thanks to God for our deliverance …

The thirtieth day, we slew twenty-six Seals and espied three white Bears. We went aboard for Shot and Powder; and coming to the Ice again, we found a she-Bear and two young ones. Master Thomas Weldon shot and killed her. After she was slain, we got the young ones, and brought them home into England, where they are alive in Paris Garden° …

[563] The fourteenth day [of June] … as we went along by the Cliffs, we got good store of Fowl. [This] made us glad and joyful because there was no hope to get aboard the Ship that day, nor the next. About a Northwest Sun, we got to the place abovesaid and found nine Bears. Three of them I slew; the other took the Sea. Those three that were slain we flayed, and [we] took their flesh and salted it in their skins, which I stowed in the Shallop for fear of a dearth … The fifteenth day, when we had ended our business and eaten some of our Bear's flesh, [we] set up an Ensign° in token of our possession of the Island …

[564] The eighteenth day, we went to the North side of the Island, and in our way we found good Sea-coals to burn: some we took with us to try° them, and found them good. And on the North side I slew two Bears … The twentieth day, I went to the North side again and slew a Bear. Thus we spent the time, sometimes on one side, sometimes on the other, never staying above one day in one place till the Ship came in: which was the seven and twentieth of June. On which day, I slew another Bear. I slew seven in all, whose flesh we ate full savoury, forgetting the oily rankness of it, for hunger is a savoury sauce …

[566] The sixth of August, I took the Skiff and seven men to fetch the Shallop to the Cove … [where we] found about five and forty as good-headed beasts° for Teeth° as ever I saw. We had no more Lances to kill them withal but two. I took one, and a lusty fellow that was our Cooper had the other. We had not killed past ten but his Lance broke. Then I slew all the rest in less than two hours, and we took their Teeth. And the next day, by a West Sun, we came aboard *The Paul* with them.

❧ ❧ ❧

° **Capstan bars**: levers.
° **Paris Garden**: Bear-baiting pit in London, managed by the actor Edward Alleyn. In 1623, a chained polar bear (likely one of these cubs) was baited with dogs while swimming in the Thames.
° **Ensign**: banner or flag, claiming the island for the Muscovy Company; Bear Island now belongs to Norway.
° **try**: assay, test their quality. An early instance of energy prospecting in the Arctic.
° **beasts**: walruses.   ° **Teeth**: ivory tusks.

MARGARET CAVENDISH
"The Hunting of the Hare" (1653)

Margaret Cavendish's anti-hunting poetry (she composed another verse on "The Hunting of a Stag") evinces a philosophical respect for animal intelligence and a keen empathy with both their physical and psychological suffering. While not as well known as Shakespeare's portrait of the "dew-bedabbled" hare in *Venus and Adonis,* this poem is far more explicit in its fierce denunciation of human arrogance and cruelty. The growing scarcity of large fauna such as the red deer and wild boar (the latter were virtually extinct in southern England by the fourteenth century and the former by the eighteenth) increasingly forced English hunters to pursue smaller game such as the fox and hare, previously regarded as unmanly quarry. Although the shifts in tense and perspective make the verse seem rough in spots (especially in the 1653 version), Cavendish prefaces it by the declaration that she favours a "wild" style that (like the hare) "runs wild about, ... a Style that Nature frames not Art." For other hare-hunting poems, see George Turberville's "Of a Hare Complaining of the Hatred of Dogs (1567, 99ᵛ), George Gascoigne's "The Hare to the Hunter" (1575, 176–8), the anonymous "Hunting of the Hare" (Brotherton MS Lt 34, 15ʳ–16ᵛ), and "The Huntsman" (in *Wit And Drollery,* 1661, 214–18). Source: *Poems and Fancies* (1664), 134–6; with emendations from 1653, 110–13.

> Betwixt two Ridges of Ploughed land sat° Wat,°
> Whose Body pressed to th'Earth lay close and squat.°
> His Nose upon his two Forefeet did lie,°
> With his grey Eyes he glared Obliquely.°
> His Head he always set against the Wind,
> His Tail when turned° his Hair blew up behind,
> And made him to get Cold; but he, being Wise,°
> Doth keep° his Coat still down, so warm he lies.
> Thus rests he all the Day till Sun doth Set,
> Then up he riseth his Relief to get,°
> And walks about until the Sun doth Rise,
> Then coming back in's former Posture lies.°
> At last poor Wat was found as he there lay,
> By Huntsmen with their Dogs which came that way;
> Whom seeing, he got up and fast did run,°
> Hoping some way the Cruél Dogs to shun;
> But they by Nature had so quick a Scent,
> That by their Nose they Traced what way he went;

10

° **sat**: lay] 1653.   ° **Wat**: a common name for a hare.
° **Whose... squat**: Pressing his Body close to Earth lay squat] 1653.
° **did lie**: close lies] 1653.
° **With ... Obliquely**: Glaring obliquely with his great grey Eyes] 1653.
° **His ... blew**: If turn his Tail, his Hairs blow] 1653.
° **And ... Wise**: Which he too cold will grow, but he is wise] 1653.
° **Doth keep**: And keeps] 1653.
° **Then ... get**: Then riseth up, his Relief for to get.] 1653.
° **Then ... lies**:] Then back returns, down in his Form he lies] 1653.
° **Whom ... run**: Seeing, gets up and fast begins to run] 1653.

And with their deep wide Mouths set forth a Cry,
20   Which answered was by Echo in the Sky.
Then Wat was struck with Terror and with Fear,
Seeing each Shadow, thought the Dogs were there,°
And running out some distance from the noise,°
To hide himself, his Thoughts he new employs.°
Under a Clod of Earth in Sandpit wide,
Poor Wat sat close, hoping himself to hide.
There long he had not been, but straight in's Ears°
The winding Horns and crying Dogs he hears;
Then starting up with fear, he Leaped, and such
30   Swift speed he made the Ground he scarce did touch;°
Into a great thick Wood he straightway gets,°
Where underneath a broken Bough he sits,°
Where every Leaf that° with the Wind did shake,
Brought him such Terror that his Heart did Ache;°
That Place he left, to Champaign Plains he went,
Winding about, for to deceive their Scent;
And while they Snuffling were to find his Track,
Poor Wat, being weary, his swift Pace did slack.
On his two Hinder-legs for ease he Sat,°
40   His Forefeet rubbed his Face from Dust and Sweat,
Licking his Feet, he wiped his Ears so clean
That none could tell that Wat had Hunted been;
But casting round about his fair grey° Eyes,
The Hounds in full Career he near him Spies;
To Wat it was so Terrible a Sight,
Fear gave him Wings and made his Body light;
Though he was Tired° before by Running long,
Yet now his Breath he never felt more Strong;
Like those that Dying are think Health returns,
50   When 'tis but a faint Blast that Life out-burns;
For Spirits seek to guard the Heart about,
Striving with Death, but Death doth quench them out.
The Hounds so fast came on, and with such Cry,°
That he no hopes had left, nor help could spy.
With that the Winds did pity poor Wat's Case,
And with their Breath, the Scent blew from that Place.
Then every Nose was busily employed,
And every Nostril was set open wide,

° **Seeing ... there**: Thinks every Shadow still the Dogs they were] 1653.
° **the noise**: 1653; their Cry] 1664.   ° **new employs**: 1653; did employ] 1664.
° **been ... Ears**: sat, but straight his Ears] 1653.
° **Then ... touch**: Starting with Fear, up leaps, and then doth run / And with such speed the
   Ground scarce treads upon] 1653.
° **he ... gets**: 1653; straightways he got] 1664.   ° **sits**: 1653; sat] 1664.
° **Where ... that**: At every Leaf what] 1653.
° **Brought ... ache**: Did bring such terror, made his heart to ache] 1664.
° **he Sat**: did sit] 1653.   ° **grey**: great] 1653   ° **he ... Tired**: weary was] 1653.
° **The ... Cry**: Thus they so fast came on, with such loud Cries] 1653.

And every Head did seek a several way,
To find the Grass or Track where the Scent lay.°　　　60
Thus Witty Industry is never Slack;°
'Tis like to Witchcraft,° and brings lost things back.
But though the Wind had tied the Scent up close,
A busy Dog thrust in his snuffling Nose
And drew it out, with that° did foremost run:
Then Horns blew loud, the rest to follow on.
The great slow Hounds, their Throats did set a Bass;
The fleet, swift Hounds, as Tenors next in place;
The little Beagles did° a Treble Sing,
And through the Air their Voices round° did Ring,　　　70
Which made such Consort as they Ran along
That, had they Spoken words, 't had been a Song.°
The Horns kept time, the Men did° shout for Joy,
And seemed most valiant, poor Wat to Destroy;
Spurring their Horses to a full Career,
Swum Rivers deep, leaped Ditches without fear,
Endangered Life and Limbs, so fast they'd ride,
Only to see how patiently Wat Died.
At last,° the Dogs so near his Heels did get,
That they their sharp Teeth in his Breech did set;　　　80
Then Tumbling down, he fell with weeping Eyes,
Gave up his Ghost,° and thus poor Wat he Dies.
Men whooping loud, such Acclamations made,
As if the Devil they imprisoned had,
When they but did a shiftless° Creature kill;
To Hunt there needs no Valiant Soldier's Skill.
But Men do° think that Exercise and Toil,
To keep their Health, is best which makes most Spoil,
Thinking that Food and Nourishment so good
Which doth proceed from others'° Flesh and Blood.　　　90
When they do Lions, Wolves, Bears, Tigers see
Kill silly Sheep, they° say they Cruèl be;
But for themselves all Creatures think too few:
For Luxury,° wish God would make more° New,

° **the ... lay**: what Grass or Track the Scent on lay] 1653.
° **witty ... Slack**: quick Industry, that is not slack] 1653.
° **'Tis ... Witchcraft**: Is like to Witchery] 1653.
° **that**: it] 1653.　　　° **did**: they] 1653.　　　° **Voices round**: Voice a round] 1653.
° **That ... Song**: If they but words could speak might sing a Song] 1653.　　　° **Men did**: Hunters] 1653.
° **At last**: For why] 1653.
° **Gave ... Ghost**: Gives ... Ghost] 1653. A phrase famously used to describe the death of Christ in Matthew 27:50.
° **shiftless**: helpless.　　　° **Men do**: Man doth] 1653.
° **Which ... others'**: And Appetite that feeds on] 1653.
° **Kill ... they**: To kill poor Sheep, straight] 1653.
° **Luxury**: indulgence.　　　° **more**: them] 1653.

As if God did make Creatures for Man's meat,
And gave° them Life and Sense for Man to eat;
Or else for Sport or Recreation's sake,
For to Destroy those Lives that God did make,°
Making their Stomachs Graves, which full they fill
100   With Murdered Bodies, which in Sport they Kill.
Yet Man doth think himself so Gentle and Mild,
When of all Creatures he's° most Cruel, Wild;
Nay, so Proud, that he only thinks to Live,°
That God a God-like Nature him did give,
And that all Creatures for his Sake alone
Were made, for him to Tyrannize upon.°

ðk ðk ðk

° **And gave**: To give] 1653.
° **For... make**: Destroy those Lives that God saw good to make] 1653.
° **When ... he's**: When he of Creatures is] 1653.
° **Nay... Live**: And is so Proud, thinks only he shall live] 1653.
° **Were ... upon**: Was made for him, to Tyrannize upon] 1653.

GEORGE TURBERVILLE
"In Commendation of Hawking" (1575)

Falconry manuals like Turberville's *Book* and *Latham's Falconry* (1614) capture the
thrill and glamour of this elite sport in Renaissance England. They also document
its cruelty. Turberville here encourages its practitioners to revel in the feeling of
mastery over (or "reclaiming" of) a wild thing. No wonder that this performance
of anthropocentric dominion could, like horse-breaking and hunting, supply disturbing metaphors for patriarchal dominance (e.g. Shakespeare's *Taming of the
Shrew*). Despite the affective bond between handler and bird (recently celebrated
in Helen Macdonald's *H is for Hawk*), Turberville shows scant concern for the
suffering of the falcons themselves, as he touts the health benefits of this sport for
humans.
Source: *The Book of Falconry or Hawking* (1611), ¶3ʳ-¶4ᵛ, 88–9, 142–3.

What sense so sad, what mind so 'mazed, but sets his sorrows by,
When once the Falcon free begins to scud° amid the sky?
To turn and wind a bird by sleight, and eke at last to slay
40   With strong encounter doves and ducks, and every other prey:
The pretty Partridge, Rails, and Quails that haunt the open field?
And from her mountee° to enforce the Heron haught° to yield,
By binding with her close in clouds, in manner out of sight?
For noble Peers and chiefest States, a passing pleasant flight:

° **scud**: dart.   ° **mountee**: apex of flight.   ° **haught**: proud.

So small a bird, so large a fowl, at such a lofty gate,°
To reach and rap, and force to fall; it is a game of state.
No fellow to the flight at Brook,° that game is full of glee;
It is a sport the stooping° of a roisting° Hawk to see.
And if she miss, to mark her how she then gets up amain,°
For best advantage to e'new° the springing fowl again,   50
Who if't be landed as it ought, then is it sure to die;
Or if she slip, a joy to see the Hawk at random fly,
And so for head° to slay the fowl: a noble sport to view.
In my conceit no pleasure like to Hawks, I tell you true.
It sets the senses all to work, there may none idle be:
The tongue it lures, the legs they leap, the eye beholds the glee;
The ears are busied eke to hear the calling Spaniel's quest.°
Do tell me then what sense it is that respite hath to rest?
And more than that, the heart it leaps and laughs for joy to think,
How such a slender hawk should cause so huge a fowl to shrink.°   60
This kind of sport doth banish vice and vile devices quite,
When other games do foster faults and breed but base delight.
No idle thought can harbour well within the Falconer's brain,
For though his sports right pleasant be, yet are they mixed with pain.°
The toil he takes to find the fowl, his greedy lust to slay,
The fowl once found cuts off conceits and drives ill thoughts away.
He lures, he leaps, he calls, he cries, he joys, he waxeth sad,
And frames his mood according as his hawk doth well or bad.
Dame Venus harbours not in holts,° no Cupid haunts the hills;
Diana dwells in open place, with bow her game she kills …   70
At cockpit some their pleasures place, to wager wealth away,
Where Falconers only force the fields, to hear their spaniels bay.
What greater glee can man desire than by his cunning skill,
So to reclaim a haggard° hawk, as she the fowl shall kill,
To make and man her in such sort, as tossing out a train,
Or bait the lure° when she is at large, to whoop her in again?
Where birds and beasts and each thing else, their freedom so embrace,
As let them loose, they will be thralled no more in any case …   80
To make her mew° when time requires, to bowse° and eke to bathe,
By cunning skill to cause her cast° such glut as breeds her scathe;
To cut her hoods, to shape her jess,° her terrets,° and her line,°
With Bells, and Bewets,° Verrels° eke, to make the Falcon fine:
Believe me is no common skill, no bate° nor base device,
But meet for civil courtly men that are reputed wise …

° **gate**: flight.
° **flight at Brook**: hunting water-fowl.   ° **stooping**: swooping.   ° **roisting**: clamorous.
° **amain**: vehemently.   ° **e'new**: drive prey into water.   ° **for head**: at last.
° **quest**: bark.   ° **shrink**: cower.   ° **pain**: exertion (of the falconer).   ° **holts**: woods.
° **haggard**: wild adult female.
° **bait the lure**: present a feathered toy resembling the bird's quarry.   ° **mew**: confine in a cage
   or hawk-house, especially when moulting..
° **bowse**: drink.   ° **cast**: disgorge.   ° **jess**: leg straps.
° **terrets**: rings through which the jesses are threaded.   ° **line**: tether.   ° **Bewets**: bell-ring.
° **Verrels**: bracelets.   ° **bate**: rough, hasty.

How to Seal a Sparrowhawk

Take a needle threaded with untwisted thread, and (casting° your Hawk) take her by the beak and put the needle through her eyelid, not right against the sight° of the eye, but [89] somewhat nearer to the beak because she may see backwards. And you must take good heed that you hurt not the web, which is under the eyelid or on the inside thereof. Then put your needle also through that other eyelid. Drawing the ends of the thread together, tie them over the beak, not with a strait knot, but cut off the threads' ends near to the knot and twist them together in such sort that the eyelids may be raised so upwards that the hawk may not see at all. And when the thread shall wax loose or untied, then the hawk may see somewhat backwards, which is the cause that the thread is put nearer to the beak …

To Use° a Hawk to the Hood

When your Hawk, being so sealed, doth feed well and will abide the Hood, and to be handled without striking or biting at your hand, then in an Evening by candlelight you shall unseal her, and with your finger and a little spittle, anoint the place where the sealing thread was drawn through. And when you have hooded her, take her on your fist, and hold her so all night until day appear again, doing off her Hood oftentimes, and handling her gently with your hand, stroking her softly about the wings and the body, hooding and unhooding of her, and giving her sometimes to feed a morsel or [143] twain … But above all things you must watch° her on the fist so many nights together, without setting her down on any perch, that she may be weary, and suffer you to hood and handle her gently without any manner of resistance, and until she have altogether left and forgotten her striking and biting at your hand. But some Hawks will be long before they leave that fault, as the more coy or ramage° that they be, the longer they will retain those ill taches,° and will not peradventure be won from them in three, four, or five days. When she is well reclaimed from it, then may you let her sit upon a perch to rest her. But every night you shall do well to keep her on the fist three or four hours, handling her and stroking her gently, and causing her to tire … And the like may you do also by daylight, but in a Chamber apart, where she may see no great light until she feed surely and eagerly without dread.

๛ ๛ ๛

° **casting**: pinning an animal on its back against the ground.   ° **sight**: pupil.   ° **Use**: accustom.
° **watch**: keep awake.   ° **ramage**: wild.   ° **taches**: habits.

Fishing

JOHN DEE
"Manifold disorder used about fry and spawn" (1577)

Now best known as a magus, Dee also took a worldly interest in politics, and was an early advocate of British imperialism. Beyond imparting nautical wisdom, his treatise on navigation makes a staunch defence of England's fishing rights in its territorial waters, sounding the alarm that incursions by the Dutch might deplete fish stocks in the Atlantic and North Sea – a topic he returned to twenty years later in his essay *British Sea-Sovereignty*. The excerpt below voices outrage over commercial fishing in the Thames, as Dee employs his considerable mathematical expertise to present one of the earliest arguments for sustainable fishing based on quantitative analysis.
Source: *The Perfect Art of Navigation* (1577), 43–6.

You may understand that in the River of Thames ... every year by the fishermen belonging to some one small town ... there is destroyed above 1,000 bushels of the young fry of diverse kinds of good fish, which in due time of their growth and by lawful order being taken would have been able to satisfy 200,000 one day ... or 4,000 men fifty days, etc. [44] What is then, I pray you, to be reckoned of the public damage of 500 cartloads of fish yearly thus destroyed? How may it (reasonably) any longer remain unreformed?°

[These] 500 cartloads ... do amount [to] only 2,400 bushels of fry yearly destroyed. But if you suppose ... thirty trink-boats° ... every day for 300 days only in every whole year, [and each] destroy but one bushel of very small fry, the sum thereof doth amount to 9,000 bushels of fry so destroyed yearly: which fry, when it should be marketable, would be ... of ten times more meat and fish than when it is so destroyed. Therefore, the craftsmen of the trink-boats on the Thames may very probably be accused, convicted, judged, and condemned as the most abominable yearly destructioners of 90,000 bushels of marketable fish. So is it now also probable that in all England by the manifold disorder used about fry and spawn destroying, there is yearly spoiled or hindered the brood of 2,000 cartloads of fresh fish. The value of the foresaid 90,000 bushels of fresh fish ... (being rated at five shillings a bushel) is £220,500° ... [This] quantity of fish also (according to our former hypotheses) would maintain for one day 1,800,000 men or 25,000 men 72 days, etc. ... What discrete subject or true member of the British or English Monarchy is there, who in his heart

---

° **unreformed**: governmental efforts to regulate fishing date back to the thirteenth century. See legislation from 1543 and 1559 in Appendix A.
° **trink-boats**: boats equipped with nets.
° **£220,500**: over 45 million in today's money.

doth not abhor this heinous enormity? And will not with his voice heartily
cry out and say, "Fie, fie on them! Away with them, away with them!" ...

God, of his infinite goodness, sendeth us yearly evident tokens of the
great abundance of this kind of good victuals, prepared purposely for this
part of British Albion. But these trinker-men cast incredible much of such
a treasure before their swine to battle° them withal; and are by that means
great hinderers, both to the wealth and relief public, and also to the Glory
of God, who would be duly glorified and praised of many a thousand of
the rich and poor who should be served, pleasured, and relieved with the
great abundance of the diverse° and wholesome fish swarming in this incomparable River of Thames ... [46] if these public enemies of God and
man did not (more than barbarously and less than Christian-like) utterly
spoil and wickedly tread under their feet such a blessing and liberal gift
of our GOD ... preferred unto us and, in a manner, put into our hands.

多 多 多

° **battle**: feed. Unsold fish were commonly used for hog-fodder, although Dee also plays on the
  biblical saying to "cast pearls before swine."
° **diverse**: 125 species of fish can be found in the Thames estuary.

THOMAS BASTARD
"There is no fish in brooks" and "De Piscatione"° (1598)

As population growth drove up food prices in the late sixteenth century, the
English began to consume larger quantities of fish, triggering a corresponding
decline in their numbers – much to the chagrin of the surly clergyman and satirist
Thomas Bastard.
Source: *Chrestoloros* (1598), 138–9.

6.13

There is no fish in brooks, little or great:
And why? For all is fish that comes to net.°
The small eat sweet, the great more daintily;
The great will seethe° or bake, the small will fry.
For rich men's tables serve the greater fish;
The small are to the poor a dainty dish.
The great are at their best, and serve for store;
The small once ta'en, keep, or you catch no more.
We must thank ponds, for rivers we have none.
The fowl swim in the brook, the fish are flown.

° ***De Piscatione***: Of Fishing.
° **For ... net**: a popular proverb, meaning one should make use of anything.   ° **seethe**: boil.

6.14

Fishing, if I, a fisher, may protest,
Of pleasures is the sweet'st, of sports the best,
Of exercises the most excellent,
Of recreations the most innocent.
But now the sport is marred, and wot° ye why?
Fishes decrease, and fishers multiply.

᷄᷄ ᷄᷄ ᷄᷄

° **wot**: know.

JOHN DENNYS
from The Secrets of Angling (1613)

Piscatorial poetry enjoyed a brief vogue in the Renaissance, with memorable examples by Jacopo Sannazaro, John Donne, and Phineas Fletcher. John Dennys's
verses convey the angler's pleasure in the outdoors, and Izaak Walton admired
them enough to include them in his perennial bestseller *The Compleat Angler*.
Embellishing on Ovid, the second section offers an etiological myth on the origin
of fishing, while lamenting that humans may have become too proficient at it.
Source: *The Secrets of Angling* (1613), B7^{r-v}, C1^r–C2^r.

O let me rather on the pleasant Brink
Of Tyne and Trent possess some dwelling place,
Where I may see my Quill and Cork° down sink,
With eager bite of Barbel, Bleak, or Dace,
And on the World and his Creator think,
While they proud Thais'° painted sheet embrace,
And with the fume of strong Tobacco's smoke,
All quaffing round are ready for to choke.

Let them that list these pastimes them pursue,
And on their pleasing fancies feed their fill,   290
So I the Fields and Meadows green may view,
And by the Rivers fresh may walk at will,
Among the Daisies and the Violets blue,
Red Hyacinth° and yellow Daffodil,
Purple Narcissus, like the morning rays,
Pale Gandergrass,° and azure Culverkeys.°

° **Quill and Cork**: float or bobber.   ° **Thais**: a prostitute.
° **Red Hyacinth**: Gerard refers to hyacinths or bluebells of a "carnation" colour, and its flowers can
   sometimes take on a pinkish tint due to mutation.   ° **Gandergrass**: early purple orchid.
° **Culverkeys**: English bluebells.

I count it better pleasure to behold
The goodly compass of the lofty Sky,
And in the midst thereof like burning gold
300   The flaming Chariot of the world's great eye;
The wat'ry clouds that in the air uprolled
With sundry kinds of painted colours fly;
And fair Aurora lifting up her head,
All blushing rise from old Tithonus'° bed;

The hills and Mountains raisèd from the Plains;
The plains extended level with the ground;
The ground divided into sundry veins;
The veins enclosed with running rivers round;
The rivers making way through nature's chain,
310   With headlong course into the sea profound;
The surging sea beneath the valleys low;
The valleys sweet and lakes that lovely flow;

The lofty woods; the forests wide and long,
Adorned with leaves and branches fresh and green,
In whose cool bowers the birds with chanting song,
Do welcome with their choir the Summer's Queen;
The meadows fair where Flora's gifts among
Are intermixed the verdant grass between;
The silver-scalèd fish that softly swim,
320   Within the brooks and Crystal wat'ry brim.

All these and many more of his creation
That made the heavens, the Angler oft doth see,
And takes therein no little delectation,
To think how strange and wonderful they be;
Framing thereof an inward contemplation,
To set his thoughts from other fancies free.
And while he looks on these with joyful eye,
His mind is rapt above the starry sky …

"The Author of Angling"

Thus was the earth replenishèd anew,
With people strange, sprung up with little pain,
Of whose increase the progeny that grew
Did soon supply the empty world again.°
But now a greater care there did ensue:
How such a mighty number to maintain?
(Since food there was not any to be found,
For that great flood had all destroyed and drowned.)

° **Tithonus**: a king of Troy, who married Aurora, the goddess of the dawn.
° **Thus … again**: in the omitted section, Dennys retells the flood myth from Ovid's *Metamorphoses*, in which the lone survivors (Deucalion and Pyrrha) repopulate the earth by throwing stones over their shoulders.

Then did Deucalion first the Art invent
Of Angling, and his people taught the same;   410
And to the Woods and groves with them he went,
Fit tools to find for this most needful game.
There from the trees the longest rinds they rent,°
Wherewith strong lines they roughly twist and frame,
And of each crook of hardest Bush and Brake,
They made them Hooks the hungry Fish to take.

And to entice them to the eager bit,
Dead frogs and flies of sundry sorts he took,
And snails and worms such as he found most fit,
Wherein to hide the close and deadly hook.   420
And thus with practice and inventive wit,
He found the means in every lake and brook
Such store of Fish to take with little pain,
As did long time this people new sustain.

In this rude sort began this simple Art,
And so remained in that first age of old,
When Saturn did Amalthea's horn° impart
Unto the world, that then was all of Gold.
The Fish as yet had felt but little smart,
And were to bite more eager, apt, and bold;   430
And plenty still supplied the place again
Of woeful want, whereof we now complain.

But when in time the fear and dread of man
Fell more and more on every living thing,
And all the creatures of the world began
To stand in awe of this usurping King,
Whose tyranny so far extended then
That Earth and Seas it did in thraldom bring;
It was a work of greater pain and skill,
The wary Fish in Lake or Brook to kill.   440

So worse and worse two ages more did pass,
Yet still this Art more perfect daily grew;
For then the slender Rod invented was,
Of finer sort than former ages knew,
And Hooks were made of silver and of brass,
And Lines of hemp and flax were framèd new,
And sundry baits experience found out more
Than elder times did know or try before.

But at the last the Iron Age drew near,
Of all the rest the hardest and most scant.   450
Then Lines were made of Silk and subtle hair,

° **rinds they rent**: stripped off bark.
° **Amalthea's horn**: cornucopia (the horn of plenty).

And Rods of lightest Cane and Hazel plant,
And Hooks of hardest steel invented were,
That neither skill nor workmanship did want.
And so this Art did in the end attain
Unto that state where now it doth remain.

⁊⮜ ⁊⮜ ⁊⮜

TIMOTHY GRANGER

Seventeen Monstrous Fishes Taken in Suffolk (1568)

On the basis of Granger's description and the engraving that accompanies it, the "monstrous fishes" were almost certainly orcas (and hence mammals). Although orcas have long inhabited the coastal waters off Scotland, the last resident pod in the UK is now endangered – only eight remain as of 2016. This Elizabethan broadside may help explain their decline, while offering a grisly example of how many early moderns reacted when they encountered unusual wildlife.
Source: *A Most True and Marvellous Strange Wonder … Of Seventeen Monstrous Fishes Taken in Suffolk* (1568).

Of these seventeen fishes there were a male and female that were more huge and monstrous than the other fifteen. For the least of these two fishes was twenty-seven feet long and as big in the middle, each of them, as three Butts° of Malmsey, and of marvellous great strength … for they tied one of these fishes to a boat to bring it to Ipswich wharf and, being so tied to the boat, [he] swam away with the boat and all the men that were in it toward the sea a marvellous swift pace for all that they could do. This was when the tide came; for they had made provision before when the water was low to tie great ropes about their tails and fins … [But] the tide coming in and the fish having water, [he] swam away with the boat so fast toward the sea that if there had not been rescue of other boats and such vessels as they had thereabout, that boat and all they in it had been utterly lost and cast away. But as God would have it, by the help of the other boasts or vessels, tying the fish also, [they] brought him by force to a convenient place, and tied him fast to a tree with strong cable ropes, and so using them one by one, found means to bring them to Ipswich wharf, where they were laid with great labour and trouble, beside breaking of their windlass and a great cable rope with hauling them up … Some of them lay upon the wharf two days and a night before they were dead, and yet they struck them with axes and other weapons to kill them. The river wherein they were taken was coloured red with the blood that issued from their wounds … There were also three butchers a whole day cutting out one of these fishes to carry it away with hand-barrels° to the town warehouse; and the butchers

---

° **Butts**: casks.   ° **hand-barrels**: wheelbarrows.

were fain to put on boots to stand in to cut it out, it was so deep and full of garbage … His mouth was wide, gaping above a yard broad, and had forty-four teeth … Upon their heads were holes, as big as a man might put in both his fists at once, out of the which they did spout a great quantity of water while they were a-taking, that they almost drowned two boats, men and all, with spouting of water; for the water would ascend upward from the fishes as high as any house, and so fall down and wet all them that were within their reach most cruelly. Also they were white beneath the eyes a hand broad, their eyes black, and no bigger than the eyes of a calf. Their backs as black as ink, so smooth and bright that one might have seen his face on it, as in a dim glass, [and] their bellies white as milk. And upon their backs they had each of them one great black fin growing … and two great black ones underneath … [As for] the male one of the two biggest … his tail was three yards long and two yards broad, very thick and black and wonderful strong; for ten tall men stood upon his tail and he, lifting his tail up, overthrew them all. Also when he had lifted up his tail it was of such monstrous weight, strength, and bigness, that when it fell the very ground would ring and shake therewith. This fish was cut out in pieces and given away to diverse in the town that did eat of it, and was very good meat, either roast or baked (so much of it as was kept sweet), and the meat of them baked tasted like red deer. And as they cut it out it was weighed by pieces so that the very body of this one fish weighed 5,200,° the bare carcass …

If the men of Ipswich had known so much betimes° while they were sweet,° as they have sense, they might have made 200 marks more of them than is now made. But now they be barrelled up to make oil of, and will not be sold for a great piece of money. And this you may see, the perfect and true description of these strange fishes, wherein is to be noted the strange and marvellous handiworks of the Lord. Blessed be God in all his gifts and holy in all his works. The Lord's name be praised, in them and for them, forever and ever. So be it.

ⁿ ⁿ ⁿ

° **5,200**: male orcas can weigh in excess of 11,000 pounds (5,000 kg).
° **betimes**: earlier.   ° **sweet**: fresh.

EDMUND WALLER
"The Battle of the Summer Islands" (1645)

Many ancient maritime cultures around the world hunted whales for subsistence. In sixteenth-century Europe, however, growing demand for oil ushered in the era of commercial whaling. The Basques, Dutch, and Germans dominated the industry, and by the late 1600s were slaughtering an average of 830 whales per year (Richards 600). In comparison, the English were relative latecomers and only dabbled in the trade. The first commercial whaling expedition out of England launched in 1594, and a second set sail in 1611 under the aegis of the Muscovy Company. Based in Hull, English whalers primarily targeted bowhead whales and walruses in the North Sea. The first whale hunt in English literature, however, is not a commercial voyage to the Arctic; instead it describes a communal assault on two whales stranded in the harbour of St George's, Bermuda, and was reportedly inspired by true events, relayed to Waller by an eye-witness (John Evelyn recorded a similar incident in his *Diary* on 3 June 1658; for more on representations of beached whales in Renaissance Europe, see Brayton 108–35). The poem might be read as an allegory in which the whales (which were designated "royal fish" and legally belonged to the Crown) represent Charles I and II, and the hunters the Parliamentarians, as Bermuda was fiercely divided during the Civil War. However, it would perhaps be more accurate to claim that, despite the mock-epic tone, Waller's royalist sympathies foster sympathy for the whales and a corresponding resentment of their would-be killers. Source: *Poems* (1645), 54–9.

Canto 2

At length two monsters of unequal size,
10   Hard by the shore a fisherman espies,
Two mighty Whales, which swellings Seas have tossed,
And left them prisoners on the rocky coast:
One as a mountain vast, and with her came
A Cub not much inferior to his Dam;
Here in a pool among the Rocks engaged,
They roared like Lions caught in toils, and raged.
The man knew what they were, who heretofore
Had seen the like lie murdered on the shore,
By the wild fury of some tempest cast,
20   The fate of ships and shipwrecked men to taste ...
The welcome news through all the Nation spread,
To sudden joy and hope converts their dread.
What lately was their public terror they
Behold with glad eyes as a certain prey;
Dispose already of th'untaken spoil,
And as the purchase of their future toil,
These share the bones and they divide the oil:
So was the Huntsman by the Bear oppressed,
Whose hide he sold before he caught the beast.
40   They man their Boats, and all their young men arm
With whatsoever may the Monsters harm:
Pikes, halberds, spits and darts that wound so far,
The tools of peace and instruments of war.
Now was the time for vig'rous lads to show
What love of honour could invite them to.
A goodly Theatre where rocks are round
With reverend age, and lovely lasses crowned:

Such was the lake which held this dreadful pair
Within the bounds of noble Warwick's° share ...

Canto 3

The Boat which on the first assault did go
Struck with a harping-iron the younger foe,
Who, when he felt his side so rudely gored,
Loud as the Seas that nourished him he roared.
As a broad Bream to please some curious taste,
While yet alive in boiling water cast,
Vexed with unwonted heat, boils, flings about
The scorching brass, and hurls the liquor out,
So with the barbèd Jav'lin stung, he raves,
And scourges with his tail the suff'ring waves;   10
Like Fairy Talus° with his iron flail,
He threatens ruin with his pond'rous tail,
Dissolving at one stroke the battered Boat,
And down the men fall drenchèd in the moat:
With every fierce encounter they are forced
To quit their boats, and fare like men unhorsed.
    The bigger Whale like some huge Carrack° lay,
Which wanteth Sea-room with her foes to play;
Slowly she swims, and when provoked she would
Advance her tail, her head salutes the mud.   20
The shallow water doth her force infringe,
And renders vain her tail's impetuous swing.
The shining steel her tender sides receive,
And there like Bees they all their weapons leave.
    This sees the Cub, and does himself oppose
Betwixt his cumbered mother and her foes;
With desperate courage he receives her wounds,
And men and boats his active tail confounds.
Their surges joined, the Seas with billows fill,
And make a tempest though the winds be still.   30
    Now would the men with half their hopèd prey
Be well content, and wish this cub away.
Their wish they have; he to direct his Dam
Unto the gap through which they thither came,
Before her swims, and quits the hostile lake:
A pris'ner there, but for his Mothers' sake.
She by the rocks compelled to stay behind,
Is by the vastness of her bulk confined.
They shout for joy, and now on her alone
Their fury falls, and all their Darts are thrown.   40

° **Warwick**: 2nd Earl of Warwick, Robert Rich, appointed commander of the fleet in 1642 by the
Long Parliament and one year later the commissioner of the colonies.
° **Talus**: the famous iron man from Book 5 of Spenser's *Faerie Queene.*   ° **Carrack**: large ship.

Their Lances spent, one bolder than the rest
With his broad sword provoked the sluggish beast:
Her oily side devours blade and heft,
And there his Steel the bold Bermudian left.
Courage the rest from his example take,
And now they change the colour of the Lake.
Blood flows in rivers from her wounded side,
As if they would prevent° the tardy tide,
And raise the flood to that propitious height,
50   As might convey her from this fatal strait.
She swims in blood, and blood does spouting throw
To heav'n, that Heav'n men's cruélties might know.
Their fixèd Jav'lins in her side she wears,
And on her back a grove of Pikes appears ...
Roaring she tears the air with such a noise ...
60   To reach the ears of her escapèd son.
He (though a league escapèd from the foe)
Hastes to her aid ...
The men amazèd blush to see the seed
Of monsters human piety exceed ...
Their courage droops and hopeless now they wish
70   For composition° with th'unconquered fish ...
Not daring to approach their wounded foe,
Whom her courageous son protected so,
They charge their musket, and with hot desire
Of fell revenge, renew the fight with fire.
Standing aloof, with lead they bruise the scales
80   And tear the flesh of the incensèd Whales.
But no success their fierce endeavours found,
Nor this way could they give one fatal wound.
Now to the Fort they are about to send
For the loud Engines° which their Isle defend;
But what those pieces framed to batter Walls
Would have effected on those mighty Whales,
Great Neptune will not have us know; who sends
A tide so high that it relieves his friends.
And thus they parted with exchange of harms,
90   Much blood the Monsters lost, and they their Arms.

                          ❧ ❧ ❧

° **prevent**: precede.   ° **composition**: truce.   ° **Engines**: cannons.

Pet-Keeping

JOHN CAIUS

"Of the delicate, neat, and pretty kind of dogs called the Spaniel Gentle, or the Comforter" (1570)

The historian Keith Thomas observes that it was "in the sixteenth and seventeenth centuries that pets seemed to have really established themselves as normal features of the middle-class household" (110). In early modern England a wide range of species could be (1) permitted inside the house, (2) given names, or (3) spared from the butcher's knife. The poet Robert Herrick had a spaniel, a cat, a sparrow, a lamb, and even a pet pig (to whom he gave sips of beer), while some kept tame falcons, monkeys, or deer (see Skelton's "Philip Sparrow," c. 1505, and Marvell's "Nymph Complaining of the Death of her Fawn," c. 1649). Then as now, pet-keeping could reflect cultural attitudes about class and gender. Whereas Tudor men were encouraged to raise large dogs for hunting or herding, it became increasingly common for city-dwelling gentlewomen to lavish affection on lapdogs. Rather than praise this attachment to a "companion species" (Haraway), Caius growls his disapproval of such attitudes as symptomatic of feminine frivolity. Caius's treatise would later be incorporated wholesale into Topsell's *History of Four-Footed Beasts*, and was favourite reading of King James, who was once accused of loving his dogs better than his subjects, and whose grandson would have a spaniel breed named after him. Shakespeare knew this book, too, as Kent assumes the alias Caius when he shows a dog-like fidelity to Lear.
Source: *Of English Dogs*, trans. Abraham Fleming (1576), 20–1.

These dogs are little, pretty, proper, and fine, and sought for to satisfy the delicateness of dainty dames, and wanton women's wills, instruments of folly for them to play and dally withal, to trifle away the treasure of time, to withdraw their minds from more commendable exercises, and [21] to content their corrupted concupiscences with vain disport (a silly shift to shun irksome idleness). These puppies the smaller they be, the more pleasure they provoke, as more meet playfellows for mincing mistresses to bear in their bosoms, to keep company withal in their chambers, to succour with sleep in bed, and nourish with meat at board, to lay in their laps, and lick their lips as they ride in their wagons. And good reason it should be so; for coarseness with fineness hath no fellowship, but featness° with neatness hath neighbourhood enough. That plausible proverb verified upon a Tyrant, namely that he loved his sow better than his son, may well be applied to these kind of people who delight more in dogs that are deprived of all possibility of reason than they do in children that be capable of wisdom and judgement.

꙳ ꙳ ꙳

° **featness**: elegance.

JOHN HARINGTON
"To his Wife, for striking her Dog" (c. 1600)

Mary Harington may be the sort of "dainty dame" Caius accused of being too
fond of lapdogs. However, her rebuking her husband – who was himself extremely
attached to his dog Bungay (see Part 11, p. 121) – for beating her dog and his subsequent penitence can be seen as illustrative of a rise in the status of domestic pets
in early modern England (Boehrer 2002).
Source: *Epigrams* (1618), D1ᵛ.

> Your little Dog that barked as I came by,
> I struck by hap° so hard, I made him cry;
> And straight you put your finger in your eye,
> And louring sat, and asked the reason why.
> "Love me, and love my Dog,"° thou didst reply.
> "Love as both should be loved." "I will," said I,
> And sealed it with a kiss. Then by and by,
> Cleared were the clouds of thy fair frowning sky.
> Thus small events great masteries may try.
> For I by this do at their meaning guess,
> That beat a Whelp afore a Lioness.

10

🐾 🐾 🐾

° **hap**: chance.   ° **Love ... dog**: proverbial.

ANONYMOUS
"The Old Woman's Legacy to Her Cat" (1695)

Scoffing headlines of huge fortunes bequeathed to pets often appear in the popular press today, and the early modern period was no different. The following
broadside attests to the intensity of cross-species attachment between humans and
pets in seventeenth-century England, and the discomfort it could occasion (see
Raber 2008, 98–9).
Source: *Great News from Southwark* (1695).

Giving an account of an old miserable woman, who lately kept a blind°
alehouse in St Tooley Street, near the Borough of Southwark; who was so
wretchedly covetous as to deny herself the common benefits of life, as to
meat and clothes; leaving at her death about £1,800 to her CAT; using to
say often, when the CAT mewed, "Peace PUSS, peace; thou shalt have all
when I am dead."

° **blind**: in a back alley, or perhaps windowless.

To the tune of "The Bleeding Heart"

In Southwark there did lately dwell,
A rich old woman, noted well,
An alehouse-keeper by her trade;
She lived alone, and had no maid.

For very poor she seemed to be,
And was maintained by charity.
Her family was very small:
A CAT she kept, and that was all.

No food herself she would afford,
But what came from her neighbours' board;   10
But for her CAT she meat would buy,
And feed her ay,° most daintily.

She lived so close° and fared so hard,
That she herself had well-nigh starved.
No clothes or victuals would she buy,
But feed her CAT most daintily.

She heapèd up her bags in store,
And pinched her guts to lay up more.
Tho' she as lean as rake did grow,
Her CAT was plump as any doe.   20

Her belly-money up she laid,
Until a handsome sum it made.
Her guttage° money it was found
To be nigh eighteen hundred pound.

For death at length began to creep,
And rock the rich old crone asleep:
Asleep she lay, to death confined,
And left her CAT and wealth behind.

❧ ❧ ❧

° **ay**: always.   ° **close**: frugally.   ° **guttage**: food.

GEORGE GIFFORD
[Witches' Familiars] (1593)

Intimacy between women and domestic pets could sometimes arouse more than mild scorn. In this theological dialogue on witchcraft, several interlocutors endorse the prevalent belief that witches kept certain animals as "familiars" or demonic servants to execute their malicious vendettas. Such speeches attest to early modern paranoia about cross-species bonds, particularly with nocturnal fauna or vermin that were thought to harm cattle, even as the Puritan Gifford, through the character of Daniel, voices scepticism towards old Popish superstitions and calls for greater inquiry into "natural causes" before pinning the blame on talking animals. Source: *A Dialogue concerning witches and witchcraft* (1593), A4^v–B1^r, B4^v–C1^r, C4^r– C4^v, E1^r.

SAMUEL They say there is scarce any town or village in all this shire, but there is one or two witches at the least in it. In good sooth, I may tell it to you as to my friend, when I go but into my closes,° I am afraid; for I see now and then a Hare, which my conscience giveth me is a witch, or some witch's spirit, she stareth so upon me. And sometime I see an ugly weasel run through my yard, and there is a foul great cat sometimes in my Barn, which I have no liking unto.

DANIEL You never had no hurt done yet, had you, by any witch?

SAMUEL Trust me I cannot tell, but I fear me I have. [B1^r] For there be two or three in our town which I like not, but especially an old woman. I have been as careful to please her as ever I was to please mine own mother, and to give her ever anon one thing or other; and yet methinks she frowns at me now and then. And I had a hog which ate his meat with his fellows and was very well to our thinking overnight; and in the morning he was stark dead. My wife hath had five or six hens even of late dead. Some of my neighbours wish me to burn something alive,° as a hen or a hog … One of mine acquaintance but two miles hence … lost two or three kine, six hogs … and a mare. He went to [a cunning man who] told him he suspected an old woman in the parish. And I think he told me that he showed him her in a Glass, and told him she had three or four imps, some call them puckerels°—one like a grey cat, another like a weasel, another like a mouse (a vengeance take them! It is great pity the country is not rid of them!)—and told him also what he should do. It is half a year ago, and he never had any hurt since … [B4^v] M. B.° What say you to this? That the witches have their spirits (some hath one, some hath more, as two, three, four, or five; some in one likeness and some in another, as like cats, weasels, toads, or mice, whom they nourish with milk, or with a chicken, or by letting them suck° now and then a drop of blood) whom they call when they be offended with any, and send them to hurt them in their bodies—yea, to kill them and to kill their cattle?

DANIEL Here is great deceit and great illusion; here the devil leadeth the ignorant people into foul errors, [C1^r] by which he draweth them headlong into many grievous sins.

° **closes**: enclosures.
° **burn … alive**: fire was regarded as a prophylactic against disease and witchcraft, although immolating animals smacked of pagan sacrifice.
° **puckerels**: imps (cf. Puck in *A Midsummer Night's Dream*).
° **M. B.**: identified in the text as a schoolmaster.
° **suck**: in a perversion of breastfeeding, witches were believed to feed their familiars through a third nipple (a protuberant mole).

M. B. Nay then, I see you are awry if you deny these things and say they be but illusions. They have been proved and proved again, even by the manifold confessions of the witches themselves. I am out of all doubt in these, and could in many particulars lay open what hath fallen out. I did dwell in a village within these five years where there was a man of good wealth; and suddenly, within ten days space, he had three kine died, his gelding worth ten pounds fell lame, he was himself taken with a great pain in his back, and a child of seven years old died. He sent to the [cunning] woman at R. H., and she said he was plagued by a witch, adding moreover that there were three women witches in that town and one man-witch: willing him to look whom he most suspected. He suspected one old woman and caused her to be carried before a Justice of Peace and examined. With much ado, at the last she confessed all. Which was this in effect: that she had three spirits: one like a cat, which she called Lightfoot; another like a Toad, which she called Lunch; the third like a Weasel, which she called Makeshift. This Lightfoot, she said, one mother Barley of W. sold her above sixteen years ago for an oven cake, and told her the Cat would do her good service; if she would, she might send her of her errand. This Cat was with her but a while, but the Weasel and the Toad came and offered their service. The Cat would kill kine; the Weasel would kill horses; the Toad would plague men in their bodies. She sent them all three (as she confessed) against this man. She was committed to the prison, and there she died before the Assizes. I could tell you of many such ... [C4ʳ] There was one old mother W. of great T. which had a spirit like a Weasel.° She was offended highly with one H. M. [and] home she went, and called forth her spirit, which lay in a pot of wool under her bed. She willed him to go plague the man: he required° what she would give him [if] he would kill H. M. She said she would give him a cock, which she did; and he went, and the man fell sick with a great pain in his belly, languished, and died. The witch was arraigned, [C4ᵛ] condemned, and hanged, and did confess all this ...

[E1ʳ] SAMUEL [Another witch confessed] she had a spirit in the likeness of a yellow dun cat. This cat came unto her, as she said, as she sat by her fire, when she was fallen out with a neighbour of hers, and wished that the vengeance of God might light upon him and his. The cat bade her not be afraid, she would do her no harm. She had served a dame five years in Kent, that was now dead, and if she would, she would be her servant. And whereas, said the Cat, such a man hath misused thee, if thou wilt I will plague him in his cattle. She sent the Cat; she killed three hogs and one Cow. The man, suspecting, burnt a pig alive; and, as she said, her cat would never go thither any more. Afterward she fell out with that M. she

---

° **Weasel**: Gifford relays this story from *The Examination and Confession of Certain Witches* (1566, B3v–B4r).

° **required**: asked.

sent her Cat, who told her that she had given him that [from] which he should never recover; and, indeed, the man died. Now do you not think the woman spake the truth in all this? Would the woman accuse herself falsely at her death? Did not the Cat become her servant? Did not she send her? Did she not plague and kill both man and beast? What should a man think of this?

ﻉﻉ ﻉ

Cooking, Feasting, Fasting, Healing

THOMAS DAWSON
from The Good Housewife's Jewel (1587)

These recipes (or receipts, as they were then called) are taken from a popular Elizabethan cookbook, reprinted over half a dozen times before 1650. The selections have been chosen to showcase the range of foods eaten in early modern England, many of which are not typically found in English markets or butchers today.
Source: *The Good Housewife's Jewel* (1587), A3ᵛ, 4ᵛ, 7ʳ-8ʳ, 10ᵛ, 14ʳ⁻ᵛ, 16ʳ, 18ᵛ, 20ᵛ–21ʳ.

To Boil Larks

Take sweetbread° and strain it into a pipkin;° and set it on the fire and put in a piece of Butter; and skim it as clean as you can and put in Spinach and Endive; and cut it a little, and so let it boil; and put in Pepper, Cloves, Mace, Cinnamon and Ginger, and a little Verjuice;° and when you serve them up, lay sops° in the dish …

[4ᵛ] To Boil a Neat's° Tongue

In primis, [boil] in fair° Water and salt, then peel it and cut it in the middle; and then boil it in red wine, and fill him full of cloves, and a little sugar; and then wash it with a little sweet broth, to do away the scent of the wine; and you must make a little red Muscadine with red wine and prunes boiled together; then strain it, and strain a little Mustard in a fine cloth together, and so serve it up …

[7ʳ] To Boil a Lamb's Head

Strain your broth into a pipkin and set it on the fire; and put in butter, and skim it as clean as you can; and put in your meat and put in endive, and [7ᵛ] cut it a little; and strain a little yeast, and put it into it, and currants and prunes; and put in all manner of spices, and so serve it upon sops …

[8ʳ] To Stew Calf's Feet

Take calf's feet fair blanched and cut them in the half; and when they be more than half-boiled, put to them great raisins, mutton broth, a

---

° **sweetbread**: pancreas or thymus gland, considered a delicacy in the Renaissance.
° **pipkin**: earthen pot. ° **Verjuice**: acidic juice of unripe fruit. ° **sops**: bread soaked with drippings or steeped in liquids.
° **Neat**: ox or cow. ° **fair**: clean.

369

little saffron, and sweet butter, pepper, sugar, and some sweet herbs finely minced. Boil calf's feet, sheep's feet, or lamb's feet with mutton broth, sweet herbs, Onions chopped fine, butter, and Pepper; and when they boil, take the yolk of an egg and strain it with verjuice; so serve it ...

[10ʳ] To Make Black Puddings°

Take great oatmeal and lay it in milk to steep; then take sheep's blood and put to it, and take Ox white° and mince into it; then take a few sweet herbs and two or three leek blades, and chop them very small, and put into it then the yolks of some eggs, and season it with cinnamon, ginger, cloves, mace, pepper and salt; and so fill them ...

[14ʳ] To Bake a Kid

Take your Kid and parboil him; and wash it in verjuice and saffron; and season it with pepper, salt, and a little mace; then lay it in your coffin° with sweet butter and the liquor it was seasoned in; and so bake it ...

[14ᵛ] To Bake Red Deer

Take a handful of thyme, a handful of rosemary, a handful of winter savoury, a handful of bay leaves, and a handful of fennel; and when your liquor seethes that you parboil your venison in, put in your herbs also and parboil your venison until it be half enough; then take it out and lay it upon a fair board that the water may run out from it; then take a knife and prick it full of holes, and while it is warm have a fair tray with vinegar therein, and so put your venison therein from morning until night, and every now and then turn it upside down; and then at night ... season it with cinnamon, ginger, nutmegs, pepper, and salt; and, when you have seasoned it, put it into your coffin, and put a good quantity of sweet butter into it; and then put it into the Oven at night when you go to bed, and in the morning draw it forth ...

[16ʳ] To Roast a Hare

You must not cut off her head, feet nor ears, but make a pudding in her belly; and put paper about her ears that they burn not; and when the Hare is roasted, you must take cinnamon and Ginger, and grated bread, and you

---

° **Black Puddings**: blood sausage.   ° **white**: milk.   ° **coffin**: pie-dish.

must make very sweet sauce; and you must put in barberries, and let them boil together ...

[18ᵛ] To Make a Veal Pie

Let your Veal boil a good while; and when it is boiled mince it by itself, and the white by itself, and season it with salt, pepper, cinnamon, ginger, sugar, cloves and mace; and you must have prunes, raisins, dates, and currants on the top ...

[20ᵛ] To Make a Tart that is a Courage° to a Man or Woman

Take two Quinces and two or three Burr roots, and a Potation; ... put them into a quart of wine and let them boil till they be tender; and put in an ounce of dates and ... draw them through a strainer, wine and all; and then put in the yolks of eight Eggs and the brains of three or four cock sparrows; [21ʳ] ... and seethe them all with Sugar, Cinnamon, Ginger, Cloves, and Mace; ... and so let it boil till it be something big.

❧ ❧ ❧

° **Courage**: aphrodisiac.

THOMAS NASHE
"Nature in England is But Plain Dame, But in Spain and Italy, Because They Have More Use of Her Than We, She is Dubbed a Lady" (1592)

In addition to defending plays against Puritan critics, Nashe also defended Lenten fasts. Here he lambastes his nation's reputation as voracious beef-eaters, and praises a Mediterranean diet.
Source: *Pierce Penniless, His Supplication to the Devil* (1592), E2ʳ⁻ᵛ.

It is not for nothing that other Countries, whom we upbraid with Drunkenness, call us bursten-bellied Gluttons; for we make our greedy paunches powdering tubs of beef, and eat more meat at one meal than the Spaniard or Italian in a month. Good thrifty men, they draw out a dinner with salads ... and make Madonna Nature their best Caterer. We must have our Tables furnished like Poulter's stalls, or as though we were to victual Noah's Ark again (wherein there was all sorts of living creatures that ever were), or else the good-wife will not [E2ᵛ] open her mouth to bid one welcome. A stranger that should come to one of our *Magnificoes'*° houses, when dinner were set on the board and he not yet seated, would think the goodman of the house were a Haberdasher of Wildfowl, or a Merchant-venturer of dainty meat that sells commodities of good cheer by the great,° and hath Factors in Arabia, Turkey, Egypt, and Barbary, to provide him of strange Birds, China Mustard, and odd patterns to make Custards by.

Lord, what a coil have we with this Course and that course, removing this dish higher, setting another lower, and taking away the third. A General might in less space remove his Camp than they stand disposing of their gluttony. And where to tends all this gourmandise, but to give sleep gross humours to feed on, to corrupt the brain, and make it unapt and unwieldy for anything?

The Roman Censors, if they lighted upon a fat corpulent man, they straightaway took away his horse, and constrained him to go afoot, positively concluding his carcass was so puffed up with gluttony or idleness. If we had such horse-takers amongst us, and that surfeit-swollen Churls who now ride on their foot-cloths might be constrained to carry their flesh budgets° from place to place on foot, the price of velvet and cloth would fall with their bellies ... Nay, we are such flesh-eating Saracens° that chaste fish may not content us, but we delight in the murder of innocent mutton, in the unpluming of poultry, and quartering of Calves and Oxen. It is horrible and detestable; no godly Fishmonger can digest it.

※ ※ ※

° ***Magnificoes***: great ones. To appreciate Nashe's critique, see the menus in Hannah Wooley's *Queen-like Closet* (354–6).
° **great**: gross.   ° **budgets**: pouches. See the theft of Falstaff's horse in *1 Henry IV*.
° **Saracens**: a derogatory term for Muslims, reputedly fond of beef.

JOHN HARINGTON
"Against Feasting" and "In Defence of Lent" (*c.* 1600)

Today, environmental advocates have begun to campaign for "Meatless Mondays." The idea would not have struck an inhabitant of Tudor England as odd. In early modern Europe, Christian communities refrained from eating beef, chicken, or pork on Fridays, Saturdays, the twelve Ember Days, and, most importantly, for the forty days of Lent. Since meat is scarce in late winter and early spring, and many animals breed during this time, the practice was ecologically attuned to the rhythms of agrarian life. After the Reformation, however, many Puritans began to brazenly defy the custom, so that Elizabeth and James had to issue frequent proclamations to punish transgressors (see Appendix A). In 1563, a bill was passed with the support of Lord Burghley to make Wednesday a "fish day" as well, and remained on the books for two decades. Rather than appeal to religious doctrine, the edict justifies the practice as in accordance with the "Law of Nature." In these verses modelled on the Roman satirist Juvenal, Harington censures the gluttony of the elite, and defends Lenten fasting with scriptural precedents.

Source: *The Epigrams* (1618), E5ʳ, G7ʳ⁻ᵛ.

"Against Feasting"

Kind Marcus me to supper lately bade,
And to declare how well to us he wishes,
The room was strewed with Roses not with Rushes,
And all the cheer was got that could be had.
Now in the midst of all our dainty dishes,
"Methinks," said he to me, "you look but sad."
"Alas," said I, "'tis to see thee so mad,
To spoil the sky of Fowls, the sea of Fishes,
The land of Beasts, and be at so much cost,
For that which in one hour will all be lost.   10
That entertainment that makes me most glad,
Is not the store of stewed, boiled, baked, or roast,
But sweet discourse, mean fare, and then believe me,
To make to thee like cheer shall never grieve me."

"In Defence of Lent"

Our belly gods dispraise the Lenten fast,
And blame the lingering days and tedious time,
And swear this abstinence too long doth last,
Whose folly I refute in this my rhyme:
Methusalem° nine hundred years was fed
With naught but herbs and berries of the field;
John the Baptist thirty years his life had led
With locusts and wild honey woods did yield;
He that the Israelites from Egypt brought,
Where they in slavish thraldom long did dwell;°   10
He whom to heav'n the fi'ry Chariot wrought;°
Yea, Christ himself (that saves us all from hell)
As those three° holy Scriptures do repeat,
In forty days did neither drink nor eat.
Why then should we against this Law repine,
That are permitted ev'ry kind of Fish?
Are not forbid the taste of costly Wine?
Are not debarred of many a dainty dish:
Both Sugar, Ginger, Pepper, Cloves, and Mace,
And Cinnamon and Spice of ev'ry kind,   20

° **Methusalem**: see Genesis 5:27.   ° **He … dwell**: Moses.   ° **He … wrought**: Elijah.
° **three**: the evangelists Mathew, Mark, and Luke tell of Christ's fast. These three, as] 1618.

And Raisins, Figs, and Almonds in like case,
To please the taste and satisfy the mind?
And yet, forsooth, we think we shall be marred
If we from flesh but forty days be barred.

ᴈᴇ ᴈᴇ ᴈᴇ

THOMAS MIDDLETON
from A Chaste Maid in Cheapside (*c.* 1613)

In this Jacobean city comedy, Middleton depicts a flourishing black-market trade in meat during Lent. Rather than endorse the Crown's policy, the staunch Protestant Middleton begrudges the restriction and satirizes the corrupt officials who seek to confiscate contraband meat to sell or eat it themselves.
Source: *A Chaste Maid in Cheapside* (1630), 21–6.

2.2

ALLWIT Ha, how now? What are these that stand so close
At the Street corner, pricking up their Ears
And snuffing up their Noses like rich men's Dogs
When the first Course goes in? By the mass, Promoters!°
'Tis so, I hold my life; and planted there
To arrest the dead Corpses of poor Calves and Sheep,
Like ravenous Creditors that will not suffer
The Bodies of their poor departed Debtors
To go to th'grave but e'en in Death to vex
And stay the Corpse with Bills of Middlesex.°
This Lent will fat the whoresons up with Sweetbreads,°
And lard their whores with Lamb-stones;° what their golls°
Can clutch goes presently to their Molls and Dolls.°
The Bawds will be so fat with what they earn,
Their Chins will hang like Udders by Easter-eve,
And being stroked will give the Milk of Witches.°
How did the Mongrels hear my wife lies in?°
  Well, I may baffle° 'em gallantly. [*To them*] By your favour, Gentlemen,
I am a stranger both unto the City and to her carnal strictness.
FIRST PROMOTER Good; your will, sir?
ALLWIT Pray, tell me where one dwells that kills this Lent?
FIRST PROMOTER How, kills? [*To Second Promoter*] Come hither, Dick.
  A Bird, a Bird!°

° **Promoters**: informers. The oath links the fast with Catholicism.
° **Bills of Middlesex**: legal pretexts.   ° **Sweetbreads**: delicacy made of animal glands.
° **stones**: testicles. Like the pancreas, regarded as an aphrodisiac.   ° **golls**: hands.
° **Molls ... Dolls**: prostitutes.
° **Milk ... Witches**: witches were believed to possess a third nipple (a mole) with which they suckled
  their familiar spirits.
° **lies in**: is pregnant.
° **baffle**: trick, but with more precise meaning of throw a hound off the scent.   ° **Bird**: easy prey.

SECOND PROMOTER What is't that you would have?

ALLWIT Faith, any Flesh; but I long especially for Veal and Green-sauce.°

SECOND PROMOTER [*Aside*] Green Goose,° you shall be sauced.°

ALLWIT I have a scornful stomach, no Fish will be admitted.

FIRST PROMOTER Not this Lent, Sir?

ALLWIT What cares Colon here for Lent?

FIRST PROMOTER You say well, Sir. Good reason that the Colon of a Gentleman, as you were lately pleased to term your worship, Sir, should be fulfilled with answerable food, to sharpen Blood, delight Health, and tickle Nature. Were you directed hither to this Street, Sir?

ALLWIT That I was, aye, marry.

SECOND PROMOTER And the Butcher, belike, should kill and sell close in some upper Room?

ALLWIT Some Apple-loft, as I take it, or Coal-house; I know not which, i'faith.

SECOND PROMOTER Either will serve. [*To First Promoter*] This Butcher shall kiss Newgate° 'less he turn up the Bottom of the Pocket of his Apron. [*To Allwit*] You go to seek him?

ALLWIT Where you shall not find him: I'll buy and walk by your Noses with my Flesh, Sheep-biting Mongrels! Hand-basket Freebooters!° My Wife lies in. A *foutre*° for Promoters!   *Exit.*

FIRST PROMOTER That shall not serve your turn! What a Rogue's this! How cunningly he came over us.

> *Enter a* Man *with Meat in a Basket*

SECOND PROMOTER Hush't, stand close!

MAN [*Aside*] I have 'scaped well thus far; they say the Knaves are wondrous hot and busy.

FIRST PROMOTER By your leave, Sir, we must see what you have under your Cloak there.

MAN Have? I have nothing.

FIRST PROMOTER No? Do you tell us that? What makes this lump stick out then? We must see, Sir.

MAN What will you see, Sir? A pair of Sheets and two of my Wife's foul Smocks going to the Washers?

SECOND PROMOTER Oh, we love that sight well! You cannot please us better. [*He grabs the meat out of the basket*] What, do you gull us? Call you these Shirts and Smocks?

MAN Now, a Pox choke you! You have cozened me and five of my Wife's kindred of a good Dinner. We must make it up now with Herrings and Milk-pottage.

FIRST PROMOTER 'Tis all Veal.

SECOND PROMOTER All Veal? Pox, the worse luck! I promised faithfully to send this morning a fat quarter of Lamb to a kind Gentlewoman in Turnbull Street° that longs; and how I'm crossed!

° **Green-sauce**: made of herbs, vinegar, and sugar.
° **Green Goose**: naïve fool.   ° **sauced**: swindled, forced to pay up.
° **Newgate**: notorious London prison.   ° **Freebooters**: pirates.
° *foutre*: fuck (accompanied by obscene gesture).   ° **Turnbull Street**: infamous for its prostitutes.

FIRST PROMOTER Let's share this, and see what hap comes next then.
                    Enter another with a Basket
SECOND PROMOTER Agreed. Stand close again: another booty. What's he?
FIRST PROMOTER Sir, by your favour.
SECOND MAN Meaning me, Sir?
FIRST PROMOTER Good Master Oliver? Cry thee mercy, i'faith! What
    hast thou there?
SECOND MAN A Rack of Mutton, Sir, and half a Lamb; you know my
    Mistress' diet.
FIRST PROMOTER Go, go, we see thee not; away, keep close!
[*To Second Promoter*] Heart, let him pass! Thou'lt never have the wit to
    know our benefactors!   [*Exit*].
SECOND PROMOTER I have forgot him.
FIRST PROMOTER 'Tis Master Beggarland's man, the wealthy Merchant
    that is in fee with us.
SECOND PROMOTER Now I have a feeling of him.
FIRST PROMOTER You know he purchased the whole Lent together,
    gave us ten groats apiece on Ash Wednesday.
SECOND PROMOTER True, true.
Enter a Wench *with a Basket, and a Child in it under a Loin of Mutton*
FIRST PROMOTER A Wench.
SECOND PROMOTER Why, then, stand close indeed.
WENCH [*Aside*] Women have need of wit if they'll shift° here,
And she that hath wit may shift anywhere.
FIRST PROMOTER Look, look! Poor Fool, she has left the Rump uncov-
    ered too, more to betray her. This is like a Murd'rer that will outface
    the deed with a bloody Band.°
SECOND PROMOTER What time of year is't, Sister?
WENCH O, sweet gentlemen, I am a poor Servant. Let me go.
FIRST PROMOTER You shall, Wench, but this must stay with us.
WENCH O, you undo me, Sir! 'Tis for a wealthy Gentlewoman that
    takes Physic, Sir. The Doctor does allow my Mistress Mutton. O, as
    you tender the dear life of a Gentlewoman, I'll bring my Master to you;
    he shall show you a true authority° from the higher powers. And I'll
    run every foot.
SECOND PROMOTER Well, leave your Basket, then, and run and spare not.
WENCH Will you swear then to me to keep it till I come?
FIRST PROMOTER Now by this light, I will.
WENCH What say you, Gentleman?
SECOND PROMOTER [*To First Promoter*] What a strange Wench 'tis! [*To
    Wench*] Would we might perish else.
WENCH Nay then, I run, Sir.   *Exit.*
FIRST PROMOTER And ne'er return I hope.
SECOND PROMOTER A politic Baggage!° She makes us swear to keep it.
    I prithee look what market she hath made.

° **shift**: make a living.
° **Band**: collar or cuff.
° **authority**: note granting permission to eat meat during Lent.
° **politic Baggage**: crafty whore.

FIRST PROMOTER *Imprimis,*° a good fat Loin of Mutton. What comes next under this Cloth? Now for a quarter of Lamb.

SECOND PROMOTER Now for a Shoulder of Mutton.

FIRST PROMOTER Done!°

SECOND PROMOTER Why done, Sir!

FIRST PROMOTER By the mass, I feel I have lost. 'Tis of more weight, i'faith.

SECOND PROMOTER Some Loin of Veal?

FIRST PROMOTER No, faith, here's a Lamb's Head, I felt that plainly. Why, I'll yet win my wager. [*He takes out the baby*]

SECOND PROMOTER Ha?

FIRST PROMOTER 'Swounds, what's here?

SECOND PROMOTER A Child!

FIRST PROMOTER A Pox of all dissembling cunning Whores!

SECOND PROMOTER Here's an unlucky Breakfast!

FIRST PROMOTER What shall 's do?

SECOND PROMOTER The Quean° made us swear to keep it too.

FIRST PROMOTER We might leave it else.

SECOND PROMOTER Villainous strange! Life, had she none to gull but poor Promoters that watch hard for a living?

FIRST PROMOTER Half our gettings must run in Sugar-sops and Nurses' wages now, besides many a pound of Soap and Tallow; we have need to get Loins of Mutton still, to save Suet to change for Candles.

SECOND PROMOTER Nothing mads me but this was a Lamb's head with you! You felt it! She has made Calves' heads° of us.

FIRST PROMOTER Prithee, no more on't. There's time yet to get it up; it is not come to Mid-Lent Sunday yet.

SECOND PROMOTER I'll watch no more today.

FIRST PROMOTER Faith, nor I neither.

SECOND PROMOTER Why, then, I'll make a motion.

FIRST PROMOTER Well, what is't?

SECOND PROMOTER Let's e'en go to the Chequer at Queenhithe,° and roast the Loin of Mutton till young Flood;° then send the child to Brentford.°   [*Exeunt.*]

❧ ❧ ❧

° ***Imprimis****:* first of all. The woman's ruse recalls a famous episode in *The Second Shepherds' Play.*
° **Done***:* a bet.   ° **Quean***:* whore.   ° **Calves' heads***:* fools.
° **Chequer ... Queenhithe***:* pub near the Thames, just south of St Paul's Cathedral.
° **young Flood***:* rising tide.   ° **Brentford***:* suburb of London with an unsavoury reputation.

THOMAS MOFFETT
"Of Fatting of Meats" (1655)

Although one might presume that battery farming originated with modern agri-business, livestock were kept in cramped pens and subjected to inhumane methods of fattening even in Roman times. By the seventeenth century some

physicians had begun to question these cruel practices on health if not humanitarian grounds.
Source: *Health's Improvement* (1655), 42–4.

Lean meat as it is unwholesome so it seemed also unsavoury in ancient times; insomuch that Q. Curtius, being a server at Caesar's table, seeing a dish of lean birds to be set at the table was not afraid to hurl them out at the window. Also the priests of Israel (yea, the Heathen Priests also of Rome and Egypt) touched no lean flesh because it is imperfect till it be fat, fitter to feed hawks and vultures than … to be eaten of men … Hereupon came trial how to fatten flesh and fish (yea, snails and tortoises, as Macrobius writeth) by feeding them with filling and forced meats, casting … livers and garbage into fishponds … Hence also came it that swine were fattened with whey and figs … Amongst the Romans it was a question who first taught the art of fattening geese … Cranes and swans were fattened in Rome with ox blood, milk, oatmeal, barley, curds, and chalk, mingled (to use Plutarch's° [43] phrase) into a "monstrous meat," wherewithal they were crammed in dark places, or else their eyes were stitched up, by which means their flesh proved both tenderer and sweeter, whiter and (as it is supposed) far wholesomer. Hens, capons, cockerels, and finches° were fattened by them of Delia° with bread steeped in milk, and feeding in a dark and narrow place, that want of scope and light might cause them to sleep and sit much, which of itself procureth fatness …

But here a question may be moved: whether this penning up of birds, and want of exercise, and depriving them of light, and cramming them so often with strange meat, makes not their flesh as unwholesome to us as well as fat?° To which I answer: that to cram Capons or any birds and to deprive them of all light is ill for them and us too. For though their body be puffed up, yet their flesh is not natural and wholesome; witness their small discoloured and rotten livers, whereas Hens and Capons feeding themselves in open and clean place with good corn have large, ruddy, and firm livers: so great is the diversity betwixt a crammed, I may say, a strangled and captive Capon, and betwixt a gentleman capon feeding himself fat without art. Wherefore the best fattening of all fowl is first to feed them with good meat (for like food, [44] like flesh). Secondly to give it them not continually, as crammers do, forcing one gobbet after another till they be fully gorged, but as often as they themselves desire it, that nature be not urged above her strength; not in a coop or close room, for then the air and themselves will smell of their own dung, but in a clean house,

---

° **Plutarch**: Roman historian and philosopher. An English translation of his essay advocating vegetarianism, "Whether it Be Lawful to Eat Flesh or No," was published in 1603.
° **finches**: such as the Ortolan bunting, which is still consumed, bones and all, as a delicacy in France.
° **Delia**: Delos, a Greek island.   ° **fat**: nourishing.

spacious enough for their little exercise; not in a dark place, or stitching up their eyes, for that will cause them to be timorous or ever sleepy, both of which are enemies to their bodies and consequently to ours. For every man knows that fear marreth concoction, and sleepiness, bereaving us of exercise, hindereth digestion. Yea, young Pigeons whilst they are in the nest (be they never so fat) are reckoned but an unwholesome meat, but when they follow and fly a little after the dam then are they of great and good nourishment. The like may be said of the fatting of beasts. For they are not to be styed or stalled so close they cannot stir, but to have sufficient room for to walk in, as well to feed in, that they may be wholesome as well as fat, and not corrupt our bodies with their own corruption. So likewise fish kept in great ponds where they may rove at pleasure are better than such as be mewed in a narrow and shallow ditch, which not only we shall find by inward digestion, but also by outward tasting. Yea, look what difference there is betwixt tame and wild Conies, betwixt Deer fed by hand and Deer fattening themselves in the Chase and Copses, the like shall you perceive betwixt forced fatness and fatness gotten by natural and good diet.

ᘒᘕ ᘒᘕ ᘒᘕ

THOMAS TRYON

"The Voice of the Dumb, or the Complaints of the Creatures, Expostulating with Man, Touching the Cruel Usages they Suffer from Him" (1691)

A prolific author of advice books on health, housewifery, education, and religion, Thomas Tryon was also the first outspoken vegetarian in English history. He first renounced meat in 1657 (and for a brief period dairy products as well) and later set forth his views in a *Treatise on Cleanness in Meats and Drinks* (1682). He restates them vehemently in his *Way to Health*, a popular dietary and lifestyle manual that went through several editions, converting Benjamin Franklin to vegetarianism and inspiring Percy Shelley's *Vindication of a Natural Diet*. Influenced by Hinduism, Pythagoreanism, Western mysticism, and natural philosophy, Tryon objects to carnivorism on spiritual grounds (it provokes violence and sloth), for medicinal reasons (those with a meat-heavy diet are "digging their graves with their own teeth," 1688, 3), and for political motives (it offers a warrant for domination). It would be only a mild exaggeration to claim that Tryon views meat-eating as the root of all evil; he even sketches a vegetarian utopia in which "all oppression, violence, controversies, and killing would cease" (333). Citing Genesis 1:29, Tryon argues that humans are not carnivorous by nature, but that custom has blunted our instinctive disgust in the same way that cannibals "will most savourly gnaw a shoulder of a man, a breast of a woman, or the haunches of a child, and think it altogether as sweet and wholesome as my Lord does his venison or my Lady her partridge" (256). The first extract below presents a stomach-turning peek inside an early modern shambles. In subsequent pages, Tryon gives a voice to animals to protest their inhumane treatment. He even makes what Marjorie Spiegel calls the "dreaded comparison" between race-based and species-based slavery (Tryon also wrote abolitionist tracts from the perspective of slaves on sugar plantations, which he witnessed on a trip to Barbados). Although his philosophy is very much shaped by the political and religious fervour of his age, his denunciation of human barbarism anticipates that of Swift's Houyhnhnms, and he can be regarded as a forerunner of the eighteenth-century "man of feeling," who helped lay the groundwork for animal rights advocacy.

Source: *The Way to Health* (1691), 330, 367–73.

Is there any comparison to be made between an Herb Market and a Flesh Market? In one ... a thousand pieces of the dead Carcasses of various Creatures lie stinking, the Channels running with Blood, and all the places full of Excrements, Ordure, Garbage, Grease, and Filthiness, sending forth dismal, poisonous Scents, enough to corrupt the very Air. In the other, you have delicate Fruits of most excellent tastes, wholesome Medicinal Herbs, savoury Grains, and most beautiful, fragrant Flowers, whose various Scents, Colours, etc., make at once a Banquet to all the Senses, and nourish the purer Spirits, and refresh the very Souls of such who pass through them, and perfume all the circumambient Air with redolent Exhalations. This was the Place and Food ordained for Mankind in the beginning.° The Lord planted a Garden for him, replenished with all manner of ravishing Fruits and Herbs. There was no Flesh-Markets nor Shambles talked of in the primitive times, but "every green Herb, Fruit, and Seed shall be for Food to Man," saith the Creator; which if it had been still observed Man had not contracted so many Diseases in his Body and cruel Vices in his Soul by making his Throat an open Sepulchre wherein to entomb the dead Bodies of Beasts. Nor should the noble Image of the Deity have been thus shamefully defiled with Brutalities.

> Creatures of Sea and Land we slay,
> And in our Maws do bury;
> And worse by half than Beasts of Prey,
> Are at their Fun'rals merry.
> How shall they but Bestial grow,
> That thus to feed on Beasts are willing?
> Or why should they a long Life know,
> Who daily practise KILLING? ...

[367] The Tyranny of Man over his Fellow-Creatures (the Root of which we have discovered in the foregoing Chapters) leads us a little more nearly to consider the sad state and condition of those inferior Animals under his savage Butcheries, and how ungrateful, as well as cruel, he is towards them. For as most of them contribute to his well-being, either by bringing him in Food (as Milk, Honey, Butter, Cheese, Eggs, etc.), or Raiment (as

---

° **beginning**: in Eden. Tryon subsequently cites Genesis 1:29.

Wool, Furs, Skins), or Ease (as the Horse to carry him, the Ox to draw for him, and the like, too tedious to enumerate); so is there scarce any of them upon whom he does not extend his Rage. And generally the more harmless and useful they are, the more barbarously he deals with them; so that as their Groans ascend up to Heaven, so their Cries fill the Earth. And methinks their inarticulate Lamentations should reach to the Ears of our Minds, and respectively vent their several Dolours in some such kind of Expostulations.

[368] The Complaint of the Cows and Oxen

Cruel and hard-hearted Man! Wert thou constituted our great Creator's Deputy and Viceroy of this Universe of sublunary Beings that thou shouldst play the Tyrant and the Epicure, and domineer with rigour over all the rest of its Inhabitants? Dost thou in any kind imitate thy Sovereign, from whom thou dost derive thy Title? Is not he good and bountiful and merciful to all the Works of his Hands, and the Preserver of the whole Creation? And darest thou take upon thee to be a Destroyer, a Killer, and daily Practiser of Cruelty? Knowest thou not that we inferior Creatures were not given thee as a Prey, that thou might'st dispose of us absolutely at thy lustful and irregular pleasure, but entrusted to thy Conduct and Oversight to be subservient unto thee, to minister to thy Necessities, to employ the Faculties of thy Soul with a devout Contemplation on our numberless Numbers, various Shapes, distinct and wonderful Natures, etc., and thereby ravish thee with Thoughts of Jehovah's infinite Wisdom,° Power, and Goodness, that hath formed, governeth, and conserveth so many Millions of wonderful Beings? And wilt thou, instead of this noble, serene, and quiet study of worthy Faculties so divine as thou art endowed with, forget thy Duty, thy Office, and all Obligations, as to be the first that disturbs this blessed Harmony, and by thy Sin and Folly and Madness set all the Creation into a Tumult and a Combustion, and exercise thy fierce Passions upon us lower Graduates in this mighty Academy, and worry, and kill, and devour us?

We are God's Creatures, and by his divine Power have our subsistence; he hath formed us, and given us Shapes suitable to our inward Natures ... [369] With patience we endure the Summer's scorching Heat and the Winter's Snow. We wear our own Cloths, even those natural Coverings bestowed upon us as the Livery of our Maker. We are not fond of Variety, when one suit answers all the Ends of Nature as well or better. Much less are we so vain to glory in our Shame, be proud of that which should reproach us with Sin, and value ourselves because we have got other Creatures' Excrements° upon our backs. Amongst us there are no quarrels

° **Wisdom**: see similar arguments advanced by John Ray in Part I, p. 84.
° **Excrements**: outgrowths.

about Gentility. Nor do we esteem or despise one another because our Coats are of different colours and our Horns not all of a length. We have all our Food in common and never grutch or grumble that one eats more or daintier than the other. We call nothing our own but what is in our mouths. We all drink out of one Cup ... The Stall and the Crib serve us as well as Palaces, and all our delight is to behold the pleasant green Fields, sprouting up their delicious Herbs and Grass into our Mouths, and view the gliding Streams or murmuring Fountains, ready to supply our Thirst.

We observe our Times and Seasons of Generation ... Nor are we tempted with Beauty, Honour, Riches, or any other thing to act contrary to the Law of Nature. [370] That troublesome Passion called Love, as it is a fond, foolish Excess of Desire or Dotage, over us has no power. Yet we love and are tender of our little Ones till they can provide for themselves ... We raise no Wars or Tumults nor contrive treacherous Plots and Sham-Plots against each other or against Men. We have no Weapons but such as God and Nature have endued us with for our particular defence. And if at any time we do fight (for which Man must justly bear the fault; for if he had not transgressed the Divine Law we never had had any such inclination at all), our Battles are sudden and not premeditated Murders ... But though we live thus innocently in the obedience to God's Law in Nature, and have not done anything whereby to awaken his Wrath or draw down Judgements on ourselves, yet we suffer many and great Miseries, Oppressions, and Tyranny, which comes to pass through the transgression and fall of our Prince and Governor (viz. Man). He has violated the divine Law in Nature, and is become disobedient, whereby he hath opened the Floodgates of Wrath and enthralled himself in many Miseries, and inured himself to all kinds of unjust Cruelties, and makes us groan under heavy Burdens; and all we can do is too little to give him satisfaction.

We COWS give him our pleasant Milk, which is not only a most Sovereign Food of itself, but being altered and variously dressed makes a great number of delicate and wholesome Dishes; but this will not content them. For after we have for several years twice a day yielded them plentiful Meals of Milk, and every year (for the most part) a Calf, which they have rended away from us before its time, to our great affliction (for 'tis unnatural to take away any Creature's young before [371] it can provide for itself); when they have thus bereaved us of the Fruit of our Wombs, and killed and eaten them, yet sometimes through Covetousness, notwithstanding all these Benefits, they will half starve us; and if it chance that any one of us do not give good store of Milk and bring them forth as many Calves as their Avarice expects, then our cruel Egyptian° Masters cry, "Hang her! Knock her o'th' head! What is she good for?" Counting nothing good but what brings in great profit to satisfy their Lusts. And when thus through many

---

° **Egyptian**: Tryon makes frequent comparisons between human enslavement of animals and the Egyptian enslavement of the Jews.

Miseries we have sustained from them diverse Years, then what Reward do they give us? Why, truly, they will put us into a good Pasture, and then we think this is pure kindness and begin to forget our former Injuries. But as soon as we have gathered our Flesh and begin to be plump and fat, then they swap us away for a little Money to the Butcher, and he knocks us o'th' Head, and cuts our Throats, and our kind Masters perhaps devour a piece of us; and if our Flesh prove not so delicate as they would have it, which is their fault, then they curse us again when we are in their Bellies ...

[372] Thus all of us live in great Slavery most part of our Lives, far below that generous Liberty wherein our great and good Creator had estated us by his grand Charter of Nature. And at last we die, both untimely and unwillingly, many of us cut off in Youth or in the prime of our strength to please the Palates of extravagant People, whose Lusts nothing but Flesh can satisfy. Have we not then just reason, O Man! to complain of thy injustice? Have we not cause to keep back and restrain those daily renewed Fountains of liquid Crystal wherewith we sustain you, to shake off your Yokes, and, inspired with Rage and Revenge, tear you to pieces with our Horns? Yet we do none of these, but continue our drudging Services and perpetual Tribute to the Milk pail, and submit ourselves to your Knives and your Axes. And yet neither your own Cruelties nor our submissive Patience can mollify you into greater Moderation. And can we choose then but send up our Complaints [373] against you in a silent eloquence to Heaven? And can you expect any thence in return but Showers of Judgements upon your Heads, since you have thus presumptuously opened the Fountains of Wrath, and brought in War and Destruction upon us?

❦ ❦ ❦

JOHN FLETCHER
"Enter Clorin the Shepherdess, sorting of herbs and telling the natures of them" (1610)

Herbal medicine was widely practised in Renaissance England, and perfectly acceptable as long as it was intended to heal rather than harm. With the development of male-dominated medical science, however, women who dispensed traditional herbal remedies could be accused of incompetence or, worse, witchcraft. No wonder Clorin, who enters with the invocation "Hail, holy earth," is quick to dissociate herself from the enchantress Medea and instead insist on the salutary powers latent in nature. The speech of Fletcher's eponymous shepherdess thus offers a counterpoint to Oberon's love potion and the demonic cookery of the weird sisters in *Macbeth*.

Source: *The Faithful Shepherdess* (1610), D1^{r-v}.

2.I

Now let me know what my best Art hath done,
Helped by the great power of the virtuous moon,
In her full light; O, you sons of earth,
You only brood, unto whose happy birth
Virtue was given, holding more of nature
40   Than man, her first-born and most perfect creature,
Let me adore you! You that only can
Help or kill nature, drawing out that span
Of life and breath, even to the end of time.
You that these hands did crop long before prime
Of day, give me your names, and next your hidden power.
This is the Clote,° bearing a yellow flower,
And this black Horehound; both are very good
For sheep or shepherd, bitten by a wood°
Dog's venomed tooth. These Rhamnus° branches are,
50   Which stuck in entries, or about the bar
That holds the door fast, kill all the enchantments, charms,
Were they Medea's verses that do harm
To men or cattle. These for frenzy be
A speedy and a sovereign remedy:
The bitter Wormwood, Sage, and Marigold;
Such sympathy with man's good they do hold.
This Tormentil, whose virtue is to part
All deadly killing poison from the heart;
And here Narcissus root, for swellings best;
60   Yellow Lysimachus,° to give sweet rest
To the faint shepherd, killing where it comes
All busy gnats, and every fly that hums.
For leprosy, Darnel and Celandine,
With Calamint, whose virtues do refine
The blood of Man, making it free and fair
As the first hour it breathed, or the best air.
Here, other two, but your rebellious use
Is not for me, whose goodness is abuse;
Therefore, foul Standergrass,° from me and mine
70   I banish thee, with lustful Turpentine.°
You that entice the veins and stir the heat
To civil mutiny, scaling the seat
Our reason moves in, and deluding it
With dreams and wanton fancies, till the fit
Of burning lust be quenched by appetite,
Robbing the soul of blessedness and light.
And thou, light Vervain,° too, thou must go after,
Provoking easy souls to mirth and laughter.
No more shall I dip thee in water now,

° **Clote**: probably yellow dock.   ° **wood**: mad.   ° **Rhamnus**: buckthorn.
° **Lysimachus**: loosestrife.
° **Standergrass**: early purple orchid (or long-purple), considered an aphrodisiac because of its phallic
    shape.
° **Turpentine**: terebinth.   ° **Vervain**: verbena.

And sprinkle every post and every bough 80
With thy well-pleasing juice, to make the grooms
Swell with high mirth, with joy all the rooms.

ک‍ ک‍ ک‍

ALETHEIA TALBOT
from Natura Exenterata (1655)

In the seventeenth century, recipe books that had predominantly circulated in manuscript began to appear in print. Judging by the titles of works such as *A Closet for
Ladies* (1608) and *The Ladies Cabinet Opened* (1639), many were being marketed to
a growing female readership. Since uneducated women who dabbled in medicine
might be branded witches, it was mainly women from the upper ranks of society,
such as Lady Talbot, the Countess of Arundel, who dared publish their remedies.
Many of Talbot's recipes, however, are attributed to others (her preface lists over
100 people who either contributed recipes or provided testimonials, forty of them
women), offering further evidence of how medicine was a collective endeavour
produced by networks rather than individuals. The selections have been chosen to
illustrate a range of common ailments in the early modern period and the arsenal
of herbs and animal parts used to treat them. Although twenty-first-century readers
may find some of the remedies disgusting, that disgust is perhaps an index of how
much further removed we are from the natural world. In contrast to the ecofemi-
nine stereotype that women are innately more compassionate and environmentally
sensitive, Talbot's recipes substantiate DiMeo and Laroche's claim that "women
were writing, collecting, and circulating medical recipes that required them to kill
(and sometimes torture) animals" (94). Hence a sinister undertone emanates from
Talbot's title, which could be translated "Nature Disembowelled."
Source: *Natura Exenterata* (1655), 4, 8, 14, 16, 68, 72, 104, 108, 110, 121–2, 174, 183,
187, 189, 201, 206, 208, 212, 223, 225, 267, 278.

[4] To Make the Green Ointment,° by Wilson's Wife of London

Take Orpine,° Columbine, the herb Mercury, Ivy, the tender crops of red
Brambles, Ribwort, Hounds-tongue, Plantain, Water-betony, Mallows,
Valerian, Rose campions, wild Tansy, Cinquefoil: of each one handful;
Wormwood, four little branches, or half an handful; half an handful of
Featherfew, and as much of Smallage;° of Rue, three little crops; Daisy
roots, leaves of Colts-foot, Privet, Sage, Hart's-tongue, Honeysuckle
leaves and flowers, Tornsorve,° Horehound, Garden-betony, Camomile,

---

° **Green ointment**: a generic name for salves used to treat a wide variety of minor complaints such
  as itches, rashes, and aches. This receipt thus offers a representative list of plants believed to
  possess healing properties.
° **Orpine**: stonecrop.   ° **Smallage**: wild celery.   ° **Tornsorve**: tutsan?

Ale-hoof, Nightshade, Tansy, Saint John's-wort and Dill: of each a good handful; of Hemlocks, whereof the stalks be speckled, half an handful. All these being clean, washed, and dried in a cloth, then shred them small and beat them small in a stone mortar. Then take four pound of clarified butter and boil your herbs therein till it wax green, and so strain it through a coarse canvas. Then put to it two ounces of Turpentine washed, and half a pound of wax clarified, one ounce of honey, one ounce of Rosin molten, and set all this on the fire a Pater Noster-while.° Then take it off, and pour it into a vessel of cold water; and when it is cold, beat it from the water, and put it into boxes, and so use it. This is a most excellent Ointment or Salve for any kind of swelling, sore, or green° wound …

[8] A Salve for the Piles or Haemorrhoids

Take the blowing of one's nose, and put it on a cloth, and lay to the place …

[14] For the Cancer in a Woman's Pap

Take Goose dung and Celandine, and bray° them together, and lay them to the sore Pap, and it will cleanse the Cancer, kill the worm,° and heal the sore …

[16] A Salve or Plaster to Stanch Blood, by Mrs. Scudamore.

Take *Bursa pastoris*, called Shepherd's purse; the dung of a Mare, not green, but dry; Spider-webs; [and] soot of a chimney tempered with whites of Eggs. Any Medicine laid to a vein or cut must lie three days without removing if you will stop the blood kindly° …

[68] A Medicine for the Toothache

Take a live Mole, and put him in a brass pot, and there let him die. Then cut him asunder and take out the guts, and dry the blood with a cloth; then cut him in quarters, and hang him on a thread drying by the fireside. When you would use it, lay the fleshy side of it with bladders of Saffron with a cloth to your sore. Take the hearts of six Moles, put them upon a new tile-stone made red hot, then lay these hearts upon this stone until they be burnt to coals. Then beat them into powder …

° **Paster Noster-while**: length of time to say the Our Father prayer. An idiomatic phrase, but suggestive of lingering pre-Reformation beliefs that prayer could improve the efficacy of medicine.
° **green**: fresh.   ° **bray**: crush.   ° **worm**: tumor.   ° **kindly**: completely

[72] For the Yellow Jaundice

Take worms, wash off the earth, and then dry them upon a tile. Then beat them into a powder, mix it with Turmeric and Saffron, of each a little quantity, and put them into two or three spoonfuls of drink: which drink morning and evening. It will add something to the speedy recovery if you slit a warm pigeon, and lay it to the soles of the feet …

[104] A Medicine to Stanch Blood

Take the dung of a hog hot, and apply it to the wound, and it will stanch the bleeding presently …

[108] A Medicine against Melancholy

Take the bone° in a Hart's heart beaten into powder and drink it in white wine …

[110] To Make Oil of Swallows,° Good for all Manner of Aches

Take ten or twelve young Swallows ready to fly, stamp them in a stone Mortar with their feathers and guts together, with Lavender-cotton, Balm, Spearmint, red Sage, Camomile, Wild Strawberry leaves, and wild Thyme: of each a handful. But let these herbs lie one day unwashed after they be gathered, and then stamp them all together with the Swallows till no feather be left whole. Put thereto a good quantity of May-butter or fresh butter, and let all stand one night in the Mortar. The next day boil all these together very softly three quarters of an hour or a whole hour; then strain it through a clean linen cloth into a clean Vessel, and keep it for your use.

[121] An Excellent Medicine for a Plague Sore

Take a Cock Pullet,° Chicken, or Pigeon, and pluck off the feathers of the tail and rump; then lay the bare of the pullet to the sore, and the pullet will gape and [122] and labour for life, and at the length die. And continue [to] lay other pullets as long as any die; for when the poison is drawn out, the

---

° **bone**: actually mineralized tissue.
° **Swallows**: this is one of three recipes in Talbot's book made from pulped baby swallows. An earlier version of it appears in Dawson's *Housewife's Jewel* (1587, 50r). Several of them mention that the birds must not touch the ground and should be mashed while still alive. For more on these recipes, see DiMeo and Laroche.
° **Pullet**: male chicken. This is one of two recipes Talbot records to cure plague by plucking live chickens to death and applying their cloaca to the sores (80–1).

chicken that is laid to it will live, the sore presently will assuage. The first pullet will make the plague sore very soft, whereas before it was very hard, and the other will draw out the venom …

[183] A Medicine for a Man that is Burned with a Harlot°

Take an old flaxen cloth that is clean washed, burn it and make powder thereof; and take oil of Eggs, anoint the sore holes therewith, and fill them full of that powder, and it will heal it in short time …

[187] To Stop the Flowers°

Take and drink the juice of *Bursa Pastoris,*° and put part of the Herbs into thy privy parts, and Waybread° together, and it shall stop them …

[189] To Know Whether a Man Shall Live or Die

Take Mouse-ear,° and let him drink it: and if he cast° it up, he shall die; if he keep it, the contrary. Also take his Urine and cast it on a green Nettle at evening: and if you find it green in the morning, he shall live; and if the Nettle be dead, he shall die …

[201] To Make a Woman Conceive

Take powder made of Boar's stones° and give it her to drink after her flowers, and she shall conceive; also take the shaving of Ivory and drink it, and it shall make her able to conceive.

To Make a Man Have Lust to a Woman

Take fennel-seeds, and skirret,° of each two ounces; grind it and mingle it with new cow's milk, and make pellets thereof as big as beans, and take three at night and three in the morning. First of all anoint thy members with oil, and the juice of morel° and vinegar, and mingle them together …

° **Burned … Harlot**: infected with syphilis, a disease often treated with mercury by Renaissance physicians.
° **Flowers**: menstruation.   ° ***Bursa Pastoris***: shepherd's purse.   ° **Waybread**: plantain.
° **Mouse-ear**: chickweed.   ° **cast**: vomit.
° **stones**: testicles; possibly referring to those of a male pig rather than a wild boar.
° **skirret**:. A kind of water parsnip.   ° **morel**: nightshade.

[206] To Make a Tooth Fall Out

Take water Frogs, and as many land Frogs, and take out their bowels, and wash their bodies clean, and boil them in fair water. When the water is cold take off the gravy, and with a little on your finger touch the tooth, and it shall fall out ...

[208] For the Deafness in the Ears

Take of a Hare new killed the Urine out of her bladder, and drop it into the Ear, and it is a speedy remedy ...

[212] To Make a Water for the Eyes

Gather in the month of May one bottle of the dew of Barley before the Sun doth rise; then put thereto half a quarter of an ounce of white Copperas,° and half a quarter of an ounce of white Salt. Boil these till it come to a quart, then let it cool and put it into a Glass, and stop it close; and when you use it, drop a drop into the sore Eye ...

[223] To Break the Stone in the Kidneys

Take a Hare and flay him quick;° receive all the blood into skin, and then burn both blood and skin. Take the ashes thereof, and put them in the patient's drink, and that will break the stone ...

[225] For the Jaundice

Take in the morning fasting, if it be a man, lice out of a female's head, and drink them with white Wine, and Sugar, and a little Nutmeg. And take in the evening powder of worms ... in white wine. Probatum° Goodwife Pelham ...

[267] For the Falling Evil°

Take the brains of a Weasel, and dry it to powder; and put it into some pure Vinegar, and temper them well together; and give that to the diseased person to drink, morning and evening first and last. Probatum. Also the skull of a dead man whereon Moss groweth, being taken and washed very

---

° **white Copperas**: proto-sulphate of zinc.   ° **quick**: alive.
° **Probatum**: proven.   ° **Falling Evil**: epilepsy.

clean and dried in an oven and then beaten to powder, will cure this infirmity, be the disease never so ancient; but the skull must be of one that hath been slain or died suddenly, or of one that was hanged. Probatum est …

[278] To Know When to Gather all Sorts of Simples in their Several Seasons

From the 25th of March till Midsummer,° the leaves and flowers are in season. From Midsummer till Michaelmas,° the crops and herbs are in season. And from St Andrew's° to the 25th of March, the roots of herbs are in force.

⁊ ⁊ ⁊

° **Midsummer**: 24 June.   ° **Michaelmas**: 29 September.   ° **St. Andrew's**: 30 November.

WILLIAM COLE
"Of the Signatures of Plants" (1656)

The "doctrine of the signatures" (botanical form reveals medicinal function) can be traced back to the ancient Greek pharmacologist Dioscorides. It informed herbal medicine throughout the Middle Ages and gained new popularity among Renaissance occultists and mystics such as Paracelsus and Jakob Böhme, the latter of whom interpreted it as "the language of nature, whence every thing speaketh out of its property and doth continually manifest, declare, and set forth itself to what it is good or profitable" (*Signatura rerum*, 1.15). For the English physician William Cole, deciphering the signatures not only could restore health but help naturalists recover a prelapsarian relationship with the earth, as revealed in the title of the work in which Cole reproduced this passage the following year: *Adam in Eden, or Nature's Paradise.*
Source: *The Art of Simpling* (1656), 88–91.

Though Sin and Satan have plunged mankind into an Ocean of Infirmities (for before the Fall Man was not subject to Diseases), yet the mercy of God, which is over all his Works, maketh Grass to grow upwards on the Mountains and Herbs for the use of Men, and hath not only stamped upon them (as upon every Man) a distinct form, but also given them particular Signatures, whereby a Man may read, even in legible Characters, the use of them.

    That Plant that is called Adder's Tongue, because the stalk of it represents one, is a sovereign wound-herb to cure the biting of an Adder or any other venomous Creature. Viper's Bugloss hath its stalks all to be speckled like a Snake or Viper, and is a most singular remedy against Poison and the stinging of Scorpions and other venomous [89] Beasts. If a Man do but rub his hands with the leaves or roots of Dragons,° no Serpent will endure to come near him, as Dioscorides writeth.

There be some Satyrions° which are just like the Stones° of a Man: one of them is full and plump and sinks it if be put in Water, and that provokes the Lust; the other swims and is lank and shrivelled, and that mortifies it, so that there is a remedy for him in both cases.

Heart's Trefoil is called not only because the Leaf is Triangular like the Heart of a man but also because each Leaf contains the perfect Icon of a Heart, and that in its proper colour, i.e. a flesh colour. It defendeth the Heart against the noisome vapour of the Spleen … And there is another Trefoil called Purplewort which is an excellent remedy against the Purples.°

Hound's Tongue hath a form not much different from its name, which will tie the [90] Tongues of Hounds so that they shall not bark at you if it be laid under the bottoms of one's feet, as Mizaldus° writeth.

If the root of Solomon's Seal be like a Seal (as some say it is) it is a good Signature, for it seals up wounds after a wonderful manner …

But Walnuts bear the whole Signature of the Head: the outward most green bark answerable to the thick skin wherewith the head is covered, and a salve made of it is singularly good for wounds in that part, as the kernel is good for the brains which it resembles, being environed with a shell which imitates the Skull. And then it is wrapped up again in a silken covering somewhat representing the Pia Mater.

The decoction of Quinces, which are a downy and hairy fruit, is accounted good for the fetching again hair that hath fallen by the French Pox. The [91] Lye where in Maidenhair is sodden or infused is good to bathe the head and make the hair come thicker in those places which are more thin and bare.

The Leaves of St John's Wort seem to be pricked or pinked very thick with little holes like the pores of a man's skin. It is a sovereign remedy for any cut in the skin and as useful also for the opening of the pores of the body when they are obstructed.

The flower of Arum or Cuckoo-pint hath the evident resemblances of the genital parts upon it and is a most powerful incentive to Lust. And I know not why Sagitaria or Arrowhead should not be good for wounds made with the head of an Arrow, and Kidney beans for diseases of the Kidneys, though I confess I have not read to that purpose in any author.

༄ ༄ ༄

° **Dragons**: dragon arum lily.
° **Satyrions**: orchids, thought to increase virility and hence named after the lusty satyr.
° **Stones**: testicles.   ° **Purples**: purpura, or HSP.
° **Mizaldus**: Antonio Mizauld, a French herbalist and occultist.

MARGARET BAKER

"Of Millefeuille or Yarrow and His Great Virtue" (*c.* 1675)

The following is taken from one of the hundreds of unpublished manuscripts currently being transcribed by the Early Modern Recipes Online Collective (EMROC). Many Renaissance women had a wide knowledge of herbal medicine, permitting them to treat their family or neighbours. A few, like Hannah Woolley, even practised medicine professionally. Almost nothing is known of Margaret Baker, apart from passing references to her relations, Lettice and Anne Corbett, with whom she exchanged recipes. The excerpt below is of particular interest as it suggests Baker conducted dissections and medical trials on animals.
Source: *Receipt Book*, Folger Va 619, 18ᵛ–19ʳ.

This herb millefeuille is well known unto most men and of many is little esteemed because it groweth so commonly amongst us. This herb being green is a miraculous and divine remedy to help any fresh-bleeding wounds. If you stamp a handful of it and lay it upon the lips,° being close joined together, within the space of twenty-four hours it shall be perfectly whole. If you drink three ounces of the juice of this herb with new milk morning and evening it will help gonorrhoea in short time. It is also an excellent remedy for those that have their liver and lungs ulcerated, the which I have proved diverse times in goats which are troubled with a certain infirmity, the which be called bisole by the goat keepers, for there are certain impostumes° that do engender in the liver and the lungs and causeth them to die.

I have, then, seeing the interior parts of the goats, made this experience:° I took millefeuille made into a powder and gave it the goats with salt; and for the most [19ʳ] part they were helped. And after that I cured a number of men and women of that disease, for of that infirmity there die a great number … Those that are eticie° and phthisic° die commonly through impostumes and ulcers that are caused in the liver, for of this I have seen above a hundred. For after they were dead I have caused them to be opened to see … Therefore the surgeon that understandeth not physic can evil help those ulcers inwardly because he cannot apply his unguents and plasters as he doth outwardly, and those kind of ulcers cannot be known but of those that have seen them … Therefore I may well discourse thereof because of them there have passed a great number through my hands, and I have seen them with mine eyes. So that if I conclude, all that I have said is two things: the one is to see things in fact; the other is to have approved medicines to help them.

° **lips:** wound's edges.   ° **impostumes**: swellings, cysts.   ° **experience**: experiment.
° **eticie**: phlegmy?
° **phthisic**: tubercular.

PART V

Environmental Problems in Early Modern England

Population

THOMAS HARRIOT

"An estimable reckoning how many persons may inhabit the whole world" (*c.* 1590)

While the Black Death had thinned the late medieval population by a third, the numbers rose dramatically throughout the early modern era. Between the reigns of Henry VIII and Charles II the population expanded from around 2.5 million to 5.5 million (Wrigley and Scofield). As London began to feel overcrowded and food prices rose (exacerbated by dearth and the converting of farmland to pasture), some advocated colonial expansion as a safety valve for demographic pressures on England's natural resources. As a mathematician and promoter of Ralegh's Virginia colony, Thomas Harriot would have understood the appeal of this argument. But this solution prompted Harriot to formulate an even bigger question: how many humans could the earth support? Sometime after his return to England, he drew up the first known calculations of the planet's carrying capacity.
Source: BL Add. MS 6782, 31^{r-v}.

Suppositions …
The compass of the Earth after the rate of 60 miles to a degree = 21,600° miles.
Ergo: The half compass = 10,300° miles.
The semi-diameter of the Earth = 3,437.747° miles
3,437.747 × 10,300 = 35,408,794.1
plano circuli quod æquat ¼ superf. terræ et aquæ. °
Ergo: 35,408,794.1 × 4 = 141,635,176.4 *superf. maris et terræ.*°
70,817,588.2 = *superf. terræ. vel maris.*°
49,987 miles square in England (*ut alibi*° by Saxton's° great map) after the rate of 60 miles to a degree, including rivers and all wastes.°
It lacketh but 13 miles of 50,000.
50,000 miles²: 5,000,000° persons supposed = 1 mile²: 100 persons.

° **21,600**: the accepted figure today is nearly 25,000 miles (40,000 km).
° **10,300**: a copying mistake for 10,800.
° **3,437**: obtained by dividing the "compass" or circumference by 2π.
° *plano … aquæ*: that [πr^2] of a circular plane equals ¼ the surface area of land and water.
° *superf. … terræ*: the surface area of sea and land. The actual number is closer to 196 million.
° *superf. … maris*: The surface area of land or sea. Harriot here generously estimates that land covers 50 per cent of the earth's surface (instead of 30 per cent).
° *ut alibi*: and elsewhere (second-hand information).
° **Saxton**: Christopher Saxton published the first detailed map of England in 1579. It seems reasonable to conclude that the rise of cartography, like whole earth photos taken from orbit, heightened awareness of scarcity and overpopulation.
° **wastes**: uncultivated land.
° **5,000,000**: recent estimates of England's population in 1600 vary, but most are slightly lower (c. 4 million).

70,817,588 miles^2: 7,081,758,800 persons in the Earth.

[Amount of land needed to support one person]

1,000,000 paces^2: 100 persons = 10,000 paces^2: 1 person.

10,000 paces^2 = 250,000 feet^2 = $5\frac{8}{11}$ acres.

6 men may stand in a pace square.

Therefore 6,000,000 in 1 mile square.

7,081,758,800 × 6,000,000 = 42,490,552,800,000,000

= The number of persons that may stand on the Earth.

[31^v] The issue from one man and one woman in 240 years may be more than can inhabit the whole Earth.

Supposing

1. That the first man and woman have a child every year: one year male and in other year female.

2. That the children when they are 20 years old and upward do also every year beget a child: one year male and another year female.

3. That all are living at the end of 240 years.°

The number of males, 5,034,303,437; females, 5,034,303,437; persons, 10,068,606,874. That in 400 years upon the former suppositions there would be more men than can stand on the face of the whole Earth.

❧ ❧ ❧

° **240 years**: this supposition suggests that Harriot wanted his calculations to unsettle.

THOMAS DEKKER AND THOMAS MIDDLETON
"The Necessity of a Plague" (1603)

In the later summer of 1603, a virulent plague swept through London. With the theatres closed, two London-born playwrights co-authored a pamphlet chronicling the horrors of the epidemic, which claimed around 30,000 lives. Dekker and Middleton offer a learned survey of contemporary medical theories regarding the plague's origin and transmission, including that it was in essence a form of atmospheric "pollution" that spread throughout the environment (so "rivers drink poisoned air / Trees shed their green and curled hair"), but hint that the ultimate cause is God's wrath against their sinful society. The grim conclusion that plagues offer a necessary check on overpopulation may sound heartless, but the Great Dearth of 1594–6 would have encouraged such proto-Malthusian logic.
Source: *News from Gravesend Sent to Nobody* (1604), F4^{r-v}.

Yet to mix comfortable words,
Though this be horrid, it affords
Sober gladness and wise joys,
Since desperate mixtures it destroys.

For if our thoughts sit truly trying°
The just necessity of dying,
How needful (though how dreadful) are
Purple Plagues or Crimson War,
We would conclude (still urging pity)
A Plague's the Purge° to cleanse a City.
Who amongst millions can deny
(In rough prose or smooth poesy)
Of Evils, 'tis the lighter brood: 1140
A dearth of people than of food!
And who knows not, our Land ran o'er
With people, and was only poor
In having too, too many living,
And wanting living!° Rather giving
Themselves to waste, deface, and spoil,
Than to increase (by virtuous toil)
The bankrupt bosom of our Realm,
Which naked° births did overwhelm.
This begets famine and bleak dearth:
When fruits of wombs pass fruits of earth.

ȝ⊱ ȝ⊱ ȝ⊱

° **trying**: considering.   ° **Purge**: with quibble on laxative.   ° **living**: employment.
° **naked**: destitute.

THOMAS FREEMAN
"London's Progress" (1614)

Between 1500 and 1700, London's population swelled from roughly 200,000 to
675,000, making it twenty times larger than the next biggest city in the realm.
When Henry VIII ascended the throne, its suburbs were still chequered with
green fields, gardens, and orchards. By the end of King James's reign, much of
the undeveloped land had been built upon (the creation of a theatre district in
Bankside is symptomatic in this regard). The following sonnet is an early humorous critique of urban sprawl, imagining London as a horizontal Tower of Babel.
Source: *Rub and a Great Cast* (1614), B3ʳ.

> *Quo ruis, ah demens?*°
> Why how now, Babel, whither wilt thou build?
> I see old Holborn, Charing Cross, the Strand,
> Are going to St Giles-in-the-Field.°

° ***Quo ... demens?***: O madman, where are you rushing? From Matteo Boiardo, *Eclogue* 4.86,
   paraphrasing Virgil, *Eclogues* 2.60.
° **St Giles-in-the-Field**: as its name suggests, this parish church was once surrounded by open
   meadows (see the 1561 Agas map) in what is now the heart of the West End.

Saint Katherine she shakes Wapping° by the hand,
And Hoxton° will to Highgate° ere't be long.
London is got a great way from the stream.°
I think she means to go to Islington,°
To eat a mess° of strawberries and cream.
The City's sure in Progress,° I surmise,
10   Or going to revel it in some disorder
Without the Walls, without the Liberties,°
Where she need fear nor Mayor nor Recorder.°
Well, say she do, 'twere pretty but 'twere pity
A Middlesex° Bailiff should arrest the City.

⁊Ꮭ ⁊Ꮭ ⁊Ꮭ

° **Saint Katherine ... Wapping**: eastern suburbs, little developed at the time of the poem.
° **Hoxton**: on the northern edge of the East End; then known for its gardens and fields.
° **Highgate**: then a remote village 4 miles north of the city walls; now an affluent suburb.
° **stream**: the River Thames.
° **Islington**: formerly a distinct village surrounded by fields and woods.
° **mess**: dish.   ° **Progress**: royal procession.
° **Liberties**: suburbs of London (outside the jurisdiction of the city).
° **Recorder**: Judge.
° **Middlesex**: a former county, now entirely engulfed by Greater London.

WALTER RALEGH
"Necessary War" (c. 1615)

Thomas Malthus's *Essay on the Principle of Population* (1798) is not the bombshell it is often thought to be. Several thinkers in early modern Europe intuited the need for limiting population growth, or finding an outlet for it abroad. In his *Utopia*, Thomas More authorizes the occupation of countries that did not practise intensive agriculture to relieve population pressures at home. Anticipating the theory of the "Malthusian check," Walter Ralegh here advances a similar environmental justification for war and conquest. Ralegh himself exploited woodlands in Ireland, and his notoriously sexist vision of Guyana as a "country that hath yet her maidenhead" reflects his fears that England's soil had lost its fertility. Interestingly, Ralegh's tutor was Thomas Harriot, who very well may have shown his patron his calculations of the earth's carrying capacity (Sokol 212). In upholding colonial expansion as preferable to warfare, Ralegh conveniently elides the fact that overseas conquest all too often required bloodshed. England's determination to build a global empire was not motivated purely by God, gold, and glory, but also by an anxiety over its depleted natural resources.
Source: *Discourse of the Original and Fundamental Cause of ... War* (1650), 4–5, 9–10.

This appeared in the Gauls, who, falling upon Italy under their Captain Brennus, told the Roman Ambassadors plainly that prevalent arms were as good as any title, and that valiant men might account to be their own as much as they could get; that they wanting Land therewith to sustain their people and the Tuscans having more than enough, it was their meaning to take what they needed by strong hand ... Now if it be well-affirmed by Lawyers that there is no taking of possession more just than *in vacuum venire*, to enter upon Land uninhabited, as our country-men have lately done in the Summer Islands,° then may it be inferred that this demand of the Gauls held more of reason than could be discerned at the first view.

[5] For if the title of occupiers be good in a Land unpeopled, why should it be bad accounted in a country Peopled over thinly? Should one family or one thousand hold possession over all the Southern, undiscovered continent because they had seated themselves in *Nova Guyana* or about the Straits of Magellan? Why not might the like be done in Africa, Europe, or Asia? If this were most absurd to imagine, let then any man's wisdom determine by lessening the Territory and increasing the number of Inhabitants, what proportion is requisite to the peopling of a Region, in such manner that the Land shall be neither too narrow for those whom it feedeth, nor capable of a greater multitude. Until this can be concluded and agreed upon, one main and fundamental cause of the most grievous war that can be imagined is not like to be taken from the Earth ...

[9] It were an endless labour to tell how the Turks and Tartars [fell] like Locusts upon that quarter of the world [Asia], having spoiled everywhere and in most places Eaten up all ... Suffice it that when any Country is overlaid by the multitude which live upon it, there is a natural necessity compelling it to disburden itself and lay the Load upon others, by right or wrong. For (to omit the danger of Pestilence often visiting those which live in a throng) there is no misery that urgeth men so violently unto desperate courses and contempt of death as the Torments or Threats of famine, whereof the War that is grounded upon this general remediless necessity [10] may be termed the general, the remediless, or the necessary War ...

[15] Were it not thus, Arithmetical progression might easily demonstrate how fast mankind would increase in multitude, overpassing as miraculous (though indeed natural) that example of the Israelites, who were multiplied in 215 years from 70 unto 600,000° able men. Hence we may observe that the very propagation of our [16] kind hath with it a strong incentive, even of those daily Wars which afflict the earth.

※ ※ ※

° **Summer Islands**: the Bermudas, settled by the English in 1609.
° **70 ... 600,000**: See Exodus 1:5–7, and Numbers 1:46–7.

GABRIEL PLATTES
from A Discovery of Infinite Treasure (1639)

An alternative solution to overpopulation and dearth was boosting crop yields. Many early modern agrarian improvers such as Gabriel Plattes were cornucopians, who believed that technological advances and new farming methods (e.g. better fertilizers, crop rotation, land reclamation, replanting woodlands as hedgerows, deterrents against insects and blight) would permit humans to overleap pre-existing limitations on population growth.
Source: *A Discovery of Infinite Treasure* (1639), C3^{r-v}.

If anyone shall calumniate these improvements with the name of innovations, let him be pleased to remember himself that such innovations as these have been accustomed in all ancient times, as the people grew more and more numerous, to be put in practice. For three several times the people growing too numerous for their maintenance, God hath given understanding to men to improve the earth in such a wonderful manner that it was able to maintain double the number. And so he that made mouths sent meat by teaching them understanding how to get it. For when there were but few, they were maintained by Fish, Fowl, Venison, and Fruits, freely provided by Nature. But when they grew too numerous for that food, they found out the Spade and used industry to augment their food by their endeavours. Then they growing too numerous again were compelled to use the plough, the chiefest of all engines ... whereby all Commonwealths have ever since been maintained. And at length this invention would not serve the turn neither without new skill in the using of it. For at the first they used to till the Land until the fatness° thereof was spent, and so to let it lie a long time to gather fatness again of itself, and in the meantime to till fresh Land. But when they grew too numerous for the food gotten that way, they were compelled to find out the fallowing and manuring of land, by which invention the land recovered more fatness in one year than before in many years: and so a Country would maintain double the number of people more than before. Now the people are grown numerous again, requiring new improvements which are discovered in this little Book, and shall be showed by irrefragable° demonstration and infallible experience. Also it shall be made manifest that by the common course of Husbandry used at this day the barrenness doth by little and little increase and the fertility decrease every year more and more, which in regard that the people do increase [C3^{v}] wonderfully,° must needs at length produce a horrible mischief, and cause the Commonwealth to be oppressed with poverty and beggary: when as by these new inventions and improvements being industriously practised, their wealth shall not be diminished, but contrary ways wonderfully increased, though the people shall grow wonderfully numerous ...

° **fatness**: fertility.   ° **wonderfully**: astonishingly.
° **irrefragable**: irrefutable.

And forasmuch as the new world called America doth for the present give aid and succour for the maintenance of the surplusage of people increased in those Countries, yet in regard that the finding of new worlds is not like to be a perpetual trade, it seemeth to agree with providence to begin to improve the Lands formerly peopled in such manner that by their industry there may be raised maintenance for double the number.

కళ కళ కళ

WILLIAM PETTY

An Essay Concerning the Multiplication of Mankind (1682)

A surveyor, anatomist, economist, and founding member of the Royal Society, William Petty was one of the first to foresee the importance of statistics for governmental and environmental policy. He inspired the demographic researches of his friend John Graunt in the 1660s, and his defence of the 1662 "Hearth Tax" may have been motivated in part by a desire to reduce coal smoke in London. His initial interest in population sprang from his less admirable commitment to English rule in Ireland. When he collated the data from parish birth and burial records in London, however, he became alarmed at what the numbers implied about the city's sustainability. If the picture of him in the National Portrait Gallery dressed in black and clutching a skull makes him appear like a Restoration Hamlet, his sobering contemplation of birth rates rather than mortality makes him a forerunner of Malthus.

Source: *An Essay Concerning the Multiplication of Mankind* (1686), 6–7, 19–21.

The Principal Points of this Discourse

1. That London doubles in forty Years, and all England in 360 Years.
2. That there be, Anno 1682, about 670,000 Souls in London, and about 7,400,000 in all England and Wales, and about 28,000,000 of Acres of profitable Land.
3. That the Periods of doubling the People are found to be in all Degrees from between ten to twelve hundred Years.
4. That the Growth of London must stop of itself before the Year 1800 ...
5. [7] That the World will be fully Peopled within the next 2,000 Years ...
6. How the City of London may be made (morally speaking) Invincible ...
7. That 'tis possible to increase Mankind by Generation four times more than at present.
8. The Plagues of London [are] the chief Impediment and Objection against the Growth of the City.
9. That an Exact Account of the People is Necessary in this Matter ...

[19] According to which Account or Measure of doubling, if there be now in England and Wales 7,400,000 People, there were about 5,526,000 in the beginning of Queen Elizabeth's Reign, Anno 1560, and about 2,000,000 at the Norman Conquest (of which consult the *Domesday Book*° and my Lord Hale's *Origination of Mankind*°).

Memorandum: that if the People double in 360 Years, that the present 320 millions computed by some learned Men (from the Measures of all the Nations of the World, their degrees of being Peopled, and good Accounts of the People in several of them) to be now upon the Face of the Earth, will within the next 2,000 years so increase as to give one [20] Head for every two Acres of Land in the Habitable part of the Earth. And then, according to the prediction of the Scriptures, there must be Wars and great Slaughter, etc.

Wherefore, as an Expedient against the above-mentioned difference between 10 and 1,200 years, we do for the present, and in this Country admit of 360 years to be the time wherein the People of England do double, according to the present Laws and Practice of Marriages.

Now if the City double its People in forty years, and the present Number be 670,000; and if the whole Territory be 7,400,000, and double in 360 years, as aforesaid; then by the underwritten Table it appears that Anno 1840, the People of the City will be 10,718,880, and those of the whole Country but 10,917,389, which is but inconsiderably more. Wherefore [21] it is Certain and Necessary that the Growth of the City must stop before the said year 1840; and will be at its utmost height in the next preceding period, Anno 1800, when the number of the City will be eight times its present number, viz. 5,359,000; and when (besides the said number) there will be 4,466,000 to perform the Tillage, Pasturage, and other Rural Works necessary to be done without the said City, as by the following Table, viz.

Annis°	Burials	People in London	People in England
1565	2,568	77,040	5,526,923
1605	5,235		
1642	11,883		
1682	22,331	669,930	7,369,230
1712	44,662		
1762	89,324		
1802	178,648	5,359,440	9,825,650
1842	357,296	10,718,880	10,917,389°

❧ ❧ ❧

° **Domesday Book**: the famous survey of England completed by the Normans in 1086; spelled "Doomsday" by Petty.
° ***Origination of Mankind***: Petty was inspired by Hale's chapter on "Correctives of the Excess of Mankind" (1677 207).   ° ***Annis***: Years.
° **10,917,389**: Demographers estimate that England's population in 1840 was closer to 14 million (Wrigley and Schofield 534–6). The current (2016) population estimate of the UK is around 65 million.

Enclosure

THOMAS MORE
"English Sheep Devourers of Men" (1516)

By the late Middle Ages, wool had become the lifeblood of the English economy. As demand increased in the early sixteenth century thanks to the booming textile industry, the market value of wool skyrocketed. As a result, farmers began to expand pastureland at the expense of arable land and woodlands, and to enclose commons. This triggered a great number of economic and social problems, as some displaced agricultural workers apparently turned to theft to survive. More's protest not only anticipates sociological theories of crime but also intuits the monstrous environmental impact of cross-species assemblages, in this case, the "landlord/sheep hybrid," that transforms England into a "Ewe-topia" (Yates).
Source: *Utopia*, trans. Ralph Robinson (1551), C6ᵛ– D1ʳ.

"But yet this is not only the necessary cause of stealing. There is another which, as I suppose, is proper° and peculiar to you Englishmen alone."

"What is that?" quoth the Cardinal.

"Forsooth," quod I, "your sheep that were wont to be so meek and tame, and so small eaters, now, as I hear say, be become so great devourers and so wild that they eat up and swallow down the very men themselves. They consume, destroy, and devour whole fields, houses, and cities. For look in what parts of [C7ʳ] the realm doth grow the finest and, therefore, dearest wool, there noblemen and gentlemen—yea, and certain Abbots, holy men, God wote°—not contenting themselves with the yearly revenues and profits that were wont to grow to their forefathers and predecessors of their lands, nor being content that they live in rest and pleasure nothing profiting—yea, much annoying—the weal-public, leave no ground for tillage. They enclose all in pastures. They throw down houses. They pluck down towns, and leave nothing standing but only the church to make of it a sheephouse. And as though you lost no small quantity of ground by forests, chases, lands, and parks, those good holy men turn all dwellings places and all glebe-land° into desolation and wilderness. Therefore that one covetous and insatiable cormorant° and very plague of his native country may compass about and enclose many thousand acres of ground together within one pale or hedge, the husbandmen be thrust out of their own, or else either by covin° [C7ᵛ] or fraud or by violent oppression they be put besides it, or by wrongs and injuries they be so wearied that they be compelled to sell all. By one means therefore or by other, either by hook or crook, they

---

° **proper**: distinctive.   ° **wote**: knows.   ° **glebe-land**: cultivated fields.
° **cormorant**: literally a water-dwelling bird regarded as gluttonous.
° **covin**: conspiracy.

must needs depart away, poor, silly, wretched souls: men, women, husbands, wives, fatherless children, widows, woeful mothers with their young babes, and their whole household, small in substance and much in number, as husbandry requireth many hands. Away they trudge, I say, out of their known and accustomed houses, finding no places to rest in. All their household stuff, which is very little worth, though it might well abide the sale, yet being suddenly thrust out, they be constrained to sell it for a thing of nought.° And when they have wandering about so spent that, what can they else do but steal, and then justly, God wote, be hanged, or else go about a-begging? And yet then also they be cast in prison as vagabonds because they go about and work not, whom [C8ʳ] no man will set a-work, though they never so willingly offer themselves thereto. For one shepherd or herdsman is enough to eat up that ground with cattle, to the occupying whereof about husbandry many hands were requisite. And this is also the cause that victuals be now in many places dearer. Yea, besides this the price of wool is so risen that poor folks, which were wont to work it and make cloth of it, be now able to buy none at all. And by this means very many be fain° to forsake work and to give themselves to idleness. For after that so much ground was enclosed for pasture, an infinite multitude of sheep died of the rot, such vengeance God took of their inordinate and insatiable covetousness, sending among the sheep that pestiferous murrain,° which much more justly should have fallen on the sheep-masters' own heads. And though the number of sheep increase never so fast, yet the price falleth not one mite because there be so few sellers. For they be almost all come into a few [C8ᵛ] rich men's hands, whom no need driveth to sell before they lust,° and they lust not before they may sell as dear as they lust. Now the same cause bringeth in like dearth of the other kinds of cattle—yea, and that so much the more—because that after farms [are] plucked down and husbandry decayed, there is no man that passeth for the breeding of young store. For these rich men bring not up the young ones of great cattle as they do lambs.° But first they buy them abroad very cheap, and afterward, when they be fatted in their pastures, they sell them again exceeding dear. And therefore (as I suppose) the whole incommodity hereof is not yet felt. For yet they make dearth only in those places where they sell. But when they shall fetch them away from thence where they be bred faster than they can be brought up, then shall there also be felt great dearth when store beginneth to fail there, where the ware is bought. Thus the unreasonable covetousness of a few hath turned that thing to the utter undoing of your island, in [D1ʳ] the which thing the chief felicity of your realm did consist.

❧ ❧ ❧

° **nought**: no value.   ° **fain**: obliged.   ° **murrain**: disease.   ° **lust**: wish.
° **For … lambs**: see Appendix A for the 1529 Act for Bringing up and Rearing of Calves.

THOMAS BASTARD
"Sheep have eat up our meadows and our downs," and *"When the great forests' dwelling was so wide"* (1598)

Like Thomas More, the Elizabethan satirist Thomas Bastard was alarmed by the impact of sheep on the economy and natural resources of the realm. How do the views expressed in the following epigrams compare with those of contemporary re-wilding advocates who decry the way the British countryside has been "sheep-wrecked" (Monbiot 153)?
Source: *Chrestoloros* (1598), 90, 136.

4.20

Sheep have eat up our meadows and our downs,
Our corn, our wood, whole villages and towns.
Yea, they have eat up many wealthy men,
Besides widows and orphan children,
Besides our statutes and our iron laws,
Which they swallowèd down into their maws.°
Till now I thought the proverb did but jest,
Which said a black sheep was a biting beast.

6.8

When the great forests' dwelling was so wide,
And careless° wood grew fast by the fire's side,
Then dogs did want° the shepherd's field to keep:
Now we want Foxes to consume our sheep.

❧ ❧ ❧

° **maws**: stomachs.   ° **careless**: uncared for.   ° **want**: lack.

JOHN HARINGTON
"Of Sheep Turned Wolves" (c. 1600)

Similar to the other anti-sheep texts, Harington's epigram transforms this meek herbivore, a time-honoured symbol of innocence, into a voracious predator.
Source: *Epigrams* (1618), H8ᵛ.

When hearts obdurate make of sin a habit,
High-frowning Nemesis° was wont to send
Bears, Lions, Wolves, and Serpents,° to this end:
To spoil the coasts° where so bad folk inhabit.

° **Nemesis**: Greek goddess of retribution.   ° **Serpents**: Tigers] 1615.
° **spoil ... coasts**: plague the place] 1615.

Now since this age,° in habit and in act,
Excels the sins of every former age,
No marvel Nemesis in her just rage
Doth like or greater punishment exact.
And for this cause a cruèl beast is sent,
10   Not only that devours and spoils the people,
But spares not house nor village, Church nor Steeple,°
And makes poor widows mourn, orphans lament.
You muse (perhaps)° what beasts they be that keep
Such beastly rule as seld was seen before.
'Tis neither Bear nor Lion, Bull nor Boar,
But beasts than all these beasts more harmful: sheep.
Lo then, the mystery from whence the name
Of Cotswold Lions° first to England came.

꙳ ꙳ ꙳

° **age**: sin] 1615.
° **spares ... Steeple**: pulls down house and cottage, Church and steeple] 1615.
° **You ... perhaps**: But will you know] 1615.
° **Cotswold Lions**: an ironic nickname for sheep (first recorded in 1537).

JOHN TAYLOR
from Taylor's Pastoral (1624)

Critics of enclosure did not invariably despise sheep. The poet John Taylor could condemn its abuses while also recognizing the vital importance of this animal to the English economy. While expounding its symbolic and mystical properties – noting that Ieova is an anagram for *Oveia* (or sheep) and the constellation Aries is placed first in the Zodiac – he inventories how many trades depend on wool, viewing sheep as heaven-sent blessings (see also Leonard Mascall's "A Praise of Sheep," 1591, O1ᵛ) rather than (as in Harington's poem) a divine scourge.
Source: *Taylor's Pastoral* (1624), C3ᵛ–C4ʳ, D2ʳ, E2ᵛ–E3ʳ.

Unto the Sheep again my Muse doth fly,
For honest safety and commodity.
He with his flesh and fleece doth feed and clad
All languages and nations, good and bad.
What can it more but die, that we may live,
And every year to us a liv'ry give?
'Tis such a bounty, and the charge so deep,
That nothing can afford the like but Sheep.
For should the world want Sheep but five whole year,
180   Ten thousand millions would want clothes to wear.
And were't not for the flesh of this kind beast,
The world might fast when it doth often feast.

There's nothing doth unto a Sheep pertain,
But 'tis for man's commodity and gain.
For men to men so much untrusty are,
To lie, to cozen,° to forswear and swear,
That oaths, and passing words, and joining hands,
Is like assurance written in the sands.
To make men keep their words and mend all this,
The silly Sheepskin turned to Parchment is ...   190
Now of the Ram, the Ewe, the Lamb, and Wether,°
I'll touch their skins as they are turned to Leather,
And made in Purses, Pouches, Laces, Strings,
Gloves, Points,° Book-covers, and ten thousand things,
And many tradesmen live and thrive thereby,
Which if I would I more could amplify.
Their Guts serve Instruments which sweetly sound;
Their Dung is best to make most fruitful ground;
Their Hooves burnt will most venomed serpents kill;
Their grated Horns are good 'gainst poison still;   240
Their Milk makes Cheese, man's hunger to prevent,
As I have seen in Sussex and in Kent;
Their Trotters,° for the healthy or the sick,
(Dressed as they should be) are good meat to pick.
The Cooks and Butchers with the joints do gain,
And poor folks eat the Gather,° Head, and Brain ...

[D2ʳ] But to consider more seriously the wonderful blessing that the whole world hath had and hath by sheep at this present, I think it not amiss to use the words of an ingenious and well-affected poet of our time, Master T. M.,° where he truly saith, "No Ram no Lamb, no Lamb no Sheep, no Sheep no Wool, no Wool no Woolman, no Woolman no Spinner, no Spinner no Weaver, no Weaver no Cloth, no Cloth no Clothier, no Clothier no Clothworker, Fuller,° Tucker,° Shearman, Draper,° or scarcely a rich Dyer."

And what infinite numbers of people, rich and poor, have lived and do live, having their whole dependence from the poor sheep's back, all men of judgement will acknowledge ...

[E2ᵛ] And should I reckon up the particulars of profits that arise from this Beast to Graziers, Butchers, Skinners, Glovers, Fell-mongers,° Leather-sellers, Felt-mongers, Tailors, and an infinite number of other trades and functions who could not live, or else live very hardly, without this commodity, I say, should I write of these things in particular, my work would never be done in general ...

° **cozen**: cheat.   ° **Wether**: castrated ram.   ° **Points**: fastenings.
° **Trotters**: feet.   ° **Gather**: heart, liver, lungs.
° **T. M.**: most likely Thomas Middleton, or perhaps a mistake for Antony Munday (both wrote for the Drapers' Company).
° **Fuller**: one who beat wool to clean and thicken it.
° **Tucker**: another name for one who processed woollen cloth.
° **Draper**: cloth-maker or merchant.   ° **Fell-mongers**: dealers in wool and sheepskins.

[E3ʳ] And now from solid Prose I will abstain,
To pleasant Poetry and mirth again.
The Fable of the Golden Fleece began
'Cause Sheep did yield such store of Gold to Man;
For he that hath great store of woolly fleeces,
May, when he please, have store of golden pieces.
Thus many a poor man dying hath left a Son
That hath transformed the Fleece to Gold, like Jason.

꙰ ꙰ ꙰

ANONYMOUS
"The Diggers of Warwickshire to all other Diggers" (1607)

In 1607, a poor harvest and skyrocketing grain prices sparked an uprising known as the Midlands Revolt. When a crowd of over 2,000 gathered in Northamptonshire to destroy enclosures (claiming to enforce legislation to preserve arable land as documented in Appendix A), local landowners organized a paramilitary force to disperse them and to execute the ringleaders. Protests also erupted in Warwickshire, where agitators compared themselves to expendable "members" of the body politic, implicitly invoking the same metaphor deployed to forestall a riot in *Coriolanus* by the Warwickshire landowner William Shakespeare (who later signed a non-resistance pact with enclosers in his hometown). The following manuscript was apparently copied in the mid-seventeenth century (perhaps from a printed broadside), and was found among the papers of William Dell, secretary of Archbishop Laud. It is unclear whether or not Dell supplied the title linking the 1607 protesters with the Digger movement of the Civil War era. For a cynical view of the Midlands Revolt, which blames the hot-headedness of the rioters on tobacco-taking, see John Deacon's *Tobacco Tortured* (1616, 96–100).
Source: Harley MS 787, 9ᵛ.

Loving friends and subjects all under one renowned prince, for whom we pray long to continue in his most royal estate, to the subjecting of all those subjects of what degree soever that have or would deprive his most true-hearted communalty both from life and living. We as members of the whole do feel the smart of these encroaching tyrants, which would grind our flesh upon the whetstone of poverty, and make our loyal hearts to faint with breathing, so that they may dwell by themselves in the midst of their herds of fat wethers. It is not unknown unto yourselves the reason why these merciless men do resist with force against our good intents. It is not for the good of our most gracious Sovereign, whom we pray God that long may he reign amongst us, neither for the benefit of the communalty, but only for their own private gain. For there is none of them but do taste the sweetness of our wants. They have depopulated and overthrown whole towns, and made thereof sheep pastures, nothing profitable for our commonwealth. For the common fields being laid open would yield us much commodity, besides the increase of corn, on which stands our life. But if it should please God to withdraw his blessing in not prospering the fruits of the earth but one year (which God forbid) there would a worse and more fearful dearth happen than did in King Edward the Second's time,° when people were forced to eat cat's and dog's flesh, and women to eat their own children. Much more we could give you to understand, but we are persuaded that you yourselves feel a part of our grievances, and therefore need not open the matter any plainer. But if you happen to show your force and might against us, we for our part neither respect life nor living. For better it were in such cases we manfully die than hereafter to be pined to death for want of that which these devouring encroachers do serve their fat hogs and sheep withal. For God hath bestowed upon us most bountiful and innumerable blessings, and the chiefest is our most gracious and religious king, who doth and will glory in the flourishing estate of his communalty. And so we leave you, commending you to the surehold and safeguard of the mighty Jehovah, both now and evermore.

From Hampton field in haste:

We rest as poor delvers and day-labourers for the good of the commonwealth till death.

A. B. C. D. etc.°

ૐ ૐ ૐ

° **Edward the Second's time**: the catastrophic dearth of 1315–17.
° **etc.**: the letters imply multiple authors or supporters, and conceal their identities.

GERRARD WINSTANLEY *ET AL.*
from The True Levellers' Standard Advanced (1649)

In April 1649 a small band of radicals founded what we would now call an agrarian commune on uncultivated land upon St George's Hill, Surrey, and sowed it with beans, peas, and carrots. In the aftermath of the Civil War, they were testing out the revolutionary belief that England was now a literal commonwealth, and called for the abolition of not only class hierarchy but also private property. Their manifesto proposes that collective ownership of the land might restore humans to an Edenic state of oneness with a maternal earth, but should also be seen in the context of agricultural improvement schemes to convert wild spaces to arable fields to feed England's swelling population during the turbulent weather and ensuing dearth of 1647–50. The names of fifteen men, who came to be known as Diggers, are subscribed to the text, although it is usually attributed to Gerrard Winstanley and William Everard. Winstanley is also credited with composing "The Diggers' Song," the first stanza of which reads as follows:

> You noble Diggers all, stand up now, stand up now,
> You noble Diggers all, stand up now,
> The wasteland to maintain, seeing Cavaliers by name
> Your digging does disdain, and persons all defame.
> Stand up now, stand up now.   (quoted in Clarke 2:221)

The Diggers would need to bolster their courage. A few weeks later the Lord of the Manor on whose land they were squatting called in the cavalry; Winstanley and Everard were arrested, and their followers dispersed.

Source: *The True Levellers' Standard Advanced* (1649), 15–18, 20–2.

Take notice that England is not a Free People till the poor that have no Land have a free allowance to dig and labour the Commons, and so live as comfortably as the Landlords that live in their Enclosures. For the People have not laid out their Money and shed their Blood [so] that their Landlords, the Norman° power, should still have its liberty and freedom to rule in Tyranny ... but [so] that the Oppressed might be set free, Prison doors opened, and the Poor people's hearts comforted by an universal Consent of making the Earth a Common Treasury, that they may live together as one House of Israel, united in brotherly love into one Spirit, and having a comfortable livelihood in the Community of one Earth, their Mother ... [16] That we begin to Dig upon George Hill, to eat our Bread together by righteous labour and sweat of our brows, it was showed us by Vision, in Dreams and out of Dreams, that that should be the Place we should begin upon. And though that Earth, in view of Flesh, be very barren, yet we should trust the Spirit for a blessing. And that not only this Common or Heath should be taken in and Manured by the People, but all the commons and waste Ground in England, and in the whole World, shall be taken in by the People in righteousness, not owning any Propriety,° but taking the Earth to be a Common Treasury, as it was first made for all ...

[17] This work to make the Earth a Common Treasury was showed [to] us by Voice, in Trance and out of Trance, which words were these: "Work together; Eat Bread together; Declare this all abroad." ... Another Voice that was heard was this: "Israel shall neither take hire nor give hire." And if so, then certainly none shall say, "This is my Land; work for me and I'll give you Wages." For the Earth is the Lord's, that is, Man's, who is Lord of the Creation ... So every particular man is but a member or branch of mankind, and mankind living in the light and obedience to Reason ... is thereby made a fit and complete Lord of the Creation. And the whole Earth is this Lord's man, subject to the Spirit and not the inheritance of covetous proud Flesh, that is selfish and [in] enmity to the Spirit. [18] And if the Earth be not peculiar° to any one branch or branches of

---

° **Norman**: Winstanley sees the Normans' afforestation of commons as a nefarious precedent for current enclosures.

° **Propriety**: private property.   ° **peculiar**: exclusive.

mankind,° but the Inheritance of all, then is it Free and Common for all, to work together and eat together.

And truly, you Counsellors and Powers of the Earth, know this: that wheresoever there is a People thus united by Common Community of livelihood into Oneness it will become the strongest Land in the World. For then they will be as one man to defend their Inheritance ...

[21] If thou wilt find mercy, "Let Israel go free."° Break in pieces quickly the Band of particular Propriety, disown this oppressing Murder, Oppression and Thievery of Buying and Selling of Land, owning of Landlords, and paying of Rents, and give thy Free Consent to make the Earth a Common Treasury without grumbling, that the younger Brethren may live comfortably upon Earth as well as the Elder, that all may enjoy the benefit of their Creation.

And hereby thou wilt Honour thy Father and thy Mother: thy Father, which is the Spirit of Community, that made all and that dwells in all; thy Mother, which is the Earth, that brought us all forth, [and] that as a true Mother loves all her Children. Therefore do not thou hinder the Mother Earth from giving all her Children suck by thy Enclosing it into particular hands, and holding up that cursed Bondage of Enclosure by thy Power ...

[22] Therefore, once more, "Let Israel go free," that the poor may labour the Waste-land, and suck the Breasts of their Mother Earth, that they starve not ... Thus we have discharged our Souls in declaring the Cause of our Digging upon George-Hill in Surrey, that the Great Counsel and Army of the Land may take notice of it: that there is no intent of Tumult or Fighting, but only to get bread to eat with the sweat of our brows, working together in righteousness and eating the blessings of the Earth in peace.

ᕱ ᕱ ᕱ

° **mankind**: in the original "manking."
° **Let ... free**: comparing the landless of England to the enslaved Israelites in Egypt.

HENRY KING
"Woe to the worldly men" (1657)

This poem by the Bishop of Chichester draws on the biblical prophecies of Isaiah (5:8) to condemn enclosure. Through sympathetic magic, the sterility of the land eventually afflicts the landowner.
Source: *Poems* (1657), 124.

> Woe to the worldly men whose covetous
> Ambition labours to join house to house,
> Lay field to field, till their enclosures edge

The Plain, girdling° a country with one hedge;
That leave no place unbought, no piece of earth
Which they will not engross, making a dearth
Of all inhabitants, until they stand
Unneighboured as unblest within their land.

This sin cries in God's ear, who hath decreed
10   The ground they sow shall not return the seed.
They that unpeopled countries to create
Themselves sole Lords, made many desolate
To build up their own house, shall find at last
Ruin and fearful desolation cast
Upon themselves. Their Mansion shall become
A Desert, and their Palace prove a tomb.
Their vines shall barren be, their land yield tares;
Their house shall have no dwellers, they no heirs.

⁂

° **girdling**: surrounding, but perhaps with quibble on stripping off a ring of bark around a tree trunk to kill it (first used in 1662).

Deforestation

ROBIN CLIDRO
"Marchan Wood" (c. 1545–1580)

The 1536–1542 Acts of Unification with England facilitated the exploitation of Welsh woodlands to supply charcoal for iron-making, silver-mining, and lead-smelting. The following extraordinary poem presumes to speak on behalf of squirrels, and imagines them, according to a prefixed description in the Welsh manuscript, journeying to London to "file and make an affidavit on the bill for the cutting down of Marchan Wood near Rhuthyn." The poem thus decries the impact of habitat loss, and implicitly links it to territorial annexation.
Source: *The Burning Tree*, trans. Gwyn Williams (1956), 163–5.

> Odious and hard is the law
> And painful to little squirrels.
> They go the whole way to London
> With their cry and their matron before them.
> This red squirrel° was splendid,
> Soft-bellied and able to read;
> She conversed with the Council
> And made a great matter of it.
> When the Book was put under her hand
> In the faith that this would shame her,   10
> She spoke thus to the bailiff:
> "Sir Bribem, you're a deep one!"
> Then on her oath she said,
> "All Rhuthyn's woods are ravaged;
> My house and barn were taken
> One dark night, and all my nuts.
> The squirrels all are calling
> For the trees; they fear the dog.
> Up there remains of the hill wood
> Only grey ash of oak trees;   20
> There's not a stump unstolen
> Nor a crow's nest left in our land.
> The owls are always hooting
> For trees; they send the children mad.
> The poor owl catches cold,
> Left cold without her hollow trunk.
> Woe to the goats, without trees or hazels,
> And to the sow-keeper and piglets!
> Pity an old red-bellied sow
> On Sunday, in her search for an acorn.   30
> The chair of the wild cats,

° **red squirrel**: Wales is one of the few places in the southern UK where the red squirrel persists, as it has been outcompeted by the invasive American grey.

I know where that was burnt.
Goodbye hedgehog! No cow-collar
Nor pig trough will come from here anymore.
If a plucked goose is to be roasted,
It must be with bracken from Rhodwydd Gap.
No pot will come to bubbling,
No beer will boil without small twigs;
And if peat comes from the mountain
40   In the rain, it's cold and dear.
Colds will exhaust the housemaid,
With cold feet and dripping nose.
There's no hollow trunk or branch,
Nor a fence for the beating of an old thin snipe.
Yes, Angharad° spoke the truth:
If we don't get coal it's goodbye to our land."

                    ✿ ✿ ✿

° **Angharad**: a Welsh feminine given name.

ANONYMOUS
"Glyn Cynon Wood" (*c.* 1600)

Throughout history, imperial expansion is all too often accompanied by environmental devastation. The following anonymous elegy mourns the clear-cutting of a wood in Glamorganshire by the English to fuel their iron furnaces. The poem accurately predicts the fate of South Wales landscape in the industrial era. The English also felled woods in Ireland (a policy recommended by Edmund Spenser), as noted by Boate and decried in the song "Lament for Kilcash" (c. 1800), which opens with the verse: "Now what will we do for timber, / With the last of the woods laid low?" The poem can be likened to Ronsard's "Against the Woodcutters of Gatine Forest" (1573), throwing into relief the absence of comparable anti-tree-felling verses in English prior to Michael Drayton.
Source: *The Burning Tree,* trans. Gwyn Williams (1956), 167–9.

        Aberdare, Llanwynno through,
        All Merthyr to Llanfabon;
        There was never a more disastrous thing
        Than the cutting of Glyn Cynon.

        They cut down many a parlour pure
        Where youth and manhood meet;
        In those days of the regular star,
        Glyn Cynon's woods were sweet.

If a man in sudden plight
Took to flight from foe,   10
For guest-house to the nightingale
In Cynon Vale he'd go.

Many a birch-tree green of cloak
(I'd like to choke the Saxon!)
Is now a flaming heap of fire
Where iron-workers blacken.

For cutting the branch and bearing away
The wild birds' habitation
May misfortune quickly reach
Rowena's treacherous children!°   20

Rather should the English be
Strung up beneath the seas,
Keeping painful house in hell
Than felling Cynon's trees.

Upon my oath, I've heard it said
That a herd of the red deer
For Mawddwy's deep dark woods has left,
Bereft of its warmth here.

No more the badger's earth we'll sack
Nor start a buck from the glade;   30
No more deer-stalking in my day,
Now they've cut Glyn Cynon's shade.

If ever a stag got into a wood
With huntsmen a stride behind,
Never again will he turn in his run
With Cynon Wood in mind.

If the flour-white girl once came
To walk along the brook,
Glyn Cynon's wood was always there
As a fair trysting nook.   40

If as in times gone by men plan
To span the mountain river,
Though wood be found for house and church,
Glyn Cynon's no provider.

° **Rowena's … children**: the Saxons. According to Geoffrey of Monmouth, Rowena was the daughter of the Saxon king Hengist, and her marriage to the British king Vortigen facilitated the Saxon incursion into Britain.

I'd like to call on them a quest°
Of every honest bird,
Where the owl, worthiest in the wood,
As hangman would be heard.

If there's a question who rehearsed
50   In verse this cruèl tale,
It's one who many a tryst has kept
In the depth of Cynon Vale.

ﺰ ﺰ ﺰ

° **quest**: inquest, jury.

WILLIAM HARRISON
"*Of Woods*" (1577)

England has the unflattering distinction of being one of the least wooded countries in the temperate world. While woodlands cover approximately 38 per cent
of the EU, only 13 per cent of the UK is forested (cf. USA 30 per cent, Canada 50
per cent, Brazil 56 per cent, and Japan 67 per cent). This commentary by Harrison
is one of the first attempts to gauge the extent of deforestation by appealing to
ancient chronicles. Although he recognizes it as a chronic problem stretching back
into prehistory, he also points a finger at contemporary architectural styles, and
at private individuals who flout the Elizabethan timber laws (see Appendix A).
Source: *Holinshed's Chronicles* (1587), 211–14.

It should seem by ancient records° and the testimony of sundry authors
that the whole countries of Logres and Cambria (now England and Wales)
have sometimes been very well replenished with great woods and groves,
although at this time the said commodity be not a little decayed in both,
and in such wise that a man [212] shall oft ride ten or twenty miles in each
of them and find very little, or rather none at all, except it be near unto
towns, gentlemen's houses, and villages, where the inhabitants have planted a few elms, oaks, hazels, or ashes about their dwellings for their defence
from the rough winds and keeping off the stormy weather from annoyance
of the same. This scarcity at the first grew (as it is thought) either by the
industry of man for maintenance of tillage (as we understand the like to
be done of late by the Spaniards in the West Indies, where they fired whole
woods of very great compass thereby to come by ground whereon to sow
their grains); or else through the covetousness of such (as in preferring of

° **ancient records**: such as the Normans' Domesday Book. A note in the margin here reads "Great
    abundance of wood sometime in England."

pasture for their sheep and greater cattle) do make small account of fire-bote° and timber; or finally by the cruelty of the enemies, whereof we have sundry examples declared in our histories. Howbeit where the rocks and quarry grounds are, I take the swart of the earth to be so thin that no tree of any greatness other than shrubs and bushes is able to grow or prosper long therein for want of sufficient moisture ... and this either is or may be one other cause wherefore some places are naturally void of wood. But to proceed. Although I must needs confess that there is good store of great wood or timber here and there even now in some places of England, yet in our days it is far unlike to that plenty which our ancestors have seen heretofore, when stately building was less in use. For albeit that there were then greater number of messuages° and mansions almost in every place, yet were their frames so slight and slender that one mean dwelling house in our time is able to countervail very many of them, if you consider the present charge with the plenty of timber that we bestow upon them. In times past men were contented to dwell in houses built of sallow, willow, plumtree, hardbeam,° and elm, so that the use of oak was in manner dedicated wholly unto churches, religious houses, princes' palaces, noblemen's lodgings, and navigation. But now all these are rejected and nothing but oak any whit regarded. And yet see the change: for when our houses were built of willow, then had we oaken men; but now that our houses are come to be made of oak, our men are not only become willow, but a great many through Persian delicacy° crept in among us altogether of straw ... which is a sore alteration ...

[213] I might here take occasion to speak of the great sales yearly made of wood, whereby an infinite quantity hath been destroyed within these few years, but I give over to travail° in this behalf. Howbeit thus much I dare affirm: that if woods go so fast to decay in the next hundred years of Grace as they have done and are like to do in this, sometimes for increase of sheepwalks, and some maintenance of prodigality and pomp (for I have known a well-burnished° gentleman that hath borne threescore at once in one pair of galligaskins° to show his strength and bravery), it is to be feared that the fenny-bote,° broom, turf, gall, heath, furze, brakes, ... ling, ... hassocks, flags, straw, sedge, reed, rush, and also sea-coal will be good merchandise, even in the city of London, whereunto some of then even now have gotten ready passage, and taken up their inns in the greatest merchants' parlours. A man would think that our laws were able enough to make sufficient provision for the redress of this error and enormity likely to ensue. But such is the nature of our countrymen that as many laws are

---

° **firebote**: firewood which tenants are entitled to take from their landlord's estate.
° **messuages**: dwellings.   ° **hardbeam**: hornbeam.
° **Persian delicacy**: Eastern luxury, which some Elizabethans regarded as emasculating, as the accompanying marginal note attests: "Desire of much wealth and ease abateth manhood."
° **travail**: spelled "travel."   ° **well-burnished**: plump.   ° **galligaskins**: loose breeches.
° **fenny-bote**: peat.

made, so they will keep none; or if they be urged to make answer, they will rather seek some crooked construction of them to the increase of their private gain than yield themselves to be guided by the same for a commonwealth and profit to their country: so that in the end, whatsoever the law saith, we will have our wills …

[214] Many moors, that in times past … have been harder ground and sundry of them well replenished with great woods … now are void of bushes … We find in our histories that Lincoln was sometime built by Lud (brother to Cassibelan), who called it *Caer Ludcoit*, of the great store of woods that environed the same. But now the commodity is utterly decayed there, so that if Lud were alive again he would not call it his "City-in-the-Wood," but rather his "Town-in-the-Plains." For the wood (as I hear) is wasted altogether about the same. The hills called the Peak were in like sort named *Mennith* and *Orcoit*, that is, the woody hills and forests. But how much wood is now to be seen in those places, let him that hath been there testify if he list. For I hear of no such store there as hath been in time past by those that travel that way.

※ ※ ※

JOHN LYLY
"The Crime of Erysichthon" (*c.* 1588)

This Elizabethan play is based on an ancient legend retold in Ovid's *Metamorphoses* (8.923–1088). A Thessalonian king named Erysichthon ("earth-tearer" in Greek) clear-cuts a grove sacred to Ceres and is punished with eternal hunger. To feed his voracious appetite he is forced to sell his shape-shifting daughter. The eco-critical moral of the tale is not hard to unravel: in the absence of a paid forestry service, prehistoric peoples guarded groves with *genii loci* or tutelary deities, and Erysichthon's misdeed thus stands as one of the oldest versions in Western culture of the "crime against nature" plot. In adapting this tale for performance by the Children of Paul's, the playwright John Lyly made several drastic changes: adding a Petrachan sub-plot and happy ending in which Ceres eventually pardons the penitent woodcutter so three of her nymphs, transformed by Cupid for scorning the love of three foresters, can be restored. Considering Lyly's penchant for political allegory, it is tempting to read Erysichthon as a parody of King Philip II (whom Lyly lampooned in his contemporaneous *Midas*), alluding to his tree-felling to build the Spanish Armada, and rumours that the Spanish fleet sought to burn the Forest of Dean. However, the quarto identifies the Thessalonian tyrant not as a king but a "boorish farmer and self-proclaimed ruler of the forest," so the wrath of Ceres may glance at Queen Elizabeth's frustration over her government's inability to protect royal forests or enforce the Timber Acts.
Source: *Love's Metamorphosis* (1601), B2v–C1r.

I.2
[*The Grove of Ceres*]

ERYSICHTHON What noise is this? What assembly? What Idolatry?° Is the modesty of virgins turned to wantonness? The honour of Ceres accounted immortal and Erysichthon, ruler of this Forest, esteemed of no force? Impudent giglots° that you are to disturb my game or dare do honour to any but Erysichthon! It is not your fair faces as smooth as jet, nor your enticing eyes, though they drew iron like Adamants, nor your filed° speeches, were they as forcible [B3ʳ] as Thessalides',° that shall make me any way flexible.

NIOBE Erysichthon, thy stern looks joined with thy stout speeches, thy words as unkempt as thy locks, were able to affright men of bold courage, and to make us silly° girls frantic that are full of fear. But know thou, Erysichthon, that were thy hands so unstated as thy tongue, and th'one as ready to execute mischief as the other to threaten it, it should neither move our hearts to ask pity or remove our bodies from this place. We are the handmaids of divine Ceres. To fair Ceres is this holy tree dedicated: to Ceres, by whose favour thyself livest, that are worthy to perish.

ERYSICHTHON Are you addicted° to Ceres that in spite of Erysichthon you will use these sacrifices? No, immodest girls, you shall see that I have neither regard of your sex, which men should tender, nor of your beauty, which foolish love would dote on, nor of your goddess, which none but peevish girls reverence. I will destroy this tree in despite of all. And that you may see my hand execute what my heart intendeth, and that no mean° may appease my malice, my last word shall be the beginning of the first blow.

[*He hacks the tree with his axe.*]

CELIA Out, alas! What hath he done?

NIOBE Ourselves, I fear, must also minister matter to his fury.

NISA Let him alone. But see, the tree poureth out blood, and I hear a voice.

ERYSICHTHON What voice? If in the tree there be anybody, speak quickly, lest the next blow hit the tale out of thy mouth.

FIDELIA Monster of men, hate of the heavens, and to the earth a burden, what hath chaste Fidelia committed? It is thy spite, Cupid, that having no power to wound my unspotted mind, procurest means to mangle my tender body and by violence to gash those sides that enclose a heart dedicate to virtue. Or is it that savage satyr, that feeding his [B3ᵛ] sensual appetite upon lust, seeketh now to quench it with blood, that, being without hope to attain my love, he may with cruelty end my life? Or doth

---

° **Idolatry**: this word may link Erysichthon with Puritan iconoclasts, who defaced or felled "gospel oaks."
° **giglots**: flirts.   ° **filed**: polished.
° **Thessalides**: witches whose incantations could draw down the moon.
° **silly**: innocent.   ° **addicted**: devoted   ° **mean**: intermediary, contrivance.

Ceres, whose nymph I have been many years, in recompense of my inviolable faith, reward me with unspeakable torments? Divine Phoebus, that pursued Daphne° till she was turned to a Bay tree, ceased then to trouble her. Aye, the gods are pitiful. And Cinyras, that with fury followed his daughter Myrrha° till she was changed to a myrrh tree, left then to prosecute her. Yea, parents are natural. Phoebus lamented the loss of his friend; Cinyras, of his child: but both gods and men either forget or neglect the change of Fidelia—nay, follow her after her change to make her more miserable. So that there is nothing more hateful than to be chaste, whose bodies are followed in the world with lust and prosecuted in the graves with tyranny; whose minds the freer they are from vice, their bodies are in the more danger of mischief. So that they are not safe when they live because of men's love; nor, being changed, because of their hates; nor, being dead, because of their defaming. What is that chastity which so few women study to keep, and both gods and men seek to violate? If only a naked name, why are we so superstitious of a hollow sound? If a rare virtue, why are men so careless of such an exceeding rareness? Go, Ladies, tell Ceres I am that Fidelia, that so long knit Garlands in her honour, and, chased with a Satyr, by prayer to the gods became turned to a tree, whose body now is grown over with rough bark and whose golden locks are covered with green leaves; yet whose mind nothing can alter: neither the fear of death nor the torments. If Ceres seek no revenge, then let virginity be not only the scorn of Savage people, but the spoil. But, alas, I feel my last blood to come, and therefore must end my last breath …
[B4ʳ] NISA   Thou monster, canst thou hear this without grief?
ERYSICHTHON   Yea, and double your griefs with my blows.
[He fells the tree.]
NISA   Ah, poor Fidelia, the express pattern of chastity, and example of misfortune!
CELIA   Ah, cruel Erysichthon, that not only defacest these holy trees, but murderest also this chaste nymph!
ERYSICHTHON   Nymph or goddess, it skilleth° not. For there is none that Erysichthon careth for but Erysichthon. Let Ceres, the Lady of your harvest, revenge when she will—nay, when she dares! And tell her this: that I am Erysichthon.
NIOBE   Thou art none of the gods.
ERYSICHTHON   No, a condemner of the gods.
NISA   And hopest thou to escape revenge, being but a man?
ERYSICHTHON   Yea, I care not for revenge, being a man and Erysichthon.

° **Phoebus .. Daphne**: To save her from the lustful Phoebus, the gods transform Daphne into a laurel tree. See Ovid, *Metamorphoses* 1.545–700.
° **Cinyras … Myrrha**: Myrrha (spelled "Miretia" in Lyly's text) conceives an incestuous passion for her father Cinyras, and is arborified by her guilt. See Ovid, *Metamorphoses*, 10.327–576.
° **skilleth**: matters.

NISA Come, let us to Ceres and complain of this unacquainted° and incredible villain. If there be power in her deity, in her mind pity, or virtue in virginity, this monster cannot escape.   *Exeunt.*

2.1
[*Enter*] Ceres, Niobe, Nisa, Tirtena.

CERES Doth Erysichthon offer force to my Nymphs, and to my deity disgrace? Have I stuffed his barns with fruitful [B4ᵛ] grain, and doth he stretch his hand against me with intolerable pride? So it is, Ceres, thine eyes may witness what thy Nymphs have told. Here lieth the tree hacked in pieces, and the blood scarce cold of the fairest virgin. If this be thy cruelty, Cupid, I will no more hallow thy temple with sacred vows; if thy cankered nature, Erysichthon, thou shalt find as great misery as thou showest malice. I am resolved of thy punishment and as speedy shall be my revenge as thy rigour barbarous. Tirtena, on yonder hill° where never grew grain nor leaves, where nothing is but barrenness and coldness, fear and paleness, lieth Famine. Go to her and say that Ceres commandeth her to gnaw on the bowels of Erysichthon, that his hunger may be as unquenchable as his fury.

TIRTENA I obey: but how should I know her from others?

CERES Thou canst not miss of her if thou remember but her name. And that canst thou not forget, for that coming near to the place thou shalt find gnawing in thy stomach. She lieth gaping, and swalloweth nought but air; her face pale and so lean that as easily thou mayest through the very skin behold the bone as in a glass thy shadow;° her hair long, black, and shaggy; her eyes sunk so far into her head that she looketh out of the nape of her neck; her lips white and rough; her teeth hollow and red with rustiness; her skin so thin that thou mayest as lively° make an Anatomy of her body as she were cut up with Surgeon; her maw° like a dry bladder; her heart swollen big with wind; and all her bowels like snakes working in her body. When this monster thou shalt behold, tell her my mind and return with speed.

TIRTENA I go, fearing more the sight of Famine than the force.

CERES Take thou these few ears of corn, but let not Famine so much as smell to them. And let her go aloof from thee. [*Exit Tirtena, with ears of grain.*] Now shall Erysichthon see that Ceres is a great goddess, as full of power as himself of pride, and as pitiless [C1ʳ] as he presumptuous. How think you, ladies? Is not this revenge apt for so great injury?

NIOBE Yes, Madam: to let men see they that contend with the gods do but confound themselves.

ॐ ॐ ॐ

° **unacquainted**: unknown, unprecedented.   ° **hill**: moorland.
° **glass ... shadow**: mirror your reflection.   ° **lively**: vividly, accurately.   ° **maw**: stomach.

JOHN HARINGTON
"Of the Growth of Trees, to Sir Hugh Portman" (*c.* 1600)

Portman was a Member of Parliament and a wealthy landowner in Somerset. While his planting trees on his estate might be construed as an act of conservation, Harington, his neighbour, takes a sardonic view of it as an investment, contrasting the slow physical growth of trees with the exponential growth of timber prices. Source: *Epigrams* (1618), H1ᵛ.

> At your rich Orchard you to me did show,
> How swift the Trees were planted there did grow:
> Namely, an Elm, that in no long abode
> Did of a twig grow up to be a load.°
> But you would quite condemn your trees of sloth
> Compared to our trees' admirable growth.
> Our planters have found out such secret skills,
> With pipe° and barrel staves, and iron Mills,
> That Oaks, for which none ten years since were willing

10
> To give ten groats, are grown worth thirty shilling.°
> At which I waxed so wood° I said in rage,
> That thirst of Gold makes this an Iron age.

⁂

° **load**: approximately 50 cubic feet of wood.   ° **pipe**: cask.
° **groats … shilling**: the former was worth 4d. and the latter 12d. In other words, timber prices increased ninefold in a decade.
° **wood**: mad, with an obvious pun; in Folger MS V. a. 249 the first person pronouns are replaced with "my muse" and "she."

JOHN NORDEN
"Articles of Inquiry from a Court of Survey" and *"Gentlemen Sell Their Woods too Fast"* (1607)

As a well-travelled chorographer and surveyor of Crown woods in Berkshire, Devon, and Surrey, John Norden is a particularly trustworthy witness of the scale of the timber crisis. Although his profession disposed him to view trees as commodities, Norden's use of the dialogue format allows the Surveyor and Bailey to consider the problem from multiple angles and propose some sensible solutions. The first extract comes from a list of questions a surveyor was expected to ask when inventorying an estate's assets. In the second selection, the speakers unfurl a granular picture of which regions had been most severely deforested, lament the abuse of the nation's forest laws, and assess the environmental impact of unregulated industry. Norden's plea for a national tree-planting campaign would soon be championed by Arthur Standish and Rooke Church, and half a century later by John Evelyn. Source: *Surveyor's Dialogue* (1607), 116–17, 211–17.

"Articles of Inquiry from a Court of Survey"

SURVEYOR Article 35: Whether doth the Lord, or may he, take in any swine to pannage° yearly into his park or woods, what is the pannage worth by year.

BAILEY Sir, you need little to inquire of that. For Oaks and Beech that have been formerly very famous in many parts of this kingdom for feeding the Farmers' venison are fallen to the ground and gone, and their places are scarcely known where they stood.

SURVEYOR It is very true. And it is pity that Lords of Manors have no more care of their posterities. For assuredly there will be greater want of timber in time to come in this Realm than may be supplied with little charge from any part else whatsoever. And therefore might Lords and Farmers easily add some supply of future hope in setting for every twenty acres of other land, one acre of acorns, which would come to be good timber in his son's age, especially where there is (and like to be) more want.

[117] BAILEY Truly, it is pity it were not enjoined to men of ability and land to do it. But I think men imagine there will be timber enough to the end of the world ...

[211] "Gentlemen Sell their Woods too Fast"

BAILEY I will tell you, sir, careless Gentlemen that have Manors and Parks well-wooded left them by their careful ancestors, that would not strip a tree for gold, are of the mind (as it seemeth) that the shadow of the high trees do dazzle their eyes; they cannot see to play the good husbands nor look about them to sell the land till the trees be taken out of their sight.

SURVEYOR Can you break a jest so boldly upon men of worth?

BAILEY You see as well as I some do it in earnest. And I think indeed it is partly your fault that are Surveyors. For when Gentlemen have sunk themselves by rowing in Vanity's boat, you blow them the bladders° of lavishing helps to make them swim again awhile, counselling first to clear the land of [212] the wood (in the sale whereof is great abuse) persuading them they shall sell the land little the cheaper. And indeed I hold it providence where necessity commands to chose of two the lesser evil: namely, to sell part of a superfluous quantity of wood, where the remnant will serve the party in use ...

SURVEYOR When you seem to have best skill and earnest desire to draw the line straight ... a man inclinable to his own will ... will rather give it into the hands of someone that feeds his conceits with flattery ... and he shall manage the building, when you have laid the foundation ... I say only this: since timber and timber trees and wood by due observation are found to decay so fast, methinks in common discretion it should behove every good husband (for all would be so accounted), both upon his own

---

° **pannage**: forage (for acorns and nuts); also the fee paid for permission to do so.
° **bladders**: floats.

and as also upon such as he holds of other men, not only to maintain and to the uttermost to preserve the timber trees and saplings likely to become timber trees (Oak, Elm, and Ash), but voluntarily to plant young. And because there is not only a universal inclination to hurl down it were expedient [213] that, since *will* will not, authority should constrain some mean of restoration: namely, to enjoin men, as well Lords as tenants, to plant for every sum of acre a number of trees, or to sow or set a quantity of ground with Acorns.

BAILEY I remember there is a Statute° made (35 Henry VIII and the 1 Elizabeth) for the preservation of timber trees: Oak, Ash, Elm, Aspen, and Beech; and that twelve storers° and standels° should be left standing at every fall, upon an acre. But methinks this Statute is deluded and the meaning abused. For I have seen in many places at the falls, where indeed they leave the number of standels and more, but instead they cut down them that were preserved before; and at the next fall, them that were left to answer the Statute, and young left again in their steads. So that there can be no increase of timber trees, notwithstanding the words of the Statute ... And therefore it were not amiss that some provision were made to maintain the meaning of the Statute in more force. But I leave that to such as see more than I see and have power to reform it.

SURVEYOR It is a thing indeed to be regarded, for indeed there is abuse in it.

BAILEY Surely it is, especially in places where little timber grows. For there is no Country, how barren of timber soever, but hath use of timber. And therefore if neither men's own wills, seeing the imminent want, nor force of justice will move and work a reformation, we may say as the Proverb is: Let them that live longest, fetch their wood farthest.

SURVEYOR But some Countries are yet well stored, and for the abundance of timber and wood were excepted in the Statute, as the Wealds of Kent, Sussex and Surrey, [214] which were all anciently comprehended under the name of Holmesdale. There are diverse places also in Devonshire, Cheshire and Shropshire, well wooded. And yet he that well observes it and hath known the Wealds of Sussex, Surrey, and Kent, the grand nursery of those kind of trees (especially Oak and Beech), shall find such an alteration within less than thirty years as may well strike a fear ... lest few years more as pestilent as the former will leave few good trees standing in those Wealds.

Such a heat issueth out of the many forges and furnaces for the making of Iron, and out of the glass kilns, as hath devoured many famous woods within the Wealds: as about Burningfold, Lopwood Green, the Minns, Kirdford, Petworth parks, Eberno e Wassal, Rusper, Balcombe, Dallington ... and some forests and other places infinite ... But the crop of this commodious

---

° **Statute**: see Appendix A.   ° **storers**: old trees spared from felling.
° **standels**: young trees spared from felling.

fruit of the earth, which nature itself doth sow, being thus reaped and cut down by the sickle of time, hath been in some plentiful places, in regard of the superfluous abundance, rather held a hurtful weed than a profitable fruit; and therefore the wasting of it held providence,° to the end that corn, a more profitable increase, might be brought in instead of it, which hath made inhabitants so fast to hasten the confusion of the one to have the other. But it is to be feared that posterities will find want where now they think is too much.

BAILEY It is no marvel if Sussex and other places you speak of be deprived of this benefit. For I have heard there are, or lately were, in Sussex near 140 [215] hammers and furnaces for Iron, and in it and Surrey adjoining, three or four glass-houses. The hammers and furnaces spend, each of them in every twenty-four hours, two, three, or four loads of charcoal, which in a year amounteth to an infinite quantity, as you can better account by your arithmetic than I.

SURVEYOR That which you say is true, but they work not all the year. For many of them lack water in the Summer to blow their bellows. And to say truth, the consuming of much of these in the Weald is no such great prejudice to the weal public as is the overthrow of wood and timber in places where there is no great quantity. For I have observed that the cleansing of many of these Weald grounds hath redounded rather to the benefit than to the hurt of the Country. For where woods did grow in superfluous abundance, there was lack of pasture for kine and of arable land for corn, without the which a Country or Country farm cannot stand or be relieved but by neighbour helps, as the Downs have their wood from the Weald. Besides, people bred amongst woods are naturally more stubborn and uncivil than in the Champaign Countries ... Yet I hold a moderation necessary, lest that the too much overthrowing of timber trees and stocking up of Woods bring such a scarcity of that most necessary commodity, as men build not for lack of timber ... which cannot but ensue if there be neither prevention for the subversion° of the present, [217] nor provision to plant or spare for the time to come. Who seeth not that the general extirpation and stocking up of copse grounds in Middlesex will breed want to them that shall succeed?

BAILEY But that may be the more tolerated because it bringeth a greater profit in tillage and pasture: the ground, being good, bringeth forth wheat and oats and other commodious grain instead of stubs and shrubs.

SURVEYOR Stubs and shrubs are also necessary. But as we desire food, we must preserve the means to prepare it for food. For as corn availeth not without Mills to grind, so other necessaries without firing are of little use. If all were arable, where were meadow and pasture? If all pasture and meadow, where corn? If all for corn and grass, it were like Midas his wish.

° **providence**: provident.   ° **subversion**: downfall.

Therefore it is good to foresee and to avoid a mischief to come by desiring or using present commodities moderately and providently. For when there is a true concurrence between the use and preservation, and increase of necessary commodities without wilful consuming, there seldom followeth too much want. But if for the overgreedy use of things present there be no regard of future occasion, it cannot be but if the earth, the mother of man and other creatures, could verbally complain, she might well say, she were even robbed of her fruits by her own children.

~~ ~~ ~~

MICHAEL DRAYTON
[Deforestation in Poly-Olbion] (1612, 1622)

By the early seventeenth century, alarms over England's depleted woodlands were reaching a shrill pitch. Troubled by the 1607 Midlands Revolt, Arthur Standish undertook a four-year journey throughout the countryside to inquire into the roots of the unrest and concluded that they sprang from the exorbitant cost of not only food but also timber in a wood-based economy. Deforestation, he believed, posed a threat to the stability of the realm: "no wood, no Kingdom" (2). One year after Norden published his dialogue, King James ordered him to participate in a massive survey of Crown woods to investigate mismanagement and determine which ones he could auction off to replenish the state coffers. Another surveyor involved in the project was Rooke Church, who was appalled by the "lamentable scarcity and exceeding abuses" (A3ʳ) in the royal forests. These environmental audits reveal the topical urgency of Drayton's literary survey of England, which echoes their dire warnings and appeared in print while James was approving the sale of several woodlands (McRae 2012). Although the references to deforestation might seem statistically insignificant given the scope of his 15,000-line chorographical epic, the persistent elegies for forests make it something of a unifying theme. The four excerpts below reflect Drayton's nostalgia for a pagan poetics of enchantment, his belief in a symbiosis between England's sylvan ecology and its literature, and his unspoken conviction that the antiquarian study of the past can nurture a sense of ethical obligation towards posterity. For Drayton, history and natural history are one.
Source: *Poly-Olbion* (1612), 1:24–5, 33–4, 42–3, 107–8, and *Poly-Olbion* (1622), 2:62.

[The Frome's Lament for Blackmore°]

60
    Then Frome (a nobler flood) the Muses doth implore,
    Her mother Blackmore's state they sadly would bewail,
    Whose big and lordly Oaks once bore as brave a sail

° **Blackmore:** forest in northern Dorsetshire, now known as Blackmore Vale.

As they themselves that thought the largest shades to spread:
But man's devouring hand, with all the earth not fed,
Hath hewed her Timber down; which, wounded when it fell,
By the great noise it made, the workmen seemed to tell
The loss that to the Land would shortly come thereby,
Where no man ever plants to our posterity;
That when sharp Winter shoots her sleet and hardened hail,
Or sudden gusts from Sea the harmless Deer assail,   70
The shrubs are not of power to shield them from the wind …
The Forests took their leave: Bere, Chute, and Buckholt bid
Adieu; so Woolmer and so Ash Holt° kindly did;
And Pamber° shook her head, as grievèd at the heart;°
When far upon her way, and ready to depart,   470
As now the wand'ring Muse so sadly went along,
To her last Farewell, thus the goodly Forests sung:°
"Dear Muse, to plead our right, whom time at last hath brought,
Which else forlorn had lain, and banished every thought,
When thou ascend'st the hills, and from their rising shrouds
Our sisters shalt command, whose tops once touched the clouds:
Old Arden when thou meet'st, or dost fair Sherwood see,
Tell them that as they waste, so every day do we.
Wish them we of our griefs may be each other's heirs;
Let them lament our fall, and we will mourn for theirs" …   480

[The Prophecy of Salisbury Plain]

"Away ye barb'rous Woods, however ye be placed:
On Mountains or in Dales, or happily be graced
With floods or marshy fells,° with pasture or with earth,
By nature made to till, that by the yearly birth
The large-bayed Barn doth fill—yea, though the fruitful'st ground.
For in respect of Plains, what pleasure can be found
In dark and sleepy shades? Where mists and rotten fogs
Hang in the gloomy thicks and make unsteadfast bogs,
By dropping from the boughs, the o'ergrown trees among,
With Caterpillars' cells° and dusky cobwebs hung,   120
The deadly Screech-owl sits, in gloomy covert hid.
Whereas the smooth-browed Plain, as liberally doth bid

° **Ash Holt**: also called Alice Holt. In 1603, the navy expropriated 1,600 loads of timber from this forest (Surrey 6729/11/102). Four years later another 500 trees were felled in Ash Holt and 400 in Pamber for shipyards (Berkshire Record Office D/EN/04/3).

° **Pamber**: deemed "well preserved" (National Archives E178/2049) in 1596, when 168 trees were sold to a shipwright named Cross, it was deforested in 1614, "the woods being sold away and the deer gone." It is now a Site of Special Scientific Interest renowned for the number of butterfly species it supports.

° **heart**: spelled "hart."

° **sung**: Drayton's spelling "song" emphasizes the rhyme but also allows for a reading of the final two words as "Forests' song."

° **fells**: bogs.

° **cells**: cocoons.

The Lark to leave her Bower, and on her trembling wing
In climbing up towards heav'n, her high-pitched Hymns to sing …
The gentle Shepherds here survey their gentler sheep;
Amongst the bushy woods, luxurious° Satyrs keep …
But Forests, to your plague, there soon will come an Age,
150   In which all damnèd sins most veh'mently shall rage.
An Age! What have I said! Nay, Ages there shall rise,
So senseless of the good of their posterities,
That of your greatest Groves they scarce shall leave a tree
(By which the harmless Deer may after sheltered be),
Their luxury and pride but only to maintain,
And for your long excess shall turn ye all to pain …

[The Destruction of Wyre]

When soon the goodly Wyre, that wonted was so high
Her stately top to rear, ashamèd to behold
Her straight and goodly Woods unto the Furnace° sold
(And looking on herself, by her decay doth see
260   The misery wherein her sister Forests be),
Of Erysichthon's° end begins her to bethink,
And of his cruël plagues doth wish they all might drink
That thus have them despoiled; then of her own despite,
That she, in whom her Town fair Bewdely took delight,
And from her goodly seat conceived so great a pride,
In Severn on her east, Wyre on the setting side,
So naked left of woods, of pleasure, and forlorn,
As she that loved her most, her now the most doth scorn;
With endless grief perplexed, her stubborn breast she strake,
270   And to the deafened air thus passionately spake:
"You Dryads that are said with Oaks to live and die,
Wherefore in our distress do you our dwellings fly,
Upon this monstrous Age and not revenge our wrong?
For cutting down an Oak that justly did belong
To one of Ceres' Nymphs, in Thessaly that grew
In the Dodonean° Grove, (O Nymphs!) you could pursue
The son of Perops° then, and did the Goddess stir
That villainy to wreak° the Tyrant did to her;
Who with a dreadful frown did blast the growing Grain,
280   And having from him reft what should his life maintain,
She unto Scythia sent for Hunger, him to gnaw,
And thrust her down his throat into his staunchless maw;°

° **luxurious**: lecherous.
° **Furnace**: much of Wyre's woodlands were felled to make charcoal to fuel ironworks founded by
   Robert Dudley, Earl of Leicester, at Cleobury Mortimer.
° **Erysichthon**: see Ovid's *Metamorphoses*, 8.923–1088, and the excerpt from Lyly, p. 418.
° **Dodonean**: Drayton here conflates Ceres's grove in Thessaly with a grove dedicated to Jove in
   Dodona.
° **son of Perops**: Erysichthon.   ° **wreak**: punish.   ° **staunchless maw**: insatiable stomach.

Who, when nor Sea nor Land for him sufficient were,
With his devouring teeth his wretched flesh did tear.
This did you for one Tree; but of whole Forests they
That in these impious times have been the vile decay
(Whom I may justly call their Country's deadly foes),
'Gainst them you move no power; their spoil unpunished goes.
How many grievèd souls in future time shall starve
For that which they have rapt° their beastly lust to serve!   290
We, sometime that the state of famous Britain were,
For whom she was renowned in Kingdoms far and near,
Are ransacked; and our Trees so hacked above the ground,
That where their lofty tops their neighbouring Countries crowned,
Their Trunks (like agèd folks) now bare and naked stand,
As for revenge to heav'n each held a withered hand;
And where the goodly Herds of high-palmed° Harts did gaze
Upon the passer-by, there now doth only graze
The galled-back carrion Jade,° and hurtful Swine do spoil
Once to the Sylvan Powers our consecrated soil …   300

[Weybridge Forest]

So travelling along upon her silent shore,
Weybridge, a neighbouring Nymph, the only remnant left
Of all that Forest kind, by Time's injurious theft
Of all that tract destroyed, with wood which did abound,
And former times had seen the goodliest Forest ground
This Island ever had; but she so left alone,
The ruin of her kind, and no man to bemoan,
The deep entrancèd Flood,° as thinking to awake,
Thus from her shady Bower she silently bespake: 1610
"O Flood in happy plight, which to this time remain'st,
As still along in state to Neptune's court thou strain'st,
Revive thee with the thought of those forepassèd hours,
When the rough Wood-gods kept, in their delightful Bowers
On thy embroidered banks, when now this Country filled
With villages, and by the labouring ploughman tilled,
Was Forest, where the Fir and spreading Poplar grew.
O let me yet the thought of those past times renew,
When as that woody kind in our umbrageous° Wild,
When every living thing, save only they exiled,   1620
In this their world of waste,° the sovereign Empire swayed.
O who would ere have thought that time could have decayed
Those trees whose bodies seemed by their so massy weight
To press the solid earth, and with their wondrous height
To climb into the Clouds, their Arms so far to shoot,

° **rapt**: seized.   ° **palmed**: antlered.
° **Jade**: contemptuous term for less valuable breed of horse.
° **Flood**: the Great Ouse.   ° **umbrageous**: shadowy.   ° **waste**: wilderness.

As they in measuring were of Acres, and their Root
With long and mighty spurs° to grapple with the land,
As Nature would have said that they should ever stand."

ɝ ɝ ɝ

° **spurs**: roots; spurns] 1622.

MICHAEL DRAYTON
"The Tenth Nymphal"° (1630)

In this poem written late in his life, Drayton bemoans that the warnings he issued in *Poly-Olbion* have gone unheeded. The dispossessed satyr is an unmistakable self-portrait of the poet laureate of England's woodlands, and the refuge he finds with Corbilus symbolizes Drayton's flight from the ravaged Weald to Knole House (now the last surviving medieval deer park in Kent), the estate of Edward Sackville, the 4th Earl of Dorset. It has been speculated that Drayton intended the poem as a dramatic entertainment, with the roles of the nymphs played by Sackville's daughters (Hiller). The title of the work from which it is taken, spelled *Muses' Elizium*, punningly conflates the abode of the blessed in Greek mythology with a nostalgic vision of Elizabeth's reign as a golden age of both literary patronage and environmental stewardship.
Source: *The Muses' Elysium* (1630), 81–5.

> A Satyr on Elysium lights,
> Whose ugly shape the Nymphs affrights,
> Yet when they hear his just complaint,
> They make him an Elysian Saint.

CORBILUS What, breathless Nymphs? Bright Virgins, let me know
What sudden cause constrains ye to this haste?
What have ye seen that should affright ye so?
What might it be from which ye fly so fast?
I see your faces full of pallid fear,
As though some peril followed on your flight;
Take breath awhile, and quickly let me hear
Into what danger ye have lately light.
NAIIS Never were poor distressèd Girls so glad,
As when kind, lovèd Corbilus we saw,
When our much haste us so much weakened had,
That scarcely we our wearied breaths could draw.
In this next Grove under an agèd Tree,
So fell° a monster lying there we found,
As till this day our eyes did never see,
Nor ever came on the Elysian ground.

10

° **Nymphal**: a meeting of nymphs (Drayton's coinage).   ° **fell**: savage.

Half-man, half-Goat he seemed to us in show;
His upper parts our human shape doth bear,
But he's a very perfect Goat below,
His crooked Cambrels° armed with hoof and hair.   20
CLAIA Through his lean Chops° a chatt'ring he doth make
Which stirs his starting,° beastly, drivelled Beard,
And his sharp horns he seemed at us to shake;
Canst thou then blame us though we were afeard?
CORBILUS Surely it seems some Satyr this should be.
Come and go back and guide me to the place;
Be not afraid, ye are safe enough with me;
Silly° and harmless be their Sylvan Race.
CLAIA How Corbilus? A Satyr do you say?
How should he over high Parnassus hit,°   30
Since to these Fields there's none can find the way,
But only those the Muses will permit?
CORBILUS 'Tis true, but oft the sacred Sisters grace
The silly Satyr,° by whose plainness they
Are taught the world's enormities to trace,
By beastly men's abominable° way.
Besides, he may be banished his own home
By this base time, or be so much distressed
That he the craggy becliffed Hill hath clome°
To find out these more pleasant Fields of rest.   40
NAIIS Yonder he sits, and seems himself to bow
At our approach. What? Doth our presence awe him?
Methinks he seems not half so ugly now
As at the first, when I and Claia saw him.
CORBILUS 'Tis an old Satyr, Nymph, I now discern;
Sadly he sits, as he were sick or lame.
His looks would say that we may eas'ly learn
How and from whence he to Elysium came.
Satyr, these Fields how cam'st thou first to find?
What Fate first showed thee this most happy shore,   50
When never any of thy Sylvan kind
Set foot on the Elysian earth before?
SATYR O never ask how I came to this place;
What cannot strong necessity find out?
Rather bemoan my miserable case,
Constrained to wander the wide world about.
With wild Silvanus and his woody crew,
In Forests I, at liberty and free,
Lived in such pleasure as the world ne'er knew,
Nor any rightly can conceive but we.   60
This jocund life we many a day enjoyed,
Till this last age those beastly men forth brought,
That all those great and goodly Woods destroyed,
Whose growth their Grandsires with such sufferance sought,
That fair Felicia° which was but of late

° **Cambrels**: thighs, or hock, the upper part of a horse's hind leg.   ° **Chops**: jaws.
° **starting**: unkempt.° **Silly**: innocent.   ° **hit**: pass.   ° **clome**: climbed.   ° **Felicia**: England.
° **Satyr**: spelled "Satyre" to play on satire.
° **abominable**: spelled "abhominable" to evoke the Latin for inhuman.

Earth's Paradise, that never had her Peer,
Stands now in that most lamentable state
That not a Sylvan will inhabit there;
Where in the soft and most delicious shade
70   In heat of Summer we were wont to play,
When the long day too short for us we made,
The sliding hours so slyly stole away;
By Cynthia's light and on the pleasant Lawn,
The wanton Fairy we were wont to chase,
Which to the nimble cloven-footed Faun°
Upon the plain durst boldly bid the base,°
The sportive Nymphs, with shouts and laughter shook
The Hills and Valleys in their wanton play,
Waking the Echoes, their last words that took,
80   Till at the last, they louder were than they.
The lofty high Wood and the lower spring,
Shelt'ring the Deer in many a sudden shower,
Where Choirs of Birds oft wonted were to sing,
The flaming Furnace° wholly doth devour;
Once fair Felicia, but now quite defaced,
Those Braveries gone wherein she did abound,
With dainty Groves, when she was highly graced
With goodly Oak, Ash, Elm, and Beeches crowned.
But that from heav'n their judgement blinded is,
90   In humane Reason it could never be,
But that they might have clearly seen by this,
Those plagues their next posterity shall see.
The little Infant on the Mother's Lap
For want of fire shall be so sore distressed,
That whilst it draws the lank and empty Pap,
The tender lips shall freeze unto the breast;
The quaking Cattle which their Warm-stall° want,
And with bleak winter's Northern wind oppressed,
Their Browse° and Stover° waxing thin and scant,
100   The hungry Crows shall with their Carrion feast.
Men wanting Timber wherewith they should build,
And not a Forest in Felicia found,
Shall be enforced upon the open Field,
To dig them Caves for houses in the ground.
The Land thus robbed of all her rich Attire,
Naked and bare herself to heav'n doth show,
Begging from thence that Jove would dart his fire

° **Faun**: goat-like forest deity, but spelled "Fawn."
° **bid the base**: invite to play the game Prisoner's Base.
° **Furnace**: of the Wealden ironworks.   ° **Warm-stall**: fires to heat barns on cold winter days.
° **Browse**: spring shoots, twigs.   ° **Stover**: winter fodder.

Upon those wretches that disrobed her so.
This beastly Brood by no means may abide
The name of their brave Ancestors to hear,　　　110
By whom their sordid slavery is descried,
So unlike them as though not theirs they were,
Nor yet they sense nor understanding have
Of those brave Muses that their Country sung:°
But with false Lips ignobly do deprave
The right and honour that to them belong.
This cruėl kind thus Viper-like devour
That fruitful soil which them too fully fed;
The earth doth curse the Age, and every hour
Again, that it these vip'rous monsters bred.　　　120
I, seeing the plagues that shortly are to come
Upon this people, clearly them forsook,
And thus am light into Elysium,
To whose strait search I wholly me betook.
NAIIS　Poor silly creature, come along with us.
Thou shalt be free of° the Elysian fields.
Be not dismayed, nor inly grievèd thus;
This place in all abundance yields.
We to the cheerful presence will thee bring
Of Jove's dear Daughters,° where in shades they sit,　　　130
Where thou shalt hear those sacred Sisters sing,
Most heavenly Hymns, the strength and life of wit.
CLAIA　Where to the Delphion God° upon their Lyres
His Priests seem ravished in his height of praise,
Whilst he is crowning his harmonious Choirs,
With circling Garlands of immortal Bays.
CORBILUS　Here live in bliss, till thou shalt see those slaves,
Who thus set virtue and desert at nought,
Some sacrificed upon their Grandsires' graves,
And some like beasts in markets sold and bought.　　　140
Of fools and madmen leave thou then the care,
That have no understanding of their state;
For whom high heav'n doth so just plagues prepare
That they to pity shall convert thy hate.
And to Elysium be thou welcome then,
Until those base Felicians thou shalt hear,
By that vile nation° captived again,
That many a glorious age their captives were.

ᘰ ᘰ ᘰ

° **sung**: Drayton here vents his bitterness over the neglect of *Poly-Olbion*.
° **free of**: legally permitted to reside in.　　° **Jove's … daughters**: the Muses.
° **Delphion God**: Apollo.　　° **vile nation**: France, or possibly Rome.

GERARD BOATE
"Woods much diminished in Ireland since the first coming in of the English" (1645)

In his 1599 *Treatise of Ireland*, John Dymmok reported that Ireland boasts "great plenty of wood, except in Leinster, where for the great inconveniences finding them to be ready harbours for the Irish rebels, they have been cut down" (6). Although revisionist historians have complicated the traditional view that the Elizabethan occupation perpetrated an "arboreal holocaust" in Ireland (Everett 11), Boate's text furnishes ample evidence as to why this narrative was already circulating in the seventeenth century. Walter Ralegh and Henry Pyne were accused of denuding Irish woods to make "pipe staves" or casks for the wine trade, and vast quantities of timber were consumed by the ironworks at Creevla and Arigna. As this iron ordnance could have been used to fight the Irish rebels, it is hardly surprising they destroyed them in 1641, an act that would be more accurately characterized as industrial sabotage rather than eco-terrorism.
Source: *Ireland's Natural History* (1657), 119–21, 130.

In ancient times, and as long as the land was in the full possession of the Irish themselves, all Ireland was very full of Woods on every side, as evidently appeareth by the writings of Gerald of Wales, who came into Ireland upon the first conquest, in the company of Henry the Second, King of England, in the year of our Saviour 1171. But the English having settled themselves in the land, did by degrees greatly diminish the Woods in all the places where they were masters, partly to deprive the Thieves and Rogues, who used to lurk in the Woods in great numbers, of their refuge and starting-holes, and partly to gain the greater scope of profitable lands. For the trees being cut down, the roots stubbed up, and the land used and tilled according to exigency,° the Woods in most part of Ireland may be reduced not only to very good Pastures but also to excellent Arable and Meadow. Through these two causes it is come to pass in the space of many years—yea, of some Ages—that a great part of the Woods which the English [120] found in Ireland at their first arrival there are quite destroyed, so as nothing at all remaineth of them at this time.

And even since the subduing of the last great Rebellion of the Irish before this, under the conduct of the Earl of Tyrone (overthrown in the last years of Queen Elizabeth ...) and during this last peace of about forty years (the longest that Ireland ever enjoyed, both before and since the coming in of the English), the remaining Woods have very much been diminished, and in sundry places quite destroyed, partly for the reason last mentioned, and partly for the wood and timber itself: not for the ordinary uses of building and firing (the which, ever having been afoot, are not very considerable in regard of what now we speak of) but to make merchandise of, and for the making of Charcoal for the Ironworks. As for the first, I have not heard that great timber hath ever been used to be sent

° **exigency**: necessity.

out of Ireland in any great quantity, nor in any ordinary way of Traffic, but only Pipe-staves,° and the like ... but never in that vast quantity nor so constantly as of late years and during the last Peace, wherein it was grown one of the ordinary merchandable commodities of the country, so as a mighty trade was driven in them, and whole ship-loads sent into foreign countries [121] yearly ... The felling of so many thousands of trees every year as were employed that way did make a great destruction of the Woods in tract of time. As for the Charcoal, it is incredible what quantity thereof is consumed by one Ironwork in a year. And whereas there was never an Ironwork in Ireland before, there hath been a very great number of them erected since the last Peace in sundry parts of every Province; the which to furnish constantly with Charcoals, it was necessary from time to time to fell an infinite number of trees, all the loppings and windfalls being not sufficient for it in the least manner ...

[130] In imitation of these have also been erected diverse Ironworks in sundry parts of the sea-coast of Ulster and Munster by persons who, having no Mines upon or near their own Lands, had the Ore brought unto them by sea out of England; the which they found better cheap than if they had caused it to be fetched by land from some of the Mines within the land. And all this by English, whose industry herein the Irish have been so far from imitating, as since the beginning of this Rebellion they have broken down and quite demolished almost all the aforementioned Ironworks, as well those of the one as of the other sort.

⁂ ⁂ ⁂

° **Pipe-staves**: wooden casks. Walter Ralegh exported pipe-staves from his Irish estates, and was accused of destroying woodlands (a charge he denied).

MARGARET CAVENDISH
"A Dialogue between an Oak and a Man cutting him°down" (1653)

Cavendish's poems often endow non-humans with a human voice. In this example, a tree protests its felling, and chafes at the woodcutter's assurances that its utility as timber will bring it greater dignity. Although the same conceit appears in George Turberville's "The Pine to the Mariner" (1567, 82ᵛ–3ᵛ), Cavendish's version is more outspoken in its denunciation of human exploitation (also see her poem "A Dialogue Betwixt Man and Nature"). In the wake of Charles II's concealment in the Boscobel oak, her comparison of this tree to a king would have an obvious

---

° **him**: it] 1664.

political resonance. Given that Cavendish was outraged by the sell-off of her husband's confiscated woodlands, whose value she estimated at £45,000 (Whitaker 243–4), the poem's politics connot be disentangled from its environmental critique. It reflects a genuine concern about deforestation in the aftermath of a devastating Civil War (see Figure 7). However, the facts that the Cavendishes built massive stately homes and that Margaret even urged her husband to fell large woodlands at Welbeck and Sherwood (Whitaker 331) to pay off debts complicates a one-sided reading of the poem that would exalt her as a proto-environmentalist. Is Man's final ultimatum an ironic indictment of the eco-hubris of Parliamentarians and men? Or a resigned acceptance of this hubris as a failing of all humans, regardless of politics and gender?

Source: *Poems and Fancies* (1653), 66–70.

> OAK Why cut you off my Boughs, both large and long,°
> That keep you from the heat and scorching Sun,°
> And did refresh your fainting Limbs from sweat?
> From thund'ring Rains I keep you free, from Wet,°
> When on my Bark your weary head would° lay,
> Where quiet Sleep did take all Cares away,
> The whilst my Leaves a gentle noise did make,
> And blew cool Winds that you fresh Air might take.
> Besides, I did invite the Birds to sing,
> 10 That their sweet voice might you some pleasure bring,
> Where everyone did strive to do their best,
> Oft changed their Notes, and strained their tender Breast.
> In Wintertime, my Shoulders broad did hold
> Off blust'ring Storms that wounded with sharp Cold,
> And on my Head the Flakes of Snow did fall,
> Whilst you under my Boughs sat free from all.
> And will you thus requite my Love, Good Will,°
> To take away° my Life, and Body kill?
> For all my Care and Service I have passed,
> 20 Must I be cut and laid on Fire at last?
> And thus° true Love you cruelly have slain,
> And tried all ways° to torture me with pain:
> First, you do peel my Bark and flay my Skin,
> Hew down my Boughs, so chop off every Limb;°
> With Wedges you do pierce my Sides to wound,
> And with your Hatchet knock me to the ground.
> I minced shall be in Chips and Pieces small;
> And thus doth Man reward good Deeds withal.
> MAN Why grumblest thou,° old Oak, when thou hast° stood

° **both .. long**: which largely bend] 1664.
° **That ... Sun**: And from the scorching Sun you do defend] 1664.
° **From ... Wet**: And kept you free from Thund'ring Rains and Wet] 1664.
° **would**: you'ld] 1664.
° **And ... Will**: And shall thus be requited my good will] 1664.
° **To ... away**: That you will take] 1664.   ° **And thus**: See how] 1664.
° **And ... ways**: 1664; Invent always] 1653.
° **Hew ... Limb**: Chop off my Limbs, and leave me nak'd and thin] 1664.
° **thou**: you] 1664.   ° **thou hast**: you have] 1664.

This hundred years, as King of all the Wood? 30
Would you forever live and not resign
Your Place to one that is of your own Line?
Your Acorns young, when they° grow big and tall,
Long for your Crown,° and wish to see your fall;
Think every minute lost whilst you do live,
And grumble at each Office you do give.
Ambition flieth° high, and is above
All sorts of Friendship strong or° Natural Love.
Besides, all Subjects do° in Change delight;
When Kings grow old, their Government they slight. 40
Although in ease and peace and wealth they° live,
Yet all those happy times for Change will° give:
Grows discontent, and Factions still do make;
What Good so e'er he doth as Evil take.
Were he as wise as ever Nature made,
As pious, good, as ever Heaven saved,
Yet when he Dies° such Joy is in their Face,
As if the Devil had gone from that place.
With Shouts of Joy they run a new to Crown,
Although next day they strive to pull him down. 50
OAK Why (said the Oak) because that they are mad,
Shall I rejoice, for my own Death be glad?
Because my Subjects all ungrateful are,
Shall I therefore my health and life impair?
Good Kings govern justly, as they ought.°
Examine not their Humours, but their Fault:°
For when their Crimes appear 'tis time to strike,
Not to examine Thoughts how° they do like.
If° Kings are never loved till they do die,
Nor wished to live till in the Grave they lie, 60
Yet he that loves himself the less because
He cannot get every man's high applause
Shall by my Judgement be condemned to wear
The Ass's ears, and Burdens for to bear.
But let me live the Life that Nature gave,
And not, to please my Subjects, dig my Grave.
MAN But here, poor Oak, thou liv'st° in Ignorance,
And never seek'st thy° Knowledge to advance.
I'll cut thee down, cause Knowledge thou mayest° gain:
Shalt be a Ship to traffic on the Main. 70
There shalt thou° swim and cut the Seas in two,
And trample down each Wave as thou dost° go.

° **they**: you] 1664.   ° **Crown**: another term for top of a tree (*OED* 21b).
° **flieth**: doth fly] 1664.   ° **strong or**: and of] 1664.   ° **do**: 1664; they] 1653.
° **they**: 1664; do] 1653.   ° **will**: they'll] 1664.   ° **he Dies**: 1664; they die] 1653.
° **govern … ought**: who Govern justly at all times] 1664.
° **their … Fault**: Men's Humours but their Crimes] 1664.
° **how**: what] 1664.   ° **If**: Though] 1664.   ° **thou liv'st**: you Live] 1664.
° **seek'st thy**: seek your] 1664.   ° **thee … mayest**: you down, that Knowledge you may]
° **thou**: you] 1664.   ° **thou dost**: you do] 1664.

Though they rise high and big are swelled with pride,
Thou° on their Shoulders broad and Back shalt ride,
Their lofty Heads shalt bow, and make them stoop,
And on their Necks shalt set thy steady Foot;°
And on their Breast thy° stately Ship shalt bear,
Till thy° sharp Keel the wat'ry Womb doth tear.
Thus shalt thou° round the World, new Land to find,
80   That from the rest is of another kind.
OAK   O (said the Oak) I am contented well,
Without that Knowledge in my Wood to dwell.
For I had rather live, and simple be,
Than dangers run, some new° strange Sight to see.
Perchance my Ship against a Rock may hit,
Then were° I straight in sundry pieces split.
Besides, no rest nor quiet I should have;
The Winds will° toss me on each troubled Wave,
The Billows rough will beat on every side,
90   My Breast will ache to swim against the Tide.
And greedy Merchants may me over-freight,
So° should I drownèd be with my own weight;
Besides with Sails and Ropes° my Body tie,
Just like° a Prisoner, have no Liberty.
And being always wet, shall take such Colds,°
My Ship may get a Pose° and leak through holes,°
Which they to mend will put me to great pain;
Besides, all patched and pieced I shall remain.
I care not for that Wealth wherein the pains
100   And trouble is° far greater than the Gains.
I am contented with what Nature gave.
I not Repine, but one poor wish would have:
Which is that you my agèd Life would save.
MAN   To build a stately House I'll cut thee° down,
Wherein shall Princes live of great renown.
There shalt thou° live with the best Company;
All their delight and pastime thou shalt° see,
Where Plays and Masques and Beauties bright will shine,
Thy° Wood all oiled with Smoke of Meat and Wine.
110   There thou shalt° hear both Men and Women sing,
Far pleasanter than Nightingale in Spring.
Like to a Ball, their° Echoes shall rebound

° **Thou**: you] 1664.
° **And … Foot**: And bow their lofty Heads, their Pride to check, / Shall set your steady Foot upon
   their Neck] 1664.
° **And … thy**: They on their Breast your] 1664.   ° **thy**: your] 1664.
° **shalt thou**: shall you] 1664.   ° **Than … new**: Than run in danger some] 1664.
° **were**: am] 1664.   ° **will**: 1664; would] 1653.   ° **So**: Then] 1664.
° **Besides … Ropes**: With Sails and Ropes men] 1664.   ° **Just like**: And I] 1664.
° **shall … Colds**: such Colds shall take] 1664.   ° **Pose**: rheum.
° **and … holes**: through Holes, and Leak] 1664.   ° **trouble is**: Troubles are] 1664.
° **thee**: you] 1664.   ° **shalt thou**: shall you] 1664.   ° **thou shalt**: you shall] 1664.
° **Thy**: Your] 1664.   ° **thou shalt**: you shall] 1664.   ° **their**: there] 1664.

Against the Wall, yet can° no Voice be found.
OAK   Alas, what Music shall I care to hear
When on my Shoulders I such burdens bear?
Both Brick and Tiles upon my Head are laid;
Of this Preferment I am sore afraid.
And many times with Nails and Hammers strong,°
They pierce my Sides to hang their Pictures on.°
My face is Smutched° with Smoke of Candle lights,   120
In danger to be burnt in Winter Nights.
No, let me here a poor Old Oak still grow.
I care not for these vain Delights° to know.
For fruitless Promises I do not care;
More Honour 'tis my own green leaves to bear.
More Honour 'tis to be in Nature's dress
Than any Shape that Men by Art express.
I am not like to Man,° would Praises have,
And for Opinion make myself a Slave.
MAN   Why do you wish to live and not to die,   130
Since you no Pleasure have but Misery?
For here you stand against the scorching Sun,°
By's fi'ry Beams your fresh green Leaves become°
Withered,° with Winter's cold you quake and shake;
Thus° in no time or season rest can take.
OAK   Yet I am happier (said the Oak) than Man.°
With my condition I contented am.°
He° nothing loves, but what he cannot get,
And soon doth surfeit of one dish of meat,
Dislikes all Company, displeased alone,   140
Makes Grief himself, if Fortune gives him none.
And as his Mind is restless, never pleased,
So is his Body sick and oft diseased.
His Gouts and Pains do make him sigh and cry,
Yet in the midst of Pains° would live, not die.
MAN   Alas, poor Oak, thou understands,° nor can
Imagine, half the misery of Man.
All other Creatures only in Sense join,
But Man hath something more, which is divine.
He hath a Mind doth to the Heav'ns° aspire,   150
A Curiosity for to° inquire,
A Wit that nimble is, which runs about

° **yet can**: and yet] 1664.
° **And ... strong**: With Nails and Hammer they will often wound] 1664.
° **on**: round] 1664.   ° **Smutched**: tarnished.
° **I ... Delights**: Such vain Delights I matter not] 1664.
° **Man**: Men] 1664.   ° **For ... Sun**: Here you the Sun with scorching Heat doth burn] 1664.
° **By's ... become**: And all your Leaves so Green to Dryness turn] 1664.
° **Withered**: Also] 1664.   ° **Thus**: And] 1664.
° **Yet ... Man**: I'm happier far, said th'Oak, than you Mankind] 1664.
° **With ... am**: For I Content in my Condition find] 1664.   ° **He**: Man] 1664.
° **Pains**: them] 1664.   ° **thou understands**: you do not know] 1664.
° **doth .. Heavens**: and doth to Heav'n] 1664.   ° **A ... to**: For Curiosity he doth] 1664.

In every Corner to seek Nature out.
For She doth hide herself,° as feared° to show
Man all her works lest he too powerful grow;
Like to a King his Favourite makes so° great,
That at the last he fears his Power he'll get.°
And what creates desire in Man's Breast,
A° Nature is divine, which seeks the best,
And never can be satisfied until°
He like a God doth in Perfection dwell.°
If you, as Man, desire like Gods to be,
I'll spare your Life, and not cut down your Tree.

160

❧ ❧ ❧

° **She ... herself**: a paraphrase of Heraclitus's maxim, *Phusis kruptesthai philei* (Nature loves to hide).
° **as feared**: afraid] 1664.
° **makes so**: waxing] 1664.   ° **That ... get**: May well suspect that he his Pow'r will get] 1664.
° **A**: That] 1664.   ° **And ... until**: For no Perfection he at all doth prize] 1664.
° **He ... dwell**: Till he therein the Gods doth Equalize] 1664.

FIGURE 7   Clement Walker, "The Royal Oak of Britain" (1649). © Trustees of the
British Museum. Creative Commons licence CC BY-NC-SA 4.0.

ABRAHAM COWLEY
[The Oak's Prophecy] (1662)

In the concluding section of a six-book poem on plants, a personified oak summons all of England's native tree species to a council in the Forest of Dean, where she prophesies of the English Civil War. Identifying the oak as a queen, Cowley inscribes the forest as a royalist space: the trees even weep for the executed King Charles I, despite the fact that it was Charles who disafforested much of Dean in the 1620s and 1630s, and sold off 18,000 acres of woodlands to the ironworks of Sir John Winter. While Cowley clearly has an aesthetic regard for the beauty of trees in and of themselves, he also recognizes that sustainable forestry plantations will be vital for Britain to maintain its navy and to achieve its ambition of forging a global empire. First composed in Latin in 1662 (and translated anonymously in 1680 and then again in 1689 by Aphra Behn), Cowley's jeremiad was greatly admired by his friend John Evelyn, who cites from it to heighten the affective impact of his *Sylva* (1664) – a treatise on state-sponsored tree-planting and a landmark work in English environmentalism. This poem thus played a part in the passage of 1668 legislation to re-afforest Dean.
Source: "Of Plants," *from Third Part of the Works of Mr. Abraham Cowley*, trans. Aphra Behn (1689), 136, 144, 150, 153–4.

"The Forest of Dean"

There is an ancient Forest known to fame,
On this side separate from the Cambrian° Plain,
By wandering Wye, whose winding Current glides
And murm'ring Leaves behind its flowery sides;
On that, 'tis washed by nobler Severn's streams,
Whose Beauties scarce will yield to famous Thames.
Of Yore 'twas Arden called, but that great name,
As like herself, diminished into Dean.°
The cursèd Weapons of destructive War   240
In all their cruèlties have made her share;
The Iron has its noblest Shades destroyed,
Then to melt Iron is its Wood employed;
And so unhappy 'tis as it presents
Of its own Death the fatal Instruments:
With Industry its ruin to improve,
Bears Minerals below and Trees above.
O Poverty, thou happiness extreme
(When no afflicting want can intervene);
And O thou subtle Treasure of the Earth,   250
From whence all Rapes and Mischiefs take their birth;
And you, triumphing Woods, secured from spoil
By the safe blessing of your barren Soil;
Here unconsumed how small a part remains
Of that rich Store that once adorned the Plains!

° **Cambrian**: Welsh.
° **Of ... Dean**: John Selden makes the same connection in his notes to *Poly-Olbion* (223), but the name more likely derives from the Anglo-Saxon "dene" (wooded vale).

Yet that small part that has escaped the Ire
Of lawless Steel and avaricious Fire,
By many Nymphs and Deities possessed,
Of all the British shades continues still the best.
260   Here the long Reverend Dryas° (who had been
Of all the shady verdant Regions Queen,
To which by Conquest she had forced the Sea
His constant tributary Waves to pay)
Proclaimed a general Council through her Court,
To which the Sylvan Nymphs should all resort.
    All the Wood-Goddesses do straight appear,
At least who could the British Climate bear.
And on a soft ascent of rising Ground
Their Queen, their charming Dryas, they surround,
270   Who all adorned was in the middle placed,
And by a thousand awful° Beauties graced.
These Goddesses alike were dressed in Green,
The Ornaments and Liv'ries of their Queen.
Had Travellers at any distance viewed
The beauteous Order of this stately Crowd,
They would not guess they'd been Divinities,
But Groves all sacred to the Deities …°
670   O Dryas, patron to th'industrious kind,
If Man were wise and would his safety find,
What perfect Bliss thy happy Shade would give,
And Houses that their Masters would outlive!
All necessaries thou affordst alone
For harmless Innocence to live upon:
Strong yokes for Oxen, handles for the Plough;
What Husbandry requires thou dost allow.
But if the madness of desiring Gain
Or wild Ambition agitate the Brain,
680   Straight to a wand'ring Ship they Thee transfer,
And none more justly serves the Mariner.
Thou cutst the Air, dost on the waves rebound,
Wild Death and Fury raging all around,
Disdaining to behold the managed Wood,
Outbrave the Storms and baffle the rude Flood …
With thee the utmost bounds of Earth w'invade,
By thee the unlocked Orb is common made.
By thee—
The great Republic of the World revives,
And o'er the Earth luxurious traffic thrives …
Oh how has Nature blessed the British Land,
720   Who both the valued Indies can command! …
But by Divine Decree the Oak no more

° **Dryas**: the Oak.   ° **awful**: sublime.
° …: Here follows a catalogue of British trees: Poplar, Alder, Willow, Elder, Birch, Maple, Elm,
Beech, Ash, Linden, Lime-tree, Wood-pear, Crab-apple, Service, Barberry, Mulberry, Cornelian,
Walnut, Hawthorn, Plum, Box-tree, Holly, Strawberry, Privet, Coral-tree, Yew, Juniper, Cypress,
Laurel, Fir, and Pine.

Declares security as heretofore,°
With words or voices, yet to the list'ning Wood
Her diff'ring Murmurs still are understood   770
For sacred Divinations, while the sound
Informs, all but Humanity, around;
Nor ere did Dryas Murmur awful truth
More clear and plain from her Prophetic mouth: …
"You see (O my companions) that the Gods
Threaten a dire Destruction of the Woods,   780
And to all humankind—the black portents
Are seen of many sinister Events;
But lest their quick Approach too much should press
(O my astonished Nymphs) your Tenderness,
The Gods command me to foretell your Doom,
And prepossess you with the Fate to come.
With heedful Rev'rence then their Will observe,
And in your Barks' deep Chinks my Words preserve: …
All that the Air surrounds the Fates decree
To Brutus'° and Aeneas' Progeny:
Aeneas all the land, and Brutus all the sea."
This said the God, from the Prophetic Oak,
Who stretching out her branches further spoke: 850
"Here fill thy Hands with Acorns from my Tree,
Which in thy tedious Toils of use shall be,
And Witnesses of all I promise thee.
And when thy painful wand'ring shall be o'er,
And thou arrived on happy Britain's shore,
Then in her fruitful Soil these Acorns sow,
Which to vast Woods of mighty use shall grow.
Not their Chaonian Mother's° sacred Name
Shall o'er the World be sung with greater Fame.
Then holy Druids thou shalt consecrate,   860
My Honour and my Rites to celebrate …
But now—
The Conquering evil Genius of the Wars,
The impious Victor all before him bears …°
On every side the groaning Earth sustains
The pond'rous weight of Stones and wondrous Beams.
Fiercely they ply their Work, with such a noise
As if some mighty Structure they would raise
For the proud Tyrant.° No, this clam'rous din   1100
Is not for building but demolishing.
When (my companions) these sad things you see,
And each beholds the dead Beams of her parent Tree,

° **But … heretofore**: Christianity caused the cessation of oracles like the sacred oak of Dodona.
° **Brutus**: mythical founder of Britain, purportedly descended of Aeneas, the founder of Rome. This
  passage suggests that Brutus imported the oak to Britain, making it a symbol of empire, while
  promoting tree-planting during the Restoration.
° **Chaonian Mother**: Venus.
° **…:** In the omitted section, the trees weep to hear of Charles I's execution.   ° **Tyrant**: Cromwell.

Long since reposed in Palaces of Kings,
Torn down by furious Hands as useless things,
Then know your Fate is come; those hands that could
From Houses tear dead Beams and long hewn Wood,
Those cruél Hands by unresisted Force,
Will for your living Trunks find no remorse.
   Religion, which was great of old, commands
1110   No Woods should be profaned by impious Hands.
Those noble Seminaries for the Fleet,
Plantations that make towns and cities great,
Those Hopes of War and Ornaments of Peace,
Should live secure from any outrages,
Which now the barb'rous Conqueror will invade,
Tear up your Roots, and rifle all your shade.
For gain they'll sell you to the cov'tous Buyer,
A Sacrifice to every common Fire.
They'll spare no Race of Trees of any Age,
1120   But murder infant Branches in their Rage:
Elms, Beeches, tender Ashes shall be felled,
And e'en the grey and reverend Bark must yield.
The soft, the murm'ring Troop shall be no more;
No more with Music charm as heretofore.
No more each little Bird shall build her house,
And sing in her hereditary boughs,
But only Philomel° shall celebrate
In mournful Notes a new unhappy Fate.
The banished Hamadryads must be gone,
1130   And take their flight with sad but silent Moan.
For a Celestial Being ne'er complains,
Whatever be her Grief, in noisy Strains.
The Wood-Gods fly, and whither shall they go?
Not all the British Orb can scarce allow
A trunk Secure for them to rest in now.
   But yet these wild Saturnals° shall not last;
Oppressing Vengeance follows on too fast.
She shakes her brandished Steel, and still denies
Length to immod'rate Rage and Cruélties.
1140   Do not despond, my Nymphs: that wicked Birth
Th'avenging powers will chase from off the Earth.
Let 'em hew down the Woods, destroy and burn,
And all the lofty Groves to Ashes turn,
Yet still there will not want a Tree to yield
Timber enough old Tyburn° to rebuild,
Where they may hang at last, and this kind one
Shall then revenge the Woods of all their Wrong.

ᘒ ᘒ ᘒ

° **Philomel**: the nightingale.   ° **Saturnals**: riots, from the Roman holiday dedicated to Saturn.
° **Tyburn**: notorious gallows in London.

JOHN AUBREY
"This whole island was anciently one great forest"
(*c.* 1656–1685)

Best known for his compendium of facts, legends, and gossip about early modern English celebrities, Aubrey also laboured for over thirty years on a chorographical study of the natural history of his native county. In the extracts below, he records the traumatic impact of deforestation on both the poor and the wildlife.
Source: *Natural History of Wiltshire*, Bodleian Aubrey MS 1, 34–5, 118, 128, 131.

The reader is to be [35] advertised° that the forest of Melksham did extend itself to the foot of this hill.° It was full of goodly oaks, which grew so near together that they say a squirrel might have leaped from tree to tree. It was disafforested° in anno 1634 or 1635, and the oaks were sold for (to my best remembrance) less than 2d. per load. Nobody then took notice of this iron-ore, which ... after a shower in a sunshine must glister in their eyes. Now there is scarce an oak left in the whole parish ... so that now this rich treasure cannot be worked for want of charcoal ...

[118] Oaks (the best of trees). We had great plenty before the disafforestations. We had in North Wiltshire, and yet have, though not in the former plenty, as good oaks as any in England. The best oaks are bred out of rocky, clayey counties as this is. The oaks in the southern part [are] ... not so tough. The best oaks that we have now (1670) are at Oaksey Park, Sir Edward Poole's, in Malmesbury hundred. And the oaks at Easton Piers (once mine) were, for the number, not inferior to them. In my great-grandfather Lyte's° time (15–) one might have driven a plough over every oak in the oak-close, which are now grown stately trees. The great oak by the dairy-house is the biggest oak now, I believe, in all the county. It is ___ in compass, ___ in diameter. The branches spread from the body ___ feet.° There is a commonwealth of rooks there. When I was a boy the two greatest oaks were: one on the hill at the park at Draycot Cerne; the other at Mr. Sadler's, at Longley Burrell. 'Twas of one of these trees, I remember, that the trough of the paper mill at Longdean in the parish of Yatton Keynell, anno 1636, was made. In Garston Park (now the Lord Ferrar's) is perhaps the finest hollow oak in England. It is not high, but very capacious, and well wainscoted, with a little table which I think eight may sit round. When an oak is felling, before it falls, it gives a kind of shrieks or groans that may be heard a mile off, as if it were the genius of the oak lamenting.

° **advertised**: notified.
° **hill**: Seend Hill, about five miles southeast of Melksham.   ° **disafforested**: sold by the Crown.
° **Lyte**: Thomas Lyte (1531–1627).
° **It ... feet**: Aubrey evidently intended to fill in the blanks with exact measurements.

E. Wyld° Esq. hath heard it several times. This gave the occasion of that expression in Ovid's *Metamorphoses* … about Erysichthon's felling of the oak sacred to Ceres: *gemitumque dedit decidua quercus*° …

[128] This whole island was anciently one great forest. A stag might have ranged from Bradon Forest to the New Forest … and not above four or five miles interval (sc.° from Bradon Forest to Grettenham and Clockwoods; thence to the forest by Boughwood Park, by Calne and Pewsham Forest, Blackmore Forest, Gillingham Forest, Cranborne Chase, Holt Forest, to the New Forest). Most of those forests were given away by King James the First. Pewsham Forest was given to the Duke of Buckingham, who gave it, I think, to his brother, the Earl of Anglesey. Upon the disafforesting° of it, the poor people made this rhyme:

> When Chip'nam° stood in Pewsham's wood,
> Before it was destroyed,
> A cow might have gone for a groat° a year
> But now it is denied.

The meter is lamentable; but the cry of the poor was more lamentable. I knew several that did remember the going of a cow for 4d. per annum. The order was, how many they could winter they might summer. And pigs did cost nothing the going. Now the highways are encumbered with cottages, and the travellers with the beggars that dwell in them …

[131] Clarendon Park was the best park in the King's dominions. Hunt and Palmer, keepers there, did aver that they knew seven thousand head of deer in that park: all fallow deer. This park was seven miles about. Here were twenty copses, and every one a mile round.

° **E. Wyld**: Edmund Wylde (1618–95), a member of the Royal Society and friend of William Petty.
° *gemitumque … quercus*: translated by Golding as "The menaced oak did quake and sigh" (8.946). In his *Remains of Gentilism and Judaism* (Lansdowne MS 231, c. 1687), Aubrey reports that superstitions still clustered around illicit tree-felling in seventeenth-century England:
"At a Wood in Surrey belonging to the Archbishop of Canterbury called Norwood in the parish of Croydon was an ancient remarkable Tree called Vicar's Oak, where four parishes met in a point. This Wood consists all of Oaks. There was one Oak that had Mistletoe, which was felled but of late years (about 1657). One did cut this Mistletoe for an Apothecary or two in London, which he sold for ten shillings a time, and left only one Branch remaining for more to sprout out. He fell lame shortly after. About fifteen years since this Tree was felled, each man lost an Eye shortly after, and he that felled the Tree being warned by these men's misfortunes, would notwithstanding adventure to do it. And shortly after he broke his Leg. As if the Hamadryads had revenged the Injury done to that sacred and venerable Tree. This story is vulgarly and credibly related all hereabout."
° **sc.**: *scire licet* (it is permitted to know).
° **disafforesting**: the sale and enclosure of the forestlands in 1624 upset local farmers, as their loss of grazing rights apparently drove up the price of cattle. The enclosure provoked riots, as described in a poem by William Davenant, "The Countess of Anglesey, Lead Captive by the Rebels at the Disforesting of Pewsam" (*Works* 1673, 288).
° **Chip'nam**: Chippenham.   ° **groat**: coin worth about 4d.

Upon these disafforestations the martens° were utterly destroyed in North Wiltshire. It is a pretty little beast, and of a deep chestnut color: a kind of polecat, lesser than a fox, and the fur is much esteemed, not much inferior to sables. It is the richest fur of our nation. Martial says of it, *Venator capta marte superbus adest.*° In Cranborne Chase and at Vernditch are some martens still remaining.

ꙮ ꙮ ꙮ

° **martens**: by the twentieth century martens had almost vanished from England; fewer than 200 now survive. Small populations still exist in Scotland and on the Continent.
° **Venator ... adest**: "Here cometh the proud hunter that hath killed a marten" (*Epigrams*, 10.37). The original Latin reads *maele*, which could also mean badger.

The Draining of the Fens

MICHAEL DRAYTON

"Holland Fen" (1622)

In the sixteenth century, a fan-shaped swathe of eastern England in the vicinity of the Wash estuary was chequered with low-lying wetlands known as fens. Inundated for much of the winter, the sparsely populated fen region encompassed almost 1,500 square miles and was one of the country's last remaining bastions of genuine wilderness. While Drayton acknowledges that outsiders sniffed at the fens as a putrid, disease-infested morass, he more emphatically praises them as a precious habitat for a teeming abundance of plants, fish, and fowl. His poetic catalogues could be compared to a recent biodiversity audit of the fens which inventoried over 13,000 species of flora and fauna, including a quarter of the rarest wildlife in Britain, of which 25 are found nowhere else on earth (Mossman et al). Drayton also glowingly depicts the bioregional economy of the fen-dwellers, who supported themselves by fishing, fowling, seasonal grazing, and harvesting sedge and peat. Appearing at a time when the fens had become the target of ecologically disastrous drainage schemes, the quarrel between Holland and Kesteven sounds almost like a parliamentary debate on the topic, in which the poet makes a tacit plea for conserving fens as part of England's environmental heritage.
Source: *Poly-Olbion*, 2.105–10.

> Now in upon the earth, rich Lincolnshire I strain,°
> At Deeping, from whose Street the plenteous Ditches drain°
> Hemp-bearing Holland's Fen,° at Spalding that do fall
> Together in their course, themselves as emptying all
> Into one general Sewer, which seemeth to divide
> Low Holland from the High, which on their Eastern side
> Th'inbending Ocean holds° ...
> From fast and firmer Earth, whereon the Muse of late
> Trod with a steady foot, now with a slower gait,
> Through Quicksands, Beach, and Ooze,° the Washes° she must wade,
> Where Neptune every day doth powerfully invade
> The vast and queachy° soil, with Hosts of wallowing Waves,

° **strain**: sing, but with connotations of clasp.
° **drain**: small ditches and sewers were common in the fens as far back as Roman times. It was the industrial scale of the seventeenth-century drainage works, developed and managed by outsiders such as Thomas Lovell (who attempted to drain Deeping Fen in the early 1600s), that incurred resentment and protest.
° **Holland's Fen**: Holland was a large district of southern Lincolnshire. The poem zooms in on South or "Low" Holland, an area east of the River Welland between Crowland and Wisbech.
° **holds**: fens do play an ecologically important role as coastal buffers that reduce encroachment of salt water into inland watersheds, but many human-made embankments also hold back the ocean from the fens, and rising sea levels may submerge fenlands in the centuries ahead.
° **Ooze**: mudbank, though the original spelling "Ouze" may play on the Great Ouse – the river that flows through Norfolk into the Wash.
° **the Washes**: a tidal floodplain in the estuary, now a large nature reserve.   ° **queachy**: mushy.

From whose impetuous force that who himself not saves,
By swift and sudden flight, is swallowed by the deep,
When from the wrathful Tides the foaming Surges sweep
The Sands, which lay all nak'd to the wide heav'n before,
And turneth all to Sea, which was but lately Shore° ...   20
She° by the Muse's aid shall happily reveal
Her sundry sorts of Fowl, from whose abundance she,
Above all other Tracts, may boast herself to be
The Mistress, and (indeed) to sit without compare;
And for no worthless soil should in her glory share,
From her moist seat of Flags,° of Bulrushes, and Reed,
With her just proper praise, thus Holland doth proceed: ...   30
"In Summer giving earth, from which I square my Peat,
And faster feedings by, for Deer, for Horse, and Neat.°   50
My various Fleets° for Fowl: O, who is he can tell
The species that in me for multitudes excel!
The Duck and Mallard first, the Falconer's only sport
(Of River-flights the chief, so that all other sort
They only Green-fowl° term), in every Mere° abound,
That you would think they sat upon the very ground,
Their numbers be so great, the waters covering quite,
That raised, the spacious air is darkened with their flight ...
And near to them you see the lesser dabbling° Teal,
In Bunches° with the first that fly from Mere to Mere,
As they above the rest were Lords of Earth and Air;
The Goosander with them my goodly Fens do show,
His head as Ebon black, the rest as white as Snow;
With whom the Wigeon goes, the Golden-eye, the Smeath;°
And in odd scattered pits, the Flags and Reeds beneath,
The Coot, bald, else clean black; that whiteness it doth bear
Upon the forehead starred, the Water-Hen° doth wear   70
Upon her little tail, in one small feather set;
The Water-ouzel° next, all over black as Jet,
With various colours, black, green, blue, red, russet, white,
Do yield the gazing eye a variable delight,
As do these sundry Fowls, whose several plumes they be;
The diving Dabchick° here among the rest you see,
Now up, now down again, that hard it is to prove,
Whether underwater most it liveth or above;

° **Shore**: Drayton feared coastal erosion was reducing the size of England. In fact, a comparison of *Poly-Olbion*'s map to modern Ordnance Survey maps reveals that much of the Wash has shrunk due to land reclamation and silt accretion.

° **She**: the fen.

° **Flags**: plants that grow in moist ground, though Drayton may have in mind the yellow or flag iris.

° **Neat**: cattle.

° **Fleets**: defined in the margin as "brooks and pools worn by the water into which the rising floods have recourse."

° **Green-fowl**: immature, applied to birds too young to hunt.   ° **Mere**: pond or small lake.

° **dabbling**: to wet by splashing.

° **Bunches**: defined in the margin as a falconry term for "a company of Teal."

° **Smeath**: plural form of smew.   ° **Water-Hen**: moorhen.   ° **Water-ouzel**: dipper.

° **Dabchick**: small grebe.

With which last little Fowl (that water may not lack,
80   More than the Dabchick doth, and more doth love the brack°)
The Puffin we compare, which coming to the dish,
Nice palates hardly judge if it be flesh or fish.°
    But wherefore should I stand upon such toys as these,
That have so goodly Fowls the wand'ring eye to please?
Here in my vaster Pools, as white as Snow or Milk,
(In water black as Styx) swims the wild Swan, the Elk,°
Of Hollanders so termed, no niggard of his breath
(As Poets say of Swans, which only sing in death),
But oft, as other Birds, is heard his tunes to rote,°
90   Which like a Trumpet comes, from his long archèd throat …
There stalks the stately Crane, as though he marched in war,
That hath by him the Heron, which (by the Fishy Carr°)
Can fetch with their long necks out of the Rush and Reed,
Snigs,° Fry, and yellow Frogs, whereon they often feed;
And under them again (that water never take,
But by some Ditch's side, or little shallow Lake
Lie dabbling night and day) the palate-pleasing Snite,°
100   The Bidcock,° and like them the Redshank,° that delight
Together still to be in some small Reedy bed,
In which these little Fowls in Summertime were bred;
The buzzing Bittern sits, which through his hollow Bill,
A sudden bellowing sends, which many times doth fill
The neighbouring Marsh° with noise, as though a Bull did roar.
But scarcely have I yet recited half my store:
And with my wondrous flocks of Wild-geese come I then,
Which look as though alone they peopled all the Fen,
Which here in Wintertime, when all is overflowed,
110   And want of solid sward enforceth them abroad,
Th'abundance then is seen that my full Fens do yield,
That almost through the Isle do pester every field;
The Barnacles° with them, which whereso'er they breed,
On Trees or rotten Ships, yet to my Fens for feed
Continually they come, and chief abode do make,
And very hardly forced my plenty to forsake,
Who almost all this kind do challenge as mine own,
Whose like, I dare aver, is elsewhere hardly known.
For sure, unless in me, no one yet ever saw
120   The multitudes of Fowl in Mooting-time° they draw,
From which to many a one, much profit doth accrue.

° **brack**: salt water (Drayton is unique in using this as a noun).
° **Puffin … fish**: see the entry by Caius in Part 11, p. 155.
° **Elk**: fenland name for the whooper swan.   ° **rote**: repeat (Drayton's coinage).
° **Carr**: pond.   ° **Snigs**: small eels.   ° **Snite**: snipe.   ° **Bidcock**: water-rail?
° **Redshank**: large sandpiper.
° **Marsh**: while this term is often used interchangeably with fen, it could also more precisely
    designate salt-marshes, coastal wetlands silted by the sea.
° **Barnacles**: geese, rumoured to be born from barnacles on trees or driftwood. In fact, they breed on
    cliffs in remote islands in the Arctic.
° **Mooting**: meeting, with wordplay on mating.

Now such as flying feed, next these I must pursue:
The Sea-mew, Sea-pie,° Gull, and Curlew here do keep,
As searching every Shoal, and watching every deep,
To find the floating Fry, with their sharp-piercing sight,
Which suddenly they take, by stooping from their height;
The Cormorant then comes (by his devouring kind),
Which flying o'er the Fen, immediat'ly doth find
The Fleet best stored of Fish, when from his wings at full,
As though he shot himself into the thickened scull,°   130
He underwater goes, and so the Shoal pursues,
Which into Creeks do fly, when quickly he doth choose
The Fin that likes him best, and rising, flying feeds;
The Osprey oft here seen, though seldom here it breeds,
Which over them the Fish no sooner do espy
But (betwixt him and them, by an antipathy)
Turning their bellies up,° as though their death they saw,
They at his pleasure lie, to stuff his glutt'nous maw.
   The toiling Fisher here is towing of his Net;°
The Fowler is employed his limèd twigs to set;   140
One underneath his Horse,° to get a shoot doth stalk;
Another over Dikes upon his Stilts doth walk;
There others with their Spades, the Peats are squaring out,
And others from their Carrs are busily about
To draw out Sedge and Reed, for Thatch and Stover° fit:
That whosoever would a Landscape rightly hit,°
Beholding but my Fens, shall with more shapes be stored
Than Germany or France or Tuscan can afford.
And for that part of me that men High Holland call,
Where Boston seated is, by plenteous Wytham's fall,   150
I peremptory° am, large Neptune's liquid field
Doth to no other tract the like abundance yield° ...
When Kesteven,° this while that certainly had thought   192
Her tongue would ne'er have stopped, quoth she: "O how I hate,
Thus of her foggy Fens to hear rude Holland prate,
That with her Fish and Fowl here keepeth such a coil,°
As her unwholesome air and more unwholesome soil,
For these of which she boasts, the more might suffered be,
When those her feathered flocks she sends not out to me ...
From that so ramish° taste of her most fulsome mud,
When the toiled Cater° home them to the Kitchen brings,
The Cook doth cast them out, as most unsavoury things.
Besides, what is she else, but a foul, oozy Marsh?

° **Sea-pie**: oyster-catcher.   ° **scull**: basket for storing fish.
° **bellies up**: a myth derived from Pliny's *Natural History*, 10.3. Ospreys were classed as vermin and
  persecuted to extinction in Britain by the 1800s. A few hundred have now returned.
° **Net**: a marginal note here reads: "The pleasures of the Fens."   ° **Horse**: stalking horse.
° **Stover**: winter food for cattle.   ° **hit**: imitate.   ° **peremptory**: confident.
° **abundance yield**: the omitted section lists thirty-two species of saltwater fish, shellfish, and
  molluscs found along the English coast. For another literary inventory of sealife in the Wash, see
  Mildmay Fane's "A Fishing Sea-Voyage from Lynn to Boston" (1633).
° **Kesteven**: hilly region of southwestern Lincolnshire.   ° **keepeth ... coil**: makes such a fuss.
° **ramish**: pungent.   ° **Cater**: provisioner.

And that she calls her grass, so blady is and harsh,
As cuts the Cattle's mouths, constrained thereon to feed,
So that my poorest trash, which mine call Rush and Reed,
For litter scarcely fit, that to the dung I throw,
210   Doth like the Penny grass,° or the pure Clover show,
Comparèd with her best; and for her sundry Fish,
Of which she freely boasts to furnish every Dish,
Did not full Neptune's fields so furnish her with store,
Those in the Ditches bred within her muddy Moor,
Are of so earthy taste, as that the Rav'nous° Crow
Will rather starve thereon her stomach than bestow."

᪲ ᪲ ᪲

° **Penny grass**: yellow rattle.   ° **Rav'nous**: spelling and capitalization puns on raven.

BEN JONSON
"The Duke of Drowned Land" (1616)

Jonson's comedy *The Devil is an Ass* reportedly offended some influential figures
at the Jacobean court, as the king himself urged Jonson to suppress it. This furore
almost certainly had to do with its scathing portrayal of land reclamation projects
in the English fens. The king had at first opposed the drainage schemes, but re-
versed course in 1614 at the behest of his favourite, Robert Carr (see Sanders 1998,
114–22). Although the drainage aimed to transform the supposedly idle wetlands
into lucrative farmland, Jonson ridicules such Baconian techno-optimism as a
form of magical thinking, and makes it clear that the schemes will not benefit the
locals or even small-scale investors such as the naïve Fitzdottrel of Norfolk, whose
name associates him with a fenland species of plover now endangered due to over-
hunting and habitat loss. By the time Jonson's play appeared in print, however,
the Dutch engineer Cornelius Vermuyden had drained Hatfield Chase, blazing
the way for future hydro-engineering works that would eventually obliterate an
estimated 99 per cent of England's fens.
Source: *The Devil is an Ass* (1631), 112, 119.

2.1
MERECRAFT Why, Engine, then
I'll tell it you. I see you ha' credit here,
And that you can keep counsel I'll not question.
He shall but be an undertaker° with me
In a most feasible business. It shall cost him
Nothing—
ENGINE Good, Sir.
MERECRAFT Except he please, but's countenance

° **undertaker**: investor.

(That I will have) t'appear in't to great men,
For which I'll make him one. He shall not draw   40
A string of's purse. I'll drive his patent° for him.
We'll take in Citizens, Commoners, and Aldermen°
To bear the charge, and blow 'hem off again,
Like so many dead flies, when 'tis carried.
The thing is for recovery of drowned land,
Whereof the Crown's to have his moiety
If it be owner; else, the Crown and Owners
To share that moiety, and the recoverers
T'enjoy the other moiety for their charge.°
ENGINE Throughout England?   50
MERECRAFT   Yes, which will arise
To eighteen millions: seven the first year.
I have computed all, and made my survey
Unto an acre. I'll begin at the Pan,°
Not at the skirts,° as some ha' done and lost
All that they wrought: their timber-work, their trench,
Their banks all borne away, or else filled up
By the next winter.° Tut, they never went
The way; I'll have it all.
ENGINE   A gallant tract
Of land it is!
MERECRAFT 'Twill yield a pound an acre.

2.3

FITZDOTTREL°   Wife, such a man, wife!
He has such plots! He will make me a Duke!
No less, by heaven! Six mares to your coach,° wife,
That's your proportion! And your coachman bald,
Because he shall be bare enough.° Do not you laugh;
We are looking for a place, and all i'the map
What to be of. Have faith, be not an Infidel.
You know I am not easy to be gulled.°   40
I swear, when I have my millions, else I'll make
Another Duchess, if you ha' not faith.

° **patent**: rights conferred by the Crown to property or commodities.
° **Aldermen**: civic leaders.
° **charge**: this passage suggests Jonson paid close attention to the actual financial arrangements of the undertakers. The first scenario outlined by Merecraft mirrors James's pact with Carr's cousin (also named Robert Carr), and the second resembles a deal struck with the Earl of Argyll.
° **Pan**: water-filled depression (the deeper pools).   ° **skirts**: edges.
° **Not ... winter**: these lines likely glance at Thomas Lovell's failure to drain the Crowland fens in the first decade of James's reign. Draining of these wetlands resumed in the 1630s (shortly after Jonson's comedy was first printed) under the direction of the Dutch engineer Philibert Vernatti. His works were completed in 1637 but floods returned two winters later, and these lands were not made dry until a mechanical pumping station was installed in 1827.
° **Fitzdottrel**: his name evokes the dotterel, a wading bird regarded as stupid because it does not flee humans. Once common in the fens, it is now endangered in the UK, with just over 400 remaining (Hayhow *et al.* 2017, 10).
° **six ... coach**: the Jacobean equivalent of a luxury car.
° **bald ... enough**: having an elderly and hatless driver was regarded as especially fashionable.
° **gulled**: duped.

MISTRESS FITZDOTTREL You'll ha' too much, I fear, in these false
spirits.
FITZDOTTREL Spirits? O, no such thing, wife! Wit, mere wit!
This man defies the Devil and all his works!
He dos't by engine and devices, he!
He has his wingèd ploughs, that go with sails,
Will plough you forty acres at once! And mills
Will spout you water ten miles off! All Crowland°
50   Is ours, wife; and the fens, from us in Norfolk
To the utmost bound of Lincolnshire! We have viewed it
And measured it within, all by the scale!
The richest tract of land, Love, i'the kingdom!

ᘐᘐ ᘐᘐ ᘐᘐ

° **Crowland**: fen in southern Lincolnshire that proved especially resistant to drainage projects.

PENNY OF WISBECH

"The Pout's Complaint Upon the Draining of the Fens in Cambridgeshire, Ely, and Wisbech" (c. 1619)

The following text is a rare species in the literary archive: a seventeenth-century environmental protest song. A version of it was printed in William Dugdale's *History of Embanking and Draining of Diverse Fens and Marshes* in 1662. While recalling efforts to drain the fens half a century earlier, Dugdale reports that, despite the king's support, the project ground to a halt for five years due to "the opposition which diverse perverse-spirited people made thereto, by bringing of turbulent suits in law … and making of libellous songs to disparage the work; of which kind I have here thought fit to insert one called 'The Powte's Complaint'" (391–2). The ballad adopts the perspective of a fish to bewail the destruction of the fenland ecology and the fen-dwellers' economy. Shockingly, it even advocates violent resistance to the developers' schemes.

Previously misidentified as an eel, the pout is in fact a bottom-dwelling, snake-like fish known as a burbot, a species now possibly extirpated from England as a result of the habitat loss the song decries (Worthington *et al.*). The song's author has also recently been identified: a manuscript in the British Library (Add. MS 2732) reports, "This was made by one Peny of wisbich 1619 about the time of the coming of some Essex knights & gentleme[n] to the undertaking of the ffenes to be drayned." Star Chamber records witness that in June 1619 a rowdy crowd of nearly 2,000 people "of the common sort" gathered in Ely to protest the draining and enclosing of fens outside Wisbech. It is possible that the song was connected with this demonstration (see Borlik and Egan), Besides summoning a riotous assembly, the pout, like Shakespeare's Caliban, curses the interlopers, who arrogantly presume a technological dominion over nature, and calls on

floods and rising water-levels to re-inundate the wetlands, a prophecy that may
be gradually fulfilled thanks to global warming.

Source: Harley MS 837, 75ᵛ–7ᵛ; with emendations from Add MS 23723, 19ᵛ–20ᵛ;
and Dugdale.

Come Brothers° of the Water, and let us all Assemble,
To treat upon° this matter, which makes us quake and tremble;
For we shall Rue if it be true that Fens be undertaken,
And where we breed in° Sedge° and Reeds they'll feed fresh° Beef and
    Bacon.

They'll Sow both Peas° and Oats, where no Man ever° thought it,
Where Men did Row with Boats, ere Undertakers bought it;
But Ceres thou look towards us° now, let wild Oats be their venture:
O° let the Frogs and Miry Bogs destroy where they do enter.

Behold this great Design, which they do now determine,
Will make our Bodies pine, a Prey for Crows and Vermin;   10
For they do mean all Fens to drain and Waters over-Master,
And they will make of Bogs and Lakes° for Essex Calves° a Pasture.

Away with Boats and Rudder,° farewell both Boots and Skatches;°
No need of th'one nor th'other,° men now make better Matches;
Stilt-makers all and Tanners shall complain of this disaster;
All will be dry and we must die 'cause Essex Calves want Pasture.

The fen-bred° Fowls have wings, to fly to other Nations,
But we have no such things, to help our Transportations;
We must give place, a° grievous Case, to Hornèd Beasts and Cattle,
Unless° that we can all agree to drive them forth with° Battle.   20

° **Brothers**: Harley; brethren] Add, Dugdale.   ° **upon**: Harley, Dugdale; of this new] Add.
° **we breed in**: Add; there grew both] Harley; we feed in] Dugdale.
° **Sedge**: Harley; fens] Add; Fen] Dugdale.
° **feed fresh**: Add; now feed] Harley; feed both] Dugdale.   ° **Peas**: Harley; Beans] Add, Dugdale.
° **no ... ever**: Add; no ... never] Harley; never man yet] Dugdale.
° **look towards us**: Harley; look towards it] Add; behold us] Dugdale.
° **O**: Dugdale; And] Harley, Add.
° **Bogs and Lakes**: Harley; each muddy lake] Add; In Dugdale, this line and the last verse of the
    next stanza ("All will be dry") are swapped.
° **Essex Calves**: literally young cows, but also early modern slang for a simpleton from this county
    (an insult first recorded in the *OED* in 1719). This may be a jab at Sir Willam Ayloffe of Essex, a
    major backer of the 1619 drainage scheme.
° **Away ... Rudder**: Add, Dugdale; Farewell both Boats and Rowers] Harley.
° **Farewell both ... skatches**: Add, Dugdale; Away with Boats and Sketches] Harley. Skatches refers
    to stilts, often worn by fen-dwellers for walking over mud or shallow water.
° **th'one nor th'other**: Add; one or others] Harley; t'one nor t'other] Dugdale.
° **fen-bred**: Harley, Add; feathered] Dugdale.   ° **a**: Harley; oh] Add, Dugdale.
° **Unless**: Harley; Except] Add, Dugdale.   ° **forth with**: Harley; out by] Add, Dugdale.

Then first° let us Entreat, our Ancient Water Nurses,
To show their power so great, as help to drain their Purses;
And send us good old Captain Flood to lead us forth° to Battle,
Then Two-penny Jack,° with scales° on's Back, will drive out° all their
 Cattle.

This noble Captain yet, was never known to fail us,
But did the Conquest get, of all that did Assail us;
His furious Rage none could assuage, but to° the world's great wonder,
He bears° down Banks and Breaks their° Ranks and Whirligigs° asunder.

God° Aelous, we thee pray, that thou wilt not be wanting;
Thou never saidst us nay,° then hearken° to our Chanting:°
Do thou deride their hope of° Pride with purpose of Delusion,°
And send a blast° that they in haste may work no good Conclusion.

Great Neptune, god of Seas, this work must needs provoke thee;
They mean thee to disease, and with fen-waters Choke thee:
But with thy Mace thou canst° deface and quite Confound their° matter,
And send the° Sand to make firm° Land when they do° want fresh water.

And last° we pray thee° Moon, that thou wilt° be propitious,
To see that nought be done, to prosper the Malicious;
Though° Summer's heat do work a feat,° whereby themselves they flatter,
Yet be so good as send a Flood lest Essex Calves want water.

30

40

☙ ☙ ☙

° **Then first**: Harley, Add; Wherefore] Dugdale. ° **forth**: Harley, Add; out] Dugdale.
° **Jack**: slang for pike fish. Two-penny might refer to the price for which it sold in Jacobean
 fish-markets.
° **scales**: Harley, Add; Skakes] Dugdale. ° **out**: Add, Dugdale; forth] Harley.
° **but to**: Harley, Dugdale; unto] Add. ° **bears**: Add, Dugdale; drives] Harley.
° **their**: Harley, Dugdale; all] Add.
° **Whirligigs**: Add, Dugdale; hurleth all] Harley. Whirligigs were mechanical devices, presumably
 windmills for pumping water, although it is not thought that these were introduced until the 1650s.
° **God**: Dugdale; Then] Harley; And] Add. Aelous was the keeper of the winds.
° **saidst us nay**: Dugdale: failed us yet] Harley, Add. ° **hearken**: Harley, Add; listen] Dugdale.
° **Chanting**: Harley; canting] Add, Dugdale. ° **of**: Harley; and] Add, Dugdale.
° **with … Delusion**: Harley; that purpose our confusion] Add, Dugdale.
° **a blast**: Add, Dugdale; do thou] Harley. ° **thou canst**: Harley, Add; do thou] Dugdale.
° **their**: Harley; this] Add, Dugdale. ° **the**: Harley; thy] Add, Dugdale.
° **firm**: Harley, Add; dry] Dugdale. ° **do**: Harley, Add; shall] Dugdale.
° **last**: Harley, Add; eke] Dugdale. ° **thee**: Dugdale; the] Harley, Add.
° **thou wilt**: Dugdale; she will] Harley; she would] Add. ° **Though**: Add, Dugale; That] Harley.
° **do work a feat**: Add; may cause a fret] Harley; hath wrought a feat] Dugdale.

ANONYMOUS

"The Draining of the Fens" (*c.* 1620–1660)

This anonymous drinking/protest song was first printed in 1661, although it may have been composed much earlier. It pokes fun at the Dutch, who, with their advanced hydro-engineering technology, had been helping supervise drainage projects in the English fens since the 1590s. The song playfully equates their eagerness to drain the wetlands with their stereotypical fondness for binge drinking. In the refrain, however, the English locals match them at that feat. Considering that alcohol was and remains a common accelerant for public disorder, the invitation to the fen-dwellers to "drink apace" in the song's chorus is not politically innocent. The song's appearance in a manuscript compiled at Cambridge, and in a miscellany alongside poems about the university, suggests a provenance in or near Cambridgeshire, where riots against the Dutch projects erupted in the late 1620s and again in 1653. The first stanza is remarkable in that it draws a link between human-caused environmental degradation and climate change: draining the fens reduces the amount of moisture evaporating into the atmosphere and may spawn a future drought. In his *Natural History of Wiltshire*, Aubrey reports similar fears that technological interference in the wetlands was altering the climate: "Since the draining of the fens in Lincolnshire it is observed that we have had dry summers, and that since that draining, Northamptonshire (heretofore very healthy) has since been aguish and feverish, and more infested with gnats" (15ᵛ). For a more sober diatribe against fen drainage as legally, economically, and environmentally dubious, see John Maynard's *The Picklock of the Old Fen Project* (1650) and *The Anti-Projector* (c. 1653).

Source: *Wit and Drollery* (1661), 231–3, with additions from Cambridge MS Add .79, 2ʳ.

> The upland people° are full of thoughts,
> And do despair of after-rain;
> Now the sun is robbed of his morning° draughts,°
> They're afraid they shall ne'er have shower again.
>
> Then apace,° apace drink, drink deep, drink deep,
> Whilst 'tis to be had let's the liquor ply;
> The drainers are up, and a coil° they keep,
> And threaten to drain the kingdom dry.
>
> Our smaller rivers are now dry land,   10
> The Eels are turned to serpents there;
> And if old Father Thames play not the man,
> Then farewell to all good English Beer.
> Then apace, apace drink, etc.

° **upland people**: country-dwellers, but upland also signifies high ground around and within the fens.
° **morning**: Cam; morning's] WD.   ° **draughts**: from evaporation.   ° **apace**: quickly.
° **coil**: disturbance, fuss.

The Dutchman hath a thirsty soul,
Our Cellars are subject to his call;
Let every man then lay hold° on his bowl,
'Tis pity the German Sea° should have all.
Then apace, apace drink, etc.

Our new Philosophers rob us of fire,°
And by reason do strive to maintain that theft;
And now that the water begins to retire,
We shall shortly have never an Element left.
Then apace, apace drink, etc.

Why should we stay here then° and perish with thirst?
To th'new world in the Moon° away let us go;
For if the Dutch colony get thither first,
'Tis a thousand to one but they'll drain that too.
Then apace, apace drink, etc.

20

※ ※ ※

° **hold**: WD; hands] Cam.   ° **German Sea**: North Sea.
° **new ... fire**: seventeenth-century astronomers questioned Aristotle's theory that a ring of fire
   bounded the upper atmosphere of the earth.
° **then**: WD; in] Cam.
° **new ... Moon**: possibly an allusion to Ben Jonson's *News from the New World Discovered in the
   Moon* (1620) or John Wilkins's *Discovery of a World in the Moon* (1638).

GERARD BOATE
"Draining of the Bogs practised by the English in Ireland"
(1645)

Wetlands reclamation was not confined to England's fen region. English colo-
nists in Ireland also set about draining bogs, which were condemned as waste-
lands and hideouts for Irish guerrilla fighters (see Spenser's depiction of the Bog
of Allen, *FQ* 2.9.16). Fen-draining has been characterized as "an inscription
of a Protestant work ethic on the land and the people" (Irvine 29), and this
commentary, by an Anglicized Dutch physician eager to promote English settlement, indicates how differently the Irish could perceive and interact with
wilderness. Tellingly, Boate himself had never visited Ireland, but relied on the
reports of his brother Arthur and colonial land expropriators such as William
Parsons.
Source: *Natural History of Ireland* (1657), 107–10, 112–15.

The places barren through superfluous moisture are bogs, called by the Irish Moones,° whereof Ireland is full. There are three or four° different sorts of them: grassy, watery, muddy, and Hassocky …

[108] The grassy Bogs are all over covered with grass, looking fair and pleasant, as if they were dry ground and goodly meadows; whereby many, who not knowing the nature of those [109] places and because of the greenness suspecting no evil, go into them to their great trouble, and many times to the extreme danger of their lives; for the earth being very spongy can bear no weight, but, as well men as beast, as soon as they set foot on it do sink to the ground: some knee-deep, others to the waist, and many over head and ears. For all or most bogs in Ireland having underneath a hard and firm gravel are not of an equal depth, which in some is only of two or three feet, in others five, six, or more; insomuch that those who fall into the deepest places of these bogs can hardly escape, but for the most part do perish, being pitifully smothered.

Some of these bogs do so dry up in the summer that they may be passed without danger; the which in particular falleth out in the great Mountains in Munster in the county of Kerry, called Slieve-Logher,° upon which all kind of cattle do graze the summer long, being everywhere full of good and sweet grass, knee-deep in most places; whereof not the tenth part being eaten … the rest is spoiled when the wet weather cometh in …

But the deepest bogs are impassable in the summer as well as in the winter. Yet most of them have firm places in narrow paths (and in some larger parcels), by the means whereof those unto whom they are known can cross them from [110] one side to another (where others who are not used to them do not know in what part to set one step); in which nimble trick, called commonly treading of the Bogs, most Irish are very expert, as having been trained up in it from their infancy. The firm places in passing, or but lightly shaking them, tremble for a great way, which hath given them the name of Shaking-Bogs …

[112] Recklessness° of the Irish, cause of most of the Bogs

Very few of the Wet-bogs in Ireland are such by any natural property or primitive constitution, but through the superfluous moisture that in length of time hath been gathered therein … [113] So that it may easily

---

° **Moones**: from the Irish *móin*.
° **four**: ecologists now divide Irish bogs into two main varieties: blanket bogs, where peat forms on waterlogged terrain in mountains and low-lying coastal plains; and raised bogs, which are dome-shaped accumulations of peat over depressions and shallow lakes. Of the estimated 908,117 hectares of blanket bog which Ireland originally possessed, only 28 per cent remains intact. Of the 308,742 hectares of raised bog which once covered Ireland, a mere 1.3 per cent survive in good ecological health (*Ireland's Peatland Conservation Action Plan 2020*). Much of the worst damage has been inflicted in the past century by industrial peat extraction.
° **Slieve-Logher**: an Anglicization of *Sliabh Luachra*.   ° **Recklessness**: Neglect.

be comprehended that whoso could drain the water, and for the future prevent the gathering thereof, might reduce most of the Bogs in Ireland to firm land and preserve them in that condition. But this hath never been known to the Irish, or if it was they never went about it, but to the contrary let daily more and more of their good land grow boggy through their carelessness, whereby also most of the Bogs at first were caused …

[114] Draining of the Bogs practised by the English in Ireland

But as the Irish have been extreme careless in this, so the English, introducers of all good things in Ireland (for which that brutish nation from time to time hath rewarded them with unthankfulness, hatred, and envy, and lately with a horrible and bloody conspiracy, tending to their utter destruction), have set their industry at work for to remedy it; and having considered the nature of the Bogs, and how possible it was to reduce many of them unto good land, did some years since begin to go about it all over the land, and that with very good success … I know gentlemen who turned into firm land three or four hundred acres of Bog, and, in case that this detestable rebellion° had not come between, in a few years there would scarce have been left one acre of Bog of what was in the [115] lands and possession of the English.

⧼ ⧼ ⧼

° **rebellion**: the 1641 uprising that lead to the formation of the Catholic Confederation.

JOHN BUNYAN
"The Slough of Despond" (*c.* 1660–1678)

Perhaps the third most-read book in the English language after the Bible and Shakespeare, *The Pilgrim's Progress* is an allegorical dream vision of the soul's journey to salvation. Nevertheless, Bunyan often modelled his spiritual topography on actual places in the English landscape. The following episode recounting the protagonist Christian's misadventures in the Slough of Despond is probably based on Squitch Fen in Bedfordshire (which Bunyan had to cross on his way to church in Elstow), or perhaps the boggy ground around nearby Stewartby. Allegorically, Help's insistence that the mire cannot be reclaimed speaks to a Puritan belief in humanity's innate corruption. On a literal level, however, it is an indirect attack on the Crown's efforts to drain fenlands, which were often breeding grounds of religious dissent as well as wildlife. In fact, many of the drainage projects enjoyed only short-term success: the drainage ditches were often so sluggish they silted up, while the now exposed peat (no longer waterlogged) gradually shrank and crumbled, lowering the ground so that it ironically became more susceptible to flooding. Source: *The Pilgrim's Progress* (1678), 9–13.

Now I saw in my Dream that ... they drew near to a very Miry Slough that was in the midst of the Plain, and they, being heedless, did both fall suddenly into the bog. The name of the Slough was Despond. Here therefore [10] they wallowed for a time, being grievously bedaubed with the dirt. And Christian, because of the burden that was on his back, began to sink in the Mire.

Then said Pliable, "Ah, neighbour Christian, where are you now?"

"Truly," said Christian, "I do not know."

At that, Pliable began to be offended and angrily said to his Fellow, "Is this the happiness you have told me all this while of? If we have such ill-speed at our first setting out, what may we expect 'twixt this and our Journey's end? May I get out again with my life, you shall possess the brave Country alone for me." And with that, he gave a desperate struggle or two, and got out of the Mire on that side of the Slough which was next to his own House. So away he went, and Christian saw him no more. Wherefore Christian was left to tumble in the Slough of Despondency alone ...

But I beheld in my Dream that a Man came to him, whose name was Help ... [Help said,] "Give me thy hand!" So he gave him his hand, and he drew him out, and set him upon sound ground, and bid him go on his way.

Then I stepped to him that plucked him out and said, "Sir, wherefore (since over this place is the way from the City of Destruction to yonder Gate) is it that this Plat° is not mended, that poor Travellers might go thither with more security?"

And he said unto me, "This Miry Slough is such a place as cannot be mended. It is the descent whither the scum and filth that attends conviction for sin doth [12] continually run, and therefore is it called the Slough of Despond. For still as the sinner is awakened about his lost condition, there ariseth in his soul many fears, and doubts, and discouraging apprehensions, which all of them get together, and settle in this place. And this is the reason of the badness of this ground.

"It is not the pleasure of the King that this place should remain so bad. His Labourers also have, by the direction of His Majesty's surveyors, been for above this sixteen hundred years° employed about this patch of ground, if perhaps it might have been mended. Yea, and to my knowledge," saith he, "here hath been swallowed up at least twenty thousand cartloads— yea, millions of wholesome instructions that have at all seasons been brought from all places of the King's dominions (and they that can tell say they are the best materials to make good ground of the place). If so be, it might have been mended, but it is the Slough of Despond still, and so will be when they have done what they can.

° **Plat**: plot (of ground), usually flat.   ° **sixteen hundred years**: since the time of Christ.

"True, there are by the direction of [13] the Lawgiver, certain good and substantial Steps placed even through the very midst of this Slough. But at such time as this place doth much spew out its filth, as it doth against change of weather, these steps are hardly seen; or if they be, Men through the dizziness of their heads step besides; and then they are bemired to purpose,° notwithstanding the steps be there. But the ground is good when they are once got in at the Gate."°

ɝ ɝ ɝ

° **to purpose**: effectively.   ° **Gate**: thought to be Wicket Gate, at Elstow Church.

SAMUEL FORTREY?

"A True and Natural Description of the Great Level of the Fens" (*c.* 1660–1680)

If the opening of this poem signals its affinity with classical epic, it is also an early example of industrial georgic, illustrating Virgil's maxim "labour conquers all." It appeared in a 1685 book on the drainage of the fens, which includes a remarkable map of the fenlands produced by the Earl of Bedford's surveyor, Jonas Moore (Figure 8). Although his cartographic mastery mirrors the poem's sense of technological dominion over the wetlands, it is unlikely that the mathematician Moore also composed these verses. In the 1890s the poem was attributed to Samuel Fortrey, author of the mercantilist tract *England's Interest and Improvement* (1663). Fortrey's name appears among the major investors in the Bedford Level scheme (with which the poet is clearly familiar), but his authorship of these verses remains highly conjectural; the preface states only they were "formerly writ by some ingenious hand." Internal evidence suggests a date around the time of the General Drainage Act of 1663. In its admiration of human industry, the poem anticipates eighteenth-century literary tributes to the drainage such as John Dyer's "Bedford Level," in which the "dreary pathless waste" is taught to "smile." Nevertheless, the triumphant tone does not drown out the persistent notes of discord, as the author seeks to justify the scheme against its outspoken detractors. For an earlier pro-drainage manifesto in prose, see H. C.'s *Concerning the Draining of the Fens* (1629).
Source: *History or Narrative of the Great Level of the Fens* (1685), 71–81.

> I Sing no Battles fought, nor Armies foiled,
> Nor Cities razed, nor Commonwealths embroiled,
> Nor any History which may move your tears,
> Or raise your Spleens, or multiply your Fears;
> But I bespeak your wonder, your delight,
> And would your Emulation° fain invite.

° **Emulation**: "ambition to equal or excel" (*OED*).

I sing Floods muzzled and the Ocean tamed,
Luxurious Rivers governed and reclaimed,
Waters with Banks confined, as in a Jail,
Till kinder Sluices let them go on Bail;　　　　　　　　　　10
Streams curbed with Dams like Bridles, taught t'obey,
And run as straight as if they saw their way.

I sing of heaps of Water turned to Land,
Like an Elixir by the Chemist's hand,
Of Dropsies cured, where not one Limb was sound,
The Liver rotted, all the Vitals drowned;
No late discovered Isle, nor old Plantation
New Christened, but a kind of new Creation.

I sing of heaps of Gold and Indian Ore,
Of private Profit and of Public Store;　　　　　　　　　　20
No fine Romance nor Fables I invent,
Nor coin Utopias, but a Scene present,
Which with such rare yet real bliss doth Swell,
As would persuade a Monk to leave his Cell.

I sing of an Achievement, from above
Both Blest and Crowned, which God and good Men Love;
Which Kings and States encourage and protect
With Prudent Power; which none can disaffect,
But the poor Fish, who now wants room to play,
Hassocks,° and Men with Heads more rough than they.　　　30

Go on, Brave Undertakers,° and Succeed
In spite of Brutish Clamours; take no heed
To those that curse your Gen'rous labours; he
That good refrains 'cause Men unthankful be
Mistakes true Virtue's aim; each worthy Act
Doth a Reward beyond Applause expect.

Make universal Plenty, and restore
What Ten-year's Wars have ruined; let the Poor
Share your wise Alms: some will, perhaps, confess
Their Obligation and your Virtues bless;　　　　　　　　　40
But if the present Age forget their friends,
Be sure Posterity will make amends.

They'll be indifferent Judges, at what Rates
And with what Arts you purchased your Estates;
They will not grudge that you took so much Land,
But wonder why you did not more demand;
They'll candidly believe that Public Zeal
Had more of influence here than Private Weal.

° **Hassocks**: clumps of matted vegetation.　　° **Undertakers**: developers.

When, by your Noble Pattern and Success
50   Taught and encouraged, all Men shall profess
A hate of Sloth, and so the Sea shall more
Feel your Example than your Skill before,
Whilst all to work that Public Tyrant's bane
At once Conspire, as if he were a Dane;°

When such as have no Wit, but to defame
All generous Works, and blast them with the Name
Of giddy Projects, are described to be
But Slaves to Custom, Friends to Popery,
And ranked with those who, lest they should accuse
60   Their Sires, no harness but the Tail will use;°

When to your Glory all your Banks shall stand
Like the immortal Pyramid, and your Land
Forget it ere was Sea; when those dull wits,
That Judge by Sense become time's Proselytes,
And such as know no other Argument,
Shall be at last confuted by th'Event;°

When Bedford's° stately Bank and noble Drain,°
Shall Parallel the Straits of Magellan,
Or Hercules his Pillars,° in due Fame,
70   Because they wear your Livery° in their Name,
And your Renown shall share the Bays° with theirs,
Who, in times past, built Amphitheaters;

When Cities shall be built, and Houses tall
As the proud Oak, which you their Founders call,
Fair Orchards planted and the Myrtle Grove
Adorned as if it were the Scene of Love,
Gardens with Flowers of such auspicious hue,
You'd swear that Eden in the Desert grew;

When it appears the all-sufficient Soil,
80   With Primitive Strength,° yields as much Corn as Oil,
To make our Hearts strong as our Faces gay,
Meadows so blessed with Grass, so charged with Hay,
With goodly Kine and Beeves° replenished so,
As if they stood upon the Banks of Po;

° **Dane**: i.e. as if the sea were a foreign power. Denmark and Britain had quarrelled (and still do) over fishing rights in the North Sea.
° **those … use**: opposed to all technological innovations.   ° **Event**: outcome.
° **Bedford**: Francis Russell, the 4th Earl of Bedford, who spearheaded the drainage of the Cambridgeshire fenlands, renamed the Bedford Level in his honour.
° **Drain**: now known as the New Bedford River.   ° **Hercules his Pillars**: straits of Gibraltar.
° **Livery**: clothing worn by servants identifying their employer. "Your" suggests the poem may be addressing the 5th Earl, William Russell, who resumed his father's drainage projects in 1649.
° **Bays**: laurels.   ° **Primitive Strength**: unfertilized.   ° **Kine … Beeves**: cows and oxen.

When all dire Vapours (if there any were,
Besides the People's breath) are turned to Air,
Pure as the Upper Region, and the Sun
Shall shine like one well pleased with what is done;
When Agues, Scurvies, Coughs, Consumptions, Wind,
All Crude Distempers here their Cure shall find;   90

When with the change of Elements suddenly,
There shall a change of Men and Manners be,
Hearts thick and tough as Hides shall feel Remorse,
And Souls of Sedge shall understand Discourse,
New hands shall learn to Work, forget to Steal,
New legs shall go to Church, new knees shall kneel;

When Ouse proves Helicon;° when the Nine° forsake
Their lofty Mountain, and themselves betake
To this delicious Vale; when Caps and Gowns
Are seen at Wisbech; when for sordid Clowns   100
And savage Scythians there succeeds a Race
Worthy the Bliss and Genius of the place,

What Trophies will you Purchase then? What Bays
Will ye acquire? What Acclamations raise?
What greater Satisfaction? What Reward
Of higher price can all the World afford,
Than in a Work of such Renown and Merit,
T'engross the Glory and the Bliss t'inherit?

Meanwhile, proceed, and Opposition slight;
Envy perhaps may bark, it cannot bite.   110
Your Cause is good; your Friends are great; your Foes
Have neither Power nor Colour to oppose.
Rubs° you may meet with; why should that displease?
Would you accomplish Vast designs with Ease?

But vainly I, with weak insinuations,
Your Wisdoms importune; such fond persuasions
Fit none but drooping Minds whom fears oppress;
No terror, no alarm can you possess,
Who, free from sinful Canaanites'° annoy,
The Land of Promise now in part enjoy.   120

Your Proudest foes begin to sue for Peace,
And with their hopes, their malice doth decrease;
They all confess that Heaven with you Combines;
Sit down, therefore, in safety: your designs,
Begun with Virtue, shall with Fortune end;
For Profit public thoughts do still attend.

° **Helicon**: mountain of the Muses, through which sacred springs flowed.
° **Nine**: the Muses, but the original spelling "Nean" puns on the River Nene.   ° **Rubs**: obstacles.
° **Canaanites**: biblical name for the ancient inhabitants of the Promised Land, displaced by the Israelites.

And now a Muse as fruitful as the Land
Assist me, whilst my too unskillful hand
Describes the Glories of this Place: a Skill
130   Which might perhaps deserve some Laureate's Quill.
But I presume the Reader's Charity
And wise Conjecture will my faults supply.

All Seeds, all Plants and Herbs, this Noble field
Doth, with a kind of Emulation, yield.
Would you see Plenty? It is stored with Grain,
Like Egypt when Rome's Pride it did maintain,
With roots of Monstrous bulk, flesh, fowl, and fish:
All that the Belly or the Taste can wish.

Here thrives the lusty Hemp, of Strength untamed,
140   Whereof vast Sails and mighty Cables framed
Serve for our Royal Fleets; Flax soft and fine
To the East Country's envy. Could we join
To England's blessings Holland's industry,
We all the World in wealth should far outvie.

Here grows proud Rape, whose price and plenty foils
The Greenland Trade, and checks the Spanish Oils,
Whose branch, thick, large, and tall, the Earth so shrouds,
As heaps of Snow the Alps, or pregnant Clouds
The azure Sky, or like that Heav'nly Bread,°
150   Which in the Wilderness God's bounty shed.

After long Tillage it doth then abound
With Grass so plentiful, so sweet, so sound,
Scarce any tract but this can Pastures show
So large, so rich; and, if you wisely Sow
The fine Dutch Clover, with such Beauty spreads,
As if it meant t'affront our English Meads.

The gentle Osier,° placed in goodly ranks
At small Expense upon the comely Banks,
Shoots forth to admiration here, and yields
160   Revenues certain as the Rents of Fields;
And for a Crown° unto this blest Plantation,
Almost in every Ditch there's Navigation.

To scan all its Perfections would desire
A Volume, and as great a Skill require
As that which Drained the Country; in one word,
It yields whate'er our Climate will afford;

° **Heavenly Bread**: manna, food God miraculously provided the Israelites in the desert (see Exodus 16:1–36).
° **Osier**: willow.   ° **for a Crown**: to top it all.

And did the Sun with kinder beams reflect,
You might Wine, Sugar, Silk and Spice expect.

Fond witless Usurer, to rest content
In that thy Money yields thee six per cent,°   170
Which thou with hazard of the Principal
Dost rigorously extort from Men in thrall:
Come here and look for gain both vast and just,
And yet so constant that thou need'st not trust.

Unhappy Farmer, that employ'st thy Skill
And wastes thy Strength upon some barren Hill,
Which, too ungrateful, scarce the borrowed Seed
At length restores, much less relieves thy need:
These Fields shall yield thee Gold, and yet require
No labour but the Alchemy of Fire.   180

Poor Curate, whom thine envious Stars prefer
To be some hidebound° Parson's Pensioner,
On such hard Terms that if thy Flock were fed
As ill as thou, their Souls might starve for Bread:
When these fair Fields are Ploughed, then cast° with me
How large, how fat, the Livings here must be.

Ye busy Gentlemen that plant the Hop,°
And dream vast gains from that deceitful Crop,
Or by manuring what you ought to Let
Thrive backwards, and too dearly purchase Wit: 190
Leave off these Lotteries and here take your Lot.
The Profit's certain, and with ease 'tis got.

Courageous Merchants, who, confronting fates,
Trust Seas and Pirates with your whole Estates:
Part in this bank methinks were far more sure.
And ye whom hopes of sudden Wealth allure,
Or wants into Virginia force to fly:
Ev'n spare your pains; here's Florida hard by.

Fair Damsels that your Portions° would advance:
Employ them on this blest Inheritance.   200
And faithful Guardians that would quit° the trust
In you reposed, like Men as wise as just:
Here, here, bestow your Orphan's Talents;° ye
Shall now no longer Friends but Fathers be.

° **six per cent**: the interest rate was reduced from eight to six percent by the Usury Act of 1660, which provides a *terminus a quo* for the poem's composition.
° **hidebound**: stingy.   ° **cast**: forecast.
° **Hop**: hop cultivation boomed in the 1650s, but it could be considered "deceitful" as it was vulnerable to cold weather.
° **Portions**: dowries.   ° **quit**: repay.
° **Talents**: money, an allusion to Christ's Parable of the Talents (Matthew 25:14–30).

All ye that Treasures either want or love
(And who is he whom Profit will not move?)
Would you repair your fortunes? Would you make?
To this most fruitful Land yourselves betake,
Where first your Money doubles in a trice,
210   And then, by new Progression, multiplies.

If therefore Gain, or Honour, or Delight,
Or care of Public Good, will Men invite
Into this fortunate Isle,° now let them enter
With confidence, since here they all concentre;°
But if all these be choked and drowned with phlegm,
Let them enjoy their Sloth, sit still, and dream.

⅔⅔ ⅔⅔ ⅔⅔

° **Isle**: Britain, but also an island in the fens, like Ely or Axholme, here conflated with the "Fortunate Isles" of Greek legend.
° **concentre**: converge.

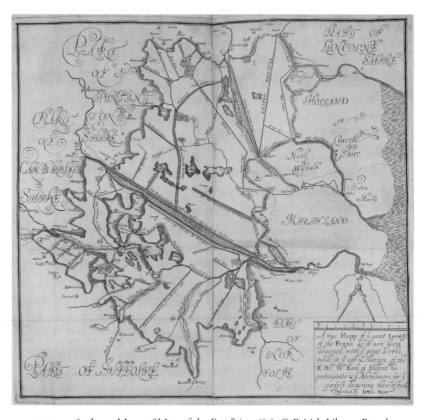

FIGURE 8   Jonas Moore, "Map of the Fens" (c. 1685). © British Library Board.

Pollution

EDMUND SPENSER

[Mammon's Delve] (1590)

While tin was mined in Britain as far back as the Bronze Age, the Elizabethan period witnessed an unprecedented push to exploit the nation's mineral wealth. In 1568, mineral rights were declared to be the exclusive property of the Crown, and the queen Set up a duopoly run by the Society of Mines-Royal and the Company of Mineral and Battery Works. Pits were soon dug or expanded to extract copper in Keswick, iron in the Weald and Forest of Dean, lead in the Peak District, zinc ore in the Mendip Hills, and silver in Cardiganshire. The following excerpt from Spenser's Legend of Temperance (Book 2, Canto 7 of *The Faerie Queene*) indicates that he took a dim view of this industrial boom, as does the imagery from Book 1 associating the fire-belching dragon with furnaces and forges. Spenser's antipathy to mining owes something to the Roman poet Ovid, but also reflects his belief that the selfish desire to strike it rich was distracting settlers in Ireland and America from farming, which he regarded as a more effective way to promote English colonization. Another factor may have been his grudge against the Lord Treasurer, William Cecil, who was a leading member of the Society of Mines-Royal and a patron of the mining engineer William Humfrey. It is entirely possible that Spenser had some knowledge of ironworks in the Weald or of mining in Cornwall (overseen by his friend Ralegh); in Book 4, he describes the River Dart as "nigh choked with sands of tinny mines" (*FQ* 4.11.31). He also would have been aware of industrialization in Ireland, such as a proposed mint near Clane, an iron forge at Enniscorthy, or a blast furnace at Mogeely Castle in Munster (Hadfield 217). Although the earliest reference to this furnace dates from 1593, it is conceivable that mining and smelting operations were occurring in the 1580s after Sir John Norreys became President of Munster, as Spenser's description has the immediacy of a first-hand account. Source: *The Faerie Queene* (1590), 272–3, 279, 281.

3

At last he° came unto a gloomy glade,
Covered with boughs and shrubs from heaven's light,
Whereas he sitting found in secret shade,
An uncouth, savage, and uncivil wight,
Of grisly hue and foul, ill-favoured sight;
His face with smoke was tanned and eyes were bleared,
His head and beard with soot were ill bedight,°
His coal-black° hands did seem to have been seared
In smith's fire-spitting forge, and nails like claws appeared.

° **he**: Sir Guyon, the Knight of Temperance.   ° **bedight**: adorned
° **coal-black**: coal could mean "charcoal" (pyrolized wood), but "pit-coal" or "sea-coal" was starting to be used as an industrial fuel at this time.

4

His iron coat, all overgrown with rust,
Was underneath envelopèd with gold,
Whose glist'ring gloss, darkened with filthy dust,
Well yet appeared to have been of old
A work of rich entail° and curious mould,°
Woven with antics° and wild imagery;
And in his lap a mass of coin he told,°
And turnèd upside down, to feed his eye
And covetous desire with his huge treasury.

5

And round about him lay on every side
Great heaps of gold, that never could be spent:
Of which some were rude ore, not purified
Of Mulciber's devouring element;°
Some others were new driven and distent°
Into great ingots° and to wedges square;
Some in round plates withouten monument:°
But most were stamped, and in their metal bare
The antique shapes of kings, and caesars strange and rare …

28

That house's form within was rude and strong,
Like a huge cave, hewn out of rocky cliff,
From whose rough vault the raggèd breaches hung,
Embossed with massy gold of glorious gift,
And with rich metal loaded every rift,
That heavy ruin they did seem to threat;
And over them Arachne° high did lift
Her cunning web, and spread her subtle net,
Enwrappèd in foul smoke and clouds more black than jet …

35

Thence forward he him led, and shortly brought
Unto another room, whose door forthright
To him did open, as it had been taught:
Therein a hundred ranges° were in pight,°
And hundred furnaces all burning bright;
By every furnace many fiends did bide,
Deformèd creatures, horrible in sight,
And every fiend his busy pains applied
To melt the golden metal, ready to be tried.

° **entail**: ornamental carving   ° **curious mould**: unusual shape.
° **antics**: grotesques.   ° **told**: counted.
° **Mulciber's … element**: fire; Mulciber was another name for Vulcan.
° **driven and distent**: beaten thin.   ° **ingots**: cast metal.
° **monument**: markings.
° **Arachne**: the spider (a weaver transformed by the goddess Minerva; see Ovid's *Metamorphoses* 6.1–145).
° **ranges**: hearths.   ° **pight**: placed.

36

One with great bellows gathered filling air,
And with forced wind the fuel did enflame;
Another did the dying brands repair
With iron° tongs, and sprinkled oft the same
With liquid waves, fierce Vulcan's rage to tame,
Who, mast'ring them, renewed his former heat:
Some scummed the dross that from the metal came;
Some stirred the molten ore with ladles great;
And everyone did swink,° and everyone did sweat.

જ઼ જ઼ જ઼

° **iron**: 1596; dying] 1590.　　° **swink**: toil.

GAWIN SMITH

"For the Cleansing and Clean Keeping and Continuing Sweet of the Ditches about the Walls of London" (*c.* 1610)

Tudor London could be a hellishly unsanitary place, as rubbish and excrement were often tossed into the muddy streets and waterways. As far back as 1390, the government took steps to clean up the Thames, and passed legislation fining polluters in 1535, 1543, and 1590. The widespread adoption of sea-coal as a domestic fuel in the final years of Elizabeth's reign compounded the sanitation crisis, since Londoners dumped the ash into the nearest ditch or sewer, choking its flow. In response, the early seventeenth century witnessed a campaign to improve the city's water quality, as attested by a series of manuscripts in the Cotton MS Titus BV collection. BV/87 contains a petition to the Earl of Northampton (d. 1614) to construct "a channel of brick or stone" to drain Tower Ditch (routinely contaminated by offal from the Smithfields meat market) so that it might "be for ever freed from annoyance and choking filth," to the benefit not only of the human inhabitants but also for the "breed and increase of fishes, and pleasing in itself." The manuscript transcribed below depicts early modern London as besieged by foul, stagnant water, and petitions the king to establish a forerunner of the Victorian sewer system. Its author was the engineer Gawin Smith, who had previously built a conduit to supply water to Edinburgh, and also submitted a proposal to James I to cleanse Fleet Ditch – promising to purge it of "all noisome things, as drowned dogs, cats, straw, rushes, rags" (BV/122; also see BV/87, 263) – which makes a fascinating counterpart to Ben Jonson's "On the Famous Voyage." Source: Cotton MS Titus BV/87, 264.

The occasions whereby the said ditches do become so noisome and offensive, and so greatly in so few years chargeable to the city as now they be are:

First, for that there is recourse unto them of so many noisome and filthy waters, thick, loathsome, gross, and corrupt, from the streets, sewers, and otherlike. As, for special instance, in Little Moorland° between the two

° **Little Moorland**: near Little Moorfields, just outside Moorgate.

posterns a channel of continual loathsomeness ... [where] such noisome waters are forward in abundance [more] than any clean or sweet waters which hath recourse or passage into the same; so it followeth of necessity that the same turneth into corrupt and stinking mud, and thereby choketh the ditches and dispossesseth and soaketh up such small quantities of clean or sweet water as have recourse thither; so as in small time there is no powerful passage or quantities of good waters to master the other, or to have convenient issue, but standeth noisome in sort aforesaid. As, for special instance, may appear by that part of the ditch that is between Cripplegate and Moorgate, where the mud is so high that grass groweth through the waters in the midst and most part of all the ditch.

Secondly, it is a common fault through all parts of the city and suburbs of [the] same that soil,° and specially sea-coal ashes, are cast as well into the common sewers as into the sweet, where in times of great rains and waters the same are carried with violence into the common sewers and ditches of the city,° where it settleth and abideth and turneth presently into noisome and choking soil, and is of nature now hard and unremoveable than any sand or other earths.

The Redress

The ditches being now in manner by the occasions aforesaid grown and choked up, and the present state of time not requiring nor having need, use, or service of the said ditches to be restored to their full breadths, depths, space, and circuit of water, but (as convenience of the present time requireth) to have the annoyance removed, both for present and future times, the presented device is that through the midst only of every of the city wall ditches there be taken and cast up, even down to the firm ground, all the noisome mud and soil, by the breadth of ten or twelve foot, as shall be found convenient; and within the same to be built of brick or stone a passage or channel of six foot of breadth within, and of four or five foot of height, open above for the continual passage away of all matter into the Thames.

Secondarily, that to keep the said passages or channels sweet and clean, and to resist all bulky thing,° as well as prevent the increase of mud and other gross matter from the said channel or passage from annoying the Thames, there may be made and settled at sundry place of convenient place and distance upon and within the said passage and channel, two or three iron grates;° and an officer appointed with some convenient allowance to attend them, and from time to time with drag° and engines, to be limited and provided for that purpose, to take up and in convenient

---

° **soil**: filth.
° **sewers .... city**: in the left-hand margin, another hand has written "And so into the Thames."
° **bulky thing**: same annotator specifies, "Dogs, cats, carrion, clouts, weeds, or any other filth."
° **grates**: a similar proposal had been made by London's Court of Common Council in 1535.
° **drag**: dragnet or dredging apparatus.

sort and place to be appointed nigh to the neighbours or passengers, and to yield free passage to the water. The said passage and channel being so provided that it shall still have descent and ready passage to the Thames, being so free as aforesaid of impediment.

Thirdly, that the said passage and channel being thus made ... it is of necessity that there should be provided some plentiful course of water to be at times let out,° suddenly to command and carry away such offensive filth or soils as naturally and of necessity (notwithstanding the removing of the foresaid greater annoyances and impediment) will grow and be moved by and out of the very waters coming from the sewers into the said passage or channel. The proprietor knoweth and assureth himself of waters to be in great plenty found and raised in place not far from the city, which by his duty, industry, and engines he will undertake to draw and gather together into some one apt and fitting place without the said city, which as it shall be let out may have forcible descent and passage in and through the said chan-nel,° and the same to be at times convenient let out, by force whereof the said channel shall be thoroughly cleansed and kept clean. Which work, as also the report and attendance of the foresaid grates, the proprietor will perform and undertake upon remuneration to be agreed upon for his service.

And if at any time hereafter it shall be held fit to reform the city ditches to the full, into nature and kind of ditches again, there will be, and out of the such gathered waters as aforesaid ... [more] ready store of water than now is ... and in better sweeter and cleaner sort by far than now they be or at any time have been.

❦ ❦ ❦

° **water ... out**: marginal annotation reads, "A thousand tons or more at once."
° **channel**: in left margin, "or common sewer."

BEN JONSON

"On the Famous Voyage" (1616)

Although John Harington invented the first flush toilet in 1596, it would be another three hundred years before indoor plumbing was widely adopted. Prior to the twentieth century, human waste, or "night-soil," was dumped in city streets and waterways. Jonson's scatological poem takes a deep whiff of the nox-ious smells of early modern London prior to modern sanitation. It recounts the journey of an intrepid duo up the Fleet River in a rowboat, from Bridewell docks (where it flows into the Thames) to Holborn. During the eighteenth and nineteenth centuries the Fleet was gradually covered over; in Jonson's day, how-ever, it was an open sewer. The opening lines frame the poem as a mock-epic that lampoons the voyage to the underworld in classical literature (cf. Book 11 of Homer's *Odyssey* and Book 6 of Virgil's *Aeneid*). With mordant wit, Jonson superimposes the infernal topographies of Greco-Roman mythology over a polluted urban ecology. It has been suggested that the poem draws on Jonson's childhood memories of living on Hartshorn Lane, through which a large sewer ran (Donaldson 67). Its nauseating depictions of excrement, dead cats, mercury, and pewter steeping in the Fleet make "The Famous Voyage" a prime example of what Lawrence Buell calls "toxic discourse," anticipating the Victorian poem "Dirty Father Thames." When situated alongside early modern legislation to protect the water quality of London's waterways, Jonson's satire has a serious environmentalist undercurrent.

Source: *The Works of Benjamin Jonson* (1616), 813–18.

> No more let Greece her bolder fables tell
> Of Hercules or Theseus going to hell,
> Orpheus, Ulysses; or the Latin Muse,
> With tales of Troy's just knight,° our faiths abuse:
> We have a Shelton° and a Heyden° got,
> Had power to act° what they to feign had not.
> All that they boast of Styx, of Acheron,
> Cocytus, Phlegeton,° ours have proved in one:
> The filth, stench, noise, save only what was there
> Subtly distinguished, was confusèd here. *(10)*
> Their wherry° had no sail, too; ours had none:
> And in it, two more horrid knaves than Charon.°
> Arses were heard to croak instead of frogs,
> And for one Cerberus,° the whole coast was dogs …
> But hold my torch while I describe the entry
> To this dire passage. Say thou stop thy nose:
> 'Tis but light pains; indeed, this Dock's no rose. *(60)*
> In the first jaws appeared that ugly monster,
> Ycleped° Mud, which, when their oars did once stir,
> Belched forth an air as hot as at the muster
> Of all your night-tubs,° when the carts do cluster
> Who shall discharge first his merd-urinous° load:
> Thorough her womb they make their famous road,
> Between two walls, where, on one side, to scar° men,
> Were seen your ugly Centaurs ye call Car-men;
> Gorgonian scolds and Harpies on the other *(70)*
> Hung stench, diseases, and old filth, their mother,
> With famine, wants, and sorrows many a dozen,

° **Troy's just knight**: Aeneas.

° **Shelton**: Presumably the Sir Ralph Shelton (1560–1628) to whom Jonson dedicates Epigram 119; he had been one of the promoters of the London Company's Bermuda voyage. It may be relevant that his father had been appointed a Commissioner of Sewers in Norfolk.

° **Heyden**: Possibly Sir Christopher Heyden (1561–1623), author of treatise defending astrology, who had participated in the raid on Cadiz. After his involvement in the Essex Revolt, he was held in the Fleet prison. Alternatively, Heyden could be an unknown friend or servant of Ralph Shelton.

° **act**: these lines imply that the journey actually took place.

° **Styx … Phlegeton**: rivers in the underworld.   ° **wherry**: rowboat.

° **Charon**: ferryman of the River Styx.   ° **Cerberus**: three-headed guard dog of Hades.

° **Ycleped**: named.   ° **night-tubs**: chamber pots.

° **merd-urinous**: faeces and urine mixed.   ° **scar**: archaic past tense of scare.

The least of which was to the plague a cousin.
But they unfrighted pass, though many a privy
Spake to 'hem louder than the ox in Livy;°
And many a sink° poured out her rage against 'hem,
But still their valour and their virtue fenced 'hem ...
"No going back; on still, you rogues, and row."
"How hight° the place?" A voice was heard: "Cocytus."°
"Row close then slaves." "Alas, they will beshite us."   90
"No matter, stinkards, row." "What croaking sound
Is this we hear? Of frogs?" "No, guts wind-bound,°
Over your heads. Well, row." At this a loud
Crack did report itself, as if a cloud
Had burst with storm, and down fell, *ab excelsis*,°
Poor Mercury,° crying out on Paracelsus° ...
For (where he was the god of eloquence
And subtlety of metals) they dispense   100
His spirits now in pills and eke in potions,
Suppositories, cataplasm, and lotions.
"But many Moons there shall not wane," quoth he,
"In the meantime let 'hem imprison me,
But I will speak (and I know I shall be heard)
Touching this cause,° where they will be afeared
To answer me." And sure it was th'intent
Of that grave fart,° late let in parliament,
Had it been seconded ...
The well-greased wherry now had got between
And bade her farewell sough° unto the lurdan:°
Never did bottom more betray her burden;
The meat-boat° of the Bears' College, Paris Garden,
Stunk not so ill; nor, when she kissed, Kate Arden.°
Yet one day in the year for sweet 'tis voiced,
And that is when it is the Lord Mayor's foist.°   120

° **Livy**: the Roman historian reported that an ox bellowed "Rome, be on thy guard!" (*History of Rome* 35.21) – an omen of warning to the state.
° **sink**: sewer.   ° **hight**: is called.   ° **Cocytus**: "river of wailing" in Hades.
° **wind-bound**: constipated.   ° *ab excelsis*: from above.
° **Mercury**: the Roman god, but primarily the chemical, a common ingredient in early modern medicines and purges, taken orally or anally, and eventually excreted into the river.
° **Paracelsus**: Swiss physician who advocated chemical treatments involving mercury for ailments such as constipation and syphilis.
° **cause**: restricting the use of chemical medicine?
° **fart**: this 1607 incident inspired many humorous quips, and Jonson here jokingly imagines the stinking sound as a voice in a legislative debate.
° **sough**: murmur, sigh.   ° **lurdan**: sluggard, alluding to the sluggishness of the river.
° **meat-boat**: baited bears at Paris Garden were fed with rotten meat.
° **Kate Arden**: a notorious prostitute.
° **foist**: annual mayoral parade on a river boat down the Thames, but with wordplay on a musty smell or silent fart.

By this time had they reached the Stygian pool,
By which the Masters swear when on the stool°
Of worship, they their nodding chins do hit
Against their breasts. Here sev'ral ghosts did flit
About the shore of farts, but late departed,
White, black, blue, green, and in more forms outstarted
Than all those Atomi ridiculous,
Whereof old Democrite° and Hill Nicholas,°
One said, the other swore, the world consists.
130   These be the cause of those thick frequent mists
Arising in that place, through which who goes
Must try the unused valour of a nose:
And that ours did. For yet, no nare° was tainted,
Nor thumb nor finger to the stop acquainted,
But open and unarmed encountered all:
Whether it languishing stuck upon the wall,
Or were precipitated down the jakes,°
And after swum abroad in ample flakes,
Or that it lay heaped like a usurer's mass:
140   All was to them the same. They were to pass,
And so they did, from Styx to Acheron,
The ever-boiling flood, whose banks upon
Your Fleet Lane Furies and hot cooks do dwell,
That with still-scalding steams make the place hell.
The sinks ran grease and hair of measled hogs,
The head, hocks, entrails and the hides of dogs.
For, to say truth, what scullion° is so nasty
To put the skins and offal in a pasty?
Cats there lay, diverse° had been flayed and roasted,
150   And, after mouldy grown, again were toasted;
Then, selling not, a dish was ta'en to mince 'hem,
But still it seemed their rankness did convince° 'hem.
For here they were thrown in with th'melted pewter,°
Yet drowned they not; they had five lives in future.

⁊ᴇ ⁊ᴇ ⁊ᴇ

° **stool**: toilet.
° **Democrite**: Democritus, Roman materialist philosopher who first proposed that the universe is composed of atoms.
° **Hill Nicholas**: Nicholas Hill, an early English promoter of atomic theory.
° **nare**: nostril.   ° **jakes**: privy.   ° **scullion**: kitchen maid.
° **diverse**: several.   ° **convince**: convict.
° **pewter**: early modern pewter had a high lead content, and was therefore toxic.

PATRICK HANNAY
"Croydon clothed in black" (1622)

Located on the southern fringe of London, Croydon became an important centre for charcoal manufacturing in the Middle Ages. Charking was regarded as a filthy trade, and the following verse from a seldom-read Jacobean poet captures the early modern tendency to demonize industrial zones as infernal places.
Source: *Songs and Sonnets* (1622), 240–4.

When curious Nature did her cunning try,
In framing of this fair terrestrial round,
Her workmanship the more to beautify,
With changed variety made it abound,
And oft did place a plot of fertile ground,
Fraught with delights, nigh to a barren soil,
To make the best seem better by a foil.

Thus first were made by Thames the motley° meads,
Wearing the livery of the Summer's Queen,
Whose flowery robe o'er them she freely spreads,   10
With colours more than are in Iris° seen,
And all the ground and hem of grassy green,
Whereon the silly sheep do fearless feed,
While on a bank the shepherd tunes his reed.

Next shady groves where Delia° hunteth oft,
And light-foot Fairies tripping still do haunt,
There mirthful Muses raise sweet notes aloft,
And wanton birds their chaste loves cheerly chant.
There no delightful pleasure e'er doth want;
There Sylvan° with his Satyrs doth remain;   20
There Nymphs do love and are beloved again.

This place doth seem an earthly Paradise,
Where on fit object every sense may feed,
And filled with dainties that do thence arise
Of superfluity, help others' need:
Yet no satiety that store doth breed;
For when the sense nigh surfeits on delight,
New objects the dulled appetite do whet.

This place I say doth border on a plain,
Which Step-dame Nature seems to have made in scorn,   30
Where hungry husbandmen have toiled in vain,
And with the share° the barren soil have torn;
Nor did they rest till rise of ruddy Morn:

° **motley**: multi-coloured.   ° **Iris**: the rainbow.   ° **Delia**: Diana.
° **Sylvan**: Silvanus, the Roman god of woods.   ° **share**: plough.

Yet when was come the harvest of their hopes,
They for their gain do gather grainless crops.

It seems of starved Sterility the seat,
Where barren downs do it environ round,
Whose parchèd tops in Summer are not wet,
And only are with snow in winter crowned;
40   Only with barrenness do they still abound,
Or if on some of them we roughet° find,
It's tawny heath, badge of the barren rind.

In midst of these stands Croydon clothed in black,
In a low bottom, sink of all these hills,
And is receipt of all the dirty wrack,°
Which from their tops still in abundance trills,
The unpaved lanes with muddy mire it fills.
If one shower fall, or if that blessing stay,
You may well smell, but never see your way.

50   For never doth the flower-perfumèd Air,
Which steals choice sweets from other blessèd fields,
With panting breast take any resting there;
Nor of that prey a portion to it yields:
For those harsh hills his coming either shields,
Or else his breath infected with their kisses,
Cannot enrich it with his fragrant blisses.

And those who there inhabit, suiting well
With such a place, do either Negroes seem,
Or harbingers for Pluto, Prince of Hell,
60   Or his fire-beaters° one might rightly deem;
Their sight would make a soul of hell to dream,
Besmeared with soot, and breathing pitchy smoke,
Which (save themselves) a living wight° would choke.

These with the demi-gods still disagreeing
(As vice with virtue ever is at jar)
With all who in the pleasant woods have being,
Do undertake an everlasting war:
Cuts down their groves, and often do them scar,°
And in a close-pent° fire their arbours burn,
70   While as the Muses can do nought but mourn.

The other Sylvans, with their sight affrighted,
Do flee the place whereas these elves resort,°

° **roughet**: coarse vegetation; spelled "roughnetle."
° **wrack**: waste.　° **fire-beaters**: stokers.　° **wight**: person.
° **scar**: archaic past tense of scare, but with pun on disfigure.
° **close-pent**: charcoal was made from wood burned slowly in earthen mounds. See Evelyn, *Sylva*, 100–3.
° **whereas ... resort**: where these imps frequent.

Shunning the pleasures which them erst delighted,
When they behold these grooms° of Pluto's court,
While they do take their spoils and count it sport,
To spoil these dainties that them so delighted,
And see them with their ugly shapes affrighted.

To all proud dames I wish no greater hell,
Who do disdain of chastely proffered love,
Than to that place confined there e'er to dwell;   80
That place their pride's dear price might justly prove:
For if (which God forbid) my dear should move
Me not come nigh her for to pass my troth,°
Place her but there and I shall keep mine oath.

ॐ ॐ ॐ

° **grooms**: servants.   ° **troth**: vow (not to have premarital sex).

HUGH PLAT
"Sea-coal sweetened and multiplied" (1603)

As timber supplies dwindled in the late sixteenth century, England gradually shifted to coal as its major energy source. At first, sea-coal or pit-coal (so-called to differentiate it from charcoal) was used mainly for industrial purposes, but economic
pressures soon made it the common fuel for domestic cooking and heating. In
comparison to charcoal, however, sea-coal has a high sulphuric content. It has
been estimated that the amount of SO_2 in London's air swelled from a medieval
baseline of 5–7 micrograms per cubic metre to around 20 micrograms by 1575; half
a century later it had approximately doubled to 40 micrograms (Brimblecombe
and Grossi 1355). This impact on London air quality did not go unnoticed. A
manuscript at the British Library (Lansdowne 67/20) reveals that a method for
creating clean coal ("to correct its sulphury nature") had been proposed to the
queen as early as 1591. The inventor is identified only as "AB," although the manuscript in support of the project appears to have passed through the hands of John
Thornborough, the Dean of York, who corresponded with Lord Burghley at this
time about exporting the more harmful, lower quality coal abroad. Just over a decade later, Hugh Plat published a similar proposal for purifying coal. Despite this
commendable plan, Plat would be better categorized as a pragmatic agrarian im-
prover rather than an environmentalist. He also praised Thomas Lovell's scheme
to drain 33,000 acres of Lincolnshire fenland, arguing that the reclaimed land
could be sown with willow trees, whose timber would resupply charcoal burners.
The dream of clean coal was still being pursued by Richard Gesling in the 1640s,
when a broadside satirized the fickleness of "fine-nosed city dames," who would
exclaim "O Husband! we shall never be well, we nor our children, whilst we live
in the smell of this city's sea-coal smoke. Pray, a country house for our health, that
we may get out of this stinking sea-coal smell." When Newcastle was blockaded
during the war, however, the same women allegedly recanted: "Would to God we
had sea-coal! O the want of fire undoes us! O the sweet sea-coal fire we used to
have, how we want them now! No fire to your sea-coal!" (*Artificial Fire* 1644, 1). As

Ken Hiltner argues, seventeenth-century London was experiencing a small-scale version of the ethical dilemma now confronting the planet: craving affordable fossil fuels that provide heat and food that help sustain human life in the short term but threaten the planet's long-term health (2011, 122).

Source: *A New, Cheap, and Delicate Fire of Coal-Balls* (1603), B3ʳ–B4ᵛ.

In the winter season, after some few frosts, gather so much loam° as will serve your house for one whole year's spending ... Half a peck, and happily a less proportion of this loam, dissolved in a little tub of water, is a sufficient quantity for the knitting up of a bushel of sea-coal into balls, and your water and loam incorporated and well-laboured together must be like a very thin pap.

Then take a bushel of the best° sea-coal, which, being strewed upon a stony or paved floor, you must break or bruise with a hammer, mallet, or some other apt tool or instrument ... Spread these coals abroad some handful thick, or thereabouts, equally upon the floor. Then sprinkle some of your thin pap all over the heap. Then turn them with a shovel or a spade, and spread them again as before, throwing more of your loamy liquor upon them. Continue this course till you have made [B4ʳ] the whole mass or lump of your coals soft enough to be wrought up into balls between your hands, according to the manner and making of snowballs ... I have found in mine own experience that such fires as consist of balls be neither so offensive in smell, nor yet in soil,° as the ordinary sea-coal fires are ...

[B4ᵛ] And therefore my opinion is that the smoke which in our usual fires doth immediately ascend from the sea-coals unprepared must needs, according to the foul and gross manner of the coal, be also foul and smutty itself. But when the smoke doth pass and become, as it were, searsed° through the loam (which is the band that knitteth the coals together), it is then so refined and subtilated° before his penetration as that it either consumeth and swalloweth up or else leaveth behind it the gross residence of his own nature, whereby that black kind of peppering or sea-coal dust (if I be not greatly deceived) is either wholly or for the most part avoided: being a matter of so great offence to all the pleasant gardens of Noblemen, Gentlemen, and Merchants of this most honourable City and the suburbs thereof, besides the discolouring and defacing of all the stately hangings and other rich furniture of their houses, as also of their costly and gorgeous apparel, as that I presume, though these my charitable and well-intentioned labours should only produce a remedy for this long and hitherto unavoidable mischief, that yet they would be received with a sufficient applause and liking of all men. Also the stirring up of common sea-coal fires after they are once caked and knit together doth make a hellish smoke and smother, dispersing the smutty substance and subtle atomies° abroad into the air, which in a fire of balls doth never happen.

ᘔ ᘔ ᘔ

° **loam**: earth, or clay moistened with water.   ° **best**: caking coal, which produced less soot.
° **soil**: soot.   ° **searsed**: strained.   ° **subtilated**: sublimated.
° **atomies**: particles.

THOMAS MIDDLETON
"The Mist of Error" (1613)

Middleton composed this pageant to celebrate the installation of a new Lord Mayor, confusingly also named Thomas Myddleton. In the following scene, an artificial hill representing London is "overspread with a thick, sulphurous darkness" (C2ʳ). Although the clouds more broadly signify moral pollution, the pageant can also be seen as an early attempt to dramatize an "urban environmental catastrophe, a toxic, disease-bearing haze" (Boehrer 2013, 33). London and Truth remind the Lord Mayor of his duty to regulate industry (Myddleton's predecessors had helped rid England of starch-works), and they advocate environmental protection as one of the chief responsibilities of government.
Source: *Triumphs of Truth* (1613), B1ʳ, B2ʳ, C2ʳ⁻ᵛ, C3ᵛ–C4ᵛ.

> LONDON Fix thy most serious Thought upon the Weight
> Thou goest to undergo: 'tis the just Government
> Of this Famed City, Me, whom Nations call
> Their brightest Eye. Then with great care and fear
> Ought I to be o'er-seen to be kept clear.°
> Spots in deformèd Faces are scarce Noted,
> Fair cheeks are stained if ne'er so little blotted.
> See'st thou this Key of Gold? It shows thy charge.
> This place is the King's Chamber; all Pollution,°
> Sin, and Uncleanness must be locked out here,
> And be kept sweet, with Sanctity, Faith, and Fear …

[B2ʳ] The Trumpet then sounding, the Angel° and Zeal° rank themselves just before his Lordship, and conduct him to Paul's-Chain,° where in the South-yard Error, in a Chariot with his infernal Ministers, attends° to assault him: his Garment of Ash-colour silk, his head rolled° in a cloud, over which stands an Owl, a Mole on one shoulder, a Bat on the other (all Symbols of blind Ignorance and Darkness), Mists hanging at his Eyes. Close before him rides Envy, his Champion, eating of a human heart, mounted on a Rhinoceros …

> [C2ʳ] TRUTH What's here? The Mist of Error? Dare his spite
> Stain this triumphant Mount, where our delight
> Hath been Divinely fixed so many Ages?
> Dare darkness now breathe forth her insolent Rages,
> And hang in poisonous Vapours o'er the Place°

° **clear**: free of mist and haze.
° **Pollution**: the word has both a moral and material sense.
° **Angel**: Truth's emissary, who protects London from Error's "subtle mists."
° **Zeal**: Truth's champion, who later burns Error's chariot. The word was associated with Puritanism, which both the poet and Mayor supported.
° **Paul's-Chain**: lane near St Paul's Cathedral. ° **attends**: awaits. ° **rolled**: enwrapped.
° **Place**: this confrontation took place at Little Conduit, which supplied many Londoners with water.

[C2ᵛ] From whence we received Love, and returned Grace?
I see if Truth awhile but turn her Eyes,
Thick are the Mists that o'er fair Cities rise.
We did expect to receive welcome here
From no deformed Shapes, but Divine and Clear:
Instead of Monsters that this place attends,
To meet with Goodness and her Glorious Friends;
Nor can they so forget me to be far;
I know there stands no other envious Bar,
But that foul Cloud to Darken this bright Day,
Which with this Fan of Stars I'll chase away.
Vanish Infectious Fog, that I may see
This City's Grace, that takes her Light from Me!   *Vanish, give way.*

At this her powerful command, the Cloud suddenly rises, and changes into a bright spreading Canopy, stuck thick with Stars and beams of Gold shooting forth round about it, the Mount appearing then most rich in Beauty and Glory; the four Monsters° falling flat at the Foot of the Hill; that grave, Feminine Shape, figuring London, sitting in greatest Honour … [C3ᵛ] The Mount thus made glorious by the Power of Truth, and the Mist expelled, London thus speaks:

> LONDON   Thick Scales of Darkness in a Moment's space
> Are fell from both mine Eyes; I see the Face
> Of all my Friends about me now most clearly …

[C4ʳ] At which Words the whole Triumph° moves in his richest glory toward the Cross in Cheap,° at which place Error, full of Wrath and Malice to see his Mist so chased away, falls into this Fury:

> ERROR   Heart of all the Fiends in Hell!
> Could her Beggarly Power expel
> Such a Thick and Poisonous Mist,
> Which I set Envy's Snakes to twist?
> Up, Monsters! Was her Feeble Frown
> Of Force to strike my Officers down?
> Barbarism, Impudence, Lies, Ignorance:
> All your Hell-bred Heads advance,
> And once again with Rotten Darkness shroud
> This Mount Triumphant, drop down Sulphurous Cloud.

[C4ᵛ] At which the Mist falls again, and hangs over all the Beauty of the Mount, not a Person of Glory seen, only the four Monsters gather courage

---

° **four Monsters**: identified as Barbarism, Ignorance, Impudence, Falsehood, "on whom hangs part of the mist for their clothing." Cf. the monster Error in Spenser (*FQ* 1.1.22).
° **Triumph**: procession, here specifically the mount.
° **Cross in Cheap**: Cheapside, a major London thoroughfare. The Eleanor Cross there was the gathering place for chimney-sweeps (see *Chimney-Sweeper's Sad Complaint*, 1663).

again and take their Seats, advancing their Clubs above their Heads;
which no sooner perceived, but Truth in her Chariot making near to the
place, willing still to rescue her Friends and Servants from the Powers of
Ignorance and Darkness, makes use of these Words:

> TRUTH Dare yet the works of Ugliness appear
> 'Gainst this Day's Brightness, and see Us so near?
> How bold is Sin and Hell, that yet it dare
> Rise against us? But know, Perdition's Heir,
> 'Tis idle to contend against our Power:
> Vanish again, Foul Mist, from Honour's Bower!

Then the Cloud dispersing itself again, and all the Mount appearing glorious, it passeth so on to the Standard,° about which place, by elaborate
action from Error, it falls again, and goes so darkened till it comes to St
Lawrence Lane's end, where, by the former words by Truth uttered, being
again chased away, London thus gratefully requites her goodness:

> LONDON Eternity's bright Sister, by whose Light
> Error's infectious Works°" still fly my Sight,
> Receive thy Servant's thanks. Now, Perfect Love,
> Whose right hand holds a Sphere, wherein do move
> Twelve blest Societies,° whose beloved increase,
> Styles it the Ring of Brotherhood, Faith, and Peace,
> From thy Harmonious Lips let them all taste,
> The Golden Counsel that makes Health long last.

⁂

° **Standard**: column and water-conduit in Cheapside.
° **Twelve ... Societies**: livery companies represented at the pageant.
° **Works:** deeds, but also factories.

WILLIAM STRODE
[The Chimney-Sweeper's Song] (c. 1640)

While most people think of the chimney-sweep as an icon of Victorian London and
the squalor of the Industrial Age, the trade first became common in the sixteenth
century (the earliest citation in the *OED* is from 1518). In the Middle Ages, very
few houses had chimneys. It was the increasing popularity of soot-producing coal
as a domestic fuel in the late Elizabethan period that made them a necessity (see
Harrison's *Description of England* 200). A character in Chapman's *May Day* (printed
1611) is "besmeared with a chimney-sweeper's resemblance," and Shakespeare seems
to acknowledge the trade's high mortality rate in the famous dirge from *Cymbeline*.
Strode's poem imitates the cries of sweeps advertising their services on the streets.
While the speaker takes a boisterous pride in his profession, the song simultaneously exposes how dangerous it is, achieving a mixture of naïvete and brashness that
rivals the complexity if not the pathos of the better-known chimney-sweep poems
of William Blake. Source: Corpus Christi College, Oxford, MS 325, 68ʳ–9ʳ.

The engraving contains the following text:

MULLD:SAKE.

I walke the Strand, and Westminster: and scorne | My smoking Pipe, Scarfe, Garter, Rose on shoe;
to march i'th' Cittie, though I beare the Horne. | showe my braue minde t' affect what Gallants doe.
My Feather, and my yellow Band accord | I singe, dance, drinke, and merrily passe the day,
to proue me Courtier: My Boote, Spurr, and; | and like a Chimney sweepe all care away.
                              sword

Are to be sold by Compton Holland, ouer against th'exchange

FIGURE 9   The Chimney-Sweep Mulled-Sack (c. 1620). Wellcome Library.

Hath Christmas furred° your Chimneys?
Or have the maids neglected?
Do Fireballs° drop from your Chimney's top?
Then Pigeon is respected.°
Look up with fear and horror,

° **furred**: coated with soot; it was customary to keep a large fire going during the twelve days of Christmas.
° **Fireballs**: due to the dreaded yet not uncommon occurrence of a chimney-fire, described in the ensuing lines.
° **respected**: regarded, noticed. Bird nests in or near chimneys can cause fires, although jackdaws are more commonly to blame than pigeons. Alternatively, Pigeon might be a nickname for the sweep, in which case respected could mean esteemed.

Oh how my mistress wonders!°
The street doth cry, the news doth fly,
The boys they think it thunders.
Then up I rush with my pole and brush,
I scour the chimney's Jacket;   10
I make it shine as bright as mine,
When I have rubbed and rak'd it.

Take heed, ten groats you'll forfeit;°
The Mayor will not have under.
In vain is dung,° so is your gun,°
When bricks do fly asunder.
Let not each faggot° fright ye,
When three pence will me call in.
The Bishop's foot° is not worse than soot,
If ever it should fall in.   20
Up will I rush, etc.

The scent, the smoke ne'er hurts me,
The dust is never minded;
Mine Eyes are glass, men swear as I pass,
Or else I had been blinded.
For in the midst of Chimneys
I laugh, I sing, I hallow;°
I chant my lays in Vulcan's praise,
As merry as the swallow.
Still up I rush, etc.   30

With Engines and devices,
I scale the proudest chimney;
The Prince's throne to mine alone
Gives place: the Stars I climb nigh.
I scorn all men beneath me,
While there I stand a-scouring;
All they below look like a Crow,
Or men on Paul's° a-tow'ring.
Then down I rush, etc.

And as I downward rumble,   40
What think you is my lot then?
A good neat's tongue° in th'inside hung,
The maid hath it forgotten.

° **O … wonders**: in MS, lines 5 and 6 are run together, as are lines 17 and 18.
° **ten … forfeit**: fine of 10 groats (totalling 40d.) imposed by the Lord Mayor, either for chimney
  fires or collapsing chimneys. Chimney-sweeps had petitioned the Lord Mayor in 1618 for stricter
  enforcement of such measures.
° **dung**: sometimes mingled with coal in the belief its smoke deposited less sooty residue.
° **gun**: fired up chimneys to scour them.
° **faggot**: bundle of wood.   ° **Bishop's foot**: slang for charred bits of burned food.
° **hallow**: shout.
° **Paul's**: St Paul's Cathedral.   ° **neat's tongue**: cow and ox tongues were smoked and eaten.

If e'er the wanton° mingled
My ink° with soot, I wist° not;
Howe'er the neat° and harmless cheat
Is worth a penny, is't not?
Still do I rush, etc.

Then clothed in soot and ashes,
50   I catch the maids that haste out;
Whos'e'er I meet with smut I greet,
And pounce° their lips and waistcoat.
But on the Sunday morning,
I look not like a Wigeon,°
So brave I stand with a point in my band°
Men ask if I be Pigeon.
Yet will I rush, etc.

Mull-sack° I dare encounter,
For all his horn and feather;
60   I'll lay him a crown I'll roar him down,
I think he'll ne'er come hither.
The Boys that climb like Crickets,
And steal my trade, I'll strip them.
By privilege I, grown Chimney high,
Soon out of town will whip them.
Then will I rush, etc.

⁊ ⁊ ⁊

° **wanton**: careless or naughty person.
° **ink**: carbon-based ink was made with soot, although it is not clear why a chimney-sweep would require ink. Possibly slang for drink?
° **wist**: know.   ° **neat**: skilful (with pun from line 42).
° **pounce**: imprint by sprinkling with powder or dust.   ° **Wigeon**: a wild duck; slang for simpleton.
° **point ... band**: silken fastening on the collar, here recalling the iridescent plumage on a pigeon's neck.
° **Mull-sack**: nickname (and favourite drink) of the highwayman John Cottington, who had been a chimney-sweep in his youth, beginning at the age of eight. See Figure 9, which depicts his "horn and feather."

ANONYMOUS

"Upon the Foggy Air, Sea-coal Smoke, Dirt, Filth, and Mire of London" (c. 1640–1660)

The following verses come from a single broadsheet held at the British Library. Anonymous and undated, it was probably composed around the time of the English Civil War.
Source: *Upon the Foggy Air, Sea-coal Smoke, Dirt, Filth, and Mire of London* (n.d.).

Each day you must here shift° or else you'll be
A shifter° counted by your livery.°
Your face, your clothes, with Sea-coal smoke and fire
Will straight put on a Chimney-sweeper's tire.°
Swan's feet are black, yet still in water be,
So are this City's Laundresses I see.
These are the scourers of this place, but they
Need scouring still themselves to make them gay.°
If that you would be comely then and fair,°
Leave quite this foggy for a Country air.

❦ ❦ ❦

° **shift**: change clothes.
° **shifter**: vagabond.
° **livery**: clothing, but more precisely the uniform worn by a servant or one of the livery companies.
° **tire**: attire.   ° **gay**: beautiful.
° **fair**: beautiful, but also "free from dirt or stains" (*OED* 11b).

WILLIAM DAVENANT
"London is smothered with sulph'rous fires" (1656)

In a poem about Queen Henrietta Maria's return to London, Davenant describes her venturing into "Mists of Sea-coal smoke, / Such as your ever-teeming Wives would choke" (1638, 74). In a subsequent entertainment performed during the Interregnum, he stages a debate between a Parisian and a Londoner about the respective cleanliness of their cities. The Parisian observes that the English appetite for beef necessitates "the plentiful exercise of your chimneys [that] makes up that canopy of smoke which covers your city; whilst those in the continent are well contented with a clear sky, [and] entertain flesh as a *regalio*" (54–5) or luxury. Davenant was ahead of his time in linking pollution not just with industry but with consumer choices.
Source: *The First Day's Entertainment at Rutland House* (1656), 84–5.

London is smothered with sulph'rous fires;
Still she wears a black Hood and Cloak
Of sea-coal smoke,
As if she mourned for Brewers and Dyers.°
CHORUS But she is cooled and cleansed by streams
Of flowing and of ebbing Thames.°
Though Paris may boast a clearer Sky,
Yet wanting flows and ebbs of Seine,
To keep her clean,
She ever seems choked when she is dry.

❦ ❦ ❦

° **Brewers and Dyers**: burning large quantities of coal, these two trades were notorious polluters.
° **Thames**: London falls within the Tideway, the hundred-mile stretch of the river subject to tides.

JOHN EVELYN
Fumifugium (1661)

The following stands as one of the first sustained polemics against air pollution, and not only diagnoses the crisis but also formulates a sophisticated urban planning scheme to combat it. Although the purging of London's air could be seen to symbolize the dispersal of the Puritan Protectorate at the Restoration, the political message is very much subservient to real environmental concerns. In fact, Evelyn even proposes a theory of climatic determinism, blaming the English Civil War on coal-smog enflaming the people's tempers. Evelyn's work was praised in the anonymous *Ballad of Gresham College* ("Let none at *Fumifugium* be scoffing / Who heard at Church our Sunday's coughing"), and literary scholars have noted that his grim sketches of beclouded and sulphur-reeking London bear a conspicuous resemblance to the hellscapes of Milton's *Paradise Lost* (McColley 2007, 80–5). Less attention, however, has been given to Evelyn's text itself as a remarkable literary and rhetorical performance in its own right, or to the fact that Evelyn's plan for a green lung (inspired by a gag from Jonson's *Volpone*) involved displacing the poor from the city's suburbs.
Source: *Fumifugium: Or the Inconveniency of the Air and Smoke of London Dissipated* (1661), 1–15, 23–6.

It is not without some considerable Analogy that sundry of the Philosophers have named the Air the Vehicle of the Soul (as well as that of the Earth and this frail Vessel of ours which contains it), since we all of us find the benefit which we derive from it, not only for the necessity of common Respiration and functions of the Organs, but likewise for the use of the Spirits and Primigene° Humours, which do most nearly approach that Divine particle. But we shall not need to insist or refine much on this sublime Subject. And perhaps it might scandalize scrupulous Persons to pursue to the height it may possibly reach (as Diogenes and Anaximenes° were wont to Deify it) after we are past the Ethereal,° which is a certain Air of Plato's denomination, as well as that of the less pure, more turbulent and dense, which for most part we live and breathe in, and which comes here to be examined as it relates to the design in hand: the City of London and the environs about it.

It would doubtless be esteemed for a strange and extravagant Paradox that one should affirm that the Air itself is many times a potent and great disposer to Rebellion, and that Insulary° people (and indeed most of the Septentrion Tracts,° where this Medium is gross and heavy) are extremely

---

° **Primigene**: primary.
° **Diogenes ... Anaximenes**: pre-Socratic philosophers who maintained air was the first and most divine of the four elements.
° **Ethereal**: ether, which Plato and other Greek philosophers regarded as a mystical fifth element, like the breath of God.
° **Insulary**: island-dwelling.
° **Septentrion Tracts**: northern climates (after the seven-starred circumpolar constellation of the Great Bear).

versatile and obnoxious° to change both in Religious and Secular affairs. Plant the foot of your Compasses on the very Pole and extend the other limb to 50 degrees of Latitude. Bring it about till it describe the Circle, and then read the Histories of those Nations inclusively and [2] make the Calculation. It must be confessed that the Air of those Climates is not so pure and defecate° as those which are nearer the Tropics, where the Continent is less ragged° and the Weather more constant and steady, as well as the Inclination and Temper of the Inhabitants ...

[3] Let it be further considered ... that the Body feeds upon Meats° commonly but at certain periods and stated times (be it twice a day or oftener) whereas upon the Air or what accompanies it ... it is always preying, sleeping or waking. And therefore doubtless the election of this constant and assiduous Food should something concern us, I affirm, more than even the very Meat we eat ... Besides, Air that is corrupt insinuates itself into the vital parts immediately, whereas the meats which we take, though never so ill conditioned, require time for the concoction, by which its effects are greatly mitigated (whereas the other, passing so speedily to the Lungs and virtually to the Heart itself, is derived and communicated over the whole mass). In a word, as the lucid and noble Air clarifies the Blood, subtilizes and excites it, cheering the Spirits and promoting digestion, so the dark and gross (on the contrary) perturbs the Body, prohibits necessary Transpiration for the resolution and dissipation of ill Vapours, even to disturbance of the very Rational faculties, which the purer Air does so far illuminate, as to have rendered some Men healthy and wise even to Miracle. And therefore the empoisoning of Air was ever esteemed no less fatal than the poisoning of Water or Meat itself, and forborne even amongst barbarians ...

[4] From these, or the like considerations ... Vitruvius° ... mentions it as a principle for the ... Architect ... [to] sedulously examine the Air and Situation of the places where he designs to build ... Now whether those who were the Ancient Founders of our goodly Metropolis had considered these particulars (though long before Vitruvius) I can no ways doubt ... For first, the City of London is built upon a sweet and most agreeable Eminency of Ground, at the North-side of a goodly and well-conditioned River ... The Fumes which exhale from the Waters and lower Grounds lying Southward, by which means they are perpetually attracted, [are] carried off or dissipated by the Sun, as soon as they are born and ascend ...

[5] I forbear to enlarge upon the rest of the conveniences which this August and Opulent City enjoys ... [to] render her the most considerable that the Earth has standing upon her ample bosom, because it belongs to the Orator and the Poet, and is none of my Institution.° But I will infer that if this goodly City ... merits all that can be said to reinforce her Praises, ...

° **obnoxious**: liable.   ° **defecate**: clarified.   ° **ragged**: uneven, mountainous.   ° **Meats**: food.
° **Vitruvius**: renowned Roman architect (fl. 30 BCE); a marginal note cites *De architectura*, Lib. I. cap. I.
° **Institution**: instruction.

she is to be relieved from that which renders her less healthy, really offends her, and which darkens and eclipses all her other Attributes. And what is all this but that Hellish and dismal Cloud of SEA-COAL? Which is not only perpetually imminent over her head— ... as the Poet [writes],

Conditur in tenebris altum caligne caelum°—

but so universally mixed with the otherwise wholesome and excellent Air that her Inhabitants breathe nothing but an impure and thick Mist accompanied with a fuliginous° and filthy vapour, which renders them obnoxious to a thousand inconveniences: corrupting the Lungs and disordering the entire habits of their Bodies, so that Catarrhs,° Phthisis,° Coughs, and Consumptions rage more in this one City than in the whole Earth besides ...

Of all the common and familiar materials which emit [smoke], the immoderate use of and indulgence to [6] Sea-coal alone in the City of London exposes it to one of the foulest inconveniences and reproaches that can possibly befall so noble and otherwise incomparable a City. And that not from the Culinary fires, which for being weak and less often fed below is with such ease dispelled and scattered above as it is hardly at all discernible, but from some few particular Tunnels and Issues° belonging only to Brewers, Dyers, Lime-burners, Salt and Soap boilers, and some other private Trades: one of whose Spiracles° alone does manifestly infect the Air more than all the Chimneys of London put together besides. And that this is not in the least hyperbole, let the best judges decide it, which I take to be our senses. Whilst these are belching it forth their sooty jaws, the City of London resembles the face rather of Mount Etna, the Court of Vulcan, Stromboli,° or the Suburbs of Hell, than an Assembly of Rational Creatures and the Imperial seat of our incomparable Monarch. For when in all other places the Air is most Serene and Pure, it is here eclipsed with such a Cloud of Sulphur as the Sun itself, which gives day to all the World besides, is hardly able to penetrate and impart it here. And the weary Traveller, at many Miles distance, sooner smells than sees the City to which he repairs. This is that pernicious Smoke which sullies all her Glory, super-inducing° a sooty Crust or fur upon all that it lights, spoiling the movables, tarnishing the Plate, Gildings, and Furniture, and corroding the very Iron bars and hardest stones with those piercing and acrimonious Spirits which accompany its Sulphur, and executing more in one year than exposed to the pure Air of the Country it could effect in some hundreds.

° ***Conditur ... caelum***: smoky fires hid the depths of heaven in darkness (Virgil, *Aeneid*, II.187).
° **fuliginous**: sooty.   ° **Catarrhs**: colds.   ° **Phthisis**: lung disease (tuberculosis).
° **Tunnels and Issues**: smokestacks and vents.   ° **Spiracles**: air shafts.
° **Etna ... Stromboli**: volcanoes in Sicily.
° **super-inducing**: depositing.

Piceaque gravatum
Foedat nube diem. °

It is this horrid Smoke which obscures our Churches and makes our Palaces look old, which fouls our Cloths and corrupts the Waters, so as the very Rain and refreshing Dews which fall in the several seasons precipitate this impure vapour, which, with its black and tenacious quality, spots and contaminates whatsoever is exposed to it.

Calidoque involvitur undique fumo. °

It is this which scatters and strews about those black and smutty Atoms upon all things where it comes, insinuating itself into our very secret Cabinets and most precious Repositories. Finally, [7] it is this which diffuses and spreads a Yellowness upon our choicest Pictures and Hangings, which does this mischief at home, is Avernus° to Fowl, and kills our Bees and Flowers abroad, suffering nothing in our Gardens to bud, display themselves, or ripen. So as our Anemones and many other choicest Flowers will by no Industry be made to blow° in London or the precincts of it, unless they be raised on a Hot-bed° and governed with extraordinary artifice to accelerate their springing, imparting a bitter and ungrateful taste to those few wretched Fruits which, never arriving to their desired maturity, seem like the Apples of Sodom,° to fall even to dust when they are but touched.

Not therefore to be forgotten is that which was by many observed: that in the year when Newcastle° was besieged and blocked up in our late wars, so as through the great Dearth and Scarcity of Coals, those fumous° works, many of them were either left off or spent but few Coals in comparison to what they now use, [and] diverse garden and orchards planted even in the very heart of London (as in particular my Lord Marquess of Hertford° in the Strand, my Lord Bridgewater,° and some others about Barbican) were observed to bear such plentiful and infinite quantities of Fruits, as they never produced the like either before or since, to their great astonishment. But it was by the Owners rightly imputed to the penury of Coals and the little Smoke ... for there is a

---

° *Piceaque ... diem*: "The dark clouds oppress the day" (Claudian, *The Rape of Proserpina*, 1.160). A description of ash spewed from Mount Etna.
° *Calidoque ... fumo*: "enveloped in scorching smoke" (Ovid, *Metamorphoses*, 2.232). A description of Phaeton choked by the burning earth.
° **Avernus**: volcanic crater in Italy regarded as an entrance to hell (derived from the Latin for "birdless").
° **blow**: bloom.
° **Hot-bed**: glass enclosure.
° **Apples of Sodom**: described by Josephus (4.8.4) and referenced in Milton's *Paradise Lost* (10.522).
° **Newcastle**: Parliament voted to cut off trade with Newcastle in 1643. See Hugh Adamson's *Sea-Coal, Small Coal, and Charcoal* (1644).
° **fumous**: smoking.   ° **Marquess of Hertford**: William Seymour.
° **Lord Bridgewater**: John Edgerton, the 1st Earl, for whom Milton composed his masque *Comus*, which complains of "rank vapours" of coal smoke in the Severn valley.

virtue in the Air to penetrate, alter, nourish—yea, and to multiply Plants and Fruits—without which no vegetable could possibly thrive …

I have strangely wondered, and not without some just indignation, when the South wind has been gently breathing, to have sometimes beheld that stately House and Garden belonging to my Lord of Northumberland,° even as far as Whitehall and Westminster, wrapped in a horrid Cloud of this Smoke, issuing from a Brewhouse or two contiguous to that noble Palace, so as coming [8] up the River that part of the City has appeared a Sea where no Land was within ken. The same frequently happens from a Lime-kiln on the Bankside near the Falcon,° which when the Wind blows Southern dilates itself all over that Point of the Thames and the opposite part of London, especially about St Paul's, poisoning the Air with so dark and thick a Fog as I have been hardly able to pass through it for the extraordinary stench and halitus° it sends forth. And the like is near Foxhall° at the farther end of Lambeth …

[10] Whether the Head and the Brain (as some have imagined) take in the ambient Air—nay, the very Arteries through the skin universally over the whole body— is greatly controverted.° But if so, of what consequence the goodness and purity of the Air is will to everyone appear. Sure we are how much the respiration is perturbed and concerned when the Lungs are prepossessed with these gross and dense vapours … Newcastle Coal, as an expert physician° affirms, causeth Consumptions, Phthisis, and the indisposition of the Lungs, not only by the suffocating abundance of Smoke but also by its Virulency. For all subterranean Fuel hath a kind of virulent or Arsenical vapour rising from it, which as it speedily destroys those who dig it in the Mines, so does it by little and little those who use it here above them. Therefore those Diseases (saith this Doctor) most afflict about London … And if indeed there is such a Venomous quality latent and sometimes breathing from this Fuel, we are less to trouble ourselves for finding out the cause of those Pestilential and Epidemical Sicknesses … which at diverse periods have so terribly infested and wasted us, or that it should be so susceptible to infection, all [12] manner of Disease having so universal a Vehicle as is that of the Smoke which perpetually invests this City. But this is also noted by the learned Sir Kenelm Digby,° in confirmation of the Doctrine of Atomical Effluvias and Emanations, wafted, mixed, and communicated by the Air, where he well observes that from the materials of our London Fires there results a great quantity of volatile Salts, which being very sharp and dissipated by the Smoke doth infect the Air, and so incorporate with it that, though the very Bodies of those corrosive particles escape our perception, yet we soon find their effects by

---

° **Lord of Northumberland**: Algernon Percy, the 10th Earl.
° **Falcon**: a tavern close to London Bridge.
° **halitus**: vapour.   ° **Foxhall**: Vauxhall.   ° **controverted**: debated.
° **expert physician**: probably William Harvey (see Calvert 80–1).
° **Kenelm Digby**: much of the ensuing passage is a direct quotation of Digby's *Late Discourse …
Touching the Cure of Wounds by the Powder of Sympathy* (1658, 38–40).

the destruction which they induce upon all things that they do but touch: spoiling and destroying their beautiful colours with their fuliginous qualities ...

But in the meantime, being thus incorporated with the very Air, which ministers to the necessary respiration of our Lungs, the Inhabitants of London and such as frequent it find it in all their Expectorations: the Spittle and other excrements which proceed from them being for the most part of a blackish and fuliginous Colour. Besides this acrimonious Soot produces another sad effect by rendering the people obnoxious° to Inflammations and comes in time to exulcerate° the Lungs, which is a mischief so incurable that it carries away multitudes by languishing and deep Consumptions ... [13] The consequences, then, of all this is that ... almost one half of them who perish in London die of Phthisical and pulmonic distempers,° [and] that the Inhabitants are never free from Coughs and importunate Rheumatisms, spitting of Impostumated and corrupt matter ...

[14] Let it be considered what a Fuliginous crust is yearly contracted and adheres to the Sides of our ordinary Chimneys where this gross Fuel is used, and then imagine if there were a solid Tentorium or Canopy over London: what a mass of Soot [15] would then stick to it which now (as was said) comes down every Night in the Streets, on our Houses, the Waters, and is taken into our Bodies ...

To talk of serving this vast City (though Paris, as great, be so supplied) with Wood were madness. And yet doubtless it were possible that much larger proportions of Wood might be brought to London and sold at easier rates ... by planting and preserving of Woods and Copses,° and by what might by sea be brought out of the Northern Countries, where it so greatly abounds and seems inexhaustible. But the Remedy which I propose has nothing in it of this difficulty, requiring only the Removal of such Trades as are manifest Nuisances to the City, which I would have placed at farther distances, especially such as in their Works and Furnaces use great quantities of Sea-coal, the sole and only cause of those prodigious Clouds of Smoke which so universally and fatally infest the Air, and would in no City of Europe be permitted where Men had either respect to Health or Ornament ...

[23] There goes a pleasant Tale of a certain Sir Politic, that in the last great Plague projected,° how by a Vessel freighted with peeled Onions which should pass along the Thames by the City when the Wind sat in a favourable quarter, to attract the pollution of the Air and sail away with the Infection to the Sea. Transplantation of diseases we sometimes read of amongst the

---

° **obnoxious**: liable.
° **exulcerate**: cover in ulcers or sores.
° **one half ... distempers**: citing Digby (1658, 40).
° **Copses**: small woodlands managed for timber. Evelyn would elaborate on this scheme in his forestry treatise *Sylva* (1664).
° **projected**: proposed. Strangely, Evelyn derived his plan to purify London's air from a joke in Ben Jonson's *Volpone* (4.1.100–25).

magnetical or rather magical cures ... But however this excellent conceit has often afforded good mirth on the Stage, and I now mention to prevent the application to what I hope [to] propound, there is yet [24] another expedient which I have here to offer ... by which the City and environs about it might be rendered one of the most pleasant and agreeable places in the world.

In order to [do] this, I propose that all low ground circumjacent to the City, especially East and Southwest, be cast and contrived into square plots or Fields of twenty, thirty, and forty Acres or more, separated from each other by Fences of double Palisades of 150 or more feet deep about each Field ... [and] that these Palisades be elegantly planted, diligently kept, and supplied with such Shrubs as yield the most fragrant and odoriferous Flowers, and are aptest to tinge the Air upon every gentle emission at a great distance: such as are (for instance amongst many others) the Sweetbrier, ... Woodbine,° the Common white and yellow Jasmine, both the Syringas or Pipe trees,° the Guelder-Rose, the Musk, and all other Roses ... [25] By which means, the Air and Winds, perpetually fanned from so many circling and encompassing Hedges, fragrant Shrubs, Trees, and Flowers ... may in Winter, on some occasions of weather and winds, be burnt, to visit the City with a more benign smoke. Not only all that did approach the Region ... but even the whole City would be sensible of the sweet and ravishing varieties of the perfumes, as well as most the delightful and pleasant objects and places of Recreation for the Inhabitants, yielding also a Prospect of noble and masculine Majesty, by reason of the frequent plantations of Trees and Nurseries, for Ornament, Profit, and Security ...

And the farther exorbitant increase in Tenements, poor and nasty Cottages near the City, [should] be prohibited, which discharge and take off from the sweetness and amenity of the Environs of London, and are already become a great Eyesore in the grounds opposite to his Majesty's palace of Whitehall, which, being converted to this use, might yield a diversion inferior to none that could be [26] imagined for Health, Profit, and Beauty, which are the three Transcendancies° that render a place without all exception.

° **Woodbine**: honeysuckle.   ° **Syringas ... trees**: lilacs.
° **Transcendancies**: supreme excellencies.

PART VI

Disaster and Resilience in the Little Ice Age

Extreme Weather, Disorder, Dearth

JOHN HEYWOOD

from The Play of the Weather (1533)

In this interlude performed before King Henry VIII, Jupiter descends to earth to determine what type of weather mortals most prefer. The answer proves to be remarkably varied, contingent on a person's profession, socio-economic status, gender, or age. A lengthy debate between a wind miller and a water miller documents the widespread practice in Tudor England of harnessing renewable energy from the elements. Yet the play also insinuates that while some trades might suffer from irregular weather patterns, others could capitalize on the resultant economic trends (a Tudor equivalent of climate-change profiteering, which Jupiter must regulate). The extract below offers a neat recapitulation of the plot. Although internal evidence suggests it was composed around 1533, the play is undeniably inspired by the meteorological trauma of the late 1520s (Ailles). The water miller complains that grain prices have been high "this seven year," which tallies with the sudden spike in late 1526 due to heavy rains and ensuing dearth. The following year, 1527, was one of the wettest ever recorded in England (rain fell almost continuously from April to June), and the next two years were not much drier. In response to soaring food costs, the king issued several proclamations around this time to prohibit grain hoarding, restrict food exports, and curtail enclosure, just as Jupiter here staves off a potential crisis. Heywood's play thus seeks to contain anxiety over climatic variability by transforming it into a metaphor for the vagaries of royal favour.
Source: *The Play of the Weather* (1533), D3ᵛ–F1ᵛ.

> MERRY REPORT Oyez!° If that any knave here,
> Be willing to appear,
> For weather foul or clear,   1060
> Come in before this flock,
> And be he whole or sickly,
> Come show his mind quickly,
> And if his tale be not likely,°
> Ye shall lick my tail in the nock!°
> All his time I perceive is spent in waste
> To wait for more suitors; I see none make haste.
> Wherefore I will show the god all this process,
> And be delivered of my simple office.
> Now lord, according to your commandment,   1070
> Attending suitors I have been diligent,
> And at beginning as your will was I should,
> I come now at end to show what each man would.
> The first suitor before yourself did appear,
> A gentleman desiring weather clear:
> Cloudy nor misty, nor no wind to blow,
> For hurt in his hunting. And then, as ye know,

° **Oyez**: Hear ye!   ° **likely**: plausible, appropriate.   ° **nock**: crack.

The merchant sued for all of that kind,
For weather clear and measurable wind,
1080   As they may best bear their sails to make speed.
And straight after this there came to me indeed
Another man, who named himself a ranger,°
And said all of his craft be far brought in danger,
For lack of living, which chiefly is windfall:°
But he plainly saith there bloweth no wind at all;
Wherefore he desireth, for increase of their fleeces,°
Extreme rage of wind, trees to tear in pieces.
Then came a water miller, and he cried out
For water, and said the wind was so stout
1090   The rain could not fall; wherefore he made request
For plenty of rain, to set the wind at rest.
And then, sir, there came a wind miller in,
Who said for the rain he could no wind win;
The water he wished to be banished all,
Beseeching your grace of wind continual.
Then came there another that would banish all this,
A goodly dame, an idle thing iwis;°
Wind, rain, nor frost, nor sunshine would she have,
But fair close° weather, her beauty to save.
1100   Then came there another that liveth by laundry,
Who must have weather hot and clear her clothes to dry.
Then came there a boy for frost and snow continual:
Snow to make snowballs and frost for his pitfall,°
For which, god wot, he sueth full greedily.
Your first man would have weather clear and not windy;
The second the same, save cools to blow meanly;°
The third desired storms and wind most extremely;
The fourth all in water and would have no wind;
The fifth no water, but all wind to grind;
1110   The sixth would have none of all these, nor no bright sun;
The seventh extremely the hot sun would have won;°
The eighth and the last for the frost and snow he prayed.
By'r Lady, we shall take shame I am afraid!
Who marketh in what manner this sort is led,
May think it impossible all to be sped° …

JUPITER As long as discretion so well doth you guide
Obediently to use your duty,
Doubt ye not we shall your safety provide.
Your griefs we have heard, wherefore we sent for ye
1160   To receive answer, each man in his degree.
And first to content most reason it is
The first man that sued, wherefore mark ye this:

° **ranger**: forester.
° **windfall**: timber blown down by storms, which the forester was legally entitled to sell.
° **fleeces**: spoils; also the crop (of timber).   ° **iwis**: truly.   ° **close**: indoor (i.e. cloudy).
° **pitfall**: bird-trap.   ° **meanly**: moderately.   ° **won**: remain.   ° **sped**: appeased.

Oft shall ye have the weather clear and still,
To hunt in for recompense of your pain.
Also you merchants shall have much your will;
For oft times when no wind on land doth remain,
Yet on the sea pleasant cools you shall obtain.
And since your hunting may rest in the night,
Oft shall the wind then rise, and before daylight

It shall rattle down the wood in such case   1170
That all ye rangers the better live may.
And ye water millers shall obtain this grace:
Many times the rain to fall in the valley,
When at the self° times on hills we shall purvey
Fair weather for your windmills, with such cools of wind,
As in one instant both kinds of mills may grind.

And for ye fair women that close weather would have,
We shall provide that ye may sufficiently
Have time to walk in and your beauty save.
And yet shall ye have that liveth by laundry   1180
The hot sun oft enough your clothes to dry.
Also ye, pretty child, shall have both frost and snow.
Now mark this conclusion, we charge you a-row.°

Much better have we now devised for ye all
Than ye all can perceive or could desire.
Each of you sued to have continual
Such weather as his craft only doth require.
All weathers in all places, if men all times might hire,
Who could live by other? What is this negligence,
Us to attempt in such inconvenience?   1190

Now, on the other side, if we had granted
The full of the some one suit and no mo,
And from all the rest the weather had forbid,
Yet who so had obtained had won his own woe.
There is no one craft can preserve man so,
But by other crafts, of necessity,
He must have much part of his commodity.

All to serve at once and one destroy another,
Or else to serve one and destroy all the rest,
Neither will we do t'one nor t'other,   1200
But serve as many or as few as we think best.
And where or what time to serve most or least
The direction of that doubtless shall stand,
Perpetually in the power of our hand.

° **self**: selfsame.
° **a-row**: successively.

Wherefore we will the whole world to attend°
Each sort of such weather as for them doth fall:
Now one, now other, as liketh us to send.
Who that hath it, ply° it, and sure we shall
So guide the weather in course to you all,
1210   That each with other ye shall whole remain
In pleasure and plentiful wealth, certain.

❧ ❧ ❧

° **attend**: await.
° **ply**: use, make the most of. Incidentally, Heywood is the first writer to record the proverb, "When the sun shineth, make hay" (1546, A4r).

ROGER ASCHAM
[The Wind on the Snow] (1545)

One would not expect to find prose resembling modern nature writing in a Tudor treatise on archery. To be sure, Ascham's agenda is nationalist (maintaining a stock of skilled archers for the English army) rather than ecological. Nevertheless, his account of the seeing the wind reflects a growing delight among sixteenth-century humanists in the meticulous observation of natural phenomena.
Source: *Toxophilus* (1545), 2.37^r–8^r.

To see the wind with a man's eyes it is impossible: the nature of it is so fine and subtle. Yet this experience of the wind had I once myself, and that was in the great snow that fell four years ago. I rode in the highway betwixt Topcliffe-upon-Swale° and Boroughbridge, the way being somewhat trodden afore by wayfaring men. The fields on both sides were plain and lay almost yard-deep with snow. The night afore had been a little frost, so that the snow was hard [37^v] and crusted above. That morning the sun shone bright and clear, the wind was whistling aloft, and sharp according to the time of the year. The snow in the highway lay loose and trodden with horse-feet, so as the wind blew it took the loose snow with it and made it so slide upon the snow in the field, which was hard and crusted by reason of the frost overnight, that thereby I might see very well the whole nature of the wind as it blew that day. And I had a great delight and pleasure to mark it, which maketh me now far better to remember it. Sometime the wind would be not past two yards broad, and so it would carry the snow as far as I could see; another time the snow would blow over half the field at once. Sometime the snow would tumble softly; by and by, it would fly wonderful

---

° **Topcliffe-upon-Swale**: Ascham was a Yorkshireman, born near Kirby Wiske, just north of Topcliffe.

fast. And this I perceived also: that the wind goeth by streams and not whole together. For I should see one stream within a score° of me; then the space of two score no snow would stir, but after so much quantity of ground another stream of snow at the same very time should be carried likewise, but not equally. For the one would stand still when the other flew apace, and so continue, sometime swiftlier, sometime slowlier, sometime broader, sometime narrower, as far as I could see. Nor it flew not straight, but sometime it crooked this way, sometime that way, and sometime it ran round about in a compass. And sometime the snow would be lifted clean from the ground up in to the air, and by and by it would be all clapped to the ground as though there [38ʳ] had been no wind at all; straightway it would rise and fly again.

And that which was the most marvellous of all: at one time two drifts of snow flew, the one out of the west into the east, the other out of the north into the east. And I saw two winds by reason of the snow, the one cross over the other, as it had been two highways. And again I should hear the wind blow in the air when nothing was stirred at the ground. And when all was still where I rode, not very far from [me] the snow should be lifted wonderfully. This experience made me more marvel at the nature of the wind than it made me cunning in the knowledge of the wind.

᠀ ᠀ ᠀

° **score**: twenty paces.

THOMAS HILL
"The End, Effect, and Signification of Comets" (1567)

Although we now think of comets as astronomical, early moderns regarded their appearance as ominous meteorological events. It was then believed that they passed beneath the moon and that their heat radiated downward to earth, adversely affecting the harvest, public health, and the mood of the populace. In the preface to the second edition of this work, first published in 1567, Hill (best known as the author of an Elizabethan gardening manual) claims he was moved to reissue it in 1574 because of "the troublesome elements these last two summers, the unseasonable weather, and last of all, the late strange and wonderful inundations," which he interprets as signs of God's anger. Hill's text reveals why the Great Comet of 1577 would provoke such consternation, moving Queen Elizabeth to summon the magus John Dee to predict the political fallout. The terrestrial and celestial were not entirely distinct in a culture that still took astrology seriously.
Source: *A Contemplation of Mysteries Containing the Rare Effects and Significations of Certain Comets* (1574), 3ᵛ–5ʳ.

1. The end of Comets is to prepare drought, the Pestilence, hunger, battles, the alteration of kingdoms, commonwealths, and the traditions of

men: also winds, earthquakes, dearth, land-floods, and great heat to follow. The said Comets portend both many other harms, and that mighty,
to men.

2. A Comet is the note° of a great drought, in that a mean° heat cannot
resolve° such matter out of the earth and drain the same up.

3. The second effect of a Comet is barrenness [4ʳ] of the earth, hunger,
and the dearth of victuals, in that the earth is caused [to be] barren through
much drought and lack of moisture. For drought is as the stepmother unto
all fruits and corn of the earth, but moisture is the apt mother unto all
fruits and crescent° things on the earth, so that such a mighty heat doth exceedingly dry up the earth and consumeth the moisture in plants and trees,
through which they decay and bear no yield nor store of fruit … A Comet
doth cause barrenness of the earth in that … a great and much exhalation
is required, by whose elevation from the earth the fatness° of the earth
is so drawn up, which, thus elevated, the earth after becometh barren of
yield, and the moisture with which the earth ought to be battened° is then
through the overmuch drought utterly deprived. For which cause a Comet
is the forenote of hunger and dearth in the same Realm which it specially
beholdeth or stretcheth the tail towards, and from whence it gathered and
took his substance.

4. Comets do portend the murrain° of [4ᵛ] beasts, in that the air ensuing
is infected and evil-disposed through the hot, gross, and cloudy exhalations, which when beasts draw thereof are then intoxicated and infected,
and so die. Also, for that the time then is exceeding hot and the radical
moisture is on such wise° drawn up by the hot air from the bodies of men
and beasts … the same beasts and other living creatures die …

5. Comets move battles and seditions, and alter Emperies and kingdoms. For that in the time of a Comet are many exhalations in the air, hot
and dry, which do dry men and kindle heat in them, by which they are
lightly provoked to ire …

6. Comets do portend the death of princes, [5ʳ] kings, governors, and
other magistrates of a commonwealth, in that these lead a more dainty
life and feed on finer meats continually, through which they sooner be infected. The death besides of princes and head governors … is of worthier
report and fame, and for that cause more observed. To these I add that
Choleric persons are then vehementer moved, through which the perturbations or troubles of mind ensue that procure seditions and battles, after
which proceed oftentimes the slaughter of many and death of princes.

❧ ❧ ❧

° **note**: token.   ° **mean**: ordinary.   ° **resolve**: liquefy.
° **crescent**: growing.   ° **fatness**: nutrients.   ° **battened**: fertilized.
° **murrain**: disease.   ° **wise**: manner.

ABRAHAM FLEMING
"A Terrible Tempest in Norfolk" (1577)

The following report describes an episode of mass hysteria induced by a thunderstorm and an astraphobic dog. In the religious climate of early modern England, storms were regarded as manifestations of divine wrath (Walsham 339–45) or omens of political upheaval. The latter view is repeatedly expressed in Shakespearean tragedy (Jones 2016) and was still prevalent in 1658 when Edmund Waller composed verses about a hurricane hitting southern England a few days before the death of Oliver Cromwell. Source: *A strange and terrible wonder wrought very late in the parish church of Bongay … in a great tempest of violent rain, lightning, and thunder … with the appearance of a horrible shaped thing* (1577), A4ᵛ–B3ᵛ.

Sunday, being the fourth of this August, in the year of our Lord 1577, to the amazing and singular astonishment of the present beholders and absent hearers, at a certain town called Bongay, not past ten miles distant from the City of Norwich, there fell from heaven an exceeding great and terrible tempest, sudden and violent, between nine of the clock in the morning and ten … This tempest took beginning with a rain, which fell with a wonderful force and with no less violence than abundance, which made the storm so much the more extreme and terrible.

This tempest was not simply of rain, but also of lightning and thunder; the flashing of the one whereof was so rare and vehement and the roaring noise of the other so forceable and violent that it made not only people perplexed in mind and at their wit's end, [B1ʳ] but ministered such strange and unaccustomed cause of fear to be conceived that dumb creatures, with the horror of that which fortuned, were exceedingly disquieted, and senseless things, void of all life and feeling, shook and trembled.

There were assembled at the same season to hear divine service and common prayer … in the parish church … the people thereabouts inhabiting, who were witnesses of the strangeness, the rareness, and suddenness of the storm, consisting of rain violently falling, fearful flashes of lightning, and terrible cracks of thunder, which came with such unwonted force and power that to the perceiving of the people … the Church did, as it were, quake and stagger, which struck into the hearts of those that were present such a sore and sudden fear that they were in a manner robbed of their right wits.

Immediately hereupon there appeared in a most horrible similitude and likeness to the congregation then and there [B1ᵛ] present a dog … of a black colour. At the sight whereof, together with the fearful flashes of fire which then were seen, moved such admiration° in the minds of the assembly that they thought doomsday was already come. This black dog,° or the devil in such a likeness (God he knoweth all, who worketh all), running all along down the body of the Church with great swiftness and incredible

---

° **admiration**: astonishment.
° **black dog**: many tales circulate in East Anglian folklore of a demonic dog known as Black Shuck.

haste ... passed between two persons as they were kneeling upon their knees, occupied in prayer, and, as it seemed, wrung the necks of them both at one instant clean backward, insomuch that even at a moment where they kneeled, they strangely died. This is a wonderful° example of God's wrath, no doubt to terrify us that we might fear him for his justice, or pulling back our footsteps from the paths of sin, to love him for his mercy ...

[B2ᵛ] At the time that these things in this order happened, the rector or curate of the Church, being partaker of the people's perplexity, seeing what was seen and done, comforted the people and exhorted them to prayer, whose counsel in such extreme distress they followed, and prayed to God as they were assembled together. Now for the verifying of this report (which to some will seem absurd, although the sensibleness of the thing itself confirmeth it to be a truth), as testimonies and witnesses of the force which rested in this strange-shaped thing, there are remaining in the stones of the Church, and likewise in the Church-door, which are marvellously renten° and torn, the marks, as it were, of his claws or talons. Besides that, all the wires, the wheels, and other things belonging to the Clock were wrung in sunder, and broken in pieces.

And ... while these storms endured, the whole church [B3ʳ] was so darkened—yea, with such a palpable darkness—that one person could not perceive another ... but only when the great flashing of fire and lightning appeared. These things are not lightly with silence to be overpassed, but precisely° and thoroughly to be considered ...

[B3ᵛ] Let us pray unto God, as it is the duty of Christians, to work all things to the best, to turn our flinty hearts into fleshy hearts, that we may feel the fire of God's mercy, and flee from the scourge of his justice.

❧ ❧ ❧

° **wonderful**: awe-inspiring. ° **renten**: ripped.
° **precisely**: scrupulously. This word carried Puritan overtones in Elizabethan English.

THOMAS NASHE
"Backwinter" (c. 1592–1600)

Modelled on the orderly state processions of which the Tudors were so fond, Nashe's interlude dramatizes the annual procession of the seasons. This pageant, however, proves to be anything but orderly. When situated in its meteorological and ecological context, this entertainment can be seen as an anxious commentary on the climatic turbulence that rocked late Elizabethan England. It was probably first performed in December 1592 at the palace of the Archbishop of Canterbury at Croydon, where much of the court had gone to escape an outbreak of plague. Interestingly, Croydon was also a hub of the charcoal industry, whose smoke-belching fires were regarded as a prophylactic against infection. Nashe likely revised the play prior to its publication in 1600 (as R. B. McKerrow and Bart van Es have both argued), as its elegies for summer would have been even more poignant in the wake of the cold summers of 1594–6. In the extract below, the cantankerous Backwinter – Nashe's coinage for a belated outbreak of wintry weather in springtime – curses the earth with apocalyptic fury to rival King Lear's. Although he is eventually banished, Nashe's lyrical meditations on the fragility of life and, more broadly, his sense of the tension between artistic structure and theatrical improvisation, teach the audience to expect disorder. The play thus recognizes a post-equilibrium ecology that it also yearns to contain.

Source: *Summer's Last Will and Testament* (1600), G4ʳ–Iʳᵛ.

AUTUMN I challenge Winter for my enemy,
A most insatiate miserable carl,°
That to fill up his garners to the brim
Cares not how he endamageth the earth,
What poverty he makes it to endure!   1530
He overbars the crystal streams with ice,
That none but he and his may drink of them.
All for a foul Backwinter he lays up.
Hard craggy ways and uncouth slippery paths
He frames, that passengers may slide and fall.
Who quaketh not that heareth but his name?
Oh, but two sons he hath worse than himself:
Christmas the one, a pinchbeck,° cutthroat churl,
That keeps no open house as he should do,   1540
Delighteth in no game or fellowship,
Loves no good deeds and hateth talk,
But sitteth in a corner turning Crabs,°
Or coughing o'er a warmèd pot of Ale;
Backwinter th'other, that's his own sweet boy,
Who like his father taketh in all points.°
An elf it is compact of envious pride;
A miscreant, born for a plague to men;
A monster that devoureth all he meets.
Were but his father dead, ° so he would reign …
WINTER Pleaseth your honour, all he says is false.
For my own part, I love good husbandry,
But hate dishonourable covetise.
Youth ne'er aspires to virtue's perfect growth
Till his wild oats be sown; and so the earth,
Until his weeds be rotted with my frosts,
Is not for any seed or tillage fit.
He must be purgèd that hath surfeited.
The fields have surfeited with Summer fruits;
They must be purged, made poor, oppressed with snow,   1580
Ere they recover their decayèd pride.

° **carl**: bad-tempered miser.   ° **pinchbeck**: miser.   ° **turning Crabs**: roasting crab-apples.
° **taketh … points**: takes after in all respects.   ° **Were … dead** : if only his father were dead.

For overbarring of the streams with Ice,
Who locks not poison from his children's taste?
When Winter reigns the water is so cold
That it is poison, present death to those
That wash or bathe their limbs in his cold streams.
The slipp'rier that ways are under us,
The better it makes us to heed our steps,
And look ere we presume too rashly on.
1590   If that my sons have misbehaved themselves,
In God's name let them answer't 'fore my Lord …
SUMMER   To weary out the time until they come,
Sing me some doleful ditty to the Lute,
1600   That may complain my near approaching death.

The Song

Adieu, farewell earth's bliss,
This world uncertain is.
Fond° are life's lustful joys,
Death proves them all but toys.°
None from his darts can fly:
I am sick, I must die.
Lord have mercy on us!°

Rich men, trust not in wealth,
Gold cannot buy you health.
1610   Physic himself must fade,
All things to end are made.
The plague full swift goes by:
I am sick, I must die.
Lord have mercy on us!

Beauty is but a flower,
Which wrinkles will devour.
Brightness falls from the air,
Queens have died young and fair.
Dust hath closed Helen's° eye:
1620   I am sick, I must die.
Lord have mercy on us!

Strength stoops unto the grave,
Worms feed on Hector° brave.
Swords may not fight with fate,
Earth still holds ope her gate.

° **Fond**: foolish.   ° **toys**: trivialities.
° **Lord … us**: echoing the *Kyrie eleison*, a common response to prayer in Christian liturgy.
° **Helen**: of Troy, a paragon of female beauty.
° **Hector**: the Trojan warrior, an exemplar of male valour.

"Come, come," the bells do cry:
I am sick, I must die.
Lord have mercy on us!

Wit with his wantonness
Tasteth death's bitterness.　　　　　　　1630
Hell's executioner
Hath no ears for to hear
What vain art can reply:
I am sick, I must die.
Lord have mercy on us!

Haste therefore each degree
To welcome destiny.
Heaven is our heritage,
Earth but a player's stage.
Mount we unto the sky:　　　　　　　1640
I am sick, I must die.
Lord have mercy on us! …

SUMMER Backwinter, stand forth.
VERTUMNUS° Stand forth, stand forth. Hold up your head; speak out.
BACKWINTER What, should I stand? Or whither should I go?
SUMMER Autumn accuses thee of sundry crimes,
Which here thou art to clear or to confess.
BACKWINTER With thee or Autumn have I nought to do.
I would you were both hangèd face to face.
SUMMER Is this the reverence that thou owest us?
BACKWINTER Why not? What art thou? Shalt thou always live?
AUTUMN It is the veriest Dog in Christendom.　　　　　　1790
WINTER That's for he barks at such a knave as thou.
BACKWINTER Would I could bark the sun out of the sky,
Turn Moon and stars to frozen Meteors,
And make the Ocean a dry land of Ice!
With tempest of my breath turn up high trees,
On mountains heap up second mounts of snow,
Which melted into water might fall down
As fell the deluge on the former world!
I hate the air, the fire, the Spring, the year,
And whatso'er brings mankind any good.　　　　　　1800
O that my looks were lightnings to blast fruits!
Would I with thunder presently might die,
So I might speak in thunder to slay men.
Earth, if I cannot injure thee enough,
I'll bite thee with my teeth; I'll scratch thee thus!
I'll beat down the partition with my heels,
Which as a mud-vault severs hell and thee!
Spirits, come up! 'Tis I that knock for you:
One that envies° the world far more than you.

° **Vertumnus**: Etruscan god of the seasons.　　° **envies**: scorns.

1810
Come up in millions! Millions are too few
To execute the malice I intend.
SUMMER   *O scelus inauditum, O vox damnatorum!*°
Not raging Hecuba,° whose hollow eyes
Gave suck to fifty sorrows at one time,
That midwife to so many murders was,
Used half the execration that thou dost.
BACKWINTER   More I will use, if more I may prevail.
Backwinter comes but seldom forth abroad,
But when he comes he pincheth to the proof.°
1820
Winter is mild; his sons are rough and stern.
Ovid could well write of my tyranny,
When he was banished to the frozen Zone.°
SUMMER   And banished be thou from my fertile bounds!
Winter, imprison him in thy dark Cell,
Or with the winds in bellowing caves of brass
Let stern Hippotades° lock him up safe,
Ne'er to peep forth, but when thou, faint and weak,
Want'st him to aid thee in thy regiment.
BACKWINTER   I will peep forth, thy kingdom to supplant.
1830
My father will I quickly freeze to death,
And then sole Monarch will I sit and think
How I may banish thee as thou dost me …
SUMMER   This is the last stroke my tongue's clock must strike,
My last will, which I will that you perform.
My crown I have disposed already of.
Item: I give my withered flowers and herbs
Unto dead corpses, for to deck them with;
My shady walks to great men's servitors,
Who in their master's shadows walk secure;
1860
My pleasant open air and fragrant smells,
To Croydon and the grounds abutting round;
My heat and warmth to toiling labourers;
My long days to bondmen and prisoners;
My short nights to young married souls;
My drought and thirst to drunkards' quenchless throats;
My fruits to Autumn, my adopted heir;
My murmuring springs, musicians of sweet sleep,
To malcontents,° with their well-tunèd cares,
Channelled in a sweet-falling quatorzain,°
1870
Do lull their ears asleep, list'ning themselves;
And finally, O words, now cleanse your course,
Unto Eliza, that most sacred Dame,
Whom none but Saints and Angels ought to name,
All my fair days remaining I bequeath

° ***O … damnatorum***: O unheard of villain, O damned voice!
° **Hecuba**: Trojan queen, who cursed when she beheld the bodies of her fifty murdered children.
° **proof**: utmost.   ° **Ovid … Zone**: the Roman poet was in fact banished to Romania.
° **Hippotades**: god of winds, Aeolus.   ° **malcontents**: murmuring malcontents] Q.
° **quatorzain**: fourteen-line verse.

To wait upon her till she be returned.
Autumn, I charge thee, when that I am dead,
Be pressed° and serviceable at her beck:
Present her with thy goodliest ripened fruits;
Unclothe no Arbours where she ever sat;
Touch not a tree thou think'st she may pass by.   1880
And Winter, with thy writhen frosty face,
Smooth up thy visage when thou look'st on her;
Thou never look'st on such bright majesty.
A charmèd circle draw about her court,
Wherein warm days may dance and no cold come.
On seas let winds make war, not vex her rest;
Quiet enclose her bed, thought fly her breast.
Ah, gracious Queen, though Summer pine away,
Yet let thy flourishing stand at a stay!
First droop this universe's agèd frame,   1890
Ere any malady thy strength should tame.
Heaven raise up pillars to uphold thy hand;
Peace may have still his temple in thy land.
Lo, I have said: this is the total sum.
Autumn and Winter, on your faithfulness
For the performance I do firmly build.
Farewell, my friends; Summer bids you farewell!
Archers and bowlers, all my followers,
Adieu, and dwell with desolation.
Silence must be your master's mansion.   1900
Slow marching thus descend I to the fiends.
Weep heavens, mourn earth: here Summer ends.
   Here the Satyrs and Wood-nymphs carry him out, singing as he came in.
Autumn hath all the Summer's fruitful treasure.
Gone is our sport; fled is poor Croydon's pleasure.
Short days, sharp days, long nights come on apace.
Ah, who shall hide us from the Winter's face?
Cold doth increase; the sickness will not cease,
And here we lie, God knows, with little ease.
From winter, plague, and pestilence, good Lord, deliver us!

London doth mourn; Lambeth is quite forlorn.   1910
Trades cry "Woe worth"° that ever they were born.
The want of Term° is town and City's harm.
Close chambers we do want to keep us warm.
Long banishèd must we live from our friends.
This low-built house will bring us to our ends.°
From winter, plague, and pestilence, good Lord, deliver us!

꙲ ꙲ ꙲

° **pressed**: enlisted, often involuntarily.   ° **worth**: befall (i.e. woe is me).
° **Term**: when law courts met; they were prorogued in times of plague.
° **low-built ... ends**: due to smoke and poor ventilation.

LUDWIG LAVATER AND WILLIAM BARLOW
"Dearth" (1596)

In early modern England it was proverbial that a bad harvest would happen every seven years. Agricultural historians have established that the rate during the Little Ice Age was closer to one in four, and many of these were severe (Hoskins 1964). England suffered calamitous harvest failures in 1501, **1521**, **1527–8**, 1535, 1545, 1551, **1555–6**, 1562, 1565, 1573, 1586–7, **1594–7**, 1608, 1622, **1629–31**, 1637, 1647–50, 1661, 1673, 1678, and **1698** (dates in bold were exceptionally dire). Originally published in Switzerland in 1571, the following dearth sermons were translated by William Barlow at the behest of the Archbishop of Canterbury in response to the Great Dearth of the mid-1590s. Rather than present a straightforward translation, however, Barlow intersperses his own commentary comparing and contrasting the Swiss predicament with England's in 1596, while formulating a specifically Protestant response to the crisis out of fear that it might rekindle nostalgia for Catholic fertility rites. Instead of greenhouse gases, early moderns viewed God, malign planets, fairies (see Titania's "forgeries of jealousy" speech in *A Midsummer Night's Dream*), or witches as the material cause of climatic anomalies. But how does Barlow also present the dearth as anthropogenic, seeking its root cause in human greed and ingratitude?
Source: *Three Christian Sermons* (1596), A3ʳ–A4ʳ, B3ᵛ, B6ʳ–B7ᵛ, C1ᵛ–C2ʳ, C3ᵛ–C4ʳ, C7ʳ–C8ʳ, D1ᵛ–2ʳ, D3ʳ, D5ᵛ–D6ʳ, D8ᵛ–E2ʳ, E4ᵛ–E5ʳ, E6ʳ⁻ᵛ, F5ᵛ–F6ʳ, F7ʳ, G7ᵛ–G8ʳ.

In Nazianzene's° time there was a Dearth much like to ours at this instant, not through the barrenness of the ground, but the destruction of the corn. The hope whereof in the beginning of the year, through the goodly seed-time and temperate Winter, made men's hearts to leap for joy and the Barns, as it were, to enlarge themselves for the receipt of this promised plenty. But on the sudden, that which the distilling dew of Heaven had comforted and brought forth, the showers immoderate and continual utterly rotted and corrupted ... Nazianzene's Son ... [A3ᵛ] in a solemn Sermon appointed of purpose, inquired into the causes which brought on, and showed the means how to turn away, this judgement. The like did Basil° in the like case of dearth, but unlike to that and ours in respect of the second causes: this in his time coming of a long drought, ours of never-ceasing rain ... the Sky over us louring and sunless. Though foreigners and travellers account [that] no strange thing in our land, being an Island compassed with the Sea (and therefore Tacitus saith we have always *Triste caelum,*° and others in their jollity have reported that they could never salute the Sun in England) ... yet who so observed our heavy heavens this [A4ʳ] present year, the like not remembered by any man living [or] by any record remaining, if he savour of any religion, he cannot ascribe it either to the Climate, or inclination of our Sky, or to the Vicinity of the sea, but

---

° **Nazianzene**: Gregory of Nazianzus. This is a reference to the Cappadocian famine (c. 370 CE).
° **Basil**: Bishop of Caesarea in Cappadocia (modern-day Turkey).
° *Triste caelum*: sorrowful skies.

cry out as they did [in] Exodus 8:19, "This is the finger, if not the heavy hand of God" …°

[B3ʳ] In the words of Dearth and Famine there is found but very small difference. Dearth is when all those things which belong to the life of man (for example, meat, drink, apparel, lodging, and other things) are rated at a high price. Famine is when all these before named are not to be got for money, though there be store of money. Indeed, this distinction rich men find, but the poor and needy feel no difference between Dearth and Famine. For they in the greatest [B3ᵛ] plenty of victuals wanting money are forced to starve and to pine with hunger. There are two sorts of Famine or Dearth: Universal, when in all countries or most there is scarcity of corn; Particular, when as any one village, city, or country, is punished that way. Now as all other calamities are sent from God, so this of Dearth and Famine. For God in his law expressly threateneth his people with this plague for disobedience to his word. [In] Leviticus 26:14 he speaketh in this sort: "If ye will not obey nor do my commandments but despise my laws … you shall sow your seed in vain." Verse 19: "I will make my heaven iron and your earth brass." Verse 26: "I will break the staff of your bread" …

[B6ʳ] For God, being the Lord of [B6ᵛ] nature, ruleth as himself pleaseth, without—yea, and against—the rules of nature … [B7ʳ] Plenty ariseth not by man's labour, sweat, or industry, but of God's blessing only: and therefore he alone to be thanked, both for Harvest and Vintage, and alone to be prayed unto to preserve the corn, both on the ground and in the barn …

[B7ᵛ] It hath been found by experience that both Summer and Harvest have answered our desires, both through the plentiful increase upon the ground and through the commodious housing into the barn, insomuch that there hath been great hope of abundance, [B8ʳ] as well of hay and corn as other fruits, and so the price to be reasonable and low; and yet on the sudden, beyond all expectation, the yield hath failed, and the price been enhanced, our sins provoking God to curse our plenty, as it fell out in the years 1525, 1530–31 in Helvetia,° and this year 1596 with us in England … [C1ᵛ] Many times the years prove unseasonable: in our time we may remember that on Midsummer Day we have been fain to use baths and stoves against the extremity of cold, and on New Year's Day again, we have dined abroad in our Terraces and open Galleries for the great heat. This is not man's, but God's doing …

It is said in [Switzerland] in a common Proverb, "Their children are never Sunburnt." Of the like nature is England, though not of the like situation. For it hath been observed (and is still kept for a rule) that a Drought in England never breedeth Dearth. "For when the sand helpeth the clay,

---

° **In Nazianzene's … hand of God**: The above paragraph is by Barlow, from his dedication to the Archbishop of Canterbury. Everything that follows is from his translation of Lavater, with Barlow's commentary interspersed.
° **Helvetia**: Switzerland.

then England cries wellaway."° There are over and besides these many other things which annoy both corn and trees: as mildews, blastings, field-mice, Locusts, Palmer,° and cankerworms,° Weasels, and such like Vermin. The frost also burneth the knots and buds of Trees, for which it is compared in the Psalm 147:16 to burning ashes. The Southwest and Northern winds, and also thick and duskish clouds, choke and kill the blossoms, and the unripe fruits of [C2ʳ] trees. And it falleth out oft that in the prime of the year the young leaves are eaten away, and the bough left as seared and bare as a dry broom. And if fruit decay there must needs be a penury of bread. For in our Country fruit is counted the best sustenance and the staff of bread. When our Infants cry for bread, we can easily please and satisfy them with an Apple or Pear. But when fruits fail us, then what remains? An Apple being sold as dear as the weight thereof in bread. Our ancestors were wont to say that if the wood, that is trees and vines, did underprop the corn it was a sign of a plentiful year. For bread and fruit is our principal nourishment ...

[C3ᵛ] But here we meet with a question often discussed and much debated, both by learned men and Idiots: whether Sorcerers or Witches,° Fairies or Spirits (call them by what name you will) can raise any tempests, or bring down such Hail as we oft see? To which we answer with a distinction: that as they have some, so they have no absolute nor self-sufficient power to hurt. For even [C4ʳ] Satan himself ... cannot hurt either man or beast, either how or when him list, much less these accursed slaves of his can have the air and winds at commandment. But God in his righteous judgement giving him leave, what may he not do? ...

[C7ʳ] Oft times again it happeneth that the cause of Dearth may come by continual Rain, the seed perishing by too much wet, as it happened this year 1596 in England, wherein God having opened his bottles, as himself speaketh (Job 38:37), hath made the clouds which should drop fatness (Psalm 65:12) to pour down the moisture of rottenness (Joel 1:17) ... It may hap also that the corn, being ripe and forward unto Harvest, even ready for the sickle, may be either burnt up or mowed down by the enemy ... or being in the barn, yet it may not perhaps answer the hope of increase, either under the flail, or in the dough, or in the oven; or else [C7ᵛ] from heaven or other mishap be set on fire; or, which is another and a greater mischief, in the securest peace, in the greatest plenty of all things, yet are there Usurers, Monopolists, Engrossers, Regrators,° Forestallers, Transporters, buying and hoarding up all kind of Grain, that when the husbandman's store is spent, they may sell it out at what price they list, and so wax rich by other men's misery.

° **wellaway**: an exclamation of sorrow. The rhyme implies that when England's clayey or fertile regions must purchase food from drier regions then there has been meagre harvest. In his *Description of England*, William Harrison records an extended version of this "old rude verse" that adds another couplet: "But when the clay doth serve the sand, / Then is it merry with England" (1577, 38v).

° **Palmer**: centipedes.   ° **cankerworms**: caterpillars.

° **Witches**: on the uptick in witchcraft accusations triggered by the Little Ice Age, see Behringer.

° **Regrators**: middle-men who buy food and other goods to resell at a profit. A marginal note here reads: "the vermin of the realm."

[C8ʳ] Wars also make a great scarcity, both for the present and afterward, all the Corn either being wasted with fire, or trampled down with Horses, or carried away by the Enemy. Yea, if there be but a rumour of War the greater Towns both keep in their own Corn and lay up what they may get elsewhere, till the certainty of peace be concluded ...

[D1ᵛ] True is that which Solomon speaketh [in] Proverbs 29:3, "He that feedeth harlots [D2ʳ] wasteth his substance." A fit text for this purpose and for these times, this sin being as our Land's Locust, a principal cause of our great want. Further, there may be a ready way to penury by ill housewifery, when wives, being made for the comfort and company of their husbands ... chide them out of doors, and so make them spend abroad lavishly which they might save at home ... [D3ʳ] The great increase of people, the abundance of all sorts of Artificers, the diverse cozenages and cony-catching deceits, may cause a scarcity ... which is God's curse.

[D5ᵛ] The Pagans and Gentiles believed that God defended both cattle and corn, and guided the seasons, and ruled the storms. Only herein they sinned: in attributing to other inferior and supposed Gods this great power of the true God, in worshipping Ceres for corn; Bacchus for wine; Flora for flowers; Robigo against blasting and vermin; and Apollo Nomius, or Pastoral, for their pastures and meadows. To all which and more than these they dedicated certain feasts, on which they made their prayers according to their several powers. They had also their sacrifices called *Ambarvalia*° ... because they went in procession about their arable grounds, called by the Latins *Arva*.° But we, though we use in good policy and in a godly acknowledgement from whom we receive these blessings the like Perambulations, [D6ʳ] have learned out of holy scripture and by that anniversary° Christian practice do confess that God alone both giveth and withdraweth fodder from cattle. How much more to and from man, for whom he hath made both beasts and other creatures? So that as long as men are persuaded that plenty and want cometh not from God, they cannot either by repentance turn to him, thus chastening them, nor will they with patience abide his punishment. And therefore it concerns us greatly to know from whence both do come ...

[D8ᵛ] It is not long since many, and they good men, have wandered from one place to another to relieve their hunger. And as many being brought to extreme poverty with their wives and children have been forced to beg from door to door in Cities, Towns, and Villages, but especially in Country Towns, where commonly is most want, who having once followed this idle trade can hardly be reclaimed to work, though there be [E1ʳ] many indeed that cannot for want of strength do any kind of labouring work, their flesh scarce cleaving to their bones ...

° ***Ambarvalia***: Roman agricultural holiday devoted to Ceres and celebrated on 29 May (after planting). It appears to derive from the Latin for "walking around the fields."
° ***Arva***: fields.   ° **anniversary**: annual.

[E1ʳ] Anno 1572 in Occitana° and along [E2ʳ] the Seacoasts, a grievous Famine arose, though the region in its own nature be very fruitful, insomuch that everywhere you shall see starved Carcasses lie in the streets. And in these cases it falleth out oft that Mice, Dogs, Horses, Asses, chaff, peels, hides, sawdust, are used for good sustenance, and at last man's flesh—yea (which is not to be spoken without trembling), the mothers have eaten for very hunger their own children ...

Second Sermon

[E4ᵛ] It followeth to inquire what should move so pitiful and merciful a God to afflict men, good and bad, old and young, Countries and Nations, with this terrible scourge ... [E5ʳ] The common multitude with one consent lay all the fault upon the oppression of Landlords enhancing their rents, the malice of Farmers grudging without cause, unmercifulness of Usurers grinding without pity, the intolerable licences of Monopolies and Sole-sales engrossing without measure, the covetousness of hoarders keeping up their grain without mercy. All which no doubt are principal outward means whereby God doth bring it to effect: but of corruption in manners, of vices and vileness of life, of the Immunity and Impunity of sinning without shame, without restraint, not one word ...

[E6ʳ] But here also we must take heed of judging amiss, entertaining false causes for the true. For in this and the like calamities, the whole fault for the most part is laid upon Religion: certain Miscreants and Varlets crying out of the Pulpit, in the open Market, at their public Feasts, that the new Religion (for so they entitle the preaching of the Gospel) is the only cause of this Dearth. Since there hath been a separation,° and that the Saints departed have not their due honour, and the old manner of worshipping God (for so they call their Romish superstition) is abandoned, the world hath been still in a Deluge of Calamity; from which, forsooth, [E6ᵛ] we should be freed if we had kept the profession of our forefathers. Thus they speak, to the end they may make the world to despise and despite us. But if they list, they may remember that it is not long since their Professors have tasted of this smart whip, as well as we ...

[F5ᵛ] The desire of private gain provoketh God his wrath, when men prefer the increase of their own commodities before the glory of God, the propagation of his word, or the public benefit ... [F6ʳ] Perjury and Oppression of the poor is this way also visited. [F7ʳ] This plague also followeth that inexpleble° and devouring gulf of greedy desire: ... "Woe unto them that join house to house and lay field to field, till there be no place that ye may be placed by yourselves in the midst of the earth"° ...

° **Occitana**: Pays d'Oc region in southern France.
° **separation**: the Protestant Reformation. The Anglican Church curtailed the Rogation processions and emptied them of their magical efficacy.
° **inexpleble**: insatiable.
° **Woe ... earth**: Isaiah 5:8. This verse was often cited to denounce enclosure.

[G7v] Like a skilful Physician that giveth his patient physic to prevent [G8ʳ] a disease to which he is inclining, so dealeth God with us ... For Plenty makes wantonness, and prosperity dissolute; which mischiefs Famine and calamities prevent, making us more instant in prayer. They that are full fed prove unthankful, who if they be but touched with want, then fly they unto him whom before they forgot.

ॐ ॐ ॐ

JOHN STRADLING
*"The Incredible Flooding of the Severn" and
"Another Poem on the Flood"* (1607)

The Bristol Channel flood of 1607 ranks as one of the worst natural disasters in British history, as an estimated 2,000 people lost their lives. One eye-witness report, entitled *Wonderful Overflowings of Waters* (see Figure 10), compares its twelve-foot surge to the biblical deluge, and echoes the widespread belief – also expressed in a 1570 ballad about floods in Bedfordshire and Lincolnshire, and in Thomas Churchyard's 1580 poem on the Dover Straits earthquake – that natural disasters should be regarded as divine punishment for human sins. Although he considers meteorological and astrological explanations (scientists have recently suggested that it may even have been a tsunami), the Oxford-educated Sheriff of Glamorganshire, John Stradling, reaches the same pious conclusion in some Latin verses he composed after narrowly escaping the flood with his life. In the first verse below, however, Stradling reverts to a pagan worldview to account for the unruly power of the ocean.
Source: *Epigrammatum* (1607), 160–2. Translated by Dana Sutton for *The Philological Museum* and reproduced with permission of the University of Birmingham.

"To Sir Edward Stradling, Knight, about the Incredible Flooding
of the Severn The Day After the Poet Began His Journey to
London, in which that Seawall Recently Built at Aberthaw was
Overcome and Wholly Torn Apart"

In vain he accuses Neptune who sails the water;
There is a certain error° amidst the uncertain tides.
Mortals pointlessly strive to restrict the outlaw waters with laws (which
    are not bound by law).
I had thought that limits had been imposed on the Ocean,°

° **error**: wandering.   ° **I ... Ocean**: a previous epigram boasted of the seawall, "What greater than to prescribe laws for Neptune, and impose new limits on his flood?"

FIGURE 10 The Bristol Channel Floods, from *Wonderful Overflowings of Waters*
(1607). © British Library Board.

With no shifting boundary, and laws understood by the goddess Vesta.°
But no fixed rule applies in fluid matters,
And quickly the driven wave swelled by with swollen blasts of wind.
With the peace broken which he had once ratified,
That oath-breaker Glaucus° went a-running to his old hostile tricks.
What had been saltwater before, he made to be saltwater everywhere;
He flowed over the fields and the wave challenged pious Ceres.
When I returned, finding what I had left firm to be rent asunder,
And that all my hope and sleepless effort, your expenses,
And the farmers' crops were ruined,
I ponder such words as these in my troubled breast:
Neptune, there is no faith in your government.
Boldly you protect the things that are yours,
And by force you snatch those that belong to others.

10

° **Vesta**: Roman goddess of hearth and home.
° **Glaucus**: Greek sea-god.

"Another Poem on the Flood, to William Stradling, Kinsman and Friend"

When lately I came to the city as a visitor,
Rescued from the new flood (scarce without loss of life),
From all sides my friends flocked together, eager to hear of the novelty,
And asked me what news I had to tell.
I said, "I have seen fish and men hanging from trees,
While the cow, sheep, and horse swam in the sea.
Where wagons used to roll, there the skiff flies along with sails unfurled,
And goes and returns by unaccustomed routes."
This is a novel subject for historians, and likewise for poets:
They can write true things which will scarce gain credence.

۩ ۩ ۩

WILLIAM BROWNE
"As Tavy creeps" (1613)

A native of Tavistock in Devon, Browne had an abiding love of the river that flows through his hometown. In this extract from his pastoral epic, he describes the destructive, implacable powers of its flood in comparison to the fragile works of human industry.
Source: *Britannia's Pastorals* (1613), 39–40.

As Tavy creeps upon
The Western vales of fertile Albion,
Here dashes roughly on an agèd Rock,
That his intended passage doth up-lock;
There intricately 'mongst the Woods doth wander,
Losing himself in many a wry Meander;
Here, amorously bent, clips° some fair Mead,
And then dispersed in rills doth measures tread
Upon her bosom 'mongst her flow'ry ranks;
There in another place bears down the banks   730
Of some day-labouring wretch; here meets a rill,
And with their forces joined cut out a Mill
Into an Island, then in jocund guise
Surveys his conquest, lauds his enterprise;
Here digs a cave at some high Mountain's foot;
There undermines an Oak, tears up his root;
Thence rushing to some Country farm at hand
Breaks o'er the Yeoman's mounds, sweeps from his land
His Harvest hope of Wheat, of Rye, or Peas,
And makes that channel which was Shepherds' leas;°   740

° **clips**: embraces. ° **leas**: fallow pasture.

Here, as our wicked age doth sacrilege,
Helps down an Abbey, then a natural bridge;
By creeping underground he frameth out,
As who should say he either went about
To right the wrong he did or hide his face,
For having done a deed so vile and base,
So ran this River on.

☙ ☙ ☙

THOMAS DEKKER?

from The Great Frost (1608)

Paleo-climatologists refer to the period between 1300 and 1850 as "the Little Ice Age," as average temperatures in Europe were several degrees lower than the modern era (Fagan). The brutal winter of 1607/8 was exceptionally frigid, and the seeming frequency of such weather anomalies sparked fears of cosmic decay or global cooling. Structured as a conversation between a Londoner and a Yorkshireman, this Jacobean pamphlet relays the different experiences of the cold spell in the city versus countryside, while also informing readers that bitterly cold weather prevailed throughout the realm. In having the two speakers commiserate with each other, the author (thought to be the playwright Thomas Dekker) gestures at the interdependence of city and country, of the human economy and the more-than-human ecology. In recalling that the Thames had frozen around the fifth year of Elizabeth's reign (c. 1563), and noting that the same has happened in the fifth year of James's reign, the text is indicative of an early modern tendency to perceive meteorological patterns as tied to political events rather than sunspot cycles or carbon emissions. Between 1500 and 1700 the Thames froze over no fewer than fifteen times (see Figure 11). The fact that it has not frozen since 1895 is due not simply to architectural modifications to London Bridge, which previously hindered the water flow, but also to climate change. Early modern texts supply crucial historical testimony (more compelling than a graph of average temperatures) that enables us to perceive the realities of our warming planet.
Source: *The Great Frost; or Cold Doings in London* (1608), A3ᵛ–B4ᵛ.

COUNTRYMAN But I beseech you tell me: is that goodly River of yours, I call it yours because you are a Citizen (and that River is the Nurse that gives milk and honey to your city), but is that Lady of fresh waters all covered over with ice?
CITIZEN All over, I assure you Father.° The Frost hath made a floor upon it, which shows like grey Marble, roughly hewn out. It is a very pavement of glass, but that it is more strong. The Thames now lies in,° or rather is turned (as some think) bankrupt, and dares not show her head. For all the water of it floats up and down now like a springtide in a cellar.

° **Father**: term of respect for a male elder. ° **lies in**: takes bed rest (before childbirth).

COUNTRYMAN   God help the poor Fishes. It is a hard world with them, when their houses are taken over their heads; they use not° to lie under such thick roofs … [A4ᵛ] You, Sir, are a man that, by your head and beard (as well as myself), should be one of Time's sons, and should therefore love his daughter Truth. Make me so much beholding to you as to receive from you the right Picture of all this your Waterworks:° how they began, and how they have grown, and in what fashion continued.

CITIZEN   Most gladly will I satisfy your request. You shall understand therefore that the Thames began to put on his Frieze-coat° (which yet he wears) about the week before Christmas, and hath kept it on till now this latter end of January; how long time soever besides to come, none but God knows.

COUNTRYMAN   Did it never thaw in thus many weeks?

CITIZEN   Only three days, or four at the most, and that but weakly to dissolve so great a hardness. The Cakes of Ice (great quantity and in great numbers) were made and baked cold in the mouth of winter, at the least a fortnight or three weeks before they were crusted and cemented together. But after they once joined their strengths in one, their backs held out and could not be broken.

COUNTRYMAN   We may make this good use even out of this watery and transformed element: that London upholdeth a state, and … that violent factions and combinations (albeit of the basest persons) in a commonwealth are not easily dissolved, if once they be suffered to grow up to a head.° On sir, I pray.

CITIZEN   This cold breakfast being given to the City, and the Thames growing more and more hard-hearted, wild youths and boys were the first Merchant-venturers that set out to discover these cold Islands of Ice upon the River. And the first path that was beaten forth to pass to the Bankside (without going over bridge or by boat) was about Cold Harbour, and in those places near the bridge …[B1ʳ] As the ice increased in hardness, so men's hearts increased in hardiness, so that at the length (the frost knitting all his sinews together, and the inconstant water by that means, being of a floating element, [B1ᵛ] changed into a firm ground, as it were), people walked on the Thames. Both men, women, and children walked over, and up and down in such companies that I verily believe, and I dare almost swear it, the one half (if not three parts) of the people in the City have been seen going on the Thames. The River showed not now (neither shows it yet) like a River, but like a field where Archers shoot at pricks,° whilst others play at football. It is a place of mastery,° where some wrestle, and some run, and he that does best is aptest to take a fall. It is an Alley to walk upon without dread, albeit under it be most assured danger. The

---

° **use not**: are unaccustomed to.
° **Waterworks**: literally, a mechanism for storing and distributing water, like the water-tower built by Bevis Bulmer beside the Thames in 1593.
° **Frieze-coat**: coarse woollen cloth (with obvious pun).   ° **head**: rebellion.
° **pricks**: targets. ° **mastery**: competition.

Gentlewoman that trembles to pass over a Bridge in the field doth here walk boldly. The Citizen's wife that looks pale when she sits in a boat for fear of drowning thinks that here she treads as safe now as in her Parlour. Of all ages, of all sexes, of all professions, this is the common path. It is the roadway between London and Westminster, and between Southwark and London …

[B2ʳ] COUNTRYMAN Your city cannot choose but be much damnified° by this strange congealing of the river.

CITIZEN Exceeding much Father. Strangers may [B2ᵛ] guess at our harms, yet none can give the full number of them but we that are the inhabitants. For the City by this means is cut off from all commerce. Shopkeepers may sit and ask, "what do you lack?"° when the passengers may very well reply, "what do you lack yourselves?" They may sit and stare on men, but not sit and sell. It was before called the "dead Term,"° and now may we call this the dead Vacation, the frozen Vacation, the cold Vacation. If it be a Gentleman's life to live idly and do nothing, how many poor Artificers and Tradesmen have been made Gentlemen then by this Frost? For a number of Occupations (like the flakes of ice that lie in the Thames) are by this malice of Winter trod clean underfoot, and will not yet be able to stir …

COUNTRYMAN This beating may make them wise: the want that this hard season drives them into may teach them to play the Ants,° and in Summer to make a provision against the wrath of Winter. There is no mischief borne alone I know: calamities commonly are by birth twins. Methinks, therefore, that this drying up of the waters should be a devourer up of wood. This cold Ague of the earth must needs have warmth to help it. That warmth must come from fire, and that fire cannot be had without cost. How then, I pray you, in this so general an affliction, did poor people shift° for fuel to comfort them?

CITIZEN Their care for fire was as great as for food. Nay, to want it was a worse torment than to be without meat. The belly was now pinched to have the body warmed. And had not the Provident Fathers of [B3ʳ] this city … dispersed a relief to the poor in several parts and places about the outer bounds of the city (where poverty most inhabiteth) by storing them beforehand with sea-coal and other firing at a reasonable rate, I verily persuade myself that the unconscionable and unmerciful raising of the prices of fuel by Chandlers, Woodmongers, etc. (who now meant to lay the poor on the Rack) would have been the death of many a wretched creature through the want of succour.

COUNTRYMAN Not unlikely, Sir.

° **damnified**: harmed, with wordplay on dammed.
° **what … lack?**: common cry of London street-vendors.
° **dead Term**: when law courts were closed; also know as the vacation.
° **Ants**: an allusion to Aesop's fable of the frugal Ant and the prodigal Grasshopper.
° **shift**: manage, provide themselves.

CITIZEN For neither could coal be brought up the River nor could wood be sent down. The Western Barges might now wrap up their smoky Sails; for albeit they had never so lofty a gale, their voyage was spoiled. The winds was with them, but the tide was clean against them. And not only hath this frost nipped away those comforts that should revive the outward parts of the body, but those also that should give strength and life to the inward. For you of the Country being not able to travel to the City with victuals, the price of victual must of necessity be enhanced, and victual itself brought into a scarcity ...

[Now] as I have discovered unto you what cold doings we have had (during this Frost) in the City, so I pray let me understand from you what kind of world you have lived in in the Country ...

COUNTRYMAN The world with us of the Country runs upon the old rotten wheels. For all the Northern cloth that is woven in our country will scarce make a gown to keep Charity warm; she goes so acold. Rich men had never more money, and Covetousness had never less pity ... Believe me, sir ... it goes as [B4ʳ] hard with us as it doth with you. The same cold hand of Winter is thrust into our bosoms; the same sharp air strikes wounds into our bodies; the same Sun shines upon us, but the same sun doth not heat us no more than it doth you. The poor Ploughman's children sit crying and blowing their nails as lamentably as the children and servants of your poor Artificers.° Hunger pinches their cheeks as deep into the flesh as it doth into yours here. You cry out here you are undone for coal, and we complain we shall die for want of Wood. All your care is to provide for your Wives, children, and servants in this time of sadness. But we go beyond you in cares: not only our wives, our children, and household servants are unto us a cause of sorrow, but we grieve as much to behold the misery of our poor Cattle (in this frozen-hearted season) as it doth to look upon our own affliction. Our beasts are our faithful servants and do their labour truly when we set them to it. They are our Nurses that give us milk; they are our guides in our journeys; they are our partners and help to enrich our state—yea, they are the very upholders of a poor Farmer's lands and livings. Alas, then, what Master that loves his servant as he ought, but would almost break his own heartstrings with sighing to see these pine and mourn as they do? The ground is bare and not worth a poor handful of grass. The earth seems barren and bears nothing, or if she doth, most unnaturally she kills it presently or suffers it through cold to perish. By which means the lusty horse abates his flesh and hangs the head, feeling his strength go from him. The ox stands bellowing, the ragged sheep bleating, the poor Lamb shivering and starving to death.

[B4ᵛ] The poor Cottager that hath but a Cow to live upon must feed upon hungry meals (God knows) when the beast herself hath but a bare

---

° **Artificers:** craftsmen.

Commons. He that is not able to bid all his Cattle home and to feast them with Fodder out of his Barns will scarce have cattle at the end of Summer to fetch home his harvest: which charge of feeding so many beastly mouths is able to eat up a countryman's estate, if his providence before time hath not been the greater to meet and prevent such storms. Of necessity our Sheep, Oxen etc. must be in danger of famishing (having nothing but what our old grandam the earth will allow them to live upon); of necessity must they pine, since all the fruits that had wont to spring out of her fertile womb are now nipped in their birth, and likely never to prosper.

ॐ ॐ ॐ

JOHN TAYLOR
"The Frozen Age" (1621)

As a waterman who ferried passengers across the Thames for a living, John Taylor was particularly aggrieved by the freezing of the river. Although his poem blames the frost on London's immorality (which the meteorological carnivalesque of the Frost Fair scarcely halts), it can also be read as an appeal for charity, decrying the tendency of environmental catastrophes to disproportionately affect the poor. The full title of the poem, meanwhile, reflects contemporary uncertainty as to whether this cold spell augured a long-term change in the English climate.
Source: *The Cold Term; or the Frozen Age: Or the Metamorphosis of the River of Thames* (1621).

> It was the time when men wore liquored boots,
> When rugged Winter murdered herbs and roots,
> When as the Heavens the Earth did all attire
> With plashes, puddles, pools, black dirt, and mire.
> Then at that time (to poor men's care and costs)
> A Christmas came to Town, betwixt two Frosts.
> Then in the numb Cold month of January,
> When as the Sun was lodged in moist Aquary,°
> When Boreas, all with Icicles bedight,°
> Worse than a Barber 'gan to shave and bite,
> Turning Thames' streams to hard congealèd flakes,
> And pearlèd water drops to Crystal cakes,
> Th'adulterate Earth, long having played the whore,
> In bearing and in breeding bastards' store:
> As Drunkards, swearers, lechers, Cheating knaves,
> Punks,° Panders, base extortionizing slaves,
> Rent-raising rascals, Villains, Thieves, Oppressors,
> Vainglorious proud fools, Gen'ral transgressors;

10

° **Aquary**: Aquarius, the water-bearer.   ° **bedight**: adorned.   ° **Punks**: prostitutes.

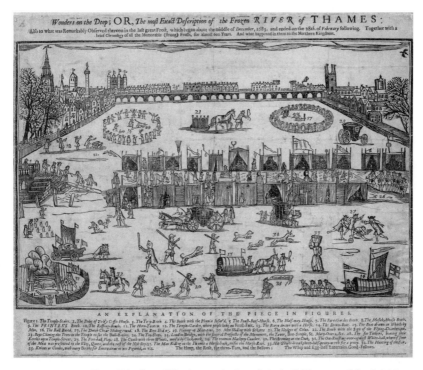

For which foul whoredom Heaven did think it meet
To make the Earth do penance in a sheet;°   20
That punishment no sooner past and gone,
But straight a Cold frieze° coat she did put on,
Which (though herself were senseless, what she ails)
It made her poorest bastards blow their nails;
Whilst many of her Rich brood did agree
To make their stony hearts as hard as she.
The liquid Thames, eachwhere° from shore to shore,
With cold-baked Paste, all pasty-crusted o'er …
Upon whose Glassy face, both to and fro,
Five hundred people all at once did go.
At Westminster there went three Horses over,
Which safely did from shore to shore recover.
There might be seen spiced Cakes and roasted Pigs;
Beer, Ale, Tobacco, Apples, Nuts, and Figs;
Fires made of Charcoals, Faggots, and Sea-coals;   70
Playing and cozening at the Pigeon-holes;°

° **whoredom … sheet**: an early modern punishment for fornication.
° **frieze**: coarse woollen fabric, spelled "freeze."   ° **eachwhere**: everywhere.
° **Pigeon-holes**: a kind of lawn bowling.

Some for two Pots at Tables,° Cards, or Dice;
Some slipping in betwixt two Cakes of Ice;
Some going on their business and affairs,
From the Bankside to Paul's, or to Trig Stairs° …
And in this gnashing age of Snow and Ice,
The Woodmongers did mount so high their price,
That many did to lie abed desire,
To save the charge of Wood, and Coal, and Fire.
Amongst the Whores there were hot comings in:
Whoever lost, they still were sure to win.
130   They in one hour so strangely did heat° men,
That all° the Frost they scarce were cool again.
The Us'rer's Bonds and Landlord's Rent came on;
Most Trades had something to depend upon.
Only the Water-men just nothing got,
And yet (by God's good help) they wanted not,
But all had coin or credit, food and fire,
And what the need of nature did require.
So farewell Frost; if Charity be living,
Poor men shall find it by the rich men's giving.

۶ٮ ۶ٮ ۶ٮ

° **Tables**: backgammon.
° **Paul's … Trig Stairs**: St Paul's Cathedral and a landing further west on the north bank of the
   Thames.
° **heat**: infect with venereal diseases that cause urinary burning.   ° **all**: despite.

WILLIAM CARTWRIGHT
"On the Great Frost, 1634" (1634)

The winter of 1634/5 was particularly harsh. The Thames was frozen over almost
continuously from 10 December to 3 February, and a series of blizzards produced
mountainous snowdrifts. Unsurprisingly, references to snow become commonplace in the poetry of this time (see Carew's "To Saxham" in Part III, p. 225). The
following specimen, composed by an admirer of Jonson and Donne, features a
number of elaborate conceits illustrating how the frigid weather creates a topsy-turvy world that melds binaries such as temperate/arctic, liquid/solid, animate/
inanimate, figurative/literal.
Source: *Comedies, Tragedies, with Other Poems* (1651), 204-6, with emendations
from Add. MS 71164, 71ʳ–2ʳ and Malone 21, 71ʳ–2ʳ.

Show me the° flames you° brag of, you that be
Armed with those two fires, Wine and Poetry.
Y'are now benumbed, spite of your Gods° and Verse,
And may° your Metaphors for Prayers rehearse;

° **the**: your] Malone.
° **you**: these lines appear to be a response to another poem by one of the tribe of Ben, possibly Robert
   Herrick's "To Live Merrily, and Trust Good Verses," which circulated in manuscript in the 1630s.
° **Gods**: God] Malone.   ° **may**: do] MS 71164 and Malone.

Whilst you,° that called° Snow "Fleece" and "Feathers," do
Wish for true Fleeces and true Feathers too.
    Waters have bound themselves, and cannot run,
Suff'ring what Xerxes' fetters° would have done.
Our Rivers are one Crystal, Shores are fit
Mirrors, being now not like to Glass, but it.   10
Our Ships stand all as planted; we may swear
They are not borne up only, but grow there;
Whilst Waters thus are Pavements, firm as Stone,
And without faith are each day walked upon.
What Parables° called folly heretofore,
Were wisdom now:° to build upon the Shore.
There's° no one dines amongst us with washed hands;
Water's as scarce here as in Afric sands,
And we expect it not but from some god
Opening a Fountain,° or some Prophet's Rod,   20
Who need not seek out where he may unlock
A stream: whate'er he struck would be true Rock.
When Heaven drops some smaller Showers, our sense
Of Grief's increased, being but deluded thence;
For while we think those drops to entertain,
They fall down Pearl, which came down half way Rain.
Green-Land's Removal° now the poor man fears,
Seeing all Waters frozen but his Tears.
We suffer Day continual, and the Snow
Doth make our Little Night become Noon now.   30
We hear of some Encrystalled, such as have
That, which procured their death, become their Grave:
Bodies that destitute of Soul yet stood,
Dead and not fallen,° drowned and without a Flood.
Nay, we who breathe still are almost as they,
And only may be styled a softer Clay.
We stand like Statues, as if Cast and fit
For life, not having, but expecting it.
Each man's° become the Stoic's wise one° hence;
For can you look for° Passion where's no Sense?   40
Which we have not, resolved to our first Stone,°
Unless it be one Sense to feel we've none.

° **you**: possibly allusions to William Strode's "Chloris in the Snow" (which describes snow as "feathered rain") and William Browne's "On one drowned in snow" (which begins with the line "Within a fleece of silent waters drowned"); both works circulated widely in seventeenth-century manuscripts.

° **called**: call] MS 71164.

° **Xerxes' fetters**: the enraged Persian king reportedly tried to fetter the Hellespont.

° **Parables**: Matthew 7:24–7.   ° **wisdom now**: now descried] MS 71164.

° **There's**: Here's] Malone.   ° **a Fountain**: some fountains] Malone.

° **Green-Land's Removal**: the browning of pastures rather than the spread of Greenland's now shrinking ice-sheet. Greenlands] MS 71164; removing] Malone.

° **fallen**: fell] Malone.

° **man's**: one's] MS 71164.

° **Stoic's wise one**: the ideal disciple of Stoicism, which taught the control of passion.

° **can ... for**: how can there be] Malone.

° **resolved ... Stone**: hardened back to the stones from which humans were created in the Deucalion myth.

Our very Smiths now work not—nay, what's more,
Our Dutchmen write° but five hours and give o'er.
We dare provoke Fate now; we know what is
That last cold Death, only by suff'ring this.
All fires are Vestal° now, and we as they,
Do in our Chimneys keep a Lasting day,
Boasting within doors this domestic Sun,
50   Adored too with our Religion.
We laugh at fire-Briefs° now, although they be
Commended to us by his Majesty;
And 'tis no Treason, for we cannot guess
Why we should pay them° for their happiness.
Each hand would be a Scaevola's;° let Rome
Call that a pleasure henceforth, not a doom.
A Fever is become a wish; we sit
And think fall'n Angels have one° Benefit:
Nor can the° thought be impious, when we see
60   Weather that Booker° durst not Prophesy,
Such as may give new Epochas and make
Another SINCE in his bold Almanac;
Weather may save his doom, and by his foe
Be thought enough for him to undergo.
We now think Alabaster° true, and look
A sudden Trump° should antedate his Book.
For whilst we suffer this, ought we not fear
The World shall not survive to a fourth year?
And sure we may conclude weak Nature old
70   And Crazed° now, being she's grown so° Cold.
     But Frost's not all our Grief: we that so sore
Suffer its stay, fear its departure more;
For when that Leaves us, which so long hath stood,
'Twill make a New Account from th'second Flood.

༆ ༆ ༆

° **write**: work (wright?) or perhaps slang for drink? The Dutch were known for their industriousness and binge drinking.
° **Vestal**: sacred fire kept burning by Roman vestal virgins.
° **fire-Briefs**: requests for financial support for victims of fires.   ° **them**: men] MS 71164.
° **Scaevola**: Roman soldier who held his hand in a flame to show his toughness.   ° **one**: a] Malone.
° **the**: your] Malone.
° **Booker**: John Booker, an almanac writer, who had correctly predicted "frosty hard weather, with snow undoubtedly" for December 1634.
° **Alabaster**: William Alabaster, playwright and author of apocalyptic tracts such as *Ecce sponsus venit tuba pulchritudim* (1633).
° **sudden Trump**: unexpected trumpet.   ° **Crazed**: crazy] MS 71164.   ° **so**: thus] MS 71164.

HENRY COVENTRY

"On the Dry Summer" (1636)

The following poem appears in the same manuscript collection as Cartwright's "Great Frost," right after a sequel to it entitled "On the Dissolution of the Frost and Snow" by Dudley Diggs. Although undated, Coventry's verse was likely composed in 1636, when no rain fell for three months straight, provoking "so great a drought that no one remembers the like" (Correr 568). The opening lines are a direct riposte to Cartwright, revealing how climatic variability can serve to mask general trends. The manuscript in which it appears was compiled by Oxford student William Holway, who also penned a Latin translation of Cartwright's poem. His collection of these weather-themed verses would seem to suggest that he took a keen interest in the instability of the climate, as no doubt many did in the 1630s. Source: British Library Add. MS 71164, 73^{r-v}.

> Where is the cold you quaked at, you that be
> Shook with two palsies, Age and Poverty?
> Covet not flames now, no Promethean° art
> Need steal from Phoebus° what we feel: his dart.
> He is too bounteous; he hath bent his bow,
> Scattered his flaming arrows, as if now
> There were new Pythons,° and the late drowned Earth
> Had bred some serpent, fearful beyond dearth.
>   The quarter° has been noontide; the whole night
> Feels the like heat with day, if not like light.   10
> Birds in the air fear stifling; poor men blow
> Their water as their pottage; we scarce know
> Cherwell° from Grief's;° Aristotle's brink°
> Yields liquor seniors may account good drink.
> All taverns are discommoned;° 'tis so hot
> Our Dutchmen,° twice well drunk, forsake the pot.
> We all live Portia's death;° our very meat
> Is roasted as soon as 'tis laid: we eat
> Nothing but heat; that which is coldest, fish,
> Comes boiled unto the shore as to the dish.   20
> The flood sunk not but vanished; the Sun's lust
> Thawed the cold ice not into drops but dust.
> The Earth now suffers Barnaby's° hard fate:
> More thirsty for her drinking, and too late
> Yawns after drink; the loathed and angry Clouds,
> For their complained of bounty, feed no floods,
> Scarce squeezed afford a dew, and that they give
> To tantalize her lips, not make her live.
> Amidst this heat no moisture there appears,
> But the fat rich man's sweat and poor man's tears.   30
> Our gliding channels are become firm land,

° **Promethean**: technological, an allusion to the mythical titan who stole fire from the gods.
° **Phoebus**: the sun.   ° **pythons**: giant serpent at Delphi slain by Phoebus (*Metamorphoses*, 1.525–40)
° **quarter**: 9 pm.   ° **Cherwell**: river near Oxford.
° **Grief's**: i.e. tears, but perhaps also alluding to Acheron, the "River of Woe" in Hades.
° **brink**: ether, mystical fifth element.
° **discommoned**: unfrequented, but also banned from trading with the university.
° **Dutchmen**: proverbially fond of drink.
° **Portia's death**: wife of Brutus; she committed suicide by swallowing hot coals.
° **Barnaby**: drunken protagonist of a series of picaresque poems by Richard Brathwaite.

Resembling Rivers only by their sand.
Without a prophet's mantle to divide,
We through our Jordans° safely walk and ride.
We have forgot the flood, begin to doubt
The element of Water: all is drought.
Now the fi'ry element we justly dare,
Spite of philosophy,° swear's below the air;
If there be any Air, for doubt we must
40   That as the other: we find nought but dust.
We are confirmed i'th faith that the world shall
From Fire, not Water, take its farewell fall.
Two elements are spent, the duller° left
Is become fuel, of its cold bereft.
Covered with flaming dust 'twill soon be brought
To ashes, if some god quench not this drought.
Agues° forget their cold fits, their frozen limbs,
[Space left blank in MS] no man swims
Unto his grave; we all with envy think
50   The River out of mercy from his false brink
Stole those two lovely brothers,° while that we
Survive to feel on earth purgatory.
If, as Elijah's body,° our souls rise,
Hurried in fi'ry raptures to the skies,
This comfort: we'll bid none take care to burn
Our bones; each grave itself will prove an urn.

☙ ☙ ☙

° **Jordan**: river marking the entrance to Canaan, the biblical Promised Land.
° **philosophy**: ancient cosmologists believed a ring of fire encircled the upper atmosphere, but this
     idea fell out of favour in the late Renaissance.   ° **duller**: i.e. earth. ° **Agues**: fevers.
° **brothers**: John and Thomas Littleton (aged thirteen and seventeen), who drowned in the Cherwell
     in 1635.
° **Elijah's body**: see 2 Kings 2:11.

GABRIEL PLATTES
"Islands of Ice" (1639)

Plattes was a polymath, interested in agriculture, chemistry, magnetism, and geology. In advocating intensive mining and other schemes to "improve" the natural
world, his writing is by no means environmentalist, but the following extract does
illustrate that – although early moderns would have feared global cooling more
than global warming – some natural philosophers understood the importance of
the frigid zones in maintaining a measure of what we would now call geoclimatic
equilibrium.
Source: *A Discovery of Subterranean Treasure* (1639), 2–3.

There is no probability that any Metals can be generated near unto the
North and South Poles of the Globe; for those can by no means have any

convenient Matrix for such a generation, being by all probabilities nothing but two Islands of Ice. For if they were anything else, the course of Nature must needs alter and change, and run presently out of order.

For as there is in the burning Zones° a continual exhalation of Water and rarefying of the same into Air, so there must needs be in the North [3] and South a continual condensation of Air into Water to supply the same again, else the motion cannot be perpetually circular. Now whereas the North and South parts, by reason of their coldness, cannot suffer the said condensed Meteors° to descend in form of Water, but in the form of Snow, Hail, or some substance of like nature, which there cannot melt in the superficies° for want of heat, it is very probable that the new Accretion this way produced doth press down still with its weight the said Islands of Ice towards the Centre, where the central heat melteth it off continually, by which means the spherical form of both Earth and Water are perpetually preserved.

⁂

° **burning Zones**: the tropics. ° **Meteors**: precipitation. ° **superficies**: outer surfaces.

JOHN EVELYN
"The Freezing of the Thames" (1684)

The winter of 1683–4 saw the worst frost ever recorded in England. The naturalist John Evelyn's account captures the clash between the meteorological carnivalesque of the Frost Fair and the lethal atmosphere of extreme cold and coal smoke.
Source: *The Diary of John Evelyn*, ed. William Bray (London: W. W. Gibbings, 1890), 454–5.

1 January. The weather continuing intolerably severe, streets of booths were set upon the Thames. The air was so very cold and thick, as of many years had not been the like. The small pox was very mortal …

6. The river quite frozen.

9. I went across the Thames on the ice, now become so thick as to bear not only streets of booths, in which they roasted meat and had diverse shops of wares, quite across as in a town, but coaches, carts, and horses passed over …

16. The Thames was filled with people and tents, selling all sorts of wares as in the city.

24. The frost continuing more and more severe, the Thames before London was still planted with booths in formal streets, all sorts of trades and shops furnished and full of commodities, even to a printing press, where the people and ladies took a fancy to have their names printed, and the day and year set down when printed on the Thames … Coaches plied from Westminster to the Temple, and from several other stairs to and fro,

as in the streets, sleds, sliding with skates, a bull-baiting, horse and coach races, puppet plays and interludes, cooks, tippling, and other lewd places, so that it seemed to be a bacchanalian triumph or carnival on the water, whilst it was a severe judgement on the land, the trees not only splitting as if by lightning struck, but men and cattle perishing in diverse places, and the very seas so locked up with ice that no vessels could stir out or come in. The fowls, fish, and birds, and all our exotic plants and greens universally perishing. Many parks of deer were destroyed, and all [455] sorts of fuel so dear that there were great contributions to preserve the poor alive. Nor was this severe weather much less intense in most parts of Europe, even as far as Spain and the most Southern tracts. London, by reason of the excessive coldness of the air hindering the ascent of the smoke, was so filled with the fuliginous steam of the sea-coal° that hardly could one see cross the streets, and this filling the lungs with its gross particles exceedingly obstructed the breast, so as one could scarcely breath. Here was no water to be had from the pipes and engines, nor could the brewers and diverse other tradesmen work, and every moment was full of disastrous accidents.

4 February. I went to Sayes Court to see how the frost had dealt with my garden, where I found many of the greens and rare plants utterly destroyed. The oranges and myrtles very sick, the rosemary and laurels dead to all appearance, but the cypress likely to endure it.

5 February. It began to thaw but froze again. My coach crossed from Lambeth to the Horse-ferry at Milbank, Westminster. The booths were almost all taken down, but there was first a map or landscape° cut in copper representing all the manner of the camp, and the several actions, sports, and pastimes thereon, in memory of so signal a frost.

૨ξ ૨ξ ૨ξ

° **sea-coal**: see Evelyn's *Fumifugium* in Part v, p. 488.   ° **landscape**: see Figure 11.

Decay

JOHN LILLIAT

"Finding few fruit upon the Oak,
This Rhyme upon the Rind he wrote" (c. 1596)

This poem appears in a manuscript collection compiled by John Lilliat, a vicar and musician at Chichester Cathedral. The aging oak symbolizes the decay of nature, a growing fear amid the Great Dearth of the mid-1590s. Acorn production does cease in old or dotard oaks, although dramatic declines in mast yields can also be caused by late frosts, a common occurrence in the Little Ice Age. The poet jestingly links nature's decline with the attempt to outdo nature in women's fashion, but seems oblivious to the actual damage he inflicts on the oak by carving verses in its bark. Source: Bodleian MS Rawlinson Poetry 148, 66^r.

> The sturdy Oak, too old to bear,
> Her ancient fruit away is worn:
> A sign the withered world doth wear,
> As weary of the burden borne;
> And agèd Atlas' back doth bend,
> As wishing all things to have end.
>
> The shadows that our dames adorn,
> Bespangled so with Acorn spots,°
> In such abundance now are worn
> That Time the Oak but few allots.   10
> And pride Dame Idle so beguiles
> That Art poor Nature quite exiles.

≈≈ ≈≈ ≈≈

° **shadows ... spots**: clothing with a "decorative design resembling an acorn in shape" (*OED* 2b).

THOMAS BASTARD

"Our fathers did but use the world before" (1598)

Aristotle taught that all living things move through three stages: growth, maturity, and decay. The world itself, however, was an exception: it had always existed and would always exist. In contrast, the Roman philosopher Lucretius believed that the earth too was mortal The rediscovery of this theory – a forerunner of entropic heat death – coincided with some the worst weather of the Little Ice Age, triggering fears in late Elizabethan England that nature was already entering its senility and ending with a protracted whimper. The trope of Nature's decay, however, is ambiguous from an environmentalist perspective. While it might foster stewardship and protection, it could also justify greater technological interference or mask human culpability. For the clergyman Thomas Bastard, however, the fault lay squarely with human mistreatment of the environment (see his poems on over-fishing and over-grazing in Parts IV and V, pp. 354 and 405). Although his contemporaries regarded him as a curmudgeon (whose career prospects were ruined when he exposed the sexual misconduct of some influential dons), his keen sense of personal injustice appears to have sharpened his sense of environmental injustice, and his caustic harangues against anthropocentric greed may have given wind to Shakespearean satirists such as Jaques, Thersites, and Apemantus. Source: *Chrestoleros* (1598), 81.

4.7

Our fathers did but use the world before,
And having used, did leave the same to us.
We spill° whatever restesth of their store.
What can our heirs inherit but our curse?
For we have sucked the sweet and sap away,
And sowed consumption in the fruitful ground.
The woods and forest clad in rich array,
With nakedness and baldness we confound.
We have defaced the lasting monuments,
And caused all honour to have end with us.
The holy temples feel our ravishments.°
What can our heirs inherit but our curse?
The world must end, for men are so accursed,
Unless God end it sooner, they will first.

10

❧ ❧ ❧

° **spill**: waste.
° **temples ... ravishments**: a reference to the dissolution of the monasteries.

EDMUND SPENSER

"Two Cantos of Mutability" (*c.* 1598)

These two cantos were published posthumously in 1609. Many readers find them to be an ideal capstone to Spenser's *Faerie Queene*, even the fragmentary state of the seventh book aptly underscores the message that all earthly ambitions are subject to imperfection. In the sixth canto, Mutability (the goddess of change) invades the palace of the moon and lays claim to the heavens. On a political level, Mutability's uprising presents a blatant allegory for the coup attempts that had threatened the reign of Elizabeth, often glorified by her courtier-poets as Cynthia or Diana. The Faunus episode bemoans the queen's withdrawing support for the Munster plantation (perhaps out of pique at Walter Ralegh's clandestine marriage to Elizabethan Throckmorton), but also reveals the poet's attachment to the Irish

landscape, while shifting blame onto the Irish for the deforestation perpetrated by the English occupation (see the extract from Boate in Part V, p. 434). An ecohistoricist reading, however, should not lose sight of the poem's philosophical profundity. According to the time-honoured Aristotelian cosmology, the supralunary realm – everything above the moon – was eternal and immutable. This theory had been literally exploded by the supernova of 1572. The Danish astronomer Tycho Brahe established that the nebulous blur was not the result of a disturbance in the earth's atmosphere but a new star (supernova) in the heavens. He later calculated that the Great Comet of 1577 must have voyaged well beyond the moon and also compiled observational data documenting the highly erratic orbit of Mars. The poem can also be read as an etiological account of an eclipse (Spenser may have witnessed one on 14 April 1595). For Spenser, then, political instability is symptomatic of a vaster cosmic instability. After all, famines caused not only by slash-and-burn warfare but also by the turbulent weather of the mid-1590s would have fuelled the unruliness of the Irish. Composed in the twilight years of the queen's reign, this poem might be considered the last stand of the embattled Elizabethan world picture, as Mutability's claim to rule the entire universe betokens the advent of a post-equilibrium ecology. Nevertheless, Spenser attempts – perhaps more successfully than Nashe – to contain disorder in the stately procession of the seasons and months, in Nature's verdict (drawing on neo-Pythagorean philosophy), and in the formal orderliness of the Spenserian stanza itself.
Source: *The Faerie Queene* (1609), 356–63.

Canto 6

38

Whilom, when IRELAND flourishèd in fame
Of wealth and goodness, far above the rest
Of all that bear the British Islands name,
The Gods then used (for pleasure and for rest)
Oft to resort thereto, when seemed them best;
But none of all therein more pleasure found
Than Cynthia, that is sovereign Queen professed
Of woods and forests, which therein abound,
Sprinkled with wholesome waters, more than most on ground.

39

But 'mongst them all, as fittest for her game,
Either for chase of beasts with hound or bow,
Or for to shroud in shade from Phoebus' flame,
Or bathe in fountains that do freshly flow,
Or from high hills, or from the dales below,
She chose this Arlo,° where she did resort
With all her Nymphs enrangèd on a row,
With whom the woody Gods did oft consort;
For with the Nymphs, the Satyrs love to play and sport.

° **Arlo**: Spenser's name for Galtymore: a mountain 30 km northeast of the poet's Irish estate in Munster. It overlooks the valley of Aherlow, from which Spenser presumably derived the fictitious name. Interestingly, the name of the Galtee mountain range is thought to derive from the Irish *Slèibhte na g Coillte*, or "Mountains of the Forests." The surrounding area is now completely treeless.

40

Amongst the which, there was a Nymph that hight°
Molanna,° daughter of old father Mole,
And sister unto Mulla,° fair and bright,
Unto whose bed false Bregog° whilom stole,
That Shepherd Colin° dearly did condole,
And made her luckless loves well known to be.
But this Molanna, were she not so shole,°
Were no less fair and beautiful than she:
Yet as she is, a fairer flood may no man see.

41

For first, she springs out of two marble Rocks,
On which a grove of Oaks high-mounted grows,
That as a garland seems to deck the locks
Of some fair Bride, brought forth with pompous shows
Out of her bower, that many flowers strows:°
So through the flowery Dales she tumbling down,
Through many woods and shady coverts flows
(That on each side her silver channel crown)
Till to the Plain she come, whose Valleys she doth drown.

42

In her sweet streams Diana used oft
(After her sweaty chase and toilsome play)
To bathe herself; and after, on the soft
And downy grass, her dainty limbs to lay
In covert shade, where none behold her may;
For much she hated sight of living eye.
Foolish God Faunus, though full many a day
He saw her clad, yet longèd foolishly
To see her naked 'mongst her Nymphs in privity.°

43

No way he found to compass his desire,
But to corrupt Molanna, this her maid,
Her to discover for some secret hire;°
So her with flattering words he first assayed,
And after pleasing gifts for her purveyed:

° **hight**: was called.
° **Molanna**: Spenser's name for the River Behanna, which has its source near Mount Galtymore.
° **Mulla**: Spenser's name for the River Awbeg.
° **Bregog**: another river near Spenser's estate in southern Ireland.
° **Colin**: In *Colin Clouts Come Home Again* (100–55), Spenser had imagined the confluence of the two rivers as a love affair.
° **shole**: shallow.   ° **strows**: scatters.
° **privity**: privacy. Curiously, a few months after Spenser's death, his patron, the Earl of Essex, infuriated Elizabeth by barging unannounced into the queen's bedchamber while she was still in her nightclothes to excuse the failure of his Irish campaign.
° **hire**: reward.

Queen-apples° and red Cherries from the tree,
With which he her allurèd and betrayed,
To tell what time he might her Lady see
When she herself did bathe, that he might secret be.

44

Thereto he promised if she would him pleasure
With this small boon, to quit° her with a better:
To wit, that whereas she had out of measure
Long loved the Fanchin,° who by nought did set her,
That he would undertake for this to get her
To be his Love, and of him likèd well;
Besides all which, he vowed to be her debtor
For many more good turns than he would tell,
The least of which this little pleasure should excel.

45

The simple maid did yield to him anon,
And eft° him placèd where he close might view
That never any saw, save only one,°
Who, for his hire to so foolhardy due,
Was of his hounds devoured in Hunter's hue.°
Tho,° as her manner was on sunny day,
Diana, with her Nymphs about her, drew
To this sweet spring; where, doffing her array,
She bathed her lovely limbs, for Jove a likely prey.

46

There Faunus saw that pleasèd much his eye,
And made his heart to tickle in his breast,
That for great joy of somewhat he did spy,
He could him not contain in silent rest,
But breaking forth in laughter, loud professed
His foolish thought. A foolish Faun indeed,
That couldst not hold thyself so hidden blessed,
But wouldest needs thine own conceit aread.°
Babblers unworthy been of so divine a meed.°

47

The Goddess, all abashèd with that noise,
In haste forth started from the guilty brook,
And running straight whereas she heard his voice,
Enclosed the bush about, and there him took,

° **Queen-apples**: probably quinces.   ° **quit**: requite.
° **Fanchin**: the River Funsheon.   ° **eft**: afterwards.
° **one**: Actaeon, the myth recounted by Ovid in *Metamorphoses* (Book 1), and upon which Spenser
   based this part of the tale.
° **hue**: clamour of the chase.   ° **Tho**: then.   ° **aread**: declare.   ° **meed**: reward.

Like darrèd° Lark, not daring up to look
On her whose sight before so much he sought.
Thence forth they drew him by the horns and shook
Nigh all to pieces, that they left him nought,
And then into the open light they forth him brought.

48

Like as an housewife that with busy care
Thinks of her Dairy to make wondrous gain,
Finding whereas some wicked beast unware
That breaks into her Dair'house there doth drain
Her creaming pans, and frustrate all her pain,
Hath in some snare or gin set close behind,
Entrappèd him, and caught into her train,
Then thinks what punishment were best assigned,
And thousand deaths deviseth in her vengeful mind:

49

So did Diana and her maidens all
Use silly Faunus, now within their bail.°
They mock and scorn him, and him foul miscall;
Some by the nose him plucked, some by the tail,
And by his goatish beard some did him hale:°
Yet he (poor soul) with patience all did bear;
For nought against their wills might countervail:
Ne ought he said, whatever he did hear,
But hanging down his head, did like a Mome° appear.

50

At length, when they had flouted him their fill,
They 'gan to cast what penance him to give.
Some would have gelt° him, but that same would spill°
The Wood-gods' breed, which must forever live;
Others would through the river him have drive,
And duckèd deep, but that seemed penance light;
But most agreed and did this sentence give:
Him in Deerskin to clad, and in that plight
To hunt him with their hounds, himself save how he might.

51

But Cynthia's self, more angry than the rest,
Thought not enough to punish him in sport,
And of her shame to make a gamesome jest;
But 'gan examine him in straiter° sort,
Which of her Nymphs, or other close consort,

° **darred**: dazzled.   ° **bail**: custody.   ° **hale**: yank.   ° **Mome**: fool.   ° **gelt**: castrated.
° **spill**: destroy.   ° **straiter**: stricter.

Him thither brought, and her to him betrayed?
He, much afeard, to her confessèd short°
That 'twas Molanna which her so bewrayed.°
Then all at once their hands upon Molanna laid.

52

But him (according as they had decreed)
With a Deerskin they covered, and then chased°
With all their hounds that after him did speed;
But he, more speedy, from them fled more fast
Than any Deer, so sore him dread aghast.
They after followed all with shrill outcry,
Shouting as they the heavens would have brast,°
That all the woods and dales where he did fly
Did ring again, and loud re-echo to the sky.

53

So they him followed till they weary were;
When, back returning to Molann' again,
They, by commandment of Diana, there
Her whelmed° with stones. Yet Faunus (for her pain)
Of her belovèd Fanchin did obtain,
That her he would receive unto his bed.
So now her waves pass through a pleasant Plain,
Till with the Fanchin she herself do wed,
And (both combined) themselves in one fair river spread.

54

Nath'less,° Diana, full of indignation,
Thenceforth abandoned her delicious brook,
In whose sweet stream before that bad occasion,
So much delight to bathe her limbs she took:
Ne only her, but also quite forsook
All those fair forests about Arlo hid,
And all that Mountain which doth overlook
The richest champaign that may else be rid,°
And the fair Shure,° in which are thousand Salmons bred.

55

Them all, and all that she so dear did weigh,
Thenceforth she left; and parting from the place,
Thereon a heavy hapless curse did lay:
To wit, that Wolves, where she was wont to space,°
Should harboured be, and all those Woods deface,

° **short**: presently.   ° **bewrayed**: exposed.
° **chased**: spelled "chast" to evoke Diana's chastity.   ° **brast**: burst.
° **whelmed**: pelted, crushed; a mythological explanation for the river's shallowness.
° **Nath'less**: nonetheless.   ° **rid**: ridden, but also perhaps cleared.
° **Shure**: the River Suir, pronounced as Spenser spells it.   ° **space**: roam.

And Thieves should rob and spoil that Coast around.
Since which, those Woods and all that goodly Chase
Doth to this day with Wolves and Thieves abound:
Which too, too true that land's indwellers° since have found.

Canto 7

Pealing,° from Jove to Nature's Bar
Bold Alteration pleads
Large Evidence: but Nature soon
Her righteous Doom° areads ...

3

Now at the time that was before agreed,
The Gods assembled° all on Arlo hill;
As well those that are sprung of heavenly seed,
As those that all the other world do fill,
And rule both sea and land unto their will:
Only th'infernal Powers might not appear;
As well for horror of their count'nance ill,
As for th'unruly fiends which they did fear;
Yet Pluto and Proserpina° were present there.

4

And thither also came all other creatures,
Whatever life or motion do retain,
According to their sundry kinds of features,
That Arlo scarcely could them all contain;
So full they fillèd every hill and Plain:
And had not Nature's Sergeant (that is Order)
Them well-disposèd by his busy pain,°
And rangèd far abroad in every border,
They would have causèd much confusion and disorder.

5

Then forth issued (great goddess) great dame Nature,
With goodly port° and gracious Majesty,
Being far greater and more tall of stature
Than any of the gods or Powers on high:
Yet certes° by her face and phys'gnomy,
Whether she man or woman inly were,
That could not any creature well descry:

° **indwellers**: inhabitants; Spenser's estate in Munster would make him an indweller.
° **Pealing**: appealing.   ° **Doom**: verdict.
° **assembled**: the assembly of the gods on the hill recalls the Irish custom of "folkmotes" described
  by Spenser in his *View of the Present State of Ireland* (54–5).
° **Pluto and Proserpina**: The Roman god and goddess of the underworld.
° **pain**: diligence.   ° **port**: bearing.   ° **certes**: truly.

For with a veil that wimpled° everywhere,
Her head and face was hid, that might to none appear.

6

That some do say was so by skill devised,
To hide the terror of her uncouth hue
From mortal eyes, that should be sore agrised;°
For that her face did like a Lion shew,
That eye of wight° could not endure to view:
But others tell that it so beauteous was,
And round about such beams of splendour threw,
That it the Sun a thousand times did pass,
Ne could be seen, but like an image in a glass.

7

That well may seemen true; for well I ween°
That this same day when she on Arlo sat,
Her garment was so bright and wondrous sheen,
That my frail wit cannot devise to what
It to compare, nor find like stuff to that,
As those three sacred Saints,° though else most wise,
Yet on Mount Tabor quite their wits forgat,
When they their glorious Lord in strange disguise
Transfigured saw: his garments so did daze their eyes.

8

In a fair Plain upon an equal° Hill,
She placèd was in a pavilion:
Not such as Craftsmen by their idle° skill
Are wont for Princes' states° to fashion,
But th'earth herself of her own motion,
Out of her fruitful bosom made to grow
Most dainty trees; that, shooting up anon,
Did seem to bow their bloss'ming heads full low,
For homage unto her, and like a throne did show.

9

So hard it is for any living wight
All her array and vestiments° to tell,
That old Dan Geoffrey° (in whose gentle sprite
The pure wellhead of Poesy did dwell)

° **wimpled**: covered in folds.   ° **agrised**: terrified.   ° **wight**: person.   ° **ween**: believe.
° **Saints**: Peter, James, and John, to whom Christ appeared on Mount Tabor in radiant clothing after
  his crucifixion .
° **equal**: level.   ° **idle**: frivolous.
° **states**: raised and canopied throne. See Robert Peake's painting of the Procession of Queen
  Elizabeth.
° **vestiments**: clothing.
° **Geoffrey**: Chaucer (1343–1400), the first great English poet and the author of *The Parliament of
Fowls*, in which Dame Nature appears.

In his *Fowls Parley* durst not with it mel,°
But it transferred° to Alain,° who he thought
Had in his *Plaint of Kind* described it well:
Which who will read set forth so as it ought,
Go seek he out that Alain where he may be sought.

10

And all the earth far underneath her feet
Was dight° with flowers, that voluntary grew
Out of the ground and sent forth odours sweet,
Ten thousand mores° of sundry scent and hue,
That might delight the smell or please the view:
The which the Nymphs from all the brooks thereby
Had gathered, which they at her footstool threw,
That richer seemed than any tapestry
That Princes' bowers adorn with painted imagery.

11

And Mole himself, to honour her the more,
Did deck himself in freshest fair attire,
And his high head, that seemeth always hoar
With hardened frosts of former winter's ire,
He with an Oaken garland now did tire,°
As if the love of some new Nymph late seen
Had in him kindled youthful fresh desire,
And made him change his grey attire to green;
Ah gentle Mole! Such joyance hath thee well-beseen° …

13

This great Grandmother of all creatures bred,
Great Nature, ever young, yet full of eld;
Still moving, yet unmovèd from her stead;°
Unseen of any, yet of all beheld;
Thus sitting in her throne as I have telled,
Before her came dame Mutability;
And being low before her presence felled,°
With meek obeisance and humility,
Thus 'gan her plaintiff Plea, with words to amplify:

14

"To thee, O greatest goddess, only great,
A humble suppliant low, I lowly fly,

° **mel**: meddle.   ° **transferred**: referred.
° **Alain**: Alain de Lille (c. 1128 – c. 1202), French theologian and author of Latin treatise *Complaint of Nature* (here translated by Spenser as *Plaint of kindes*), in which a personified Nature appears in a magnificent gown embroidered with the image of every living creature. As she walks, the gown's shimmering creates the illusion that the animals are moving.
° **dight**: decked.   ° **mores**: plants.   ° **tire**: attire.
° **hath … well-beseen**: becomes thee well.   ° **stead**: place.   ° **felled**: prostrated.

Seeking for Right, which I of thee entreat;
Who Right to all dost deal indifferently,
Damning all Wrong and tortious Injury,
Which any of thy creatures do to other
(Oppressing them with power, unequally),
Since of them all thou art the equal mother,
And knittest each to each, as brother unto brother.

15

"To thee therefore of this same Jove I plain,°
And of his fellow gods that feign to be,
That challenge to themselves the whole world's reign;
Of which the greatest part is due to me,
And heaven itself by heritage in Fee:°
For heaven and earth I both alike do deem,
Since heaven and earth are both alike to thee;
And gods no more than men thou dost esteem:
For even the gods to thee, as men to gods do seem.

16

"Then weigh, O sovereign goddess, by what right
These gods do claim the world's whole sovereignty;
And that is only due unto thy might,
Arrogate to themselves ambitiously.
As for the gods' own principality,
Which Jove usurps unjustly, that to be
My heritage Jove's self cannot deny:
From my great-Grandsire Titan unto me,
Derived by due descent, as is well known to thee.

17

"Yet maugre° Jove, and all his gods beside,
I do possess the world's most regiment:
As if ye please it into parts divide,
And every parts inholders to convent,°
Shall to your eyes appear incontinent.°
And first, the Earth (great mother of us all)
That only seems unmoved and permanent,
And unto Mutability not thrall,
Yet is she changed in part, and eke in general.

18

"For all that from her springs and is ybred,
However fair it flourish for a time,
Yet see we soon decay; and, being dead,
To turn again unto their earthly slime:

° **plain**: complain. ° **Fee**: absolute possession of a heritable estate.   ° **maugre**: despite.
° **inholders … convent**: tenants to convene.   ° **incontinent**: immediately.

Yet out of their decay and mortal crime,
We daily see new creatures to arise,
And of their Winter spring another Prime,°
Unlike in form and changed by strange disguise:
So turn they still about, and change in restless wise.°

19

"As for her tenants; that is, man and beasts,
The beasts we daily see massacred die,
As thralls and vassals unto men's behests;
And men themselves do change continually,
From youth to eld, from wealth to poverty,
From good to bad, from bad to worst of all.
Ne do their bodies only flit and fly,
But eke their minds (which they immortal call)
Still change and vary thoughts, as new occasions fall.

20

"Ne is the water in more constant case,
Whether those same on high or these below:
For th'Ocean moveth still, from place to place;
And every River still doth ebb and flow;
Ne any Lake, that seems most still and slow,
Ne Pool so small that can his smoothness hold,
When any wind doth under heaven blow;
With which the clouds are also tossed and rolled:
Now like great Hills, and straight° like sluices them unfold.

21

"So likewise are all wat'ry living wights
Still tossed and turnèd with continual change,
Never abiding in their steadfast plights.°
The fish, still floating, do at random range,
And never rest, but evermore exchange
Their dwelling places, as the streams them carry.
Ne have the wat'ry fowls a certain grange°
Wherein to rest, ne in one stead do tarry,
But flitting still do fly and still their places vary.

22

"Next is the Air, which who feels not by sense
(For of all sense it is the middle mean)°
To flit still? And with subtle influence
Of his thin spirit, all creatures to maintain
In state of life! Oh weak life! That does lean

° **Prime**: spring.   ° **wise**: manner.   ° **straight**: straightaway.   ° **plights**: conditions.
° **grange**: residence, literally a country house.
° **middle mean**: medium through which stimuli travel to the senses.

On thing so tickle° as th'unsteady Air,
Which every hour is changed and altered clean°
With every blast that bloweth foul or fair:
The fair doth it prolong; the foul doth it impair.

23

"Therein the changes infinite behold,
Which to her creatures every minute chance:
Now boiling hot, straight freezing deadly cold;
Now fair sunshine, that makes all skip and dance,
Straight bitter storms and baleful countenance,
That makes them all to shiver and to shake;
Rain, hail, and snow do pay them sad penance,
And dreadful thunderclaps (that make them quake)
With flames and flashing lights that thousand changes make.

24

"Last is the fire, which, though it live forever,
Ne can be quenchèd quite; yet every day
We see his parts, so soon as they do sever,
To lose their heat and shortly to decay:
So makes himself his own consuming prey.
Ne any living creatures doth he breed,
But all that are of others bred doth slay,
And with their death his cruèl life doth feed,
Nought leaving but their barren ashes without seed.

25

"Thus all these four (the which the groundwork be
Of all the world and of all living wights)
To thousand sorts of Change we subject see;
Yet are they changed (by other wondrous sleights)
Into themselves, and lose their native mights:
The Fire to Air, and th' Air to Water sheer,
And Water into Earth; yet Water fights
With Fire, and Air with Earth approaching near:
Yet all are in one body, and as one appear.

26

"So in them all reigns Mutability;
However these, that Gods themselves do call,
Of them do claim the rule and sovereignty:
As Vesta° of the Fire ethereal,
Vulcan° of this with us so usual,
Ops° of the Earth, and Juno of the Air,
Neptune of Seas, and Nymphs of Rivers all;

° **tickle**: volatile.   ° **clean**: completely.   ° **Vesta**: Roman goddess of the hearth and celestial fire.
° **Vulcan**: Roman god of metallurgy and terrestrial fire.   ° **Ops**: Roman fertility goddess.

For all those Rivers to me subject are,
And all the rest, which they usurp, be all my share.

27

"Which to approven true as I have told,
Vouchsafe, O goddess, to thy presence call
The rest which do the world in being hold:
As times and seasons of the year that fall.
Of all the which, demand in general,
Or judge thyself, by verdict of thine eye,
Whether to me they are not subject all."
Nature did yield thereto; and by and by,
Bade Order call them all before her Majesty.

28

So forth issued the Seasons of the year:
First, lusty Spring, all dight° in leaves of flowers
That freshly budded and new blossoms did bear
(In which a thousand birds had built their bowers,
That sweetly sung to call forth Paramours);°
And in his hand a javelin he did bear,
And on his head (as fit for warlike stours)°
A gilt engraven morion° he did wear:
That as some did him love, so others did him fear.

29

Then came the jolly Summer, being dight
In a thin silken cassock° coloured green,
That was unlinèd all, to be more light;
And on his head a garland well-beseen
He wore, from which, as he had chafèd° been,
The sweat did drop; and in his hand he bore
A bow and shafts, as he in forest green
Had hunted late the Leopard or the Boar,
And now would bathe his limbs, with labour heated sore.

30

Then came the Autumn, all in yellow clad,
As though he joyèd in his plenteous store,
Laden with fruits that made him laugh, full glad
That he had banished hunger, which tofore
Had by the belly oft him pinchèd sore.
Upon his head a wreath, that was enrolled°
With ears of corn° of every sort, he bore;
And in his hand a sickle he did hold,
To reap the ripened fruits the which the earth had yold.°

° **dight**: clad.   ° **Paramours**: lovers.   ° **stours**: combat.   ° **morion**: helmet.
° **cassock**: cloak.   ° **chafed**: heated.   ° **enrolled**: enfolded.   ° **corn**: grain.
° **yold**: yielded.

31

Lastly came Winter, clothèd all in frieze,°
Chattering his teeth for cold that did him chill,
Whilst on his hoary beard his breath did freeze,
And the dull drops that from his purplèd bill,°
As from a limbeck,° did adown distill.
In his right hand a tippèd staff he held,
With which his feeble steps he stayèd still;
For he was faint with cold, and weak with eld,
That scarce his loosèd limbs he able was to weld° ...

47

When these° were past, thus 'gan the Titaness:
"Lo, mighty mother, now be judge and say,
Whether in all thy creatures more or less
CHANGE doth not reign and bear the greatest sway:
For who sees not that Time on all doth prey?
But times do change and move continually,
So nothing here long standeth in one stay:
Wherefore this lower world who can deny
But to be subject still to Mutability? ...

55

"Besides, the sundry motions of your Spheres,°
So sundry ways and fashions as clerks feign,
Some in short space, and some in longer years,
What is the same but alteration plain?
Only the starry sky doth still remain:
Yet do the Stars and Signs therein still move,
And even itself is moved, as wizards sain.°
But all that moveth doth mutation love:
Therefore both you and them to me I subject prove.

56

"Then since within this wide great Universe
Nothing doth firm and permanent appear,
But all things tossed and turnèd by transverse,°
What then should let,° but I aloft should rear
My Trophy, and from all the triumph bear?
Now judge then (O thou, greatest goddess true!)
According as thyself dost see and hear,
And unto me adoom° that is my due:
That is the rule of all, all being ruled by you."

° **frieze**: coarse, woollen cloth (with pun).   ° **bill**: nose.
° **limbeck**: glass vessel.   ° **weld**: wield.
° **these**: In stanzas 32–46, Spenser depicts the procession of the twelve months (beginning with March), followed by Day, Night, the Hours, Life, and Death.
° **Spheres**: the omitted stanzas describe the lunar phases and erratic orbits of the planets.
° **wizards sain**: sages say.   ° **transverse**: topsy-turvy.   ° **let**: hinder.   ° **adoom**: adjudge.

57

So having ended, silence long ensued,
Ne Nature to or fro spake for a space,
But with firm eyes affixed, the ground still viewed.
Meanwhile, all creatures looking in her face,
Expecting th'end of this so doubtful case,
Did hang in long suspense what would ensue,
To whether side should fall the sovereign place:
At length, she looking up with cheerful view
The silence broke, and gave her doom in speeches few.

58

"I well consider all that ye have said,
And find that all things steadfastness do hate
And changèd be: yet being rightly weighed,
They are not changèd from their first estate,
But by their change their being do dilate;
And turning to themselves at length again,
Do work their own perfection so by fate:
Then over them Change doth not rule and reign,
But they reign over change, and do their states maintain.

59

"Cease therefore daughter further to aspire,
And thee content thus to be ruled by me:
For thy decay thou seekst by thy desire;
But time shall come that all shall changèd be,
And from thenceforth, none no more change shall see."
So was the Titaness put down and whist,°
And Jove confirmed in his imperial see.°
Then was that whole assembly quite dismissed,
And Nature's self did vanish, whither no man wist.°

Canto 8, Imperfect°

1

When I bethink me on that speech whilere°
Of Mutability, and well it weigh,
Meseems that though she all unworthy were
Of the Heav'n's Rule; yet very sooth to say
In all things else she bears the greatest sway:
Which makes me loathe this state of life so tickle,°
And love of things so vain to cast away,
Whose flowering pride, so fading and so fickle,
Short Time shall soon cut down with his consuming sickle.

° **whist**: silenced.   ° **see**: throne.   ° **wist**: knew.   ° **Imperfect**: incomplete.
° **whilere**: earlier.   ° **tickle**: precarious.

2

Then 'gin I think on that which Nature said,
Of that same time when no more Change shall be,
But steadfast rest of all things firmly stayed
Upon the pillars of Eternity,
That is contraire to Mutability:
For all that moveth doth in Change delight:
But thenceforth all shall rest eternally
With Him that is the God of sabbath° hight:
O thou° great Sabbath God, grant me that sabbaoth's sight.

ᘓ ᘓ ᘓ

° **sabbath**: rest, but the original spelling "sabbaoth" plays on the Greek for Lord of hosts or armies
   (Romans 9:29).
° **thou**: that] 1609.

JOHN DONNE
from An Anatomy of the World (1611)

Donne was commissioned to write this poem to commemorate the death of
Elizabeth Drury, the daughter of one of his patrons. Later editions renamed it "The
First Anniversary" to differentiate it from Donne's second elegy for her published
the following year. Instead of penning a wooden tribute to a fourteen-year-old girl
whom he likely never met, Donne instead seized the occasion to mourn the shatter-
ing of the traditional human-centred cosmology. Embodying the cosmic force that
brings harmony, correspondence, and beauty to the universe, Elizabeth – whose
first name happens to be identical with that of England's former monarch – could
also be compared to the World Soul (see Part 1) of Roman philosophy, and the
poem riffs on the metaphysical conceit of its "anatomy" or autopsy. As for the
cause of its demise, Donne famously accuses "new philosophy" or scientific developments, particularly in astronomy. Fittingly, Donne composed the poem one year
after Galileo discovered the phases of Venus, proving the heliocentric model correct.
The *Anatomy* also bristles with Calvinist pessimism about the human condition,
with which Donne deflates the hubris of Renaissance humanists. Like Spenser's
"Mutability Cantos" and Shakespeare's *King Lear*, its literary power derives from its
perception of a radical discontinuity with the past during the onset of modernity.
On the one hand, Donne voices a wistful yearning for an orderly, anthropocentric
universe. Yet the poem also presents a blistering critique of species-ism, a satire on
our supposed intellectual mastery over the earth, a prophetic vision of an indi-
vidualistic, capitalist culture out of kilter with its environment, and a memorable
account of climate change during the Little Ice Age. The traumatic lessons of the
Anatomy are ones that industrialized civilization has resisted. We "know" that the
earth revolves around the sun, but do not act in accordance with the implications
of that discovery spelled out here by Donne. Can environmentalists promoting
eco-humility learn something from the spirituality of the early modern period?
Source: *An Anatomy of the World* (1611), A6ʳ–B5ʳ.

There is not now that mankind which was then,
When as the Sun and man did seem to strive
(Joint tenants of the world) who should survive;

When Stag, and Raven, and the long-lived tree,
Compared with man, died in minority;°
When if a slow-paced star had stol'n away
From the observer's marking, he might stay
Two or three hundred years to see't again,
120   And then make up his observation plain;
When as the age was long the size was great,
Man's growth confessed and recompensed the meat,
So spacious and large that every soul
Did a fair Kingdom and large Realm control;
And when the very stature thus erect
Did that soul a good way towards heaven direct.
Where is this mankind now? Who lives to age
Fit to be made Methuselah his page?°
Alas, we scarce live long enough to try
130   Whether a new made clock run right or lie.
Old Grandsires talk of yesterday with sorrow,
And for our children we reserve tomorrow.
So short is life that every peasant strives,
In a torn house or field, to have three lives.°
And as in lasting, so in length is man
Contracted to an inch, who was a span.°
For had a man at first in Forests strayed,
Or shipwrecked in the Sea, one would have laid
A wager that an Elephant or Whale
140   That met him would not hastily assail
A thing so equal to him. Now, alas,
The Fairies and the Pygmies well may pass
As credible; mankind decays so soon,
We're scarce our Fathers' shadows cast at noon.
Only death adds t'our length;° nor are we grown
In stature to be men till we are none.°
But this were light, did our less volume hold
All the old Text, or had we changed to gold
Their silver, or disposed into less glass
150   Spirits of virtue, which then scattered was.
But 'tis not so: w'are not retired, but damped.
And as our bodies, so our minds are cramped.
'Tis shrinking, not close-weaving, that hath thus
In mind and body both bedwarfèd us.
We seem ambitious God's whole work t'undo.
Of nothing he made us, and we strive too

° **There … minority**: Donne here draws on scriptural accounts that humans before the Flood had a lifespan of several hundred years.

° **Methuselah … page**: the oldest of the biblical patriarchs, reported to have lived to the age of 969 (Genesis 5:27). Pages were usually young boys.

° **three lives**: a lease for three generations. Estimates of childhood mortality rates in Tudor England range from 25 per cent to around 40 per cent. Elizabeth Drury had died at fourteen.

° **span**: distance from the thumb to pinky when fingers are fully extended.

° **only … length**: due to the bloating of the body after death.

° **nor … none**: we reach our full size only in death.

To bring ourselves to nothing back; and we
Do what we can to do't so soon as he.
With new diseases on ourselves we war,
And with new physic,° a worse engine far.   160
Thus man, this world's Vice-Emperor, in whom
All faculties, all graces are at home,
And if in other Creatures they appear,
They're but man's ministers and Legates° there,
To work on their rebellions and reduce
Them to Civility and to man's use;
This man, whom God did woo, and loth t'attend
Till man came up, did down to man descend;
This man, so great, that all that is, is his,
Oh, what a trifle and poor thing he is!   170
If man were anything he's nothing now.
Help, or at least some time to waste, allow
T'his other wants: yet when he did depart
With her° whom we lament, he lost his heart.
She of whom th'Ancients seemed to prophesy
When they called virtues by the name of she;
She in whom virtue was so much refined,
That for Alloy unto so pure a mind
She took the weaker Sex; she that could drive
The poisonous tincture and the stain of Eve   180
Out of her thoughts and deeds, and purify
All by a true religious Alchemy;
She, she is dead; she's dead. When thou know'st this,
Thou know'st how poor a trifling thing man is.
And learn'st thus much by our Anatomy:
The heart being perished, no part can be free.
And that except thou feed (not banquet) on
The supernatural food, Religion,
Thy better Growth grows witherèd and scant;
Be more than man, or thou'rt less than an Ant.   190
Then as mankind, so is the world's whole frame
Quite out of joint, almost created lame;
For before God had made up all the rest,
Corruption entered and depraved the best:
It seized the Angels, and then first of all
The world did in her Cradle take a fall,
And turned her brains, and took a general maim,
Wronging each joint of th'universal frame.
The noblest part, man, felt it first, and then
Both beasts and plants, cursed in the curse of man.°   200
So did the world from the first hour decay,
That evening was beginning of the day.

° **physic**: medicines, like the chemical elixirs of Paracelsus.   ° **Legates**: delegates.
° **her**: Elizabeth Drury.
° **curse of man**: in accordance with religious belief that violence and predation in the natural world
resulted from human sin. A marginal note here reads "Decay of Nature in other parts." For
another meditation on decay informed by religious anti-humanism, see Godfrey Goodman's *The
Fall of Man* (1616).

And now the Springs and Summers which we see,
Like sons of women after fifty be.
And new Philosophy° calls all in doubt:
The Element of fire is quite put out;°
The Sun is lost,° and th'earth, and no man's wit
Can well direct him where to look for it.
And freely men confess that this world's spent,
210   When in the Planets and the Firmament
They seek so many new;° they see that this
Is crumbled out again to his Atomies.
'Tis all in pieces, all coherence gone;
All just supply, and all Relation:
Prince, Subject, Father, Son, are things forgot,
For every man alone thinks he hath got
To be a Phoenix,° and that there can be
None of that kind, of which he is, but he.
This is the world's condition now, and now
220   She that should all parts to reunion bow;
She that had all Magnetic force alone,
To draw and fasten sundered parts in one;
She whom wise nature had invented then
When she observed that every sort of men
Did in their voyage in this world's Sea stray,
And needed a new compass for their way;
She that was best and first original
Of all fair copies, and the general
230   Steward to Fate; she whose rich eyes and breast
Gilt the West Indies and perfumed the East,
Whose having breathed in this world did bestow
Spice on those Isles and bade them still smell so,
And that rich Indie which doth gold inter
Is but as single money, coined from her;
She to whom this world must itself refer
As Suburbs, or the Microcosm of her;
She, she is dead; she's dead. When thou know'st this,
Thou know'st how lame a cripple this world is.
And learn'st thus much by our Anatomy:
240   That this world's general sickness doth not lie
In any humour or one certain part,
But as thou saw'st it rotten at the heart,
Thou see'st a Hectic° fever hath got hold
Of the whole substance, not to be controlled.
And that thou hast but one way not t'admit
The world's infection: to be none of it.
For the world's subtl'st immaterial parts

° **Philosophy**: natural philosophy (science).
° **fire … out**: classical cosmology had imagined a ring of fire encircling the earth's upper atmosphere.
° **Sun … lost**: due to debates over geocentric versus heliocentric systems.
° **new**: in 1610, Galileo had discovered the four largest moons of Jupiter.
° **Phoenix**: legend claimed only one phoenix could exist at a time.   ° **Hectic**: consumptive.

Feel this consuming wound and age's darts.
For the world's beauty is decayed or gone:
Beauty, that's colour and proportion.   250
We think the heavens enjoy their Spherical,
Their round proportion embracing all.
But yet their various and perplexèd course,
Observed in diverse ages doth enforce
Men to find out so many Eccentric parts,
Such diverse downright lines, such overthwarts,°
As disproportion that pure form. It tears
The Firmament in eight and forty shares,°
And in those constellations then arise
New stars,° and old do vanish from our eyes,   260
As though heav'n suffered earthquakes, peace, or war,
When new towers rise and old demolished are.
They have impaled within a Zodiac
The free-born Sun, and keep twelve signs awake
To watch his steps; the Goat and Crab° control
And fright him back, who else to either pole
(Did not these Tropics fetter him) might run:
For his course is not round; nor can the Sun
Perfect a Circle or maintain his way
One inch direct; but where he rose today   270
He comes no more, but with a cozening line,
Steals by that point, and so is Serpentine;
And seeming weary with his reeling thus,
He means to sleep, being now fall'n nearer us.
So of the stars, which boast that they do run
In Circle still, none ends where he begun.
All their proportion's lame, it sinks, it swells.
For of Meridians and Parallels,
Man hath weaved out a net, and this net thrown
Upon the Heavens, and now they are his own.   280
Loth to go up the hill, or labour thus
To go to heaven, we make heaven come to us.
We spur, we rein the stars, and in their race
They're diversely content t'obey our pace.
But keeps the earth her round proportion still?
Doth not a Tenerife° or higher Hill
Rise so high like a Rock that one might think
The floating Moon would shipwreck there and sink?
Seas are so deep that Whales, being struck° today,
Perchance tomorrow, scarce at middle way   290
Of their wished journey's end, the bottom, die.
And men to sound depths so much line untie,

° **overthwarts**: slanted or transverse lines in the planetary orbits.
° **shares**: Ptolemaic cosmology recognized forty-eight constellations.
° **New stars**: references to the supernovas of 1572 (in Cassiopeia) and 1604 (in Ophiuchus). The new
  stars came to be associated, respectively, with Tycho Brahe and Johannes Kepler.
° **Goat and Crab**: Capricorn and Cancer.
° **Tenerife**: in the Canary Islands, dominated by 12,000-foot-tall Mount Teide.
° **struck**: the spelling "strook" might suggest, besides hit, killed or lowered with a rope.

As one might justly think that there would rise
At end thereof, one of th'Antipodes° …
Nor in ought more this world's decay appears,
Than that her influence the heav'n forbears,
Or that the Elements do not feel this:

380 The father or the mother barren is.
The clouds conceive not rain, or do not pour
In the due birth-time down the balmy shower.
Th'Air doth not motherly sit on the earth,
To hatch her seasons and give all things birth.
Springtimes were common cradles, but are tombs;
And false conceptions fill the general wombs.°
Th'Air shows such Meteors as none can see,
Not only what they mean, but what they be;
Earth such new worms, as would have troubled much

390 Th'Egyptian Mages° to have made more such.
What Artist° now dares boast that he can bring
Heaven hither, or constellate° anything,
So as the influence of those stars may be
Imprisoned in an Herb, or Charm, or Tree,
And do by touch all which those stars could do?°
The art is lost, and correspondence too.
For heaven gives little, and the earth takes less,
And man least knows their trade and purposes.
If this commerce 'twixt heaven and earth were not

400 Embarred, and all this traffic quite forgot,
She, for whose loss we have lamented thus,
Would work more fully and pow'rfully on us.
Since herbs and roots by dying lose not all,
But they, yea Ashes too, are medicinal,
Death could not quench her virtue so, but that
It would be (if not followed) wondered at;
And all the world would be one dying Swan,
To sing her funeral praise and vanish then.
But as some Serpents' poison hurteth not,

410 Except it be from the live Serpent shot,
So doth her virtue need her here to fit
That unto us: she working more than it.
But she in whom to such maturity
Virtue was grown past growth, that it must die;
She from whose influence all Impressions came,
But by Receivers' impotencies lame,
Who though she could not transubstantiate
All states to gold, yet gilded every state,

° **Antipodes**: legendary lands on the opposite side of the earth from Europe.
° **clouds … wombs**: an allusion to the turbulent weather of recent decades. England had
   experienced a severe frost and dearth in 1607–8 (see *The Great Frost*, p. 518).
° **Egyptian Mages**: in Exodus 7:11, Pharaoh's sages transformed their staffs into snakes to duplicate
   Aaron's miracle.   ° **Artist**: astrologer.   ° **constellate**: cast a horoscope.
° **So … do**: early moderns believed starlight also contributed to the growth of plants and infused
   medicinal properties into them. Hence to deny astrology meant diminishing the amount of energy
   reaching the earth – a belief that may in part account for the reluctance to abandon it.

So that some Princes have some temperance;
Some Counsellors some purpose to advance   420
The common profit; and some people have
Some stay,° no more than Kings should give, to crave;
Some women have some taciturnity;
Some Nunneries some grains of chastity;
She that did thus much and much more could do,
But that our age was Iron, and rusty too;
She, she is dead; she's dead. When thou knows't this,
Thou know'st how dry a Cinder this world is.
And learn'st thus much by our Anatomy.

३ॡ ३ॡ ३ॡ

° **stay**: scruple.

Resilience

JOACHIM DU BELLAY
"Then I beheld the fair Dodonian tree" (1558)

The following sonnet demonstrates the Renaissance's conception of itself as an age of resilience. It was originally composed by a French poet during a sojourn in Rome, anthologized in a collection of visionary poetry by a Dutch Protestant writer, and then translated into English by a seventeen-year-old Edmund Spenser. The poem can be read as an example of *translatio studii* (the transfer of culture from Troy to Rome to France to England), or an allegory for the Reformation. The correspondence between Roman ruins and the decrepit tree is even more explicit in another Du Bellay poem that Spenser translated ("He that hath seen a great Oak dry and dead"), placing great emphasis on the oak's decay. Although these verses influenced Spenser's "February" (see Part 11, p. 177), the sonnet below ends on a more hopeful note with an image of coppicing – cutting trees down to the stump and allowing them to regenerate – an important strategy for preserving England's woodlands in response to the Elizabethan timber crisis.
Source: *A Theatre for Worldlings*, trans. Edmund Spenser (1569), C3ᵛ.

> Then I beheld the fair Dodonian° tree,
> Upon seven hills° throw forth his gladsome shade,
> And Conquerors bedeckèd with his leaves
> Along the banks of the Italian stream.°
> There many ancient Trophies° were erect,
> Many a spoil and many goodly signs,
> To show the greatness of the stately race,
> That erst descended from the Trojan blood.
> Ravished I was to see so rare a thing,
10> When barbarous villains in disordered heap,
> Outraged the honour of these noble boughs.
> I heard the trunk to groan under the wedge.
> And since I saw the root in high disdain
> Send forth again a twin of forkèd trees.

❧ ❧ ❧

° **Dodonian**: Dodona was the site of a temple to Zeus, known for its sacred grove of oaks.
° **seven hills**: of Rome.   ° **Italian stream**: Tiber.
° **Trophies**: during their triumphs, Romans decorated trees with spoils of war.

GEORGE WITHER

"A Posteritati:° *He that delights to Plant and Set, Makes After-Ages in his Debt*" (c. 1620)

A 1611 Dutch emblem book by Gabriel Rollenhagen includes a memorable image of a man planting a tree. In the original, the emblem is accompanied by Latin glosses, encouraging readers to have children who will bless the names of their progenitors and worship God. The version below is not a translation but a radical rewriting of its moral. Inverting the trajectory of the metaphor, Wither turns it into a call for a tree-planting initiative to regenerate England's depleted woodlands. Source: *A Collection of Emblems* (1635), 35.

When I behold the Havoc and the Spoil,
Which (ev'n within the compass of my Days)
Is made through every quarter of this Isle
In Woods and Groves (which were this Kingdom's praise);
And when I mind° with how much greediness,
We seek the present Gain in every thing,
Not caring (so our Lust we may possess)
What Damage to Posterity we bring;
They do, methinks, as if they did foresee,
That some of those whom they have cause to hate   10
Should come in Future-times their Heirs to be:
Or else why should they such things perpetrate?
For if they think their Children shall succeed,
Or can believe that they begot their Heirs,
They could not, surely, do so foul a Deed,
As to deface the Land that should be theirs.
What our Forefathers planted, we destroy;
Nay, all Men's labours, living heretofore,
And all our own we lavishly employ
To serve our present Lusts, and for no more.   20
But let these careless Wasters learn to know,
That as Vain Spoil is open Injury,
So Planting is a Debt they truly owe,
And ought to pay, to their Posterity.
Self-love for none but for itself doth care,
And only for the present taketh pain,
But Charity for others doth prepare,
And joys in that which Future-time shall gain.
If After-ages may my Labours bless,
I care not much how Little I possess.   30

ॐ ॐ ॐ

° ***A Posteritati***: To Posterity.   ° **mind**: consider.

GEORGE HAKEWILL
"Of this Pretended Decay" (1627)

Despite the flurry of apocalyptic prophecies in the early seventeenth century, not everyone was convinced that doomsday was near. Inquiring into the cause of this unhealthy paranoia, the Oxford clergymen George Hakewill here identifies three culprits: (1) slavering, self-important poets enamoured with dramatic spectacles of destruction; (2) cantankerous old men who idealize their lost childhood; and (3) greedy farmers who deplete the fertility of their soil by refusing to let fields lie fallow. In addition to worrying that the Lucretian vision of cosmic decay would weaken religious faith, Hakewill voices concern that such anxiety will make societies over-consume their resources and disregard their obligations to posterity. How does the early modern debate over nature's decay compare with the controversial status of apocalyptic rhetoric in contemporary environmentalist discourse? (see Garrard 96–116) Does it function as a wake-up call to amend human behaviour, or might it, by instilling despair, become a self-fulfilling prophecy? If Hakewill's *Apology* failed to stem the tide of apocalyptic prophecies unleashed during the English Civil War, his eloquence did persuade many. Among them was the young John Milton. While still a student at Cambridge, Milton composed a Latin poem on this theme, entitled *Natura non pati senium* (*Nature is Not Subject to Old Age*).
Source: *An Apology of the Power and Providence of God … and Censure of the Common Error Touching Nature's Perpetual and Universal Decay* (1627), 19–22, 31–2.

As the opinion of the world's universal decay quails the hopes and blunts the edge of men's endeavours, so doth it likewise of our exhortations and threatenings, when men are persuaded that famines, pestilences, unseasonable weather and the like, are not the scourges of God for sin, but rather the diseases of wasted and decrepit Nature, not procured so much by the vices and wickedness of men, as by the old age and weakness of the world. And this opinion being once thoroughly rooted and settled in them, they neither care much for repentance nor call upon God for grace …

[20] Besides the same opinion serves to make men more careless, both in regard of their present fortunes and in providing for posterity. For when they consider how many thousand years nature hath now been, as it were, in a fever hectic,° daily consuming and wasting away by degrees, they infer that in reason she cannot hold out long. And therefore it were to as little purpose to plant trees or to erect lasting buildings, either for Civil, Charitable, or Pious uses, as to provide new apparel for a sick man that lies at death's door and hath already one foot in the grave …

[21] How long this age shall last, it is still doubtful, it being one of those secrets which the Almighty hath locked up in the cabinet of his own counsel, a secret which is neither possible [nor] profitable for us to know, as being not by God revealed unto us in his Word, much less then in the book of Nature …

° **hectic**: consumptive.

Let not, then, the vain shadows of the World's fatal decay keep us either from looking backward to the imitation of our noble Predecessors or forward in providing for posterity. But as our predecessors worthily provided for us, so let our posterity bless us in providing for them, it being still as uncertain to us what generations are yet to ensue as it was to our predecessors in their ages. I will shut up this reason with a witty Epigram made upon one who in his writings undertook to foretell the very year of the World's consummation.

> Ninety-two years the World as yet shall stand,
> If it do stand or fall at your command.
> But say, why placed you not the World's end nigher?
> Lest ere you died you might be proved a liar.°

[22] The fifth and last reason which moved me to the undertaking of this Treatise was the weak grounds which the contrary opinion of the World's decay is founded upon. I am persuaded that the fictions of Poets was it which first gave life unto it. Homer hath touched upon this string, with whom Virgil accords, and they are both seconded by Juvenal and Horace. But above all that pretty invention of the Four Ages of the World, compared to four metals (Gold, Silver, Brass, and Iron) hath wrought such an impression in men's minds that it can hardly be rooted out ...

That which above all (as I conceive) hath made way for this opinion is the morosity and crooked disposition of old men, always complaining of the hardness of the present times, together with an excessive admiration of Antiquity, which is in a manner natural and inbred in us: *vetera extollimus, recentium incuriosi.*° For the former of these, old men, for the most part being much changed from that they were in their youth in complexion and temperature,° they are filled with sad melancholy thoughts, which make them think the World is changed, whereas in truth the change is in themselves ...

[31] There is no fear, then, of the natural decay of the Elements in regard of their quantity and dimensions. All the controversy is in regard of their quality, whether the air and water be so pure and wholesome, and the earth so fertile and fruitful, as it was some hundreds or thousands of years since. Touching the former, I think I shall make it appear that the World in former ages hath been plagued with more droughts, excessive rains, winds, frosts, snows, hails, famines, earthquakes, pestilences, and other contagious diseases, than in latter times. All which should argue a greater distemper in the Elements. And for the fruitfulness of the earth, I will not compare the present with that before the fall or before the flood. I know and believe that the one drew on a curse upon it (though some great Divines° hold that curse was rather in regard of man's ensuing labour

---

° **Ninety-two ... liar**: from John Owen's *Epigrammata* (1606), a spoof of John Napier's *Plain Discovery of the Whole Revelation of St John* (1593), which predicted that the world would end in 1688 or 1700.

° **vetera ... incuriosi**: "The ancient we extol, being careless of our own times" (from Tacitus, *Annals*, 2.88.4).

° **temperature**: humoral temperament.   ° **Divines**: a marginal note identifies the Jesuit Benedict Pereira (1536–1610).

° **fatness**: fertility.   ° **Upon ... lawful**: marginal note cites Genesis 9:3.

in dressing it than of the Earth's ensuing barrenness); and the other, by washing away the surface and fatness° thereof, and by incorporating the salt waters into it, much abated the native and original fertility thereof, and consequently the vigour and virtue of plants as well in regard of nourishment as medicine. Upon which occasion it seems after the Flood man had leave given him to feed upon the flesh of beasts and fowls and fishes, which before the Flood was not lawful° …

And for grounds which are continually rent and wounded with the ploughshare, worn and wasted with tillage, it is not to be wondered if they answer not the fertility of former ages. But for such as have time and rest given to recover their strength, and renew their decayed forces, or such as yet retain their virginity without any force offered unto them, I doubt not but experience and trial will make it good that they have lost nothing [32] of their primitive goodness, at leastwise since the Flood; and, consequently, that there is in the earth itself by long-lasting no such perpetual and universal decay in regard of the fruitfulness thereof, as is commonly imagined.

And if not in the earth itself, then surely not in the trees and herbs, and plants and flowers, which suck their nourishment from thence as so many infants from their mother's breast. Let any one kind of them that ever was in any part of the world since the Creation be named that is utterly lost.° No, God and Nature have so well provided against this that one seed sometimes multiplies in one year many thousands of the same kind. Let it be proved by comparing their present qualities with those which are recorded in ancient writers, that in the revolution of so many ages they have lost anything of their wonted colour, their smell, their taste, their virtue, their proportion, their duration. And if there be no such decay as is supposed to be found in the several kinds of vegetables, what reason have we to believe it in beasts, especially those that make vegetables their food?

If Aristotle were now alive, should he need to compose some new treatise *De historia animalium* in those things where he wrote upon certain grounds and experimental observations? Have the beasts of which he wrote anything altered their dispositions? Are the wild become tame, or the strong feeble? … Hath the Lion forgotten his majesty? Or the Elephant his sagacity? Or the Tiger his fierceness? Or the Stag his swiftness? Or the Dog his fidelity? Or the Fox his wiliness? Were the Oxen then of the same Country stronger for labour, the Horses better featured or more serviceable than now? Doubtless these lessons, as their Mistress cannot but teach them, so these scholars cannot but learn them: neither is it in their power to forget them.

※ ※ ※

° **lost**: Although the concept of extinction was proposed by Robert Hooke during the Restoration, it was not widely accepted until Georges Cuvier's work in the 1790s.

MICHAEL DRAYTON
from "Noah's Flood" (1630)

Early modern Christians not only believed that fire would consume the earth on Judgement Day, but also that a global flood had once nearly obliterated all life from it. In Genesis 6, God repents creating humans and tells Noah he will "destroy them with the earth." It is not hard to fathom the appeal of the flood myth for Michael Drayton. Alienated from the Stuart court, embittered by the tepid reception of *Poly-Olbion*, and alarmed at the environmental devastation of England, the aging Drayton had become increasingly pessimistic – about the fate of his own work, of England, and of the human race. Significantly, in the first edition in which it appeared "Noah's Flood" immediately follows the "Tenth Nymphal" [see Part v, p. 430], Drayton's attack on an unsustainable society that has consumed its natural resources.

It would be misleading, however, to frame the poem as nothing but a spiteful fantasy of God pressing the reset button. Over a third of it (seven pages) consists of a lively account of the procession of the embarking animals. The poem also vividly depicts the animals' joy when the dove returns with the olive branch and when, released from their year-long confinement, they "salute the ground" (1011). The "terror-preaching" Noah is more than a righteous prophet of doom. Drayton compares him to an innkeeper and even a forester: "as within the strong pale of a Park, / So were they altogether in the Ark" (359–60). The poem also opposes sceptics who dismiss the flood story as an improbable fiction. To those who claimed no ship could be large enough to house every single species, Drayton points to modern argosies. Since the human crew aboard the ark numbered only eight, Drayton contends there would have been more than enough room to stable the comparatively small number of species known in the seventeenth century, even accounting for those whose "kind decayed [are] now unknown to men" (354). Besides recognizing the reality of extinction long before Cuvier, Drayton even suggests that species evolve as they adapt to their surroundings: "by the soil they often altered be, / In shape and colour as we daily see" (556–8). Although largely based on Genesis (with flourishes borrowed from Ovid's retelling of the Deucalion and Pyrrha myth), Drayton's flood story makes some revealing departures from its biblical source. While Drayton's Noah does perform an animal sacrifice to give thanks for their deliverance, he is not given the right to subdue and butcher other creatures. Instead of God making a covenant with Noah not to destroy the earth, Noah addresses the animals directly. How do Drayton's catalogues of creatures in both this poem and *Poly-Olbion* function like verbal arks?
Source: *The Muses' Elysium* (1630), 105–9, 112–13, 116–17.

> By this the Sun had sucked up the vast deep,
> And in gross clouds like Cisterns did it keep.
> The Stars and signs by God's great wisdom set,
> By their conjunctions waters to beget,
> Had wrought their utmost, and even now began
> Th'Almighty's justice upon sinful man.
> From every several quarter of the sky,

640 The Thunder roars, and the fierce Lightnings fly
One at another and together dash,
Volley on volley, flash comes after flash.
Heaven's lights look sad, as they would melt away;
The night is com'n i' th' morning of the day.
The Card'nal Winds he makes at once to blow,
Whose blasts to buffets with such fury go
That they themselves into the Centre shot
Into the bowels of the earth and got,
Being condensed and strongly stiffened there,
650 In such strange manner multiplied the air,
Which turned to water,° and increased the springs
To that abundance, that the earth forth brings
Water to drown herself, should heaven deny
With one small drop the Deluge to supply,
That through her pores the soft and spongy earth,
As in a dropsy or unkindly birth,
A Woman, swollen, sends from her fluxive° womb
Her oozy springs, that there was scarcely room
For the waste waters which came in so fast,
660 As though the earth her entrails up would cast.°
But these seemed yet but easily let go,
And from some Sluice came softly in and slow,
Till God's great hand so squeezed the boist'rous clouds
That from the spouts of heaven's embattled shrouds,
Even like a Floodgate plucked up by the height,
Came the wild rain, with such a pond'rous weight,
As that the fierceness of the hurrying flood
Removed huge Rocks and rammed them into mud,
Pressing the ground with that impetuous power,
670 As that the first shock of this drowning shower
Furrowed the earth's late plump and cheerful face
Like an old Woman, that in little space
With rivelled° cheeks and with bleared, blubbered eyes,
She wistly° looked upon the troubled skies.
Up to some Mountain as the people make,
Driving their Cattle till the shower should slake,°
The Flood o'ertakes them, and away doth sweep
Great herds of Neat° and mighty flocks of Sheep.
Down through a valley as one stream doth come,
680 Whose roaring strikes the neighbouring Echo dumb,
Another meets it, and whilst there they strive,
Which of them two the other back should drive,
Their dreadful currents they together dash,

° **water**: a marginal note here reads, "Water is but air condensed."   ° **fluxive**: flowing.
° **cast**: vomit.   ° **rivelled**: shrivelled.   ° **wistly**: mournfully.
° **slake**: slacken.   ° **Neat**: cattle.

So that their waves like furious Tides do wash
The head of some near hill, which falleth down
For very fear, as it itself would drown.
Some back their Beasts, so hoping to swim out,
But by the Flood encompassèd about
Are overwhelmed; some clamber up to Towers,
But these and them the Deluge soon devours; 690
Some to the top of Pines and Cedars get,
Thinking themselves they safely there should set,
But the rude Flood that over all doth sway,
Quickly comes up and carrieth them away.
The Roe's much swiftness doth no more avail
Nor help him now than if he were a Snail.
The swift-winged Swallow and the slow-winged Owl,
The fleetest Bird and the most flagging Fowl,
Are at one pass; the Flood so high hath gone,
There was no ground to set a foot upon. 700
Those Fowl that followed moistness now it fly,
And leave the wet Land to find out the dry;
But by the mighty tempest beaten down,
On the blank° water they do lie and drown.
The strong-built Tower is quickly overborne;
The o'er-grown Oak out of the earth is torn:
The subtle° shower the earth hath softened so,
And with the waves the trees tossed to and fro,
That the roots loosen and the tops down sway,
So that whole Forests quickly swim away. 710
Th'offended heaven had shut up all her lights,
The Sun nor Moon make neither days nor nights.
The waters so exceedingly abound
That in short time the Sea itself is drowned:
That by the freshness of the falling rain,
Neptune no more his saltness doth retain,
So that those scaly creatures used to keep
The mighty wastes of the immeasured deep,
Finding the gen'ral and their natural brack°
The taste and colour everywhere to lack, 720
Forsake those Seas wherein they swam before,
Strangely oppressèd with their wat'ry store.°
The crooked Dolphin on those Mountains plays,
Whereas before that time not many days
The Goat was grazing; and the mighty Whale
Upon a Rock out of his way doth fall,
From whence before one eas'ly might have seen
The wand'ring clouds far under to have been.
The Grampus° and the Whirlpool,° as they rove,
Lighting by chance upon a lofty Grove 730
Under this world of waters, are so much

° **blank**: vacant. ° **subtle**: treacherous. ° **brack**: salt water. ° **store**: abundance.
° **Grampus**: orca. ° **Whirlpool**: spouting whale.

Pleased with their wombs each tender branch to touch,
That they leave slime upon the curlèd Sprays,°
On which the Birds sung their harmonious Lays.
As huge as Hills still waves are wallowing° in,
Which from the world so wondrously do win,
That the tall Mountains which on tiptoe stood,
As though they scorned the force of any flood,
No eye of heav'n of their proud tops could see

740   One foot from this great inundation free.
As in the Chaos ere the frame was fixed,
The Air and Water were so strongly mixed,
And such a Bulk of Grossness do compose,
As in those thick Clouds which the Globe enclose,
Th'all-working Spirit were yet again to wade,
And heav'n and earth again were to be made …
     Never such joy was since the world began,
As in the Ark, when Noah and his behold
The Olive leaf, which certainly them told
The flood decreased; and they such comfort take
That, with their mirth, the Birds and Beasts they make
Sportive, which send forth such a hollow noise
As said they were partakers of their joys:
The Lion roars, but quickly doth forbear,

880   Lest he thereby the lesser Beasts should fear;
The Bull doth bellow and the Horse doth neigh;
The Stag, the Buck, and the shag-haired Goat do bray;
The Boar doth grunt; the Wolf doth howl; the Ram
Doth bleat, which yet so faintly from him came,
As though for very joy he seemed to weep;
The Ape and Monkey such a chatt'ring keep
With their thin lips, which they so well expressed,
As they would say, "We hope to be released!";
The silly Ass set open such a throat

890   That all the Ark resounded with the note;
The watchful Dog doth play and skip and bark,
And leaps upon his Masters in the Ark;
The Raven croaks and the carrion Crow doth squall;
The Pie° doth chatter and the Partridge call;
The jocund Cock crows as he claps his wings;
The Merle° doth whistle and the Mavis° sings;
The Nightingale strains her melodious throat,
Which of the small Birds being heard to rote°
They soon set to her, each a part doth take,

900   As by their music up a Choir to make;
The Parrot lately sad, then talks and jeers,
And counterfeiteth every sound he hears;
The purblind Owl which heareth all this do,
T'express her gladness cries, "Too-whit, too-whoo!"

° **Sprays**: branches.   ° **wallowing**: surging.   ° **Pie**: magpie.
° **Merle**: blackbird.   ° **Mavis**: thrush.   ° **rote**: repeat.

No Beast nor Bird was in the Ark with Noy,°
But in their kind expressed some sign of joy ...
When the almighty God bade Noah to set
Open the Ark, at liberty to let
The Beasts, the Birds, and creeping things, which came
Like as when first they went into the same,
Each male comes down, his female by his side,
As 'twere the Bridegroom bringing out his Bride,
Till th'Ark was emptied; and that mighty load,
For a whole year that there had been bestowed
(Since first that forty-days' still-falling rain
That drowned the world, was then dried up again),   1010
Which with much gladness do salute the ground:
The lighter sort some caper, and some bound;°
The heavier creatures tumble them,° as glad
That they such ease by their enlargement had;
The creeping things together fall to play,
Joyed beyond measure for this happy day;
The Birds let from this Cage do mount the Sky
To show they yet had not forgot to fly,
And sporting them upon the airy plain,
Yet to their master Noah they stoop again,   1020
To leave his presence and do still forbear
Till they from him of their release might hear;
The Beasts each other woo; the Birds they bill,
As they would say to Noah they meant to fill
The roomy earth, then altogether void,
And make, what late the deluge has destroyed ...
When to these living things quoth righteous Noah,
"Now take you all free liberty to go,
And every way do you yourselves disperse,
Till you have filled this globy universe
With your increase; let every soil be yours.
He that hath saved thee faithfully assures
Your propagation.° And dear wife," quoth he,
"And you my children, let your trust still be
In your preserver, and on him rely,
Whose promise is that we should multiply
Till in our days, of nations we shall hear
From us poor few in th'Ark that lately were."
To make a new world, thus works everyone;
The Deluge ceaseth, and the old is gone.

° **Noy**: Noah.   ° **bound**: leap.
° **them**: themselves.   ° **propagation**: see Genesis 9:10–11.

Industrialization and Environmental Legislation in the Early Anthropocene: A Timeline

1490   First blast furnace at Queenstock, Buxted.

1496   Blast furnace at Ashdown Forest in the Weald.

1503   c. 11 Act against Deer-hays and Buckstalls.
        Outlaws the use of ditches and nets in forests, chases, and parks and
        blames them for the "destruction of red deer and fallow."

1511   c. 11 Act for the Appointing of Physicians and Surgeons.
        Prohibits unlicensed physicians from dispensing medicines and ac-
        cuses "ignorant persons" who do so, such as "smiths, weavers, and
        women," of "sorceries and witchcraft."

1512   c. 8 Strode's Act.
        Exonerates Richard Strode, an MP from Devon (himself a tinner)
        who was imprisoned by the tinners' Stannaries court for attempting
        to introduce legislation restricting mining rights and calling "for
        the reformation of the perishing, hurting, and destroying of diverse
        ports, havens, and creeks."

1513   Construction of Henry VIII's great warship, *Henry Grace à Dieu*,
        consumes 1,752 tons of timber (*State Papers Henry VIII*, 8, fol. 146.)
        It has been estimated that Tudor warships required 2,000 mature
        oaks or 50 acres of woodlands (Perlin 175–6), and a fleet like the
        Spanish Armada would need 6 million cubic metres of timber
        (McNeil 398).

1522   c. 12 Act against Unlawful Hunting the Hare.
        Complains that the "game is now decayed and almost utterly de-
        stroyed" due to overhunting.

1523   c. 10 Henry VIII renews treaty with Denmark (first negotiated
        by Henry VII in 1490) to grant English fishing rights in Icelandic
        waters, suggesting that the demand for fish was exceeding supply.
        Disputes over these fishing rights created friction with Denmark
        throughout the Tudor era.
        Letter urges Cardinal Wolsey (recently appointed Bishop of Dur-
        ham) to delve more coal pits in Northumberland (Cotton Titus

B/I, fol. 301). Parliament debates a bill allowing mine-shafts to be drained onto another person's land.

1527 Proclamation Ordering Enclosures Destroyed and Tillage Restored (MS Harley 442/42).
A response to dearth. The proclamation provoked anti-enclosure riots.

1529 c. 8. Act for the Bringing up and Rearing of Calves to Increase the Multitude of Cattle.
Prohibits farmers from slaughtering newborn cattle to inflate the price of meat. Renewed in 1532 as Act "Against Killing of Calves … and Weanlings," and enlarged in 1609.

1530 c. 11 Act Concerning Powdike in Marshland.
Condemns the "perverse and malicious cutting down and breaking up" of dikes and banks for draining and enclosing fens in Norfolk and Cambridge, and criminalizes such acts as felonies.

1531 c. 5 Statute of Sewers.
Empowers the Commission of Sewers to inspect drains and embankments to prevent flooding, and impose fines on those who fail to maintain them.
c. 8 Act for Havens in the West Parts.
Condemns tin-miners for "choking" water-ways with "earth, slime, and filth" and forbids their "stream-works" in Devonshire and Cornwall "nigh to any of the said fresh-waters, rivers, or low places." Reissued due to non-compliance in 1535, despite a Stannaries statute of 1533 agreeing that all stream-works must deposit their "gravel, rubble, sands, in old hatches, tippets, miry places, or other convenient places, from the said great rivers" (D2ᵛ).
c. 18 Act for Pulling Down and Avoiding of Fish Garths … Set in the River and Water of Ouse and Humber.

1532 c. 10 Act for the Destruction of Crows, Rooks, and Choughs.
With England reeling from a recent dearth, Parliament places a bounty on seed-eating birds, similar to Mao Zedong's 1958 "Kill a Sparrow" campaign. Strengthened in 1566.

1533 c. 6 Act against Buggery.
Declares it a felony to commit buggery "with mankind or beast." Renewed in 1536, 1540, 1548; repealed 1553; reinstated 1563.
c. 7 Act against Catching Young Spawn or Fry of Eels and Salmon.
Imposes a ten-year moratorium on fishing during spawning season; penalized by a £5 fine and destruction of one's nets.
c. 11 Act against Destruction of Wild Fowl.
Punishes the stealing of bird eggs with one-year imprisonment and fine (excepting those identified as vermin in the 1532 Act).

c. 12 Concerning the Number of Sheep One Should Keep.
Caps number at 2,400 amidst concerns that sheep pasture reduced arable land and displaced dairy farming.

1534 Proclamation Punishing Grain-hoarders.

1535 c. 18 Act for the Preservation of the River Thames.
Imposes 100 shilling fine for "mining, digging, casting of dung and rubbish" in the river. City Council adds 1s. 8d. fine, and requires each ward to install grates to sift out waste.
c. 22 Act Restoring Tillage.
Crown to receive a moiety of profits from lands converted from tillage to pasture within the past three years until they are reconverted.

1536 c. 26 Laws in Wales.
Officially placing Wales under English jurisdiction, this act facilitates trade and makes it easier for England to extract resources. It abolishes the feudal Welsh Marches and the Welsh custom of partible inheritance, consolidating estates and farms in fewer hands.
John Leland observes rampant deforestation in Wales, and that a lead mine in Cardiganshire has "ceased because the wood is sore wasted" (3:118–23).

1538 Proclamation annulling the "law and custom of abstaining from white meats" (milk, butter, eggs, cheese) during Lent (Harley MS 442/115). Issued in 1542.

1539 c. 2 Act against Poaching in Fishponds.
c. 12 Act against Stealing of Hawks' Eggs and Poaching Deer and Conies.
Ironworks built by the Crown at Stumbletts; William Sidney erects ironworks at Robertsbridge Abbey (and adds a second three years later near Panningridge woods).

1541 Proclamation permitting consumption of meat on St Mark's Day (25 April).
Proclamation enlarging Hatfield Chase (Harley MS 442/137).

1542 c. 3 Act for Assize of Coal and Wood.
c. 8 The Herbalists' Charter.
Permits persons who are not surgeons but have "knowledge and experience of the nature of herbs, roots and waters" to practise medicine. Overturns 1511 legislation.
Proclamation Protecting Hawks.
"No person or persons of what estate, degree, nation, or condition soever he or they be ... shall steal, ... take, [or] keep ... any egg or eggs, bird or birds, of any goshawks, tercels, or lannerets within this

realm or other the King's dominions. Nor during the space of one whole year next after this present proclamation … [shall they] keep or bring up, or cause to be kept or brought up, any sore [under one-year old] hawk of any of the kinds of hawks above remembered, upon hand, in mew or otherwise, within this realm … upon pain to lose and forfeit for every such offence £100 sterling, whereof one tenth to the discoverers and takers, the rest to the King's highness" (Harley MS 442/141).

1543   c. 7 Act Prohibiting Fishing out of Season.
A Royal Proclamation from this year likewise warns that the use of nets and other engines will bring about the "utter destruction, spoil, and decay of the small fish and fry" in the Thames.
c. 9 Act for Reclaiming Wapping Marsh.
Drained the following year by Cornelius Vanderelf.
c. 10 Act Concerning London's Water Supply.
c. 17 Act for the Preservation of Woods.
Known as the "Statute of Woods," this bill represents the first major legislative effort to protect England's beleaguered woodlands. It had five provisions: (1) in any copsed (i.e. managed) woods "felled at twenty-four years growing or under, there shall be left standing and unfelled … twelve standels or storers of oak" per acre or the owner to pay a fine of 3s. 4d. per tree; (2) any copsed woods felled within fourteen years or under must be enclosed for four years to keep deer from devouring new growth – a similar law had been passed in 1483; (3) any woods cut between fourteen and twenty-four years to be enclosed for six years; (4) no woods or copses larger than two acres or farther than two furlongs from the owner's residence could be converted into farmland or pasture; (5) anyone felling woods or copses older than twenty-four years must leave twelve standels per acre and let them grow another twenty years or pay a fine of 6s. 8d. per tree.

1545   Proclamations for Preservation of Game in Combe Park and Westminster.
Earl of Rutland re-establishes ironworks at Rievaulx Abbey, adding a blast furnace in 1577.

1546   Bill introduced to permit Sir Nicholas Strelley to drain coal pits and pump out water onto the land of Sir John Willoughby, noting "there would be dearth of fuel in the county of Nottingham but for the kind called sea-coal" (SP 1/445, fol. 241).

1547   Proclamation permits export of grain due to abundant harvest.
Proclamation for the Preservation of Game in the Manor of Grafton.

1548   c.11 Act for Restraint on the Exportation of Leather and Salt Hides. Proclamation calls for continuance of Lenten fast as a "worldly and civil policy … to spare flesh and use fish for the benefit for the commonwealth" (Grafton 10ᵛ).

1549   The Lord Protector orders a commission headed by Thomas Cawarden, Master of the Revels, to investigate "the hurts done by iron mills and furnaces" in Sussex by depleting woodlands. The report identifies 53 mills and furnaces operating in Sussex and declares each one "spendeth at the least yearly 1,500 [later estimated at 3,000] loads of great wood made into coals," and complains of "the great and noisome spoil of the said woods … for lack of cherishing of the increase of the same so felled to the use of the iron mills." The report further blames the mills for driving up prices in the region due to the "scanty" supply of timber, and warns "many a thousand not yet born [will] feel with their parents the great hurt and incommodity engendered by their continuance" (*Calendar of the Manuscripts of the Most Hon. the Marquess of Salisbury*, 13, 20–4).
Proclamation Enforcing Previous Statutes against Enclosures.
Emboldened by King Edward's denunciation of enclosure, some 16,000 protestors lead by Robert Kett destroy hedges, fill in ditches, and pillage parks and chases in Norfolk. While Edward sympathized with their grievances (issuing a pardon if they desisted), he condemned their brash attempt to redress the "over-exploitation of communal resources" (Wood 2007, 66) as mob rule. Within a month, the Norfolk Rising was crushed and Kett executed.

1550   Proclamation for Avoiding of Sole Persons out of the City of London. All unemployed non-native Londoners who arrived in the city within the past three years ordered to leave immediately.

1552   c. 7 Act to Bring Down the Price of Wool.
The most restrictive of several early modern acts to discourage wool speculators, this legislation marks the end of the high wool prices that prevailed in the first half of the century, which had led to sheep pasture gobbling up fields and woodlands.

1553   c. 7 Act on Assize of Fuel.
Imposes a fine on fuel merchants for selling false-sized bundles of firewood and charcoal, and regulates the weights, measures, and costs of fuel. Revised and reissued in 1601.
Proclamation calls for greater provision of firewood for London; Citizens of York promote a bill to forbid destruction of woods within a sixteen-mile radius of the city (York Civic Records 24:87).

1554   c. 5 Act to Restrain Carrying of Corn, Victuals, and Wood Over the Sea.
Proclamation Enlarging Rockingham Forest.

1556 Proclamation Prohibiting Hunting at Greenwich.
Richard Showard's Chancery case against Thomas and William Tropnell for polluting the stream at Chilcompton with their dye or woad-house, which "hath so corrupted the water of the same river or brook that thereby is … the fish within the same [and] the great fish ponds … destroyed but also is the same water become so unwholesome that your said orator nor any of his men or tenants … can use the same for dressing of their meat, making of their drink, as for any other necessaries" (National Archives, Chancery Records C1/1474/26–27).

1559 c. 15 An Act that Timber Shall Not Be Felled to Make Coals for Burning of Iron.
Known as the "Timber Act," it forbids ironworks within fourteen miles of the sea, but exempts major iron-manufacturing centres in Sussex and Surrey. A bill was debated in Parliament the following year proposing ironworks should be banished the realm.
c. 17 Act to Punish Unlawful Fishing, and Preserve the Spawn of Fish and Fry.
In his *Art of Navigation* (1577), John Dee estimates that failure to abide by these laws destroyed over 200,000 cartloads of fish per year, enough to feed 300,000 people for six days (44–5).
Proclamation Enforcing Abstinence from Meat.
Imposes £ 20 fine for selling meat during Lent. Those unable to pay must "stand one market day in the market time openly upon the pillory during the space of six hours." Reissued 1560–2, 1568, 1573–5, 1579, 1584–5, 1587–9, 1594–5, 1598, 1600.

1562 Bevis Bulmer delves lead mines in Mendip Hills.
Queen grants patent to manufacture salt from evaporated sea-water. Inland salt-making in Cheshire was blamed for the "great and notable destruction of wood" (Leland 2:94).

1563 c. 5 Act Touching Politic Constitutions for the Maintenance of the Navy.
Raises the number of fish days to three per week (adding Wednesday to Friday and Saturday), although the decision was apparently unpopular and difficult to enforce (repealed 1585 c.11); requires farmers to devote one acre out of sixty to flax and hemp, used in manufacture of rope and sailcloth – a revision of 27 Henry VIII c. 4.
c. 36 Act for the Inning [Reclamation] of Erith and Plumstead Marsh.
First mentioned in a 1530 Act; updated in 1580 and 1584.
c. 21 Act for Punishing of Unlawful Taking of Fish, Deer, and Hawks.

1564   Survey of Forest of Radnor reports "800 acres of land, roots, and bushes of small hazel and thorns utterly destroyed by reason the same have been hewn and cut down by the inhabitants" (Rees 881).

1565   William Humfrey, William Cecil, and Christopher Schütz establish mines and erect a blast furnace at Tintern for smelting ore to make brass and iron (for metal combs for carding wool).

1566   c. 15 The Second Tudor Vermin Act.
A "defining point" in English attitudes towards wildlife (Lovegrove 81). Whereas the 1532 Act specifically targeted seed-eating birds, the 1566 legislation brands a large number of birds and mammals undesirable pests and places bounties on their heads: Starlings and Mice (1 penny for twelve heads); Crows, Jackdaws, Magpies, Rooks, Rats (1 penny for three); Moles (halfpenny a head); Woodpeckers, Jays, Ravens, Kites, Kingfishers, Bullfinches, Stoat, Weasel, Polecat or Wildcat (1 penny a head); Harrier Hawk, Bustard, Cormorant, Otter, Hedgehog (2 pence a head); Sea-eagle and Osprey (four pence a head); Fox and Badger (12 pence a head). The Act was renewed in 1572 and 1598, and not repealed until 1863! Compliance would have varied widely, but by the end of the seventeenth century around 50 per cent of parishes list payments for the killing of vermin (Lovegrove 84).

1567   Patent to manufacture window glass granted to Jean Carré and Anthony Becku on condition they teach English craftsmen (passed to Venetian Jacob Verzelini in 1574). Glasshouses consume vast quantities of timber.

1568   All mines of gold and silver in the realm declared to be the property of the queen, who grants a joint monopoly on mining to two companies: the Company of Mineral and Battery Works and the Society of Mines-Royal.

1570   William Humfrey develops first water-powered lead-smelting furnace at Beauchief Abbey, near Sheffield.

1571   c. 19 Wool Cap Act.
Requires every male commoner over the age of six to wear a wool cap on Sundays and holidays to support the wool trade. Reissued in 1590, 1597.

1574   Survey of "woods felled within these twenty years last past in diverse clothing parishes, which have been the best wooded in the Weald of Kent" estimates the loss at 6,542 acres. While much of this was copsed, only 607 acres were untouched. A survey by the Privy Council finds 51 furnaces and 50 forges in operation in the Weald, and stipulates they must have permission to cast guns or face a fine of £200 (SP 12/93, fol. 148).

1575   Commission of Sewers orders James Clifford to remove rubbish excavated from his coal pit (near Broseley, Shropshire) that he had dumped in the River Severn.

1576   Mayors and aldermen of Sussex write a letter to Lord Buckhurst complaining of the deforestation caused by his ironworks.

1577   Elizabeth grants the Muscovy Company a monopoly on whaling.

1578   Brewers of London promise to burn no more sea-coal near Westminster but wood only (SP 12/127, fol. 117).
        Lord Burghley considers profits to be made by manufacturing oil from seeds (Lansdowne 26/48).
        Proposal to punish soap-makers who use fish oil and tallow (Lansdowne 26/54).
        Thomas Danby purchases former monastic woodlands around Kirkstall Abbey to supply ironworks near Leeds.

1580   c. 5 Act Touching Iron Mills.
        Forbids sale of trees growing within twenty-two miles of London or the Thames to the iron industry (exempting the Weald). Thomas Norton serves on a committee to investigate loss of woodlands.
        c. 7 An Act for the Increase of Mariners.
        Outlaws importing of fish to encourage England's domestic fishing industry to send "two hundred sail and more" into Icelandic waters.
        Burghley reportedly creates oak nursery at Windsor Great Park.
        William Overton establishes glasshouses in Staffordshire that decimate Bishop's Wood.
        Royal Proclamation forbids building of new houses or tenements within three miles of the city of London (to discourage urban sprawl and spread of plague).
        Inquiry into "encroachment and spoil" in the Forest of Pickering. It is subsequently estimated that there are 5,000 sheep in the forest for every red deer (NA DL 44/287).

1582   Peter Morbis devises a system to convey water into Londoners' homes via lead pipes.

1584   c. 19 Act for Preservation of Timber
        Forbids erection of new iron mills in the Weald and imposes £300 fine for felling timber trees to make charcoal.
        Orders issued for the conservation of the Thames (Lansdowne MS 41/15). Aims to preserve navigation on the Thames, specifies that "no dung, rubbish, or other filth be cast into" the river, and regulates the fishing trade.
        Bill to suppress glasshouses cites concern over "preservation of timber." In 1589 George Longe proposes moving all glassworks to Ireland.

1585   Bill to prohibit starch-manufacturing debated in House of Commons.

Glassworks operating at Knole House (owned by Thomas Sackville) denudes Hookwood in two years.

Proclamation against the Sowing of Woad.

Prohibits it with four miles of cities and market towns. Used as a dye, woad was profitable but reduced the acreage devoted to food production, and the queen found its smell offensive. Strengthened in 1600 so that offenders were immediately imprisoned.

Walter Ralegh appointed Lord Warden of the Stannaries (courts governing the tin-mining industry in Devon and Cornwall). Succeeded in 1604 by William Herbert, Earl of Pembroke.

1586   Considerations for the Relief of the People in the Time of the Dearth (Lansdowne MS 48/52).

1587   Queen grants mining rights in North Wales to painter Nicholas Hilliard (who transfers them to Richard Grosvenor).

John Spillman operates the first English paper mill (making paper from rag pulp), near Dartford – commemorated in Thomas Churchyard's poem *A Spark of Friendship*.

1588   c. 7 Erection of Cottages Act.

Outlaws construction of squatters' cottages on commons, and stipulates new dwellings must be attached to four acres of land (extended in 1593 to areas surrounding London to prevent urban sprawl).

Earl of Hertford petitions queen for grant to dig and sell "moor-coal" or peat as alternative fuel to timber, following "the method of Mr. Topcliffe" (Lansdowne MS 57/60; 59/74).

1589   1,000 marks collected for cleansing of Fleet Ditch, but according to John Stow "the effect failed; so that the brook … is now become worse cloyed than ever it was before" (10).

Sir Fulke Greville obtains twenty-one-year lease of two iron forges, two furnaces, and timber in Staffordshire; over the next two decades he obliterates the Cannock Chase woodlands.

Letter to Burghley proposes fuelling blast furnaces with coal instead of charcoal (Lansdowne MS 59/71), and patent granted to T. Proctor (59/73). The process was eventually perfected at Coalbrooke Dale in 1709.

1590   Proclamation Enforcing the Statute against Water Pollution.

Reviving a 1390 sanitation statute that targeted the keepers of the Bear Gardens, who were dumping animal carcasses in the river, it orders Londoners to "forbear to cast or put forth any entrails of beasts or other filth or noisome thing whatsoever" into the waterways of the city and suburbs.

Sir Francis Willoughby, whose family owned lucrative coal pits near Wollaton, erects blast furnace at ironworks in Middleton and at Oakamoor in Staffordshire.

Bess of Hardwick acquires glassworks at South Wingfield to build her show-house ("Hardwick Hall, more glass than wall"). She also managed ironworks and coalmines, inherited from her four husbands. (Chatsworth House Hardwick MS 10, 25ᵛ.)

Destruction of smelting mill on Holywell Brook, Flintshire.

Accused of destroying a mill belonging to William Ratcliff, the defendants insist polluted water had harmed people and cattle (NA E 134/32 and 33 Eliz/Mich6).

1591　Proposal to purify pit-coal and free it from noxious smell (Lansdowne MS 67/20).

1592　John Taverner reports to Lord Burghley of "disorders committed in the Queen's woods" (Lansdowne MS 69/89).

1593　Bill presented in House of Commons for the "maintenance of clothing in the parish of Cranbrook."

Seeks to prohibit the construction of new ironworks and require ironmasters use only wood from their own lands, but does not pass.

Letter to Lord Burghley complains that Mr Hanley's ironworks at Tintern "hath utterly wasted more than the one half of the woods in Monmouthshire" (Lansdowne MS 75/90).

Earliest extant reference to ironworks and blast furnace in Munster near Spenser's Irish estate.

1594　Aldermen of Gloucester complain to Burghley of the "havoc made of their timber allowed them out of the Forest of Dean" (Lansdowne MS 76/64).

1595　Letter to Burghley advocates prohibiting export of non-caking coal (Lansdowne MS 65/9). Coal prices rise sharply, as shipments cannot meet demand, and the City of London appoints Christopher Lewen to inquire into abuses and increase output from Newcastle pits.

Scottish mining engineer Sir George Bruce constructs the moat pit at Culross, the first coalmine to tunnel under the sea. King James visits in 1617 and the poet John Taylor in 1619 (see his *Penniless Pilgrimage*, E1ʳ–E3ʳ).

1596　Proclamation Enforcing Orders against Dearth.

Condemns the "unreasonable increase of prices" for grain, and forbids manufacture of starch without patent. Sir John Pakington had been awarded the patent in 1593 (later acquired by Robert Cecil).

Jerome Bowes opens glassworks in Blackfriars, near the site of the theatre. Shut down in 1615.

1597　c. 2 Tillage Act.

Declares arable land converted to pasture during Elizabeth's reign must be converted back and farmed. Repealed in 1624 when the grain supply was deemed sufficient.

1598   Anthony Bradshaw presides over swainmotes in Duffield Frith, and fines "vert trespassers" (illegal woodcutters).

1600   Proclamation prohibits export and hoarding of grain.
        Founding of The East India Company.
        At Ingatestone, Essex, anyone caught stealing firewood to be whipped, and purchasers forced to sit in the stocks all Sunday (Rackham 1986, 190).

1601   c. 7 "An Act to Avoid and Prevent Diverse Misdemeanours"
        Punishes "illicit cutting and mischievous spoiling of woods, trees, or poles."
        c. 11 Act for Recovery of Many Hundred Thousand Acres of Marshes and other Grounds.
        The "Drainage Act" kickstarts serious investment in wetlands "reclamation."
        Parliament debates a bill "to restrain the excessive use of coaches within this realm."
        "Propositions for enclosing diverse parcels of the moors and commons belonging to the forest of Pickering" to prevent "encroachments" (SP 12/277/101).

1602   Roger Mostyn acquires rights to colliery in Flintshire, sinking more pits and increasing production (£700 annually by 1619).
        Richard Carew writes *Survey of Cornwall*, urging Ralegh, the Lord Warden of the Stannaries (tin-miners' court), to redress some environmental problems caused by tin-mining.

1603   c. 22 Act Concerning Tanners.
        Limits felling oak trees with bark worth over 2s. a cartload to between 1 April and 30 June.
        c. 27 Act ... for Preservation of the Game of Pheasants and Partridges, and Against Destroying Hares with Hare-pipes and Tracing Hares in the Snow.
        Renewed 1609 since this act "hath not yielded that good success ... as was hoped."
        Proclamation Against Unlawful Hunting.
        Shortly after ascending the throne, James strengthens anti-poaching laws and begins campaign to replenish depleted game stocks in royal forests.
        Enfield Chase Riots: an assembly of women prevent servants of Robert Cecil from taking firewood from Enfield Chase, claiming his rights had expired after the death of Queen Elizabeth and the wood must be burned in the king's house or given to the poor (SP 14/1/25).
        Brigstock Park Riots: Robert Cecil acquires rights to enclose deer park at Brigstock (formerly part of royal forest of Rockingham),

depriving people of hunting and timber rights. When Cecil ordered trees to be felled and carted away, a "tumultuous assembly" including a "troop of lewd women" began to harass the woodcutters, and deer were poached (SP 14/1/76).

Surveyor John Taverner decries felling of 2,000 oak trees in Pembrokeshire as a violation of timber laws.

1604   Edward Winter receives royal licence to fell trees for charcoal to fuel his ironworks in parishes of Newland and Lydney.

Coalmine in Griff, Warwickshire, records sales of £693 since August of previous year.

1605   Proclamation forbids timber fit for building to be used as firewood, and orders all buildings in and about London to be fronted with brick.

James grants licence to Jeffrey Duppa, the royal brewer, to fell 500 beeches in his park at King's Langley for firewood.

Ironworks at Sowley and Titchfield developed by the Earl of Southampton in the 1590s blamed for local timber shortage (SC/6).

c. 12 Act for the Better Preservation of Sea-fish.

c. 13 Act Against Unlawful Hunting.

Renews 5 Eliz. c. 21.

c. 18 Act for the Bringing in of a Fresh Stream of Water to the North Parts of the City of London.

Beginning of the New River project, completed 1613, and commemorated in Thomas Middleton's *Honorable Entertainments* (1621).

Fisherman Robert Ashwell "set openly in the stocks in Cheapside with a paper over his head containing these words: viz. 'for destroying of roaches great with spawn in the river of Thames at unseasonable times'" (Repertory of the London Court of Aldermen, vol. 26.2, fol. 343).

1606   c. 13 Act for the Draining of Certain Fens and Low Grounds in the Isle of Ely (the Waldersea Drainage Act).

Anonymous letter to King James denounces the draining of the fens by "covetous bloody Popham" (Chief Justice of the King's Bench), blames glasshouses and iron mills for driving up the price of timber tenfold (claiming they "shortly will consume all the timber and wood in England"), decries woad-growing and starch-manufacturing for exacerbating dearth, and calls for stricter enforcement of the Lenten fast. It concludes by unfavourably comparing James to Queen Elizabeth, boldly stating, "Your majesty wanteth some of her knowledge, breeding, and stomach" (MS State Papers Domestic, James I, SP 14/19, fol. 97).

Thomas Chaloner, an Oxford-educated courtier with an interest in alchemy, launches the English chemical industry by setting up the first alum works in Ravenscar on the North Yorkshire coast. To manufacture alum (a fixative for wool-dying), shale must be stacked in towers nearly 100 feet high and fired for nine months consecutively, then tipped into pools of water and mixed with urine and seaweed. The aroma would have been pungent, and the ecological impact severe: the mining pits scarred the landscape, the fires consumed massive quantities of timber, and ash and chemical by-products such as sulphuric acid contaminated the waterways. Founding of the Virginia Company.

1607   The Midlands Revolt. James dispatches troops to suppress an anti-enclosure riot in Northamptonshire. The "Diggers" of Warwickshire issue a statement defending the protests: "we as members of the whole do feel the smart of these encroaching tyrants, which would grind our flesh upon the whetstone of poverty, and make our loyal hearts to faint with breathing, so that they may dwell by themselves in the midst of their herds of fat wethers" (Harley MS 787, 9ᵛ). Sir George Hay erects ironworks in Ross-shire, which operated for three years "until the wood of it was spent." With commission from King James, Hay then founded the first glassworks in Scotland.

1608   Proclamation for Remedying Dearth of Grain.
King James orders survey of royal forests to determine the compliance with timber preservation laws and increase acres of copsed woodlands. Survey of forests south of the Trent finds 52,743 acres of woodlands remaining, of which 44,432 were in forests, 5,889 in parks, and 2,442 in chases. Thomas Hampton's survey of the New Forest puts its bounds at 75,000 acres, "whereof 15,000 are woods which are greatly destroyed without lawful warrant by the officers or by their permission. And yet the king's woods there are worth £15,000 to be sold" (BL Add. MS 38444).
Lord Mayor petitions Privy Council to outlaw starch-making in England, which exacerbated dearth by consuming bran. Richard Brown, a former starch-maker, supports the motion, adding, "the issue of their sour waters, if it happen to run into ponds … empoisoneth and killeth all the fish in them. And if it touch the root of any tree they never carry fruit nor leaf after" (Cotton MS Titus BV/113, fol. 315).
James imports wild boar (locally extinct in southern England) from France and releases them in Windsor Great Park; another sounder was imported and released three years later (McGregor).
James orders Dame Katherine Corbet of Woodbastwick, Norfolk, to preserve for his use an eyrie of hawks breeding in her woods.
James greenlights felling of trees to build hunting lodges at the New Forest and Chapel Hainault.

James employs Anthony Dias and Paulo Pineto, Portuguese importers of Brazil wood and sugars, in his "mineral works."

Nicholas Romero and Jas. Jackson receive patent to build machine-frames with metal and stone instead of wood to save fuel.

1609   Proclamation against Hunters, Stealers, and Killers of Deer within any of the King's Majesty's Forests, Chases, or Parks.

c. 9 Act for Bringing of Fresh Streams of Water from Hackney Marsh to Chelsea.

c. 17 Act against the Burning of Ling and Heath.

Prohibits the burning of moorlands in spring and summer, lamenting the "great destruction of the Brood of Wild-fowl and Moor-game" by the "multitude of gross vapours, and Clouds arising from those great fires," which "blast [the] fruits of the earth."

c. 20 Act for Speedy Recovery of Many Thousand Acres of Marsh Ground ... within Norfolk and Suffolk, Lately Surrounded by the Rage of the Sea.

1610   Proclamation forbids the manufacturing of starch without royal patent (reissued 1620).

William Slingsby receives patent to use sea-coal as an industrial fuel instead of timber.

1611   Hopelessly in debt, King James agrees (after resisting similar proposals in 1604 and 1609) to disafforest Crown woodlands and assarts, and sell them off to raise 3 million pounds. A licence is issued to fell 1,800 oaks, mostly from the New Forest.

1612   As newly appointed Warden of Forest of Dean, the 3rd Earl of Pembroke acquires rights to sell 12,000 cords of wood per year to iron mills.

1614   Proclamation Forbidding the Importation of Whale-fins into his Majesty's Dominions by any Apart from the Muscovy Company (reissued 1619; updated 1645).

Proclamation Prohibiting the Importation of Alum.

To encourage domestic alum production, on which the Crown had a monopoly. The major alum-works on the continent were owned by the Pope. Reissued in 1618 and 1625.

1615   Proclamation Touching Glasses.

Forbids use of wood-burning furnaces.

Proclamation for Due Execution of Forest Laws.

Proclamation for Restraining the Abuses in Tin.

1616   Sir George Hay seeks a twenty-one-year patent to export Scottish coal to Paris, but the scheme never materializes.

1617   King James's "Declaration of Sports" permits hunting, dancing, and other rural recreations on Sundays and holidays. Animal-baiting, however, is forbidden on the Sabbath. (Reissued by Charles I in 1633 as "The Book of Sports" and publicly burned by Puritans a decade later.)

        Giles Mompesson acquires commission to sell old and decaying trees in nine counties.

1618   200 chimney-sweeps petition the King to make regular chimney-cleaning compulsory to prevent fires.

1619   Proclamation to Restrain Killing and Eating of Flesh in Lent (reissued 1621–5).

1622   King James authorizes Baron Cranfield to sell off Bernwood and Feckenham Forests.

        Proclamation Commanding Nobles to Return to their Country-houses and Keep Hospitality (reissued 1624).

1624   Proclamation Concerning Royal Mines.

        Proclamation Concerning Buildings in and about London.

        Proclamation for Preservation of Grounds for Making of Saltpetre.

        Breweries Bill complains that their smoke diminishes "the health and soundness" of the city and tries to ban the use of coal in Westminster and much of West London (Calvert 53). Although it failed to pass the House of Commons, Archbishop Laud subsequently sued coal-burning brewers for damages to St Paul's Cathedral.

1625   Proclamation Touching the Surveying of Sea-coals of Newcastle, Sunderland, and Blythe.

1626   Order against Alum Works. Endorsed by six doctors from the College of Physicians, the order bans new alum works in the city and forbids the dumping of waste into the Thames, requiring manufacturers to "bury the same in the night-time in some convenient place, where it might not breed any infection or annoyance." It seems the manufacturers did not comply. A petition presented to the Privy Council the following year accuses the alum makers of having "poured or caused the said filthy dregs or excrement to fall into the ponds or ditches leading to the Thames, whereby some of the petitioners have found their wells of water appointed for brewing so tainted with the taste and savour of alum excrement, as that within a very short space the fish have been poisoned, and the water altogether unwholesome for brewing or any other use" (PC 2/36, fol. 134).

        Dutch engineer Cornelius Vermuyden launches project to drain approximately 70,000 acres of fenlands in Hatfield Chase, and is knighted for his efforts in 1629.

1633   Star Chamber Decree Concerning Soap-boilers.
Regulates soap-making and requires the industry to use vegetable oil instead of "very noisome" whale or fish oil.

1637   Thomas Bushell, a servant of Francis Bacon, acquires rights to royal silver mines in Cardiganshire, and further deforests much of the Tal-y-bont valley. Three years later, he convenes an emergency meeting of miners, smelters, and refiners, to determine whether turf can be burned instead of timber.

1640   c. 16 Act for the Limitation of Forests.
Parliament shrinks the boundaries of royal forests and would eventually sequester many Royalists estates, selling off their timber.

1649   Act for Draining the Great Level of the Fens.
Spearheaded by the 1st Duke of Bedford and supported by fenland native Cromwell, it encourages more aggressive draining to keep fens dry even during winter. Known as the "Pretended Act" because it never received royal approval. One year later, Vermuyden declared 40,000 acres had been successfully reclaimed.

1656   Parliament voids timber rights of royalist and iron magnate Sir John Winter (reinstated by Charles in 1660).
c. 18 Act for the Encouraging and Increasing of Shipping.
Prohibits importing timber and pitch from Netherlands and Germany in a bid to encourage timber plantations in England and North American colonies.

1662   John Graunt analyses bills of mortality and concludes the death rate is much higher in the city (1:32) compared to the country (1:50), due to "fumes, steams, and stenches," and the "suffocations" caused by coal smoke (65–6).
c. 10 Hearth Tax.
Following publication of Evelyn's *Fumifugium*, Charles agrees to Petty's proposal to assess households a fee of one shilling per chimney. Brathwaite's "Chimney's Scuffle" registers public resistance to the measure.
c. 28 Pilchard Fishery Act.

1663   c. 2 Act for Unlawful Cutting and Stealing or Spoiling of Wood or Underwoods.
c. 7 General Drainage Act.
Declares Earl of Bedford head of corporation administering 95,000 acres of fenland.

1664   John Evelyn's *Sylva* (first presented as a paper at the Royal Society in 1662) calls for massive tree-planting campaign to repair damages of

the Civil War and furnish the nation with sustainable timber stocks (republished in 1670 and 1679).
c. 11 Draining Deeping Fen Act.

1666   c. 8 Rebuilding of London Act.
Levies shilling tax per ton of coal to finance reconstruction of the city after the Great Fire. In the rush to rebuild, John Evelyn's plan to include more green space in and around London is rejected in favor of an ad hoc, market-driven approach.

1667   Inquiry into woodlands management in the Forest of Dean reports, "Of the said 30,233 trees sold to John Winter, there remained only about 200 in the forest, and of the 11,335 tons of ship timber reserved to the king, not more than 1,100 had been delivered" ("Third Report of the Commissioners" 15).

1668   c. 8 Act for the Increase and Preservation of Timber within the Forest of Dean.
Dean re-afforested, 11,000 acres set aside as a "nursery for wood and timber."

1676   Robert Hooke estimates smoke cloud over London at a mile high and twenty miles wide (Cockayne 208).

1678   c. 9 Act for the Preservation of Fishing in the River Severn.

1689   c. 30 Mines Royal Act.
Ends duopoly on mining established in 1568 and decriminalizes alchemy.

1709   First coke-fired blast furnace at Coalbrookdale ironworks.

Further Reading: A Bibliography of Environmental Scholarship on the English Renaissance

Ecocritical Theory

Buell, Lawrence. *Writing for an Endangered World: Literature, Culture, and the Environment in the U.S. and Beyond.* Cambridge, MA: Harvard University Press, 2001.

The Future of Environmental Criticism. Oxford: Wiley, 2005.

Clark, Timothy. *The Cambridge Introduction to Literature and the Environment.* Cambridge University Press, 2011.

Ecocriticism on the Edge: The Anthropocene as Threshold Concept. London: Bloomsbury, 2015.

Cohen, Jeffrey (ed.). *Prismatic Ecology: Ecotheory Beyond Green.* Minneapolis: University of Minnesota Press, 2013.

Garrard, Greg. *Ecocriticism.* New York: Routledge, 2011.

The Oxford Handbook of Ecocriticism. Oxford University Press, 2014.

Glotfelty, Cheryl and Harold Fromm (eds.). *Ecocriticism Reader: Landmarks in Literary Ecology.* Athens: University of Georgia Press, 1996.

Haraway, Donna. *Staying with the Trouble: Making Kin in the Cthulucene.* Durham: Duke University Press, 2016.

Heise, Ursula. "Hitchhiker's Guide to Ecocriticism." *PMLA,* 121/2 (2006): 503–16.

Sense of Place, Sense of Planet: The Environmental Imagination of the Global. Oxford University Press, 2008.

Iovino, Serenella and Serpil Opperman (eds.). *Material Ecocriticism.* Bloomington: Indiana University Press, 2014.

Mortimer-Sandilands, Catriona and Bruce Erikson. *Queer Ecologies: Sex, Nature, Politics, Desire.* Bloomington: Indiana University Press, 2010.

Morton, Timothy. *Ecology without Nature: Rethinking Environmental Aesthetics.* Cambridge, MA: Harvard University Press, 2007.

Dark Ecology: For a Logic of Future Coexistence. New York: Columbia University Press, 2016.

Westling, Louise (ed.). *Cambridge Companion to Literature and the Environment.* Cambridge University Press, 2013.

Renaissance Ecocriticism and English Environmental History

Boehrer, Bruce. *Environmental Degradation in Jacobean Drama*. Cambridge University Press, 2013.

Borlik, Todd Andrew. *Ecocriticism and Early Modern English Literature: Green Pastures*. New York: Routledge, 2011.

Bowerbank, Sylvia. *Speaking for Nature: Women and Ecologies of Early Modern England*. Baltimore, MD: Johns Hopkins University Press, 2004.

Bruckner, Lynne and Dan Brayton (eds.). *Ecocritical Shakespeare*. Burlington, VT: Ashgate, 2011.

Egan, Gabriel. *Green Shakespeare: From Ecopolitics to Ecocriticism*. London: Routledge, 2006.

Shakespeare and Ecocritical Theory. London: Bloomsbury, 2015.

Egerton, Frank. *Roots of Ecology: From Antiquity to Haeckel*. Berkeley: University of California Press, 2012.

Estok, Simon. *Ecocriticism and Shakespeare: Reading Ecophobia*. New York: Palgrave Macmillan, 2011.

Feerick, Jean and Vin Nardizzi (eds.). *The Indistinct Human in Renaissance Literature*. New York: Palgrave Macmillan, 2012.

Gruber, Elizabeth. *Renaissance Ecopolitics from Shakespeare to Bacon*. New York: Routledge, 2017.

Hallock, Thomas, Ivo Kamps and Karen Raber (eds.). *Early Modern Ecostudies: From the Florentine Codex to Shakespeare*. New York: Palgrave Macmillan, 2008.

Hiltner, Ken (ed.). *Renaissance Ecology: Imaging Eden in Milton's England*. Pittsburgh, PA: Duquesne University Press, 2008.

What Else is Pastoral? Renaissance Literature and the Environment. Ithaca, NY: Cornell University Press, 2011.

Hoskins, W. G. *The Making of the English Landscape*. London: Hodder & Stoughton, 1977.

Jones, Gwilym. "Environmental Renaissance Studies." *Literature Compass*, 14/10 (2017): e12407.

Laroche, Rebecca and Jennifer Munroe. *Shakespeare and Ecofeminist Theory*. London: Bloomsbury, 2017.

Lovegrove, Roger. *Silent Fields: The Long Decline of a Nation's Wildlife*. Oxford University Press, 2007.

MacFaul, Tom. *Shakespeare and the Natural World*. Cambridge University Press, 2015.

Martin, Randall. *Shakespeare and Ecology*. Oxford University Press, 2015.

McColley, Diane. *Poetry and Ecology in the Age of Milton and Marvell*. Burlington, VT: Ashgate, 2007.

Munroe, Jennifer, Edward Geisweidt, and Lynne Bruckner (eds.). *Ecological Approaches to Early Modern English Texts: A Field Guide to Reading and Teaching*. Burlington, VT: Ashgate, 2015.

Munroe, Jennifer and Rebecca Laroche (eds.). *Ecofeminist Approaches to Early Modernity*. New York: Palgrave Macmillan, 2011.

Nardizzi, Vin. *Wooden Os: Shakespeare's Theatres and England's Trees.* University of Toronto Press, 2013.

Rackham, Oliver. *The History of the Countryside: The Classic History of Britain's Landscape, Flora, and Fauna.* London: Dent, 1986.

Richards, John F. *The Unending Frontier: An Environmental History of the Early Modern World.* Berkeley: University of California Press, 2005.

Thomas, Keith. *Man and the Natural World: Changing Attitudes in England, 1500–1800.* London: Allen Lane, 1983.

Watson, Robert. *Back to Nature: The Green and the Real in the Late Renaissance.* Philadelphia: University of Pennsylvania Press, 2006.

Williams, Linda. "Seventeenth-Century Concepts of the Non-human World: A Nascent Romanticism?" *Green Letters*, 21/2 (2017): 122–37.

I. Cosmologies

Bruckner, Lynne. "N/nature and the Difference 'She' Makes." In Jennifer Munroe and Rebecca Laroche (eds.), *Ecofeminist Approaches to Early Modernity*, 15–36. New York: Palgrave Macmillan, 2011.

Harrison, Peter. *The Bible, Protestantism, and the Rise of Natural Science.* Cambridge University Press, 1998.

Johnson, Nicholas. "Anima-tion at Little Gidding: Thoughtful Inconsistency as Ecological Ethos in an Early Modern Bible Harmony." In Thomas Hallock, Ivo Kamps and Karen Raber (eds.), *Early Modern Ecostudies: From the Florentine Codex to Shakespeare*, 145–65. New York: Palgrave Macmillan, 2008.

Marcus, Leah. "Ecocriticism and Vitalism in *Paradise Lost.*" *Milton Quarterly*, 49/2 (2015): 96–111.

McColley, Diane. "Milton's Environmental Epic: Creature Kinship and the Language of *Paradise Lost.*" In Karla Armbruster and Kathleen Wallace (eds.), *Beyond Nature Writing: Expanding the Boundaries of Ecocriticism*, 57–74. Charlottesville: University of Virginia Press, 2001.

Merchant, Carolyn. *The Death of Nature: Women, Ecology, and the Scientific Revolution.* San Francisco: HarperSanFrancisco, 1989.

Philips, Bill. "The Rape of Mother Earth in Seventeenth Century English Poetry." *Atlantis*, 26 (2004): 49–60.

Ralph, Laura E. "'Why are we by all creatures waited on?' Situating John Donne and George Herbert in Early Modern Ecological Discourse." *Early English Studies*, 3 (2010): www.uta.edu/english/ees/fulltext/ralph3.html.

Rudrum, Alan. 'For then the Earth shall be all Paradise': Milton, Vaughan, and the Neo-Calvinists on the Ecology of the Hereafter." *Scintilla*, 4 (2000): 39–52.

Walsham, Alexandra. *The Reformation of the Landscape.* Oxford University Press, 2011.

Watson, Robert. "Thomas Traherne: The World as Present." In Watson, *Back to Nature: The Green and the Real in the Late Renaissance*, 297–323. Philadelphia: University of Pennsylvania Press, 2006.

White, Lynn. "The Historical Roots of our Ecologic Crisis." *Science*, 155 (1967): 1203–7.

Whitney, Elspeth. "Lynn White, Ecotheology, and History." *Environmental Ethics*, 15/2 (1993): 151–69.

II. The Tangled Chain

Human Animal, Beasts, Birds, Fish, Insects

Bach, Rebecca Ann. *Birds and Other Creatures in Renaissance Literature.* London: Routledge, 2017.

Boehrer, Bruce. *Shakespeare Among the Animals: Nature and Society in the Drama of Early Modern England.* New York: Palgrave Macmillan, 2002.

  Animal Characters: Nonhuman Beings in Early Modern Literature. Philadelphia: University of Pennsylvania Press, 2010.

Botelho, Keith and Joseph Campana (eds.). *Lesser Living Creatures: Insect Life in the Age of Thomas Moffett.* Pennsylvania State University Press, forthcoming.

Campana, Joseph. "The Bee and the Sovereign: Political Entomology and the Problem of Scale." *Shakespeare Studies*, 41 (2013): 94–113.

  "Humans: Exceptional Humans, Human Exceptionalism, and the Shape of Things to Come." *Shakespearean International Yearbook*, 15 (2015): 39–63.

Cuneo, Pia (ed.). *Animals and Early Modern Identity.* London: Routledge, 2017.

Dugan, Holly. "'To Bark With Judgment': Playing Baboon in Early Modern London." *Shakespeare Studies*, 41 (2013): 77–93.

Dugan, Holly and Karen Raber (eds.). *Routledge Handbook to Shakespeare and Animals.* New York: Routledge, forthcoming.

Egan, Gabriel. "Gaia and the Great Chain of Being." In Lynne Bruckner and Dan Brayton (eds.), *Ecocritical Shakespeare*, 57–69. Burlington, VT: Ashgate, 2011.

Fudge, Erica. *Brutal Reasoning: Animals, Rationality, and Humanity in Early Modern England.* Ithaca, NY: Cornell University Press, 2006.

  (ed.). *Renaissance Beasts: Of Animals, Humans, and Other Wonderful Creatures.* Champaign: University of Illinois Press, 2004.

Harrison, Peter. "The Virtues of Animals in Seventeenth-Century Thought." *Journal of the History of Ideas*, 59 (1998): 463–84.

Hoeninger, F. David and J. F. M. Hoeninger. *The Development of Natural History in Tudor England*. Boston: MIT Press, 1969.

MacInnes, Ian. "The Politic Worm: Invertebrate Life in the Early Modern English Body." Jean Feerick and Vin Nardizzi (eds.), *The Indistinct Human in Renaissance Literature*, 253–73. New York: Palgrave Macmillan, 2012.

Raber, Karen. *Animal Bodies, Renaissance Culture*. Philadelphia: University of Pennsylvania Press, 2013.

Shakespeare and Posthumanist Theory. London: Bloomsbury, 2018.

Raber, Karen and Monica Mattfeld (eds.). *Performing Animals: History, Agency, Theater*. State College: Pennsylvania State University Press, 2017.

Raven, Charles. *English Naturalists from Neckham to Ray*. Cambridge University Press, 1947.

Roberts, Jeanne Addison. "Animals as Agents of Revelation." In Roberts, *The Shakespearean Wild: Geography, Genus, and Gender*, 55–116. Lincoln: University of Nebraska Press, 1991.

Shannon, Laurie. *The Accommodated Animal: Cosmopolity in Shakespearean Locales*. University of Chicago Press, 2013.

Werth, Tiffany, "Introduction: Shakespeare and the Human." *Shakespearean International Yearbook*, 15 (2015): 1–20.

Plants

Calhoun, Joshua. "Ecosystemic Shakespeare: Vegetable Memorabilia in the Sonnets." *Shakespeare Studies*, 39 (2011): 64–73.

Knight, Leah. *Of Books and Botany: Sixteenth-Century Plants and Print Culture*. Burlington, VT: Ashgate, 2009.

Reading Green in Early Modern England. Burlington, VT: Ashgate, 2014.

Laroche, Rebecca. *Shakespeare, the Herbal, and the Intimate History of Plants*, forthcoming.

Mabey, Richard. *The Cabaret of Plants*. New York: W. W. Norton, 2015.

McColley, Diane. "Hylozoic Poetry: The Lives of Plants." In McColley, *Poetry and Ecology in the Age of Milton and Marvell*, 109–38. Burlington, VT: Ashgate, 2007.

Rosenberg, Jessica. "Poetic Language, Practical Handbooks, and the Virtue of Plants." In Jennifer Munroe, Edward Geisweidt, and Lynne Bruckner (eds.), *Ecological Approaches to Early Modern English Texts: A Field Guide to Reading and Teaching*, 61–70. Burlington, VT: Ashgate, 2015.

Swann, Marjorie. "Vegetable Love: Botany and Sexuality in Seventeenth-Century England." In Jean Feerick and Vin Nardizzi (eds.), *The Indistinct Human in Renaissance Literature*, 139–58. New York: Palgrave Macmillan, 2012.

Gems, Metals, Elements, Atoms

Clucas, Stephen. "Poetic Atomism in the Seventeenth Century: Henry More, Thomas Traherne, and the Scientific Imagination." *Renaissance Studies*, 5/3 (1991): 327–40.

Cohen, Jeffrey. *Stone: An Ecology of the Inhuman.* Minneapolis: University of Minnesota Press, 2015.

Cohen, Jeffrey and Lowell Duckert. *Elemental Ecocriticism: Thinking with Air, Water, Earth, Fire.* Minneapolis: University of Minnesota Press, 2015.

Kargon, Robert. *Atomism in England from Hariot to Newton.* Oxford University Press, 1966.

Waldron, Jennifer. "Of Stones and Stony Hearts." In Jean Feerick and Vin Nardizzi (eds.), *The Indistinct Human in Renaissance Literature*, 205–27. New York: Palgrave Macmillan, 2012.

Watson, Robert. "Ecology of Self in *A Midsummer Night's Dream*." In Lynne Bruckner and Dan Brayton (eds.), *Ecocritical Shakespeare*, 33–56. Burlington, VT: Ashgate, 2011.

III. Time and Place

Seasons

Bradford, Alan. "Mirrors of Mutability: Winter Landscapes in Tudor Poetry." *ELR*, 4 (1974): 3–39.

Buell, Lawrence. "Nature's Face, Mind's Eye: Realizing the Seasons." In Buell, *The Environmental Imagination: Thoreau, Nature Writing, and the Formation of American Culture*, 219–51. Cambridge, MA: Harvard University Press, 1995.

Olwig, Kenneth. "Liminality, Seasonality, and Landscape." *Landscape Research*, 30/2 (2005): 259–71.

Woodbridge, Linda. "Green Shakespeare." In Woodbridge, *The Scythe of Saturn: Shakespeare and Magical Thinking*, 152–205. Urbana: University of Illinois Press, 1994.

Country Houses

Bennett, S. and M. Polio (eds.). *Performing Environments: Site-Specificity in Medieval and Early Modern English Drama.* New York: Palgrave Macmillan, 2014.

Marcus, Leah. *Politics of Mirth: Jonson, Herrick, Marvell, and the Defense of Old Holiday Pastimes.* University of Chicago Press, 1989.

Markley, Robert. "'Gulfes, Deserts, Precipices, Stone': Marvell's 'Upon Appleton House' and the Contradictions of Nature." In Gerald

MacLean *et al.* (eds.), *The Country and the City Revisited*, 89–105. Cambridge University Press, 1999.

McColley, Diane. "Perceiving Habitats: Marvell and the Language of Sensuous Reciprocity." In McColley, *Poetry and Ecology in the Age of Milton and Marvell*, 13–42. Burlington, VT: Ashgate, 2007.

Noble, Louise. "'Bare and desolate now': Cultural Ecology and 'The Description of Cookham.'" In Jennifer Munroe, Edward Geisweidt, and Lynne Bruckner (eds.), *Ecological Approaches to Early Modern English Texts: A Field Guide to Reading and Teaching*, 99–108. Burlington, VT: Ashgate, 2015.

Remien, Peter. "Home to the Slaughter: Noah's Ark and the Seventeenth-Century Country House Poem." *Modern Philology*, 113/4 (2016): 507–29.

Rogers, William. "Sacramental Dwelling with Nature: Jonson's 'To Penshurst' and Heidegger's 'Building Dwelling Thinking.'" *Postscript*, 14 (1997): 43–55.

Tigner, Amy. "The Ecology of Eating in Jonson's 'To Penshurst.'" In Jennifer Munroe, Edward Geisweidt, and Lynne Bruckner (eds.), *Ecological Approaches to Early Modern English Texts: A Field Guide to Reading and Teaching*, 109–20. Burlington, VT: Ashgate, 2015.

Yoch, James. "Subjecting the landscape in Pageants and Shakespearean Pastoral." In David Bergeron (ed.), *Pageantry in the Shakespearean Theatre*, 194–246. Athens: University of Georgia Press, 1995.

Gardens

Bushnell, Rebecca. *Green Desire: Imagining Early Modern English Gardens.* Ithaca, NY: Cornell University Press, 2003.

Johnson, Bonnie L. "Visions of Soil and Body Management: The Almanac in *Richard II*." In Hillary Eklund (ed.), *Ground-work: English Renaissance Literature and Soil Science*, 59–78. Pittsburgh, PA: Duquesne University Press, 2017.

Munroe, Jennifer. *Gender and the Garden in Early Modern English Literature.* Burlington: Ashgate, 2008.

Samson, Alexander. *Locus Amoenus: Gardens and Horticulture in the Renaissance.* Chichester: Wiley, 2012.

Strong, Roy. *The Renaissance Garden in England.* London: Thames & Hudson, 1979.

Tigner, Amy. *Literature and the Renaissance Garden from Elizabeth I to Charles II.* Burlington, VT: Ashgate, 2012.

Pastoral

Bowden, Peter. *The Wool Trade in Tudor and Stuart England.* London: Macmillan, 1971.

Gifford, Terry. *Pastoral.* New York: Routledge, 1999.

Hiltner, Ken. "What Else is Pastoral?" In Hiltner, *What Else is Pastoral? Renaissance Literature and the Environment*, 34–48. Ithaca, NY: Cornell University Press, 2011.

Montrose, Louis. "'Eliza, Queen of Shepherds,' and the Pastoral of Power." *ELR*, 10 (1980): 153–82.

Nardizzi, Vin. "Shakespeare's Queer Pastoral Ecology: Alienation around Arden." *ISLE*, 23 (2016): 564–82.

Watson, Robert N. "As You Liken It: Simile in the Forest." In Watson, *Back to Nature: The Green and the Real in the Late Renaissance*, 77–107. Philadelphia: University of Pennsylvania Press, 2006.

Williams, Raymond. *The Country and the City.* Oxford University Press, 1973.

Georgic

Dolan, Frances, "Compost/Composition." In Hillary Eklund (ed.), *Ground-work: English Renaissance Literature and Soil Science*, 21–40. Pittsburgh, PA: Duquesne University Press, 2017.

Eklund, Hillary (ed.). *Ground-work: English Renaissance Literature and Soil Science.* Pittsburgh, PA: Duquesne University Press, 2017.

Hiltner, Ken. "Empire, the Environment, and the Growth of Georgic." In Hiltner, *What Else is Pastoral? Renaissance Literature and the Environment*, 156–73. Ithaca, NY: Cornell University Press, 2011.

Leslie, Michael and Timothy Raylor (eds.). *Culture and Cultivation in Early Modern England: Writing and the Land.* Leicester University Press, 1992.

Lowe, Antony. *The Georgic Revolution.* Princeton University Press, 1985.

McRae, Andrew. *God Speed the Plough: Representations of Agrarian England 1500–1660.* Cambridge University Press, 1990.

Overton, Mark. *Agricultural Revolution in England: The Transformation of the Agrarian Economy 1500–1800.* Cambridge University Press, 1996.

Scott, Charlotte. *Shakespeare's Nature: From Cultivation to Culture.* Oxford University Press, 2014.

Thirsk, Joan (ed.). *The Agrarian History of England and Wales*, vol. IV: *1500–1640*. Cambridge University Press, 1967.

"Plough and Pen: Agricultural Writers in the Seventeenth Century." In T. H. Aston *et al.* (eds.), *Social Relations and Ideas: Essays in Honour of R. H. Hilton*, 295–318. Cambridge University Press, 1983.

Waage, Frederick. "Shakespeare Unearth'd." *ISLE*, 12/2 (2005): 139–64.

Forests, Woods, Parks

Falvey, Heather. "The Articulation, Transmission, and Preservation of Custom in the Forest Community of Duffield." In Richard Hoyle (ed.), *Custom, Improvement and the Landscape in Early Modern Britain*, 65–100. New York: Routledge, 2017.

Harrison, Robert Pogue. *Forests: The Shadows of Civilization.* University of Chicago Press, 1992.

Marienstras, Richard. *The Forest, the Wild, and the Sacred: New Perspectives on the Shakespearean World.* Trans. Janet Lloyd. Cambridge University Press, 1985.

McNeil, J. R. "Woods and Warfare in World History." *Environmental History*, 9/3 (2004): 388–410.

Mitchell, F. J. G. "How Open were European Primeval Forests?" *Journal of Ecology*, 93 (2005): 168–77.

Nardizzi, Vin and Miriam Jacobson. "The Secrets of Grafting in Wroth's *Urania*." In Jennifer Munroe and Rebecca Laroche (eds.), *Ecofeminist Approaches to Early Modernity*, 175–94. New York: Palgrave Macmillan, 2011.

Perlin, John. *A Forest Journey: The Story of Wood and Civilization.* Woodstock: Countryman, 2005.

Pitmann, Susan. *Elizabethan and Jacobean Deer Parks in Kent.* PhD Thesis. University of Kent. 2011. Web.

Rackham, Oliver. *Trees and Woodlands in the British Landscape.* London: Phoenix, 2001.

Scott, Charlotte. "Dark matter: Shakespeare's Foul Dens and Forests." *Shakespeare Survey*, 64 (2011): 276–89.

Skipp, Victor. *Crisis and Development: An Ecological Case Study of the Forest of Arden 1570–1674.* Cambridge University Press, 1978.

Theis, Jeffrey S. *Writing the Forest in Early Modern England: A Sylvan Pastoral Nation.* Pittsburgh, PA: Duquesne University Press, 2009.

Heaths, Moors

Atkins, William. *The Moor: Lives, Landscape, Literature.* London: Faber and Faber, 2014.

Di Palma, Vittoria. *Wasteland: A History.* New Haven, CT: Yale University Press, 2014.

Steffes, Michael. "Medieval Wildernesses and *King Lear*: Heath, Forest, Desert." *Exemplaria*, 28/3 (2016): 230–47.

Vales, Downs, Hills, Mountains, Prospects

Duckert, Lowell. "Earth's Prospects." In Jeffrey Cohen and Lowell Duckert (eds.), *Elemental Ecocriticism*, 237–68. Minneapolis: University of Minnesota Press, 2015.

Fitter, Chris. *Poetry, Space, Landscape: Toward a New Theory.* Cambridge University Press, 1995.

Nicolson, Marjorie Hope. *Mountain Gloom and Mountain Glory: The Development of the Aesthetics of the Infinite.* Ithaca, NY: Cornell University Press, 1959; 2nd edn Seattle: University of Washington Press, 1997.

Oakley-Brown, Liz. "Writing on Borderlines: Anglo-Welsh Relations in Thomas Churchyard's *The Worthiness of Wales.*" In Stewart Mottram (ed.), *Writing Wales,* 39–58. London: Routledge, 2016.

Whyte, Ian. "Early Modern Landscapes." In Ian Whyte (ed.), *Landscape and History since 1500, 27–69.* London: Reaktion, 2002.

Lakes, Rivers, Oceans

Brayton, Dan. *Shakespeare's Ocean: An Ecocritical Exploration.* Charlottesville: University of Virginia Press, 2012.

Comito, Terry. "Beauty Bare: Speaking Waters and Fountains in Renaissance Literature." In Elisabeth MacDougall (ed.), *Fons Sapientiae: Renaissance Garden Fountains,* 15–58. Washington: Dumbarton Oaks, 1978.

Corbin, Alain. *The Lure of the Sea: The Discovery of the Seaside in the Western World 1750–1840.* Berkeley: University of California Press, 1994.

Duckert, Lowell. *For All Waters: Finding Ourselves in Early Modern Wetscapes.* Minneapolis: University of Minnesota Press, 2017.

Herendeen, William. *From Landscape to Literature: The River and the Myth of Geography.* Pittsburgh, PA: Duquesne University Press, 1986.

Mentz, Steve. *At the Bottom of Shakespeare's Ocean.* London: Continuum, 2009.

Shipwreck Ecology: Ecologies of Globalization 1550–1719. Minneapolis: University of Minnesota Press, 2015.

Sanders, Julie. "Liquid Landscapes." In Sanders, *The Cultural Geography of Early Modern Drama 1620–1650,* 18–64. Cambridge University Press, 2011.

Foreign Climes and Colonies

Allewaert, Monique. *Ariel's Ecology: Plantations, Personhood, and Colonialism in the American Tropics.* Minneapolis: University of Minnesota Press, 2013.

Branch, Michael (ed.). *Reading the Roots: American Nature Writing Before Walden.* Athens: University of Georgia Press, 2004.

Duckert, Lowell. "Walter Ralegh's Liquid Narrative: *The Discoverie of Guiana.*" In Christopher Armitage (ed.), *Literary and Visual Ralegh,* 217–41. Oxford University Press, 2016.

Gillies, John. *Shakespeare and the Geography of Difference.* Cambridge University Press, 1994.

Grove, Richard. *Green Imperialism: Colonial Expansion, Tropical Island Edens, and the Origins of Environmentalism 1600–1800*. Cambridge University Press, 1995.

Roberts, Jeanne Addison. "Confronting the Female Wild." In Roberts, *The Shakespearean Wild: Geography, Genus, and Gender*, 117–82. Lincoln: University of Nebraska Press, 1991.

Sweet, Timothy. *American Georgics: Economy and Environment in American Literature 1580–1864*. Philadelphia: University of Pennsylvania Press, 2001.

Woolway-Grenfell, Joanne. "Significant Spaces in Edmund Spenser's *View of the Present State of Ireland*." *Early Modern Literary Studies*, 4/2 (1998): 6:1–21.

IV. Interactions

Animal-Baiting

Fudge, Erica. "Screaming Monkeys: The Creatures in the Bear Garden." In Fudge, *Perceiving Animals: Humans and Beasts in Early Modern English Culture*, 11–33. Basingstoke: Macmillan, 2000.

Höfele, Andreas. *Stage, Stake, and Scaffold: Humans and Animals in Shakespeare's Theatre*. Oxford University Press, 2011.

Scott-Warren, Jason. "When Theatres Were Bear-Gardens, Or What's at Stake in the Comedy of Humors." *Shakespeare Quarterly*, 54/1 (2003): 63–82.

Hunting, Hawking, Fishing

Bates, Catherine. *Masculinity and the Hunt: From Wyatt to Spenser*. Oxford University Press, 2013.

Berry, Edward. *Shakespeare and the Hunt*. Cambridge University Press, 2001.

Duckert, Lowell. "Exit Pursued by a Polar Bear: More to Follow." *Upstart: A Journal of English Renaissance Studies*, 4 June 2013, https://upstart.sites.clemson.edu/Essays/exit-pursued-by-a-polar-bear/exit-pursued-by-a-polar-bear.xhtml.

Manning, Roger. *Hunters and Poachers: A Social and Cultural History of Unlawful Hunting in England 1484–1630*. Oxford: Clarendon Press, 1993.

MacGregor, Arthur. "Animals and the Early Stuarts: Hunting and Hawking at the Court of James I and Charles I." *Archives of Natural History*, 16/3 (1989): 305–18.

Swann, Marjorie. "Introduction" to Izaak Walton, *The Compleat Angler*, ed. Swann, xv–xxii. Oxford University Press, 2014.

Watson, Robert. "Protestant Animals: Puritan Sects and English Animal-Protection Sentiment 1550–1650." *ELH*, 81/4 (2014): 1111–48.

Pet-Keeping

Boehrer, Bruce. "Shylock and the Rise of the Household Pet: Thinking Social Exclusion in *The Merchant of Venice.*" *Shakespeare Quarterly*, 50/2 (1999): 152–70.

Fudge, Erica. "The Dog is Himself: Humans, Animals, and Self-Control in *The Two Gentlemen of Verona.*" In Laurie Maguire (ed.), *How To Do Things With Shakespeare*, 185–209. Malden, MA: Blackwell, 2008.

Raber, Karen. "How to Do Things with Animals: Thoughts on/with the Early Modern Cat." In Thomas Hallock, Ivo Kamps, and Karen Raber (eds.), *Early Modern Ecostudies: From the Florentine Codex to Shakespeare*, 93–114. New York: Palgrave Macmillan, 2008.

Cooking, Feasting, Fasting, Healing

Appelbaum, Robert. *Aguecheek's Beef, Belch's Hiccup, and Other Gastronomic Interjections: Literature, Culture, and Food among the Early Moderns.* University of Chicago Press, 2006.

Clement, Jennifer. "Thomas Tryon's Reformed Stewardship." In Clement, *Reading Humility in Early Modern England*, 107–26. Burlington, VT: Ashgate, 2015.

DiMeo, Michelle and Rebecca Laroche. "On Elizabeth Isham's 'Oil of Swallows': Animal Slaughter and Early Modern Women's Medical Recipes." In Jennifer Munroe and Rebecca Laroche (eds.), *Ecofeminist Approaches to Early Modernity*, 87–104. New York: Palgrave Macmillan, 2011.

DiMeo, Michelle and Sara Pennell (eds.). *Reading and Writing Recipe Books, 1500–1800.* Manchester University Press, 2013.

EMROC: Early Modern Recipes Online Collective. https://emroc.hypotheses .org/.

Fitzpatrick, Joan. *Food in Shakespeare: Early Modern Dietaries and the Plays.* Burlington, VT: Ashgate, 2007.

Fudge, Erica. "On Saying Nothing Concerning the Same: On Dominion, Purity, and Meat in Early Modern England." In Erica Fudge (ed.). *Renaissance Beasts: Of Animals, Humans, and Other Wonderful Creatures*, 70–86. Champaign: University of Illinois Press, 2004.

Goldstein, David. "Woolley's Mouse: Early Modern Recipe Books and the Uses of Nature." In Jennifer Munroe and Rebecca Laroche (eds.), *Ecofeminist Approaches to Early Modernity*, 105–28. New York: Palgrave Macmillan, 2011.

Eating and Ethics in Shakespeare's England. Cambridge University Press, 2013.

Laroche, Rebecca. *Medical Authority and Englishwomen's Herbal Texts.* Burlington, VT: Ashgate, 2009.

Paster, Gail Kern. "Melancholy Cats, Lugged Bears, and Early Modern Cosmology: Reading Shakespeare's Psychological Materialism across the Species Border." In Gail Kern Paster *et al.* (eds.), *Reading the Early Modern Passions: Essays in the Cultural History of Emotion,* 113–29. Philadelphia: University of Pennsylvania Press, 2004.

Raber, Karen. "Animals at the Table: Performing Meat in Early Modern England and Europe." In Karen Raber and Monica Mattfeld (eds.), *Performing Animals: History, Agency, Theater,* 14–27. State College: Pennsylvania State University Press, 2017.

Wall, Wendy. *Recipes for Thought: Knowledge and Taste in the Early Modern English Kitchen.* Philadelphia: University of Pennsylvania Press, 2015.

Zysk, Jay. "You Are What You Eat: Cooking and Writing Across the Species Barrier in Ben Jonson's *Bartholomew Fair.*" In Jean Feerick and Vin Nardizzi (eds.), *The Indistinct Human in Renaissance Literature,* 67–84. New York: Palgrave Macmillan, 2012.

Magic and Science

Cless, Downing. "Ecologically Conjuring Doctor Faustus." *Journal of Dramatic Theory and Criticism,* 20/2 (2006): 145–68.

Clucas, Stephen. "'Wondrous force and operation': Magic, Science, and Religion in the Renaissance." In Philippa Berry and Margaret Tudeau-Clayton (eds.), *Textures of Renaissance Knowledge,* 35–57. Manchester University Press, 2003.

Crane, Mary Thomas. *Losing Touch with Nature: Literature and the New Science.* Baltimore, MD: Johns Hopkins University Press, 2014.

Daston, Lorraine and Katherine Park. *Wonders and the Order of Nature.* New York: Zone, 1998.

Debus, Allen. *Man and Nature in the Renaissance.* Cambridge University Press, 1978.

Eamon, William. *Science and the Secrets of Nature.* Princeton University Press, 1994.

Edwards, Karen. *Milton and the Natural World: Science and Poetry in Paradise Lost.* Cambridge University Press, 1999.

Eggert, Katherine. *Disknowledge: How Alchemy Transmuted Ignorance in Renaissance England.* Philadelphia: University of Pennsylvania Press, 2015.

Gatti, Hillary. *Giordano Bruno and Renaissance Science.* Ithaca, NY: Cornell University Press, 2003.

Gaukroger, Stephen. *The Emergence of a Scientific Culture: Science and the Shaping of Modernity 1210–1675.* Oxford University Press, 2006.

Guerini, Anita. "The Ethics of Animal Experimentation in Seventeenth-Century England." *Journal of the History of Ideas*, 50/3 (1989): 391–407.

Harkness, Deborah. *The Jewel House: Elizabethan London and the Scientific Revolution.* New Haven, CT: Yale University Press, 2007.

"Natural History." In Peter Harrison *et al.* (eds.), *Wrestling with Nature: From Omens to Science*, 117–48. University of Chicago Press, 2011.

Henry, John. "Atomism and Eschatology." *British Journal for the History of Science*, 15 (1982): 211–39.

Kassell, Lauren. *Medicine and Magic in Elizabethan London.* Oxford University Press, 2005.

Newman, William. *Promethean Ambitions: Alchemy and the Quest to Perfect Nature.* University of Chicago Press, 2005.

Ogilvie, Brian. *The Science of Describing: Natural History in Renaissance Europe.* University of Chicago Press, 2006.

Preston, Clare. *Thomas Browne and the Writing of Early Modern Science.* Cambridge University Press, 2005.

Sarasohn, Lisa. "A Science Turned Upside Down: Feminism and the Natural Philosophy of Margaret Cavendish." *HLQ*, 47 (1984): 289–307.

Shapin, Steven. A *Social History of Truth: Civility and Science in Seventeenth-Century England.* University of Chicago Press, 1994.

Shapiro, Barbara. *A Culture of Fact: England 1550–1720.* Ithaca, NY: Cornell University Press, 2003.

Yates, Frances. *Giordano Bruno and the Hermetic Tradition.* London: Routledge, 1964.

Industry

Bascoe, Tasmin. "Carew and Matters of the Littoral." In Hillary Eklund (ed.), *Ground-work: English Renaissance Literature and Soil Science*, 41–58. Pittsburgh, PA: Duquesne University Press, 2017.

Bertram, Benjamin. *War and Ecology in the Early Modern Period: Iago's Dream.* New York: Routledge, 2017.

Buckley, Allen. *The Tudor Tin Industry.* Camborne: Penhellick, 2009.

Coleman, D. C. *Industry in Tudor and Stuart England.* London: Macmillan, 1975.

Emery, F. V. "England Circa 1600." In H. C. Darby (ed.), *A New Historical Geography of England Before 1600*, 248–302. Cambridge University Press, 1976.

Godfrey, Eleanor. *The Development of English Glass-Making 1560–1640.* Oxford: Clarendon Press, 1975.

Hatcher, John. *The History of the British Coal Industry: Before 1700.* Oxford: Clarendon Press, 1993.

Johnson, Bonnie L. and Bethany Dubow. "Allegories of Creation: Glass-making, Forests, and Fertility in Webster's *Duchess of Malfi*." *Renaissance Drama*, 45/1 (2017): 107–37.

Jones, A. C. and C. J. Harrison. "The Cannock Chase Ironworks, 1590." *English Historical Review*, 93 (1978): 795–810.

Kok, Su Mei. "'How Many Arts From Such a Labour Flow': Thomas Middleton and London's New River." *Journal of Medieval and Early Modern Studies*, 43/1 (2013): 173–90.

Martin, Randall. "Gunpowder, Militarization, and Threshold Ecologies in *Henry IV Part Two* and *Macbeth*." In Martin, *Shakespeare and Ecology*, 78–111. Oxford University Press, 2015.

Mendels, F. F. "Proto-Industrialization." *Journal of Economic History*, 32 (1972): 241–61.

Nef, J. U. "Industrial Revolution Reconsidered." *Journal of Economic History*, 3 (1943): 1–31.

Tomory, Leslie. *The History of the London Water Industry 1580–1820*. Baltimore, MD: Johns Hopkins University Press, 2017.

Zell, Michael. *Industry in the Countryside: Wealden Society in the Sixteenth Century*. Cambridge University Press, 1994.

V. Environmental Problems in Early Modern England

Population

Anderson, Michael (ed.). *British Population History: From the Black Death to the Present Day*. Cambridge University Press, 1996.

Briggs, Chris *et al.* (eds.). *Population, Welfare, and Economic Change in Britain 1290–1834*. Martlesham: Boydell & Brewer, 2014.

Geiswedt, Edward. "'The Bastard Bomb': Illegitimacy and Population in Thomas Middleton's *A Chaste Maid in Cheapside*." In Jennifer Munroe, Edward Geisweidt, and Lynne Bruckner (eds.), *Ecological Approaches to Early Modern English Texts: A Field Guide to Reading and Teaching*, 121–30. Burlington, VT: Ashgate, 2015.

Sokol, B. J. "Thomas Harriot – Sir Walter Ralegh's Tutor – on Population." *Annals of Science*, 31 (1974): 205–12.

Sweet, Timothy. "Would Thomas More Have Wanted to Go to Mars? Colonial Promotion and Bio-power." In Thomas Hallock, Ivo Kamps, and Karen Raber (eds.), *Early Modern Ecostudies: From the Florentine Codex to Shakespeare*, 269–89. New York: Palgrave Macmillan, 2008.

Wrigley, E. A. and Paul Scofield. *The Population History of England: 1541–1871*. Cambridge University Press, 1981.

Enclosure

Manning, R. B. *Village Revolts: Social Protest and Popular Disturbance in England, 1509–1640*. Oxford University Press, 1988.

McDonagh, Briony. "Making and Breaking Property: Enclosure and Common Rights in Sixteenth-Century England." *History Workshop Journal*, 76/1 (2013): 32–56.

Whitney, Charles. "Green Economics and the English Renaissance: From Capital to the Commons." In Cary DiPietro and Hugh Grady, *Shakespeare and the Urgency of Now: Criticism and Theory in the 21st Century*, 103–25. Basingstoke: Palgrave Macmillan, 2013.

Wood, Andy. *The 1549 Rebellions and the Making of Early Modern England*. Cambridge University Press, 2007.

Yates, Julian. "Counting Sheep: Dolly does Utopia (again)." *Rhizomes*, 8 (2004), www.rhizomes.net/issue8/yates2.htm.

Deforestation

Appuhn, Karl. *A Forest on the Sea: Environmental Expertise in Renaissance Venice*. Baltimore, MD: Johns Hopkins University Press, 2009.

Dasgupta, Sukanya. "Drayton's Silent Spring: *Poly-Olbion* and the Politics of Landscape." *Cambridge Quarterly*, 39/2 (2010): 152–71.

McRae, Andrew. "Tree-Felling in Early Modern England: Michael Drayton's Environmentalism." *Review of English Studies*, 63 (2012): 410–30.

Nardizzi, Vin. *Wooden Os: Shakespeare's Theatres and England's Trees*. University of Toronto Press, 2013.

Sanders, Julie. "Ecocritical Readings and the Seventeenth-Century Woodland: Milton's *Comus* and the Forest of Dean." *English*, 50 (2001): 1–18.

Theis, Jeffrey. "Marvell's 'Upon Appleton House' and Tree-felling: A Political Woodpecker." In Jennifer Munroe et al. (eds.), *Ecological Approaches to Early Modern English Texts*, 193–204. Burlington, VT: Ashgate, 2015.

Warde, Paul. "Early Modern 'Resource Crisis': The Wood Shortage Debates in Europe." In N. Brown *et al.* (eds.), *Crisis in Economic and Social History*, 137–60. Woodbridge: Boydell & Brewer, 2015.

Williams, Michael. *Deforesting the Earth: From Prehistory to Global Crisis*. University of Chicago Press, 2006.

The Draining of the Fens

Ash, Eric H. *The Draining of the Fens*. Baltimore, MD: Johns Hopkins University Press, 2017.

Borlik, Todd A. "Caliban and the Fen Demons of Lincolnshire: The Englishness of Shakespeare's *Tempest*." *Shakespeare*, 9/1 (2013): 21–51.

Borlik, Todd A. and Clare Egan. "Angling for the Powte: A Jacobean Environmental Protest Poem." *ELR*, 48/2 (2018): 256–89.

Eklund, Hillary. "Wetlands Reclamation and the Fate of the Local in Seventeenth Century England." In Hillary Eklund (ed.), *Ground-work: English Renaissance Literature and Soil Science*, 149–70. Pittsburgh, PA: Duquesne University Press, 2017.

Irvine, Richard D. G. "East Anglian Fenland: Water, the Work of Imagination, and the Creation of Value." In Kirsten and Frida Hastrup (eds.), *Waterworlds: Anthropology in Fluid Environments*, 23–45. New York: Berghahn, 2015.

Rotherham, Ian. *The Lost Fens*. Stroud: History Press, 2013.

Pollution

Brimblecombe, Peter. *The Big Smoke: A History of Air Pollution in London since Medieval Times*. London: Metheun, 1987.

Brimblecombe, Peter and C. M. Grossi. "Millennium-Long Damage to Building Materials in London." *Science of the Total Environment*, 407/4 (2009): 1354–61.

Calvert, William. *The Smoke of London: Energy and Environment in the Early Modern City*. Cambridge University Press, 2016.

Cockayne, Emily. *Hubbub: Filth, Noise, and Stench in England, 1600–1770*. New Haven, CT: Yale University Press, 2007.

Hiltner, Ken. "Representing Air Pollution in Early Modern London." In Hiltner, *What Else is Pastoral? Renaissance Literature and the Environment*, 95–124. Ithaca, NY: Cornell University Press, 2011.

Jenner, Mark. "The Politics of London Air: John Evelyn's *Fumifugium* and the Restoration." *Historical Journal*, 38/3 (1995): 535–51.

Jørgensen, Dolly. "The Metamorphosis of Ajax, Jakes, and Urban Sanitation." *Early English Studies*, 3 (2010): 1–31.

Knight, Leah. "Breathing Green: Airs, Pollution, and the Green Solution." In Knight, *Reading Green in Early Modern England*, 37–60. Burlington, VT: Ashgate, 2014.

VI. Disaster and Resilience in the Little Ice Age

Weather, Disaster, and Dearth

Ailles, Jennifer. "Ecocritical Heywood and *The Play of the Weather*." *Early Theatre*, 16/2 (2013): 185–96.

Archer, Jayne Elizabeth, Howard Thomas, and Richard M. Turley. "Reading Shakespeare with the Grain: Sustainability and the Hunger Business." *Green Letters*, 19/1 (2015): 8–20.

Behringer, Wolfgang. "Climatic Change and Witch-hunting: The Impact of the Little Ice Age on Mentalities." *Climate Change*, 43/1 (1999): 335–51.

Bruckner, Lynne. "Consuming Means Soon Preys Upon Itself: Political Expedience and Environmental Degradation in *Richard II*." In Cary DiPietro and Hugh Grady, *Shakespeare and the Urgency of Now: Criticism and Theory in the 21st Century*, 126–47. Basingstoke: Palgrave Macmillan, 2013.

Egan, Gabriel. "Supernature and the Weather." In Egan, *Green Shakespeare: From Ecopolitics to Ecocriticism*, 132–71. London: Routledge, 2006.

Fagan, Brian. *The Little Ice Age: How Climate Made History, 1300–1850*. New York: Basic, 2000.

Hindle, Steve. "Dearth and the English Revolution: The Harvest Crisis of 1647–50." *Economic History Review*, 61 (2008): 64–98.

Hoskins, W. G. "Harvest Fluctuations and English Economic History, 1480–1619." *Agricultural History Review*, 12/1 (1964): 28–46.

"Harvest Fluctuations and English Economic History, 1620–1759." *Agricultural History Review*, 16/1 (1968): 15–31.

Jones, Gwilym. *Shakespeare's Storms*. Manchester University Press, 2015.

Markley, Robert. "Summer's Lease: Shakespeare in the Little Ice Age." In Thomas Hallock, Ivo Kamps, and Karen Raber (eds.), *Early Modern Ecostudies: From the Florentine Codex to Shakespeare*, 131–44. New York: Palgrave Macmillan, 2008.

Martin, Craig. *Renaissance Meteorology: From Pomponazzi to Descartes*. Baltimore, MD: Johns Hopkins University Press, 2011.

Mentz, Steve. "Strange Weather in *King Lear*." *Shakespeare*, 6/2 (2010): 139–52.

Morgan, John E. "Understanding Flooding in Early Modern England." *Journal of Historical Geography*, 50 (2015): 37–50.

Mukherjee, Ayesha. *Penury into Plenty: Dearth and the Making of Knowledge in Early Modern England*. London: Routledge, 2014.

Decay and Resilience

Kolb, Justin. "'Rather an impotencie' : *Richard II* and the Decay of Nature as Ecology and Common-wealth," *Early Modern Culture*, 13 (2018): 79–90.

Mukherjee, Ayesha. "'Manured with the Starres': Recovering an Early Modern Discourse of Sustainability." *Literature Compass*, 11/9 (2014): 602–14.

Warde, Paul. *The Invention of Sustainability: Nature and Destiny, c. 1500–1870*. Cambridge University Press, 2018.

Woodward, Donald. "'Swords into Ploughshares': Recycling in Pre-Industrial England." *Economic History Review*, 38/2 (1985): 175–91.

Additional Works Cited

Adorno, Theodor. *Aesthetic Theory*. Trans. Robert Hullot-Kenter. London: Bloomsbury, 2004.

Aubrey, John. *Brief Lives.* Ed. Oliver Dick. London: Penguin, 1978.

Böhme, Jakob. *Signatura rerum; or The Signature of All Things.* London, 1651.

British Hedgehog Preservation Society. *State of Britain's Hedgehogs 2015.* www.britishhedgehogs.org.uk/pdf/SoBH_2015.pdf.

Burton, Robert. *Anatomy of Melancholy.* New York Review of Books, 2001.

Byrne, M. St. Clare. *Elizabethan Life in Town and Country.* London: Metheun, 1925.

Calvin, John. *A commentary of John Calvin upon the first book of Moses, called Genesis.* Trans. Thomas Tymme. London, 1578.

Carey, John. *John Donne: Life, Mind, Art.* London: Faber and Faber, 1981.

Cauchi, Simon (ed.). *The Sixth Book of Virgil's Aeneid: Translated and Commented by Sir John Harington.* Oxford: Clarendon Press, 1991.

Chakrabarty, Dipesh. "The Climate of History: Four Theses." *Critical Inquiry,* 35 (2009): 197–222.

Church, Rooke. *An Old Thrift, Newly Revived.* London, 1612.

Clarke, William. *The Clarke Papers.* London, 1894.

Correr, Anzolo. "Venice: 30 May 1636." Allen B. Hinds (ed.), *Calendar of State Papers Relating To English Affairs in the Archives of Venice,* vol. XXIII: *1632–1636.* London, 1921.

Cotton, Charles. *Wonders of the Peak.* London, 1681.

Davenant, William. *Madagascar.* London, 1638.

Works. London, 1683.

Diamond, Jared. *The World Until Yesterday: What We Can Learn from Traditional Societies.* New York: Penguin, 2013.

Digby, Kenelm. *Two Treatises.* London, 1644.

Donaldson, Ian. *Ben Jonson: A Life.* Oxford University Press, 2012.

Dugdale, William. *History of Embanking and Draining of Diverse Fens and Marshes.* London, 1662.

Dymmok, John. *A Treatise of Ireland.* Dublin, 1842.

Eaton, Mark. "State of Nature 2016: A Summary of the Report." *RSPB.* https://ww2.rspb.org.uk/community/ourwork/b/biodiversity/archive/2016/09/14/state-of-nature-2016-summary-of-the-report.aspx.

Evans, Robert C. "Anne Kemp and a New Allusion to 'Will' Shakespeare." *Ben Jonson Journal,* 14/1 (2008): 88–90.

Everett, Nigel. *The Woods of Ireland: A History, 700–1800.* Dublin: Four Courts, 2015.

Fludd, Robert. *Mosaical Philosophy.* London, 1659.

Forest Research. *Forestry Statistics 2017: International Forestry.* www.forestresearch.gov.uk/tools-and-resources/statistics/forestry-statistics/forestry-statistics-2017/international-forestry.

Foster, Charles. *Being a Beast.* London: Profile, 2016.

Foucault, Michel. *The Order of Things: An Archaeology of the Human Sciences.* London: Routledge, 2002.

Francis (Pope). *Encyclical Letter: 'Laudato Si' of the Holy Father Francis: On Care for our Common Home.* 2015. http://w2.vatican.va/content/francesco/en/encyclicals/documents/papa-francesco_20150524_enciclica-laudato-si.html.

Gervinus, Georg Gottfried. *Shakespeare Commentaries.* Trans. F. E. Bunnett. London, 1875.

Goldstein, David. "'Manuring Eden." In Hillary Eklund (ed.), *Groundwork,* 171-94. Pittsburgh, PA: Duquesne University Press, 2017.

Gesling, Richard. *Artificial Fire, or Coal for Rich and Poor.* London, 1644.

Grafton, Richard (ed.). *All such proclamations as have been set forth by [Edward VI].* London, 1551.

Graunt, John. *Natural and Political Observations.* London, 1662.

Hadfield, Andrew. *Edmund Spenser: A Life.* Oxford University Press, 2012.

Hall, Joseph. *Occasional Meditations.* London, 1630.

Hayhow, D. B. *et al.* "State of Nature 2016." *State of Nature Partnership.* http://nora.nerc.ac.uk/id/eprint/516567.

Hayhow, D. B. *et al. The state of the UK's birds 2017.* RSPB, BTO, WWT, DAERA, JNCC, NE and NRW. www.bto.org/research-data-services/publications/state-uk-birds/2017/state-uk-birds-2017.

Heywood, John. *A Dialogue Containing … all the Proverbs in the English Tongue.* London, 1546.

Hiller, Geoffrey. "Drayton's *Muses Elizium*: 'A New Way Over Parnassus.'" *Review of English Studies,* 21/81 (1970): 1–13.

Hughes, J. Donald. *Pan's Travail: Environmental Problems of the Ancient Greeks and Romans.* Baltimore, MD: Johns Hopkins University Press, 1994.

Hughes, Paul and James Larkin (eds.). *Tudor Royal Proclamations.* 3 vols. New Haven, CT: Yale University Press, 1964–9.

Irish Peatland Conservation Council. *Ireland's Peatland Conservation Action Plan 2020.* Rathangan: Irish Peatland Conservation Council, 2009.

Jefferies, Richard. *Beloved Land.* Ed. Colin McKelvie. Shrewsbury: Swan Hill, 1994.

Jørgenson, Dolly. "Rethinking Rewilding." *Geoforum,* 65 (2015): 482–8.

Kossoff, David *et al.* "Industrial Mining Heritage and the Legacy of Environmental Pollution in the Derbyshire Derwent Catchment." *Journal of Archaeological Science,* 6 (2016): 190–9.

Leland, John. *The Itinerary of John Leland.* Ed. Lucy Smith. 5 vols. London: G. Bell, 1910.

Levinson, Marjorie. *Wordsworth's Great Period Poems.* Cambridge University Press, 1986.

Lewis, Simon and Mark Maslin. "Defining the Anthropocene." *Nature,* 519 (2015): 171–80.

Long, Percy. "Spenser and the Bishop of Rochester." *PMLA,* 31/4 (1916): 713–35.

Mabey, Richard. *Common Ground: A Place for Nature in Britain's Future.* London: Orion, 1980.

Macfarlane, Robert. *The Old Ways: A Journey on Foot.* London: Penguin, 2013.

Landmarks. London: Penguin, 2015.

Mackenzie, Louisa. "Sustainability." In Vin Nardizzi and Tiffany Werth (eds.), *Premodern Ecologies in the Modern Literary Imagination.* University of Toronto Press, 2019.

Mann, Michael E. "The Little Ice Age." In Michael McCracken and John Perry (eds.), *The Earth System: Physical and Chemical Dimensions of Global Environmental Change,* 504–9. Chichester: Wiley, 2002.

Markam, Gervase. *Cavelarice, or the English Horseman.* London, 1607.

Mascall, Leonard. *The Government of Cattle.* London, 1591.

McGrade, Arthur (ed.). *Of the Laws of Ecclesiastical Polity.* Oxford University Press, 2013.

McKibben, Bill. *The End of Nature.* New York: Anchor, 1989.

McRae, Andrew and Stephen Bending. *The Writing of Rural England: 1500–1800.* New York: Palgrave Macmillan, 2003.

Mills, A. D. *A Dictionary of British Place Names.* Oxford University Press, 2011.

Monbiot, George. *Feral: Rewilding the Land, the Sea, and Human Life.* University of Chicago Press, 2014.

Moryson, Fynes. *An Itinerary.* London, 1617.

Mossman, H. L., C. J. Panter, and P. M. Dolman. *Fens Biodiversity Audit 2012.* www.cperc.org.uk/downloads/5_Fens_Biodiversity_Audit_FINAL_Report_24-10-2012.pdf.

Nelson, Bryant. *The Gannet.* London: A & C Black, 1978.

Nixon, Rob. *Slow Violence and the Environmentalism of the Poor.* Harvard University Press, 2011.

Norbrook, David and H. R. Woudhuysen (eds.). *The Penguin Book of Renaissance Verse.* London: Penguin, 1992.

O'Callaghan, Michelle. "Browne, William (1590/91–1645?)." Brian Harrison *et al.* (eds.) *Oxford Dictionary of National Biography.* Oxford University Press, 2004. Subscription website.

Onarheim, Ingrid and Marius Arhun. "Toward an Ice-Free Barents Sea." *Geophysical Research Letters,* 44/16 (2017): 8387–95.

Parkinson, John. *Paradisi in Sole, Paradisus Terrestris.* London, 1629.

Pettet, E. C. *Of Paradise and Light: A Study of Vaughan's Silex Scintillans.* Cambridge University Press, 1960.

Rees, Thomas. *The Beauties of England and Wales: South Wales.* London, 1815.

Royal Society for the Protection of Birds. *State of UK's Birds, 2017.* www.rspb.org.uk/our-work/conservation/centre-for-conservation-science/state-of-the-uks-birds/.

Sanders, Julie. *Ben Jonson's Theatrical Republics.* Basingstoke: Palgrave Macmillan, 1998.

Spiegel, Marjorie. *The Dreaded Comparison: Human and Animal Slavery.* London: Mirror, 1996.

Standish, Arthur. *The Commons' Complaint.* London, 1611.

Tryon, Thomas. *Modest Observations on the Present Extraordinary Frost.* London, 1684.

Monthly Observations for the Preserving of Health. London, 1688.

Tyson, Edward. *Orang-outang, sive, Homo sylvestris, or, The anatomy of a pygmy compared with that of a monkey, an ape, and a man.* London, 1699.

Vera, Frans. "Can't See the Trees for the Forest." In Ian Rotherham (ed.), *Trees, Forested Landscapes, and Grazing Animals,* 99–121. London: Routledge, 2013.

Watson, Robert N. "Tell Inconvenient Truths But Tell Them Slant." In Jennifer Munroe, Edward Geisweidt, and Lynne Bruckner (eds.), *Ecological Approaches to Early Modern English Texts: A Field Guide to Reading and Teaching,* 17–28. Burlington, VT: Ashgate, 2015.

Westphal, Lynne M. *et al.* "Models for Renaturing Brownfield Areas." In Marcus Hall (ed.). *Restoration and History: The Search for a Usable Environmental Past,* 208–10. London: Routledge, 2010.

Whitaker, Katie. *Mad Madge: Margaret Cavendish: Duchess of Newcastle, Royalist, Writer, and Romantic.* London: Chatto & Windus, 2002.

Wilson, E. O. *Biophilia.* Cambridge, MA: Harvard University Press, 1984.

Wohlleben, Peter. *The Hidden Life of Trees.* London: HarperCollins, 2017.

Wooley, Hannah. *The Queenlike Closet.* London, 1670.

Worthington, T. et al. "Former distribution and decline of the burbot in the UK." *Aquatic Conservation,* 20 (2010): 371-77.

Wotton, Henry. *Elements of Architecture.* London, 1624.